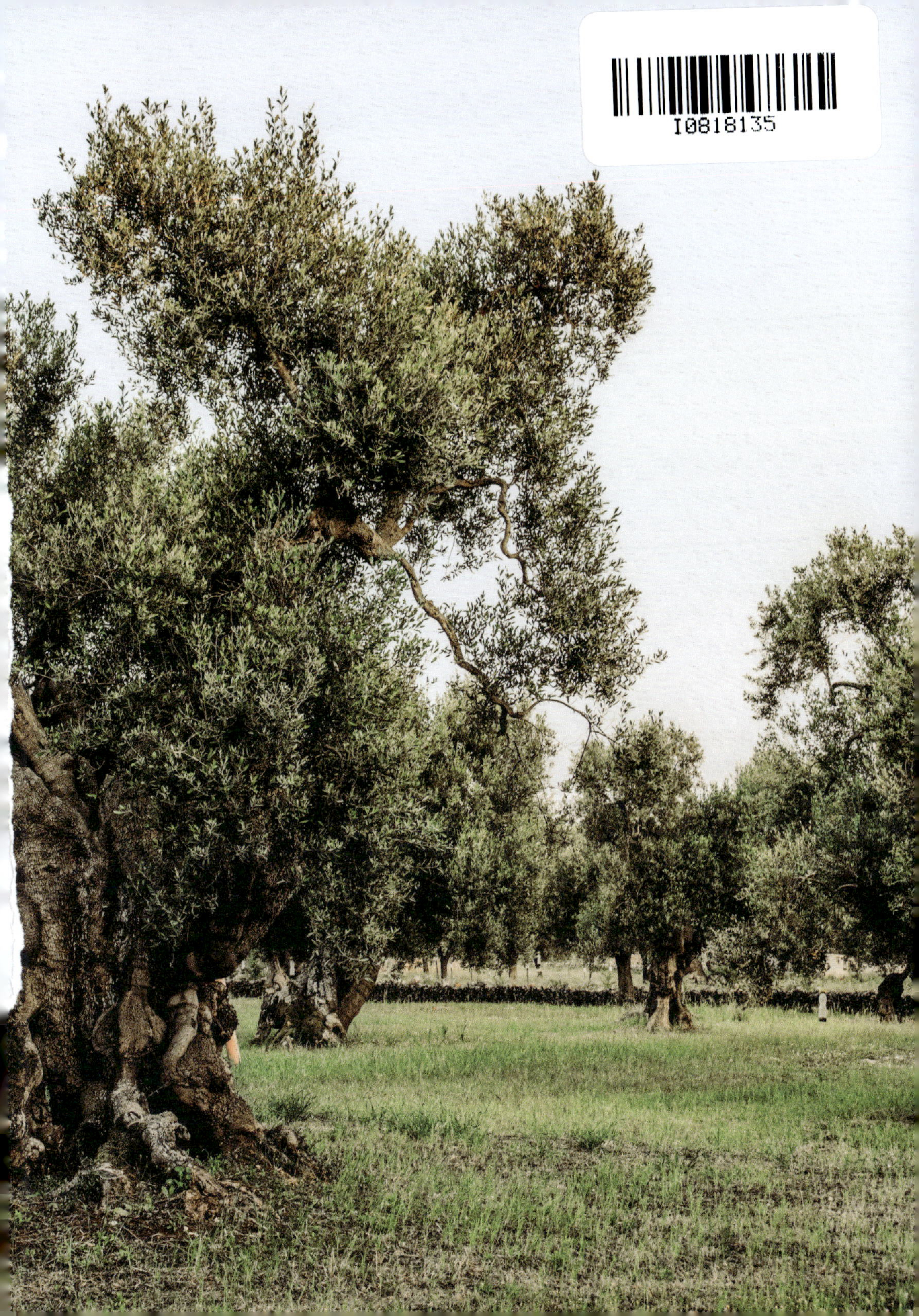
I0818135

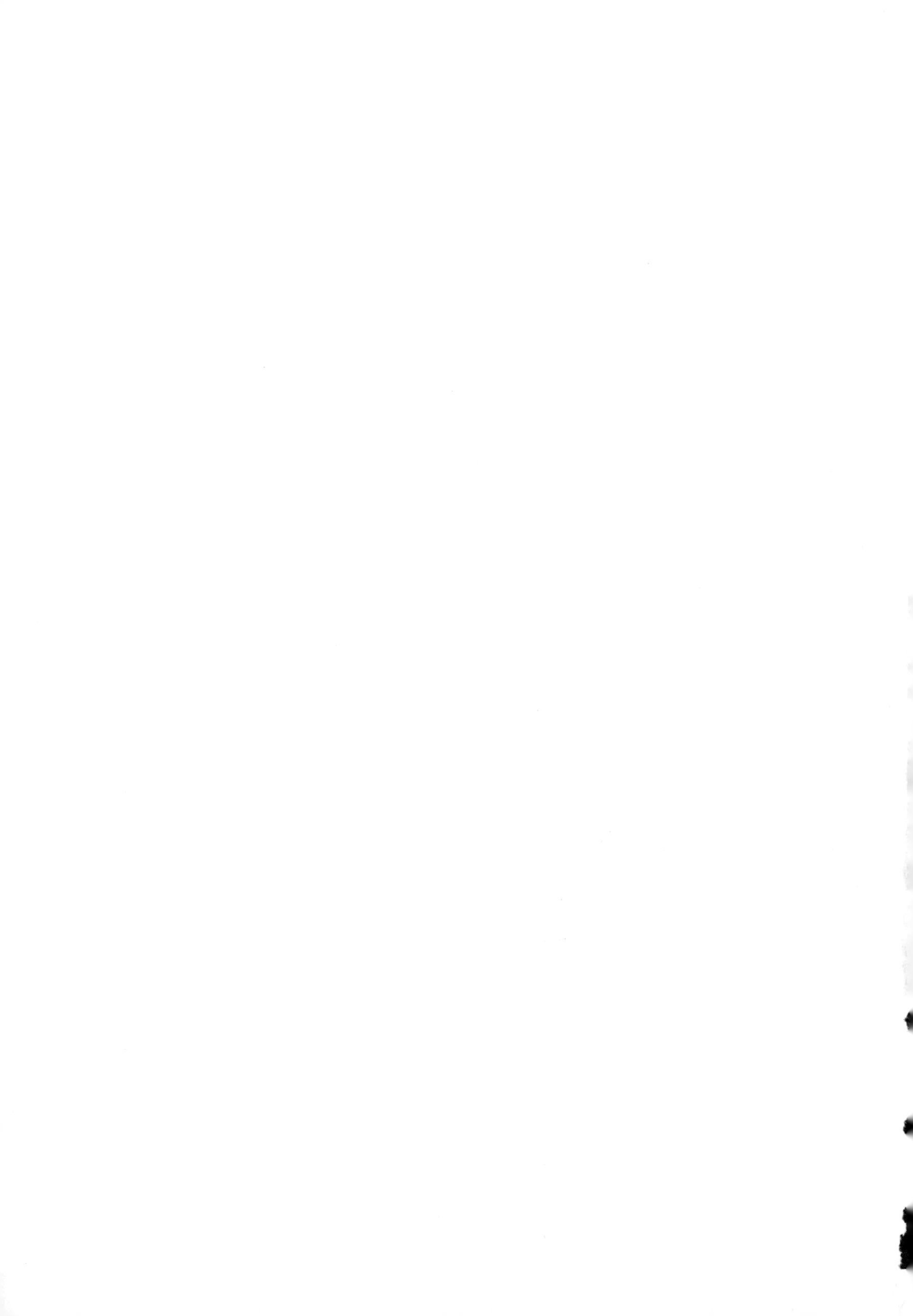

ITALY

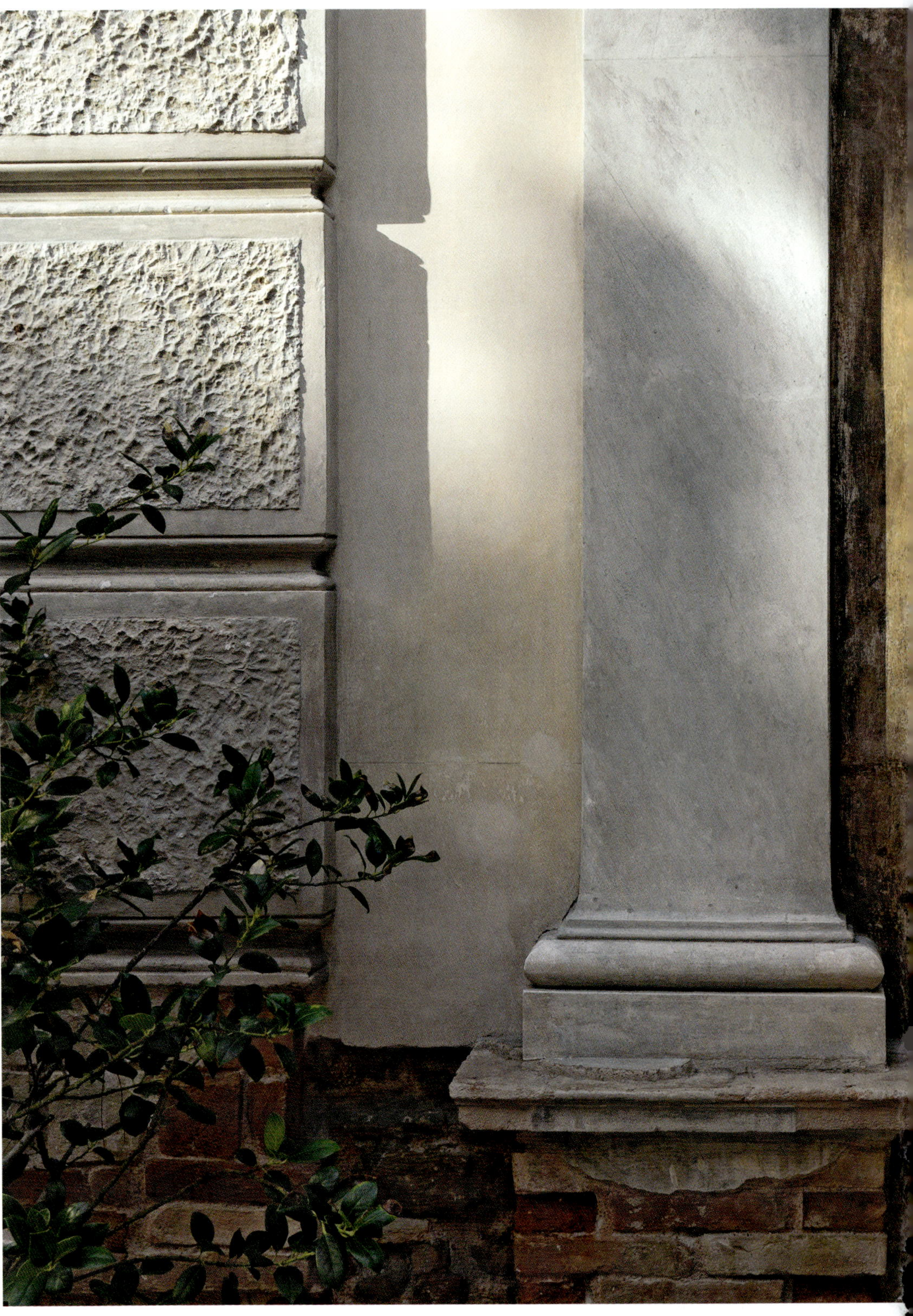

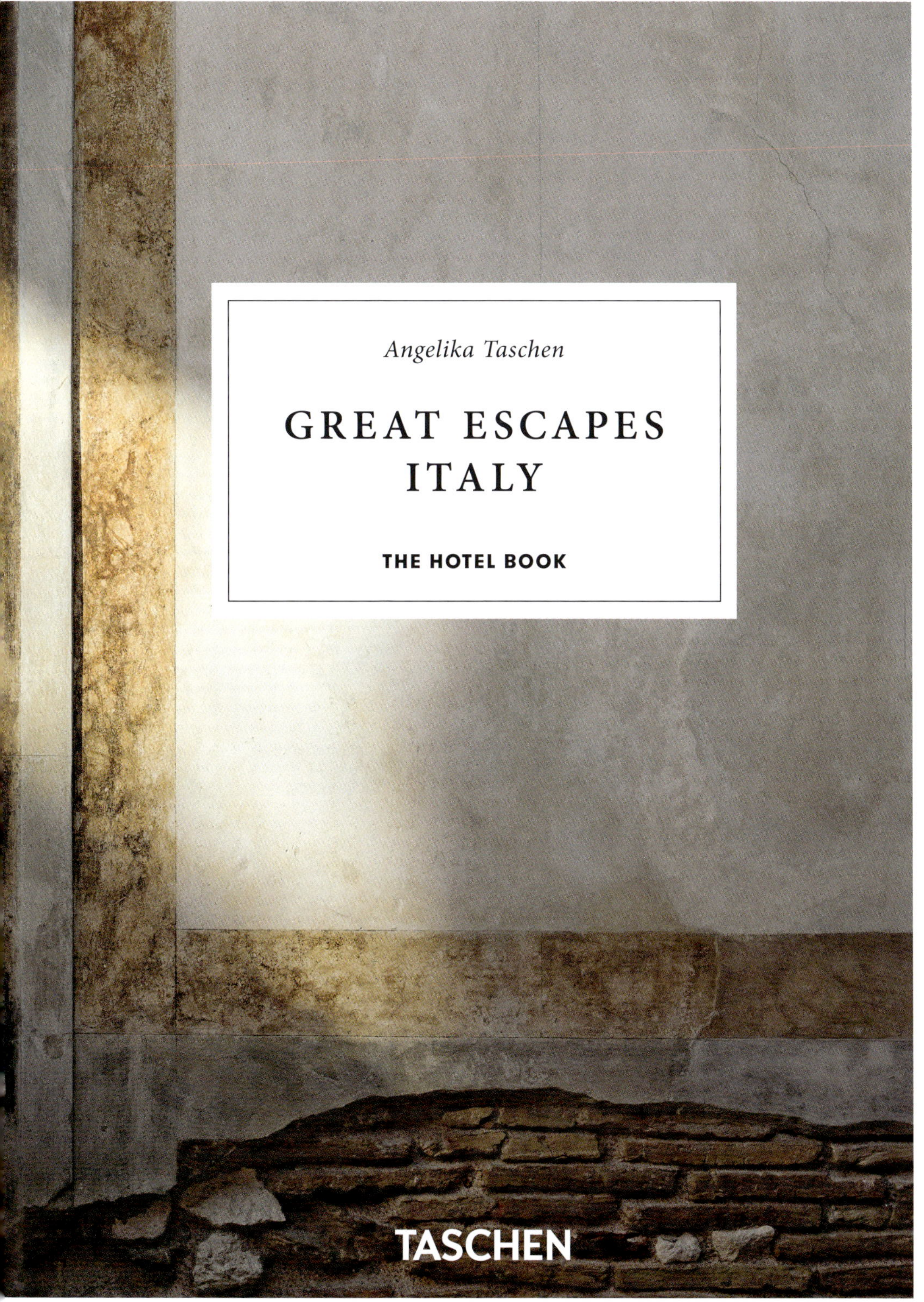
Angelika Taschen
GREAT ESCAPES
ITALY
THE HOTEL BOOK
TASCHEN

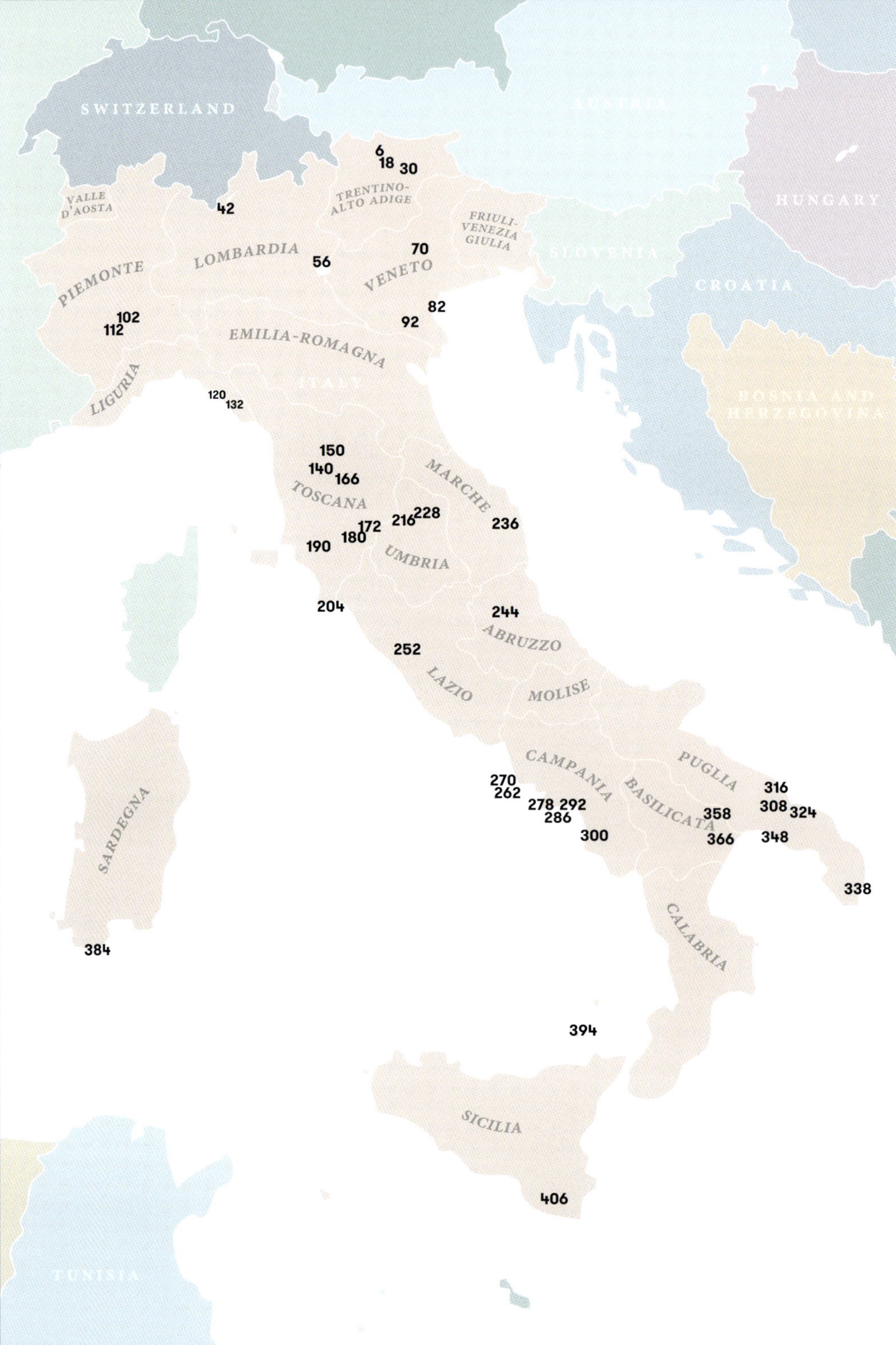
SWITZERLAND
AUSTRIA
HUNGARY
SLOVENIA
CROATIA
BOSNIA AND HERZEGOVINA
TUNISIA
ITALY
VALLE D'AOSTA
PIEMONTE
LOMBARDIA
TRENTINO-ALTO ADIGE
FRIULI-VENEZIA GIULIA
VENETO
EMILIA-ROMAGNA
LIGURIA
TOSCANA
MARCHE
UMBRIA
ABRUZZO
LAZIO
MOLISE
CAMPANIA
PUGLIA
BASILICATA
CALABRIA
SARDEGNA
SICILIA
6
18
30
42
56
70
82
92
102
112
120
132
150
140
166
172
180
190
216
228
236
204
244
252
270
262
278
292
286
300
316
308
324
358
366
348
338
384
394
406

CONTENTS

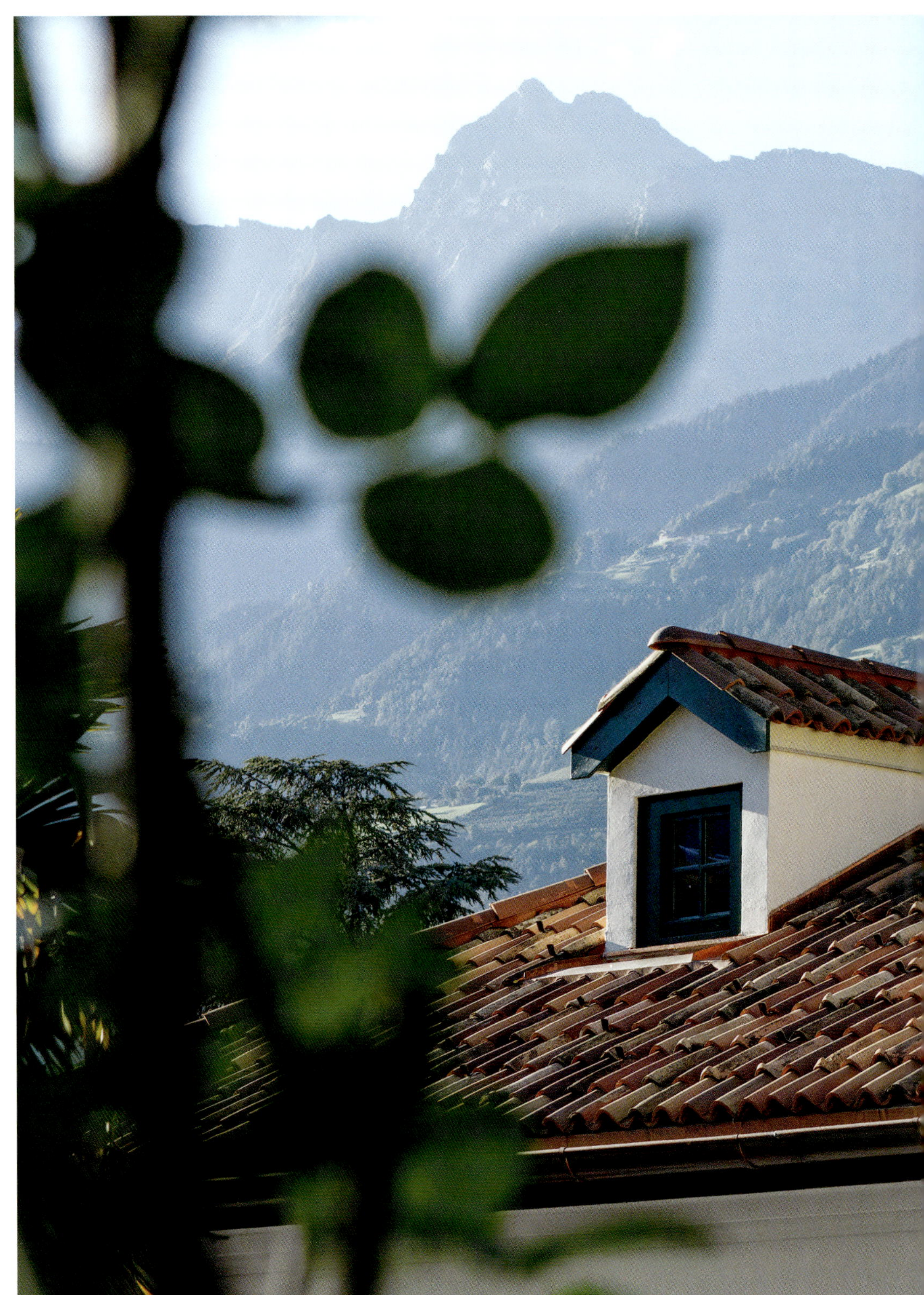

ALTO ADIGE

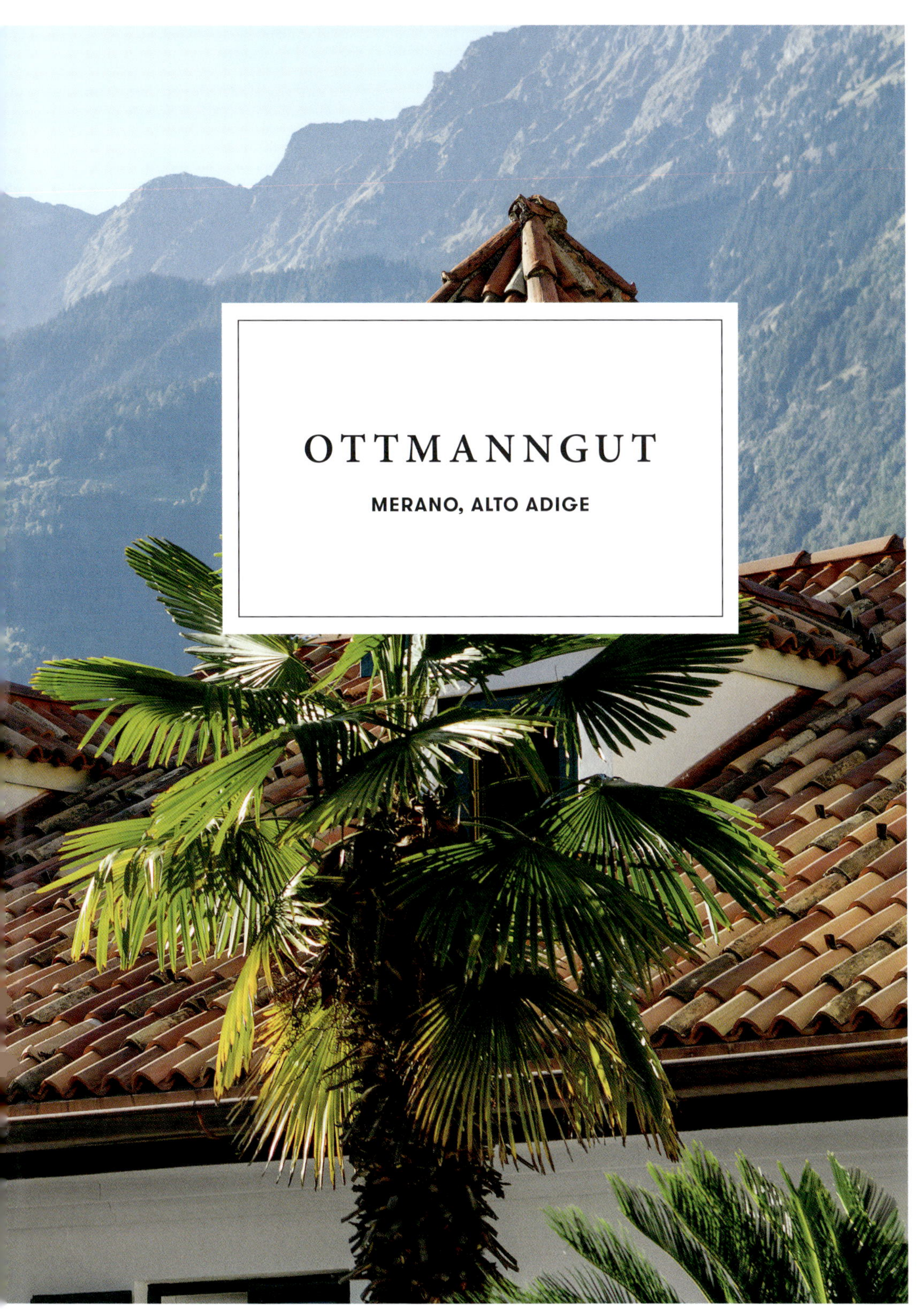

OTTMANNGUT

MERANO, ALTO ADIGE

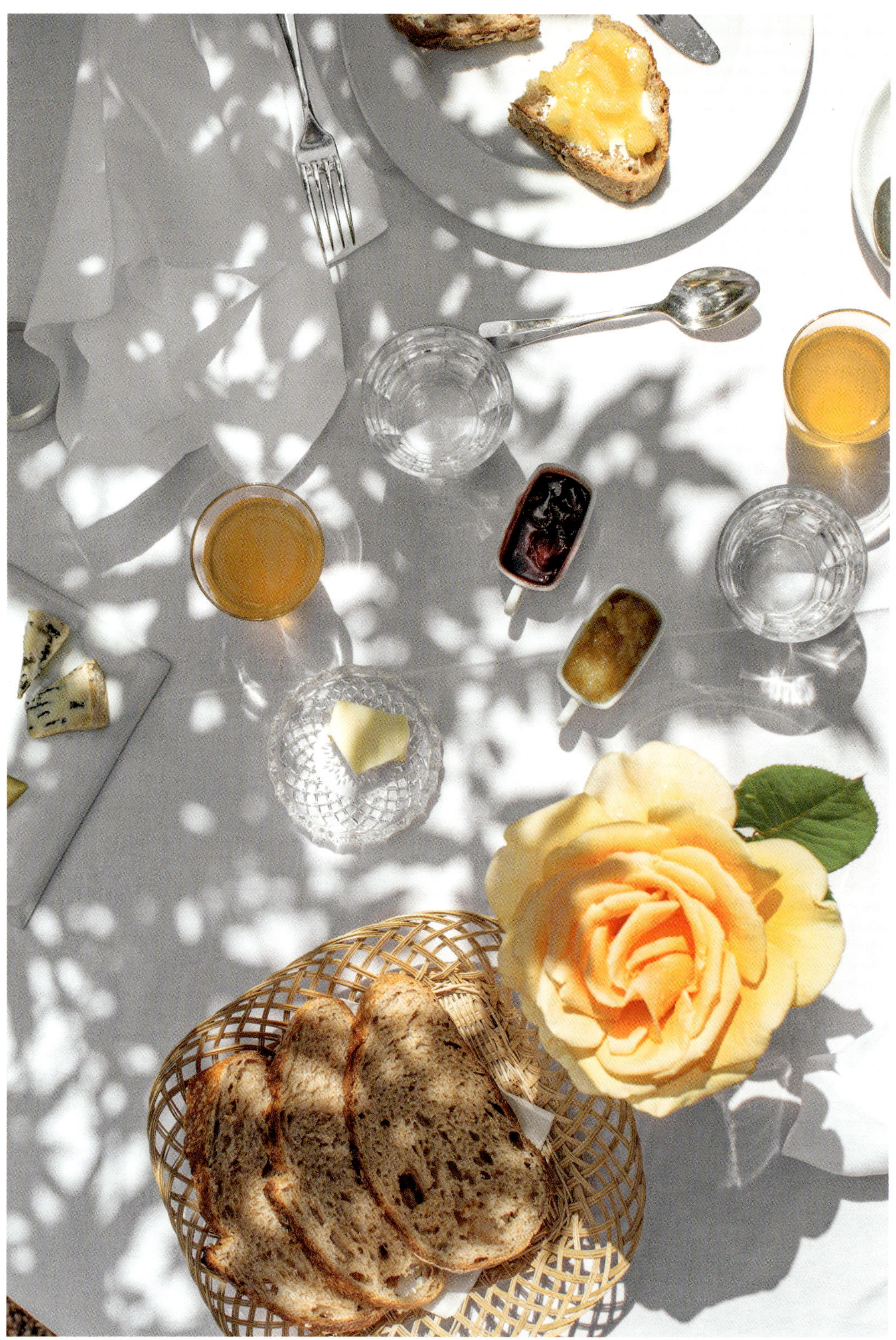

ALTO ADIGE

OTTMANNGUT

Via G. Verdi 18, 39012 Merano
Tel. +39 0473 449 656 · info@ottmanngut.it
www.ottmanngut.it
Open from late March to early January

A HOUSE STEEPED IN HISTORY The title was a bit long-winded, but it became a bestseller: "On the town of Merano in Tyrol, its surroundings and its climate, along with remarks on milk, dairy and grape health cures and nearby mineral springs". A small volume written in 1836 by a Viennese general practitioner which triggered a huge southbound avalanche amongst European aristocratic and artistic circles and established Merano as the most famous spa in the Alps. Here, in the following decades, visitors could encounter Empress Sisi of Austria with her sickly daughter, Franz Kafka with his lung complaint and Arthur Schnitzler, who was beset by undying love for a married woman during his stay. One of the first spa guests was Friedrich Wasmann, a Biedermeier painter from Hamburg who resided in the summer home of his acquaintances the Kirchlechner family and captured their Mediterranean garden on canvas. The Kirchlechners still own the house, and transformed it over the years into a wine tavern, a guest house and finally the Ottmanngut. A copy of the garden painting adorns a wall in the Wasmann Room, and each of the other rooms has its own story to tell: The Mitzi Martha Suite, for example, commemorates two flirtatious young ladies who stayed there in the last century and turned the heads of the male guests. In wonderful harmony with the history of the house, the rooms are fitted with old floorboards, tiled stoves and Biedermeier furniture, making the Ottmanngut one of the most charming and authentic places to stay in Merano. ◆ Book to pack: "Love That Died before Its Time" by Arthur Schnitzler and Olga Waissnix.

EIN HAUS VOLLER HISTORIE Sein Titel war ein wenig sperrig, doch es wurde ein Bestseller: Das 1836 von einem Wiener Leibarzt verfasste Büchlein „Über die Stadt Meran in Tirol, ihre Umgebung und ihr Klima. Nebst Bemerkungen über Milch-, Molken- und Traubenkuren und nahe Mineralquellen" löste in Europas Adels- und Künstlerkreisen eine Reiselawine in Richtung Süden aus und etablierte Meran als berühmtesten Kurort der Alpen. Hier traf man in den folgenden Jahrzehnten Kaiserin Sisi mit ihrer leidenden Tochter, den lungenkranken Franz Kafka sowie Arthur Schnitzler, der sich während seines Aufenthaltes unsterblich in eine verheiratete Frau verliebte. Einer der ersten Kurgäste war der Hamburger Biedermeiermaler Friedrich Wasmann, der im Sommerhaus der befreundeten Familie Kirchlechner Quartier fand und deren mediterranen Garten auf Leinwand bannte. Die Kirchlechners besitzen das Haus noch immer und verwandelten es im Lauf der Zeit in einen Weinauschank, eine Pension und schließlich in das heutige Ottmanngut. Im „Wasmannzimmer" schmückt eine Kopie des Gartengemäldes eine Wand, und auch jedes weitere Zimmer erzählt seine eigene Geschichte: Die „Mitzi-Martha-Suite" etwa erinnert an zwei Soubretten, die im letzten Jahrhundert dort nächtigten und den männlichen Bewohnern den Kopf verdrehten. Wunderbar passend zur Historie des Hauses sind die Räume mit alten Dielen, Kachelöfen und Biedermeiermöbeln ausgestattet und machen das Ottmanngut zu einer der charmantesten und authentischsten Adressen Merans. ◆ Buchtipp: „Liebe, die starb vor der Zeit. Ein Briefwechsel" von Arthur Schnitzler und Olga Waissnix.

UNE MAISON REMPLIE D'HISTOIRE Devenu un best-seller en dépit de son titre un peu compliqué, le petit livre écrit en 1836 par un médecin viennois « Über die Stadt Meran in Tirol, ihre Umgebung und ihr Klima, nebst Bemerkungen über Milch-, Molke- und Traubenkuren und nahe Mineralquellen » (La ville de Merano au Tyrol, ses environs et son climat, avec des observations sur les cures de lait, de petit-lait et de raisin et les sources minérales proches) a déclenché une avalanche de voyages vers le sud dans les milieux aristocratiques et artistiques européens, faisant de Merano la station thermale la plus célèbre des Alpes. Dans les décennies qui suivirent, elle accueillit l'impératrice Sissi et sa fille souffrante, Franz Kafka, malade des poumons, et Arthur Schnitzler qui tomba éperdument amoureux d'une femme mariée pendant son séjour. Friedrich Wasmann de Hambourg, peintre du Biedermeier, a été l'un des premiers hôtes de la station thermale. Séjournant dans la maison d'été de ses amis, la famille Kirchlechner, il a immortalisé leur jardin méditerranéen sur la toile. La famille Kirchlechner est toujours propriétaire de la maison et l'a transformée au fil du temps en buvette, en maison d'hôtes avant d'ouvrir l'Ottmanngut. Une copie de la peinture du jardin orne un mur de la « Wasmannzimmer », et chaque chambre raconte sa propre histoire : la « Mitzi Martha Suite », par exemple, rappelle deux soubrettes du siècle dernier qui tournaient la tête des habitants masculins. Les pièces abritent des planchers anciens, des poêles en faïence et des meubles Biedermeier, en accord parfait avec l'histoire de la maison : l'Ottmanngut est l'une des adresses les plus charmantes et authentiques de Merano.
◆ À lire : « Journal (1923–1926) » d'Arthur Schnitzler.

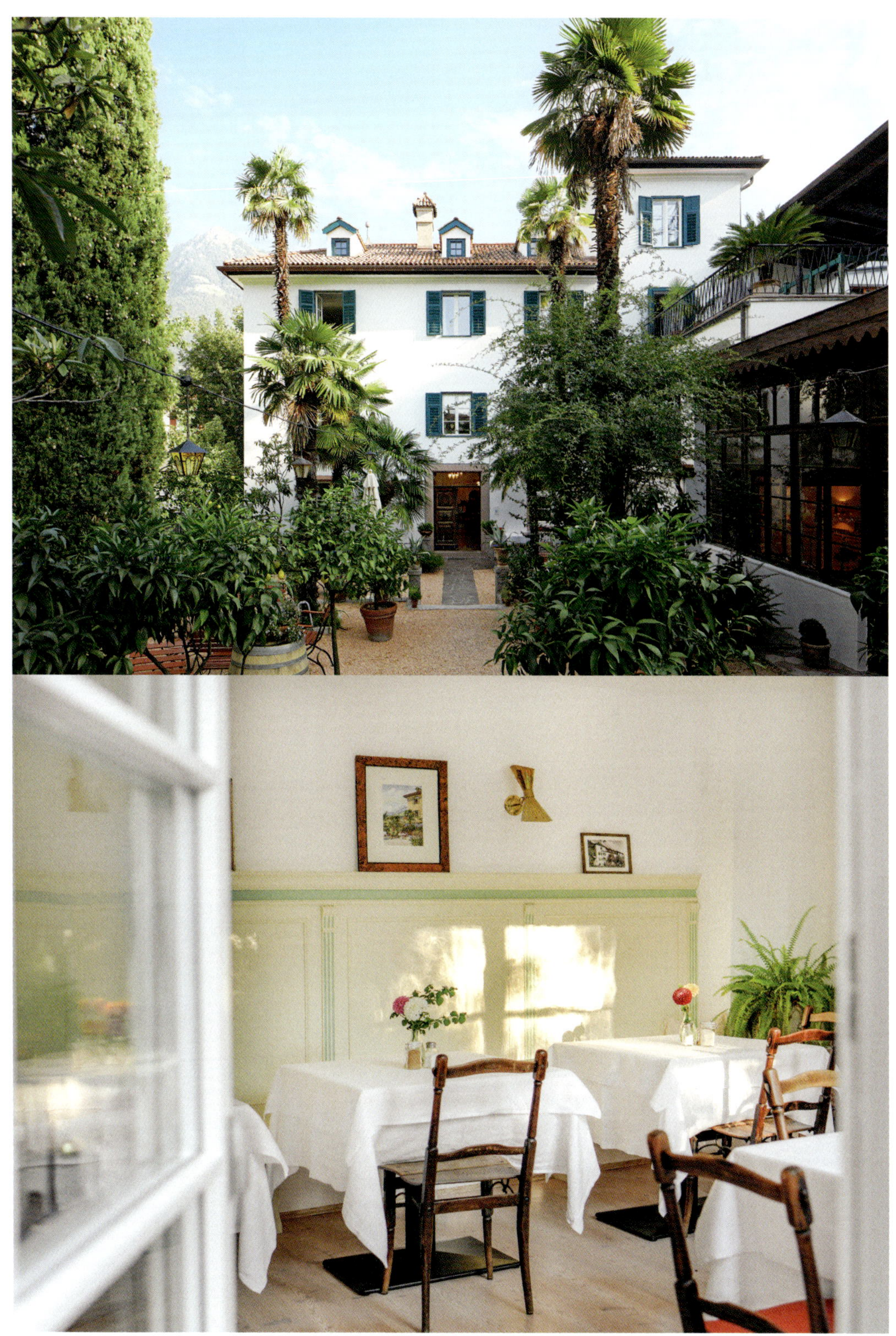

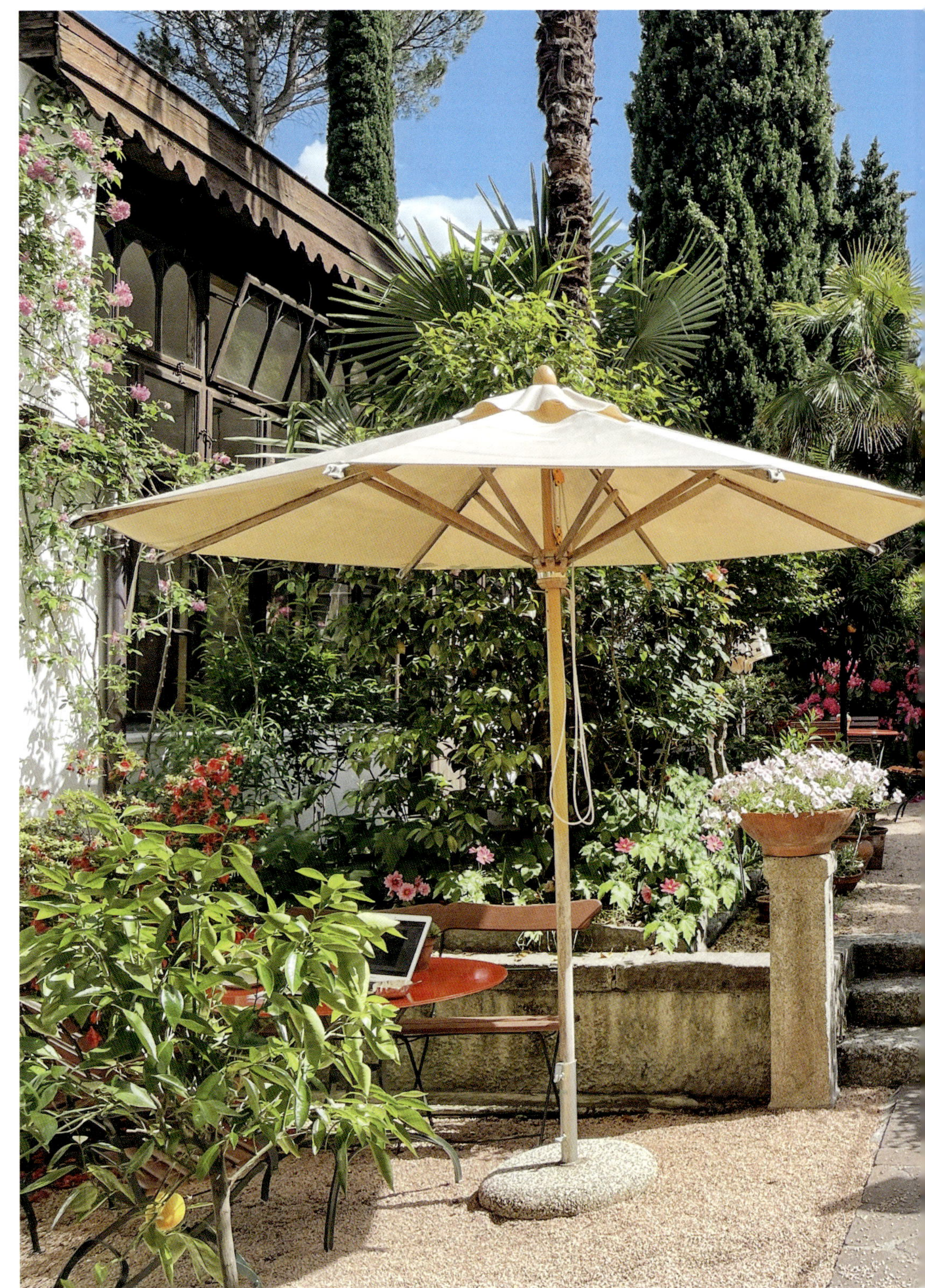

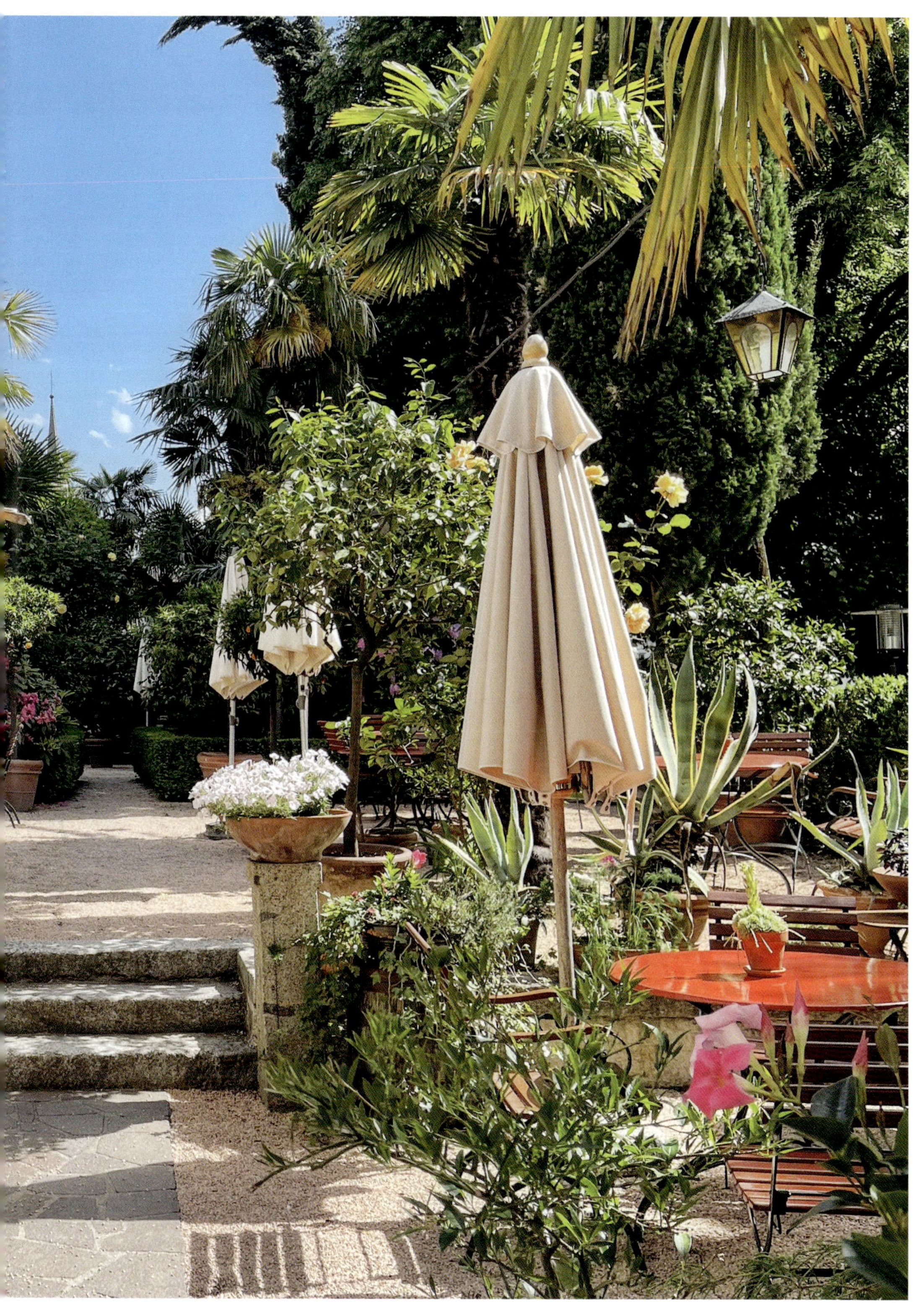

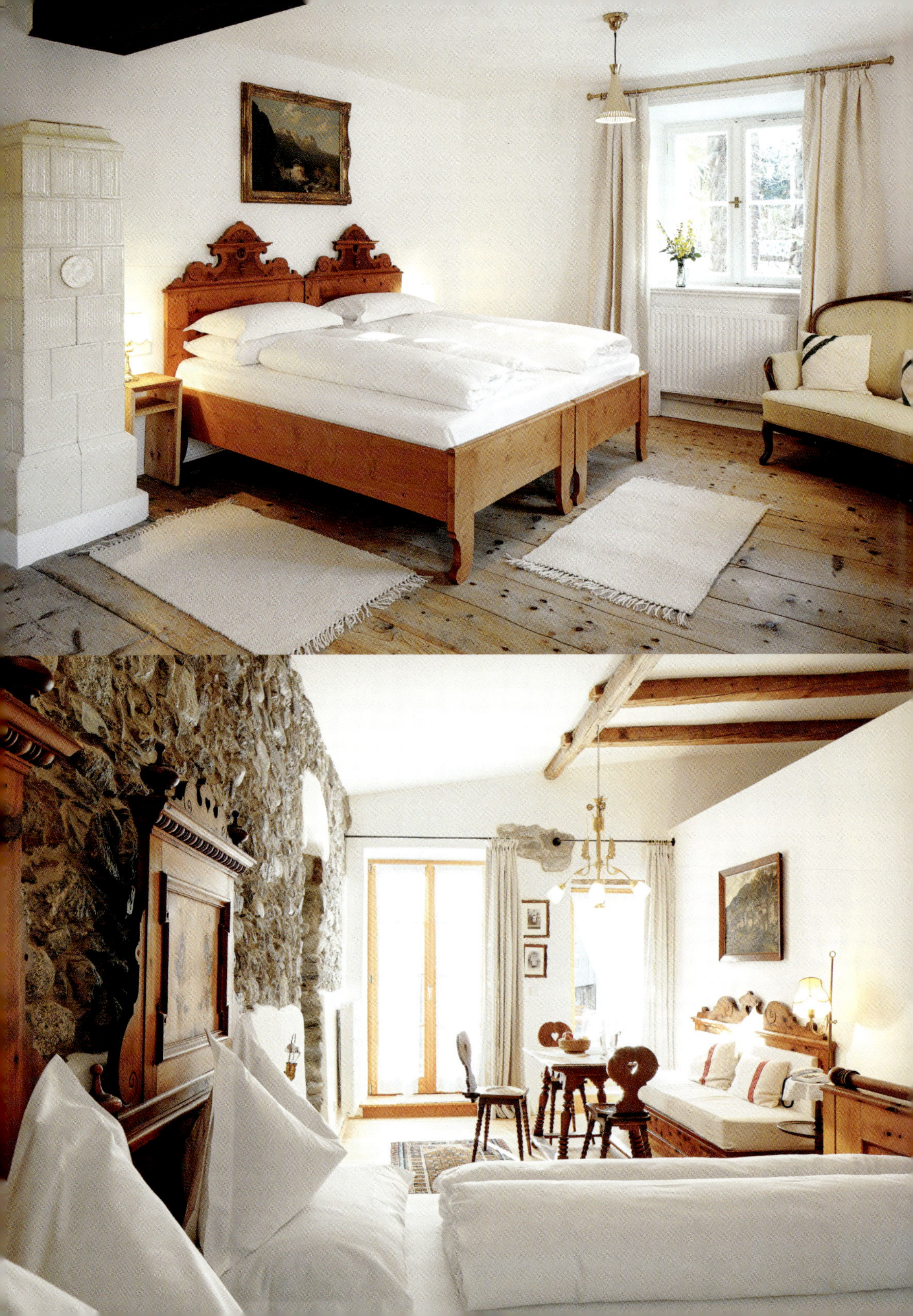

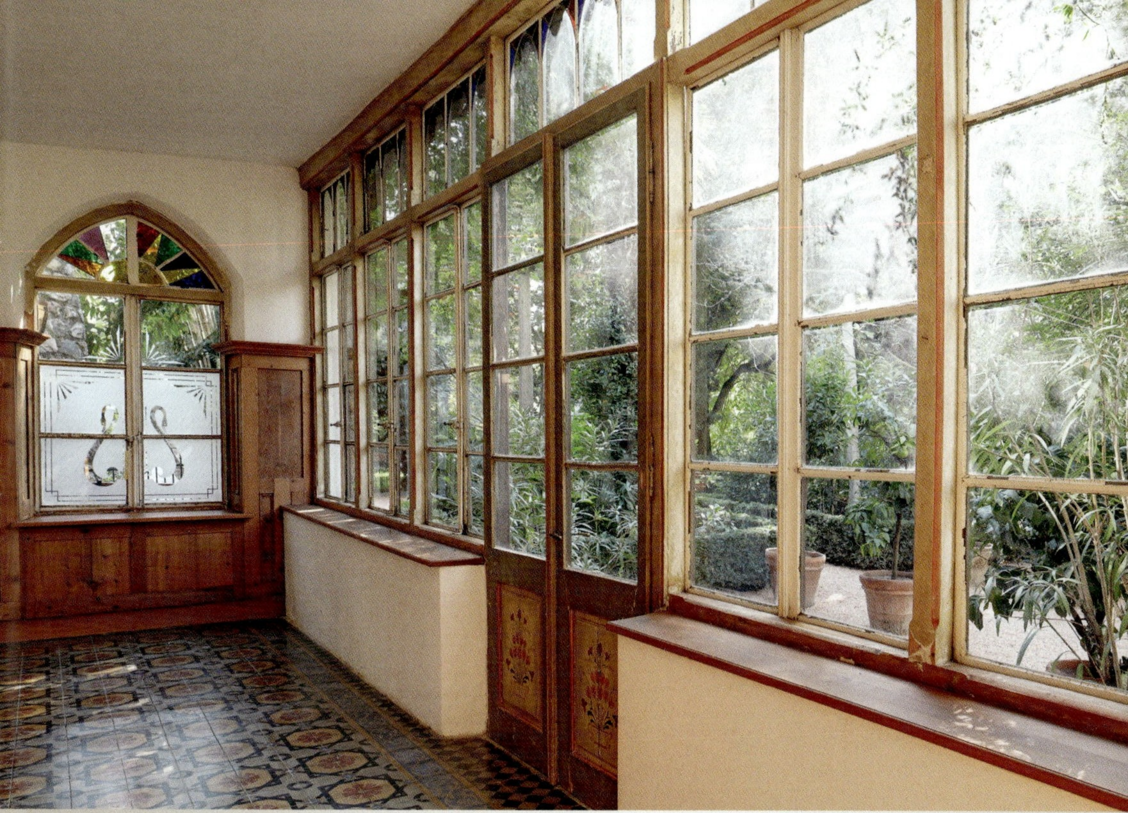

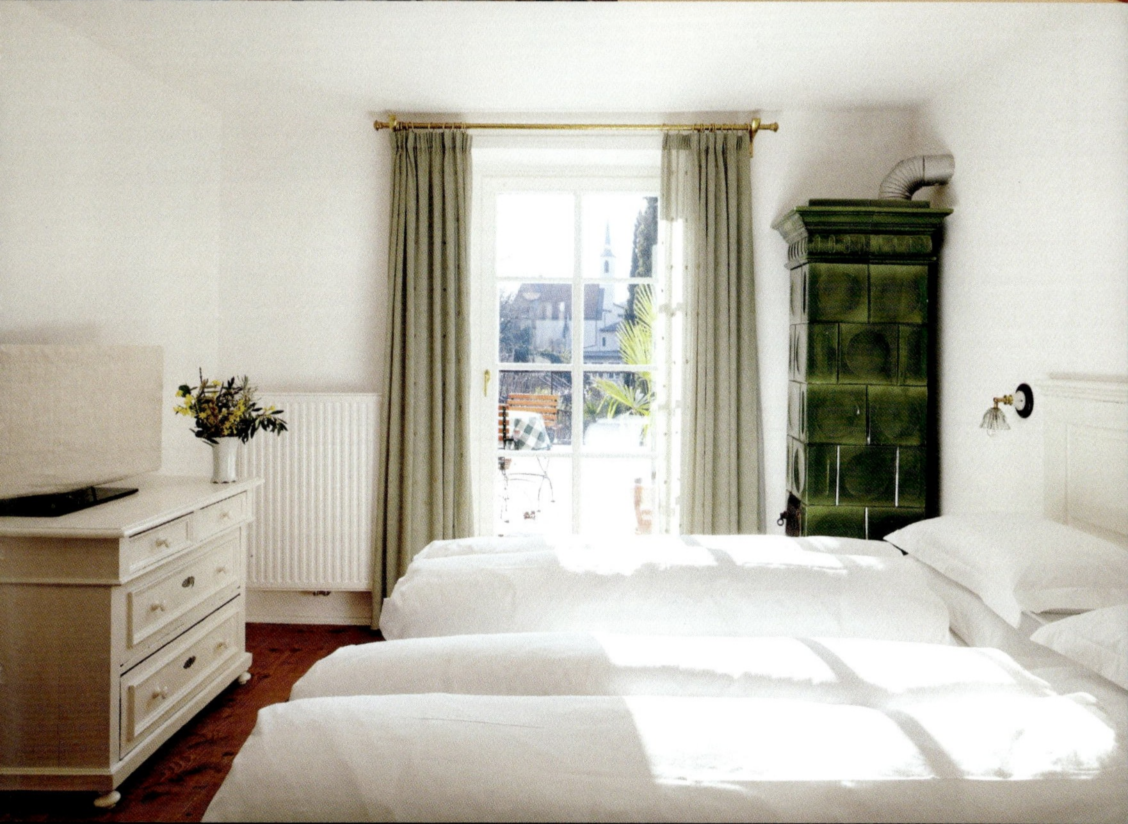

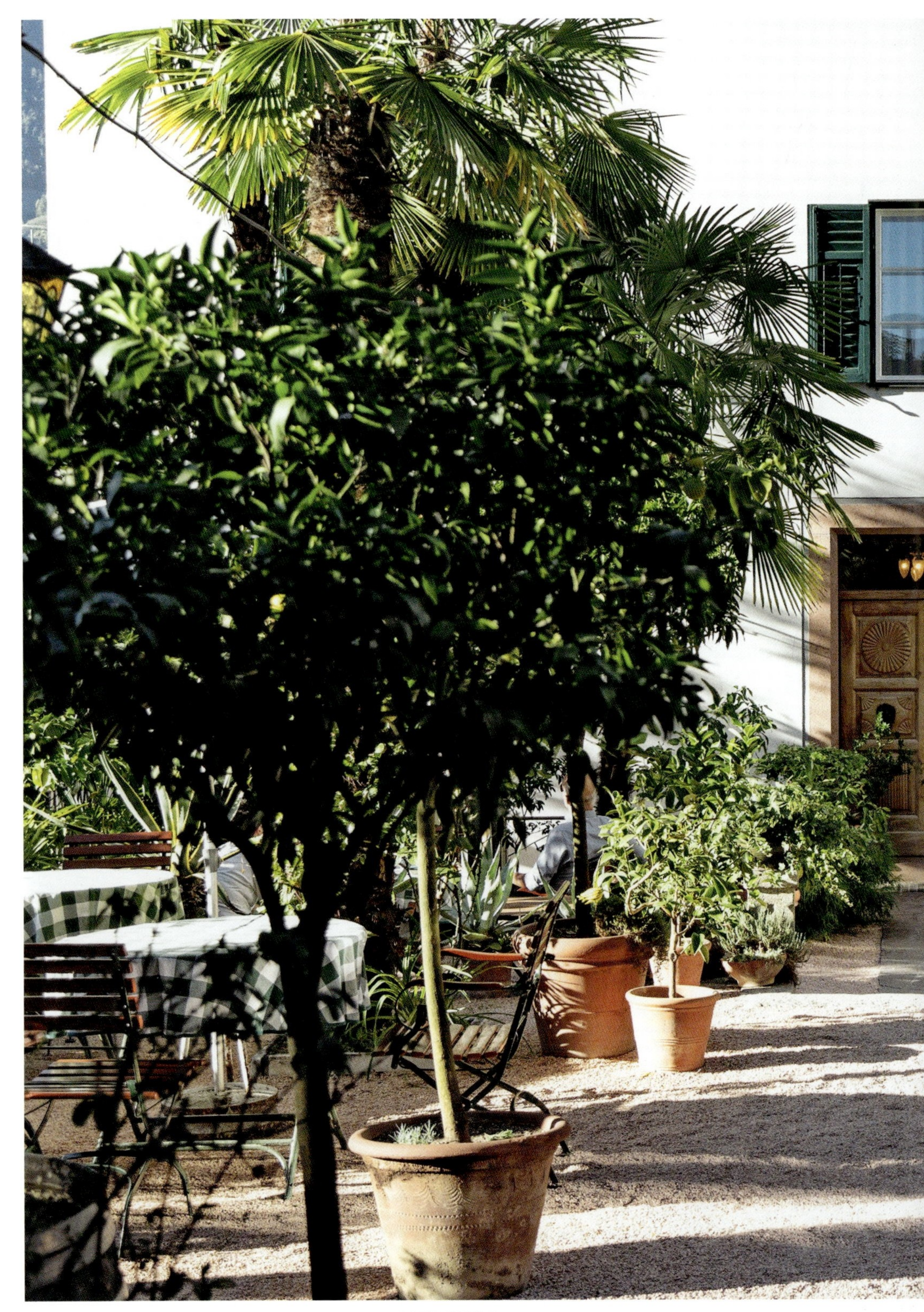

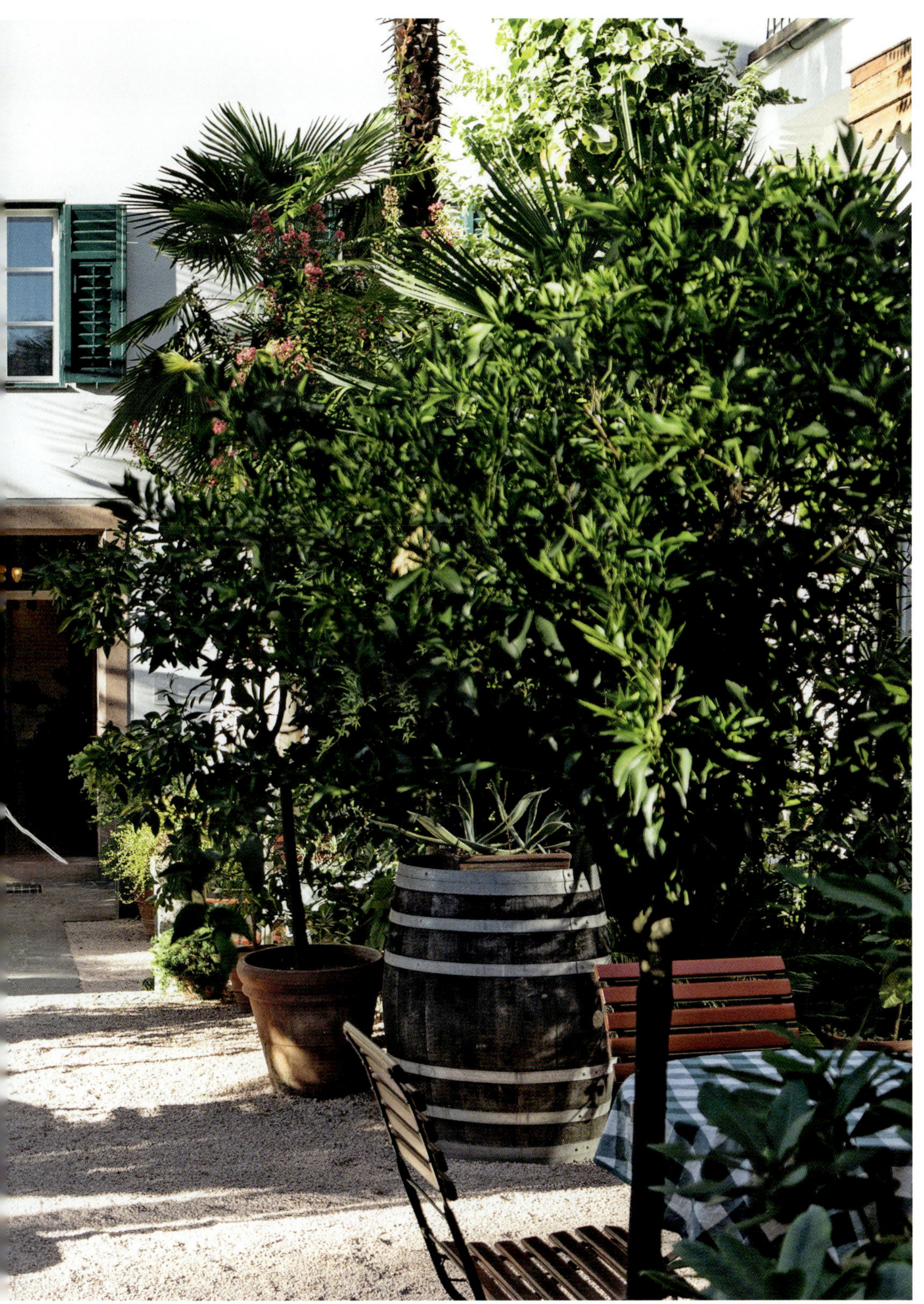

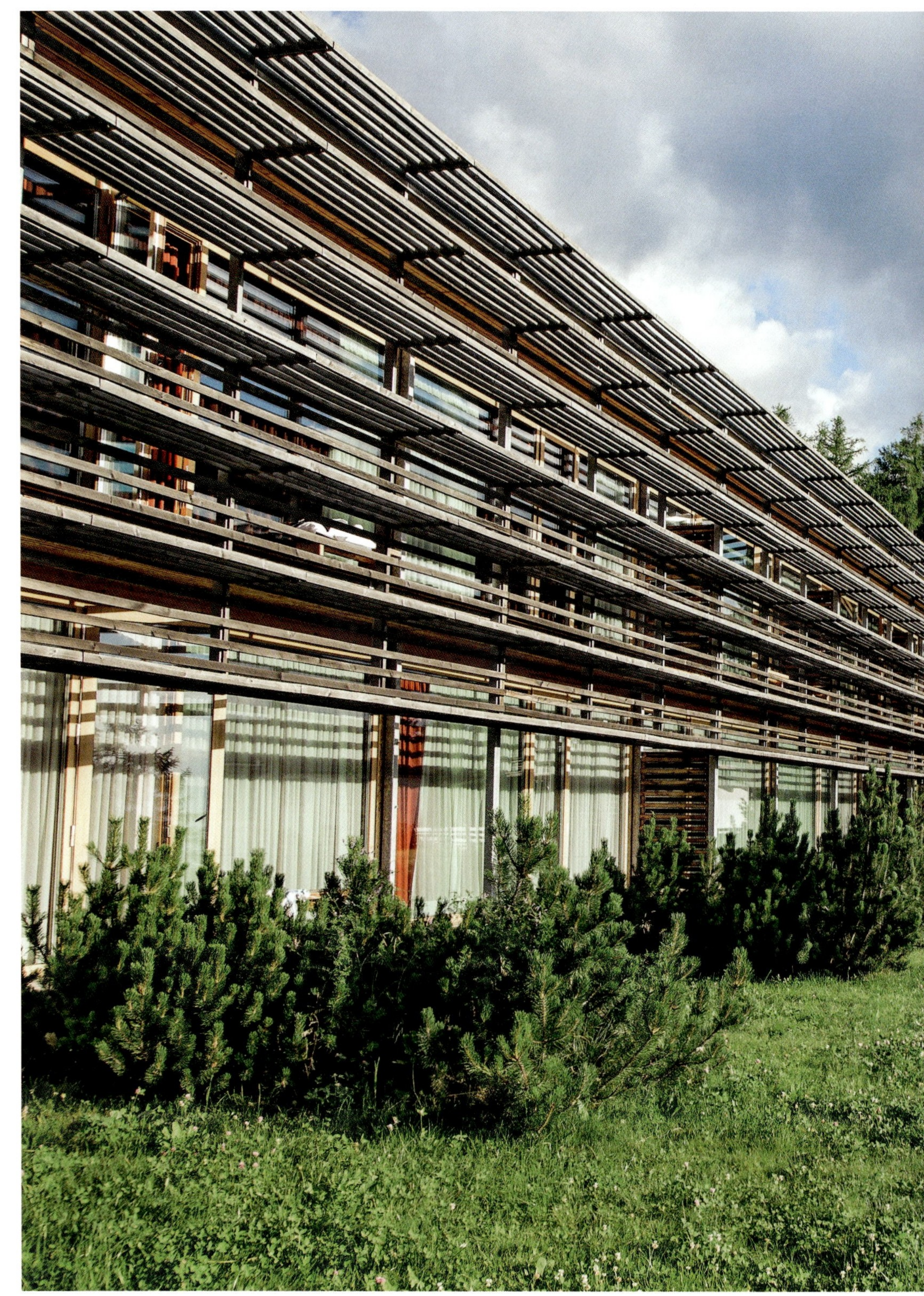

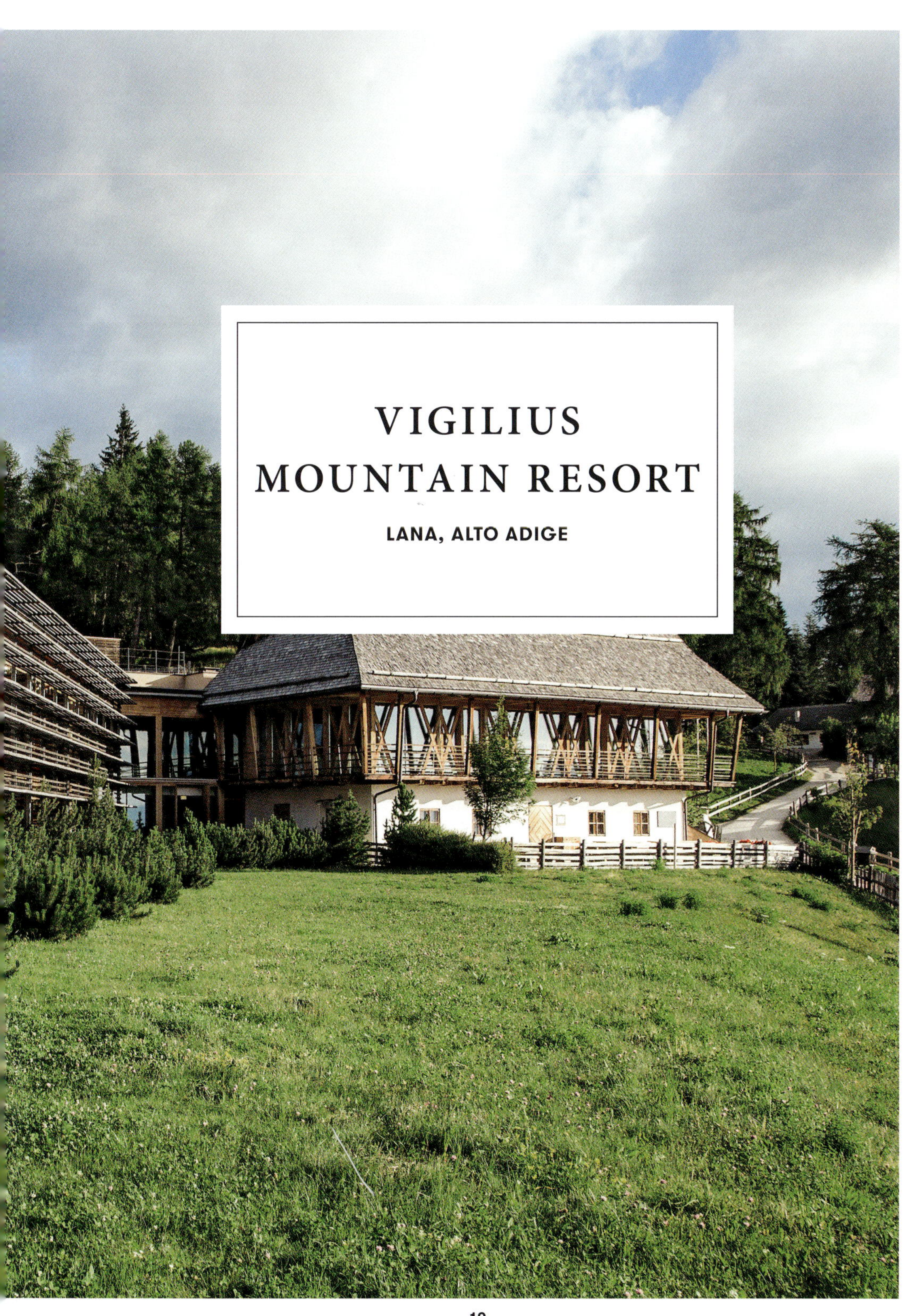

VIGILIUS MOUNTAIN RESORT

LANA, ALTO ADIGE

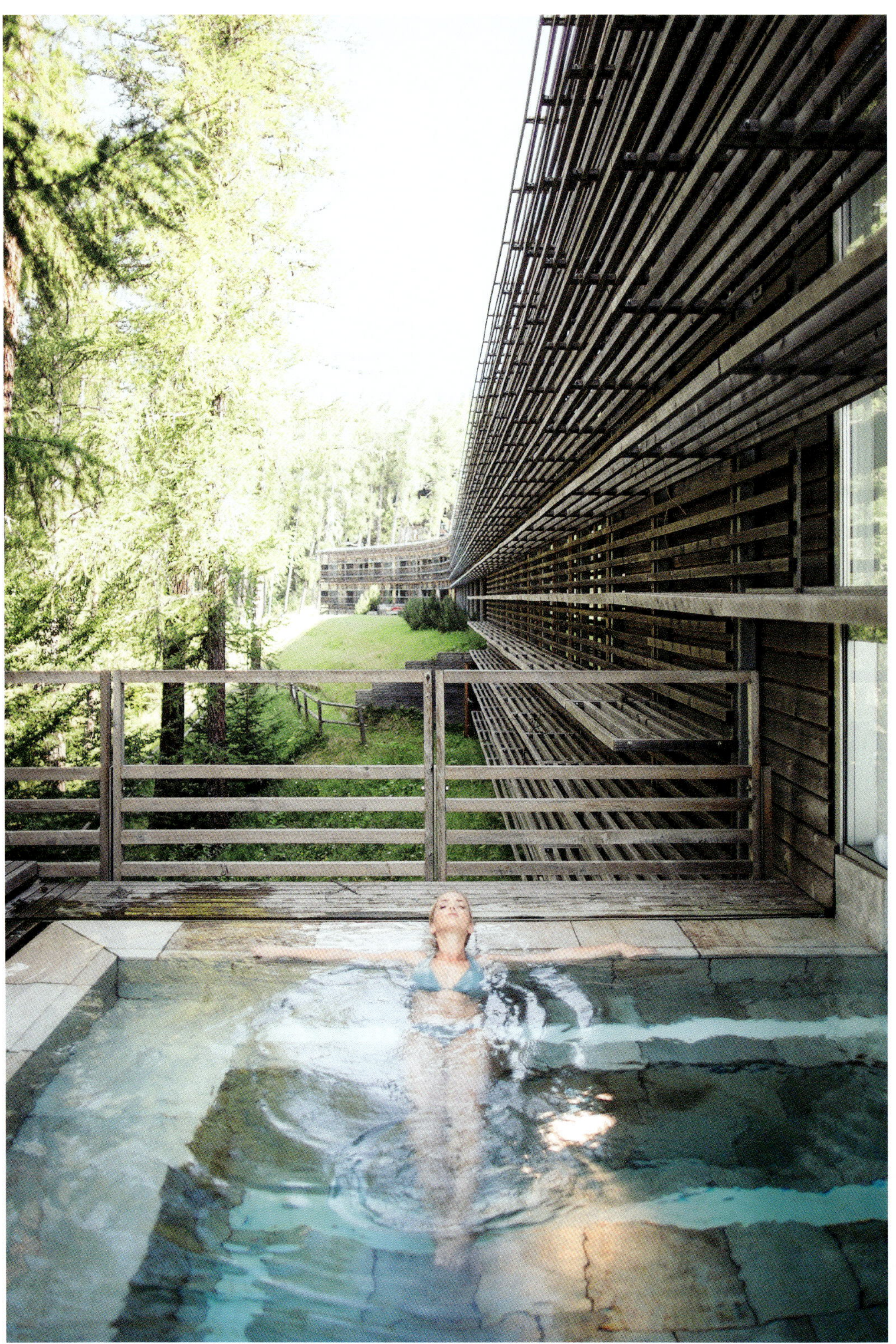

VIGILIUS MOUNTAIN RESORT

Via Villa 3, 39011 Lana
Tel. +39 0473 556 600 · info@vigilius.it
www.vigilius.it

PERFECT PEACE Seven minutes is all you need to travel to a different world. That's how long the cable car takes to glide from Lana in the valley to a height of 4,921 feet – to the Vigiljoch, where there are no cars, no traffic noise, no open-plan offices and no supermarkets. Those who escape here from everyday cares can enjoy a view of the Tyrolean peaks, breathe air that seems to tingle with the aroma of larch forests and walk over meadows where gentians flower. Back in the mists of time a pious giant is said to have lived in this mountain idyll and built a church. At the start of the third millennium Matteo Thun took his cue from these first architectural traces and designed the Vigilius Mountain Resort. Born in Alto Adige (South Tyrol) himself, Thun wanted to give his homeland a hotel whose architecture took up and evolved the forms of nature, a hotel that combined tradition with modern standards. The building lies on the slope like a huge tree trunk, made from wood, stone and glass. It was thought out down to the last detail: the flat roof was greened thanks to a layer of soil, and in the simply designed rooms a heated clay wall separates the living area from the bathroom – a wonderful source of warmth, especially in winter! And a natural source of water – a spring – supplies the spa, where the simple bodycare products are real treasures: a mountain herbal massage or a Tyrolean hay bath bring guests even closer to heaven than they already are at 4,921 feet. ◆ Book to pack: "The Cantos" by Ezra Pound.

IN ALLER RUHE Die Reise in eine andere Welt dauert nur sieben Minuten. So lange braucht die Seilbahn, um von der Talstation in Lana auf 1500 Meter Höhe zu schweben – aufs Vigiljoch, wo es keine Autos und keinen Straßenlärm gibt, keine Großraumbüros und keine Supermärkte. Weit weg vom Alltag genießt man hier stattdessen den Blick auf Südtirols Gipfel, atmet prickelnde Luft mit Lärchenwaldaroma und läuft über Wiesen, auf denen der Enzian blüht. In dieser Bergidylle soll vor Urzeiten ein frommer Riese gelebt und eine Kirche gebaut haben – Anfang des dritten Jahrtausends folgte Matteo Thun diesen ersten architektonischen Spuren und entwarf das Vigilius Mountain Resort. Selbst in Südtirol geboren, wollte Thun für seine Heimat ein Hotel errichten, dessen Architektur die Formen der Natur aufgreift und fortschreibt und das alte Traditionen mit modernen Ansprüchen verbindet. Wie ein mächtiger Baumstamm liegt das Gebäude am Hang – aus Holz, Stein sowie Glas konstruiert und mit durchdachten Details versehen: So wurde das Flachdach dank einer Humusschicht begrünt, und in den schnörkellos designten Zimmern werden Wohnbereich und Bad durch eine beheizte Lehmwand getrennt – vor allem im Winter eine herrliche Wärmequelle! Eine Wasserquelle speist das Spa, in dem sich schlichte Pflegeprodukte als wahre Schätze erweisen: Eine Bergkräuter-Massage oder ein Südtiroler Heubad bringen den Gast dem Himmel noch näher, als man in 1500 Metern Höhe ohnehin schon ist. ◆ Buchtipp: „Der Himmel über Meran“ von Joseph Zoderer.

EN TOUTE QUIÉTUDE Il suffit de sept minutes pour arriver dans un autre monde, le temps nécessaire à la télécabine partie de la station de la vallée à Lana pour rejoindre le Vigiljoch à 1 500 mètres d'altitude, là où il n'y a ni voitures ni bruits de circulation, ni bureaux paysagers ni supermarchés. Loin du quotidien, on jouit ici de la vue sur les sommets du Tyrol du Sud, on respire un air vivifiant qui embaume le mélèze et on foule des prairies où fleurit la gentiane. On raconte qu'un géant très croyant aurait vécu il y a bien longtemps dans cette région idyllique et qu'il aurait construit une église – Matteo Thun a suivi son exemple en concevant au début du troisième millénaire le Vigilius Mountain Resort. Natif du Tyrol du Sud, Thun voulait doter sa région d'un hôtel dont l'architecture reprendrait les formes de la nature et marierait les traditions anciennes et les exigences modernes. Tel un énorme tronc d'arbre, le bâtiment, construit en bois, en pierre et en verre et doté de détails sophistiqués, repose sur le flanc de la montagne. Le toit plat a ainsi été recouvert d'une couche d'humus pour le végétaliser et, dans les chambres au décor sobre, un mur en argile chauffé sépare la salle de bains et la partie séjour – rayonnant d'une sublime chaleur en hiver. Nature encore – de l'eau de source énergisante alimente le spa dans lequel des produits de soin tout simples s'avèrent très précieux : un massage aux plantes des montagnes ou un bain de foin sud-tyrolien nous emmène au septième ciel. ◆ À lire : « L'Hiver tyrolien » d'Elisabeth Demaison.

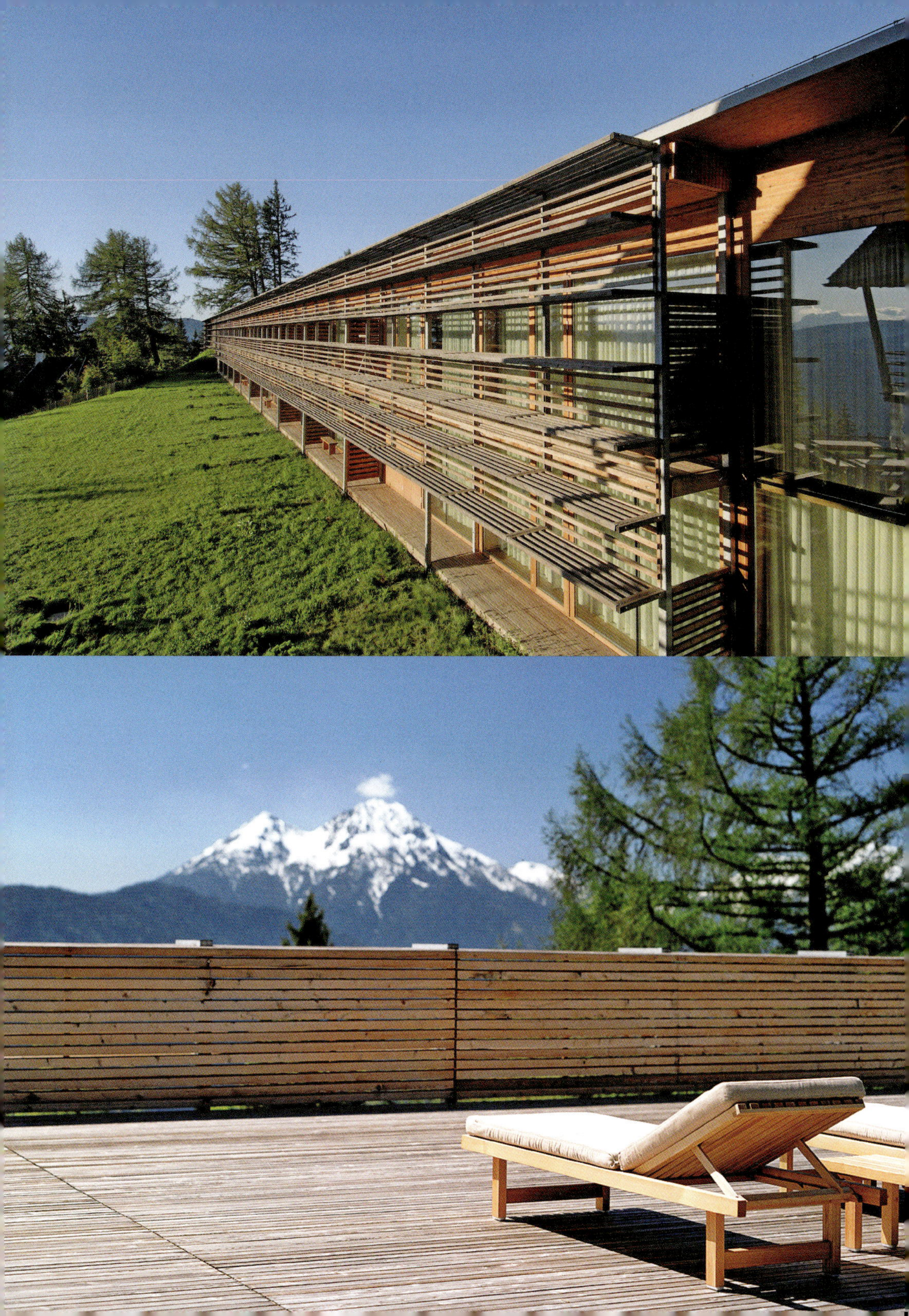

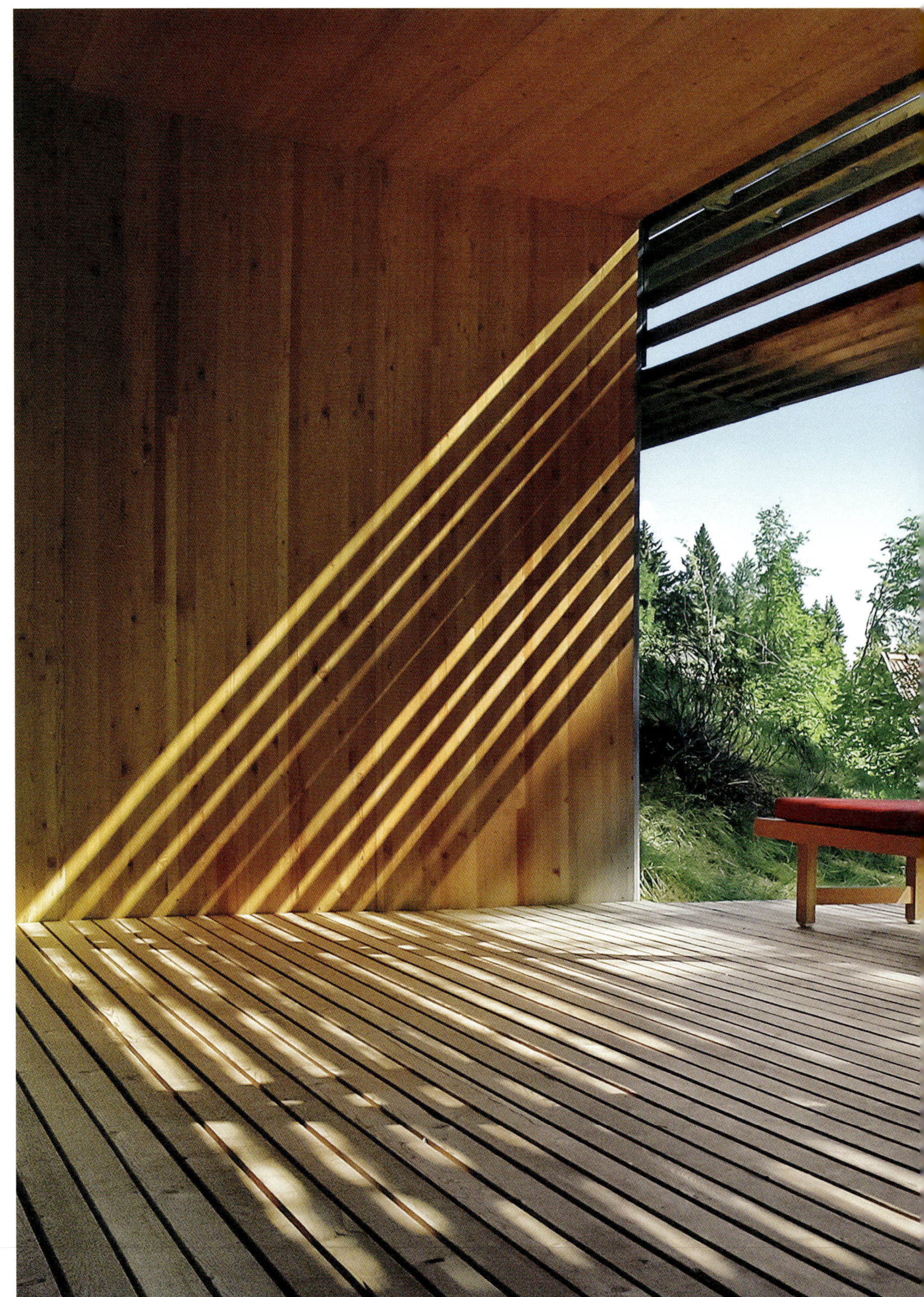

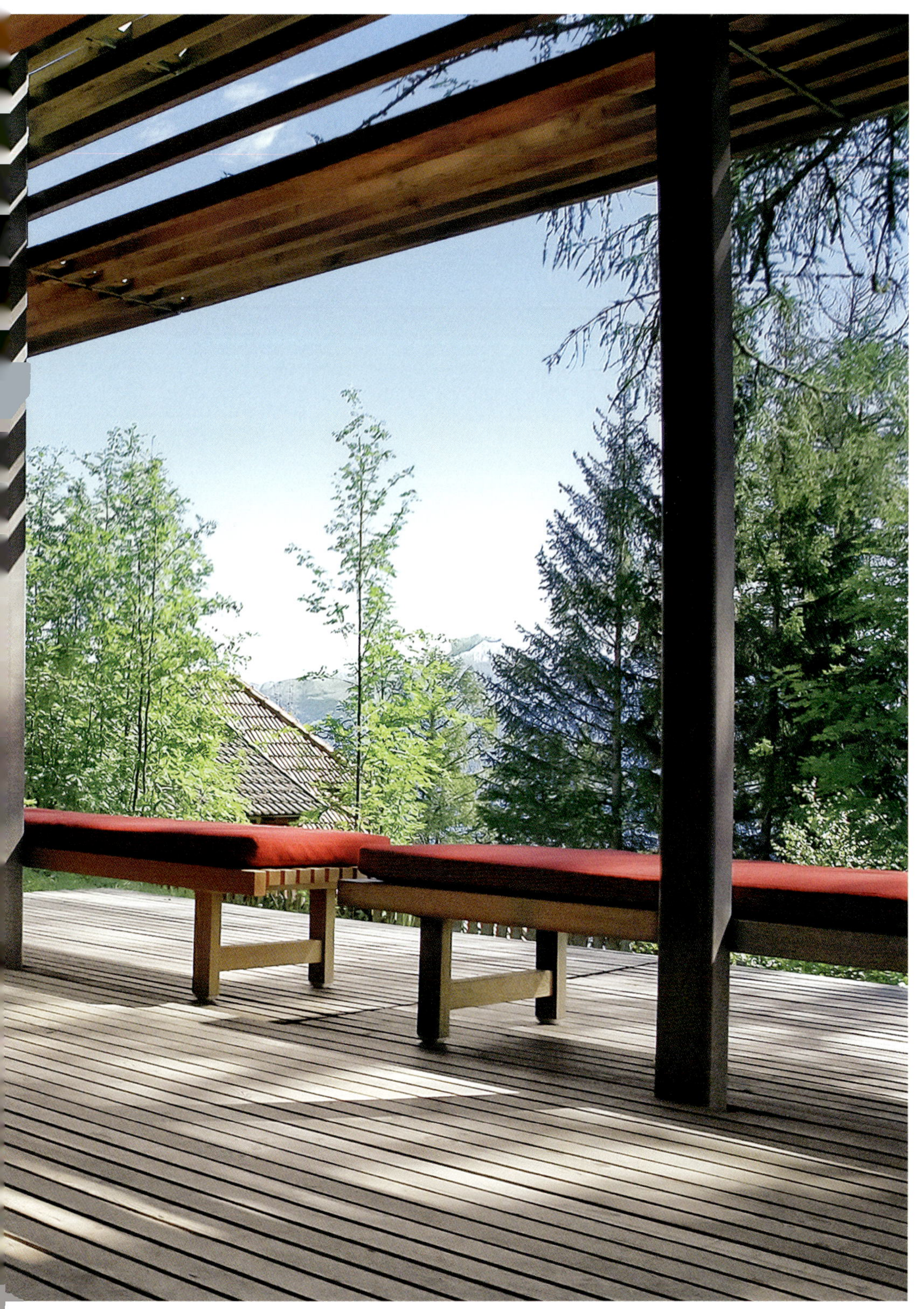

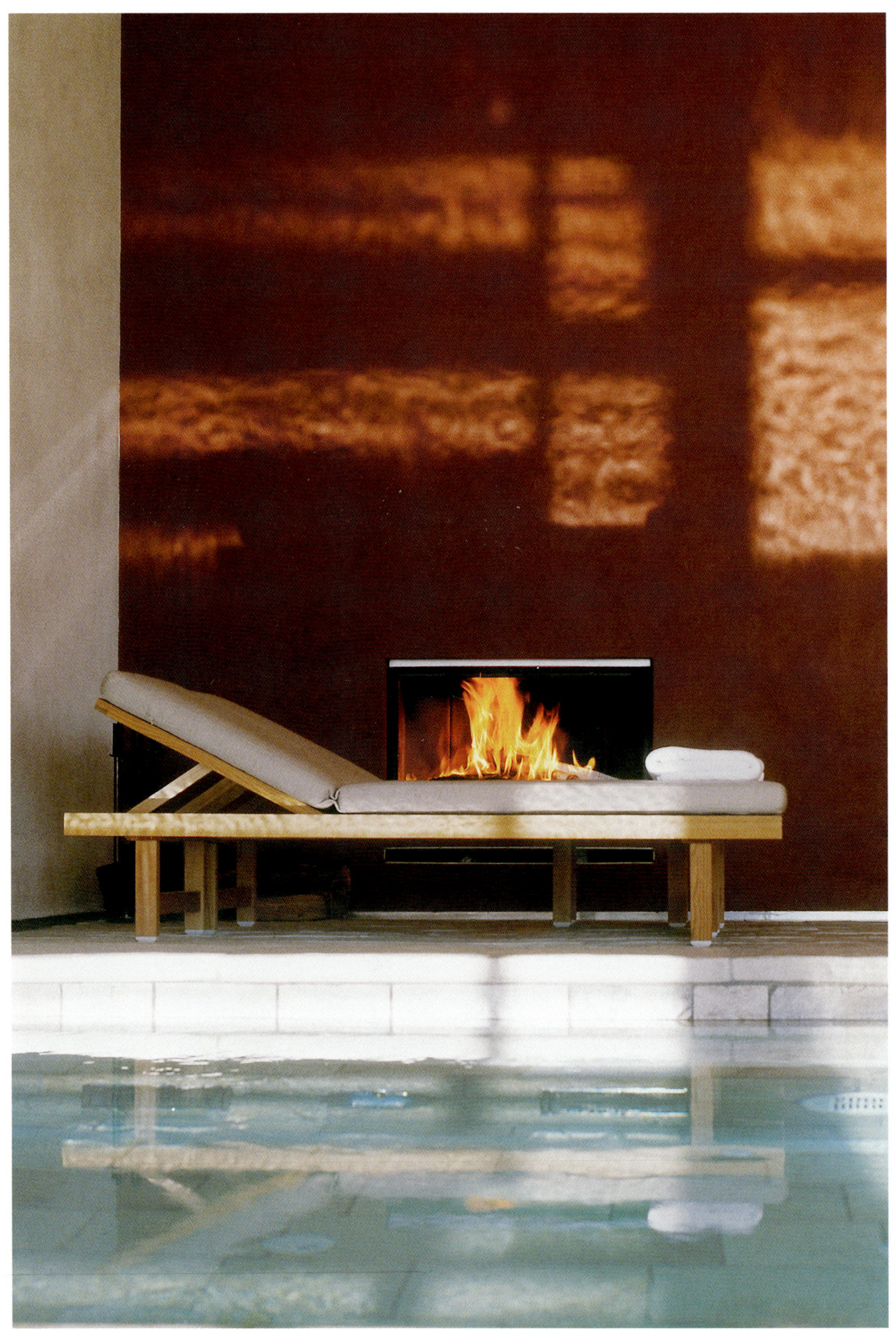

ALTO ADIGE

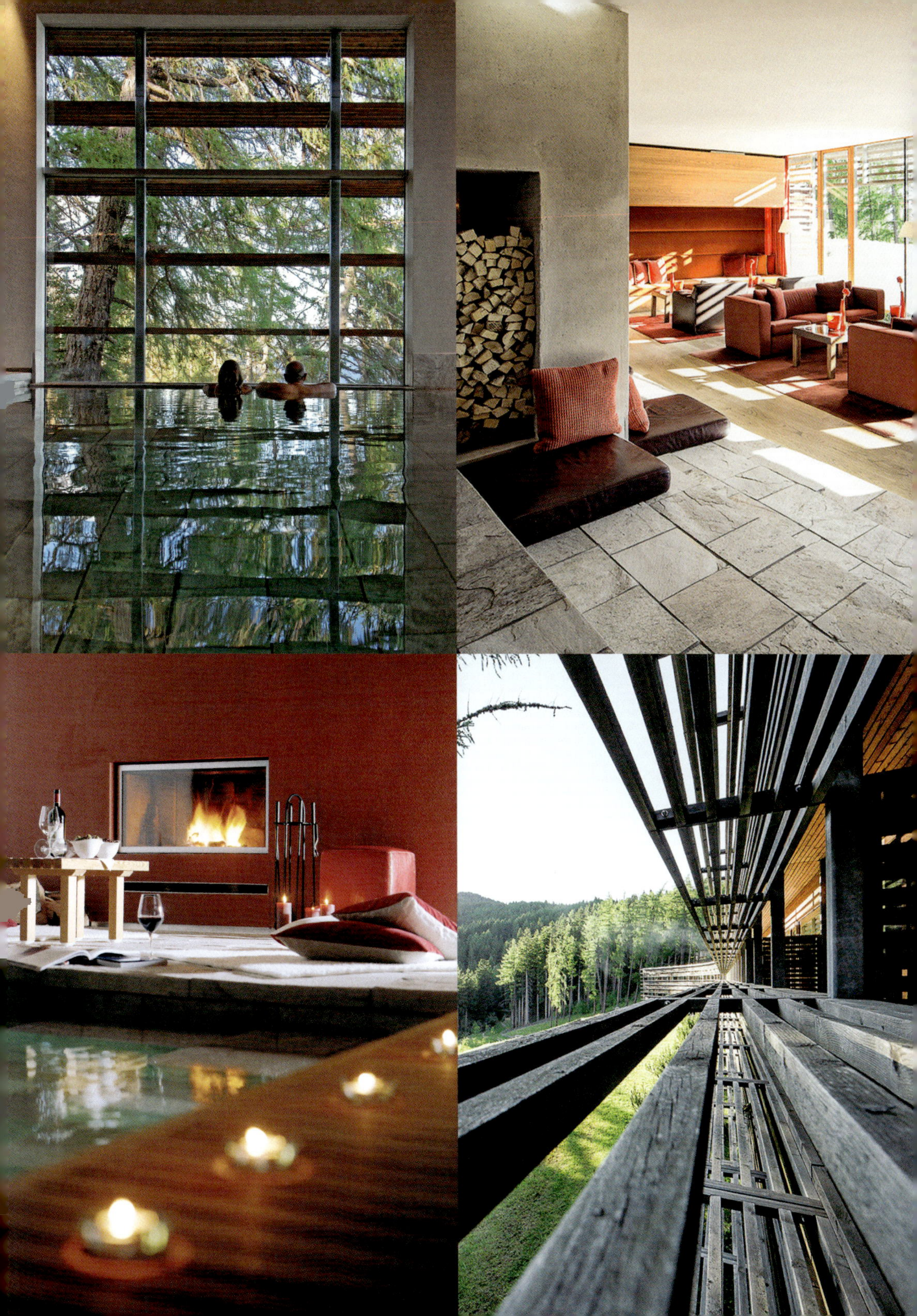

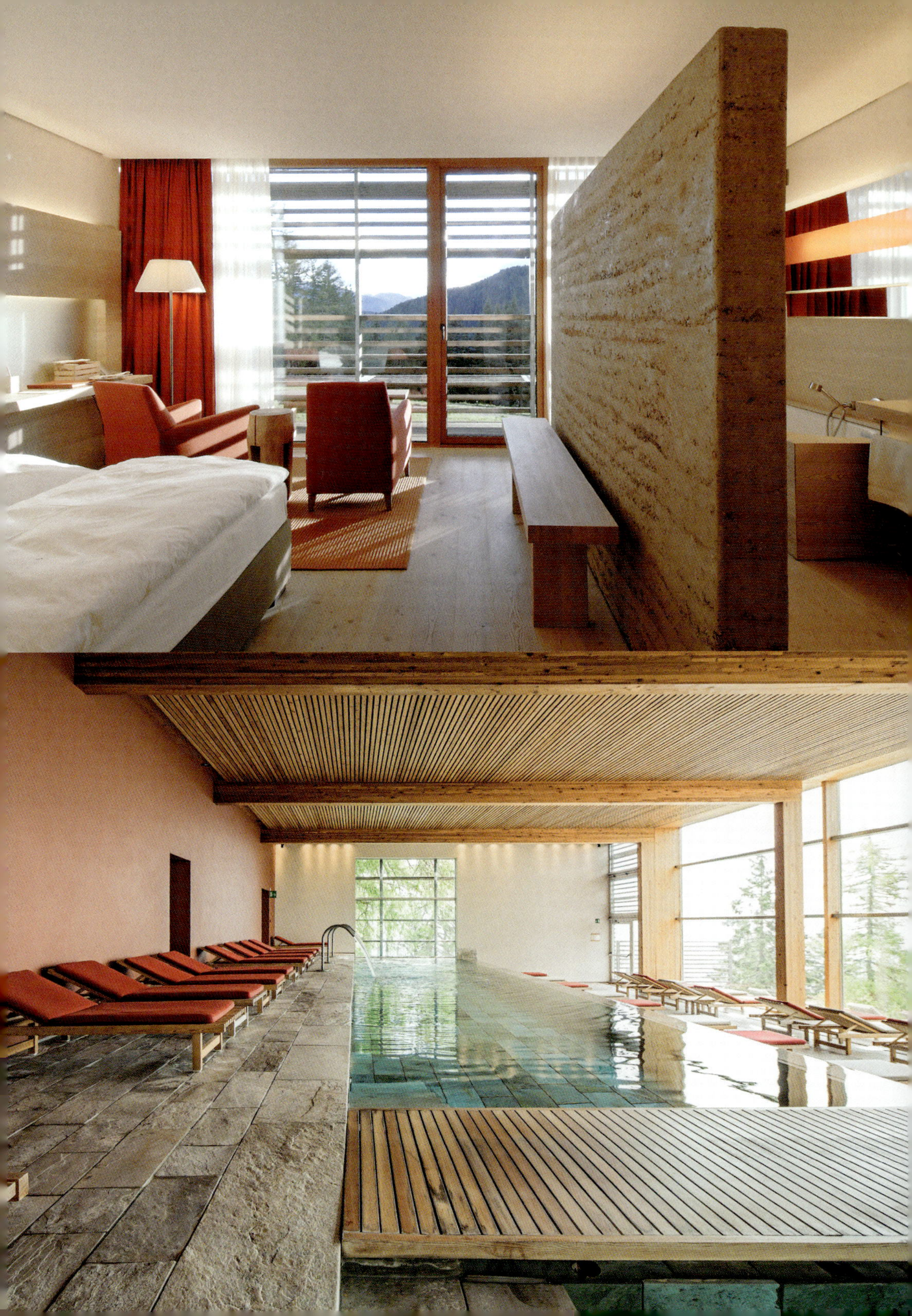

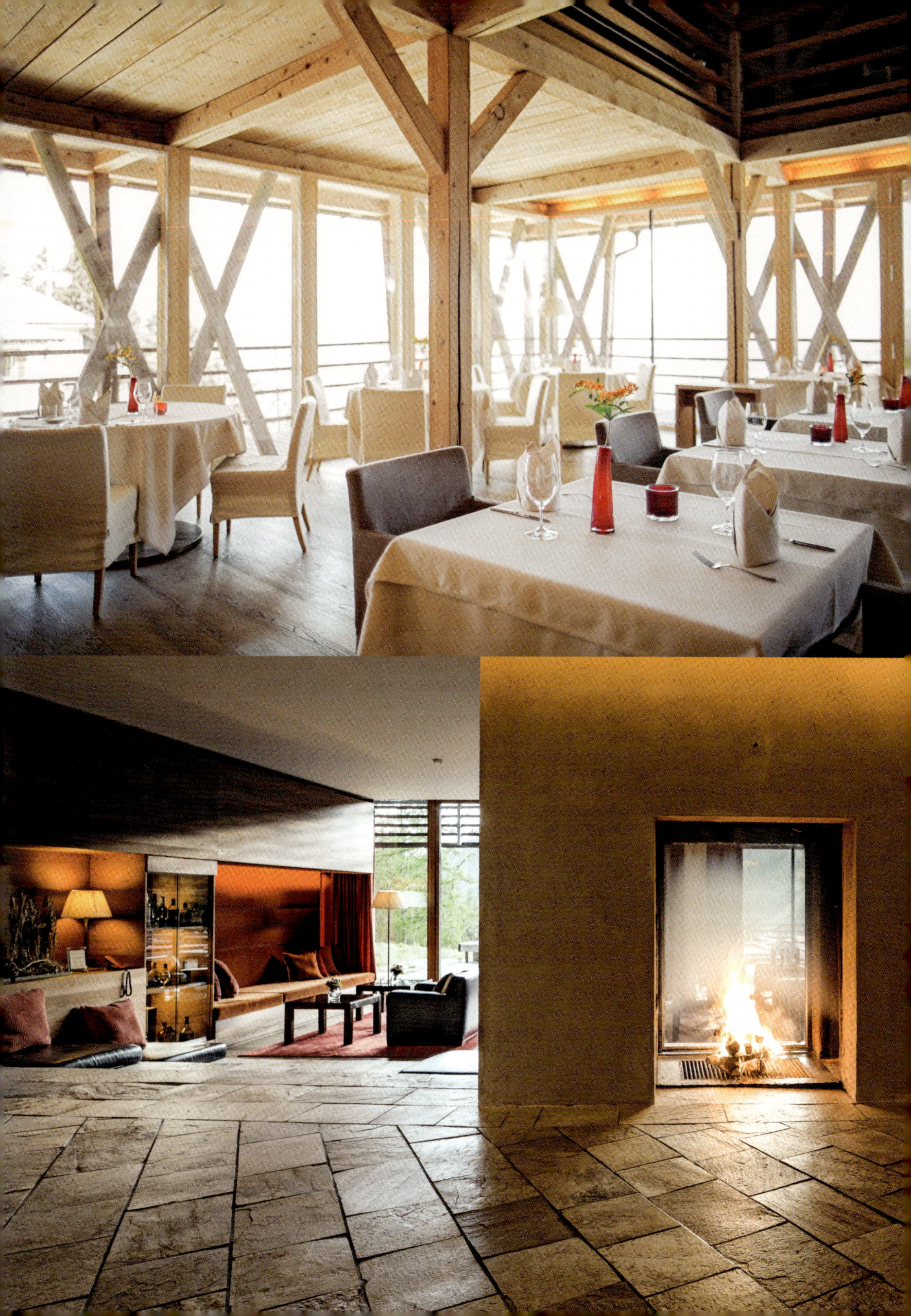

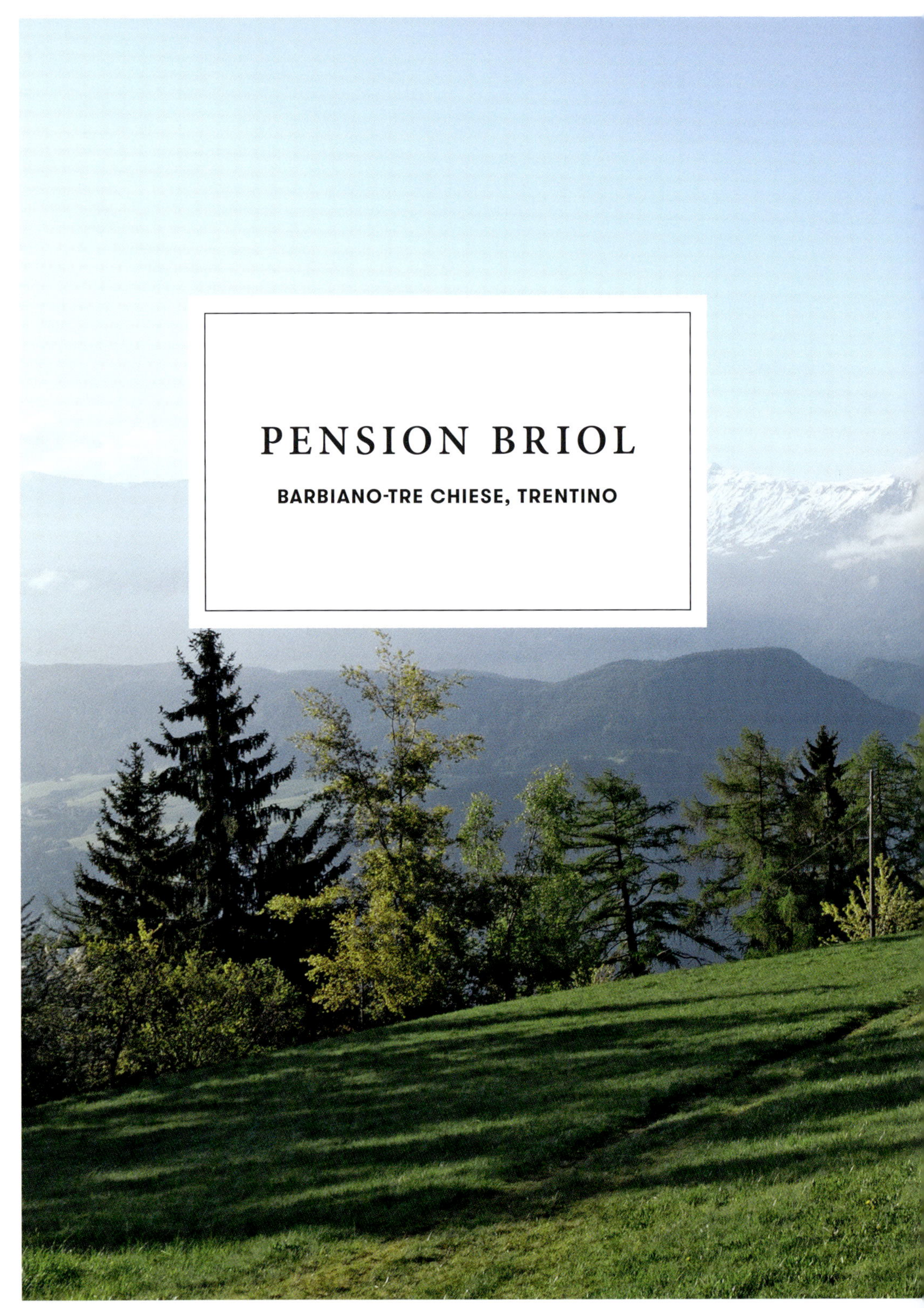

PENSION BRIOL

BARBIANO-TRE CHIESE, TRENTINO

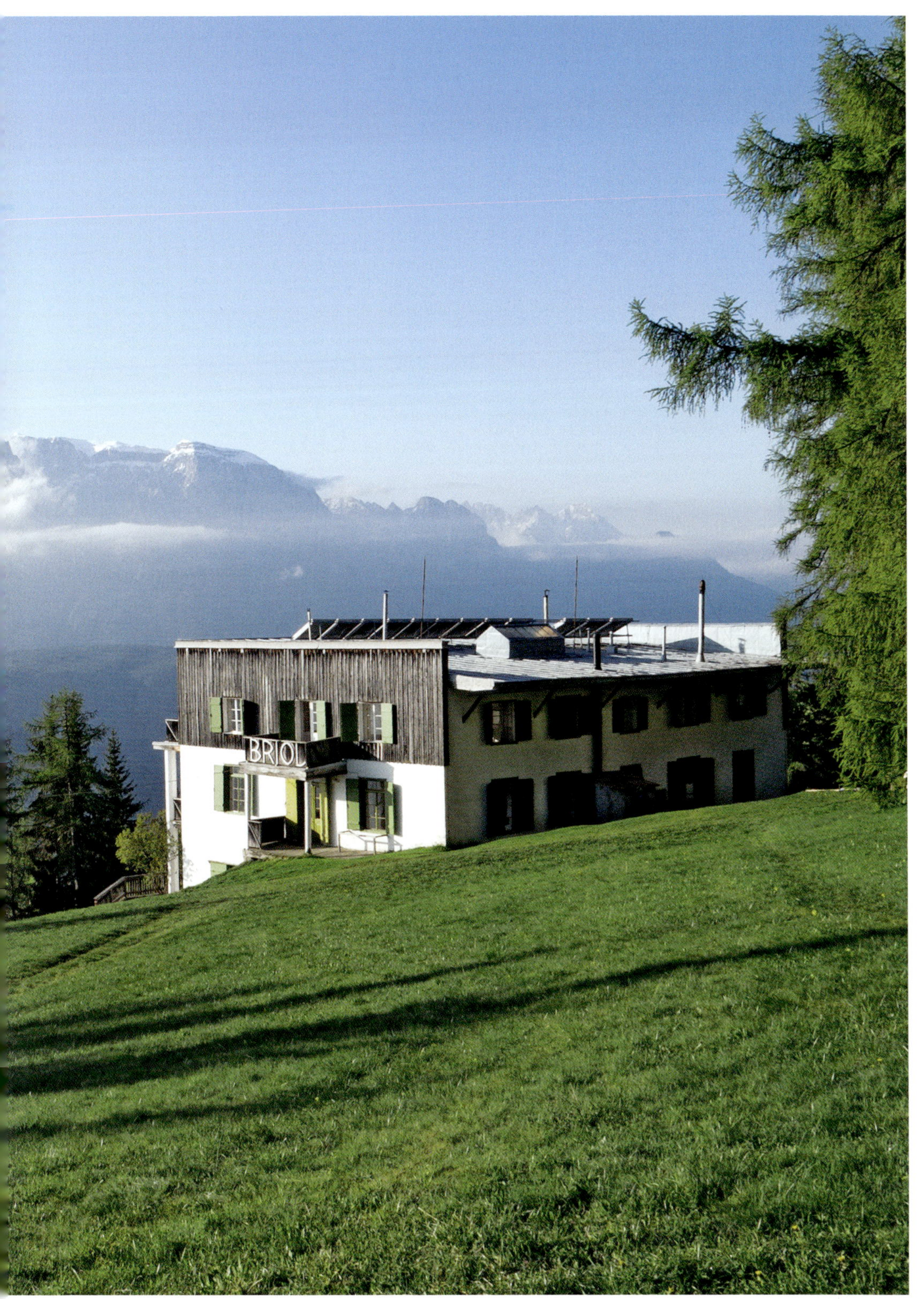
BRIOL

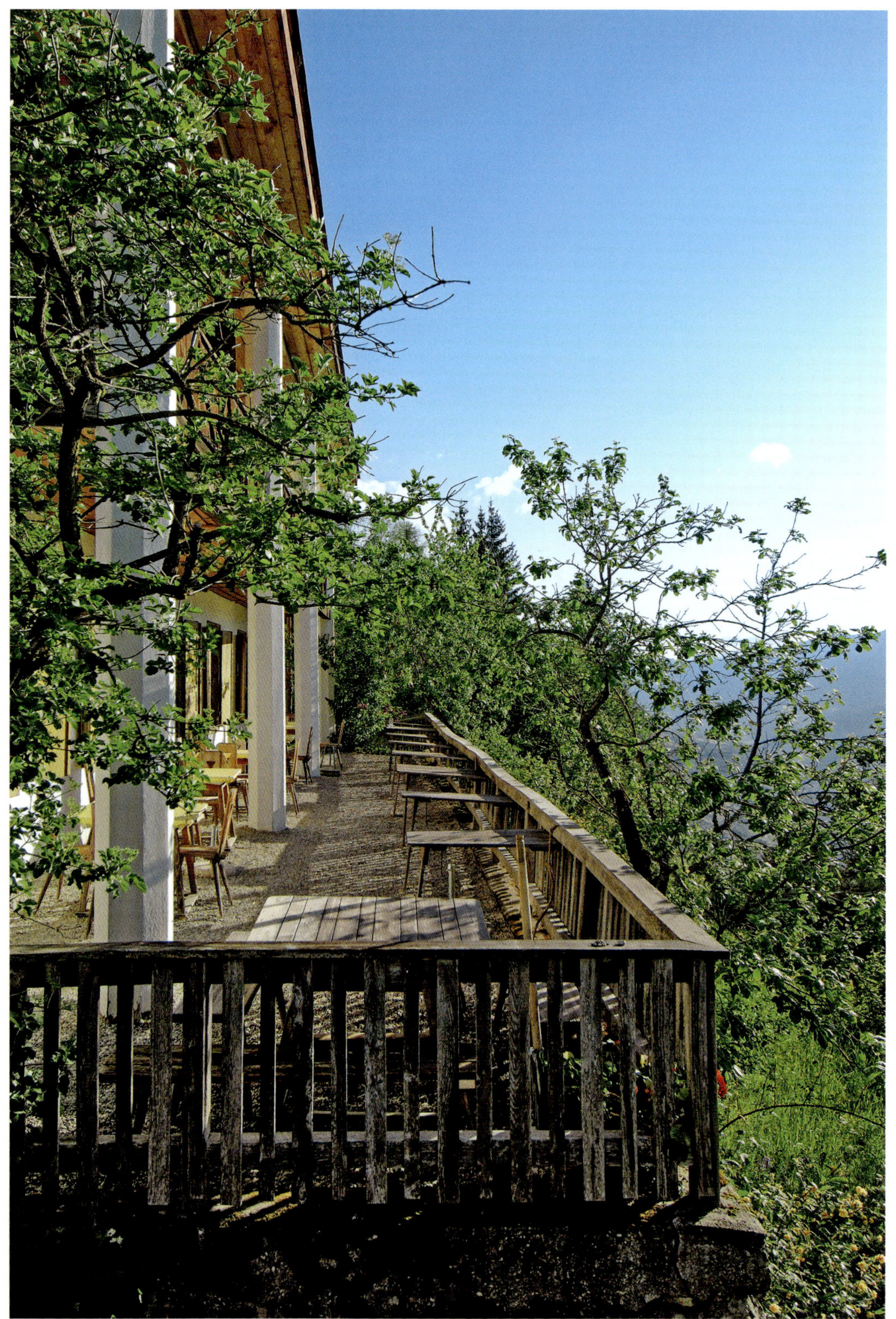

PENSION BRIOL

39040 Barbiano-Tre Chiese
Tel. +39 0471 650 125 · info@briol.it
www.briol.it

HOLIDAYS FROM GRANDMOTHER'S DAYS A high-carat ring, a beautiful dress, or fine porcelain for special occasions – the classic gifts from a husband to his wife after the birth of their child were not what Johanna Settari dreamed of. The wish that she expressed while still in childbed was more unusual: a plot of land "on the mountain" was what she wanted, a property above the Valle Isarco in South Tyrol, the homeland that she loved above all else. And since Johanna was married to a wealthy Bolzano merchant, who made her wish come true for every child, and since she gave birth to eleven girls and a boy, she eventually ultimately owned a considerable amount of land. The extended family enjoyed wonderful summers here, and soon had the company of tourists: visitors who took a break from their everyday routine at Pension Briol, which was designed in 1928 by the artist Hubert Lanzinger, Johanna's son-in-law. In the plain Bauhaus style he produced an all-round work of art in which every detail is both beautiful and functional, and harmonizes ideally with the whole. To this day these surroundings have remained unchanged. The rooms are fitted with larch wood and have no curtains in order to leave the view of the Dolomites unobstructed. Guests use the original washbasins and are treated to specialties from the Settaris' old recipe book. The outbuildings, too, are now used for accommodation, including the pretty "Mutterhäusl" (mother's cottage), where Johanna once lived, "Haus Settari," previously the sphere of the children, and "Einäugl" (One-Eye), a circular building by the architect Theo Gallmetzer that opened in 2022. The whole estate is run with heart and soul by Johanna's great-granddaughter: like all the properties "on the mountain," the house has stayed in family ownership, which was a further wish of the resolute lady who founded it.
◆ Book to pack: "The Pope's Daughter" by Dario Fo.

URLAUB WIE ZU URGROSSMUTTERS ZEITEN Ein hochkarätiger Ring, ein traumhaftes Kleid oder feines Sonntagsporzellan – mit den Klassikern, die Ehemänner ihren Frauen nach der Geburt eines Babys schenken, konnte man Johanna Settari nicht begeistern. Sie äußerte vom Wochenbett aus einen ungewöhnlichen Wunsch: Ein Stück Land „am Berg" wollte sie gerne haben, ein Grundstück oberhalb des Eisacktals – ihrer Südtiroler Heimat, die sie über alles liebte. Und da Johanna mit einem wohlhabenden Kaufmann aus Bozen verheiratet war, der ihr diesen Wunsch bei allen Kindern erfüllte, und sie elf Mädchen sowie vier Jungen zur Welt brachte, gehörte ihr schließlich ein sehr ansehnliches Areal. Hier verbrachte die Großfamilie herrliche Sommer – und bekam bald Gesellschaft von Touristen: Die Besucher nahmen ihre Auszeit vom Alltag in der Pension Briol, die Johannas Schwiegersohn, der Künstler Hubert Lanzinger, 1928 gestaltet hatte – im schnörkellosen Bauhausstil und als Gesamtkunstwerk, in dem alle Details so schön wie funktional und ideal aufeinander abgestimmt sind. Bis heute wurde das Ambiente im Haupthaus nicht verändert. Man wohnt in Zimmern, die mit Lärchenholz ausgestattet sind und zugunsten eines freien Dolomitenblicks auf Vorhänge verzichten, benutzt die originalen Waschschüsseln und schwelgt in Spezialitäten aus dem alten Rezeptbuch der Besitzer. Auch die Nebengebäude dienen inzwischen als Urlaubsunterkünfte – darunter das hübsche „Mutterhäusl", in dem Johanna einst wohnte, das „Haus Settari", ehemals Reich der Kinder, sowie das 2022 eröffnete „Einäugl", ein moderner Rundbau des Architekten Theo Gallmetzer. Mit viel Herz geführt wird das gesamte Anwesen von Johannas Urenkelin, denn Häuser und Grundstücke „am Berg" sind stets im Besitz der Familie geblieben – auch dies einer der Wünsche der resoluten Dame. ◆ Buchtipp: „Wo ist dein Haus" von Sepp Mall.

COMME AU TEMPS D'ARRIÈRE-GRAND-MAMAN Ce que les maris offrent habituellement à leur épouse après la naissance d'un enfant – une bague de prix, une robe magnifique ou de la porcelaine fine – ne subjuguait pas Johanna Settari qui, à peine relevée de couches, exprima un souhait insolite : ce qu'elle voulait, elle, c'était un terrain sur la montagne, au-dessus de la vallée de l'Isarco (Eisacktal), sa patrie sud-tyrolienne qu'elle aimait plus que tout. Mariée à un riche marchand de Bolzano qui ne songeait qu'à la satisfaire, Johanna mit au monde onze filles et quatre garçons, ce qui fait que, finalement, elle se retrouva propriétaire d'un domaine de taille respectable. La famille passait ici des étés merveilleux – et bientôt elle ne fut plus la seule à profiter de la beauté des paysages. Les touristes venaient se détendre à la pension Briol que le gendre de Johanna, l'artiste Hubert Lanzinger, avait meublée et décorée en 1928 dans un style Bauhaus dépouillé, créant une œuvre d'art totale dont tous les détails sont aussi beaux que fonctionnels et s'harmonisent parfaitement. L'ambiance n'a pas changé. On loge dans des chambres abritant des parquets et des meubles en épicéa et dépourvues de rideaux, ce qui permet d'admirer les Dolomites dans toute leur splendeur ; on utilise les cuvettes d'origine et on savoure les spécialités cuisinées d'après les recettes du vieux livre des propriétaires. Les dépendances servent aussi de logements de vacances – notamment le charmant « Mutterhäusl », où Johanna a vécu autrefois, le « Haus Settari », l'ancien domaine des enfants, et le « Einäugl », un bâtiment circulaire moderne conçu par l'architecte Theo Gallmetzer, qui a ouvert en 2022. La pension est dirigée avec une grande cordialité par l'arrière-petite-fille de Johanna, car les maisons et les terrains « sur la montagne » sont restés en possession de la famille, ainsi que l'avait imposé l'énergique ancêtre. ◆ À lire : « L'essence du mal » de Luca D'Andrea.

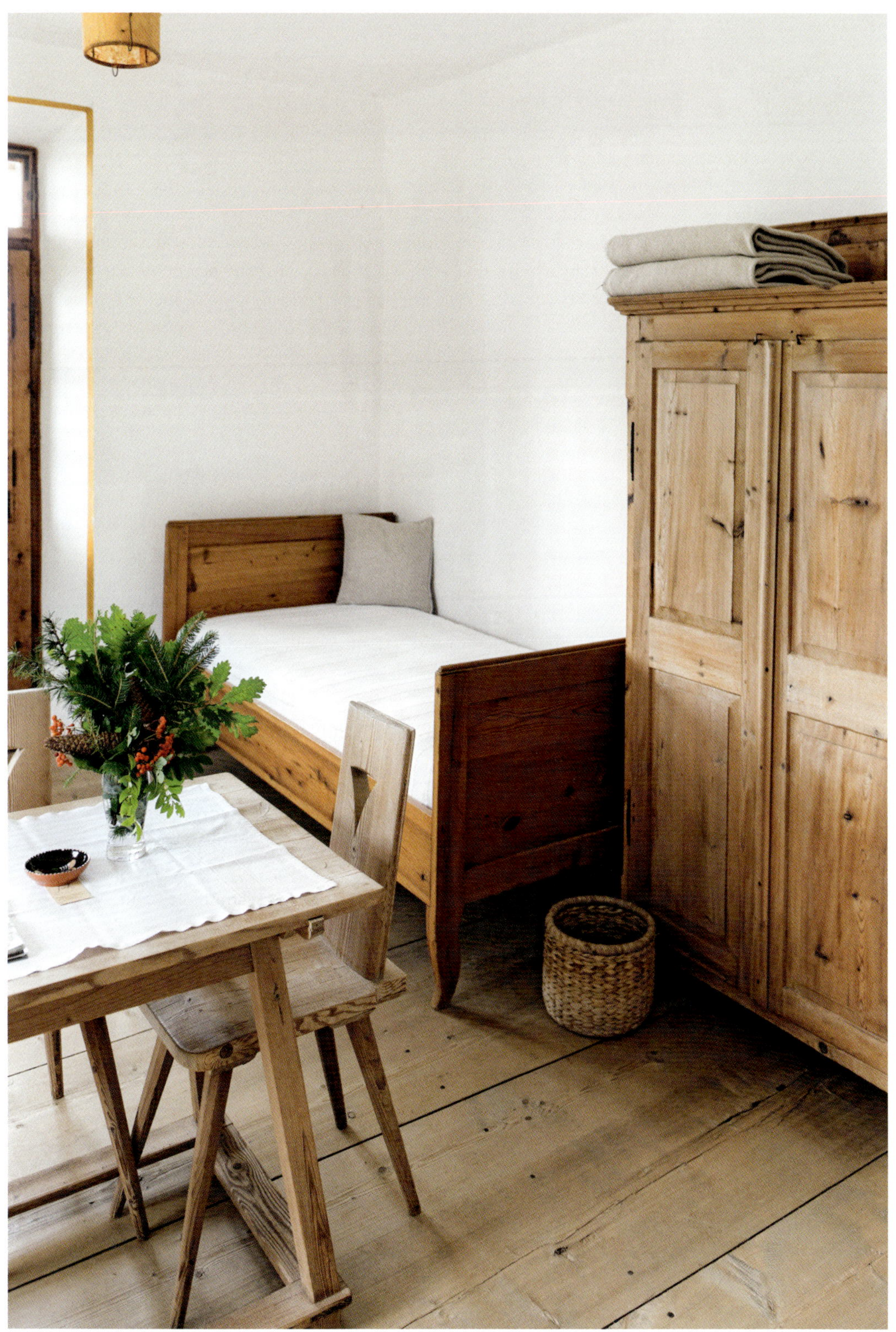

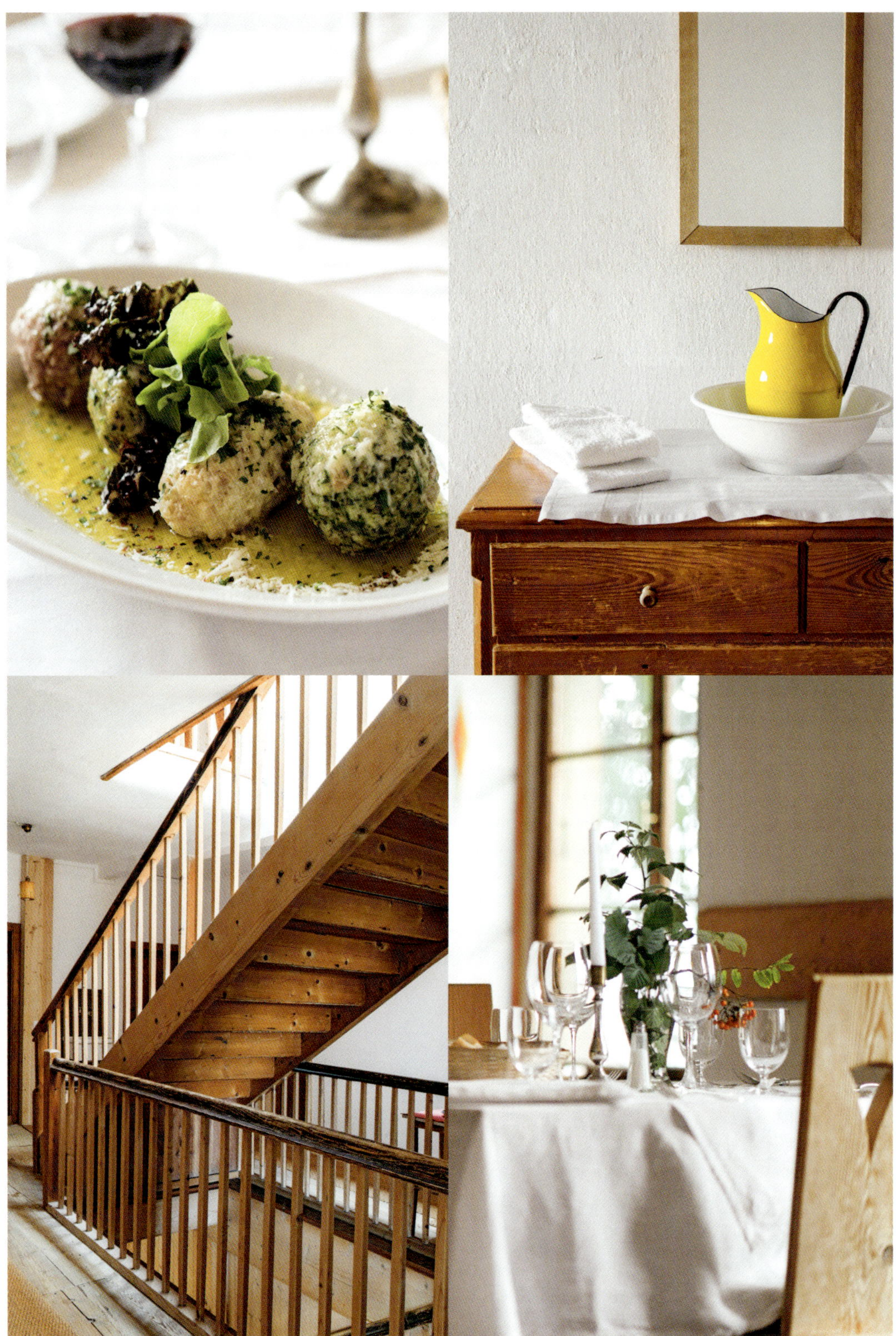

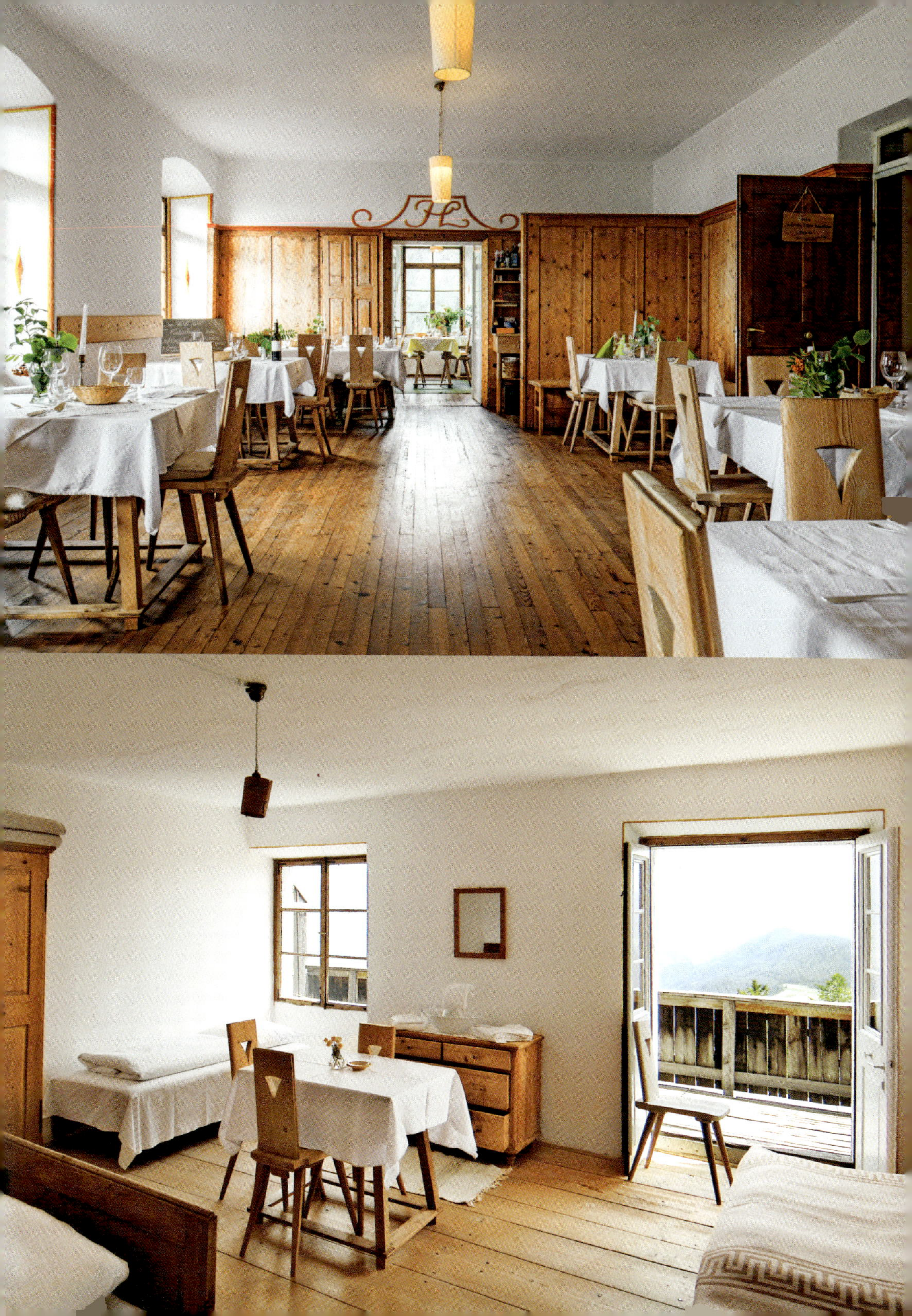

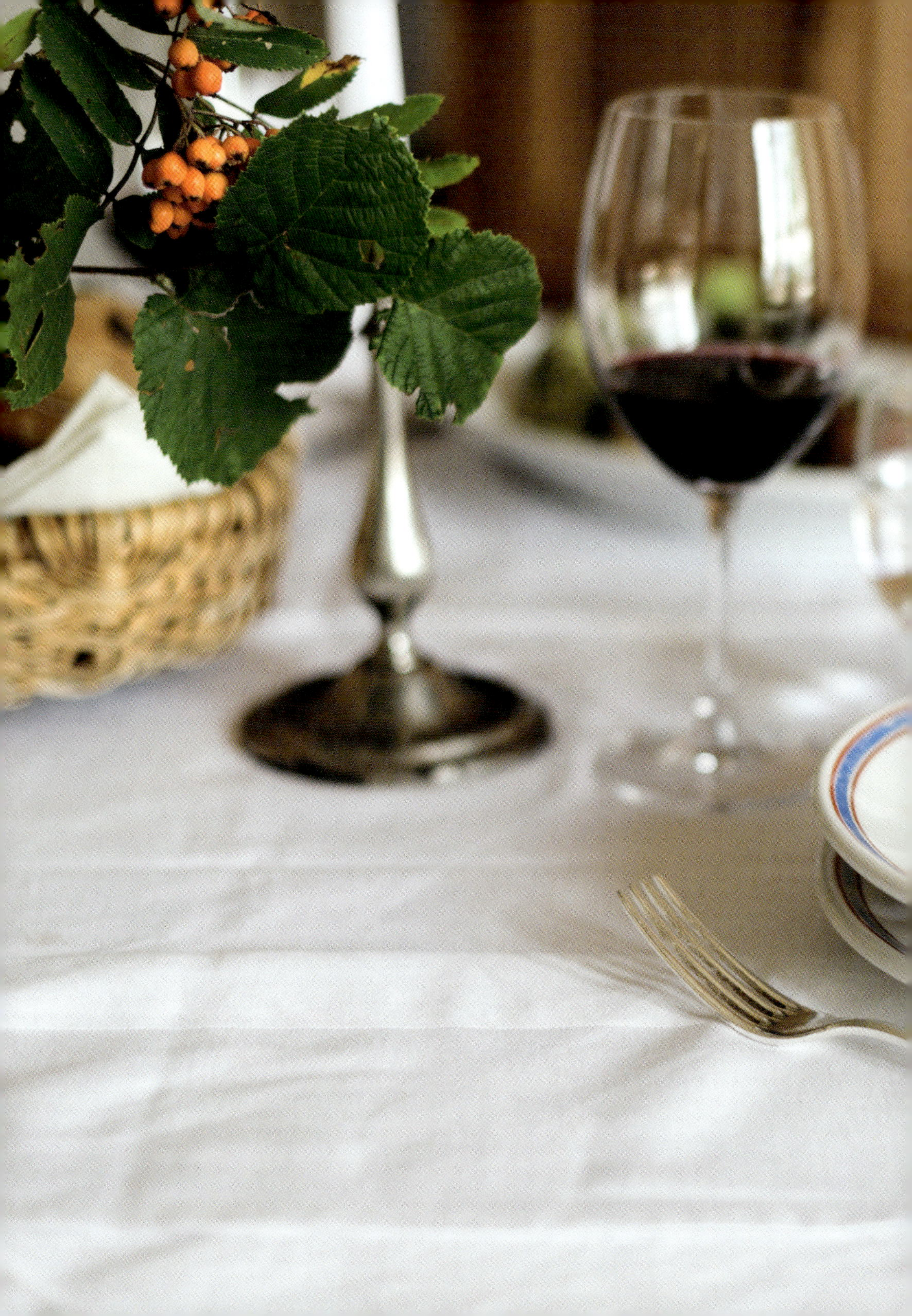

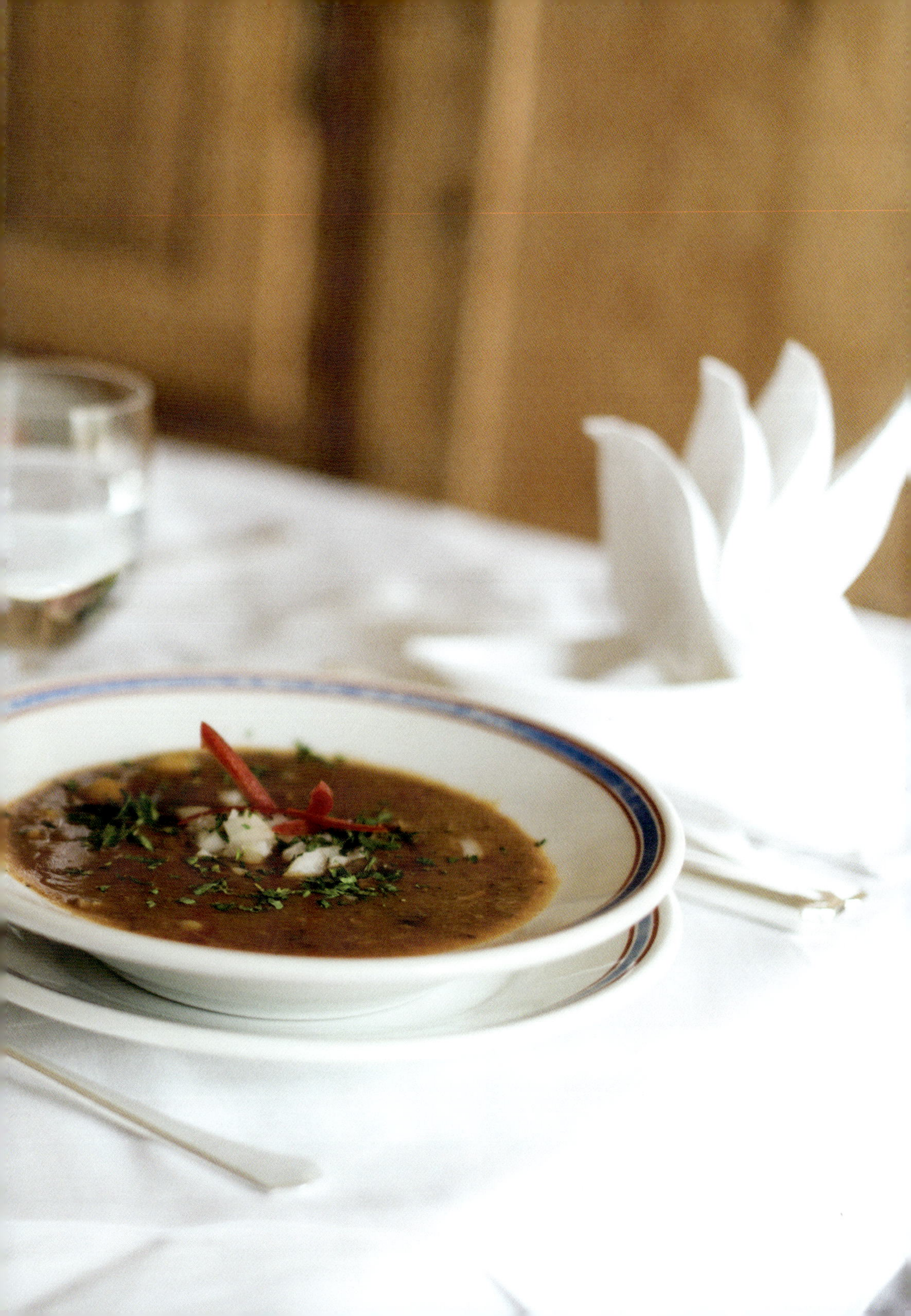

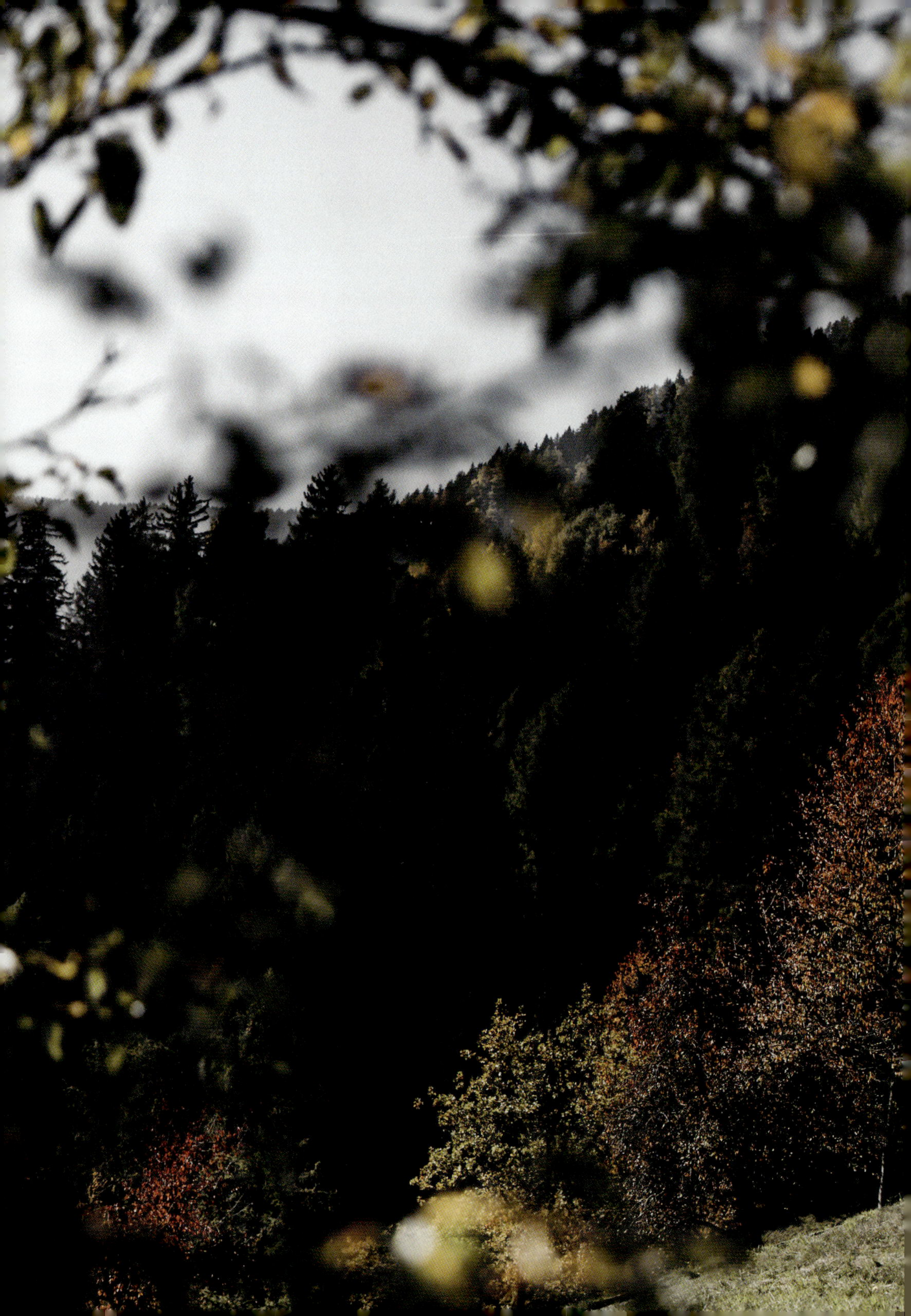

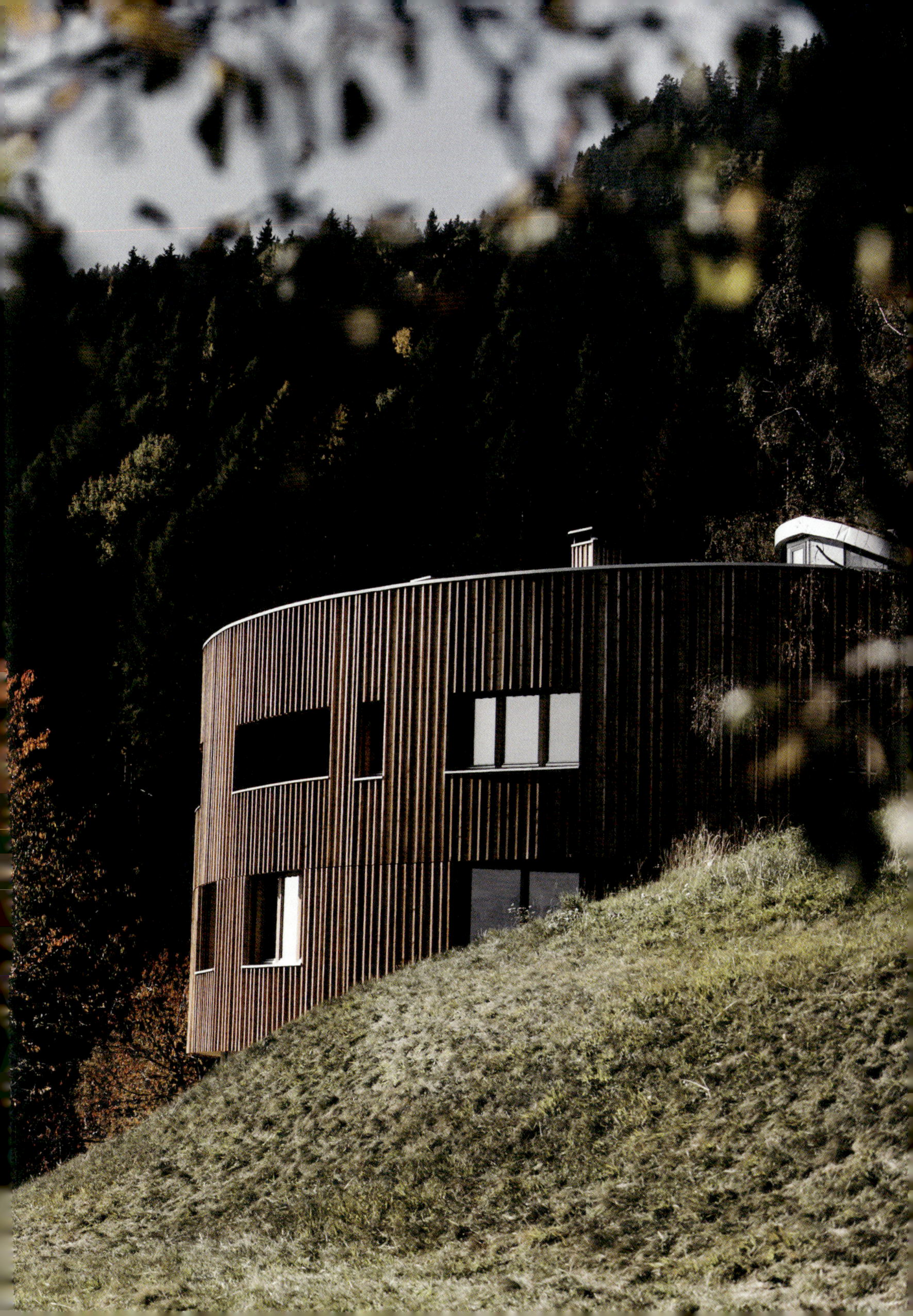

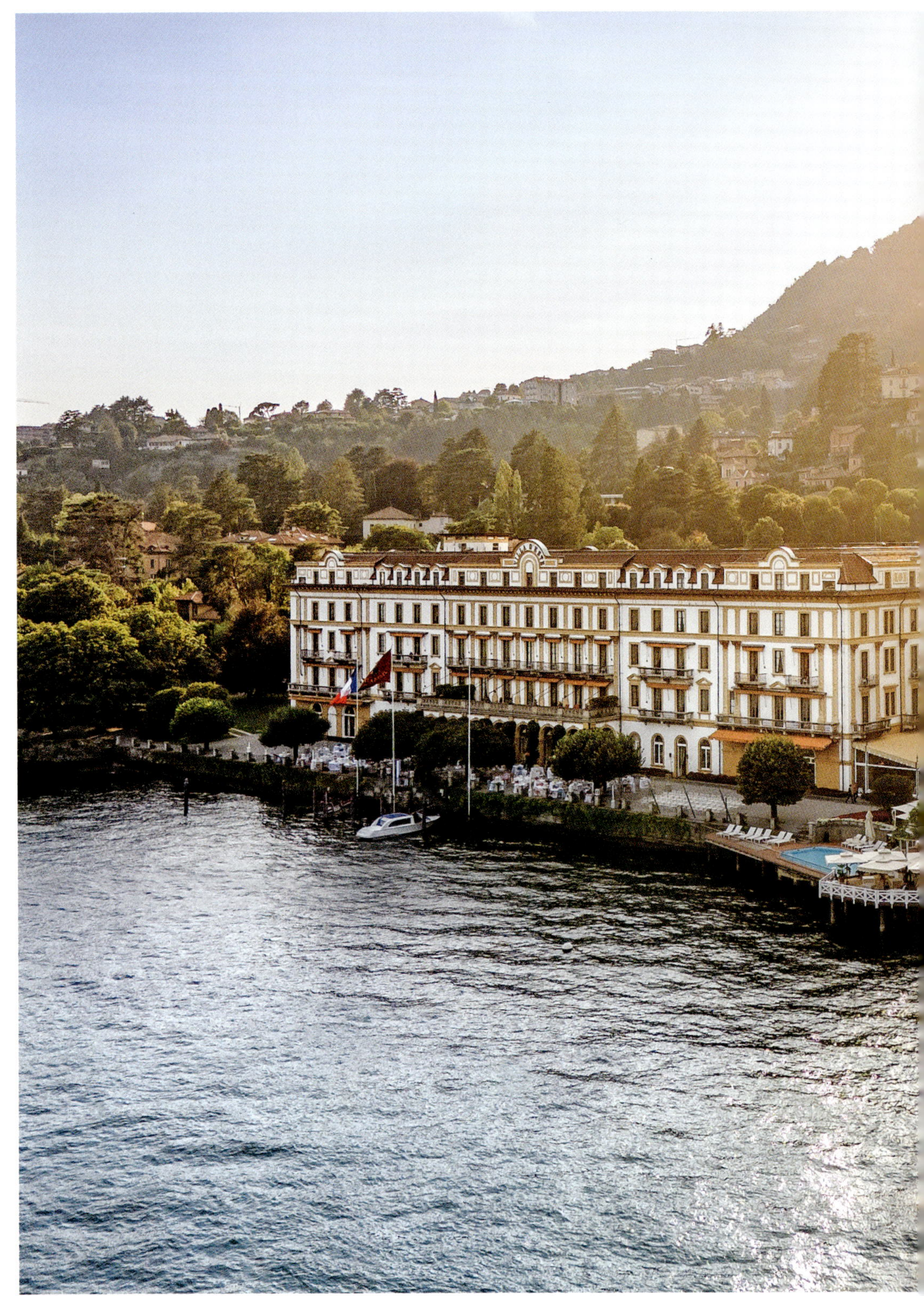

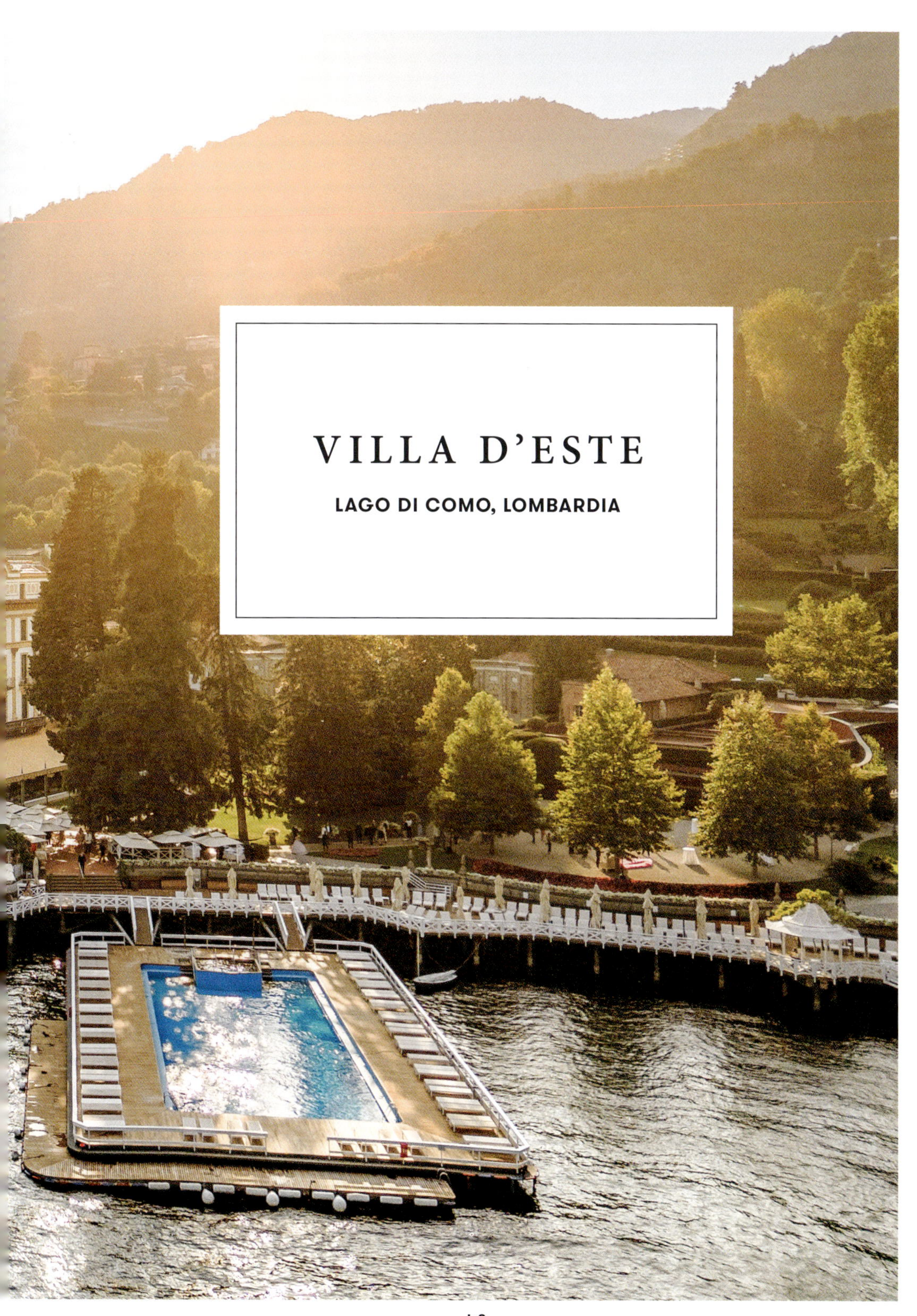

VILLA D'ESTE

LAGO DI COMO, LOMBARDIA

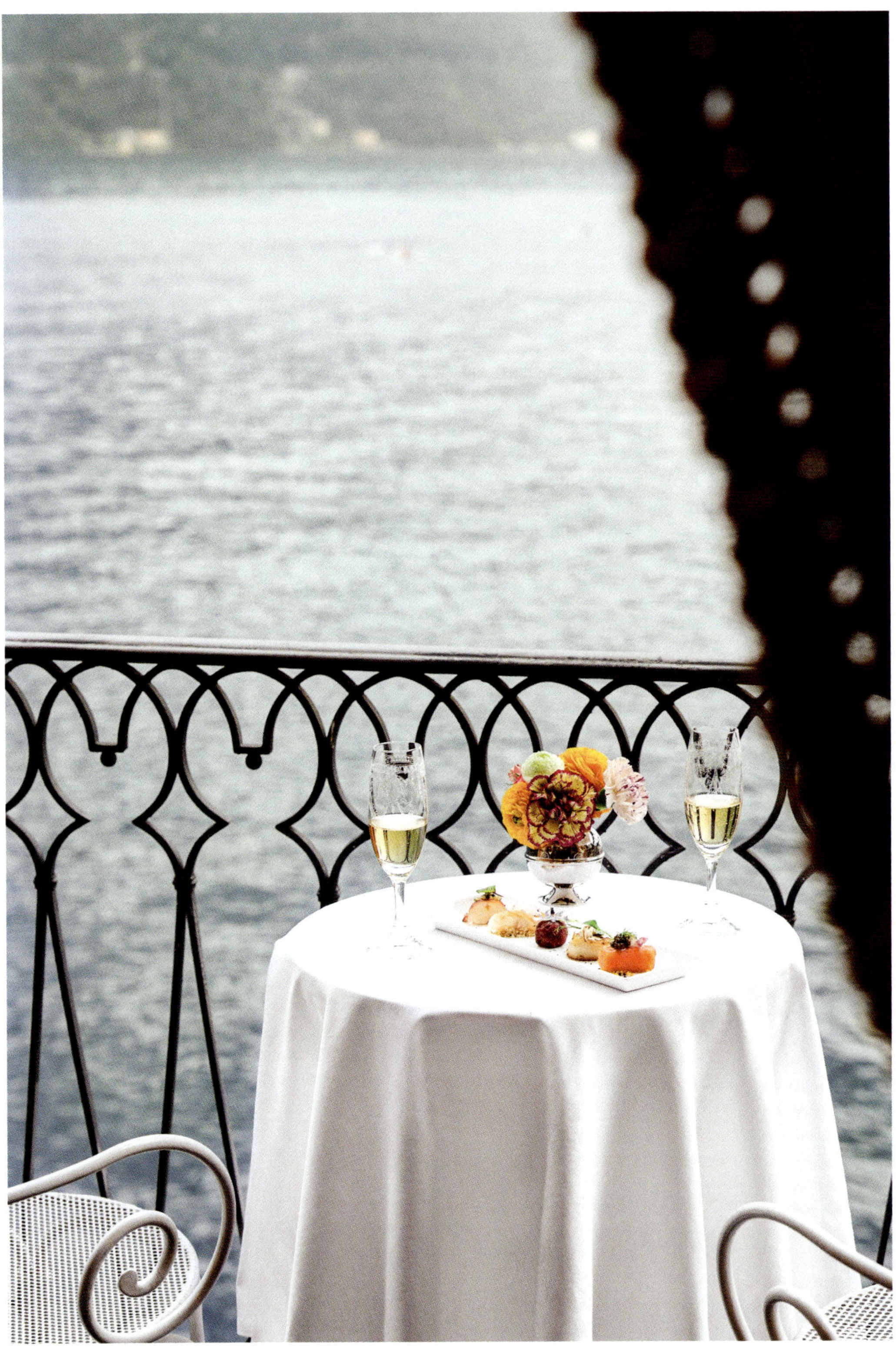

VILLA D'ESTE

Via Regina 40, 22012 Cernobbio
Tel. +39 031 3481 · info@villadeste.it
www.villadeste.com
Open from mid-March to early January

A LAKESIDE JEWEL They were cardinals, kings and artists, rich and refined, extravagant and eccentric, and consumed with a passion for Lago di Como, one of Italy's most romantic lakes: they were the owners of Villa d'Este. From the mid-16th to the mid-19th century this noble estate belonged to, among others, the Italian Cardinal Tolomeo Gallio, the ballerina Vittoria Peluso, who performed her pirouettes on the stage of La Scala in Milan, Domenico Pino, a Napoleonic general who played war games on the shores of the lake with his cadets, and Caroline of Brunswick, who took refuge here from her unhappy marriage to George IV of England. The memory of their glamour and the opulent charm of the Old World live on in Villa d'Este, which is today one of the most luxurious hotels in Italy. All rooms are furnished with antiques, rustling silk from nearby Como and original works of art, and no two rooms are alike. Guests reside particularly stylishly in the Queen's Pavilion wing, a trompe l'œil masterpiece. Those who are unable to book one of the coveted rooms with a balcony delight in the lake view from the floating pool deck and from the terrace at dinner. And a stroll through the perfectly manicured park is a chance to see faces known from Hollywood films: many of today's guests at Villa d'Este are no less famous than its owners of old.
◆ Book to pack: "The Charterhouse of Parma" by Stendhal.

EIN SCHMUCKSTÜCK AM SEE Sie waren Kardinäle, Könige und Künstler, reich und raffiniert, extravagant und exzentrisch – und voller Leidenschaft für den Comer See, der zu den romantischsten Seen Italiens gehört: die Besitzer der Villa d'Este. Zwischen Mitte des 16. und Mitte des 19. Jahrhunderts gehörte das noble Anwesen unter anderem dem italienischen Kardinal Tolomeo Gallio, der Ballerina Vittoria Peluso, die auf der Bühne der Mailänder Scala ihre Pirouetten drehte, dem General Napoleons, Domenico Pino, der mit seinen Kadetten auf dem Ufergrundstück Krieg spielte, sowie Caroline von Braunschweig-Wolfenbüttel, die hier Zuflucht vor ihrer unglücklichen Ehe mit Georg IV. von Großbritannien suchte. Die Erinnerung an diese schillernden Persönlichkeiten und der opulente Charme der Alten Welt sind in der Villa d'Este – heute eines der luxuriösesten Hotels des Landes – noch immer lebendig. Alle Zimmer wurden mit Antiquitäten, knisternder Seide aus dem nahen Como sowie originaler Kunst ausgestattet, und kein Raum gleicht dem anderen – besonders schön wohnt man im Reginapavillon, einem Meisterwerk des Trompe-l'Œil. Wer keines der begehrten Zimmer mit Balkon bekommen kann, bewundert den See vom schwimmenden Pooldeck aus und beim Dinner auf der Terrasse. Und beim Spaziergang durch den perfekt gestalteten Park kann man durchaus auf Gesichter treffen, die man aus Hollywood-Filmen kennt – viele heutige Gäste der Villa d'Este sind ebenso berühmt wie deren einstige Eigentümer. ◆ Buchtipp: „Die Kartause von Parma“ von Stendhal.

LE JOYAU DU LAC Princes de l'Église, monarques, artistes, personnages riches et raffinés, extravagants et excentriques – les propriétaires de la Villa d'Este aimaient tous passionnément le lac de Côme, l'un des lacs les plus romantiques d'Italie. Entre le milieu du XVIe et le milieu du XIXe siècle, le noble domaine appartint, entre autres, au cardinal italien Tolomeo Gallio, à la ballerine Vittoria Peluso qui évoluait sur la scène de la Scala de Milan, à Domenico Pino, un général de Napoléon qui jouait à la guerre avec ses soldats sur les berges du lac, ainsi qu'à Caroline de Brunswick qui tenta ici d'échapper à son mariage malheureux avec George IV d'Angleterre. Le souvenir de ces personnages hauts en couleur et le charme du Vieux Monde sont encore bien vivants à la Villa d'Este, devenue l'un des hôtels les plus luxueux du pays. Toutes les chambres sont meublées et décorées d'antiquités, de soieries froufroutantes originaires de Côme ainsi que d'œuvres d'art originales, et aucune pièce n'est semblable à l'autre. Le Pavillon Regina, un chef-d'œuvre du trompe-l'œil, est particulièrement intéressante. Celui qui n'a pas la chance de séjourner dans une des chambres avec balcon très convoitées admirera le lac depuis la piscine flottante ou depuis la terrasse en dînant. Et les promenades dans le superbe parc réservent des surprises : on peut y rencontrer des stars de Hollywood – nombre des clients actuels de la Villa d'Este sont aussi célèbres que ses anciens propriétaires. ◆ À lire : « La Chartreuse de Parme » de Stendhal.

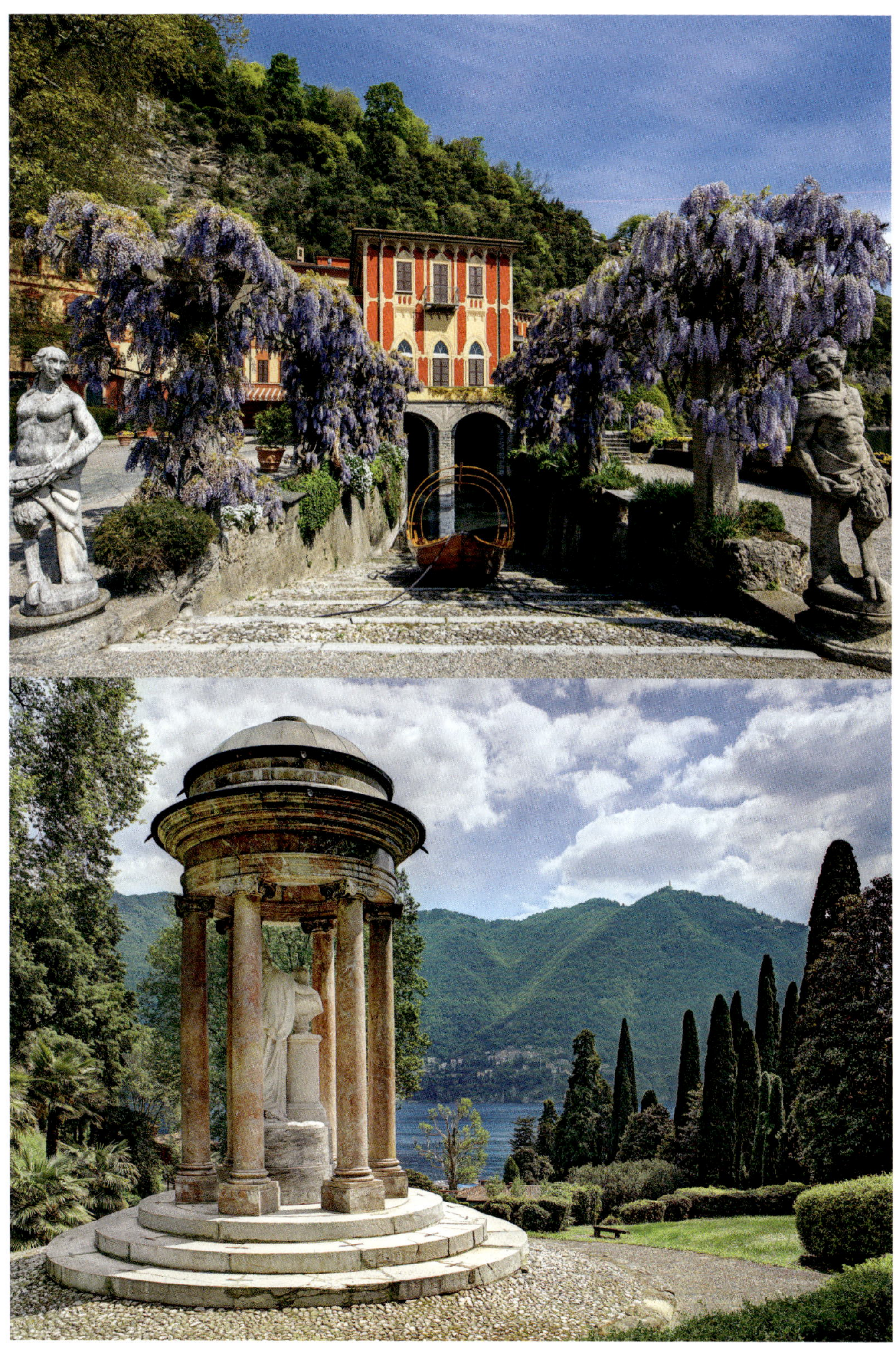

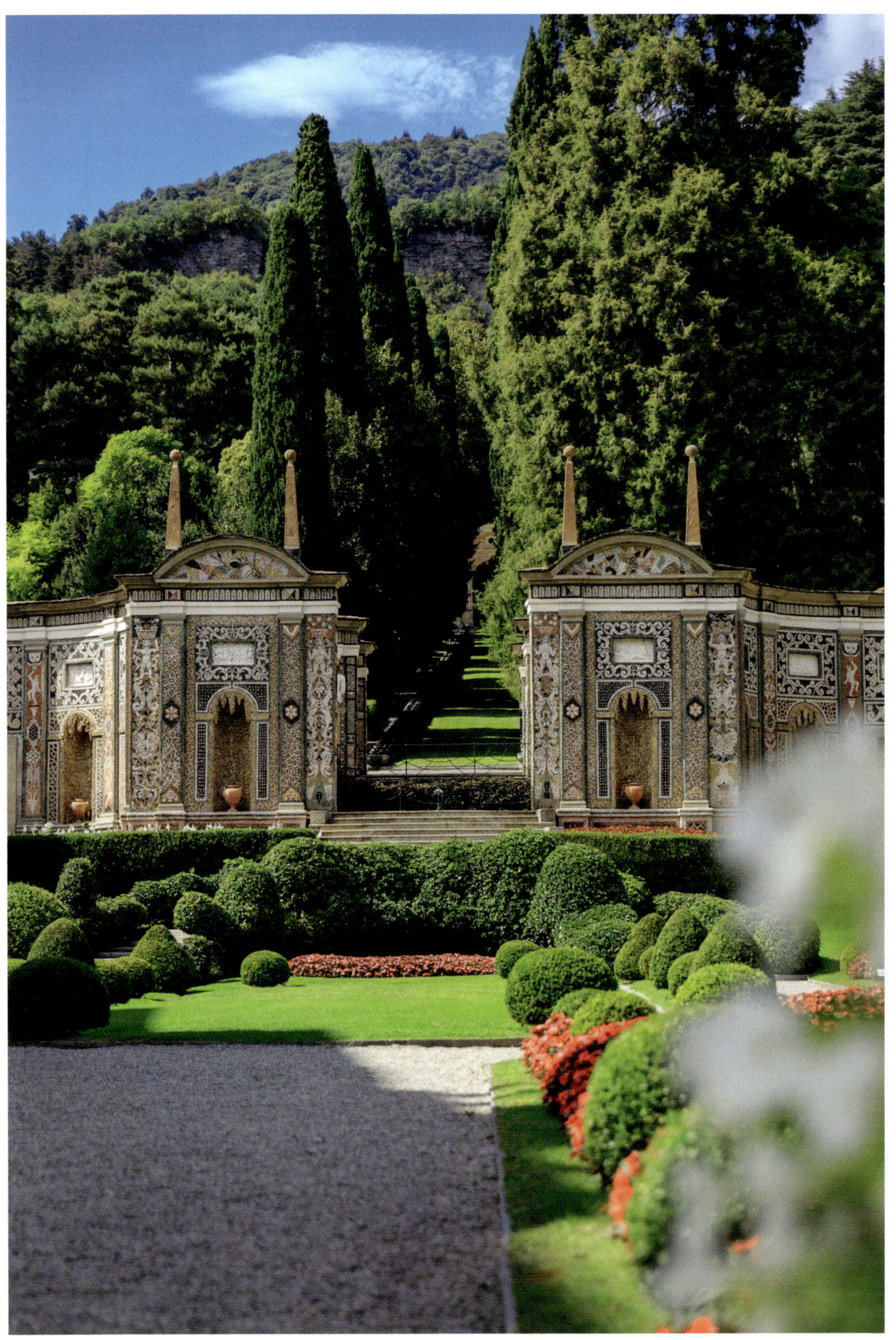

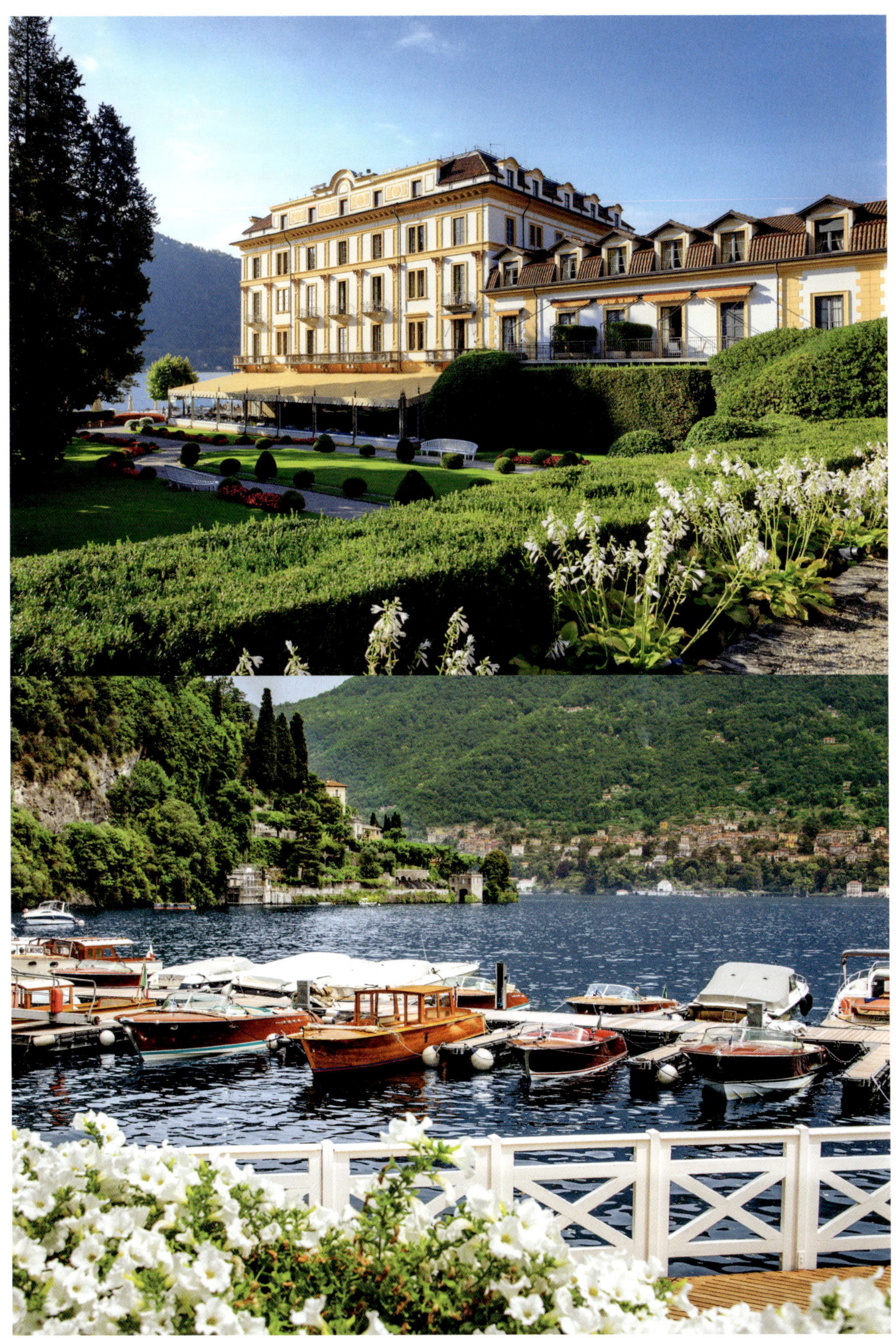

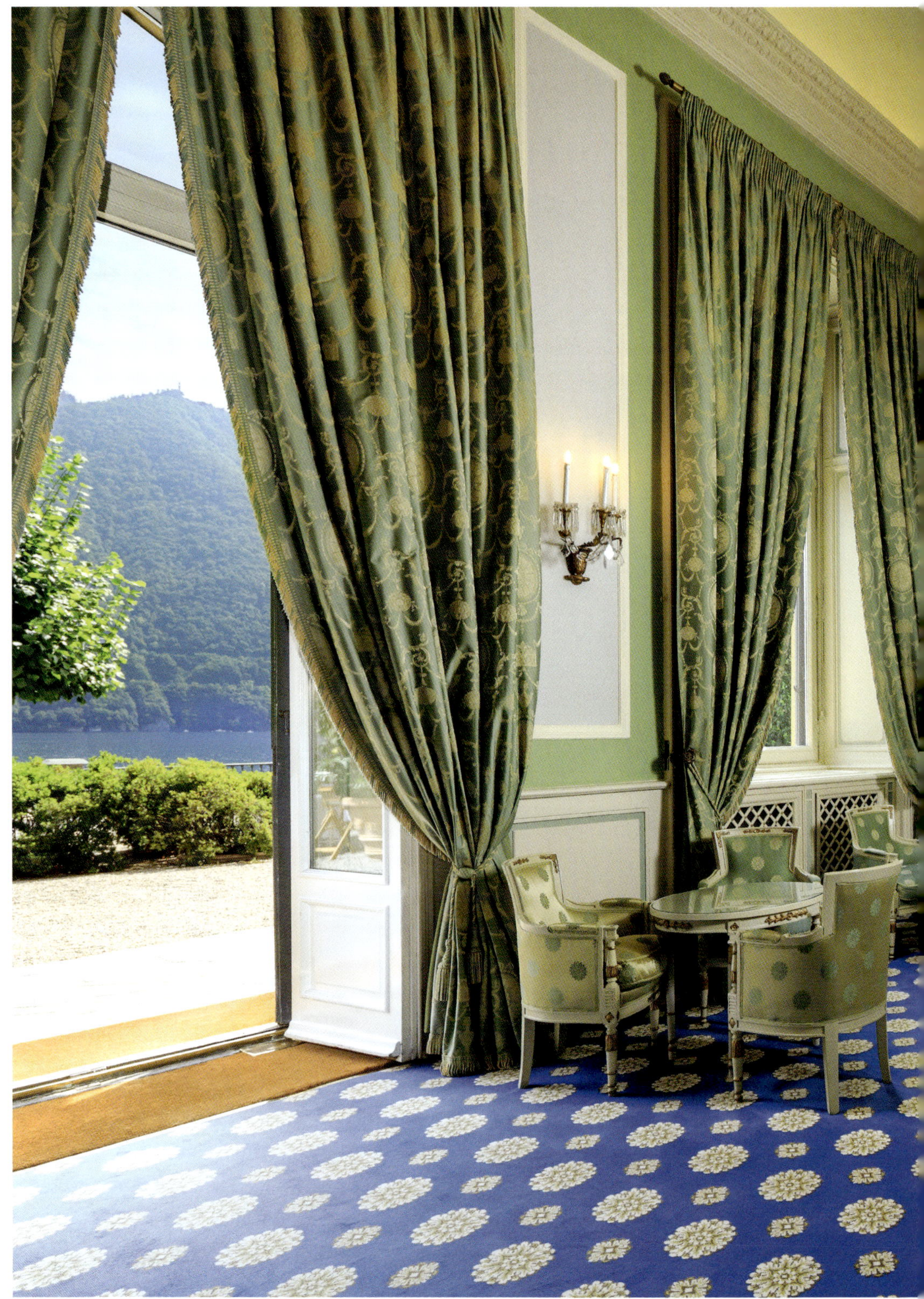

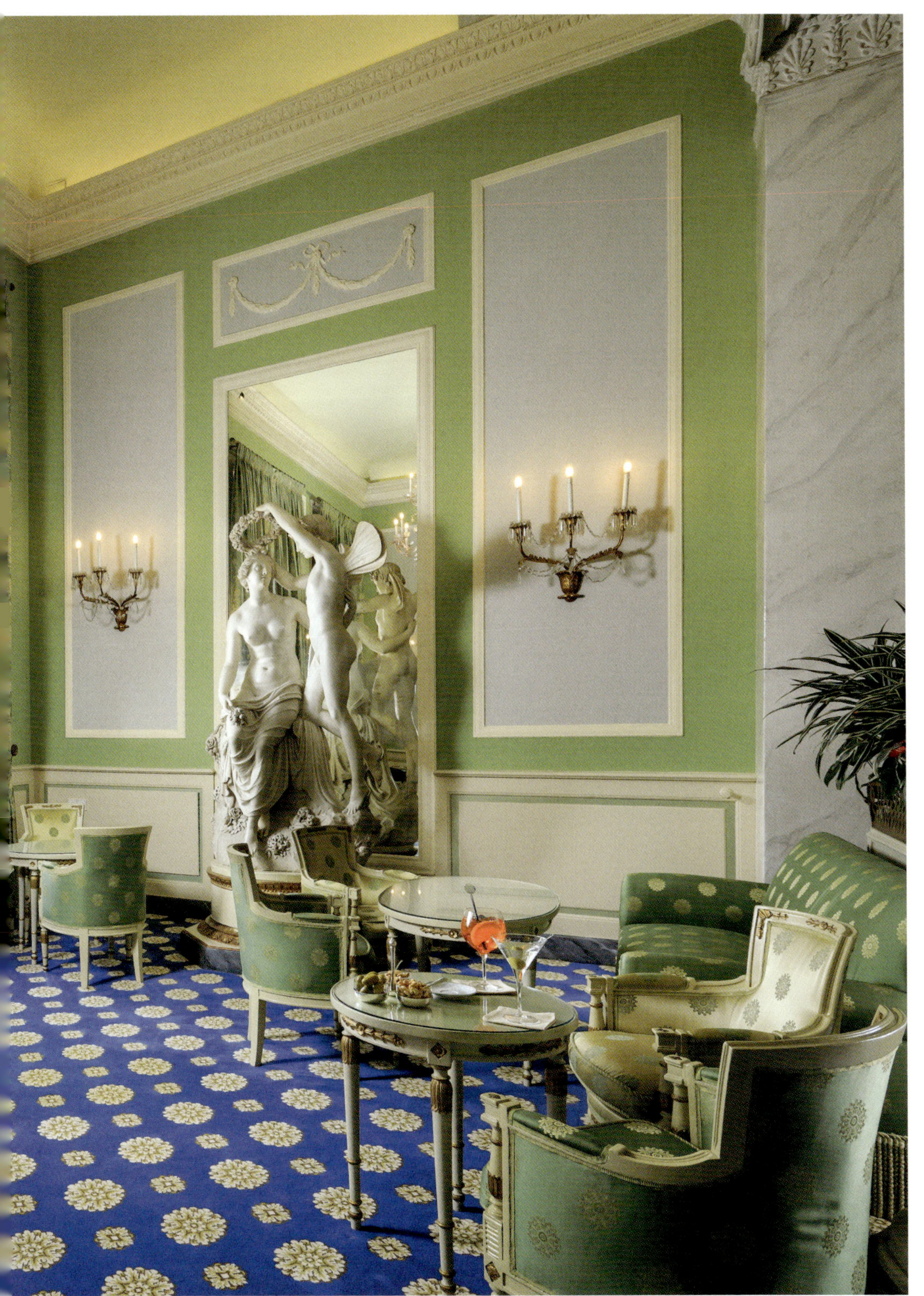

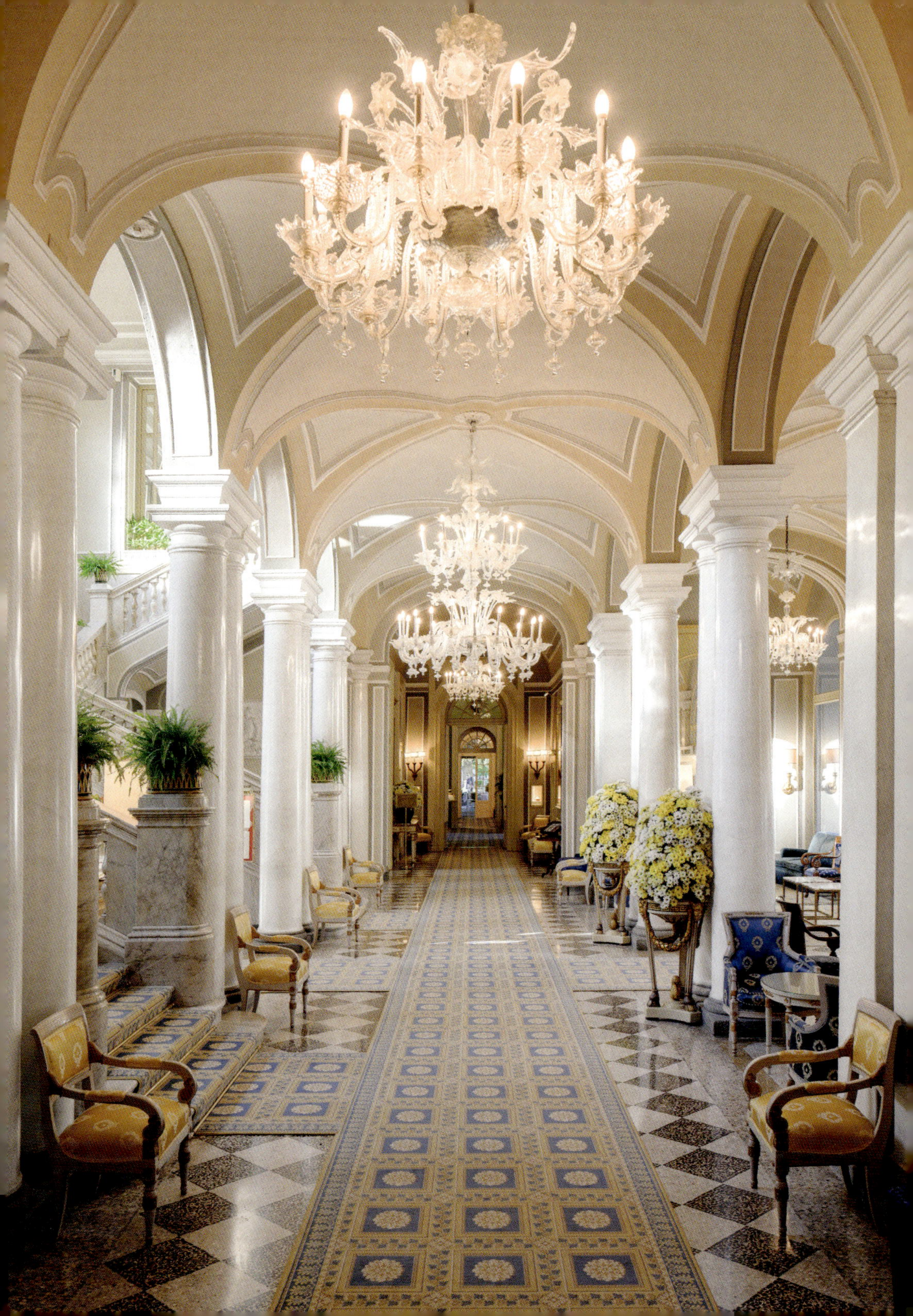

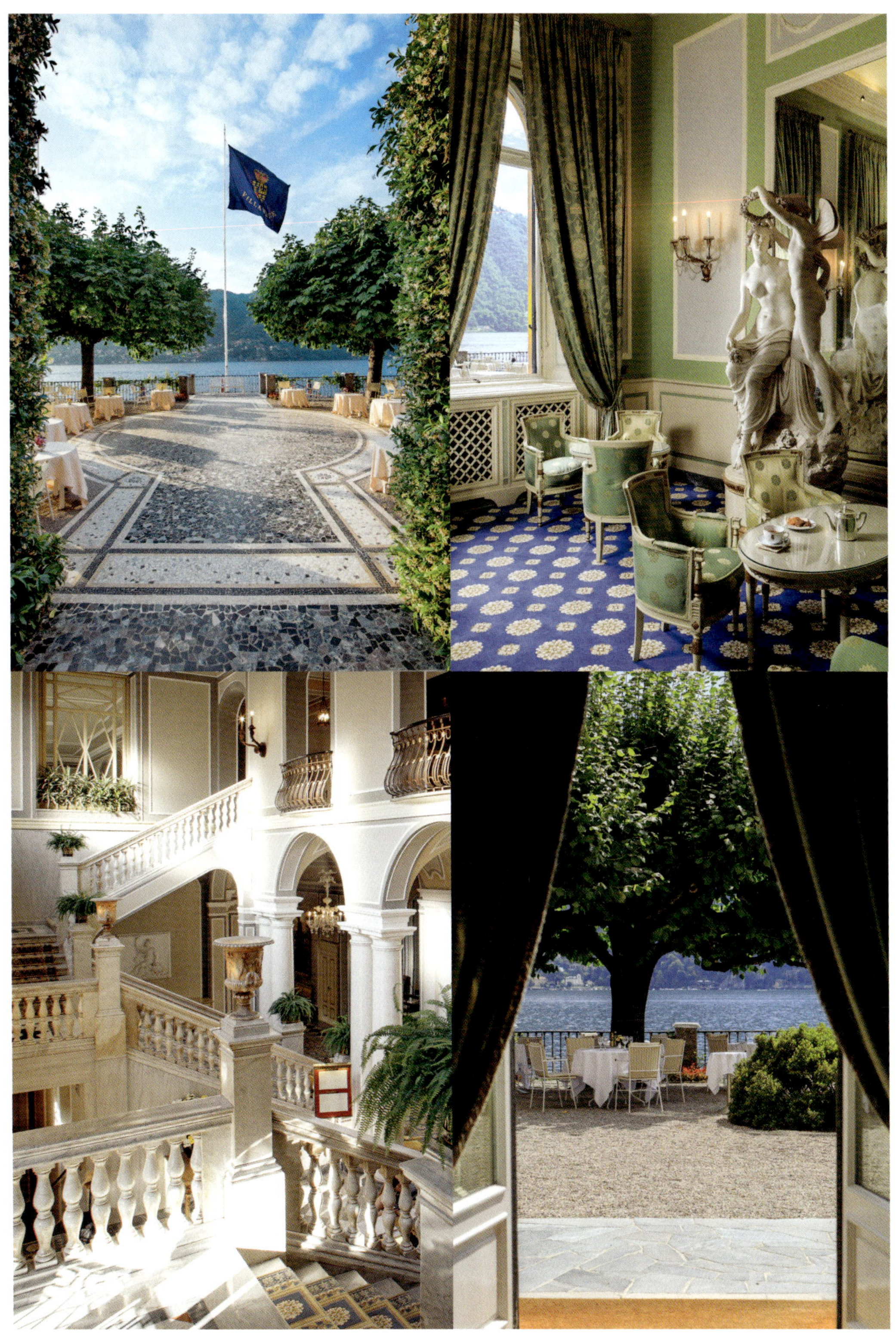

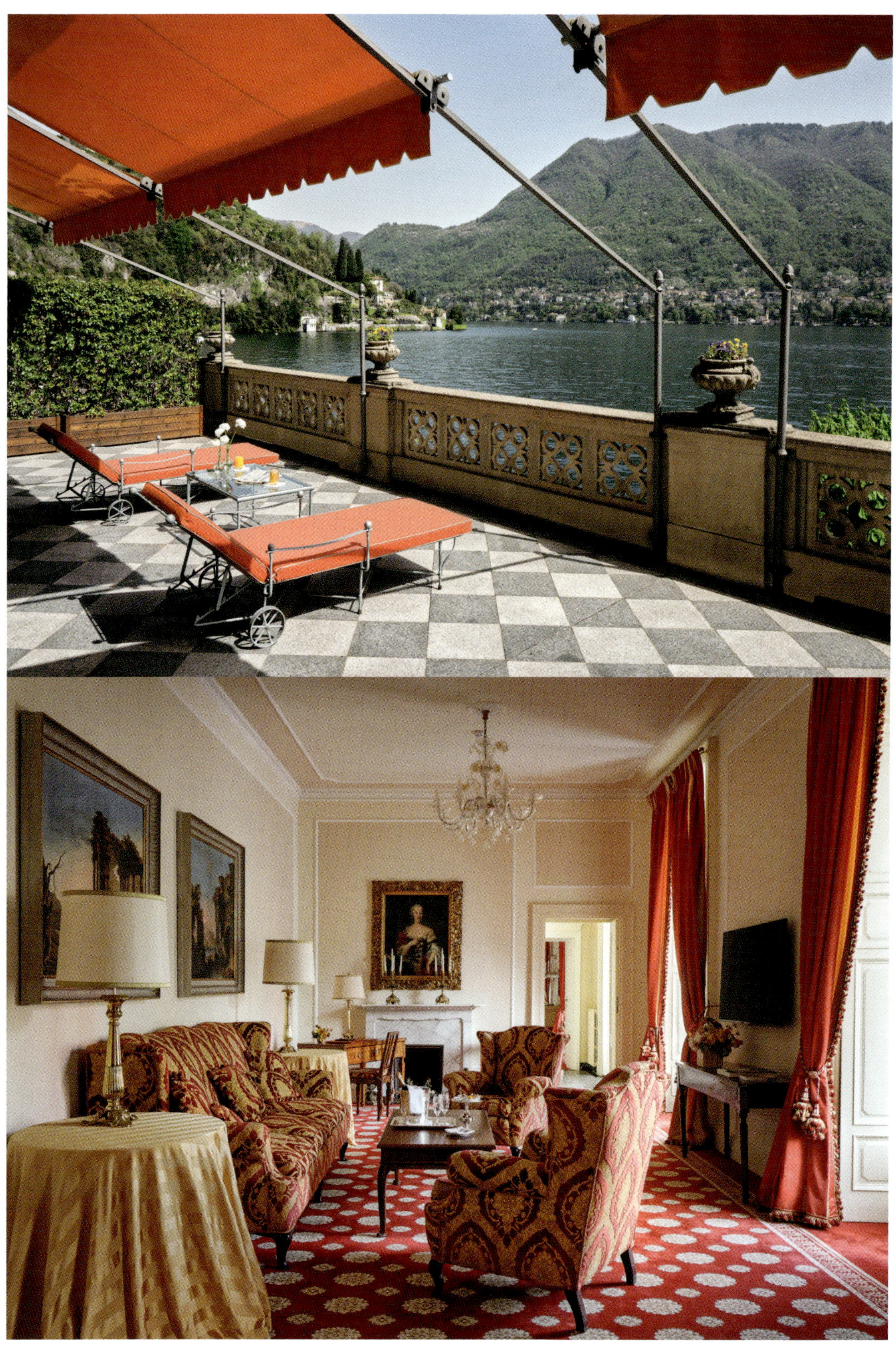

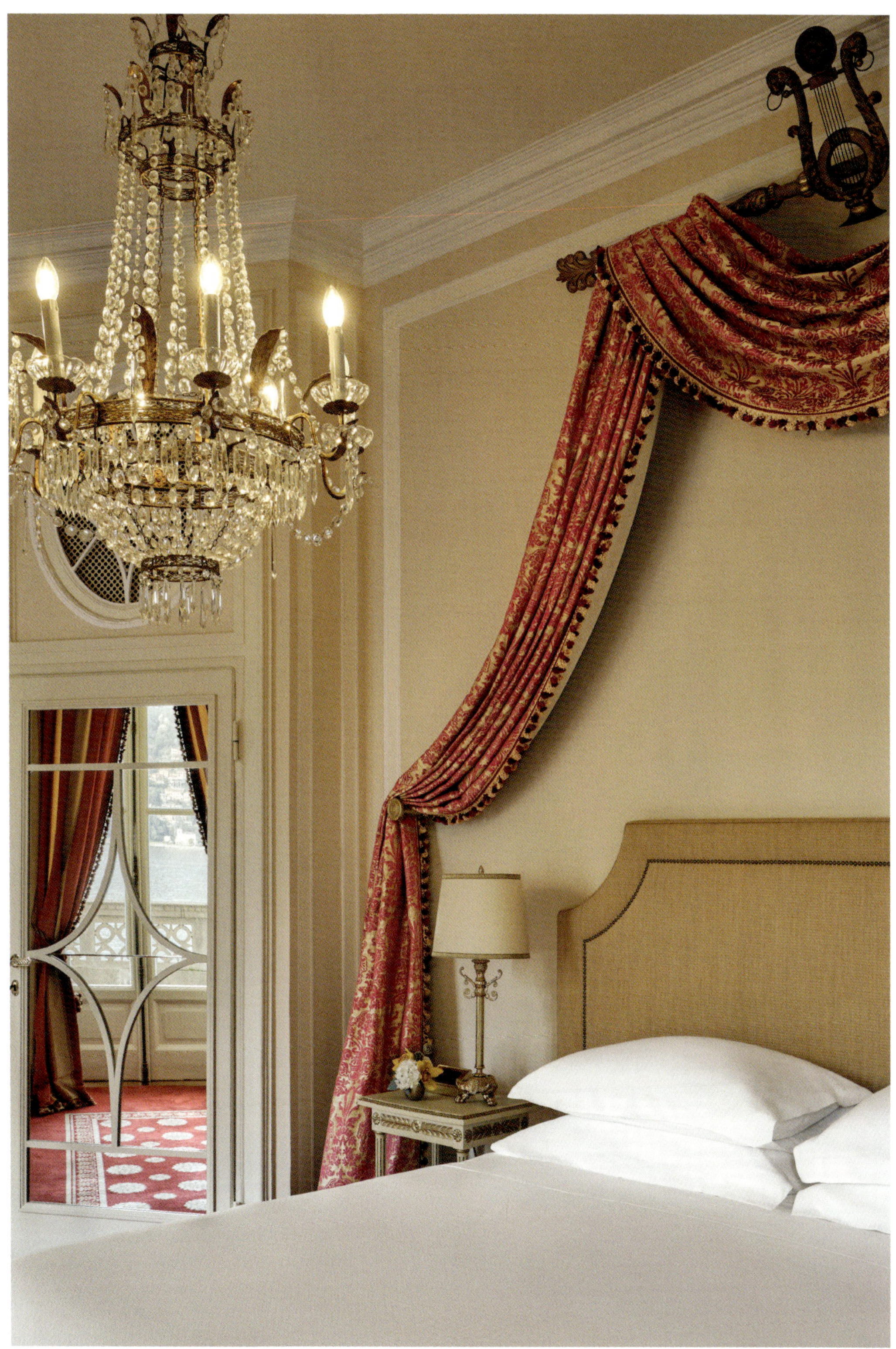

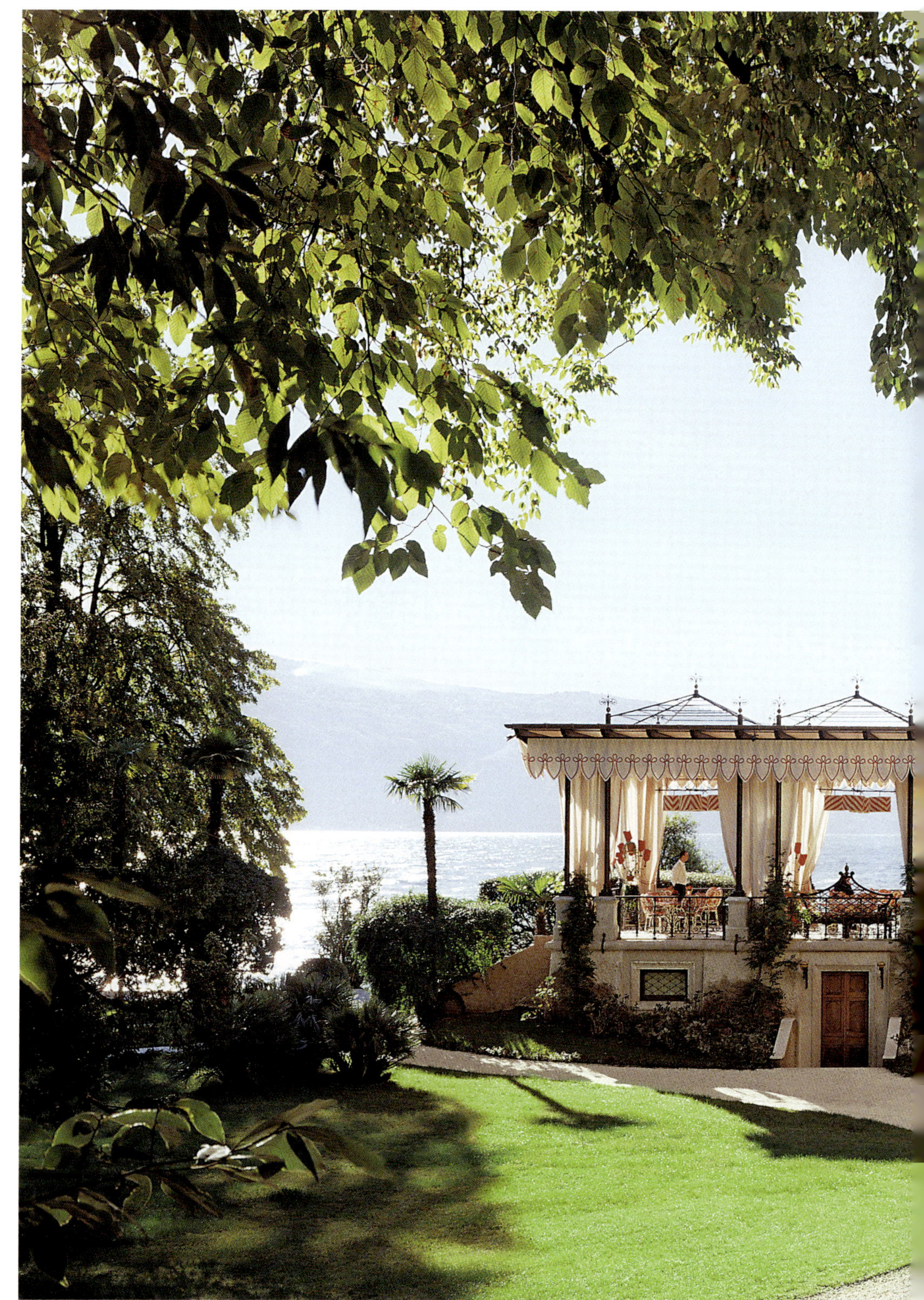

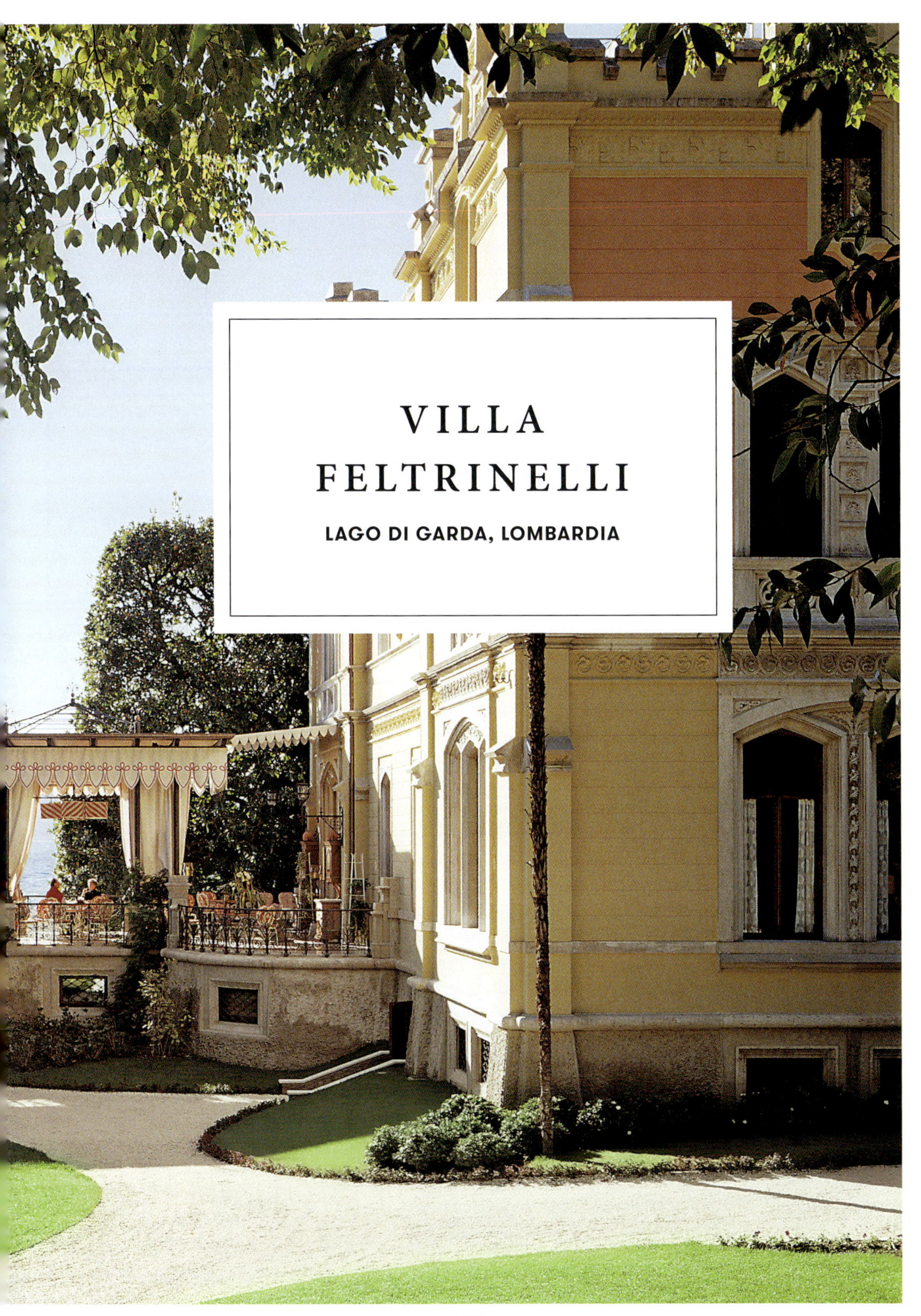

VILLA FELTRINELLI

LAGO DI GARDA, LOMBARDIA

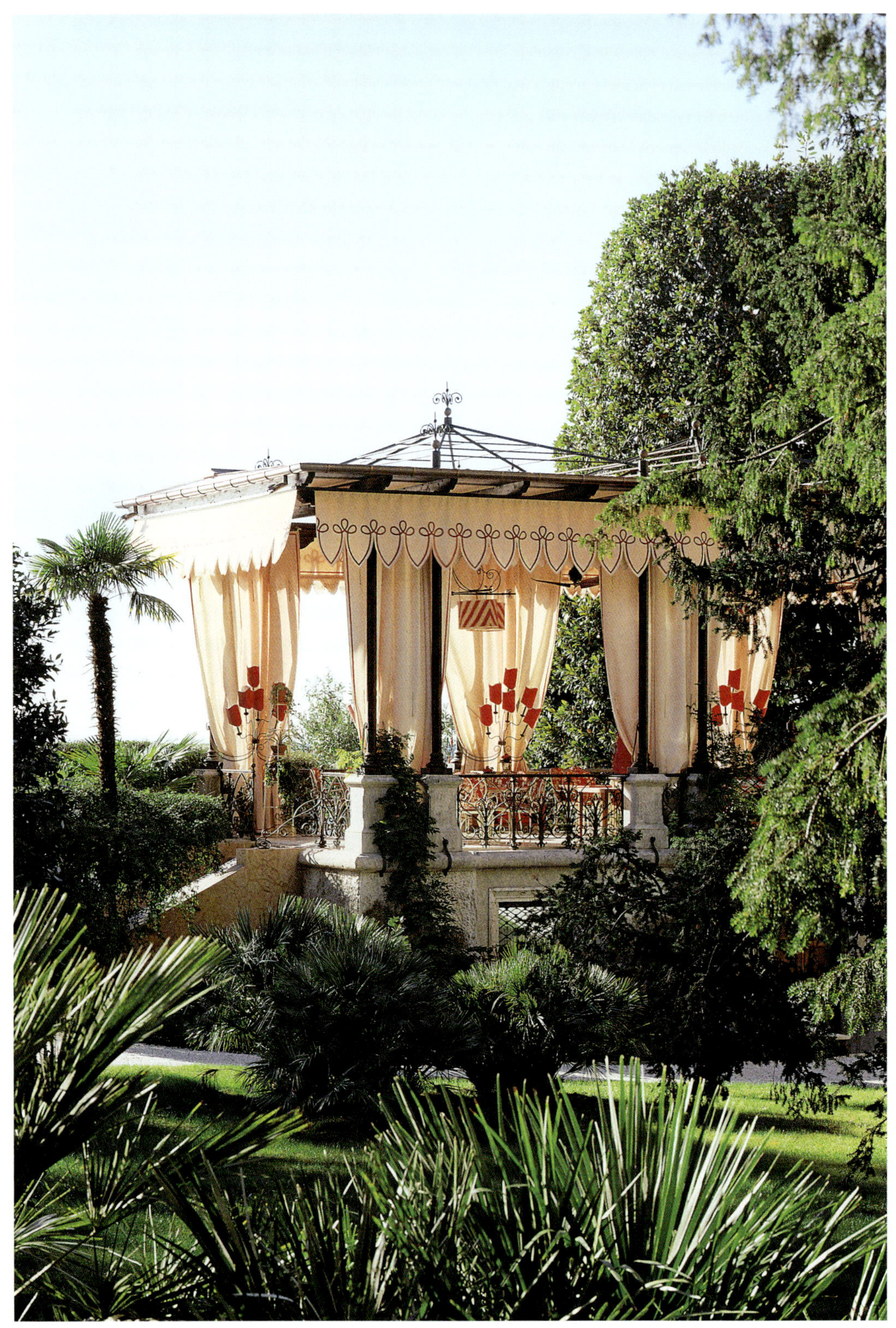

VILLA FELTRINELLI

Via Rimembranza 38–40, 25084 Gargnano
Tel. +39 0365 798 000 · grandhotel@villafeltrinelli.com
www.villafeltrinelli.com
Open from mid-April to mid-October

HISTORY AND GRANDEUR A palazzo in "Stile Liberty" (Italian Art Nouveau), the scent of lemon and olive trees in the garden and Lago di Garda sparkling right outside the door. That ought to be paradise. But Benito Mussolini took little pleasure in the magic of Villa Feltrinelli when he lived there from October 1943 to April 1945. It was not just that Hitler's generals had downgraded the once-powerful Duce to be head of a puppet regime. Mussolini hated water and thus the lake too, and had to adhere to an insipid diet as a result of stomach trouble and divide his private life between his wife and his mistress. Fortunately this kind of trouble, political or otherwise, has no place today – Villa Feltrinelli, originally built as the summer residence of the timber and publishing dynasty of the same name, has been converted into a hotel that strikes a perfect balance between luxurious elegance and a relaxed family atmosphere. With a feeling for history, architecture, and art Babey Moulton Jue & Booth have restored the house and furnished it with the finest antiques. Venetian mirrors, tall fireplaces and lamps of mouth-blown glass adorn the rooms, seven of which even have ceiling frescoes by the Lieti brothers from the 1890s. Vintage editions of "National Geographic" are in the library and at the bar drinks are served in 1950s glasses. In the evenings guests indulge in Italian cuisine of such refinement that two Michelin stars twinkle above it – to be sure, the days of Mussolini and his diet are over once and for all.
◆ Book to pack: "Twilight in Italy" by D. H. Lawrence.

GESCHICHTE UND GRANDEZZA Ein Palazzo im italienischen Liberty-Stil, duftende Zitronen- und Olivenbäume im Garten und den glitzernden Gardasee direkt vor der Tür – ein Paradies, sollte man meinen. Doch Benito Mussolini hatte wenig vom Zauber der Villa Feltrinelli, als er von Oktober 1943 bis April 1945 hier lebte. Nicht nur, dass Hitlers Generäle den einst so mächtigen Duce zum Kopf eines Marionettenregimes degradierten – Mussolini hasste zu allem Überfluss das Wasser und damit den See, musste wegen Magenbeschwerden eine fade Diät halten und sein Privatleben zwischen Frau und Geliebter aufteilen. Mussolinis politische (wie private) Nöte spielen heute glücklicherweise keine Rolle mehr – die Villa Feltrinelli, einst als Sommersitz der gleichnamigen Holz- und Verlegerdynastie erbaut, wurde in ein Hotel verwandelt, das perfekt zwischen luxuriöser Eleganz und entspannt-familiärer Atmosphäre balanciert. Mit viel Sinn für Geschichte, Architektur und Kunst haben Babey Moulton Jue & Booth das Haus restauriert und mit den schönsten Antiquitäten ausgestattet. Venezianische Spiegel, hohe Kamine und mundgeblasene Glaslampen schmücken die Räume (sieben Zimmer besitzen sogar Deckenfresken der Brüder Lieti aus den 1890ern), in der Bibliothek liegen Vintage-Ausgaben des „National Geographic", und an der Bar werden die Drinks in Gläsern aus den 1950ern serviert. Abends lässt man sich mit italienischer Küche verwöhnen, die so fein ist, dass über ihr zwei Michelin-Sterne strahlen – ja, Mussolini und seine Diät gehören definitiv der Vergangenheit an. ◆ Buchtipp: „Italienische Dämmerung" von D. H. Lawrence.

VIVRE L'UTOPIE Un palais dans le style Liberty italien, des oliviers et des citronniers odorants dans les jardins, et les eaux scintillantes du lac de Garde au pied de la porte – le paradis, direz-vous. Benito Mussolini, qui vécut à la Villa Feltrinelli d'octobre 1943 à avril 1945, avait sûrement un autre avis sur la question. Non seulement les généraux de Hitler avaient mis le Duce autrefois si puissant à la tête d'un régime fantoche, mais, en plus, Mussolini détestait l'eau et donc le lac, devait suivre un régime strict à cause de ses maux d'estomac et partager sa vie entre son épouse et sa maîtresse. Mais le temps a passé et tout cela n'a plus guère d'importance – la Villa Feltrinelli, jadis résidence d'été des membres de la dynastie du bois et de l'édition du même nom, a été transformée en un hôtel dont l'élégance luxueuse n'exclut pas l'atmosphère familiale et détendue. Babey Moulton Jue & Booth, qui ont le sens de l'Histoire, ont restauré la maison dans les règles de l'art et de l'architecture et l'ont décorée des plus belles antiquités. On trouve ici des miroirs vénitiens, de hautes cheminées et des lampes en verre soufflé (sept chambres possèdent même des fresques de plafond réalisées par les frères Lieti au cours des années 1890). La bibliothèque offre des éditions vintage du « National Geographic » et, au bar, les boissons sont servies dans des verres datant des années 1950. Le soir, on se régale d'une cuisine italienne si subtile qu'elle a même deux étoiles au Michelin – on le voit : Mussolini et son régime, tout cela est bien loin. ◆ À lire : « Crépuscule sur l'Italie » de D. H. Lawrence.

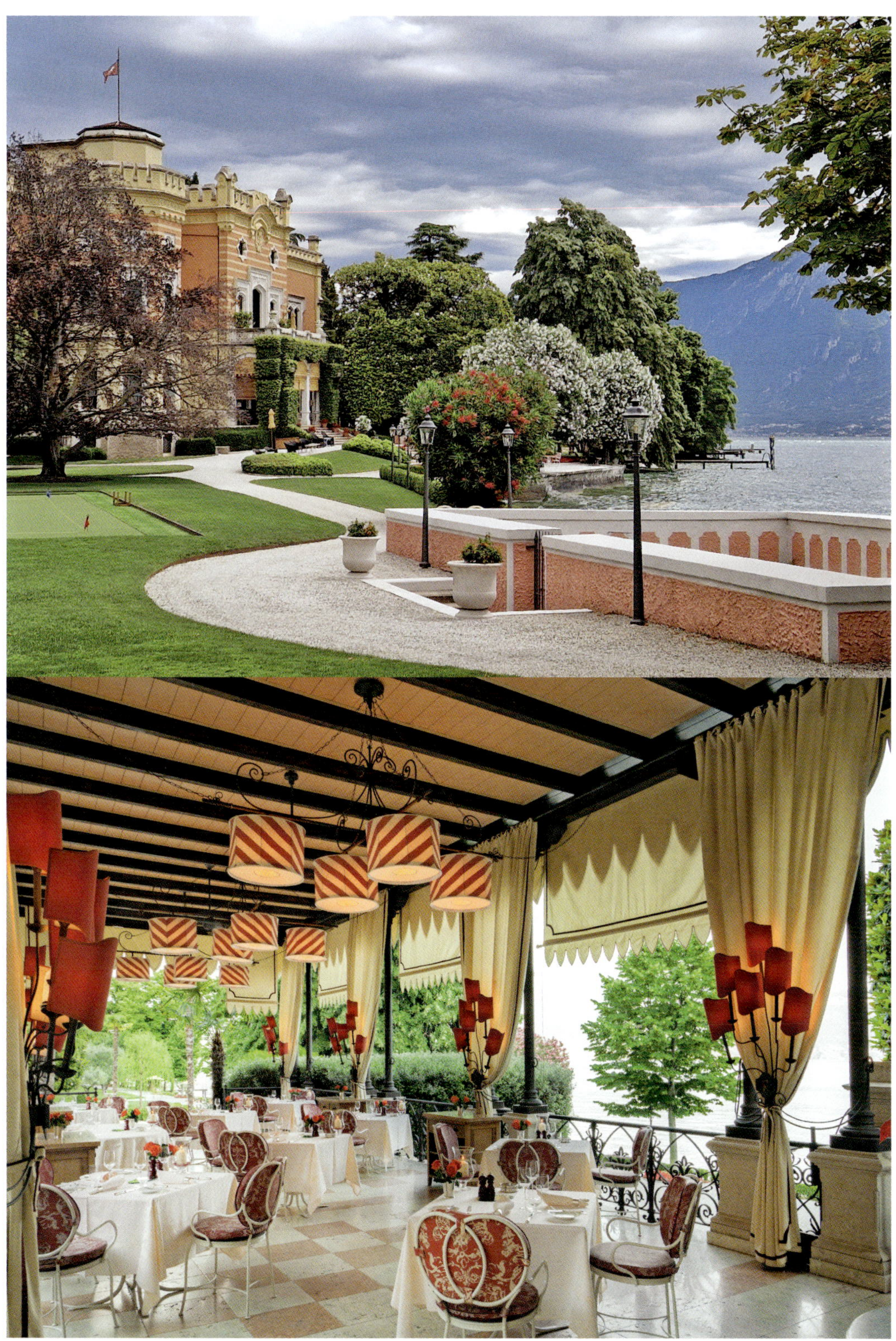

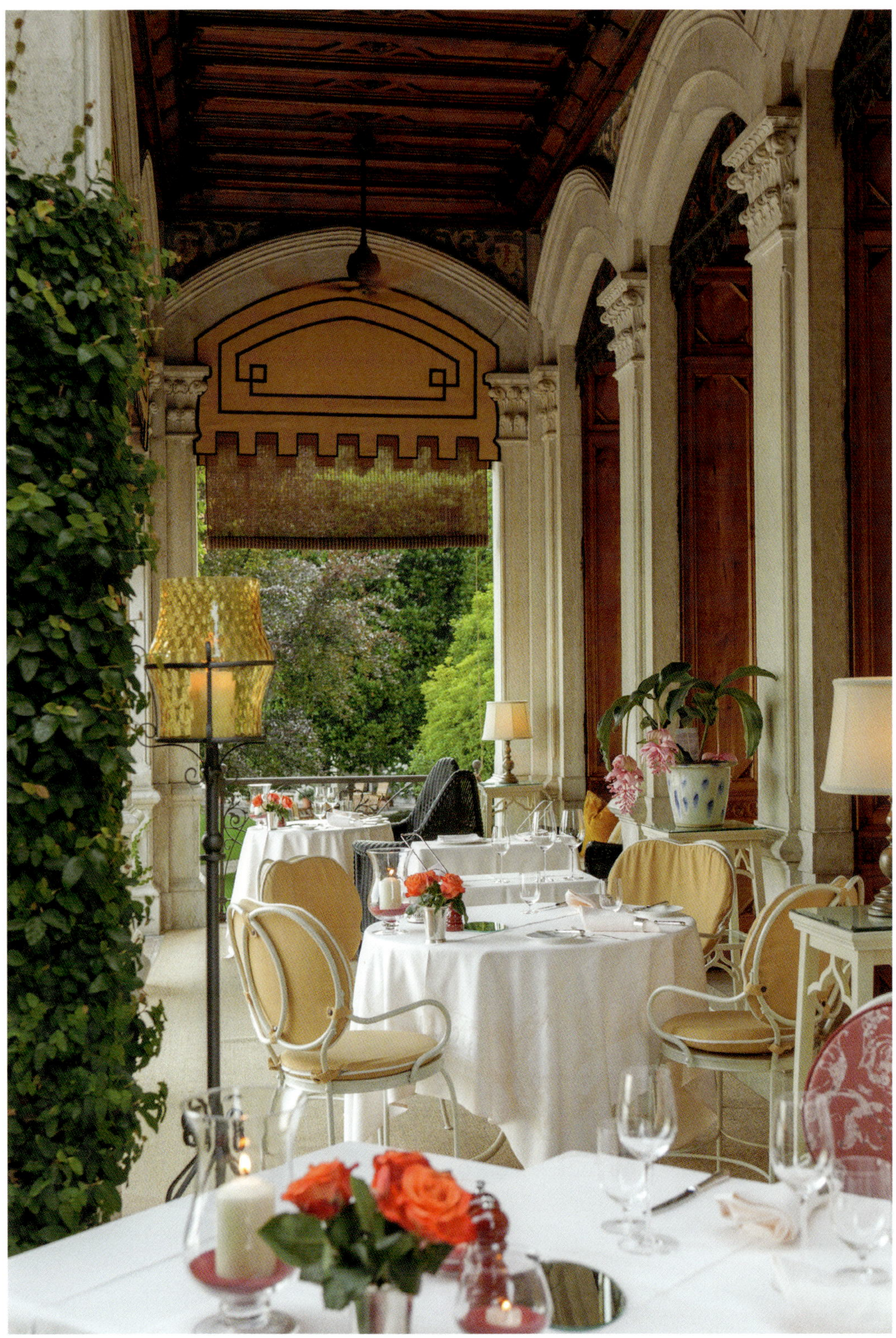

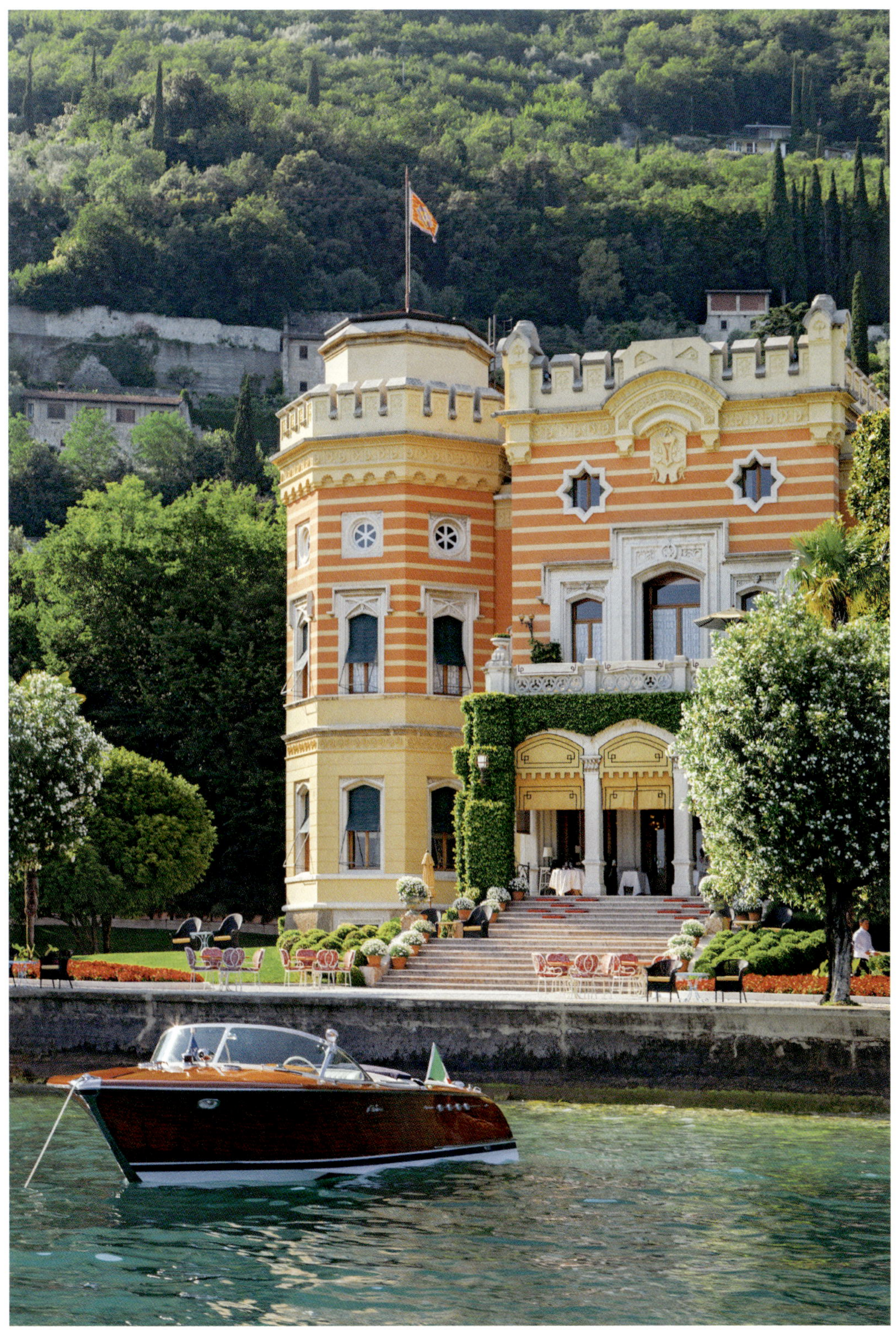

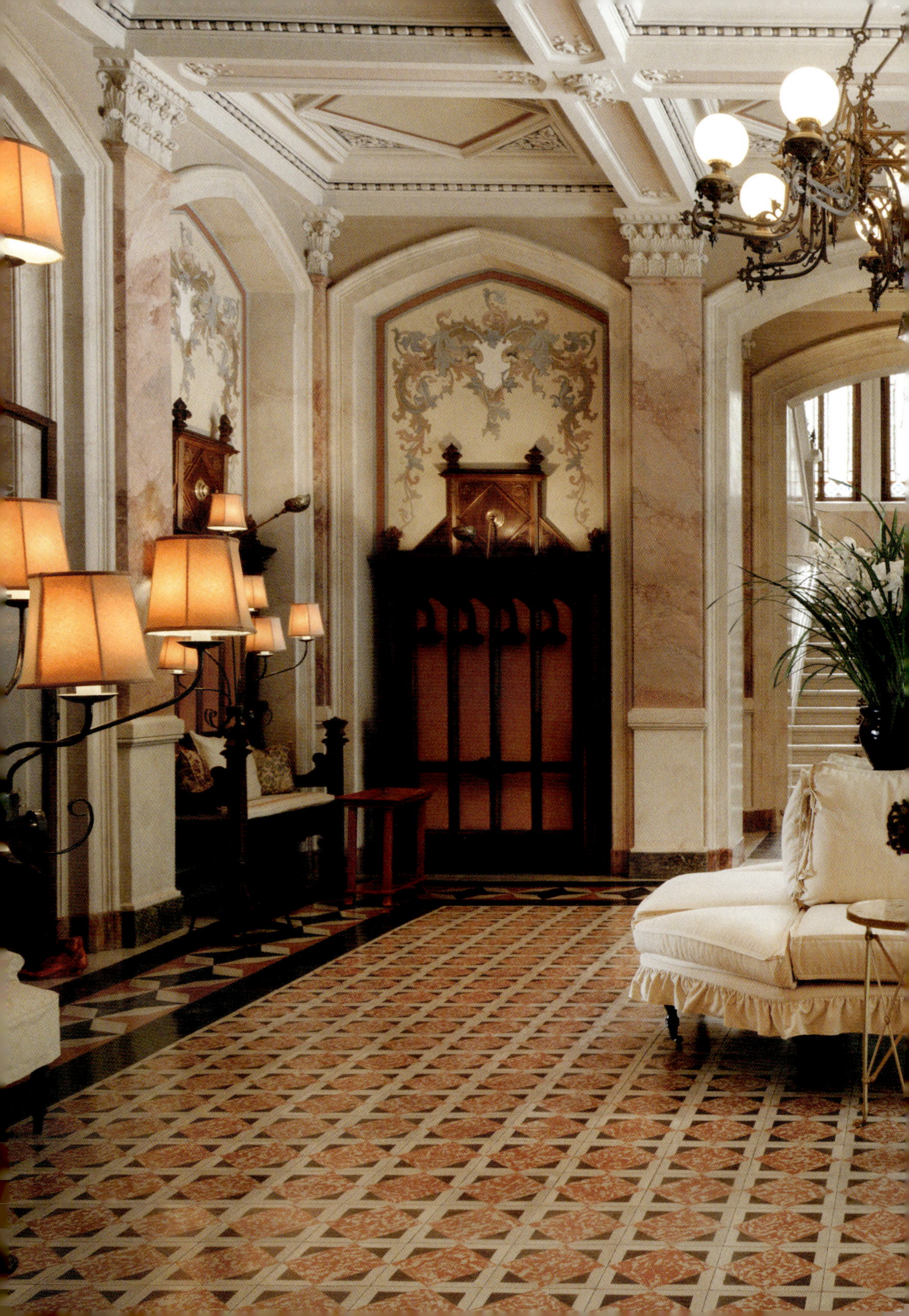

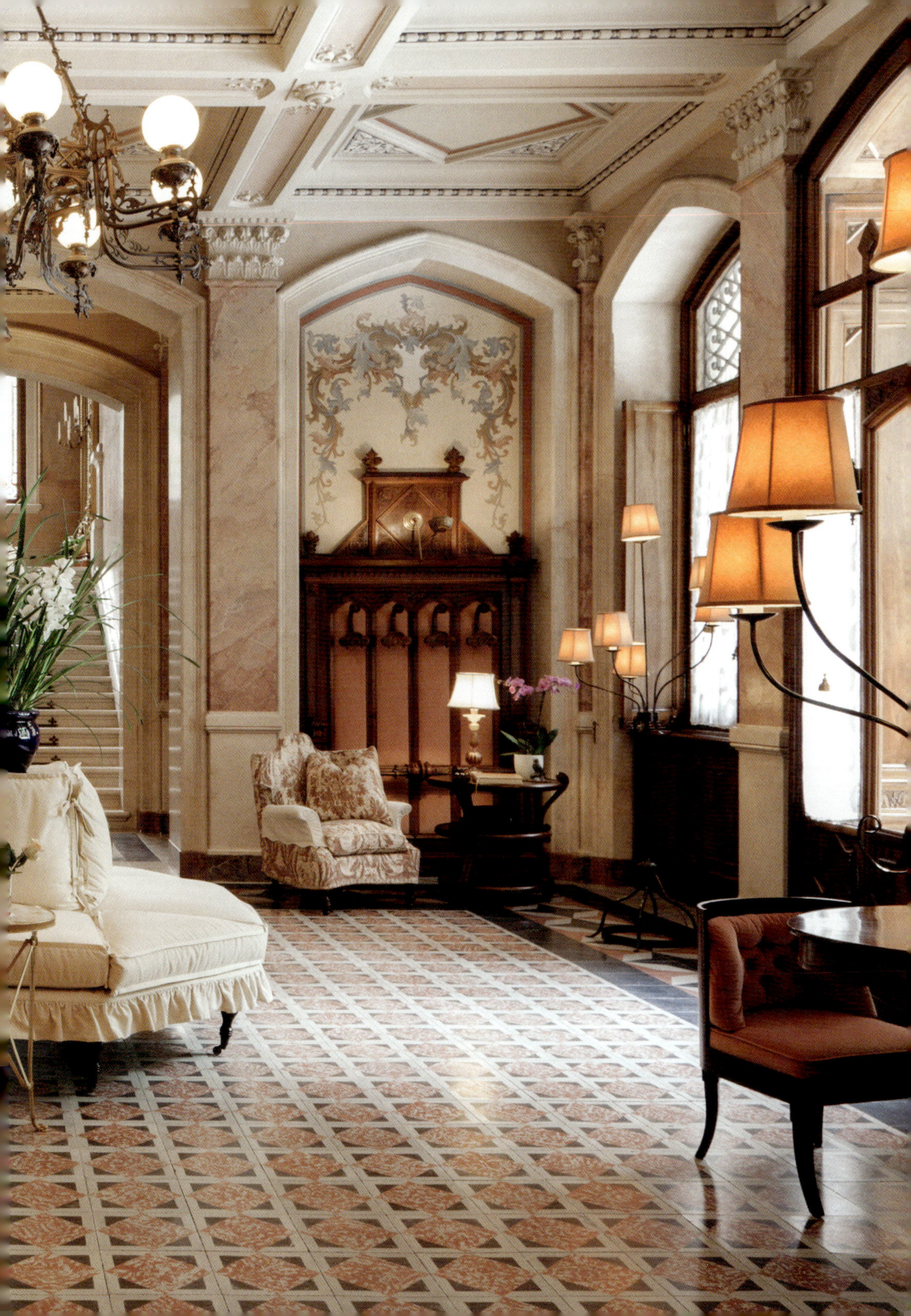

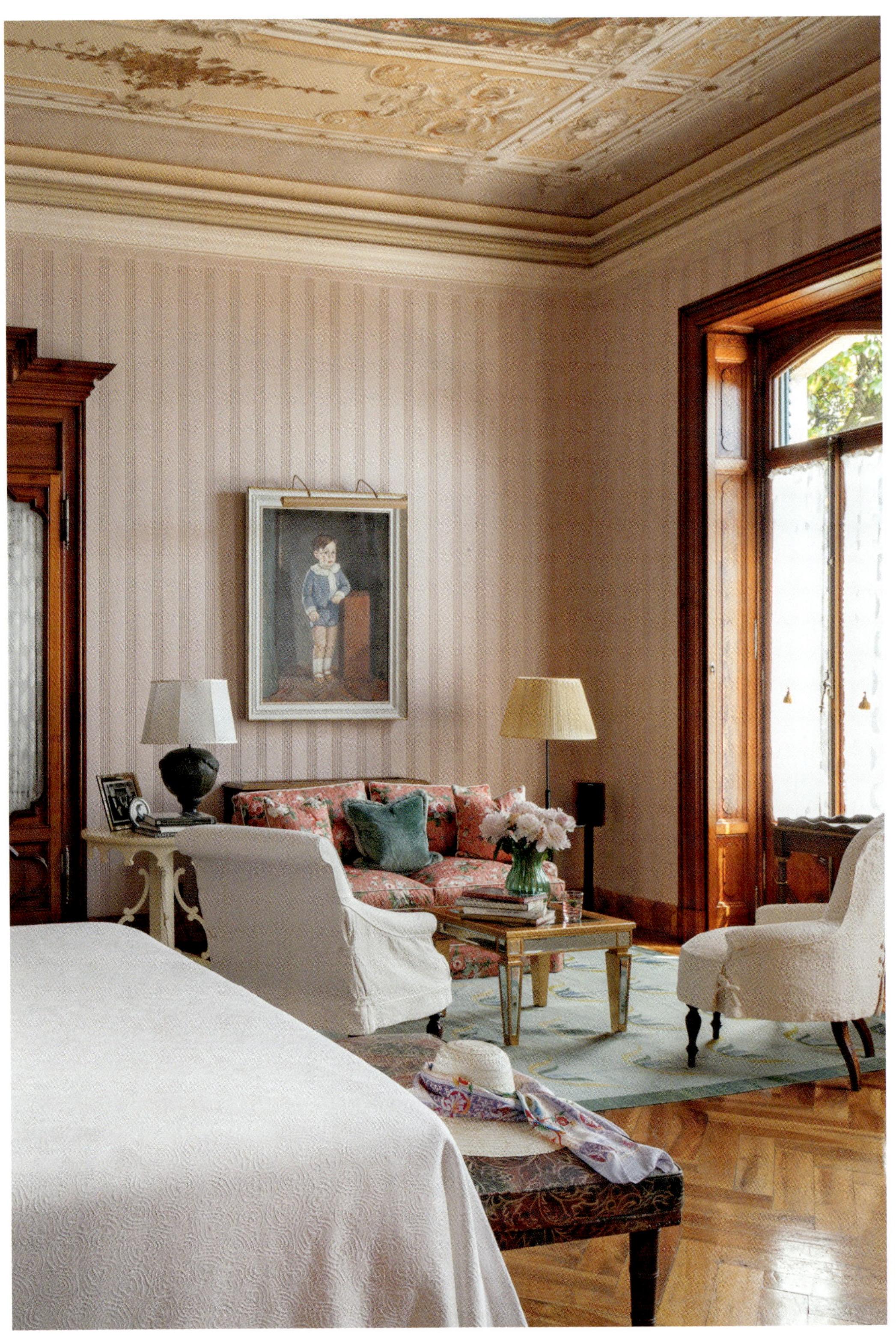

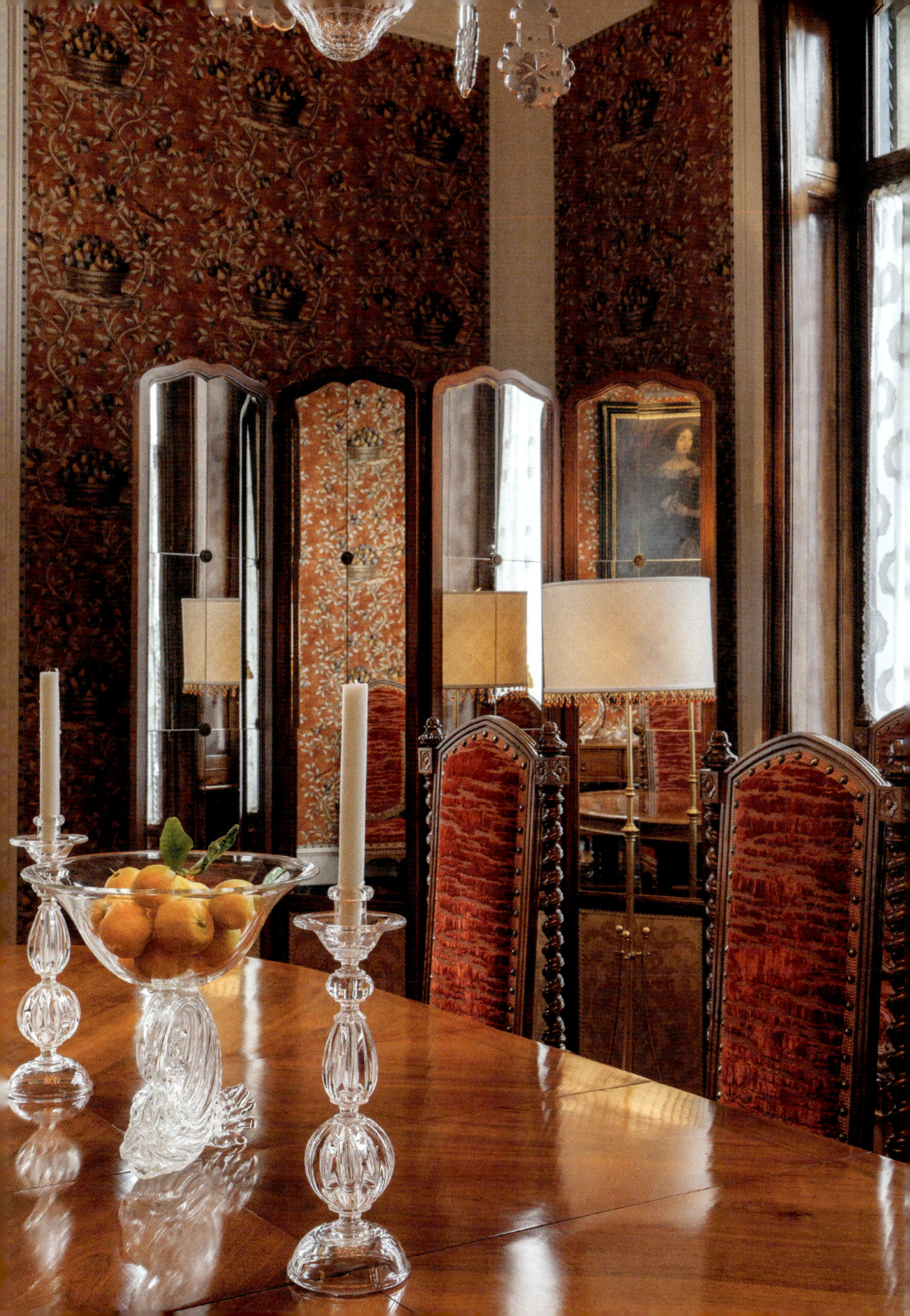

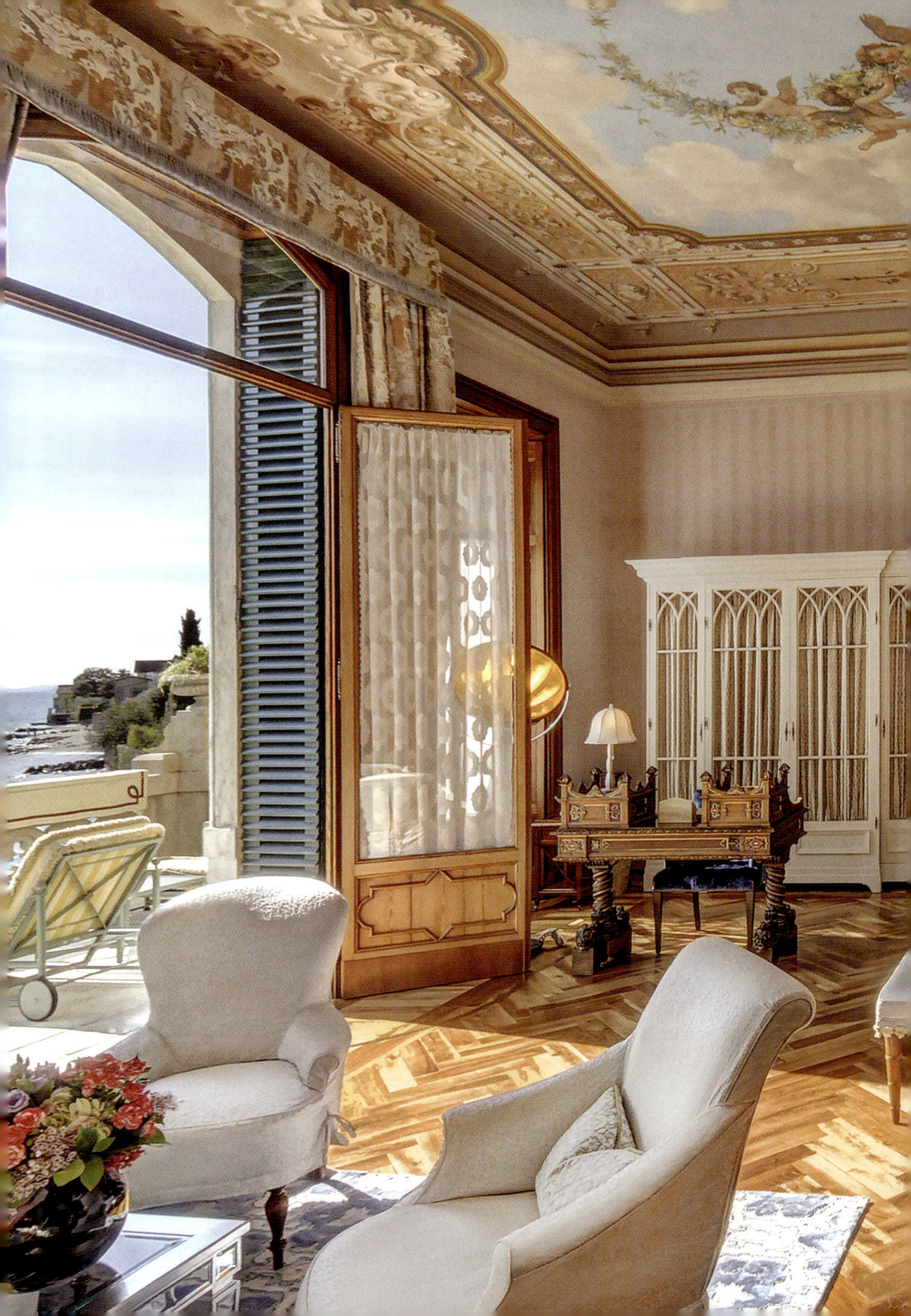

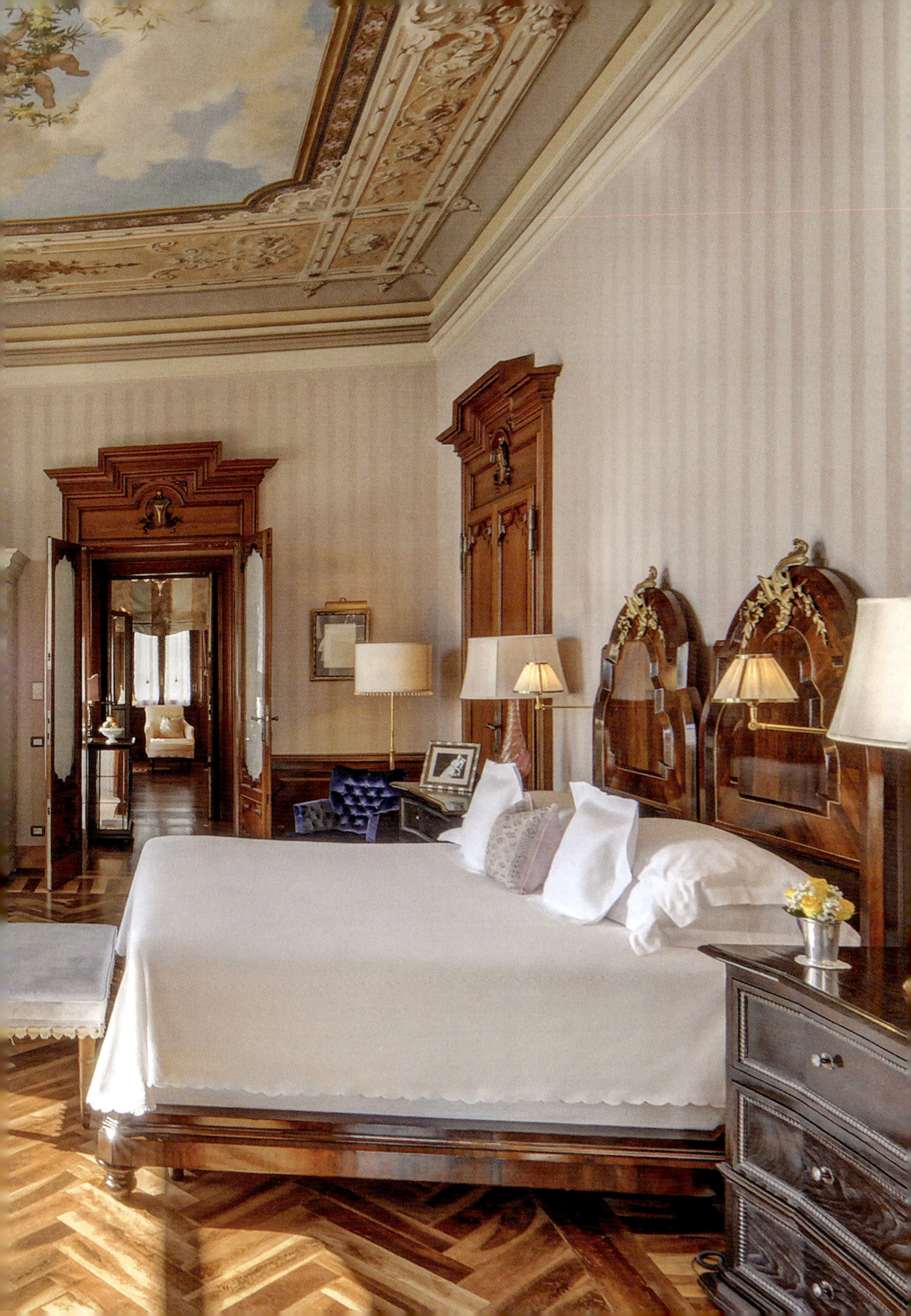

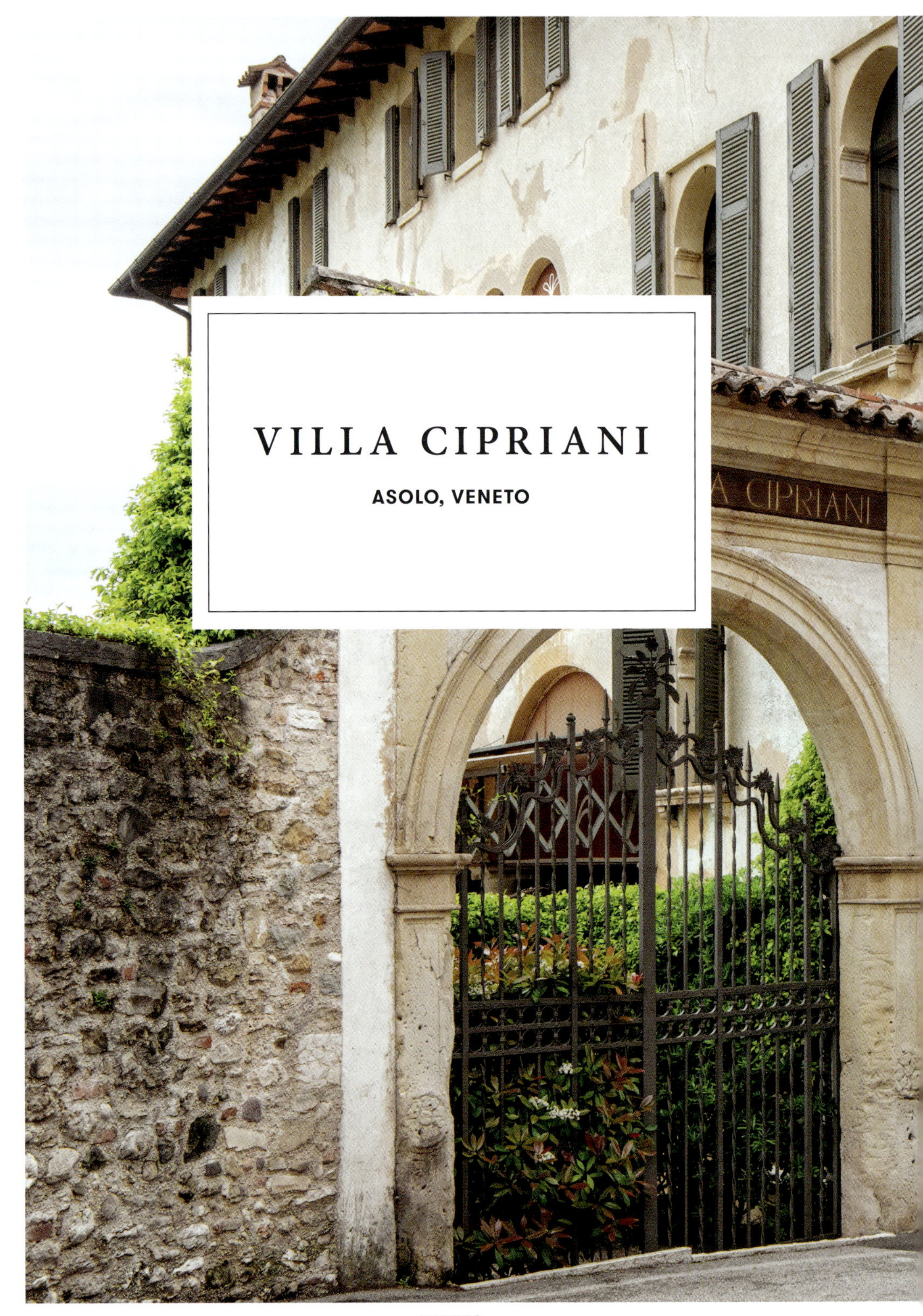

VILLA CIPRIANI

ASOLO, VENETO

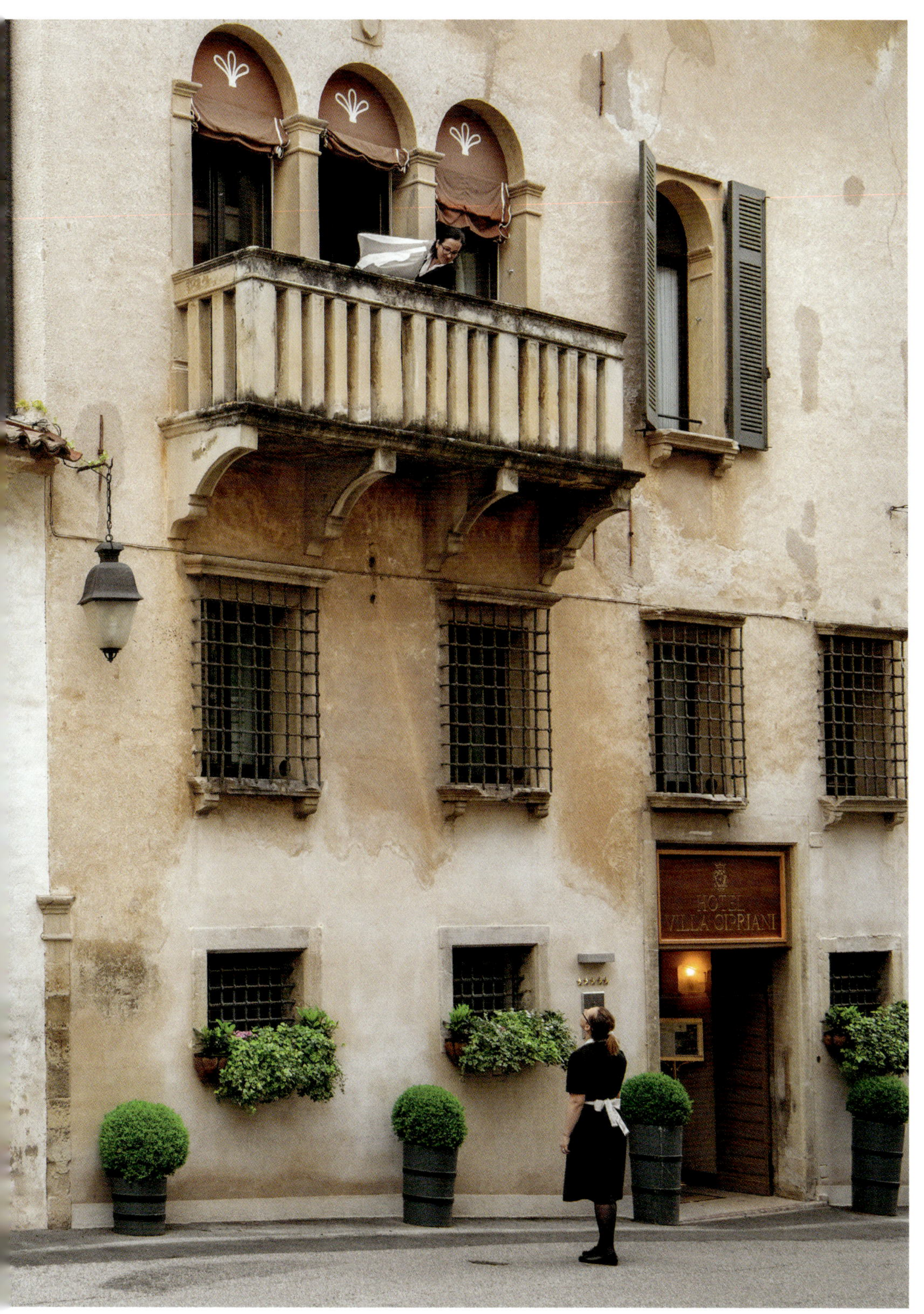
HOTEL
VILLA CIPRIANI

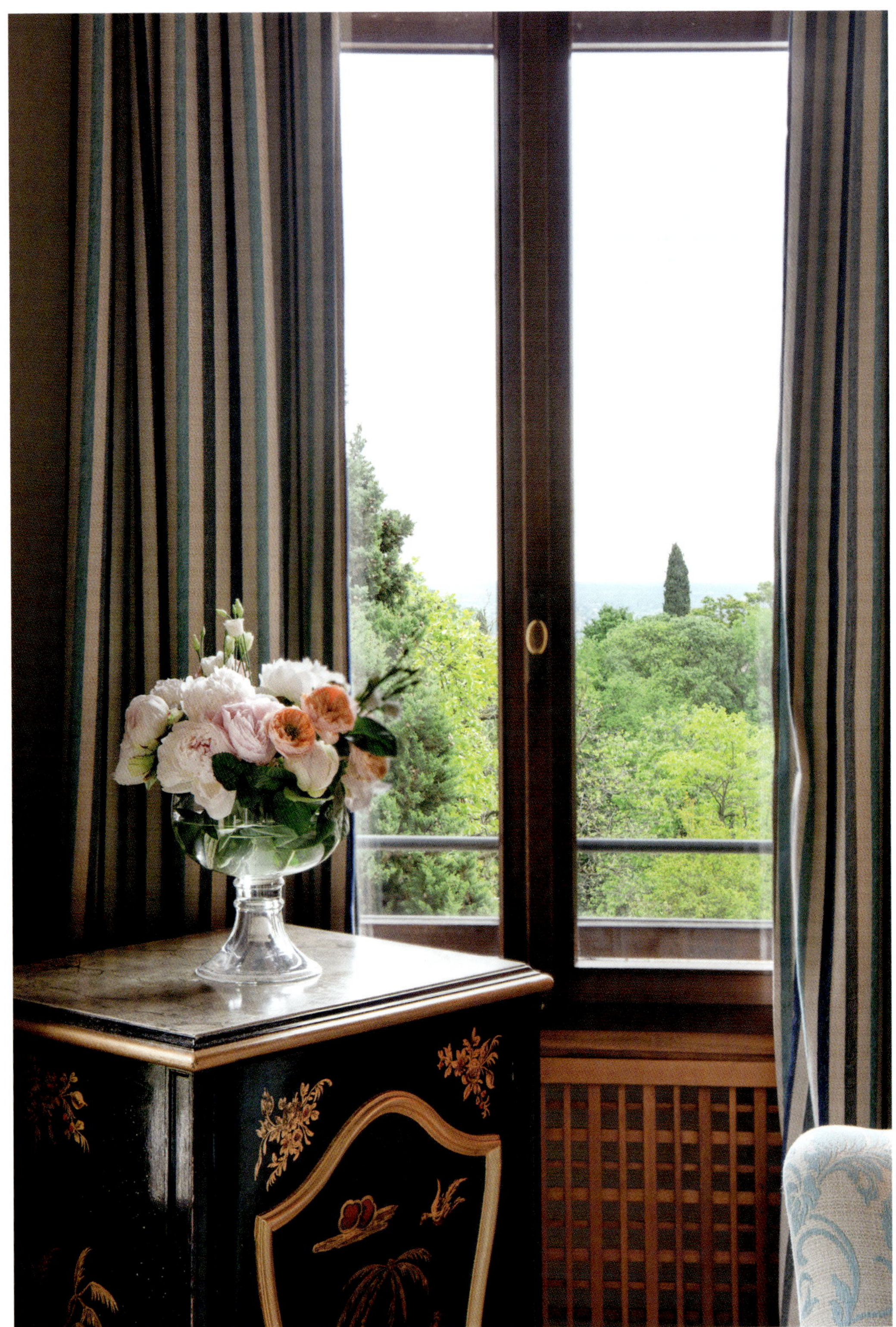

VILLA CIPRIANI

Via Canova 298, 31011 Asolo
Tel. +39 0423 523 411 · villacipriani@villacipriani.it
www.villacipriani.it
Open from mid-March to late January

LIKE A POEM The English poet Robert Browning loved Asolo so much that he named his last work, published in 1889, "Asolando". In the same year he bought this villa, but was only able to live there himself for a short time – he died on 12 December 1889. After his death, the house saw a whole series of rich and illustrious owners. A wealthy engineer from Treviso presented it to his daughter on her wedding, the Cimetta brothers converted it into a country hotel, and the Irish Guinness clan gave it the name it has today: the family commissioned Giuseppe Cipriani, who had opened Harry's Bar in Venice, to remodel and manage the estate. Villa Cipriani is owned by Massimo Zanetti, proprietor of the Segafredo coffee empire, and his wife Sigrid Guillion-Mangilli Zanetti. Their guests reside in rooms of exquisite understatement, stroll in the perfectly manicured garden and are treated to a service whose immaculate reputation was spread far beyond Asolo by such eminent visitors as the English Queen Mother with her son-in-law Prince Philip, as well as by Marcello Mastroianni and Catherine Deneuve. But no one should come here only for a spot of people-watching: the view from Villa Cipriani over the cypress hills of the Veneto region is to die for, and around Asolo stand villas by Palladio, consummate architecture of which you cannot see enough. ◆ Book to pack: "Asolando" by Robert Browning.

WIE EIN GEDICHT Der englische Dichter Robert Browning liebte Asolo so sehr, dass er sein letztes, 1889 erschienenes Werk „Asolando“ nannte. Im selben Jahr kaufte er diese Villa, konnte sie aber nur noch kurze Zeit selbst bewohnen – er starb am 12. Dezember 1889. Nach seinem Tod erlebte das Haus eine ganze Reihe reicher und illustrer Eigentümer: Ein wohlhabender Ingenieur aus Treviso schenkte es seiner Tochter zur Hochzeit, die Brüder Cimetta bauten es zum Landhotel um, und der irische Guinness-Clan gab ihm seinen aktuellen Namen – die Familie beauftragte Giuseppe Cipriani, der in Venedig „Harry's Bar“ eröffnet hatte, mit der Neugestaltung und dem Management des Anwesens. Die Villa Cipriani gehört Massimo Zanetti, dem Besitzer des Kaffeeimperiums Segafredo, und seiner Frau Sigrid Guillion-Mangilli Zanetti. Ihre Gäste wohnen in Zimmern von exquisitem Understatement, flanieren durch den perfekt manikürten Garten und genießen einen Service, dessen tadellosen Ruf prominente Besucher wie Queen Mum samt Schwiegersohn Prinz Philip, Marcello Mastroianni und Catherine Deneuve weit über die Grenzen Asolos hinaustrugen. Nur zum Leuteschauen sollte jedoch niemand herkommen: Der Blick von der Villa Cipriani über die Zypressenhügel des Veneto ist zum Niederknien schön, und rund um Asolo stehen zahlreiche Palladio-Villen, an deren vollendeter Architektur man sich kaum sattsehen kann. ◆ Buchtipp: „Asolando“ von Robert Browning.

COMME UN POÈME Le poète anglais Robert Browning aimait tellement Asolo qu'il intitula sa dernière œuvre, publiée en 1889, « Asolando ». Il a acheté cette villa la même année, mais n'a pu y vivre que peu de temps – il est mort le 12 décembre 1889. Par la suite, la maison a connu de nombreux propriétaires riches et illustres : un ingénieur fortuné de Trévise l'a offerte à sa fille pour son mariage, les frères Cimetta l'ont transformée en hôtel de campagne et le clan irlandais Guinness lui a donné son nom actuel – la famille a chargé Giuseppe Cipriani, qui avait ouvert « Harry's Bar » à Venise, de réaménager et de gérer la propriété. La Villa Cipriani appartient à Massimo Zanetti, propriétaire de l'empire du café Segafredo, et à son épouse Sigrid Guillion-Mangilli Zaneti. Ses invités vivent dans des chambres d'une élégance discrète et raffinée, se promènent dans le jardin parfaitement entretenu et bénéficient d'un service dont la réputation irréprochable a été propagée bien au-delà des frontières d'Asolo par des visiteurs de renom tels que la Reine mère et son gendre le prince Philip, Marcello Mastroianni et Catherine Deneuve. Mais personne ne devrait venir ici pour « regarder les gens » : vues de la Villa Cipriani, les collines de cyprès de la Vénétie sont belles à s'agenouiller, et on ne saurait se lasser d'admirer l'architecture parfaite des nombreuses villas palladiennes autour d'Asolo. ◆ À lire : « Asolando » de Robert Browning.

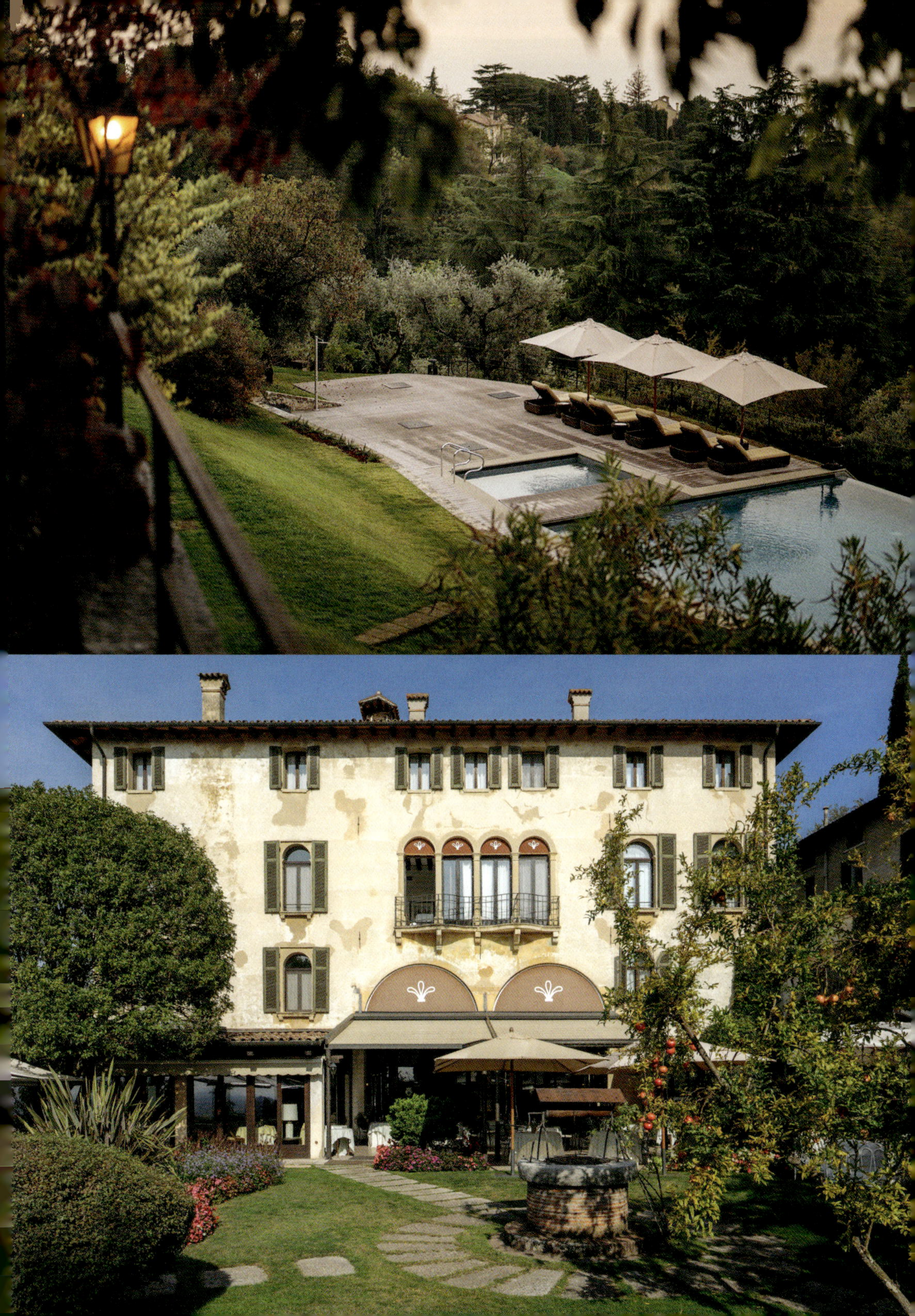

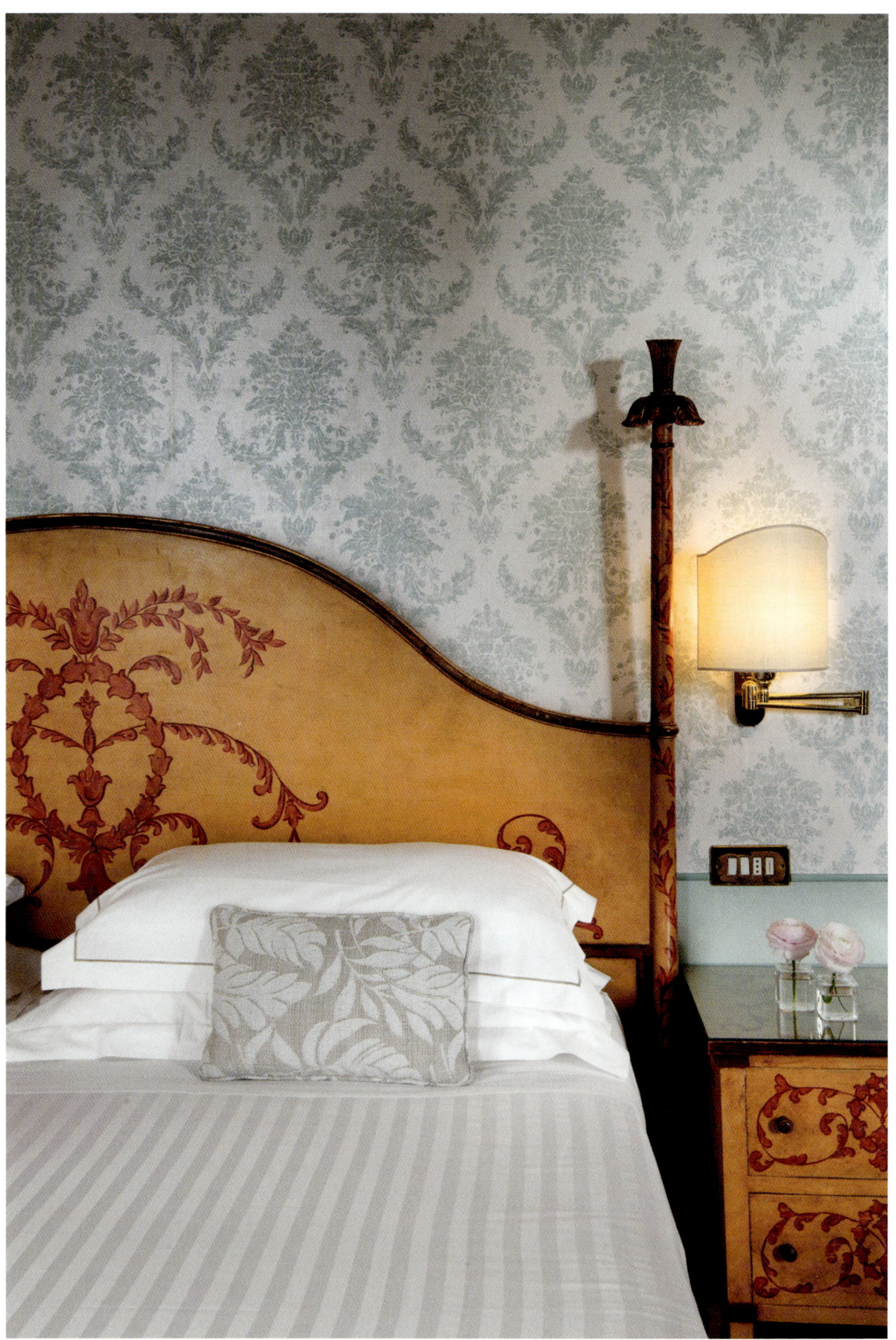

VENETO

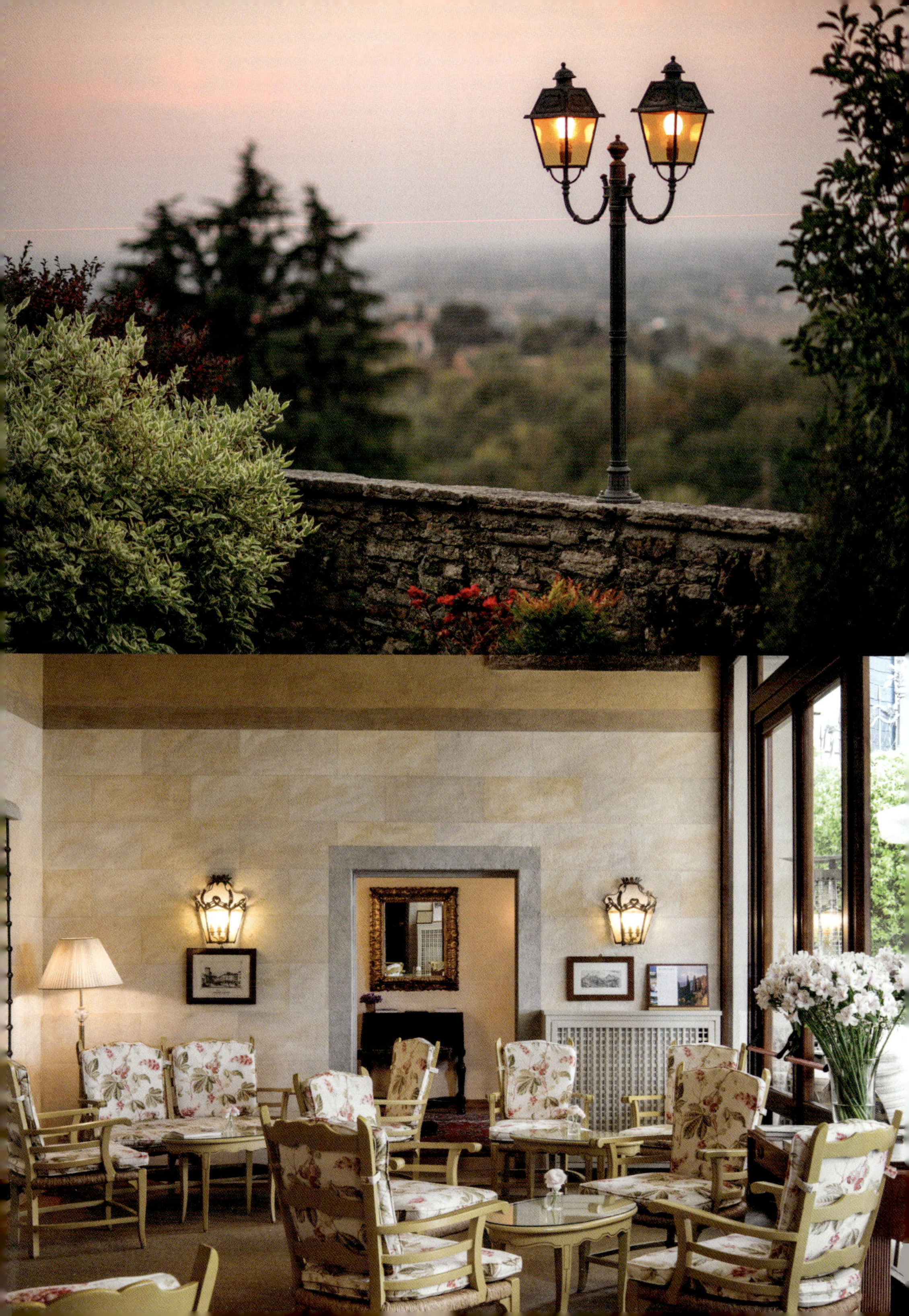

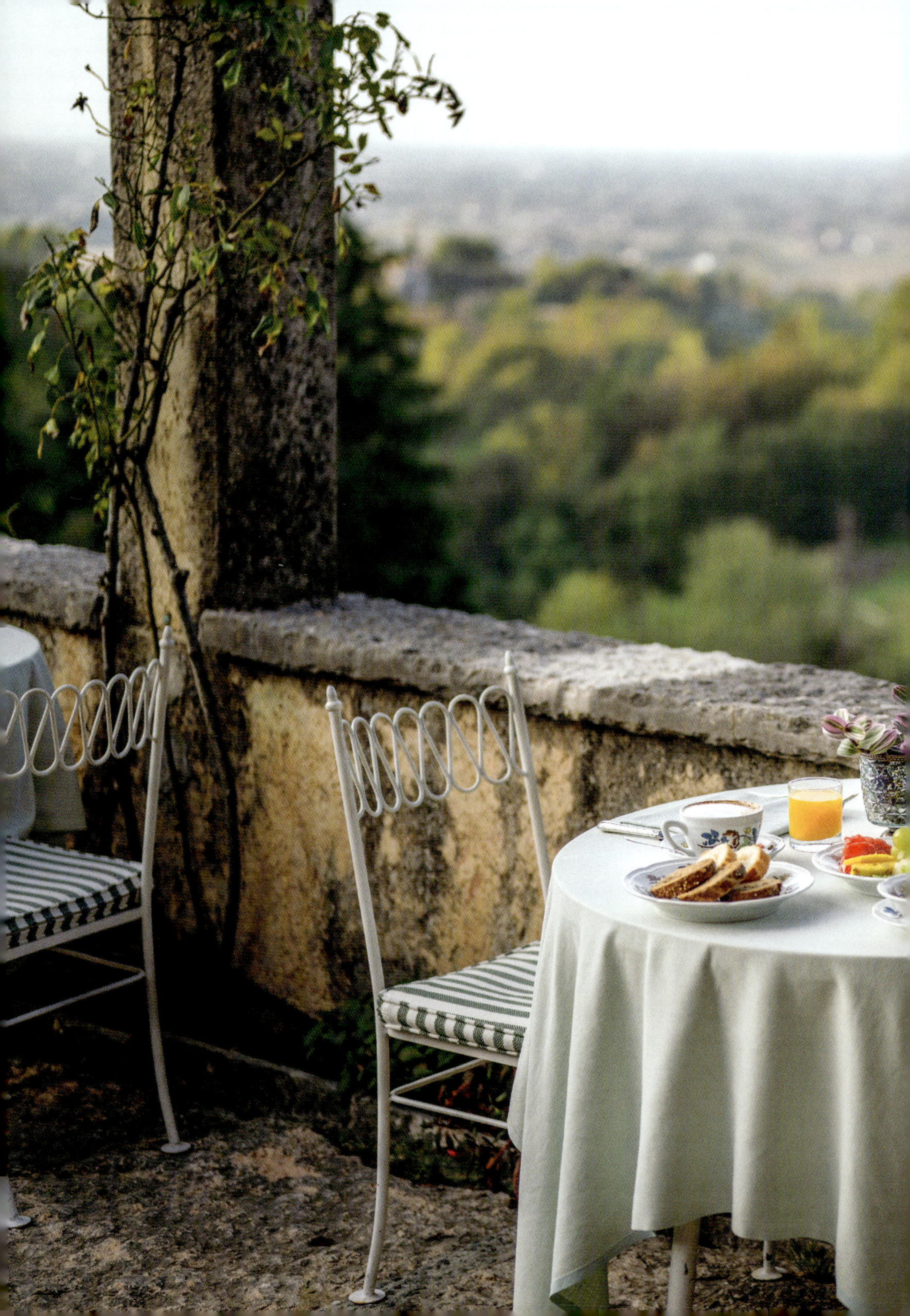

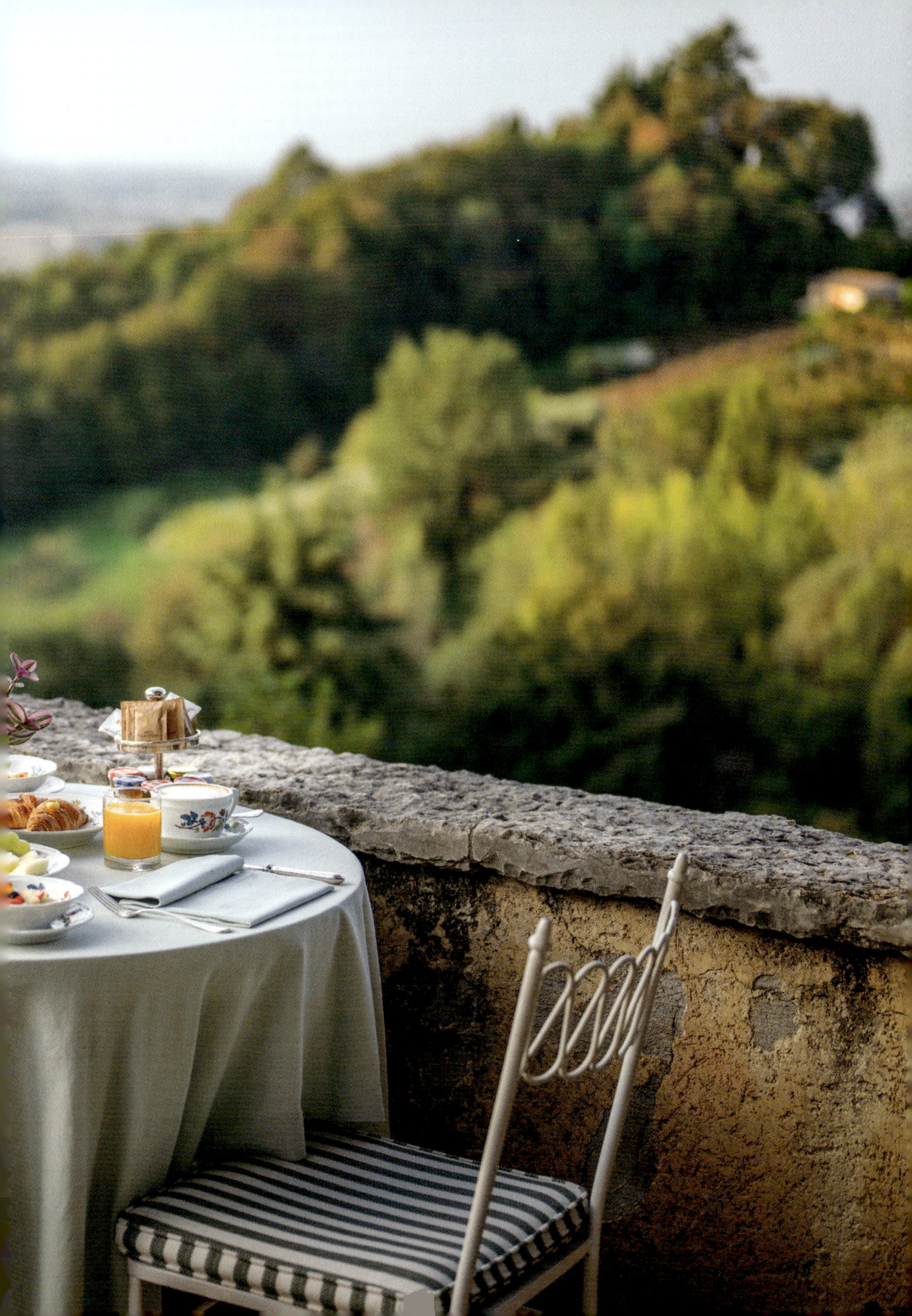

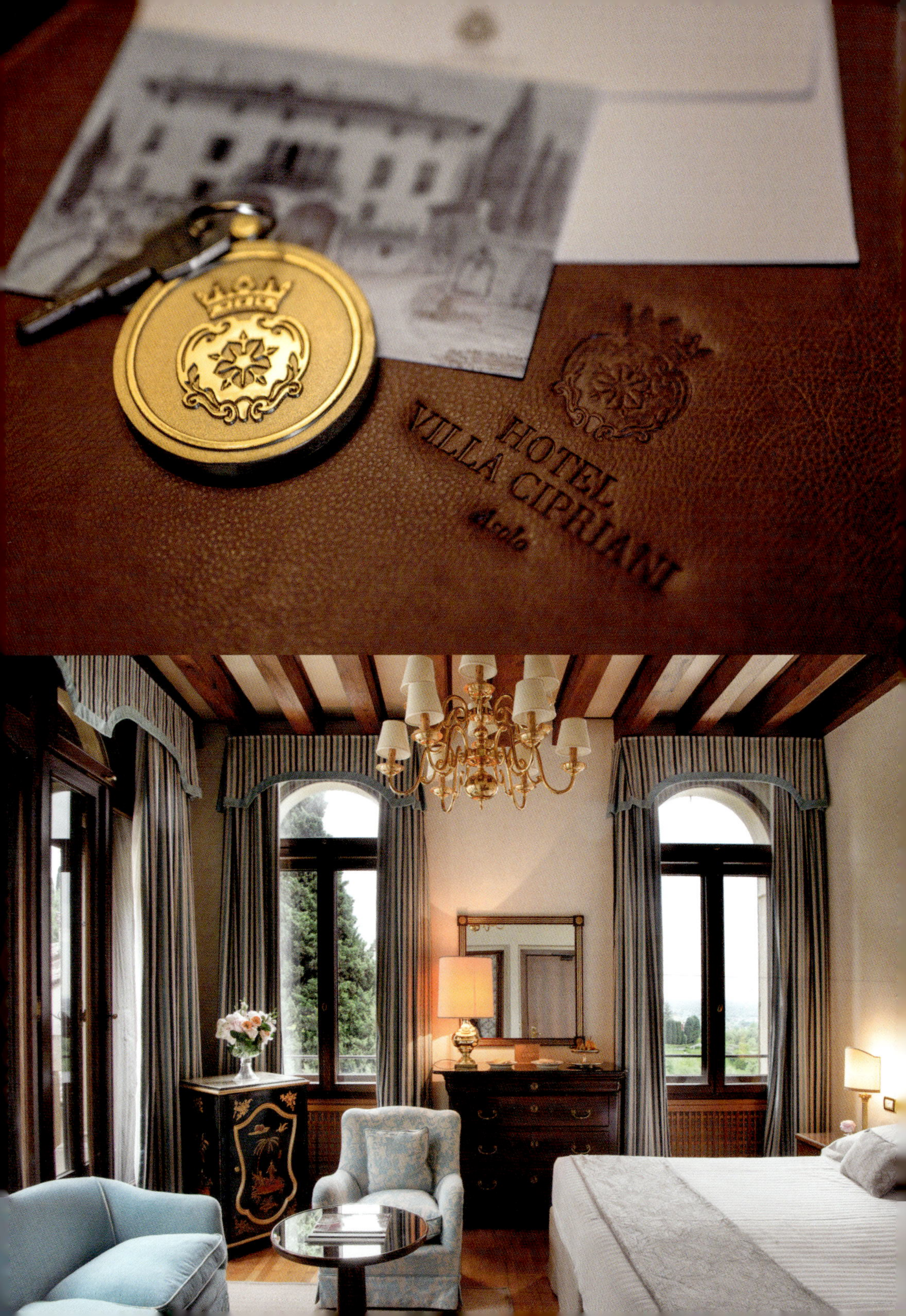
HOTEL
VILLA CIPRIANI
Asolo

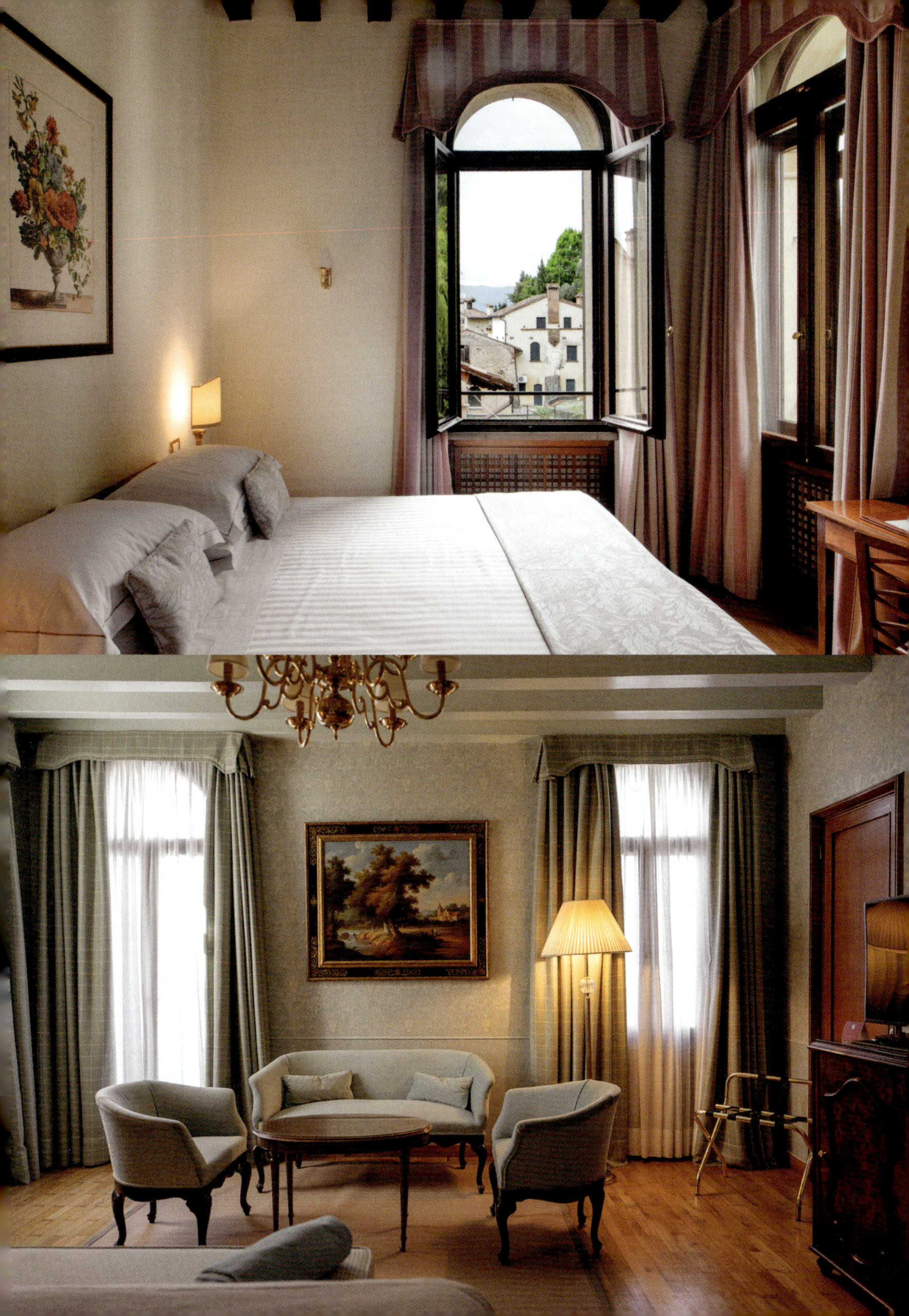

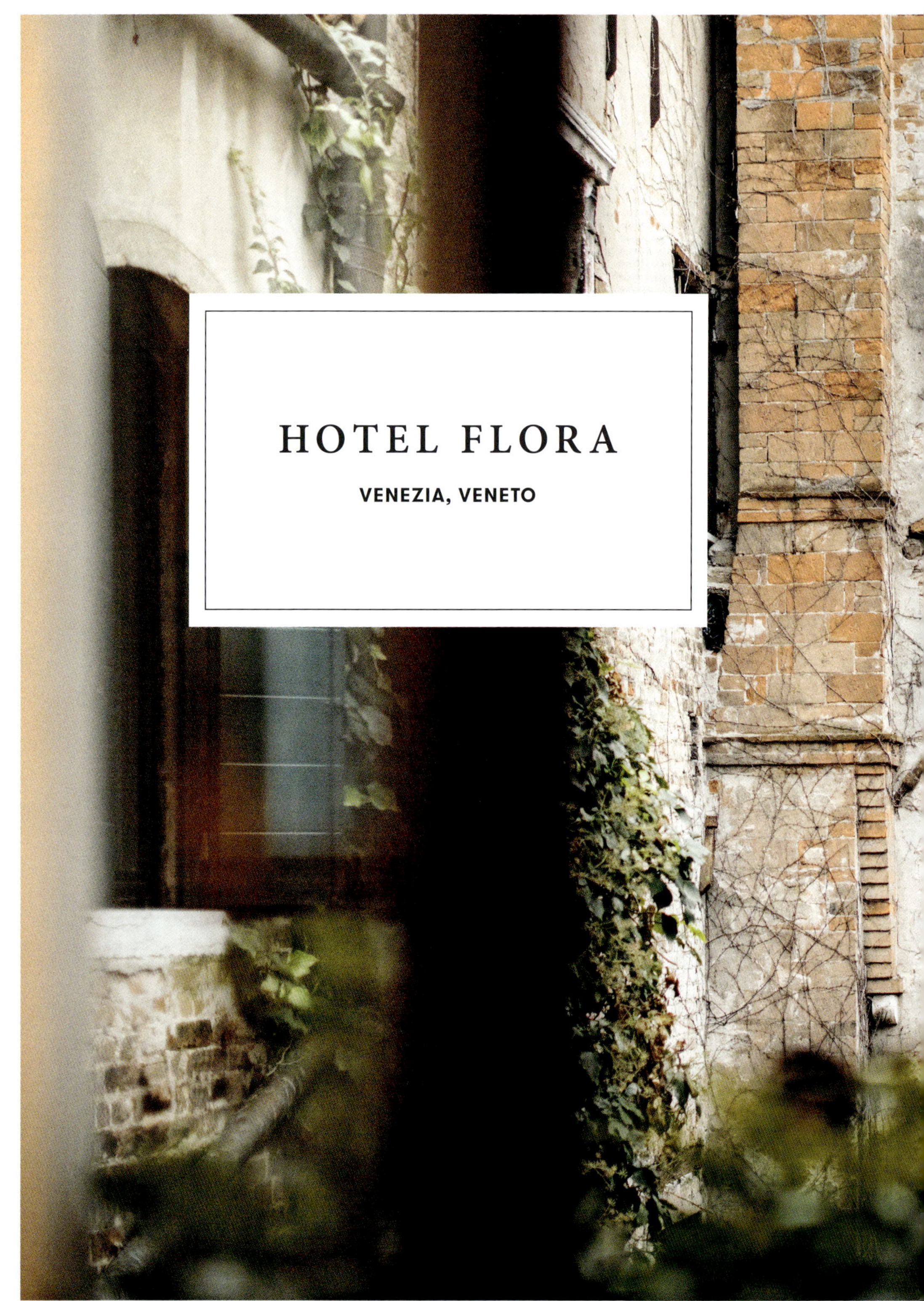

HOTEL FLORA

VENEZIA, VENETO

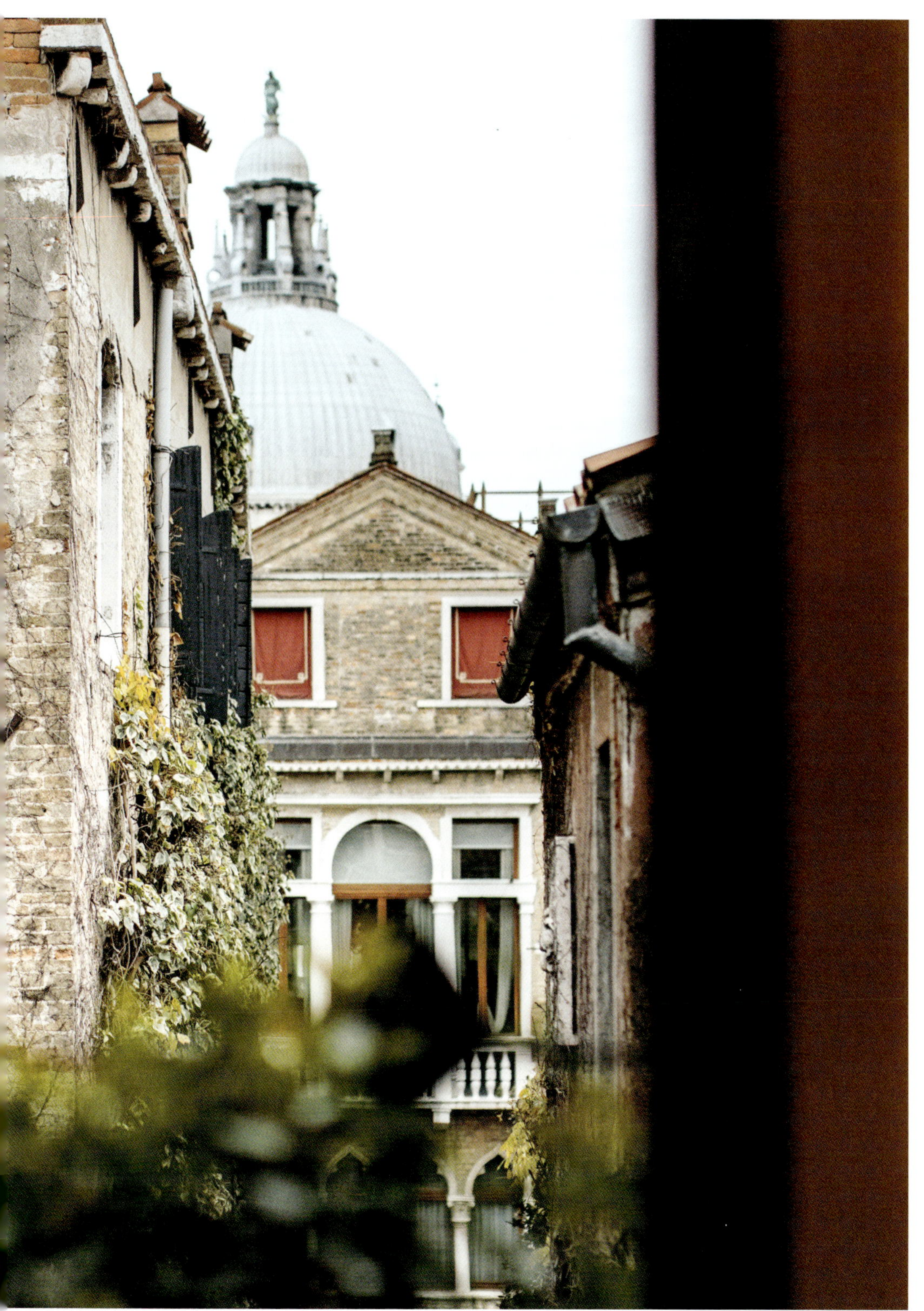

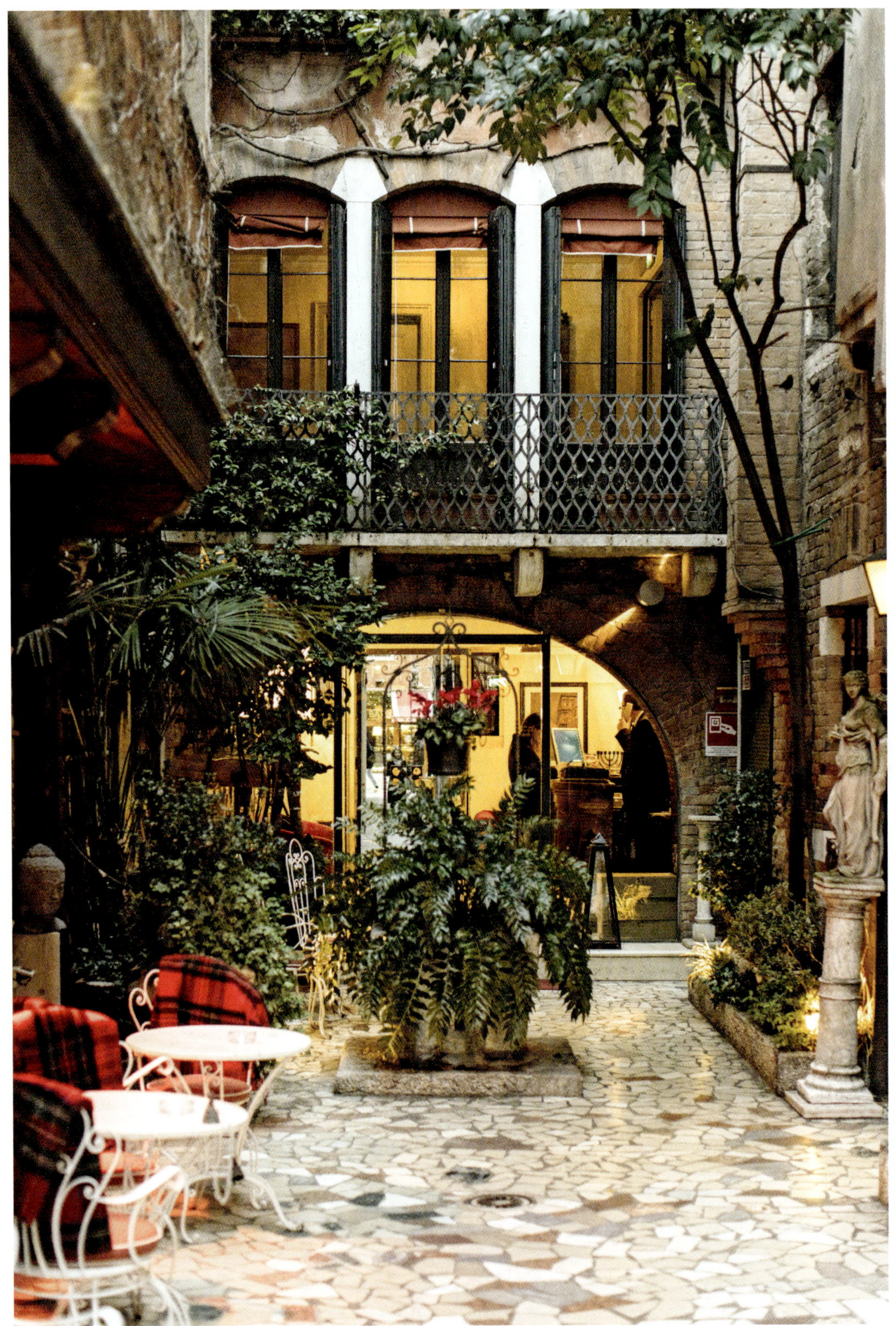

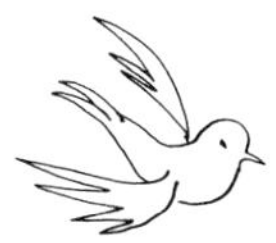

HOTEL FLORA

Calle Larga XXII Marzo, San Marco 2283/A, 30124 Venezia
Tel. +39 041 520 58 44 · info@hotelflora.it
www.hotelflora.it

IN THE HEART OF VENICE "What could I tell you about Venice that you don't already know?", as the painter Paul Signac once asked. Indeed, we are not just acquainted with the fine palazzi, magnificent churches and famous museums, we even know little details too: that Venice is also called "La Serenissima", that the Grand Canal is called Canal and not Canale, that a total of over 400 bridges span the canals and that the city has sunk by almost 9 inches in the last 100 years. But does that mean that we really know Venice? Probably not. Venice is a theater where you have to look behind the scenes; a treasure chest to which you need the key. The Venetians have this key – the Romanelli family, for example, who run the pretty Hotel Flora. For their guests a journey to the heart of Venice begins in their own four walls: in the 17th century the palazzo was a school of painting whose master is said to have known the great Titian personally. The hotel interior with its stucco, ceiling beams, mahogany beds, damask wallpaper and chandeliers also tells a story of art and culture, and right next door in Palazzo Contarini Fasan there lived a lady called Desdemona, who inspired Shakespeare to write "Othello". Those who take advice from the Romanellis before they go sightseeing will explore the lagoon on board a fishing boat, go shopping in hidden galleries or enjoy Italian cooking "alla mamma" in a trattoria. The icing on the cake is to spend some time in the sequestered courtyard of Hotel Flora – the most enchanting oasis in the city. ◆ Book to pack: "Death in Venice" by Thomas Mann.

IM HERZEN VENEDIGS „Was könnte ich Ihnen über Venedig erzählen, was Sie nicht schon wüssten?“, fragte der Maler Paul Signac einmal. Und wirklich: Wir wissen nicht nur von den edlen Palazzi, prachtvollen Kirchen und berühmten Museen, sondern kennen sogar kleine Details – dass Venedig auch „La Serenissima“ heißt und der Canal Grande nicht Canale Grande, dass sich über alle Kanäle mehr als vierhundert Brücken spannen und dass der Boden der Stadt in den letzten hundert Jahren um fast 25 Zentimeter gesunken ist. Aber bedeutet das, dass wir Venedig auch wirklich kennen? Wahrscheinlich nicht. Venedig ist ein Theater, bei dem man hinter die Kulissen sehen muss, eine Schatztruhe, zu der man den passenden Schlüssel braucht. Ihn besitzen Einheimische wie die Familie Romanelli, die das hübsche Hotel Flora führt. Für ihre Gäste beginnt die Reise zum Herzen Venedigs in den eigenen vier Mauern – im 17. Jahrhundert war der Palazzo eine Malschule, deren Leiter den großen Tizian persönlich gekannt haben soll. Von Kunst und Kultur erzählt auch das Interieur mit Deckenbalken oder Stuck, Mahagonibetten, Damasttapeten und Lüstern; und gleich nebenan steht der Palazzo Contarini Fasan, in dem einst eine Dame namens Desdemona lebte, die Shakespeare zu seinem „Othello“ inspirierte. Wer sich von den Romanellis vor dem Sightseeing beraten lässt, entdeckt die Lagune an Bord eines Fischkutters, kauft in versteckten Galerien ein oder genießt in einer Trattoria italienische Küche „alla mamma“. Gekrönt wird das Glück von Momenten im verwunschenen Hof des Flora – die zauberhafteste Oase der Stadt. ◆ Buchtipp: „Der Tod in Venedig“ von Thomas Mann.

AU CŒUR DE VENISE « Que pourrais-je vous dire de Venise que vous ne sachiez déjà ? », disait le peintre Paul Signac. Et il avait raison : non seulement nous connaissons l'existence des nobles palais, des superbes églises et des musées célèbres, mais nous savons aussi que Venise est nommée la Sérénissime et que le Grand Canal la traverse, qu'elle compte plus de 400 ponts et que le niveau du sol de la ville a baissé de près de 25 centimètres au siècle dernier. Mais cela suffit-il ? Non, sans doute. Venise est un théâtre et il faut voir ce qui se passe derrière les décors, elle est une malle aux trésors dont il faut la clé. Les gens nés ici la possèdent, par exemple la famille Romanelli qui dirige le bel hôtel Flora. Pour ceux qui y séjournent, le voyage au cœur de la cité des doges commence ici – au XVIIe siècle, le palais abritait une école de dessin dont le directeur aurait personnellement connu le grand Titien. Les poutres et les stucs, les lits d'acajou, les tentures de damas et les lustres étincelants nous parlent aussi d'art et de culture. Et juste à côté se dresse le palais Contarini Fasan, dit « Maison de Desdémone », celle-là même qui inspira à Shakespeare l'histoire d' « Othello ». Bien inspiré est celui qui écoute les conseils des Romanelli avant de visiter la ville : il découvre la lagune à bord d'un chalutier, fait ses achats dans des galeries bien cachées et déguste dans une trattoria la cuisine vénitienne « alla mamma ». Les instants passés dans la végétation luxuriante de la cour, l'oasis enchanteresse de la ville, ne pourront qu'ajouter à son bonheur. ◆ À lire : « La Mort à Venise » de Thomas Mann.

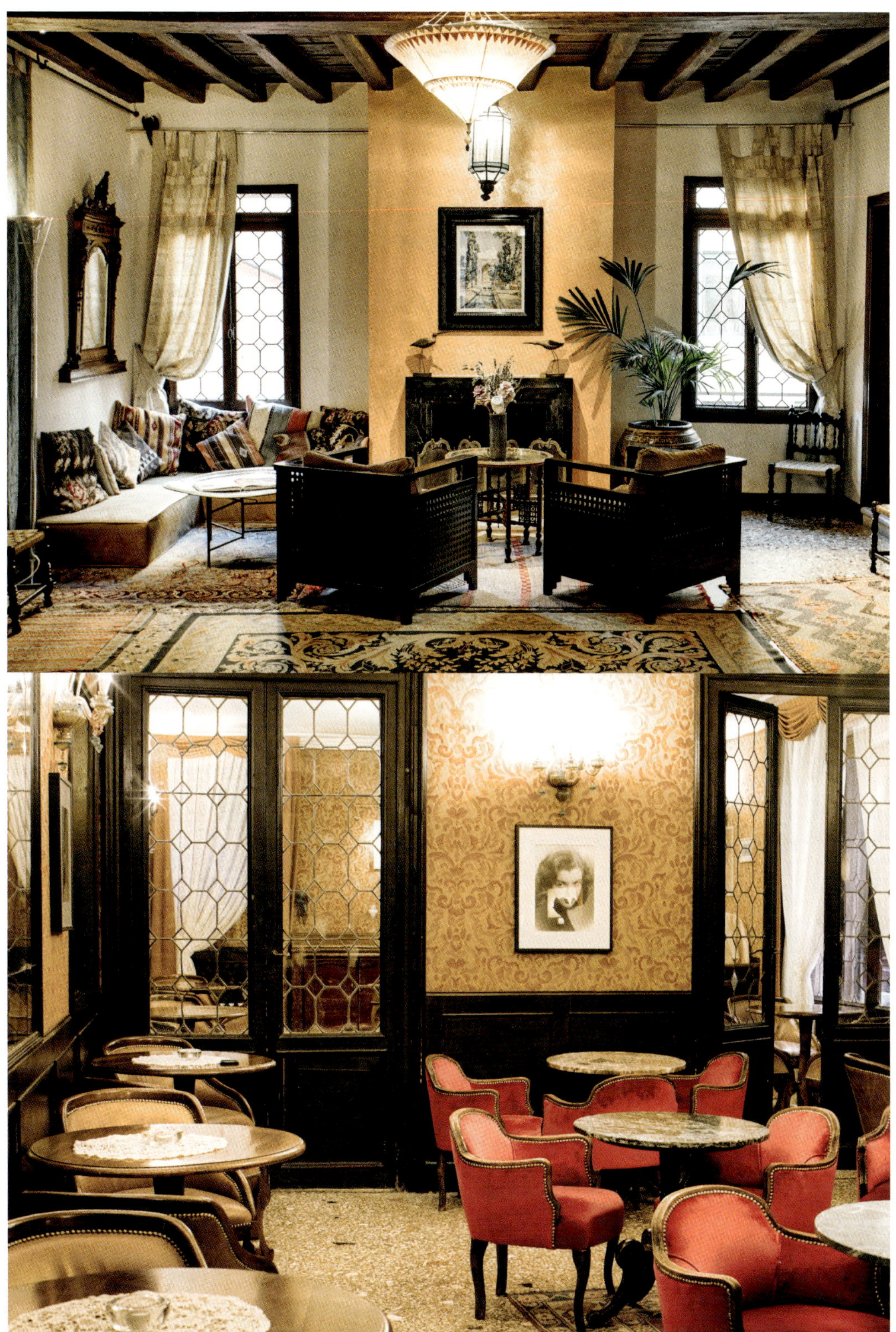

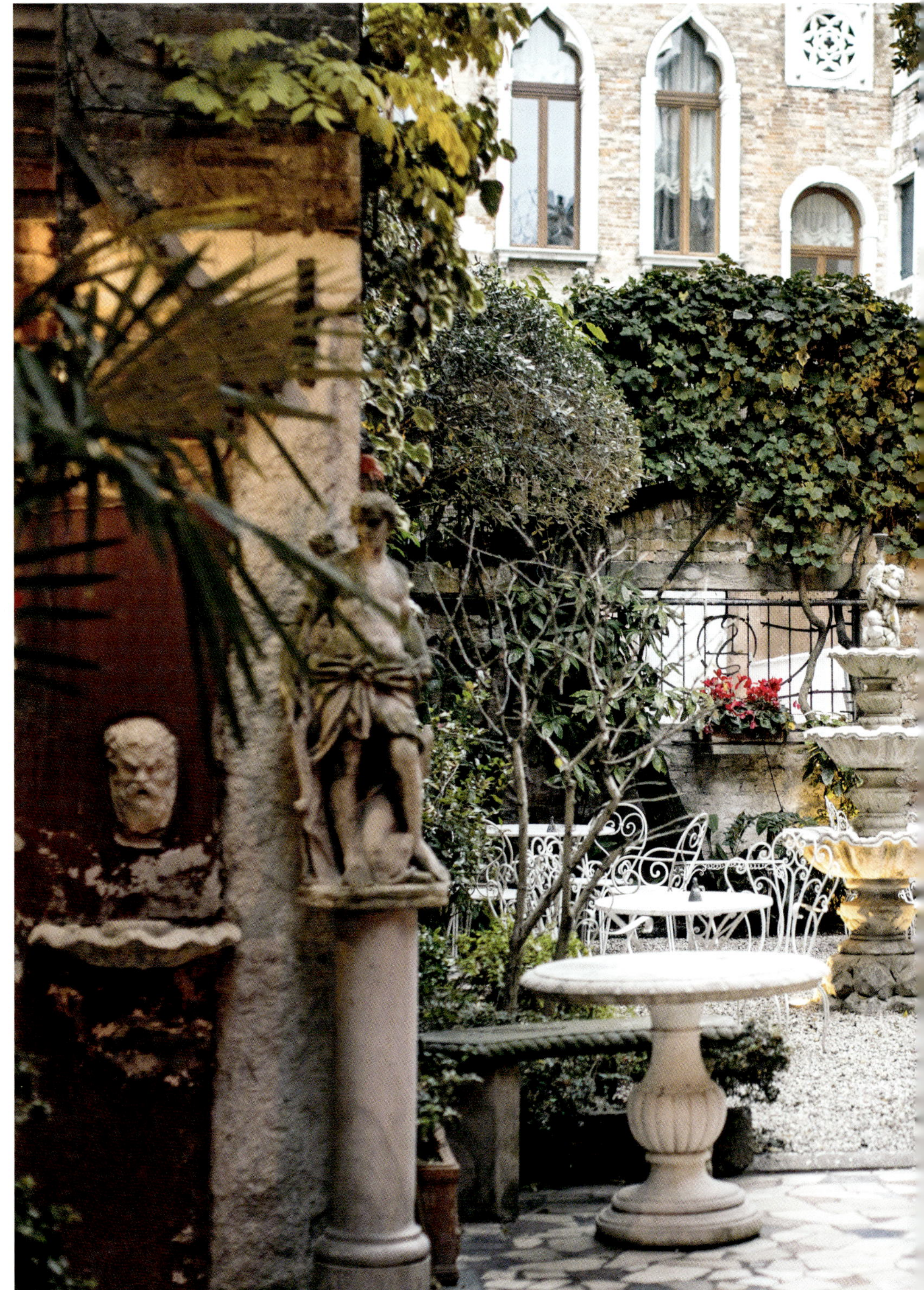

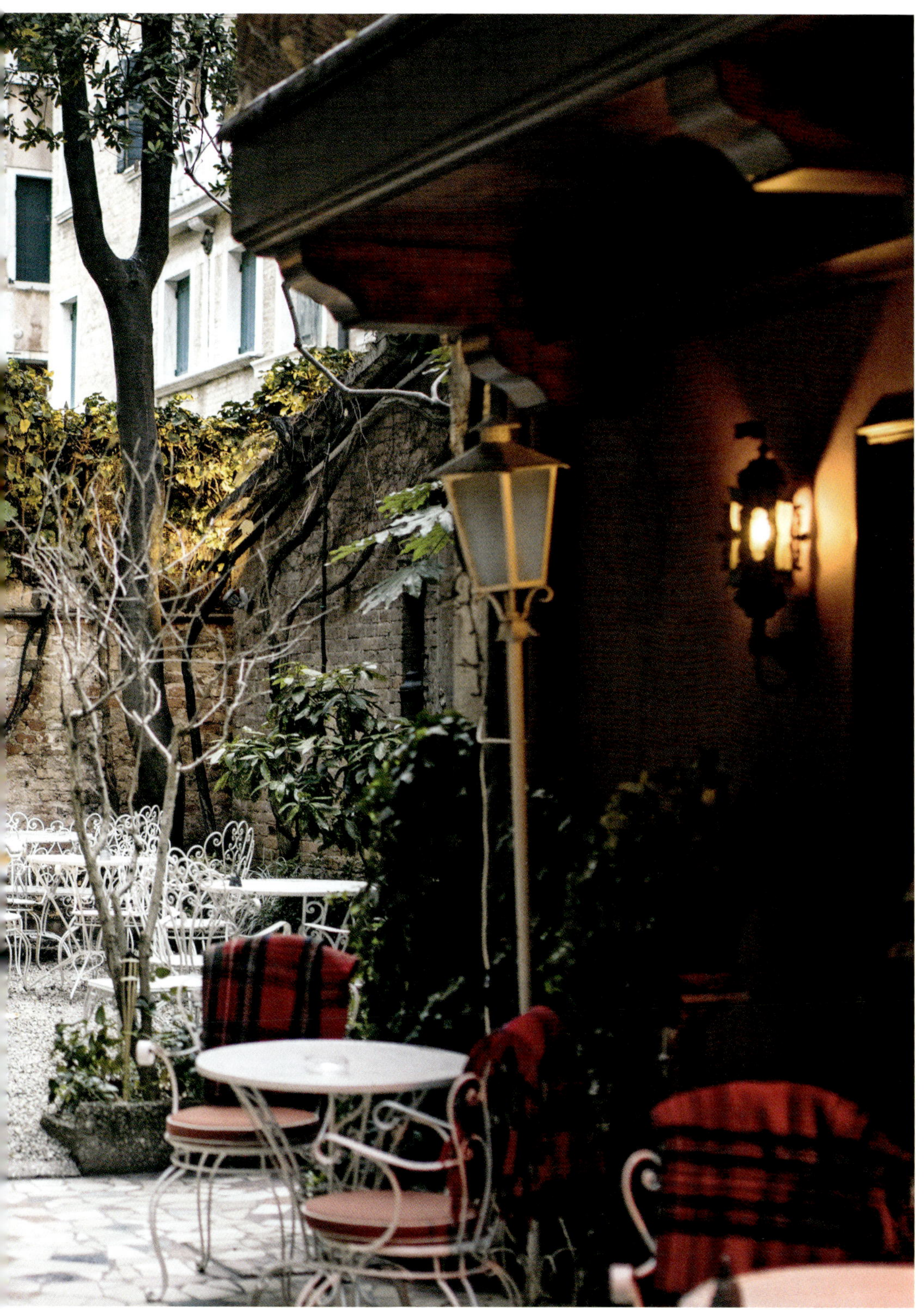

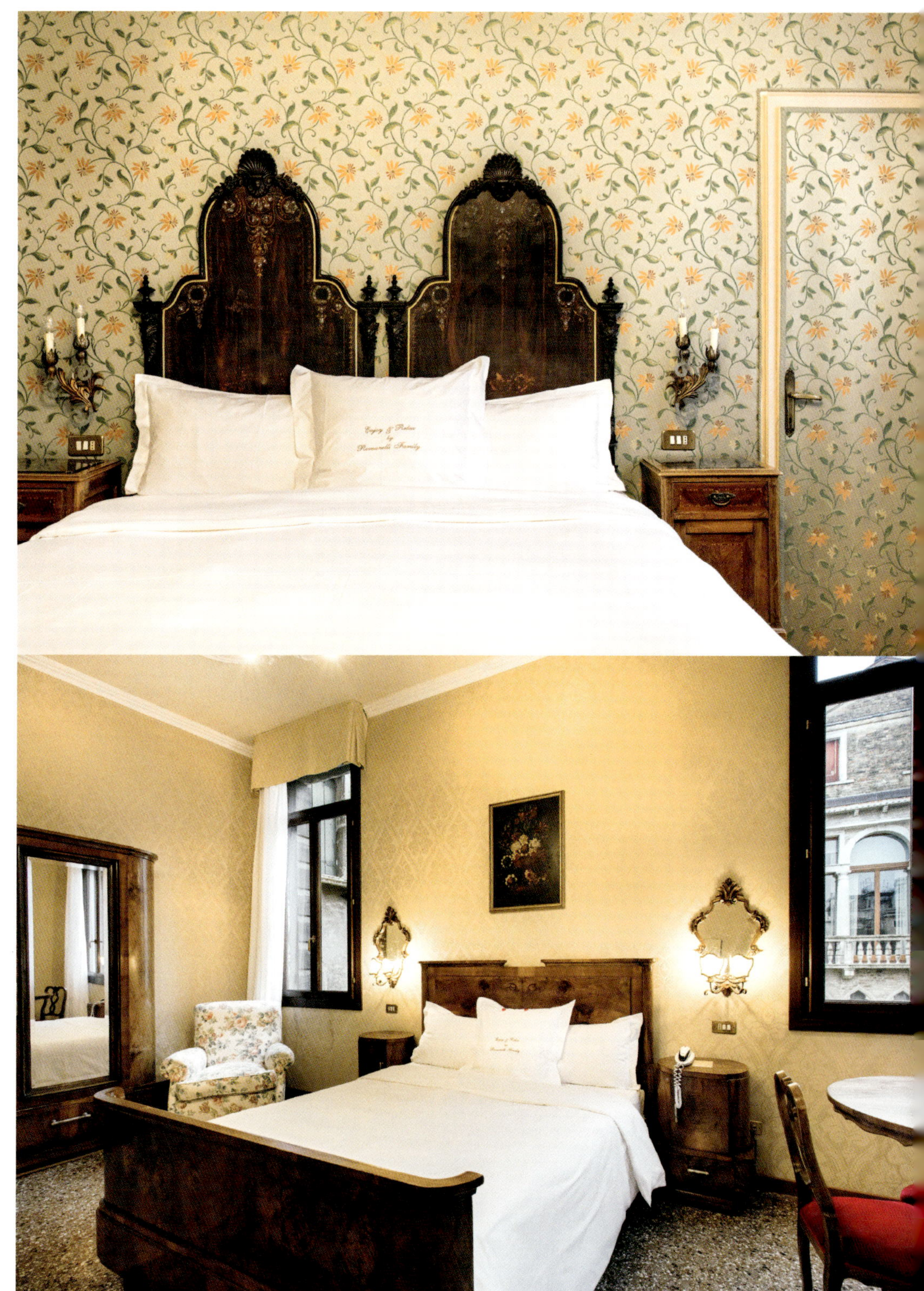

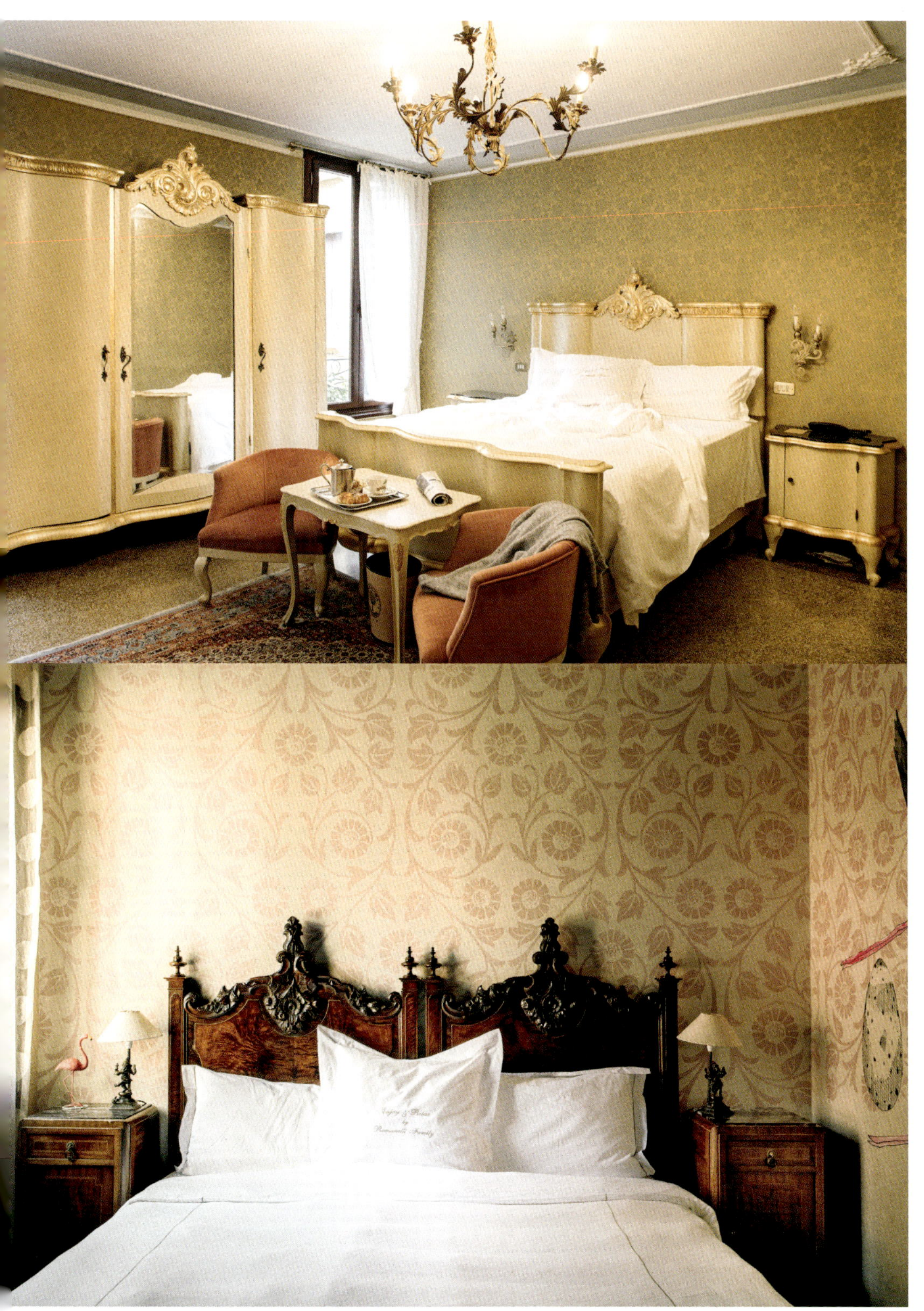

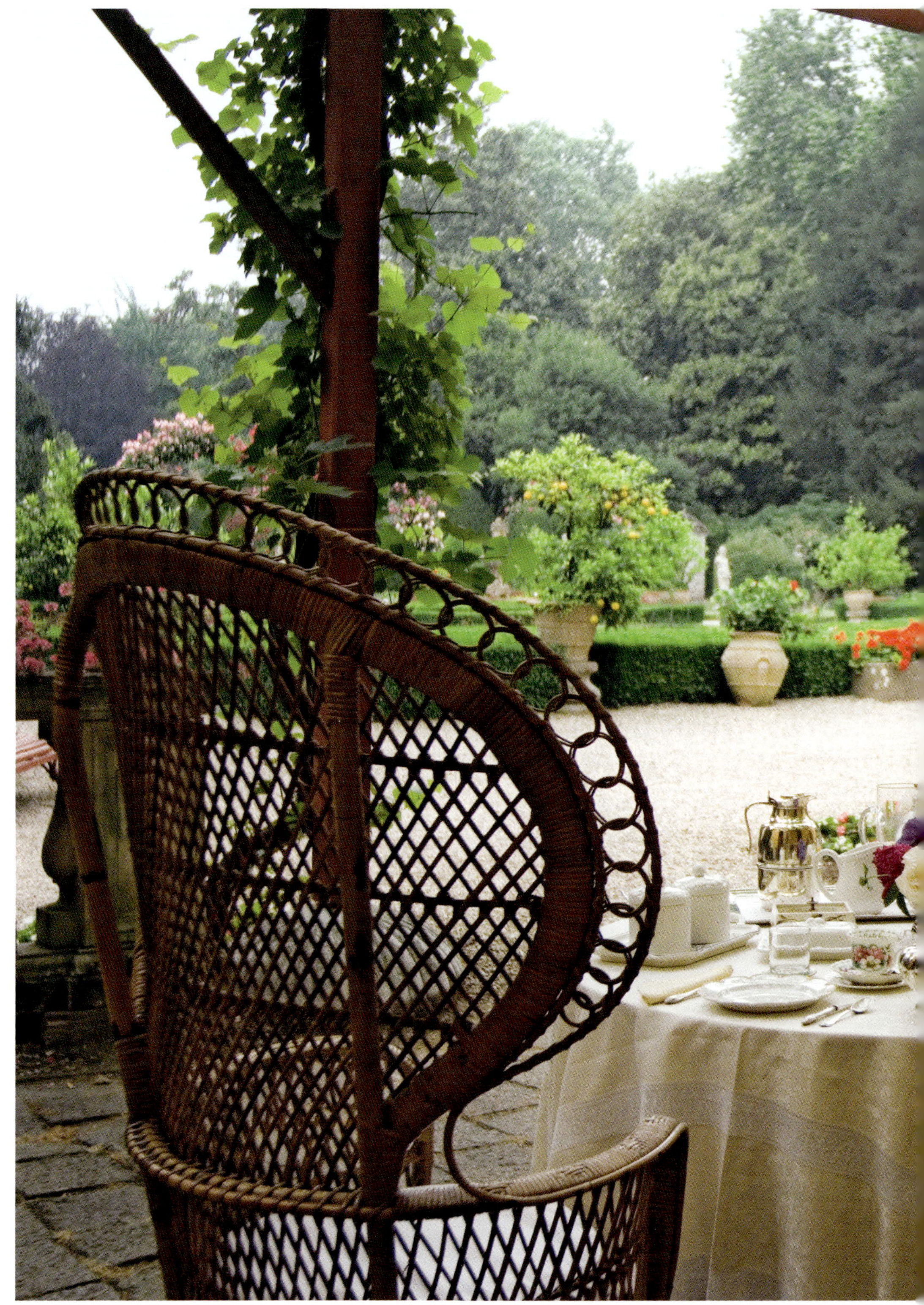

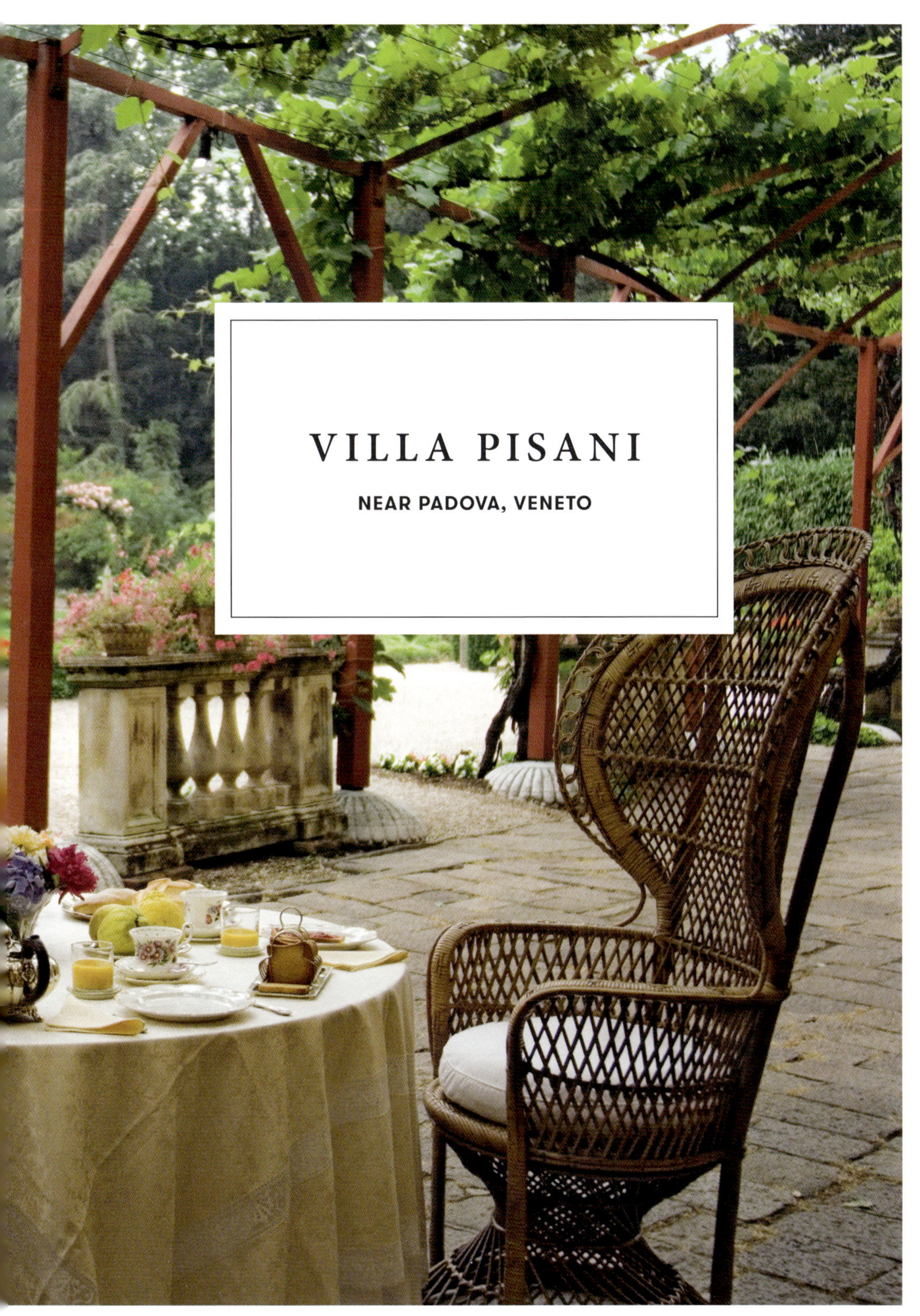

VILLA PISANI

NEAR PADOVA, VENETO

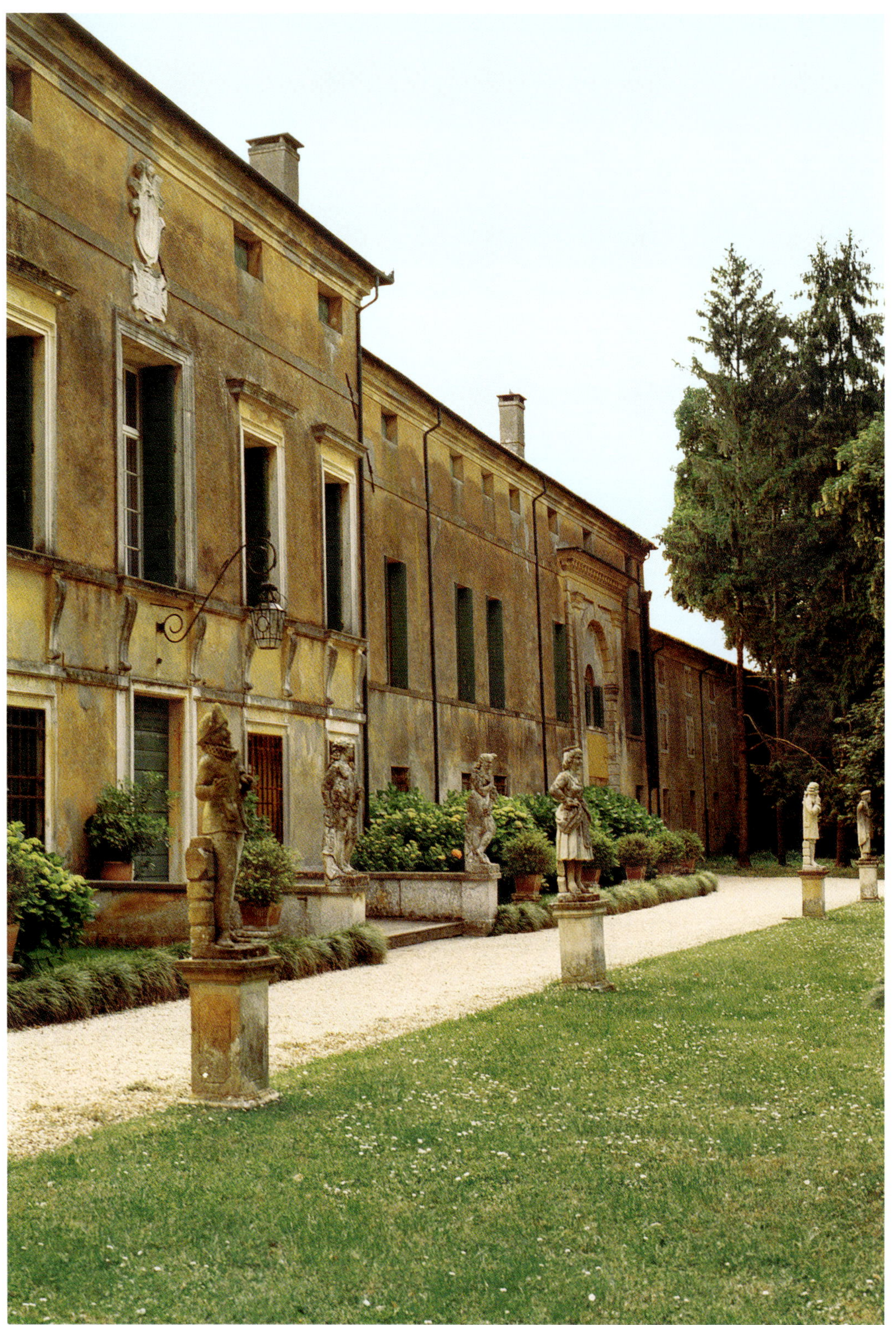

VILLA PISANI

Via Roma 25, 35040 Vescovana
Tel. + 39 0425 154 71 91 · info@villapisani.it
www.villapisani.it

EVELINA'S RICH LEGACY Her father was an English doctor whose patients included Lord Byron; her mother was French and had grown up in the harem of the Turkish sultan. Evelina van Millingen herself was brought up in Istanbul and Rome, with a multicultural and exotic background that she proudly displayed – her first appearance at "La Fenice" in Venice in an oriental robe was the talk of the town and opened the doors of the Italian aristocracy to her. In these circles she met Almoro Pisani III, the heir of one of the richest and noblest Venetian clans. In 1852 they married and moved into Villa Pisani, one of the most magnificent villas inspired by Palladio in the Veneto. Today guests can reside in the very same surroundings in which Evelina once received such notables as Queen Victoria. When the estate was renovated and converted into a high-class guest house, the original frescoes by such superb painters as Paolo Veronese and Giovanni Battista Zelotti were preserved. The rooms are furnished with antiques and have an unimpeded view of the lovely park, which Evelina laid out herself, thus combining Victorian and Italian garden design in keeping with her way of life. She so loved this green paradise that her spirit has remained there: every September, so it is said, the former lady of the house walks through the park. She cannot necessarily be seen, but can always be heard: the silk of her dress rustles softly like the leaves on the trees.
◆ Books to pack: "The Fugitive" by Massimo Carlotto and "Days Spent on a Doge's Farm" by Margaret Symonds (the author dedicated this work to Villa Pisani).

EVELINAS REICHES ERBE Ihr Vater war ein englischer Arzt, zu dessen Patienten Lord Byron gehörte, ihre Mutter eine Französin, die im Harem des türkischen Sultans aufgewachsen war, sie selbst wurde in Istanbul und Rom erzogen: Evelina van Millingen besaß so multikulturelle wie exotische Wurzeln, die sie selbstbewusst zur Schau stellte – ihr erster Besuch in Venedigs „La Fenice" in einer orientalischen Robe sorgte in der ganzen Stadt für Gesprächsstoff und öffnete ihr die Türen zum italienischen Adel. In diesen Kreisen lernte sie Almorò III. Pisani kennen, den Erben einer der nobelsten und reichsten venezianischen Familien. Sie heiratete ihn 1852 und zog mit ihm in die Villa Pisani – eine der prachtvollsten von Palladio inspirierten Villen des Veneto. Im selben Ambiente, in dem Evelina einst Berühmtheiten wie Queen Victoria empfing, kann man noch heute residieren. Bei der Renovierung des Anwesens in ein herrschaftliches Gästehaus wurden die Originalfresken von großartigen Malern wie Paolo Veronese und Giovanni Battista Zelotti erhalten, die Räume sind mit Antiquitäten eingerichtet und blicken direkt in den verwunschenen Park. Ihn hatte Evelina persönlich angelegt und dabei ihrem Lebensstil entsprechend viktorianische und italienische Gartenkunst verbunden. Sie liebte dieses grüne Wunderland so sehr, dass ihr Geist dort noch immer präsent ist: Jedes Jahr im September, so erzählt man sich, wandelt die einstige Hausherrin durch den Park. Dabei ist sie nicht immer zu sehen, aber immer zu hören: Die Seide ihres Kleides raschelt so sanft wie die Blätter der Bäume. ◆ Buchtipps: „Wo die Zitronen blühen" von Massimo Carlotto und „Days Spent on a Doge's Farm" von Margaret Symonds (die Autorin widmete dieses Werk der Villa Pisani).

L'HÉRITAGE D'EVELINA Son père était un médecin anglais dont lord Byron avait été le patient, sa mère une Française qui avait grandi dans le harem du sultan turc – elle-même fut élevée à Istanbul et à Rome : Evelina van Millingen possédait des racines multiculturelles et exotiques qu'elle savait mettre en valeur – sa première apparition en robe orientale à « La Fenice » de Venise défraya la chronique et lui ouvrit les portes de la noblesse italienne. Elle fit alors la connaissance d'Almorò III Pisani, héritier d'une des familles les plus nobles et les plus fortunées de Venise. Elle l'épousa en 1852 et s'installa avec lui dans la Villa Pisani, une des plus splendides villas palladiennes de Vénétie. On peut résider aujourd'hui encore dans ce cadre où ont été reçues des célébrités comme la reine Victoria. Lorsque la propriété a été transformée en hôtel seigneurial, les fresques originales de peintres comme Paul Véronèse et Giovanni Battista Zelotti ont été conservées ; les pièces abritent des antiquités et s'ouvrent directement sur la verdure du parc. Evelina avait conçu personnellement celui-ci, mariant selon son mode de vie l'art des jardins victorien et italien. Elle aimait tant ce séjour enchanteur que son esprit y est encore présent : on raconte que l'ancienne maîtresse des lieux se promène dans le parc chaque année en septembre. On ne la voit pas toujours, mais on entend la soie de sa robe bruisser aussi doucement que les feuilles des arbres. ◆ À lire : « Padana City » de Massimo Carlotto et Marco Videtta et « Days Spent on a Doge's Farm » de Margaret Symonds (dédié à la Villa Pisani).

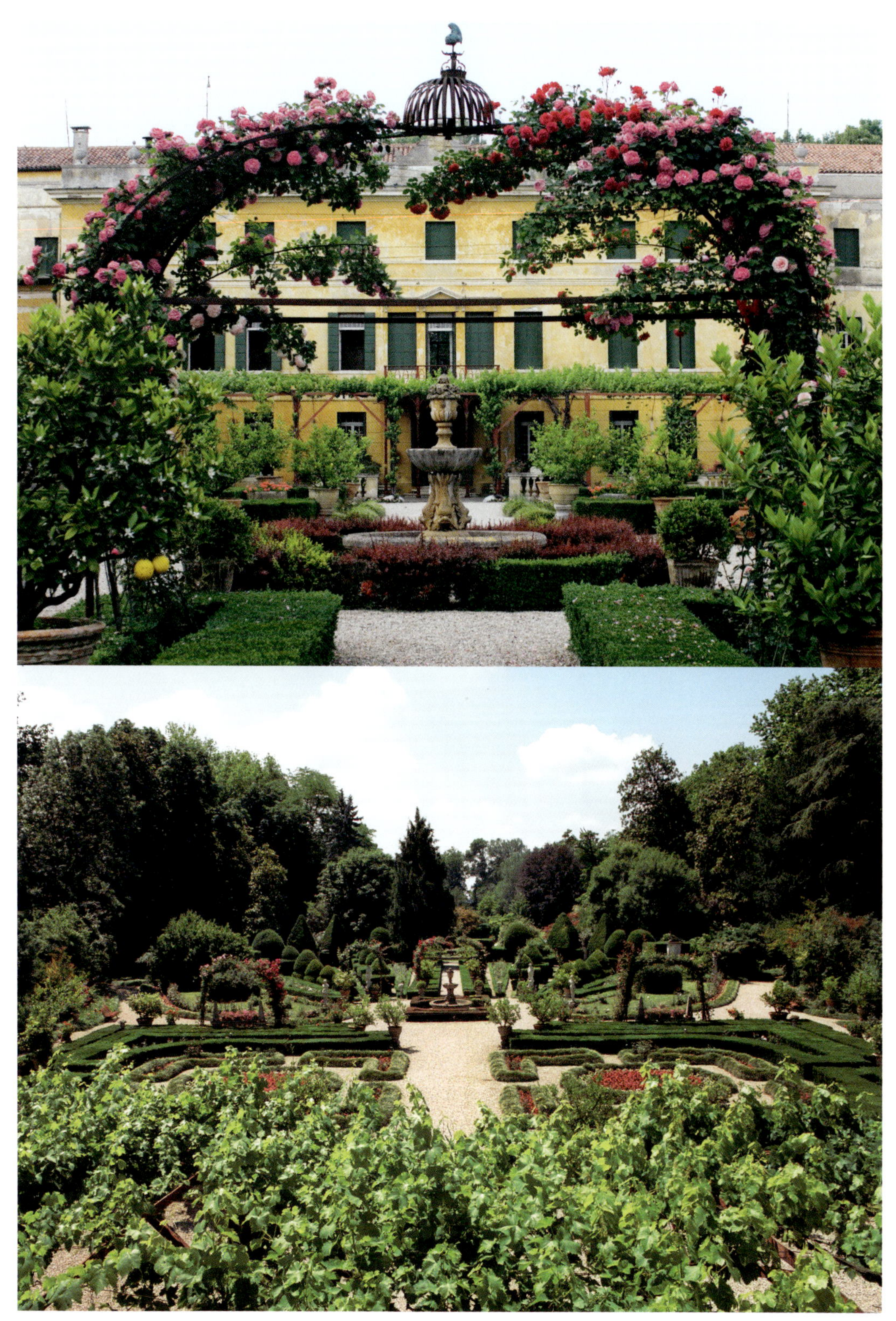

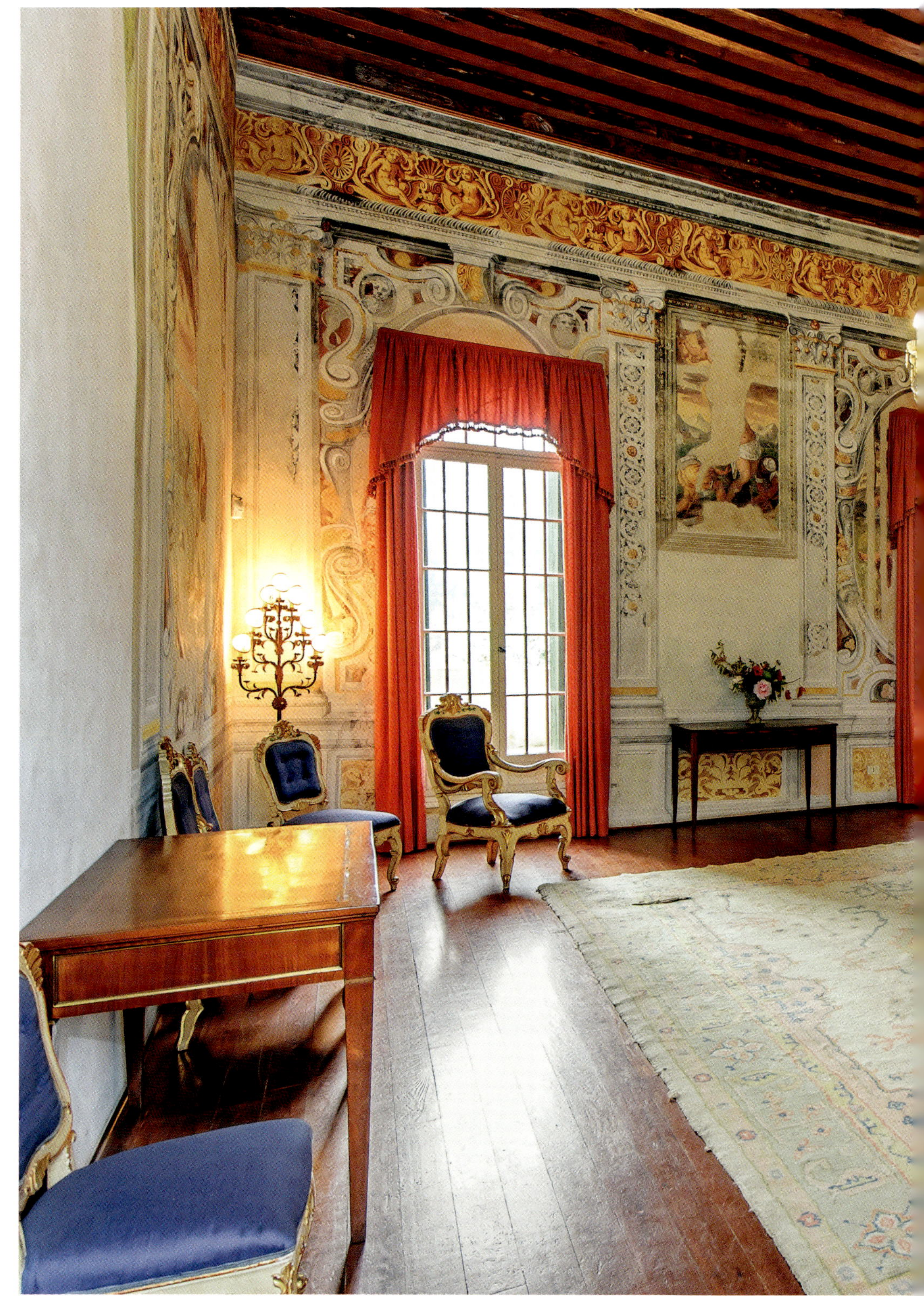

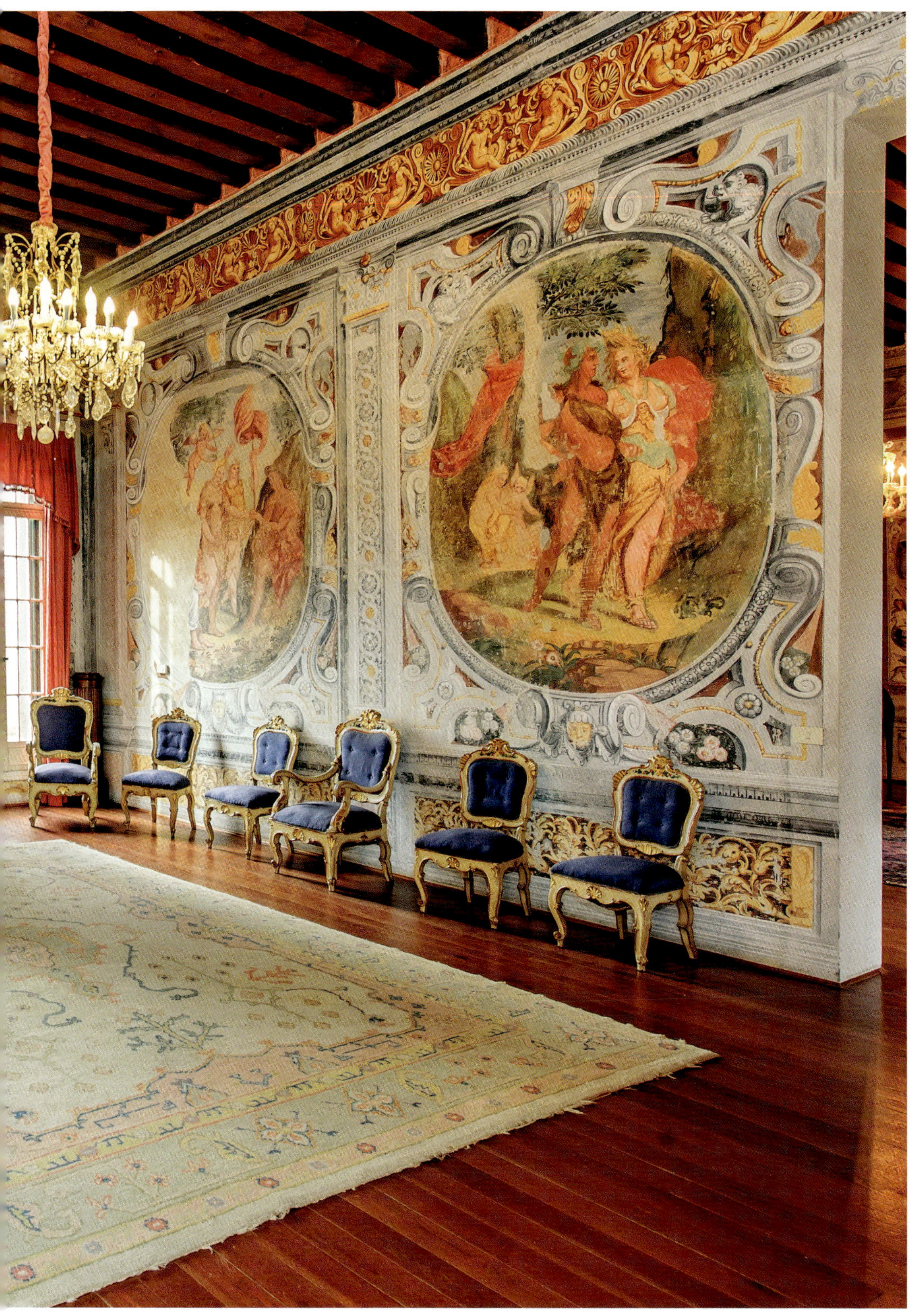

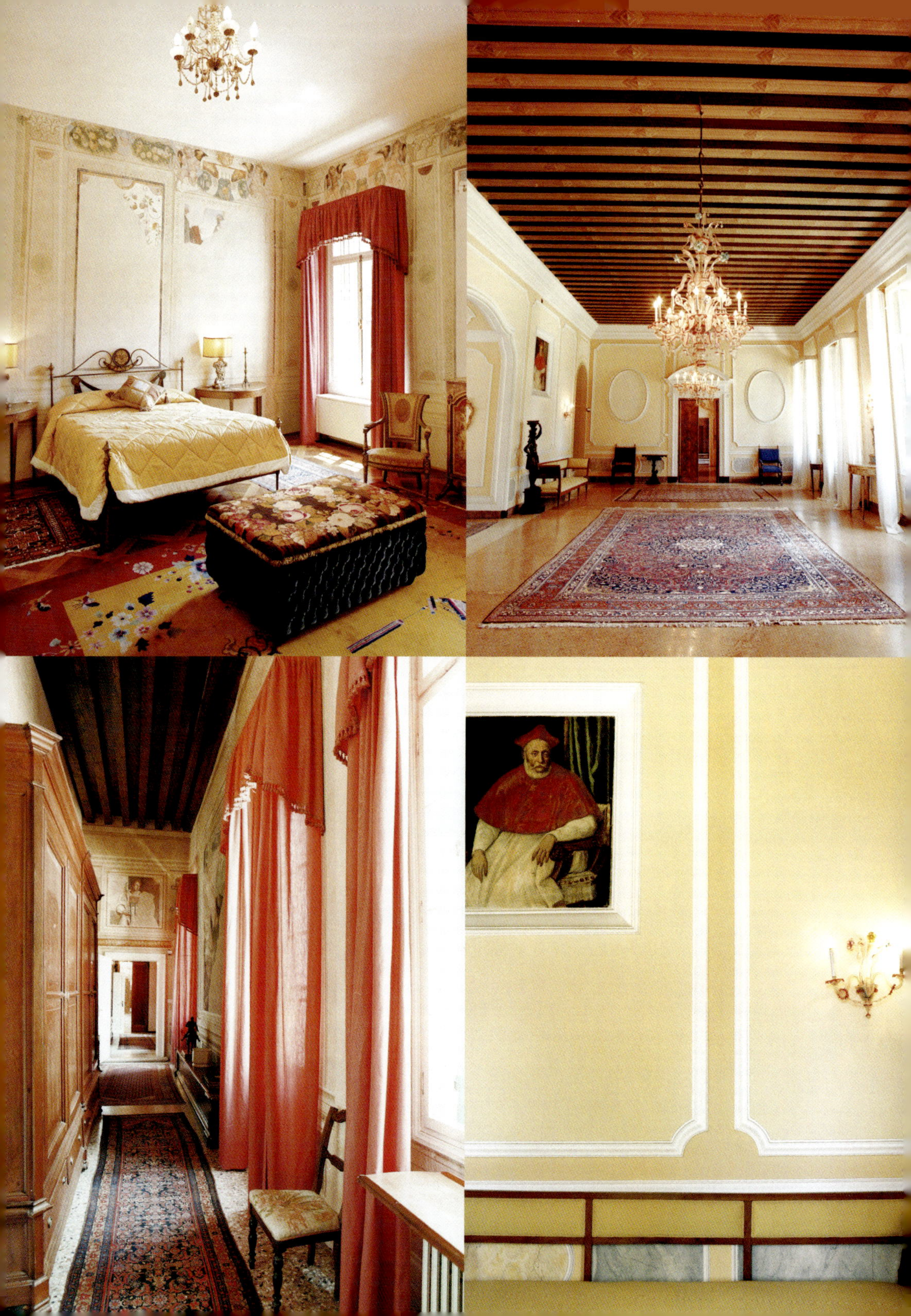

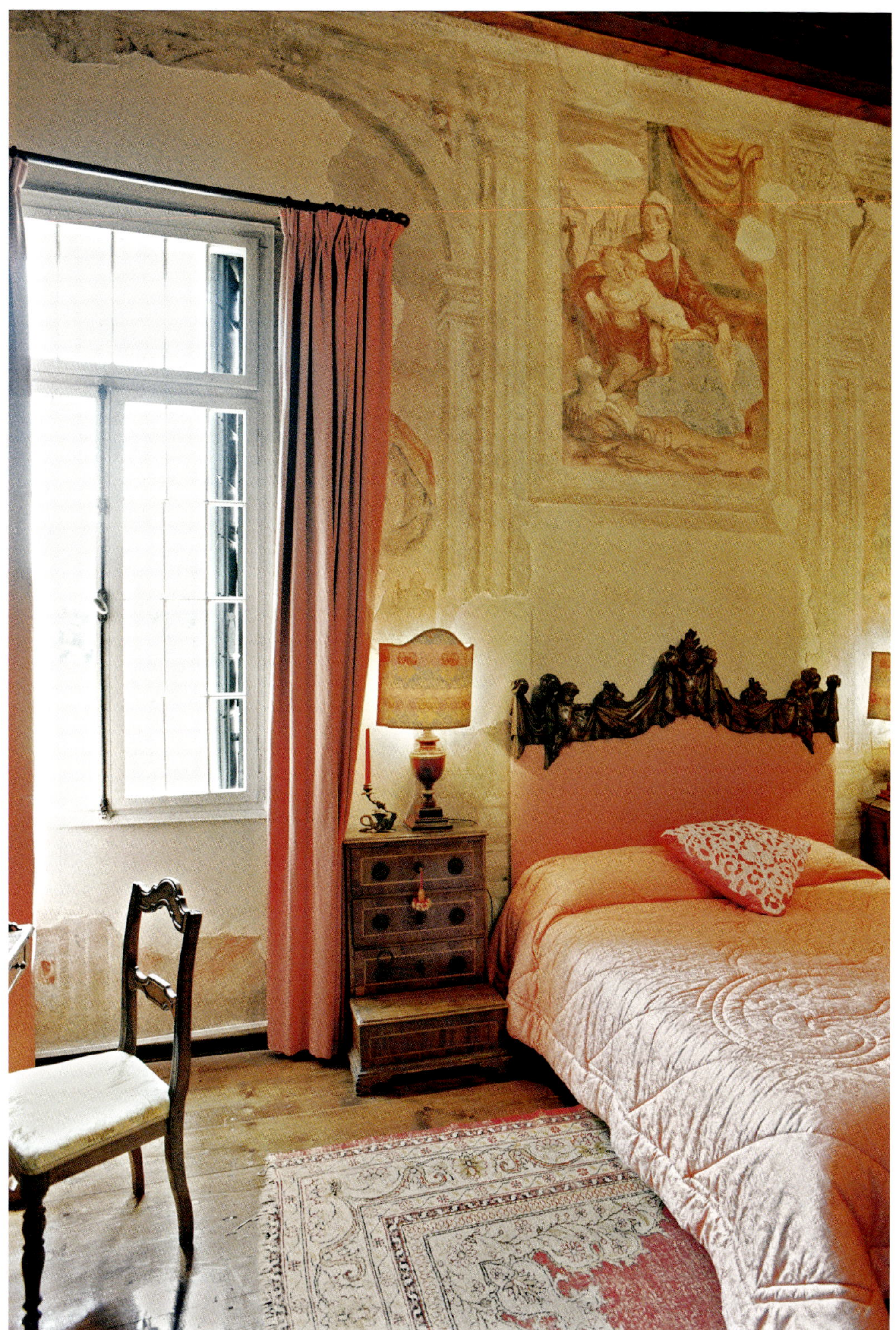

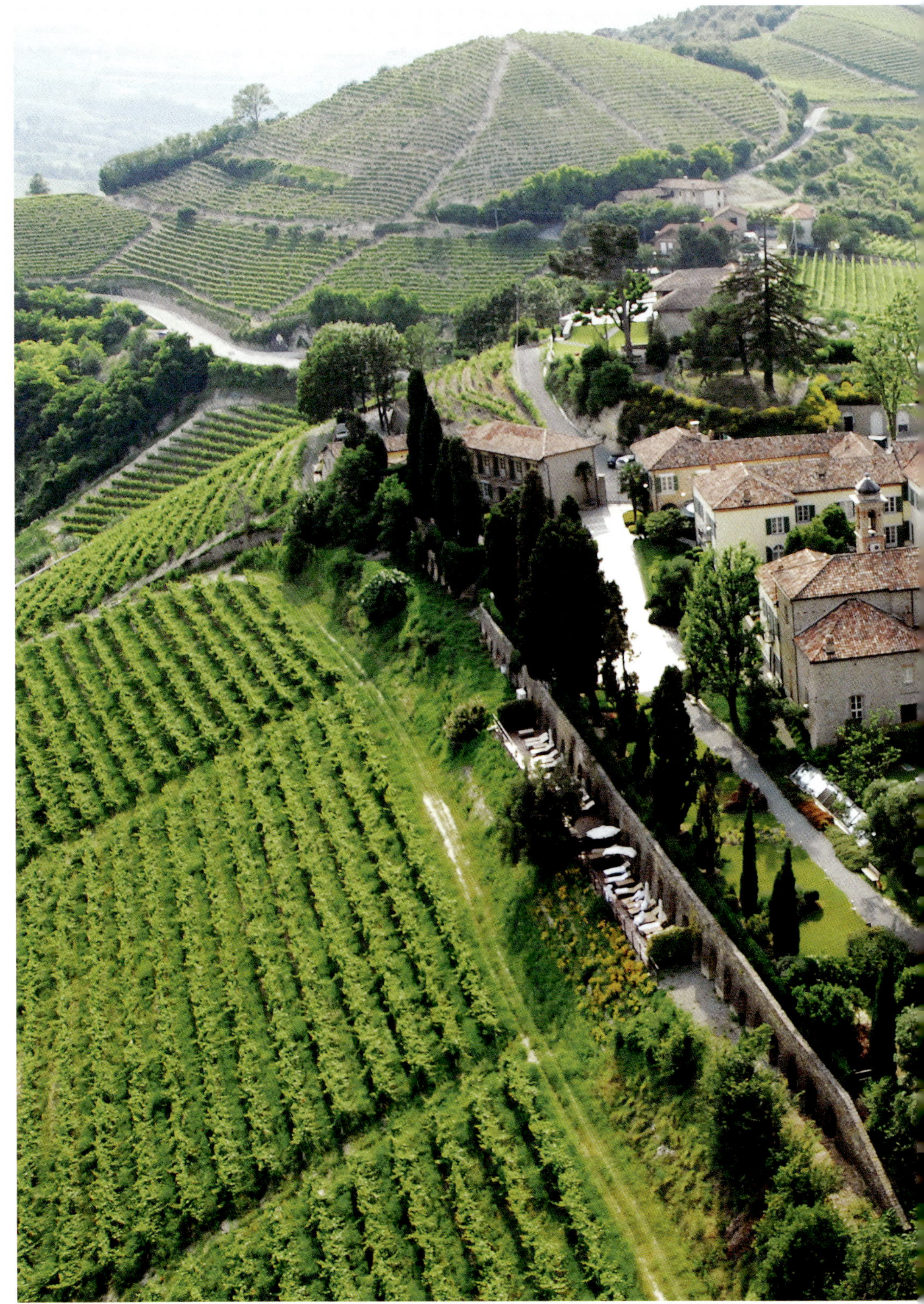

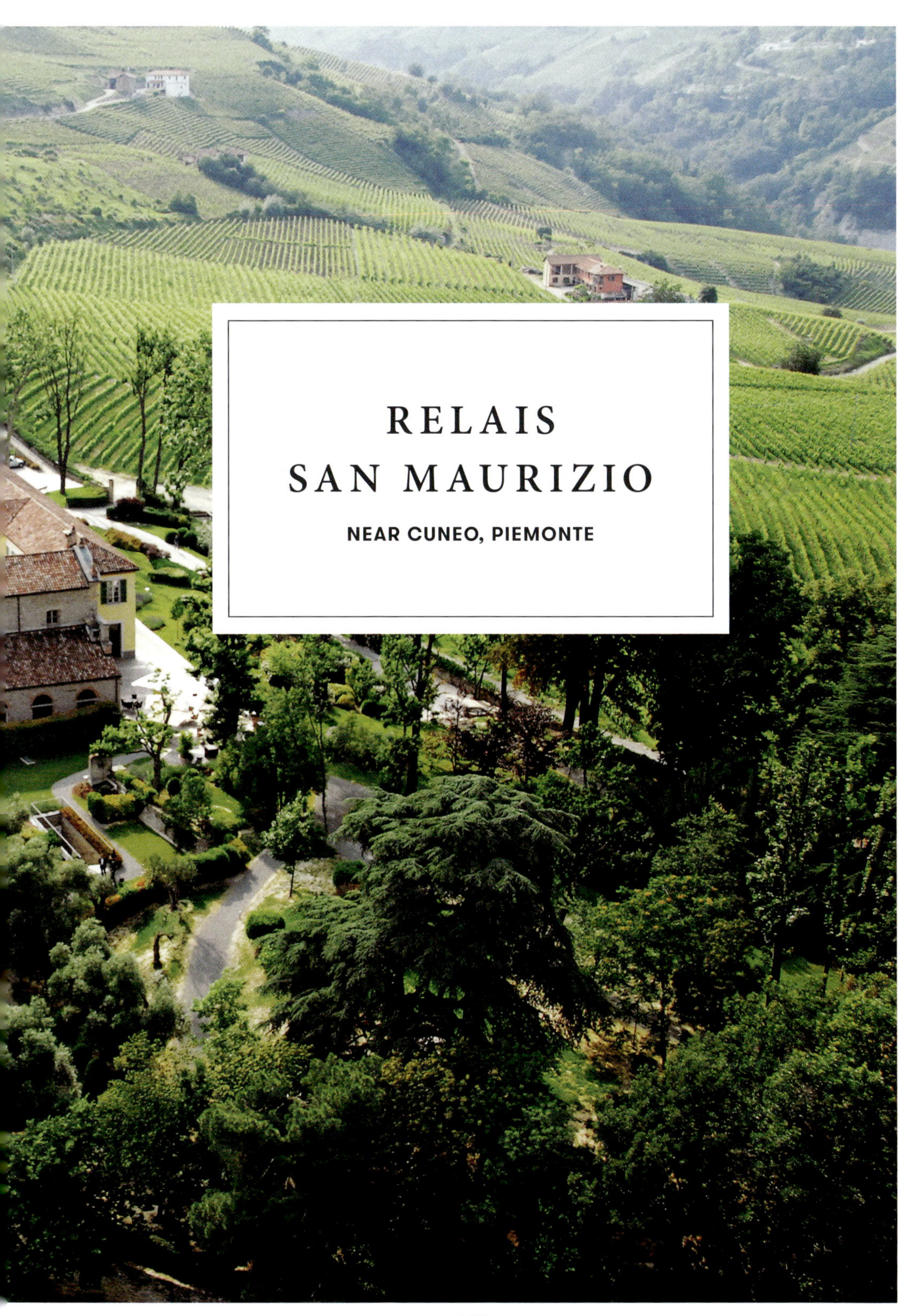

RELAIS SAN MAURIZIO

NEAR CUNEO, PIEMONTE

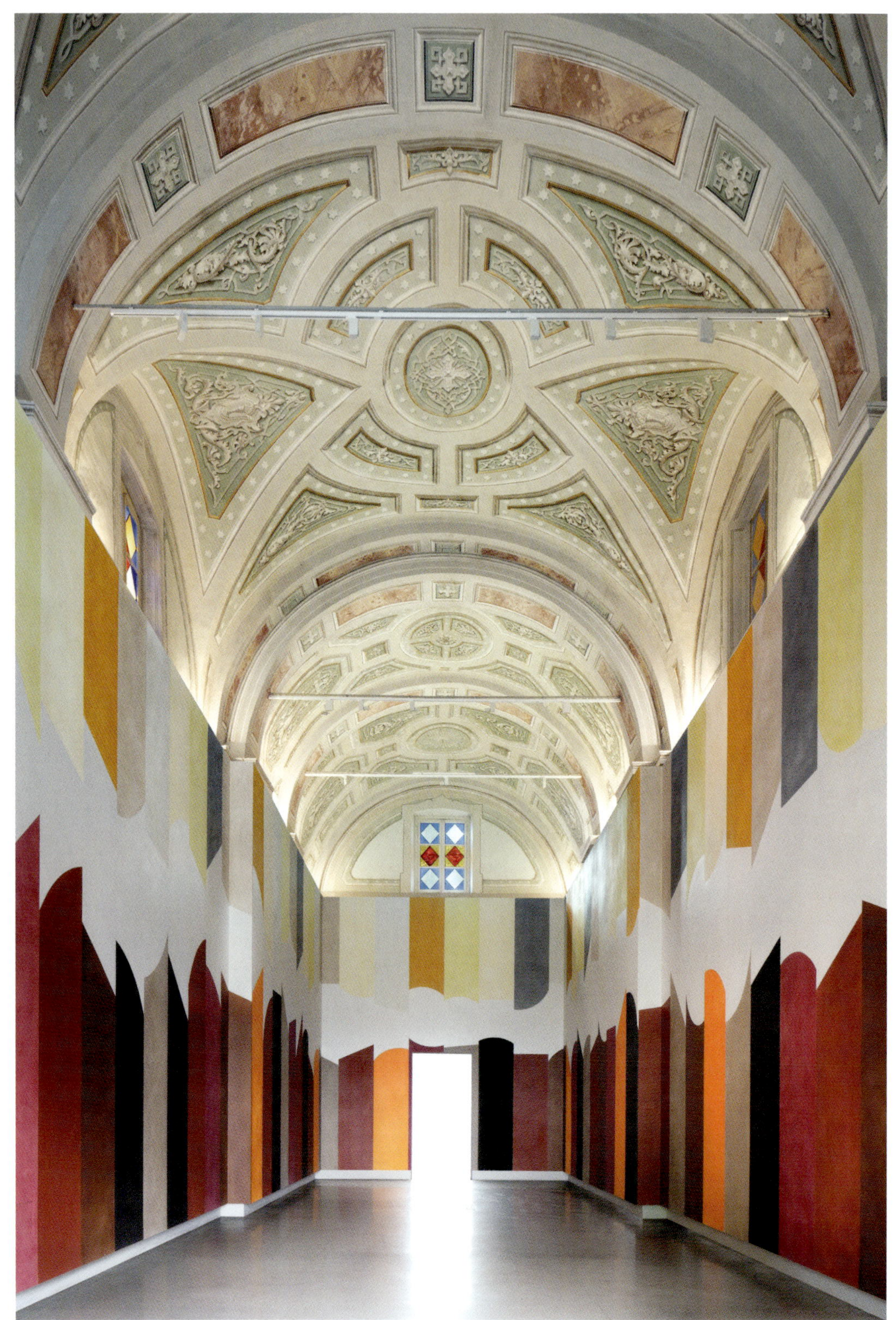

PIEMONTE

RELAIS SAN MAURIZIO

Località San Maurizio 39, 12058 Santo Stefano Belbo
Tel. +39 0141 841 900 · info@relaissanmaurizio.it
www.relaissanmaurizio.it

LAND OF PLENTY You only have to say the name, and the eyes of bon viveurs and gourmets light up: the Langhe is the culinary heart of northern Italy, a luxurious land of plenty. On its hills grow the Nebbiolo grapes, whose name tells of autumn mist ("nebbia") in the valleys; these are the grapes from which the ruby-red Barolo and Barbaresco wines are pressed. In the woods of the Langhe the "tuber magnatum pico" lies hidden: the white Alba truffle that Cicero enthused about long ago and European crowned heads have prized for centuries. Thanks to their seductive aroma, these tubers in mottled colors of cream and nut transform even the simplest dish into a delicacy. They are considered the best and most expensive truffles in the world – in 2007 a fanatical gourmet bought a 750-gram truffle for 143,000 euros at auction in Alba. This "white gold" can be enjoyed in the Michelin-starred restaurant of Relais San Maurizio, a former Cistercian monastery that is today home to a wonderful family-owned hotel. The culinary treats are served in a vaulted cellar that is every bit as atmospheric as the rooms, which were created from former monks' cells. For all its creature comforts, the estate has preserved its contemplative peace: guests can walk beneath ancient trees in the park, enjoy floating in relaxing salt pools in the spa and gaze across the vineyards. A stay in the Langhe could not offer more enjoyment. ◆ Book to pack: "This Business of Living" by Cesare Pavese.

IM SCHLARAFFENLAND Man muss nur einmal ihren Namen aussprechen – und schon bekommen Genießer und Gourmets glänzende Augen: Die Langhe sind das kulinarische Herz Norditaliens, ein Schlaraffenland de luxe. Auf ihren Hügeln wachsen die Nebbiolo-Trauben, die vom herbstlichen Nebel („nebbia") in den Tälern erzählen und aus denen die rubinroten Weine Barolo und Barbaresco gekeltert werden. Und in ihren Wäldern versteckt sich der „Tuber magnatum Pico" – der weiße Alba-Trüffel, von dem schon Cicero schwärmte und den Friedrich I. von Preußen höchstpersönlich suchte. Die creme- und nussfarben marmorierten Knollen verwandeln dank ihres verführerischen Aromas selbst die schlichtesten Speisen in Delikatessen; sie gelten als die besten und teuersten Trüffeln der Welt – im Jahr 2007 ersteigerte ein fanatischer Feinschmecker in Alba einen 750-Gramm-Trüffel für 143.000 Euro. Das „weiße Gold" lässt sich auch im mit einem Michelin-Stern ausgezeichneten Restaurant des Relais San Maurizio genießen. Einst war der Bau ein ehemaliges Zisterzienserkloster, heute beherbergt er ein wunderschönes Hotel in Familienbesitz. Die kulinarischen Köstlichkeiten weden im Gewölbekeller serviert – er ist ebenso stimmungsvoll wie die Zimmer, die aus den einstigen Mönchszellen entstanden sind. Bei allem Komfort hat sich das Anwesen eine kontemplative Ruhe bewahrt: Im Park wandelt man unter uralten Bäumen, im Spa entspannt der Salzwasserpool, und der Blick schweift über die Weinberge – genussvoller kann ein Aufenthalt in den Langhe nicht sein. ◆ Buchtipp: „Das Handwerk des Lebens" von Cesare Pavese.

LE PAYS DE COCAGNE Rien que leur nom fait briller les yeux des gourmets et des bons vivants : les Langhe sont le cœur gastronomique de l'Italie du Nord, une région où règne l'abondance. Sur ses collines pousse le nebbiolo, un cépage dont le nom (« nebbia ») évoque la brume automnale et qui composera le barolo et le barbaresco couleur de rubis. Et dans les forêts se cache la « tuber magnatum pico », la truffe blanche du Piémont, dont Cicéron chantait déjà les louanges et que Frédéric Ier de Prusse allait chercher en personne. L'arôme subtil de l'« enfant de la terre » aux marbrures crème et noisette transforme les plats les plus sobres en mets exquis ; elle est la meilleure truffe du monde et la plus chère – en 2007, un amateur d'Alba n'a pas hésité à débourser 143 000 euros pour une truffe de 750 grammes. Cet « or blanc » est bien sûr à la carte du restaurant étoilé du Relais San Maurizio, un ancien monastère cistercien qui abrite aujourd'hui un merveilleux hôtel familial. Les mets sont servis sous les voûtes, dans un cadre aussi impressionnant que celui des chambres qui étaient autrefois les cellules des moines. En dépit des changements apportés pour assurer le confort des clients, le domaine a su conserver son atmosphère paisible, propice à la méditation : les hôtes se promènent à l'ombre des arbres ancestraux du parc, se relaxent dans les bassins d'eau salée du spa, d'où ils admirent les vignobles du domaine. Un séjour dans les Langhe ne saurait être plus agréable. ◆ À lire : « Le Métier de vivre » de Cesare Pavese.

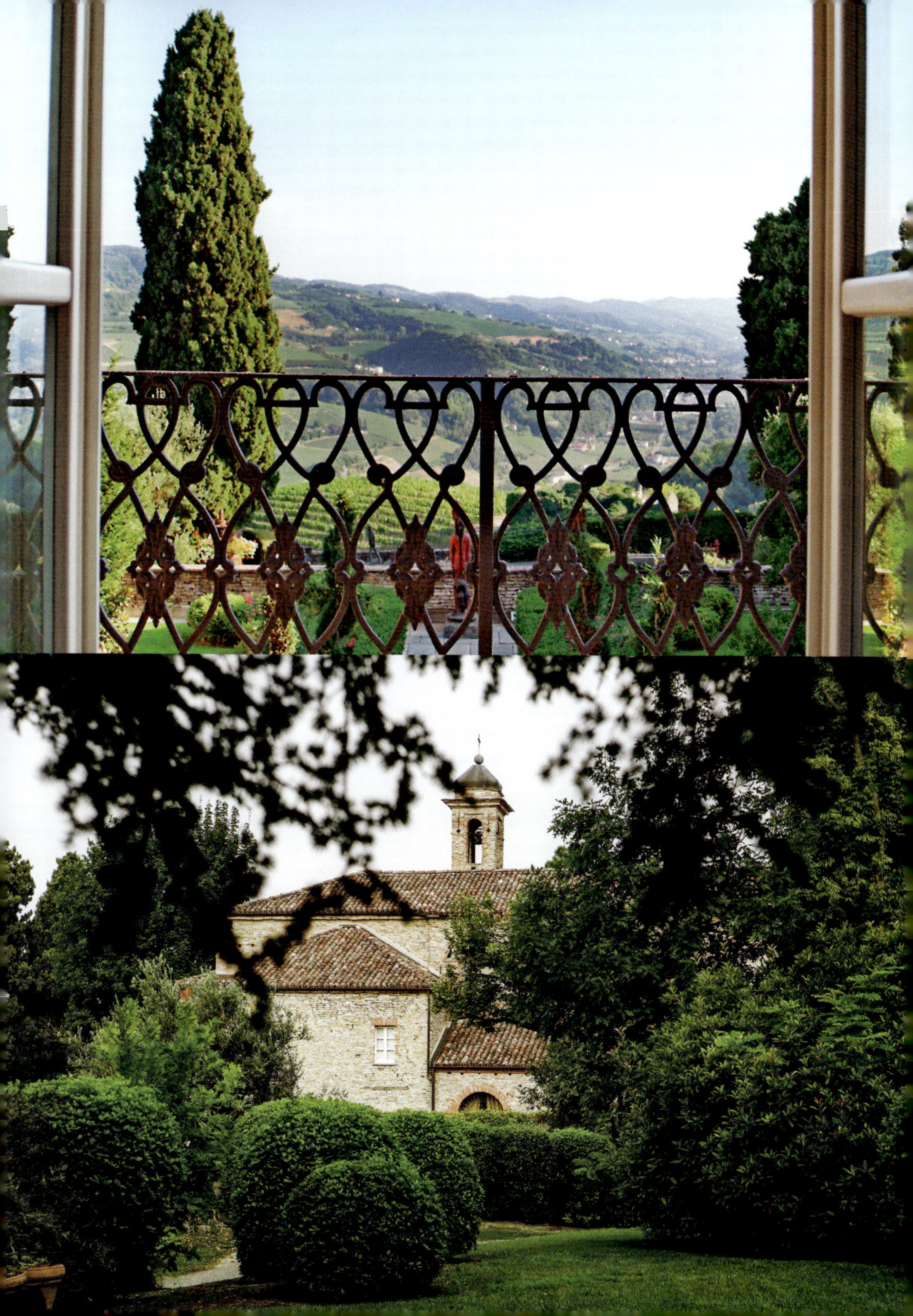

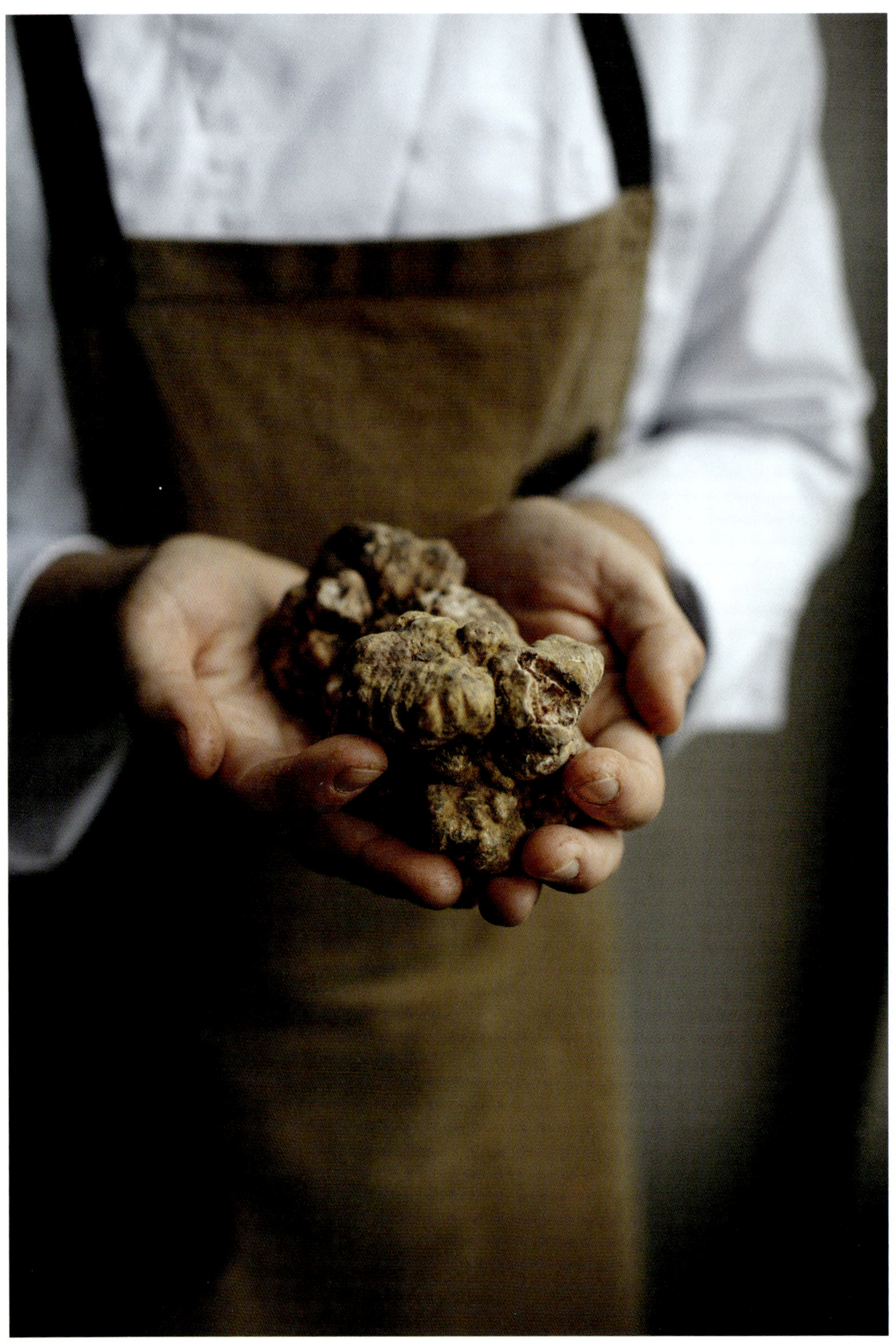

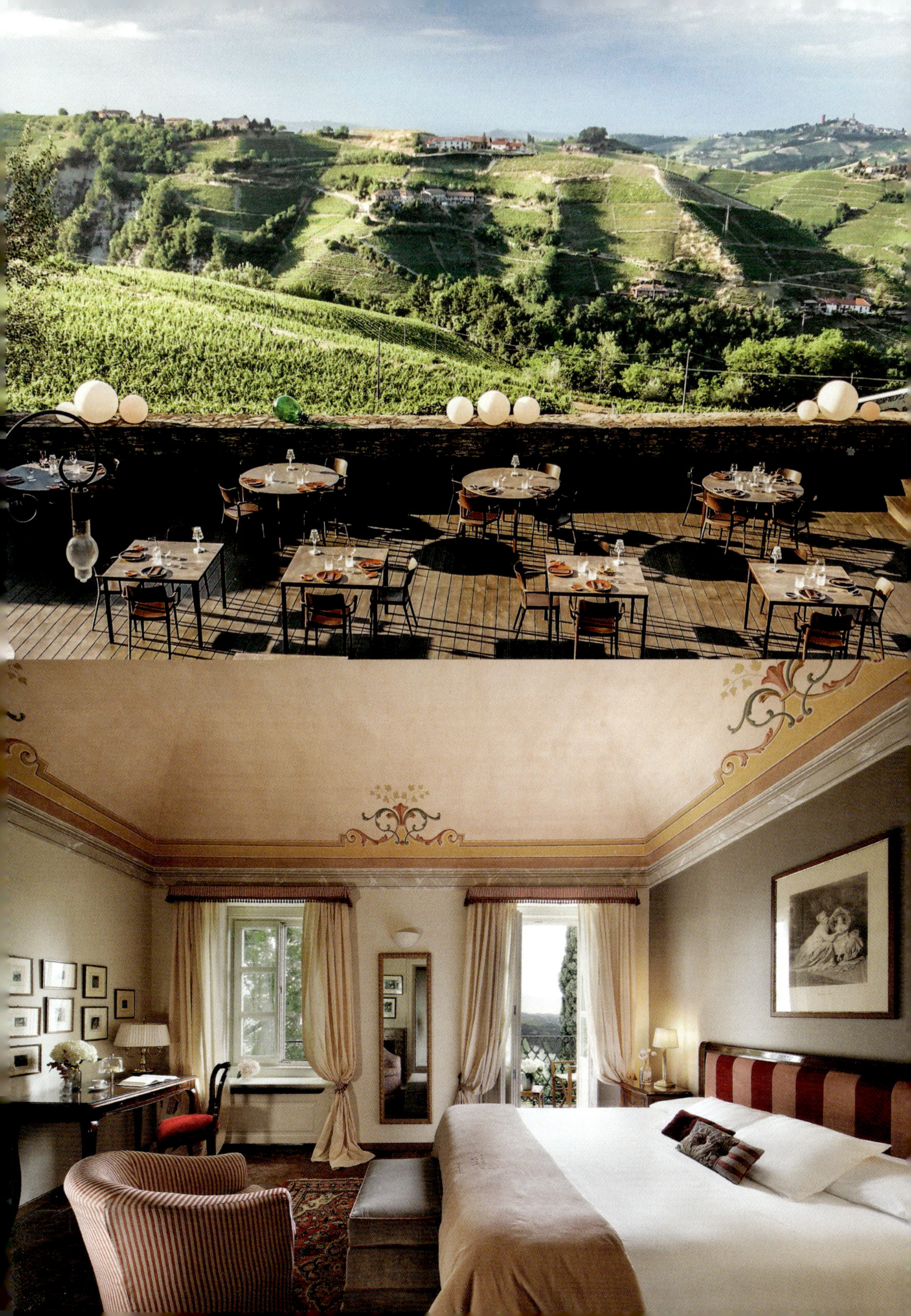

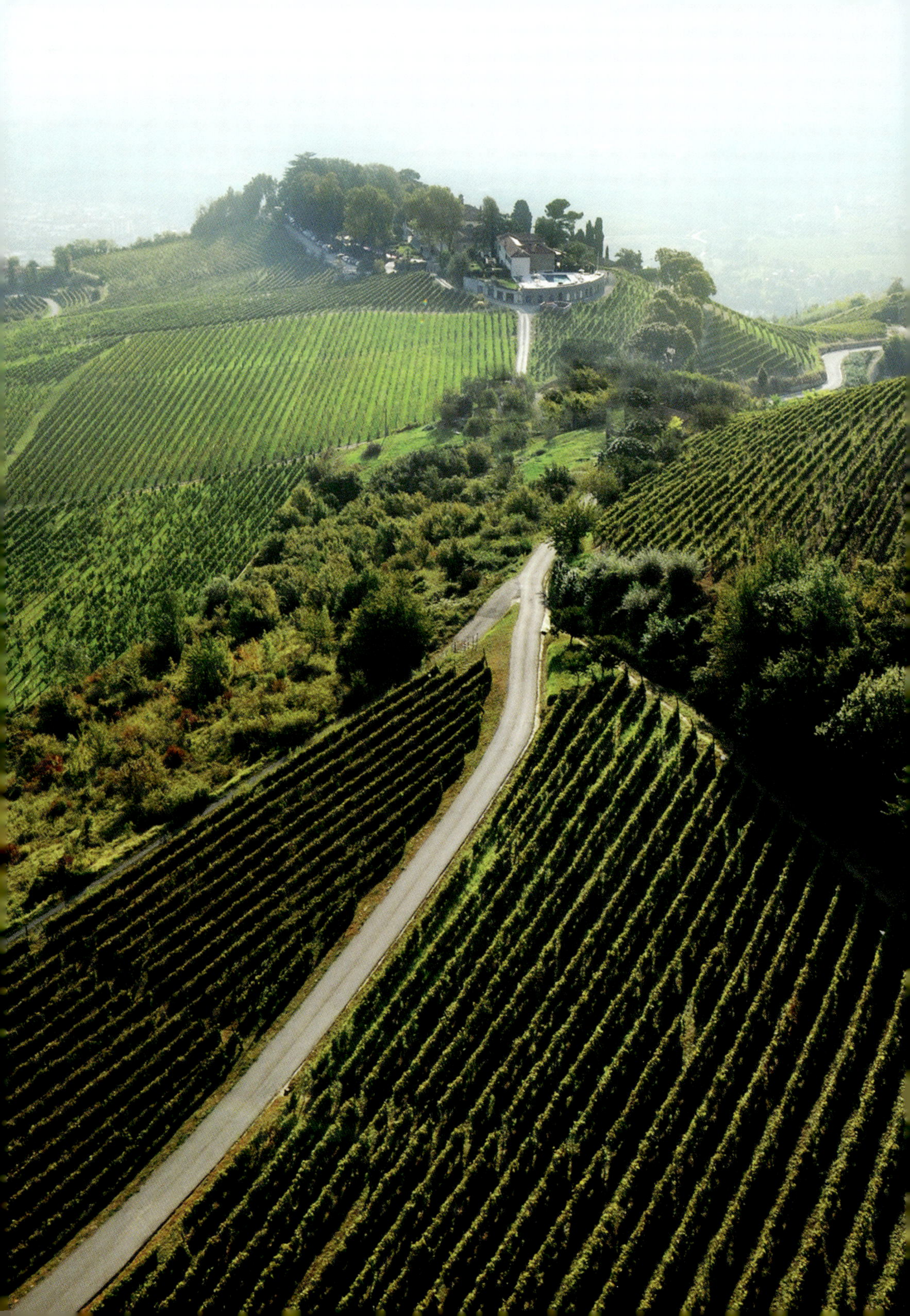

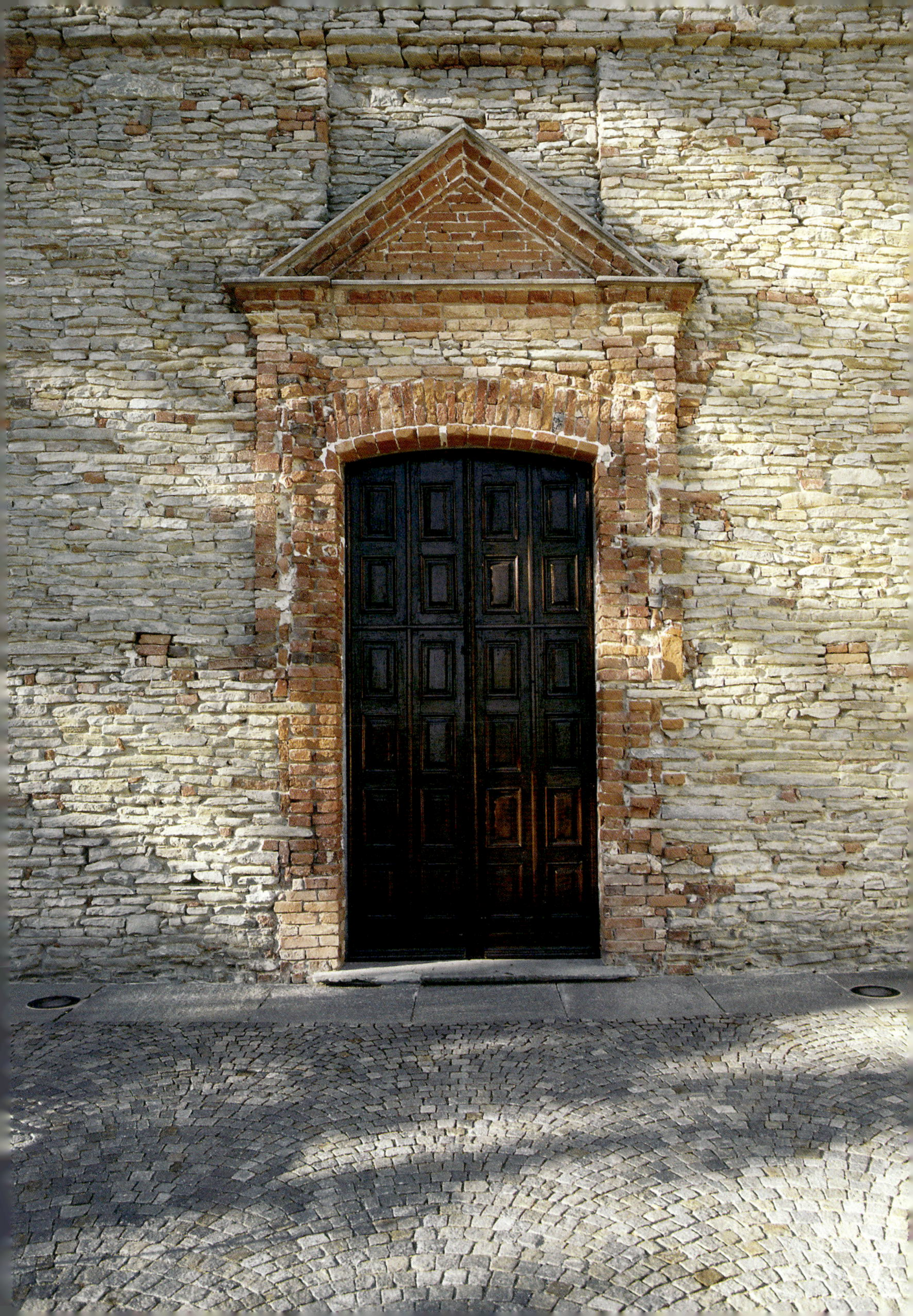

ANTICO BORGO DEL RIONDINO

NEAR CUNEO, PIEMONTE

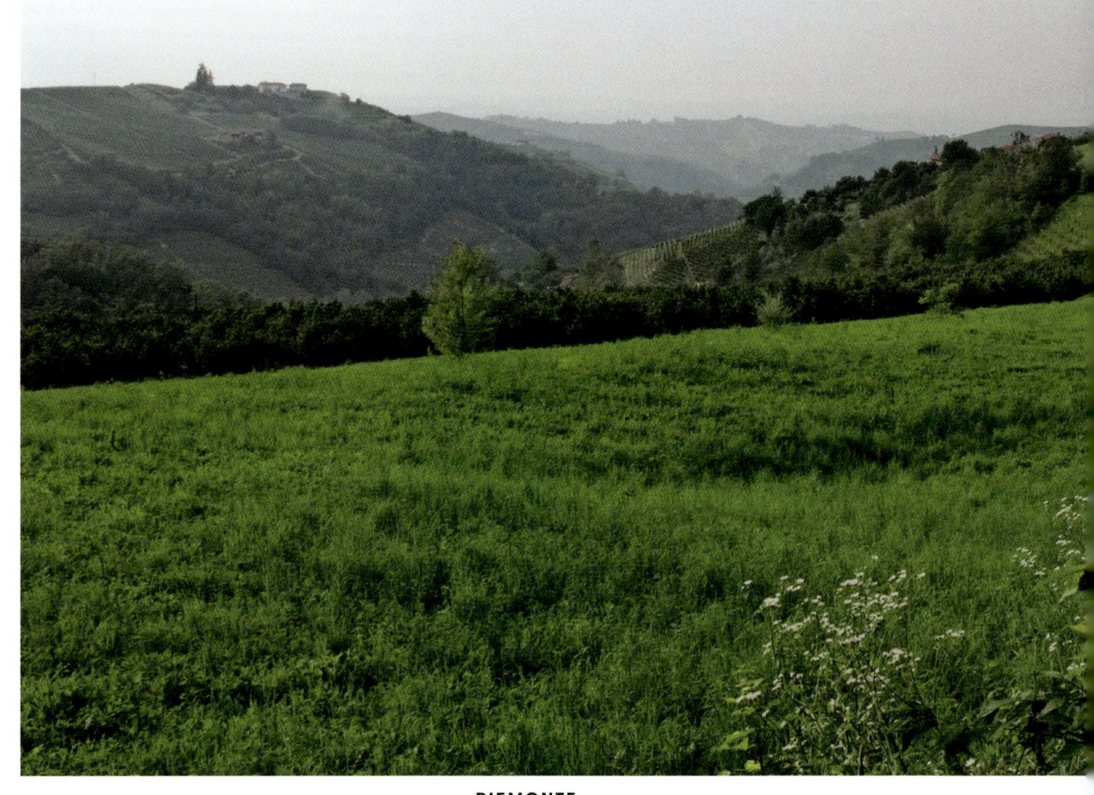

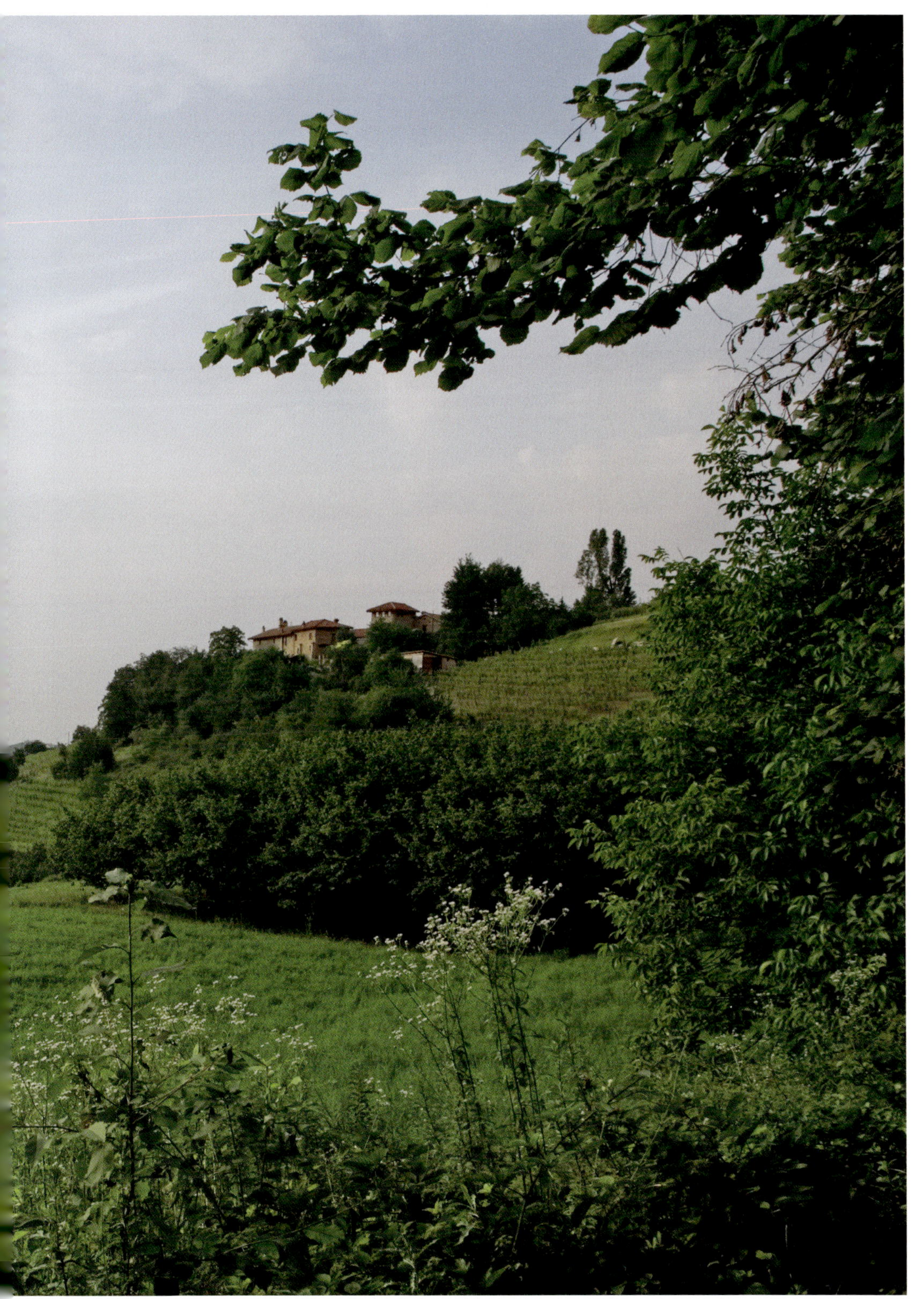

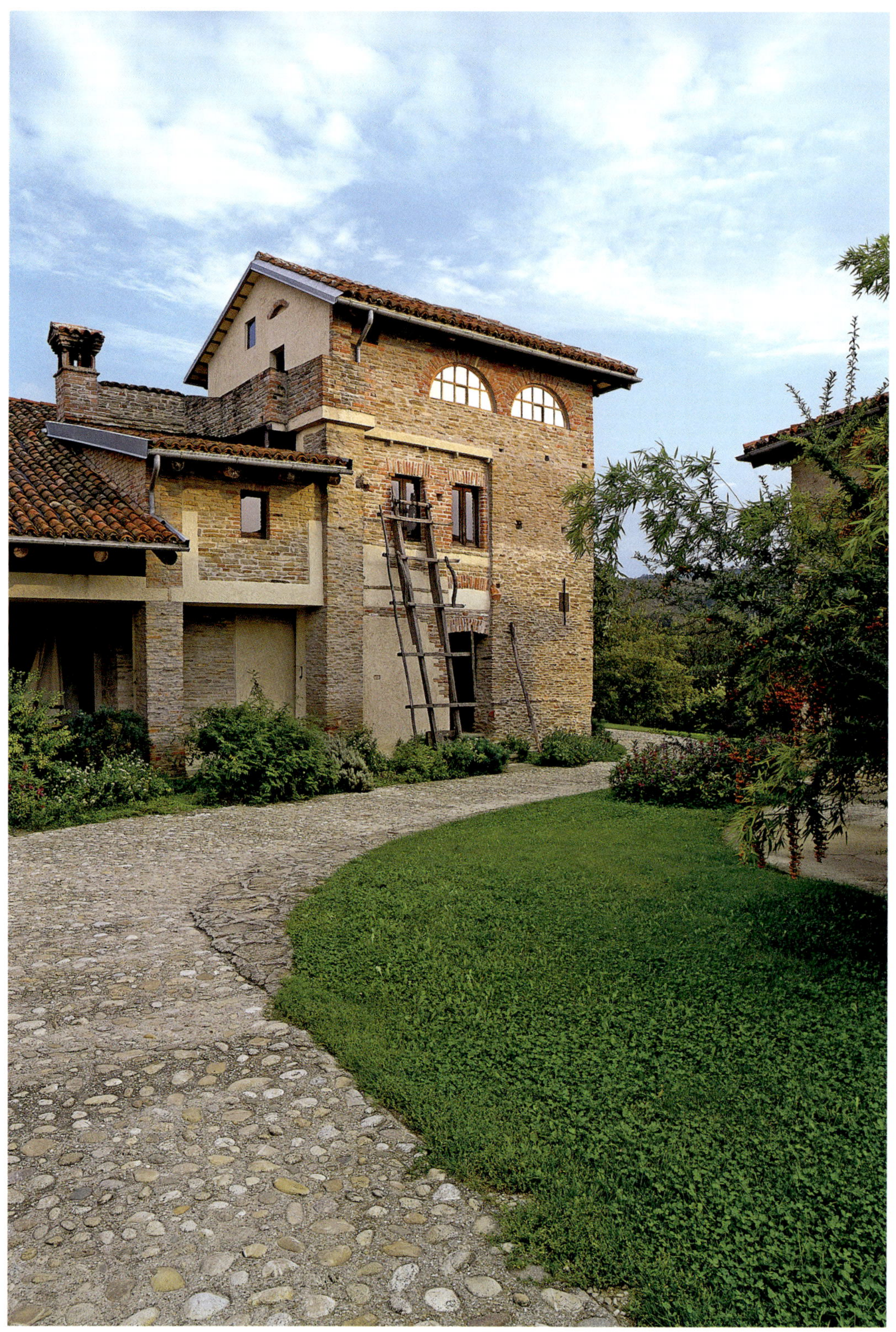

ANTICO BORGO DEL RIONDINO

Via dei Fiori 13, 12050 Trezzo Tinella
Tel. +39 0173 630 313 · info@riondino.it
www.riondino.it
Open from April to November

HOMAGE TO A LANDSCAPE Some settlements seem always to have existed. They fit into the countryside as a matter of course, so that the boundaries between nature and architecture are blurred. They possess such timeless beauty that past and present seem to merge. Antico Borgo del Riondino is just such a place – a grouping of medieval houses on a hill in the Langhe region, which the architect Marco Poncellini has converted into his studio and an agriturismo. In doing so he used traditional methods wherever possible, preserving historic masonry and ceiling joists but at the same time combining the old structure with modern elements. Façades of tall windows let in plenty of light, black ceramic tiles accentuate ancient stone or wooden floors, crystal chandeliers are suspended above heavy beds and designer washbasins collect the water from old-fashioned taps. The interior is both simple and sophisticated, highly sensuous and sometimes almost poetic – and it matches the exterior perfectly. The ten-hectare park, a wonderland of meadows, woods and vineyards, extends across the hills of three valleys. Aromatic nuts, figs and rosemary thrive here – specialities of the Langhe that are used in the agriturismo's own kitchen. Marco Poncellini's father gave up his career as a banker to be the chef here and cook to regional recipes. So even the food fits in with the overall concept and makes the Riondino an all-round work of art – and an act of homage to the landscape. ◆ Book to pack: "A Private Affair" by Beppe Fenoglio.

HOMMAGE AN EINE LANDSCHAFT Es gibt Siedlungen, die schon immer da gewesen zu sein scheinen, die sich so selbstverständlich in eine Landschaft einfügen, dass die Grenzen zwischen Natur und Architektur verwischen, und die so zeitlos schön sind, dass auch Geschichte und Gegenwart ineinander übergehen. Solch ein Ort ist der Antico Borgo del Riondino – eine Sammlung mittelalterlicher Häuser auf einem Hügel der Langhe, die der Architekt Marco Poncellini zu seinem Atelier und zu einem Agriturismo umgebaut hat. Wo immer möglich, arbeitete er dabei nach traditionellen Techniken und erhielt historische Mauern sowie Deckenbalken – gleichzeitig kombinierte er die alte Struktur aber mit modernen Elementen. So lassen hohe Fensterfronten viel Licht in die Räume, schwarze Keramikkacheln akzentuieren antike Stein- oder Holzböden, über schweren Betten schweben Kristalllüster, und unter altmodischen Wasserhähnen stehen Designerbecken. Das Interieur ist schlicht und raffiniert zugleich, sehr sinnlich und manchmal fast poetisch – und passt damit perfekt zum Exterieur: Der zehn Hektar große Park verläuft über die Hügel dreier Täler und ist ein Wunderland aus Wiesen, Wäldern und Weinbergen. Hier gedeihen aromatische Nüsse, Feigen und Rosmarin – Spezialitäten der Langhe, die im hauseigenen Restaurant Verwendung finden. Marco Poncellinis Vater gab seine Karriere als Banker auf, um hier am Herd zu stehen und nach regionalen Rezepten zu kochen. Selbst die Küche fügt sich also ins Konzept und macht den Riondino zu einem Gesamtkunstwerk – und zu einer Hommage an eine Landschaft.
◆ Buchtipp: „Eine Privatsache“ von Beppe Fenoglio.

HOMMAGE À UN PAYSAGE Certaines agglomérations rurales semblent avoir toujours existé. Elles sont si naturellement intégrées au paysage que les limites entre la nature et l'architecture s'estompent, et d'une beauté si intemporelle que le passé et le présent se marient sous nos yeux. L'Antico Borgo del Riondino – un bourg médiéval implanté sur une colline des Langhe, que Marco Poncellini a transformé en atelier et centre agrotouristique – est l'un de ces endroits. Les techniques traditionnelles ont été utilisées partout où cela était possible, les murs historiques et les poutres des plafonds on été conservés, mais en combinant la structure ancienne à des éléments modernes. De vastes baies vitrées laissent la lumière pénétrer dans les pièces, des carreaux de céramique noirs accentuent l'effet des sols anciens en pierre ou en bois, des lustres de cristal sont suspendus au-dessus de lits massifs et des robinets vieillots surplombent des lavabos design. L'intérieur est à la fois sobre et sophistiqué, très sensuel et parfois presque poétique, en parfaite harmonie avec le paysage qui l'entoure : le parc de dix hectares qui s'étend sur les collines de trois vallées est une merveille de prairies, de forêts et de vignes. On y récolte des noix, des figues et du romarin, spécialités des Langhe que propose le restaurant de la maison. Le père de Marco Poncellini a abandonné une carrière de banquier pour passer derrière les fourneaux et cuisiner des recettes de la région. Ainsi, même la cuisine est partie du concept et fait du Riondino une œuvre d'art totale et un hommage au paysage. ◆ À lire : « Une Affaire personnelle » de Beppe Fenoglio.

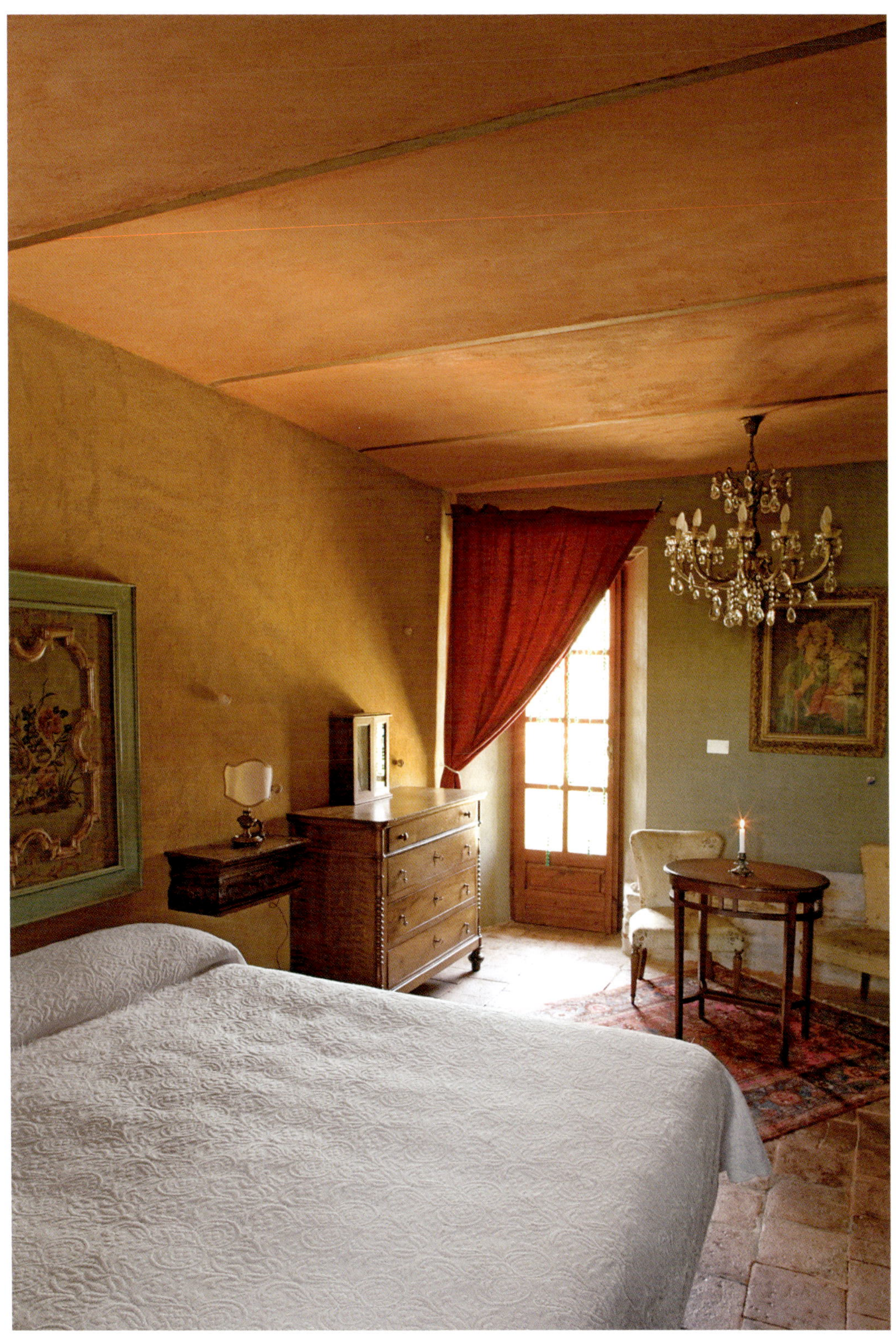

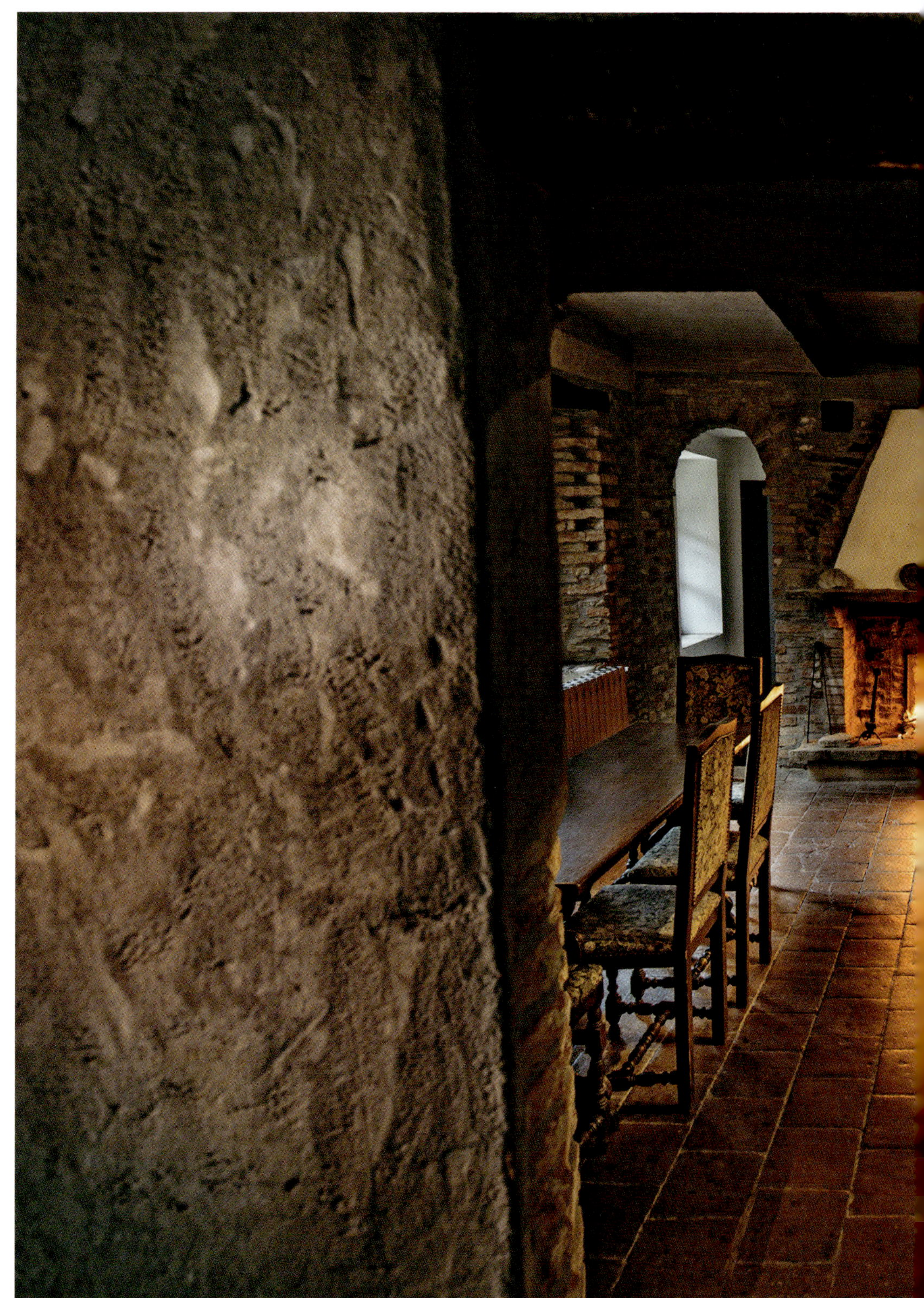

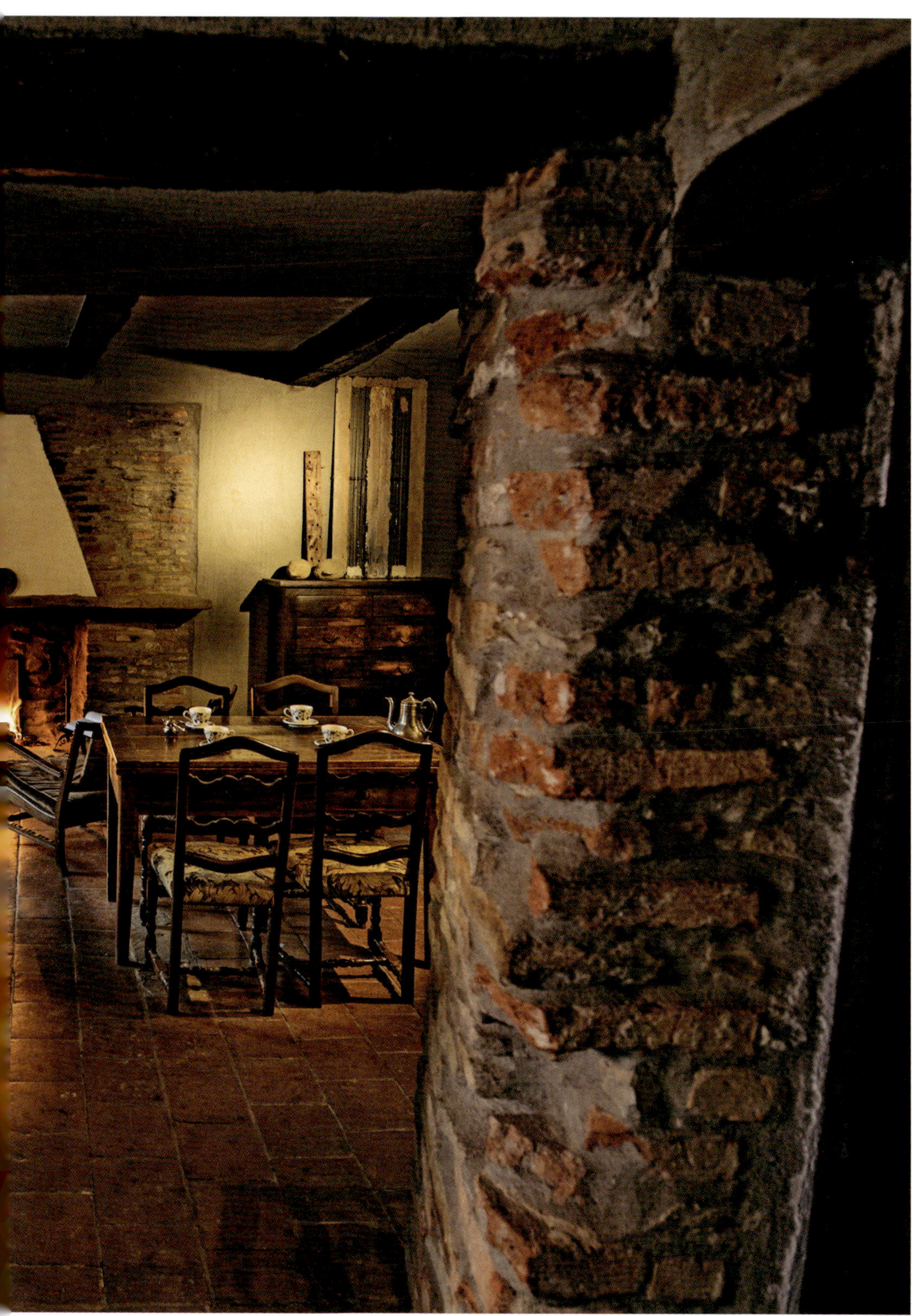

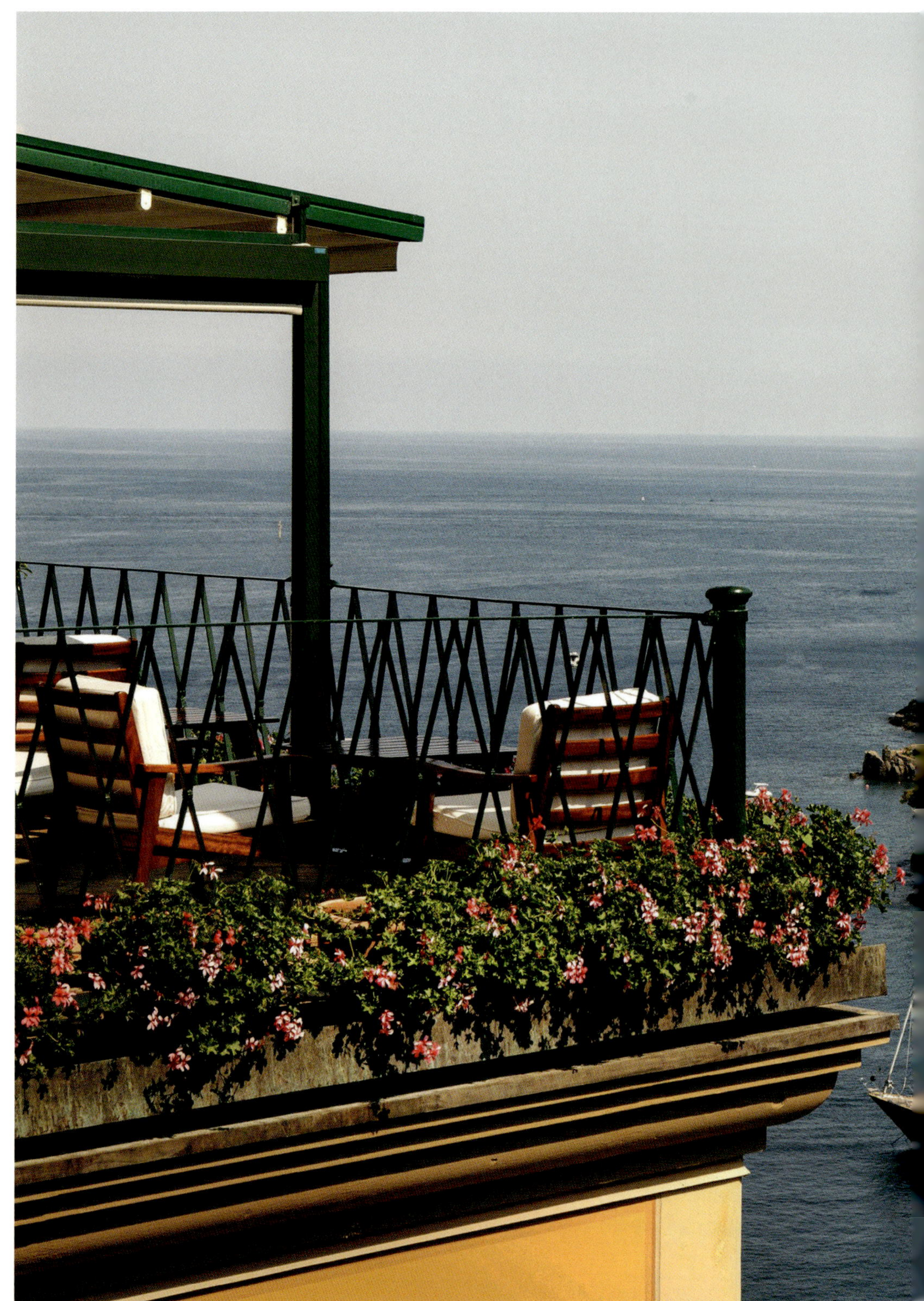

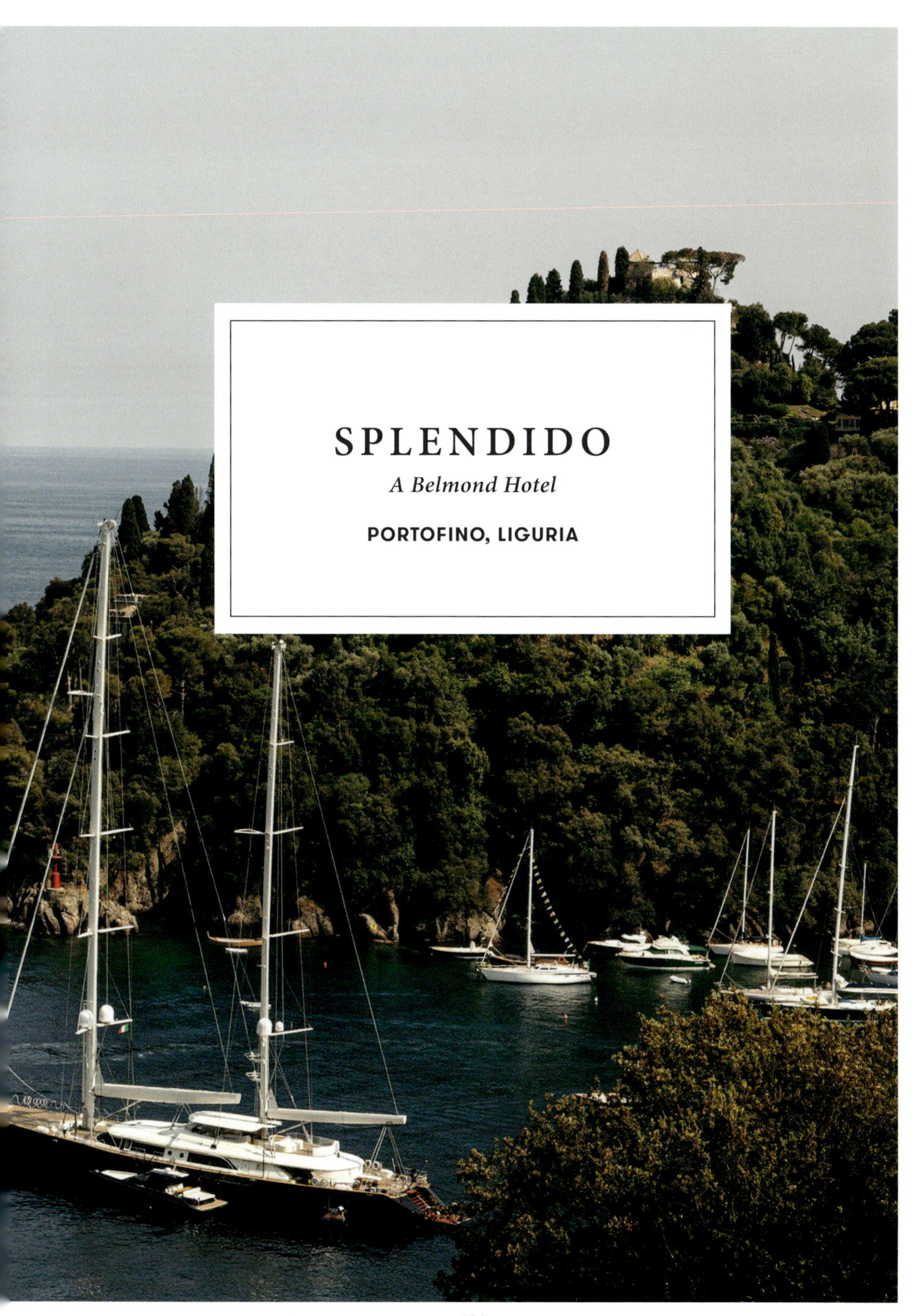

SPLENDIDO

A Belmond Hotel

PORTOFINO, LIGURIA

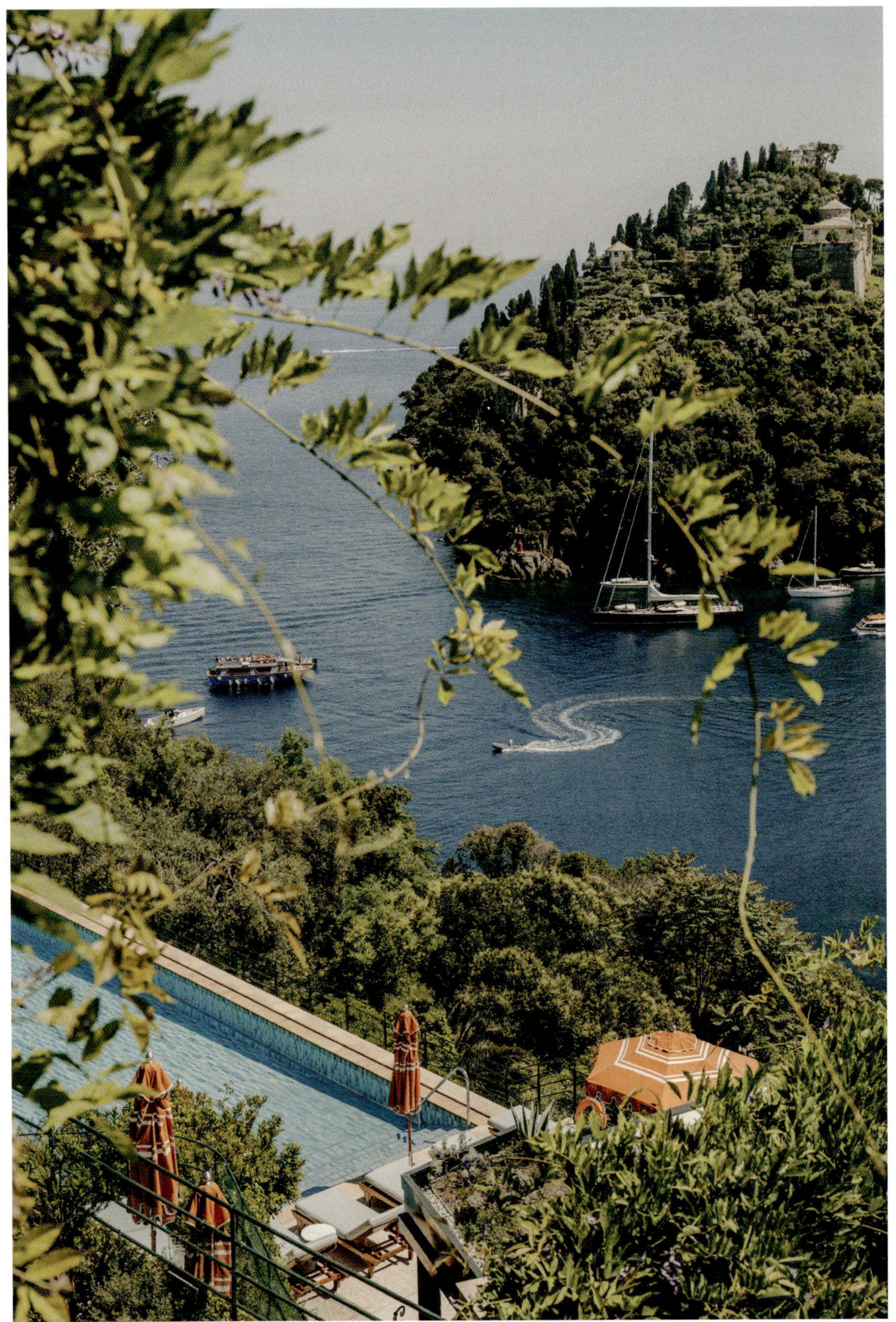

LIGURIA

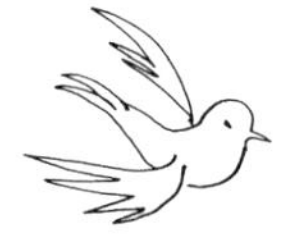

SPLENDIDO

A Belmond Hotel

Salita Baratta 16, 16034 Portofino
Tel. +39 0185 2678 00 · reservations.spl@belmond.com
www.belmond.com
Open from May 1 to November 2

CIAO BELLA! All they wanted was to pray and work here, but the monks who had constructed this building high above the fishing village of Portofino in the 16th century were raided by Saracen pirates so often that they eventually fled to the hills of the hinterland. The monastery decayed – until it was converted to the summer residence of the aristocratic Baratta family and was opened by the pioneers of tourism in Portofino in 1901 as the first grand hotel in the place. Since then the opposite of monastic asceticism has prevailed at the Splendido: this hotel stands for glamour, grandeur, sensuality and style – the Italian Riviera at its very finest. Here, as a matter of course, everything blends to form a harmonious composition: from the rooms and suites, where Martin Brudnizki has recently created a glamorous ambience in pastel colors, to the pool, reimagined by landscape architect Marco Bay and filled with salt water instead of the standard chlorination. At dinner in the exquisite restaurant with its unforgettable sea view, it is by no means unusual to sit next to someone whose face is familiar from the cinema screen or a glossy magazine: since the Duke of Windsor was the first to sign the golden guest book, the Splendido has been a popular place to stay for celebrities. One reason for this is the service, which is both immaculate and personal. Many of the staff have worked at the hotel for decades and would do anything for the Splendido and its guests – even handle an attack by pirates. ◆ Books to pack: "Satura" by Eugenio Montale and "The Path to the Spiders' Nests" by Italo Calvino.

CIAO BELLA! Sie wollten hier nur beten und arbeiten – doch die Mönche, die dieses Gebäude hoch über dem Fischerdorf Portofino im 16. Jahrhundert errichtet hatten, wurden so oft von Sarazenen-Piraten überfallen, dass sie schließlich in die Hügel des Hinterlandes flohen. Ihr Kloster verfiel – bis es zur Sommerresidenz der Adelsfamilie Baratta umgebaut und 1901 von den Tourismuspionieren Portofinos als erstes Grandhotel des Ortes eröffnet wurde. Seitdem herrscht im Haus das Gegenteil der einstigen klösterlichen Askese: Das Splendido steht für Glamour und Grandezza, Sinnlichkeit und Stil – schöner kann man die italienische Riviera nicht erleben. Hier fügt sich alles wie selbstverständlich zu einer harmonischen Komposition zusammen: von den Zimmern und Suiten, denen Martin Brudnizki ein glamouröses Ambiente in Pastelltönen verliehen hat, über den von Marco Bay neu gestalteten Pool, der nicht schnöde gechlort, sondern mit Salzwasser gefüllt ist, bis hin zu den erlesenen Restaurants mit unvergesslichem Blick aufs Meer. Dass am Dinnertisch nebenan jemand sitzt, dessen Gesicht man aus Kinofilmen oder Hochglanzmagazinen kennt, kann dabei durchaus vorkommen: Seit sich der Herzog von Windsor als erster Gast ins Goldene Buch eintrug, gilt das Splendido als Lieblingsadresse der Prominenz. Zu verdanken ist dies auch dem Service, der so formvollendet wie persönlich ist. Viele Mitarbeiter sind schon seit Jahrzehnten im Hotel tätig und würden für das Splendido und seine Gäste alles tun – selbst einem Piratenangriff hielten sie stand. ◆ Buchtipps: „Satura“ von Eugenio Montale und „Wo Spinnen ihre Nester bauen“ von Italo Calvino.

CIAO BELLA ! Les moines qui ont édifié au XVIe siècle ce bâtiment surplombant le village de pêcheurs de Portofino voulaient seulement prier et travailler, mais ils furent si souvent attaqués par les Sarrasins qu’ils finirent par s’enfuir dans les collines de l’arrière-pays. Le monastère tomba en ruine, jusqu’à ce que le baron Baratta le fasse transformer en résidence d’été pour sa famille ; plus tard, en 1901, il devint le premier Grand Hôtel de Portofino. L’ascèse monacale est bien oubliée depuis : le Splendido est aujourd’hui synonyme de glamour et de grandeur, de sensualité et d’élégance – il n’y a pas de meilleur endroit pour apprécier la Riviera italienne. Ici, tout se fond naturellement en une composition harmonieuse : des chambres et suites, auxquelles les teintes pastel récemment choisies par Martin Brudnizki confèrent une nouvelle élégance, à la piscine répensée par l’architecte paysagiste Marco Bay, remplie d’eau salée plutôt que chlorée. Le restaurant, exquis, offre une vue inoubliable sur la mer, et il n’est pas rare d’y dîner à côté d’un visage connu, vu sur grand écran ou en couverture des magazines. Depuis que le duc de Windsor a signé le premier son livre d’or, c’est un lieu prisé des célébrités. Il faut dire que le personnel est aussi courtois qu’attentionné : une grande partie travaille à l’hôtel depuis des décennies et ferait tout pour le Splendido et ceux qui y séjournent – même tenir tête aux Sarrasins. ◆ À lire : « Satura » d’Eugenio Montale et « Le Sentier des nids d’araignée » d’Italo Calvino.

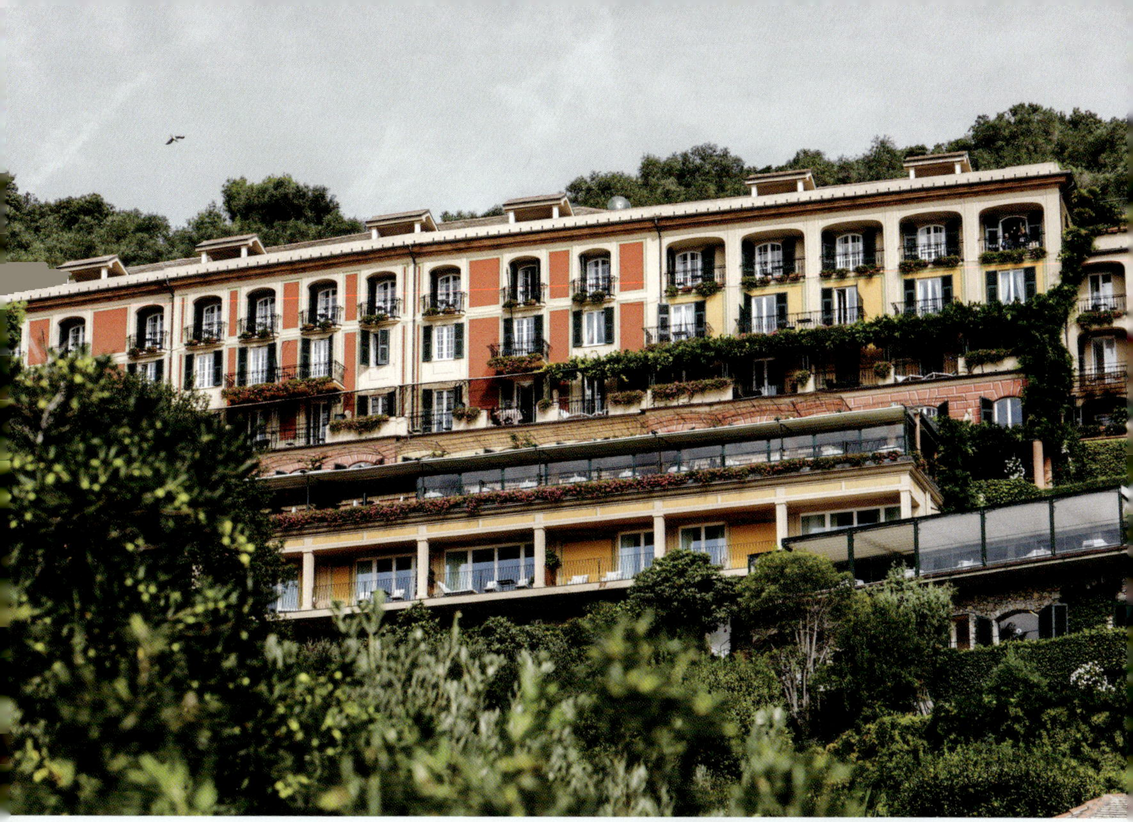

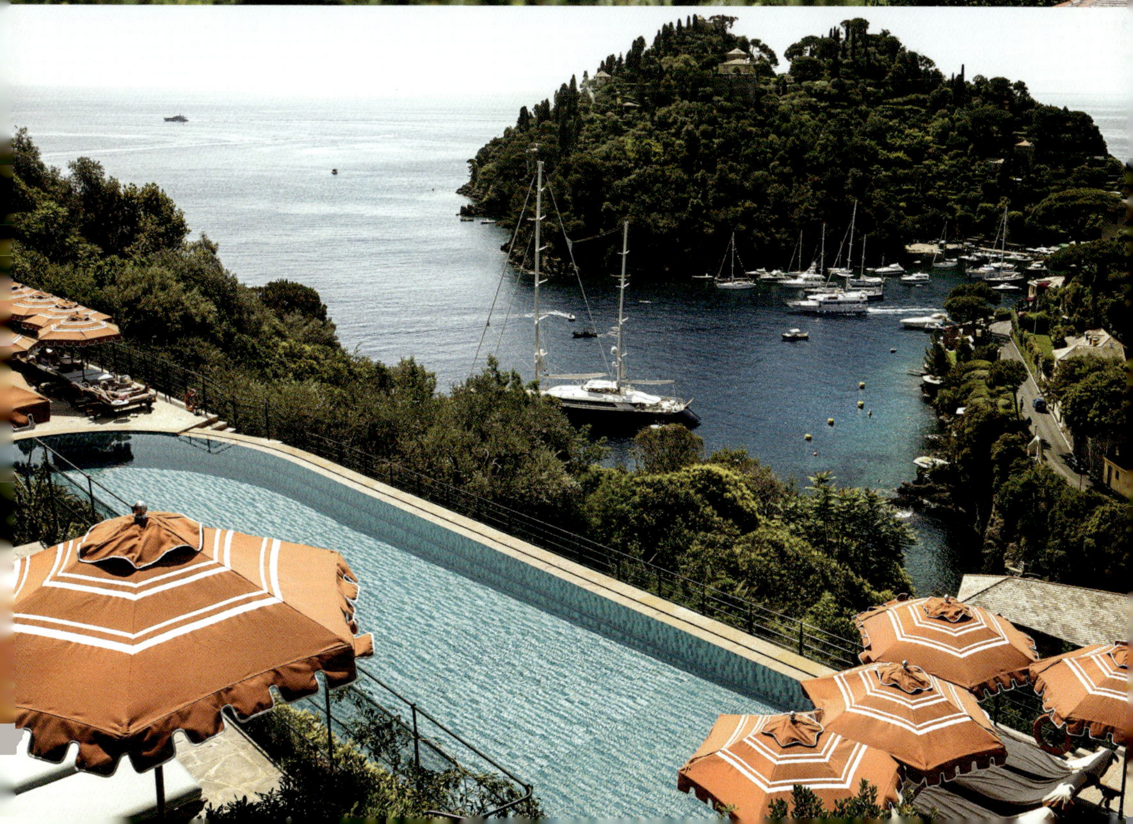

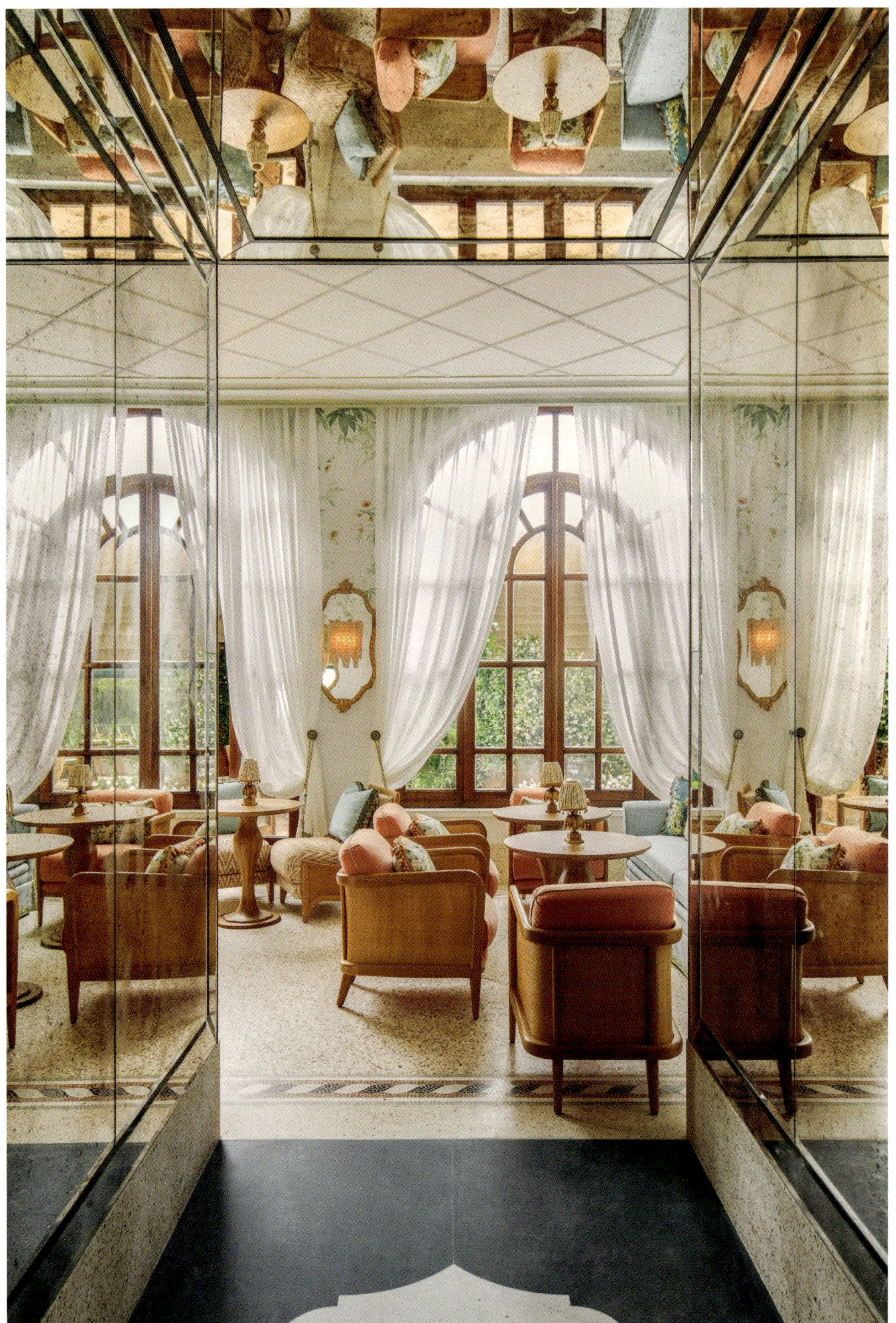

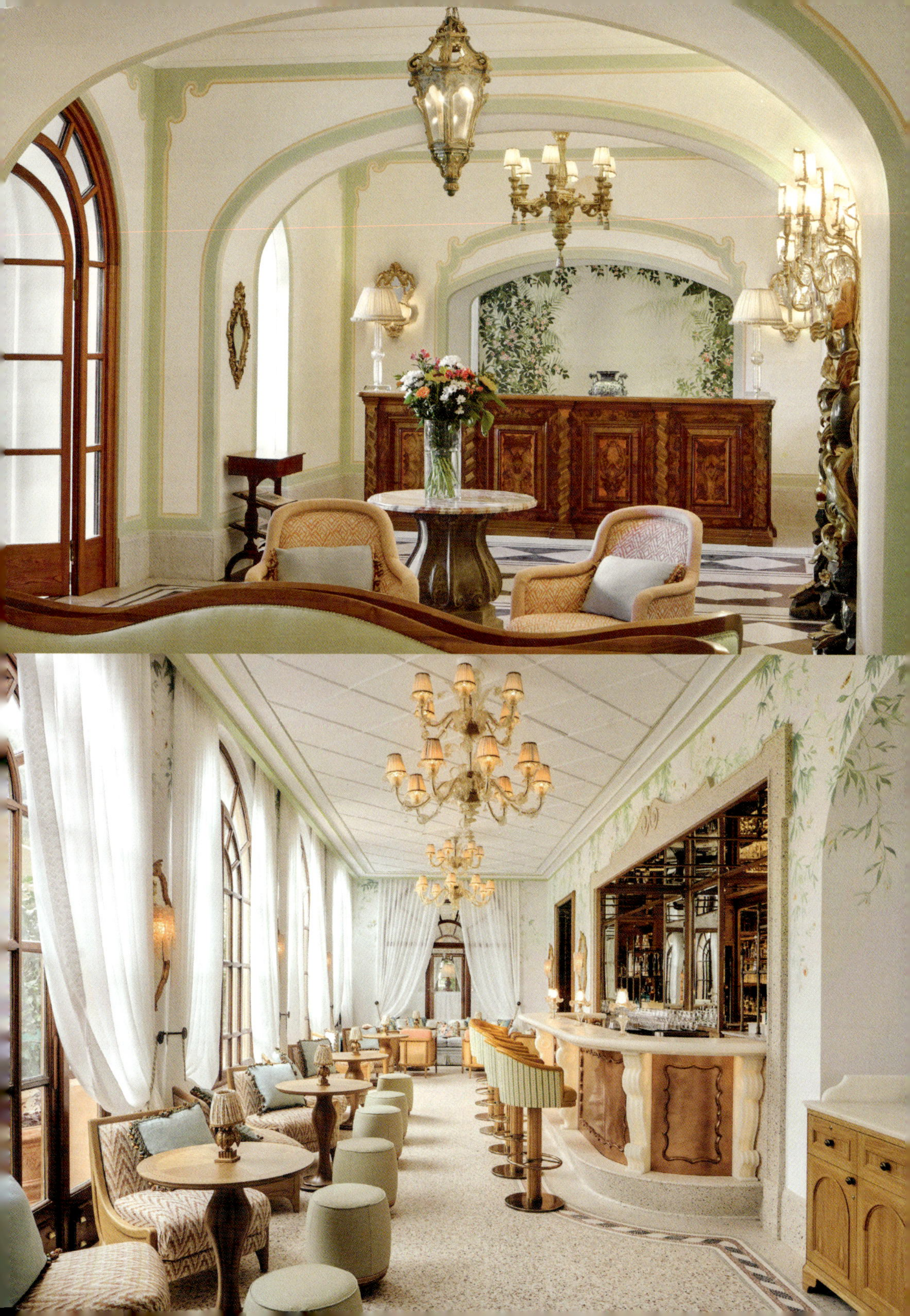

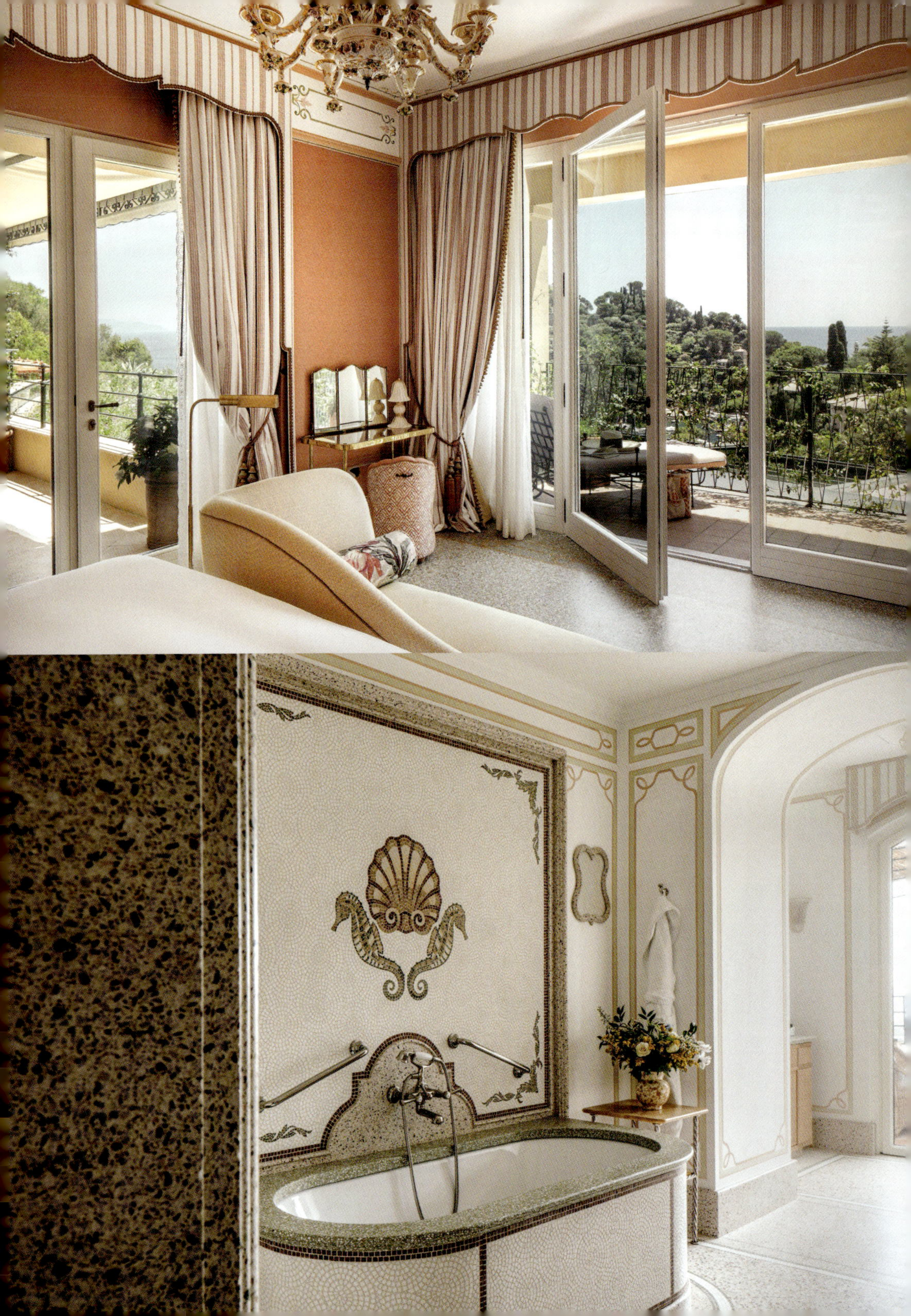

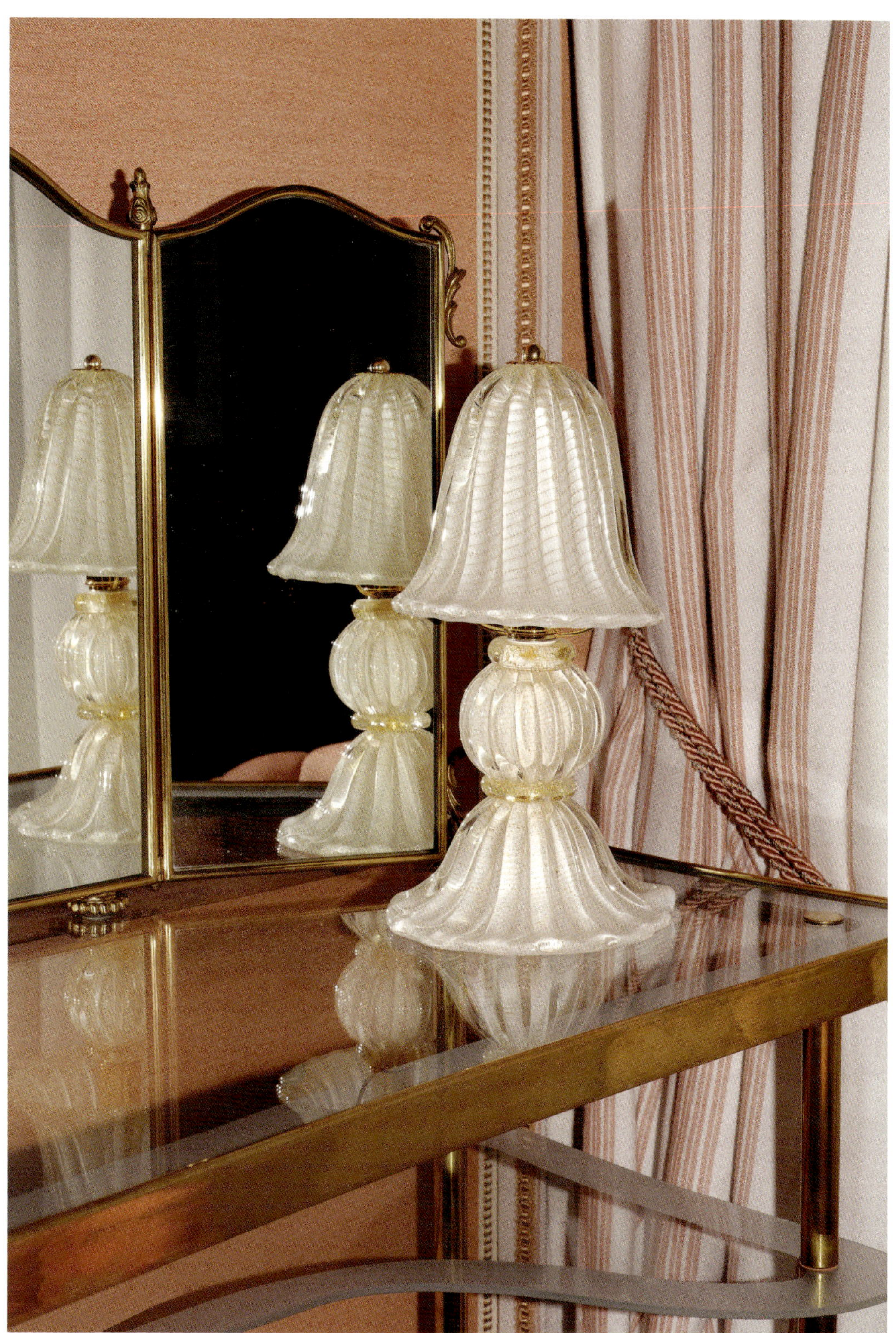

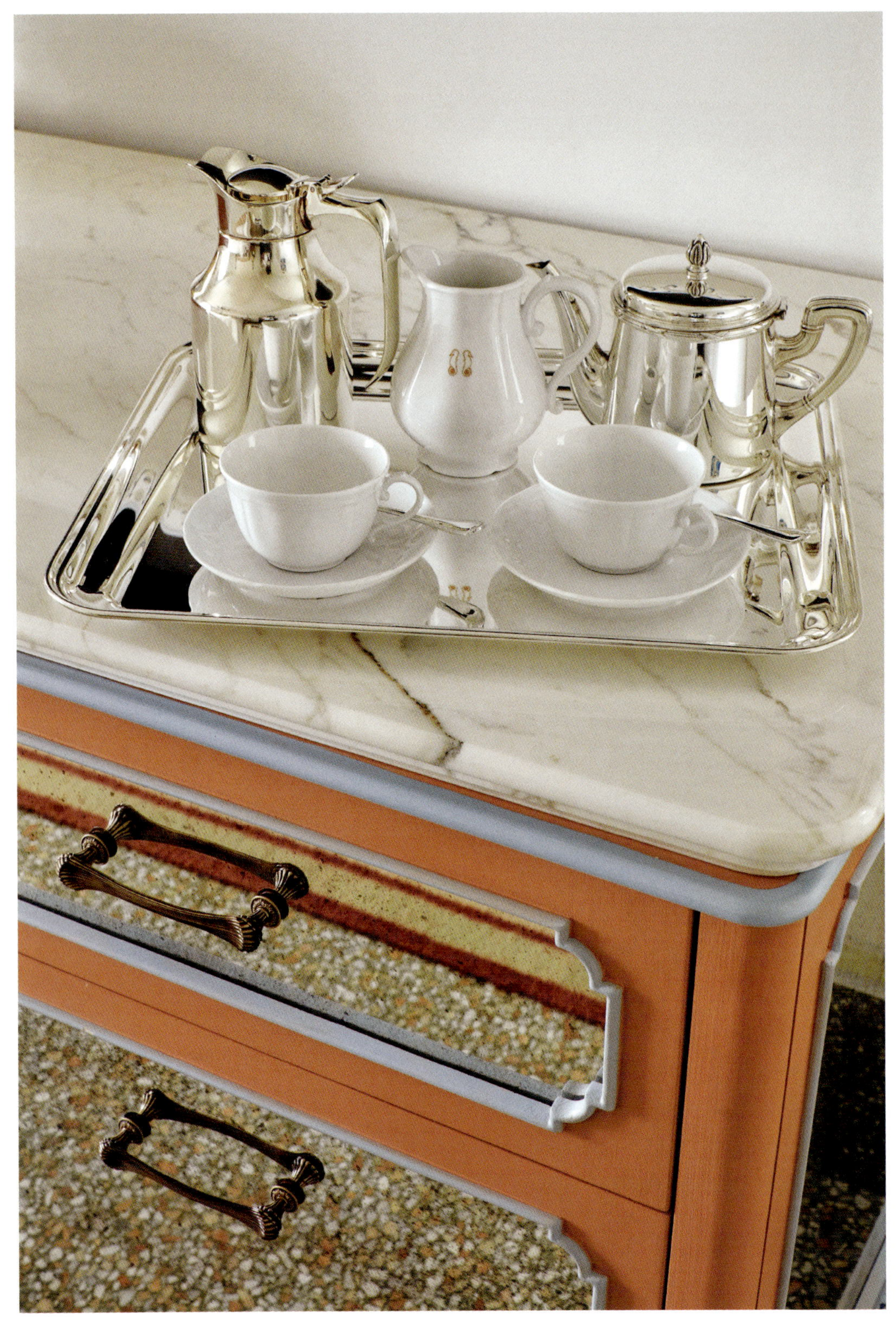

LIGURIA

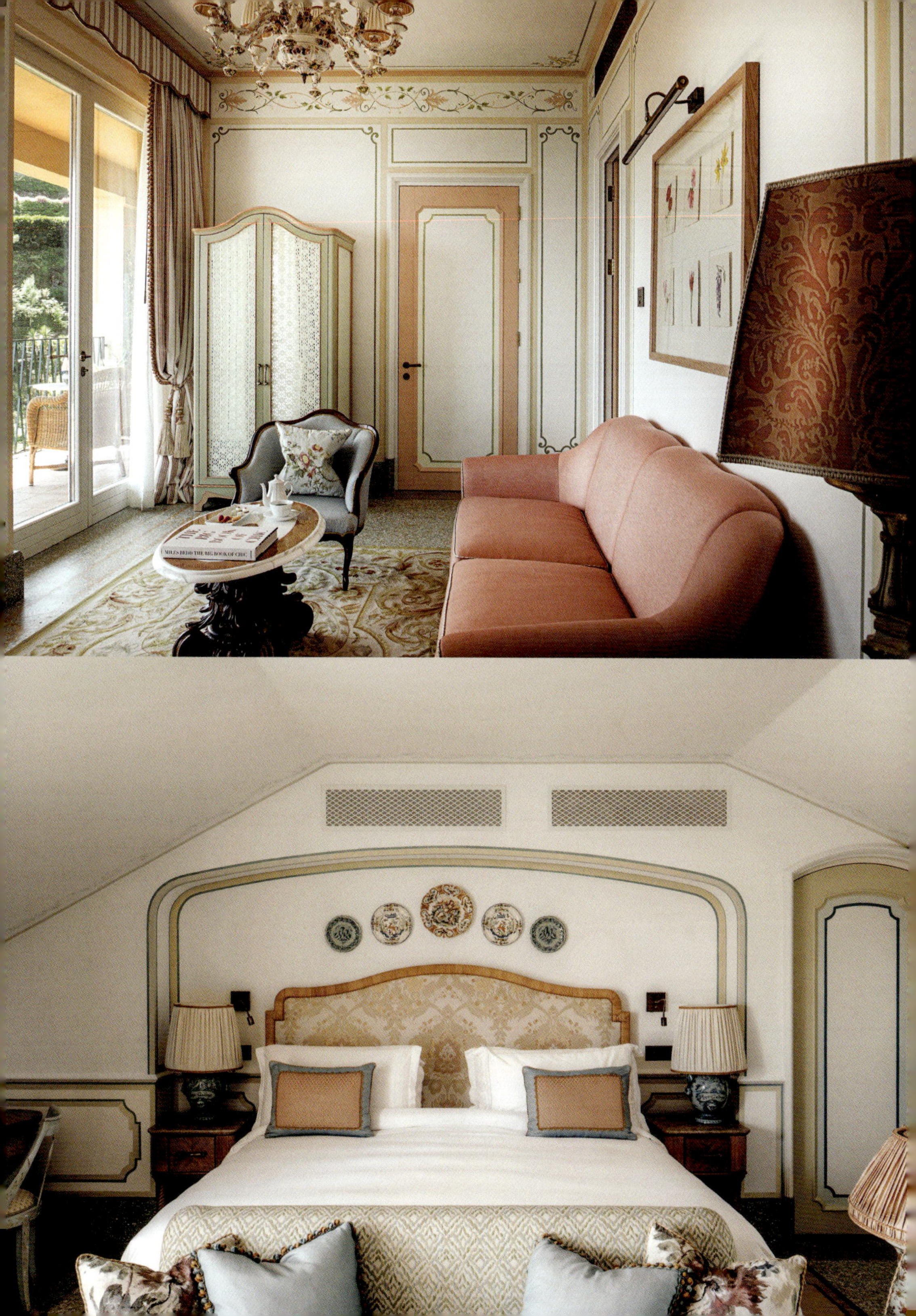
MILES REDD THE BIG BOOK OF CHIC

LA SOSTA DI OTTONE III

LEVANTO, CINQUE TERRE, LIGURIA

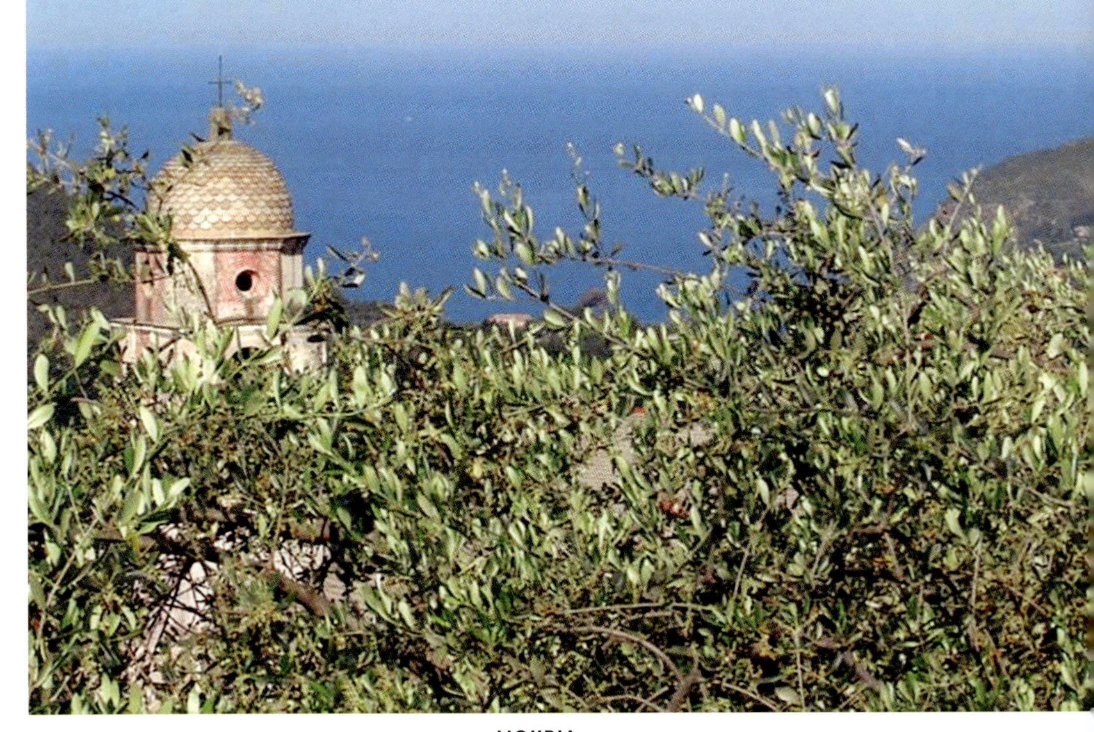

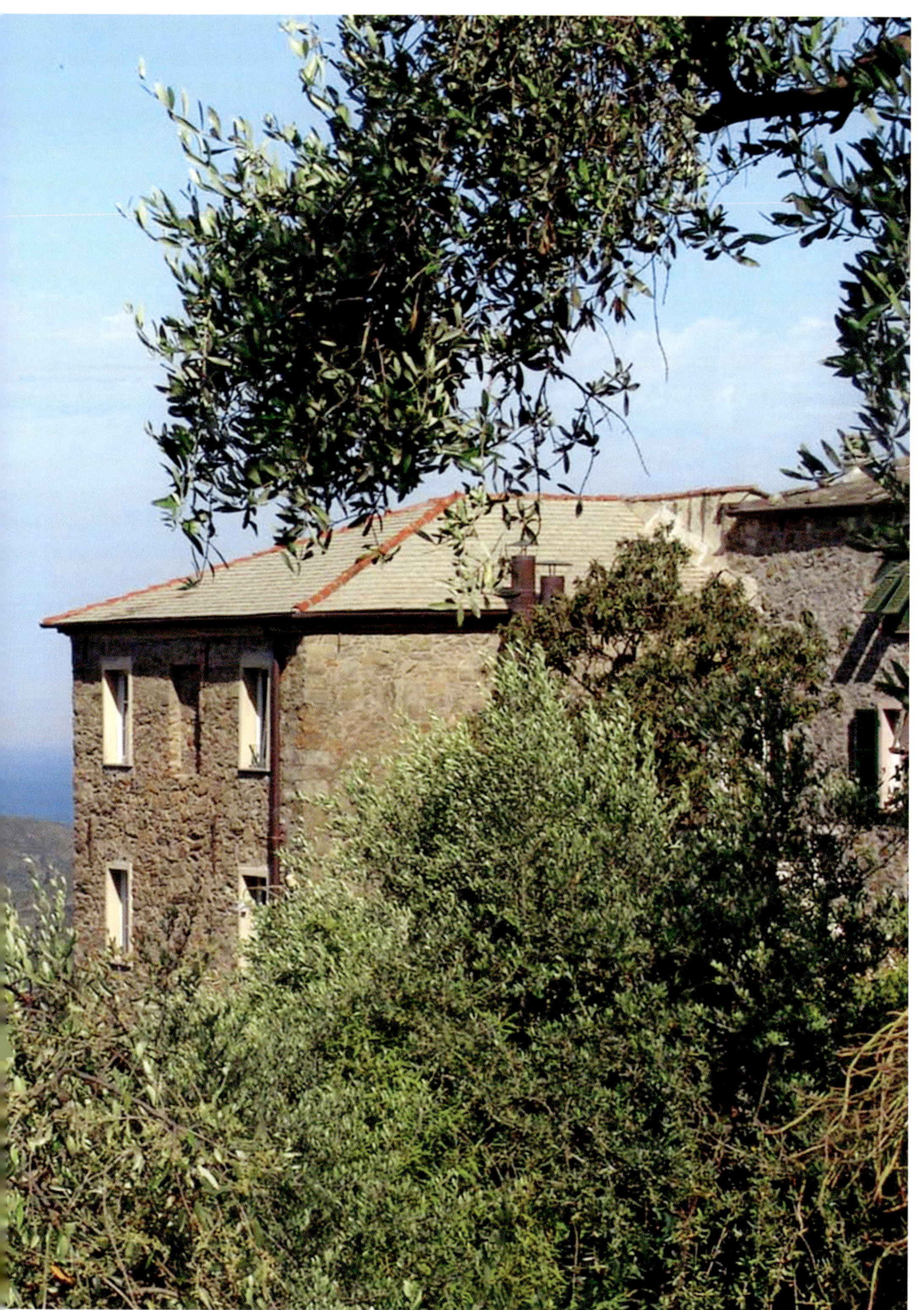

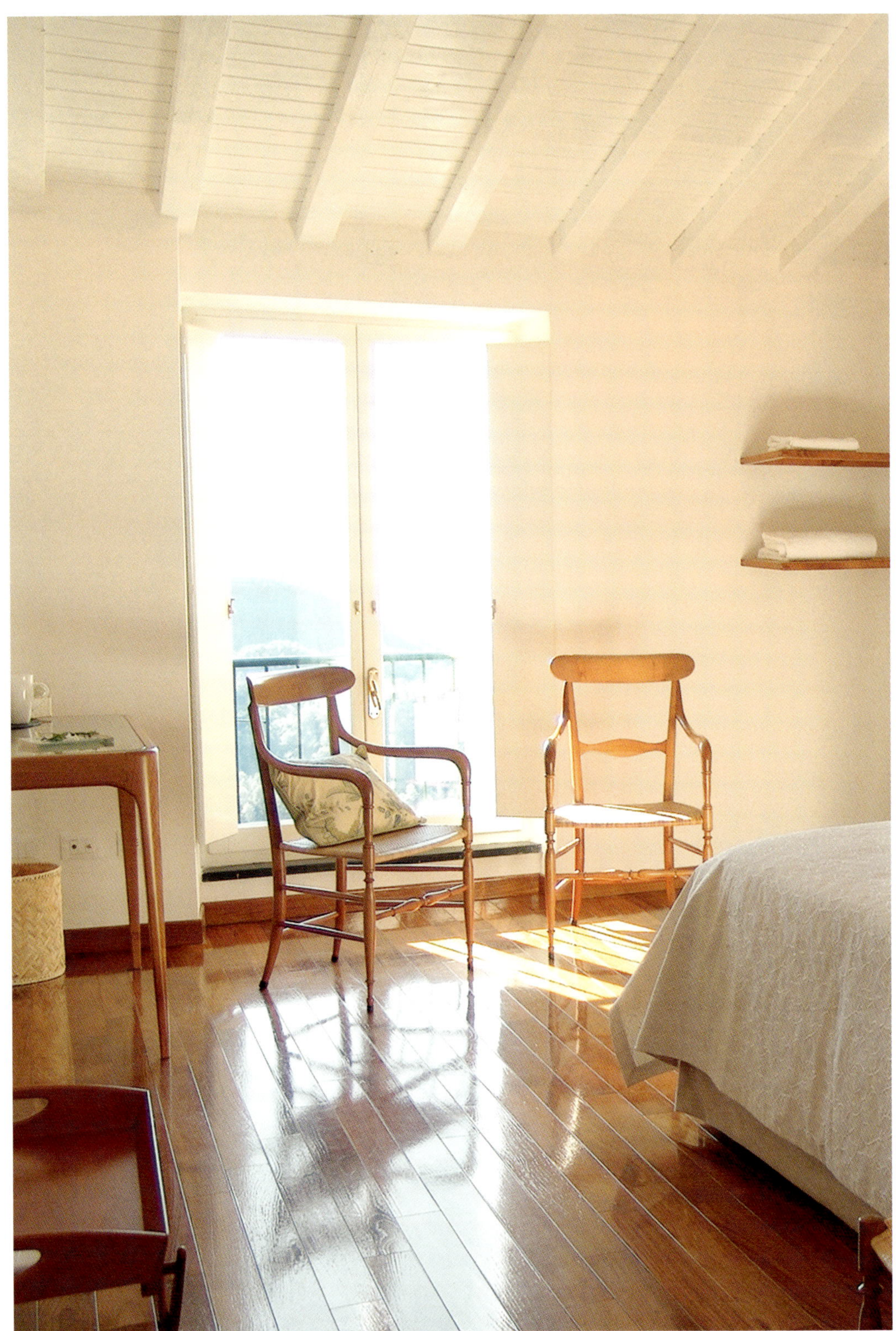

LA SOSTA DI OTTONE III

Località Chiesanuova 39, 19015 La Spezia
Tel. +39 351 886 02 51 · lasosta@lasosta.com
www.lasosta.com
Open from late March to early November

GROUNDED His father ruled the Holy Roman Empire, and his mother was a Byzantine princess. His childhood in Aachen, marked equally by Germanic laws and oriental luxury, was extremely short: at the age of three, Otto III was crowned king at Christmas 983 (although his grandmother and mother attended to ruling the empire). When he was 16, the pope gave him the status of emperor – and on his way to Rome for the ceremony, he is said to have stopped in this building, today the home of La Sosta di Ottone III ("sosta" means "stop" or "break"). Apart from its name, however, La Sosta has nothing royal about it, let alone imperial airs and graces. On the contrary, the idea is that guests should discover the Cinque Terre, their idyllic scenery and age-old culture with directness and authenticity. Angela Fenwick and Fabio Graziani have renovated the building with the help of local artisans and fitted out the six rooms simply in shades of pastel and white with rustic furnishings. The cook at La Sosta, also a native of the area, uses local ingredients to create menus that are even worth a recommendation in the Michelin Guide. The concierge, too, who is called a "day designer" here, is a local who organises walks through the Cinque Terre and extras such as a private visit to a nearby vineyard. ◆ Book to pack: "Absence" by Joanna King.

CINQUE TERRE Sein Vater war der deutsche Kaiser, seine Mutter eine byzantinische Prinzessin. Seine Kindheit in Aachen wurde von germanischen Gesetzen ebenso wie von orientalischem Luxus geprägt und war reichlich kurz: Schon als Dreijähriger wurde Otto III. an Weihnachten 983 zum römisch-deutschen König gekrönt (wenn auch seine Großmutter und Mutter die Regierungsgeschäfte führten). Als er 16 war, ernannte ihn der Papst zum Kaiser – und auf dem Weg zur Zeremonie nach Rom soll er in diesem Gebäude Rast gemacht haben, das heute La Sosta di Ottone III beherbergt („sosta" bedeutet „Stopp", „Halt"). Mit Ausnahme seines Namens hat das Haus jedoch nichts mit könglichen oder gar kaiserlichen Attitüden am Hut, ganz im Gegenteil: Wer eincheckt, soll die Cinque Terre, ihre idyllische Landschaft und lange Kultur, unmittelbar und unverfälscht erleben. Angela Fenwick und Fabio Graziani haben das Haus mithilfe örtlicher Handwerker renoviert und die sechs Zimmer in Weiß- und Pastelltönen simpel mit rustikalem Mobiliar ausgestattet. Die Köchin der Sosta stammt ebenfalls aus der Gegend und zaubert aus lokalen Zutaten Menüs, die sogar dem „Guide Michelin" eine Empfehlung wert sind. Und auch die Concierge, die hier „Day Designer" heißt, ist eine Einheimische und stellt Wanderungen durch die Orte der Cinque Terre zusammen oder organisiert Extras wie den Privatbesuch bei einem örtlichen Winzer. ◆ Buchtipp: „Vier Schwestern" von Joanna King.

TERRES RÉUNIES Son père était l'empereur allemand, sa mère une princesse byzantine. Marquée par les lois germaniques autant que par le luxe oriental, son enfance à Aix-la-Chapelle a été brève : dès l'âge de trois ans, le 25 décembre 983, Otton III est couronné roi des Romains (même si sa grand-mère et sa mère tiennent les rênes du gouvernement). Il a 16 ans quand le pape le nomme empereur – et se rendant à Rome pour se faire couronner, il se serait reposé dans ce bâtiment, qui abrite aujourd'hui la Sosta di Ottone III (« sosta » signifie « arrêt »). Abstraction faite de son nom, la maison n'a rien de royal ni d'impérial, bien au contraire : ceux qui s'installent ici doivent découvrir les Cinque Terre, leur paysage idyllique et leur culture ancestrale, de manière directe et authentique. Angela Fenwick et Fabio Graziani ont rénové la maison avec l'aide d'artisans locaux et sobrement garni de meubles rustiques les six chambres aux tonalités de blanc et pastel. Également originaire de la région, la cuisinière de la Sosta propose des menus à base de produits locaux jugés dignes d'être recommandés au Guide Michelin. Et la concierge, appelée ici « Day Designer », est aussi de la région et organise des promenades dans les villages des Cinque Terre ou des extras tels qu'une visite privée chez un vigneron local. ◆ À lire : « Absence » de Joanna King

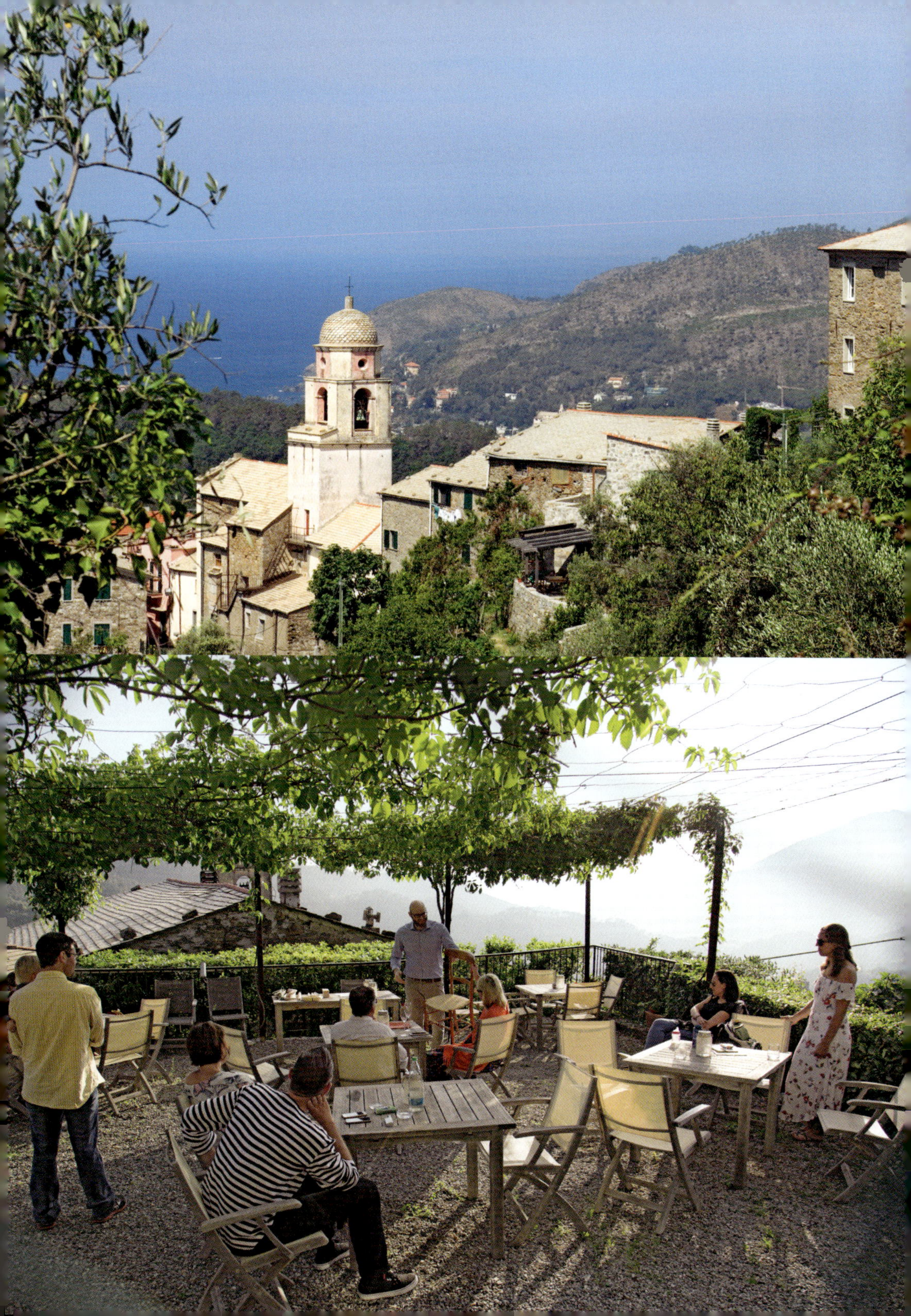

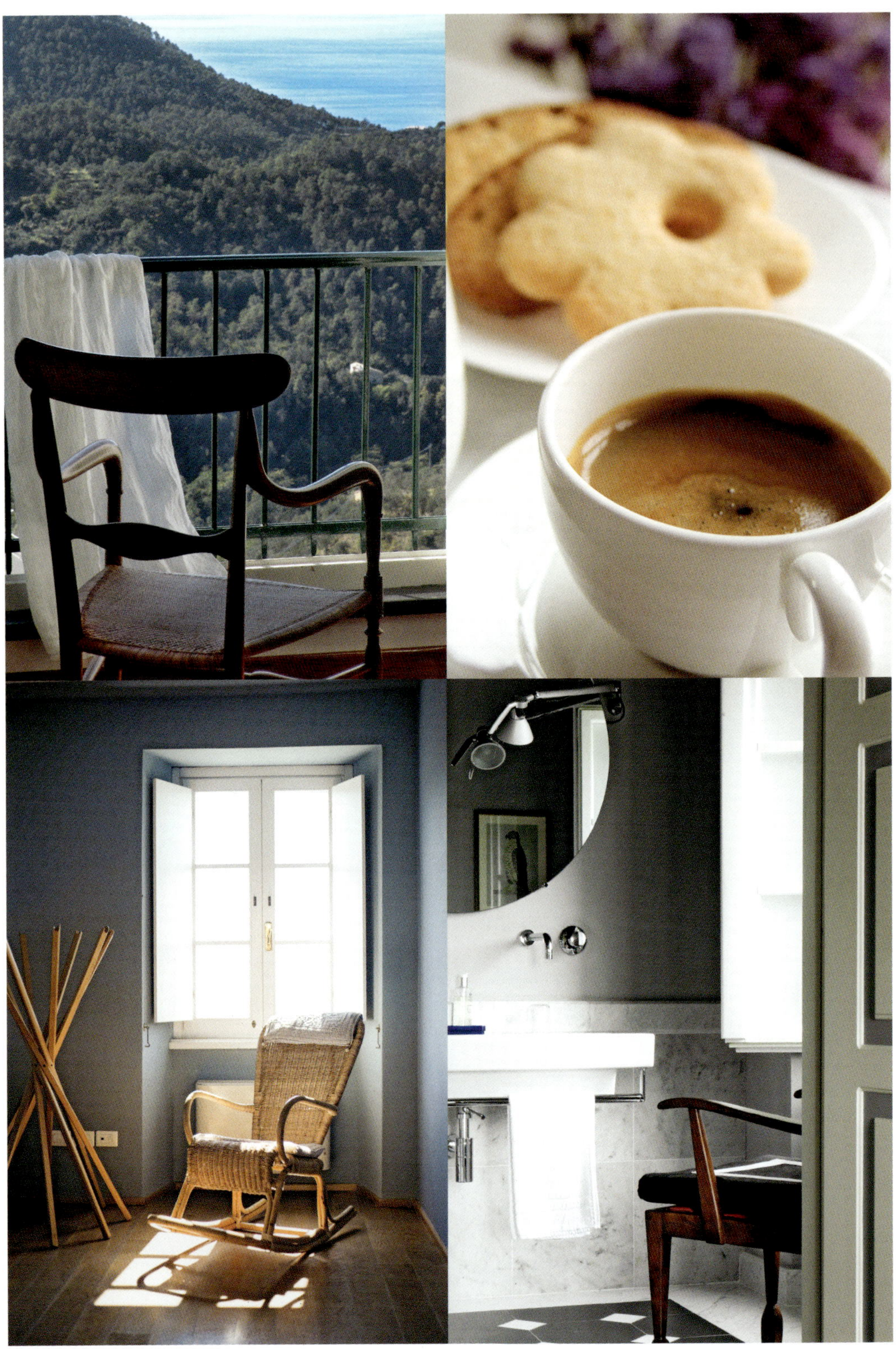

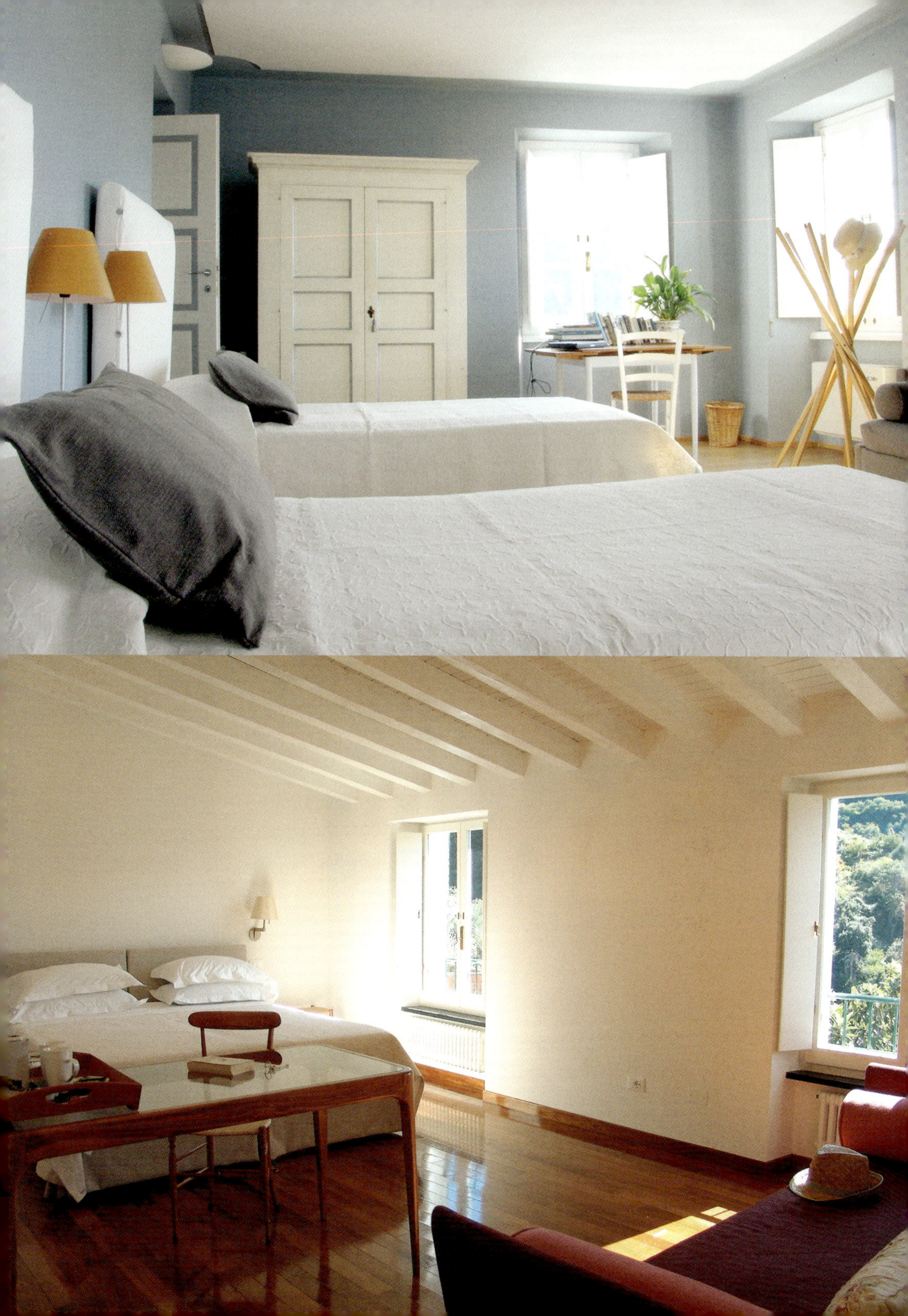

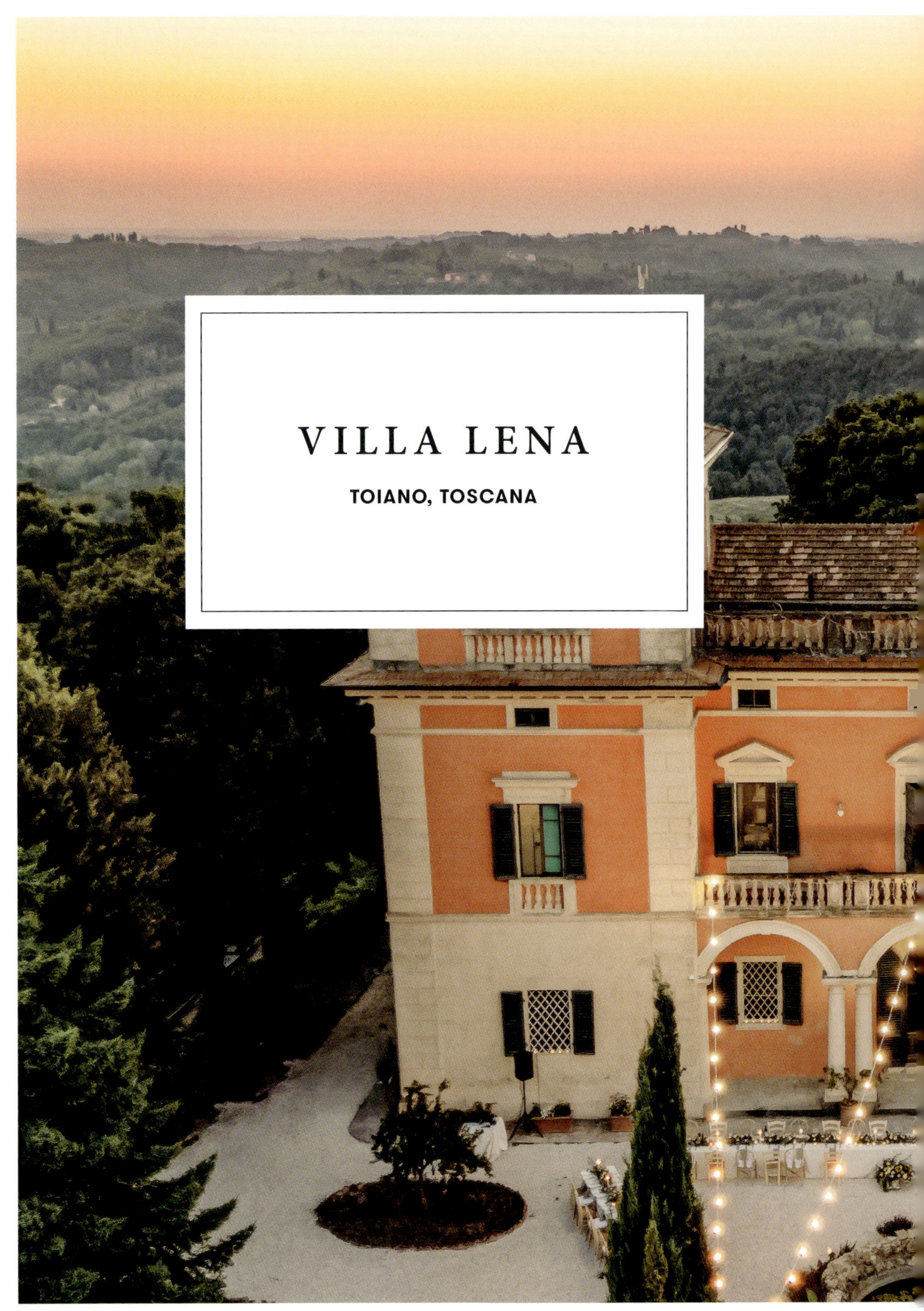

VILLA LENA

TOIANO, TOSCANA

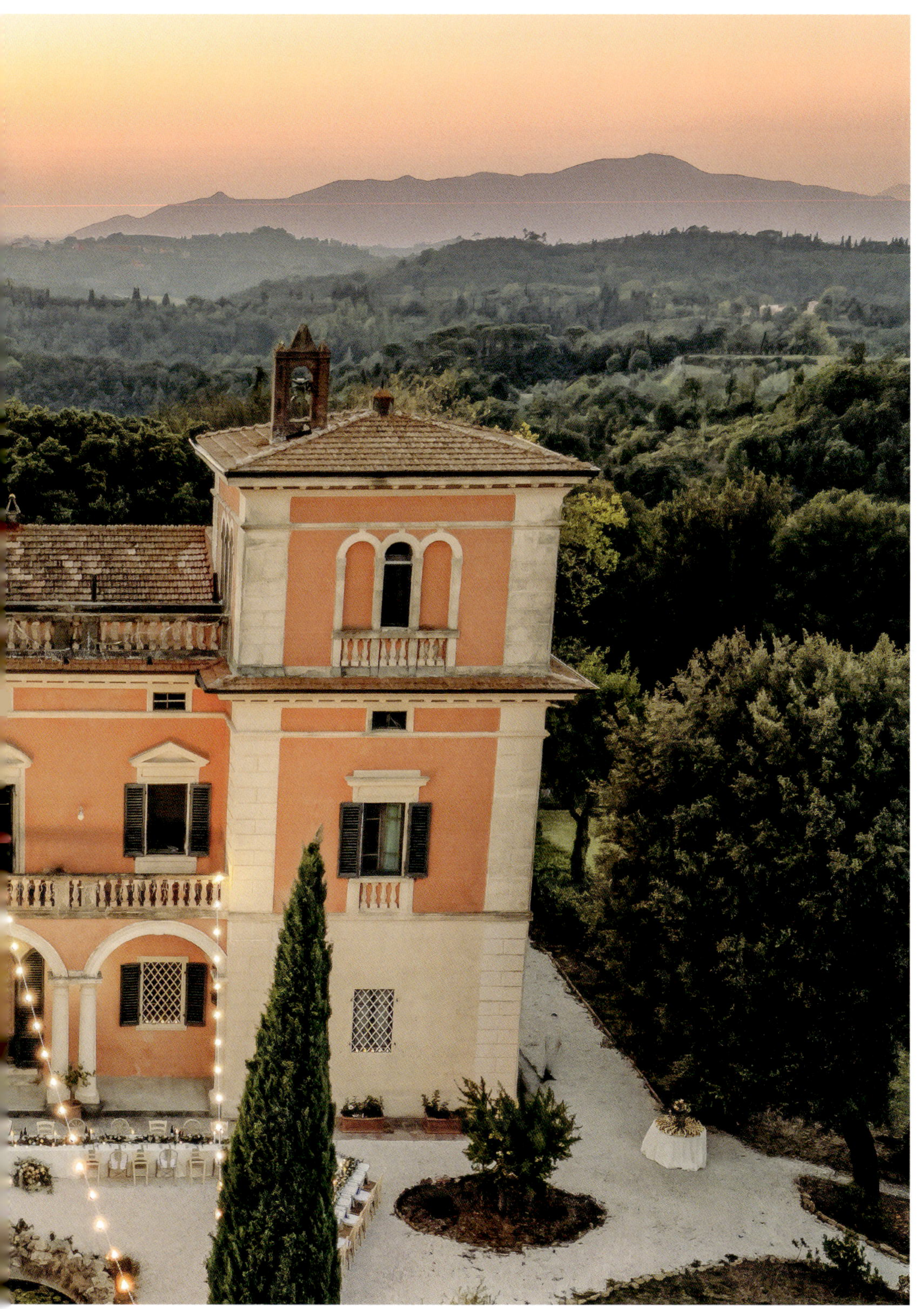

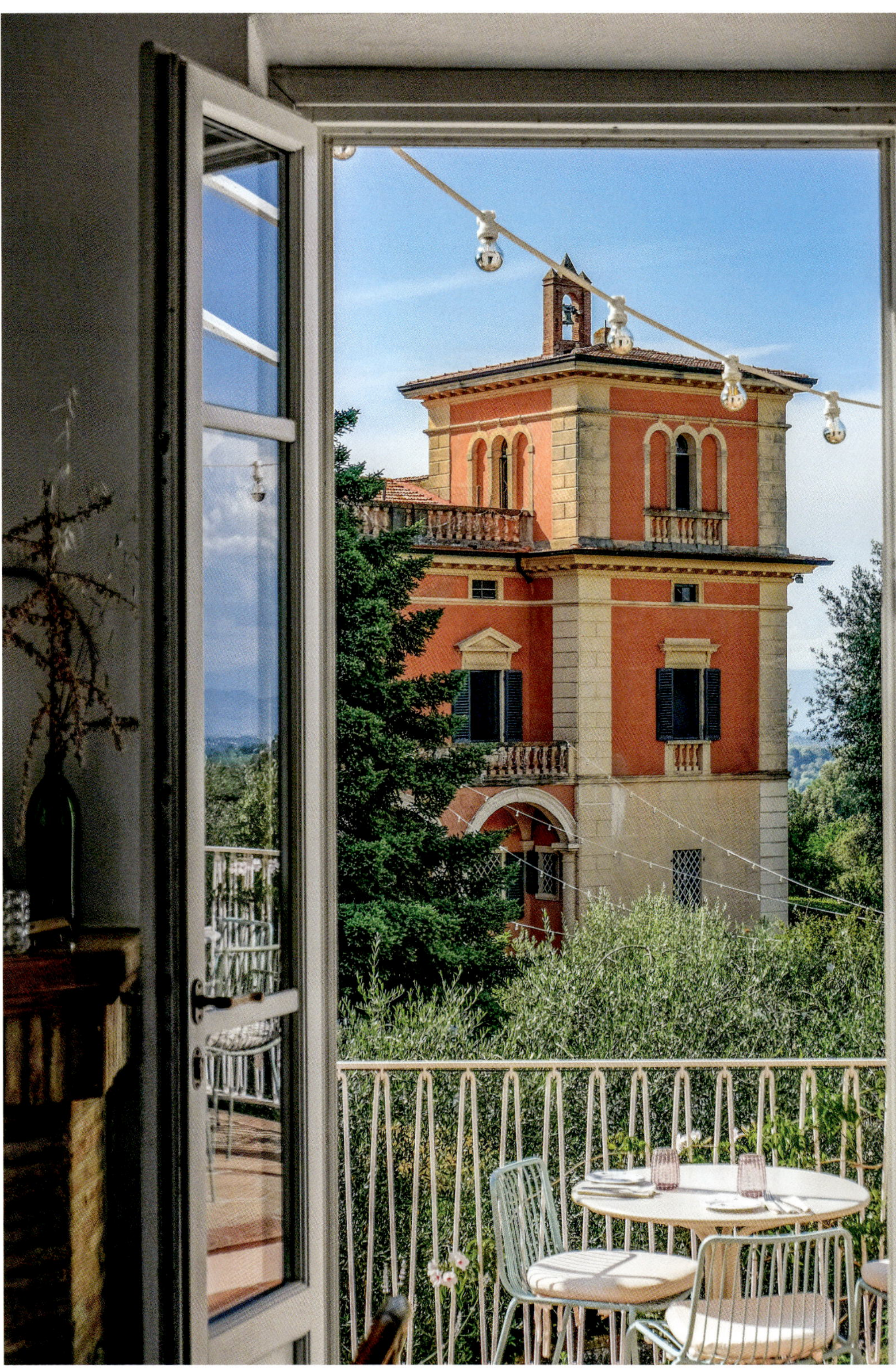

VILLA LENA

Strada comunale di Toiano 25, 56036 Toiano, Palaia
Tel. +39 0587 083 111 · host@villa-lena.it
www.villa-lena.it

ARTS FOR HEARTS' SAKE In the late 19th and early 20th centuries, this picture-postcard villa in the Tuscan hills belonged to an aristocratic Italian dynasty that held glittering parties, organized legendary gatherings for the hunt, and immortalized the women of the family on ceiling frescoes. Then came the lean years, when banks and owners came and went – but today Villa Lena is once again all about encounters with many different kinds of people, about shared passions, and about art. The curator Lena Evstafieva, after whom the villa is named, and the musician Jérôme Hadey have turned the beautifully located estate into a cross between a creative workshop, a country seat, and an organic farm. Artists from all over the world find inspiration here, and every season the artists-in-residence are joined by writers, curators and yogis, who teach asanas and breathing techniques to the guests, go truffle-hunting with them, or divulge the secret of perfect pasta to them. Participants in the workshops, or those who simply come to indulge in some time out, stay in one of the converted farmhouses, stables, or hunting lodges, which are even older than the villa itself and have been restored in the style of agriturismo. Every room is different from the others, and in each of them Lena and designers have done their work so unobtrusively, combining classic furniture with finds from antique markets, and engaging in recycling and upcycling, that the rooms have the atmosphere of private vacation apartments. To dine in the Osteria San Michele, where wine from the estate's own grapes accompanies well-loved Tuscan dishes, is to feel you are part of a big family. ◆ Book to pack: "Michelangelo" by Irving Stone.

EIN KUNSTSTÜCK Ende des 19. und Anfang des 20. Jahrhunderts gehörte diese Bilderbuchvilla in den Hügeln der Toskana einer italienischen Adelsfamilie, die hier zu rauschenden Partys lud, legendäre Jagdgesellschaften ausrichtete und ihre weiblichen Mitglieder auf den Deckenfresken verewigen ließ. Dann kam eine Durststrecke, in der sich Banken und Besitzer die Klinke in die Hand gaben – doch inzwischen geht es in der Villa Lena wieder um die Begegnung ganz unterschiedlicher Menschen, um gemeinsame Leidenschaften und um Kunst. Die Namensgeberin und Kuratorin Lena Evstafieva und der Musiker Jérôme Hadey haben das herrlich gelegene Anwesen zu einer Mischung aus Kreativwerkstatt, Landsitz und Biohof gemacht. Bei ihnen finden Künstler aus aller Welt Inspiration, und neben Artists in Residence geben jede Saison Autoren, Kuratoren und Yogis Gastspiele. Sie bringen den Gästen Asanas und Atemtechniken bei, gehen mit ihnen auf Trüffelsuche oder weihen sie in das Geheimnis der perfekten Pasta ein. Wer an einem Workshop teilnimmt oder sich einfach eine kurze Auszeit gönnt, wohnt in einem der ehemaligen Bauernhäuser, Ställe oder Jagdlodges, die noch älter als die Villa selbst sind und im Agriturismo-Stil renoviert wurden. Kein Zimmer gleicht dem anderen, und in jedem haben Lena und die Designer so unauffällig Hand angelegt, Möbelklassiker und Antikmarktfunde kombiniert, Recycling und Upcycling betrieben, dass die Räume das Flair privater Ferienwohnungen besitzen. Wie in einer großen Familie fühlt man sich auch im Restaurant Osteria San Michele, wo es zu toskanischen Lieblingsgerichten Wein aus gutseigenen Trauben gibt. ◆ Buchtipp: „Michelangelo“ von Irving Stone.

L'ART DE RECEVOIR À la fin du XIXe et au début du XXe siècle, cette villa de carte postale située dans les collines de Toscane appartenait à une famille de l'aristocratie italienne qui y organisait des fêtes grandioses, des parties de chasse légendaires, et qui fit immortaliser ses membres féminins sur les fresques du plafond. Puis vint une période de vaches maigres, pendant laquelle on vit défiler les banques et les propriétaires. Aujourd'hui, la Villa Lena est à nouveau le lieu de rencontre de personnes très différentes, qui se retrouvent autour de passions communes et d'œuvres d'art. La commissaire d'exposition Lena Evstafieva, qui a donné son prénom à l'établissement, et le musicien Jérôme Hadey ont fait de cette propriété magnifiquement située un mélange d'atelier créatif, de résidence campagnarde et de ferme biologique. Chez eux, des artistes du monde entier trouvent l'inspiration et, outre les artistes en résidence, des écrivains, des conservateurs et des yogis sont invités chaque saison. Ils enseignent aux hôtes des asanas et des techniques de respiration, les emmènent chercher des truffes ou les initient aux secrets de la parfaite préparation des pâtes. Les personnes qui participent à un atelier ou qui s'accordent simplement une petite pause séjournent dans l'une des fermes, écuries ou pavillons de chasse, encore plus anciens que la villa et rénovés dans le style agritouristique. Aucune chambre ne ressemble à une autre : ici, Lena et les designers ont œuvré de manière si discrète, combinant les meubles classiques et les trouvailles du marché d'antiquités, pratiquant le recyclage et l'upcycling, que les pièces ont l'ambiance d'appartements de vacances privés. On a aussi l'impression de faire partie d'une grande famille à l'Osteria San Michele, où les meilleurs plats toscans sont accompagnés de vins provenant des vignes du domaine. ◆ À lire : « La Vie ardente de Michel-Ange » d'Irving Stone.

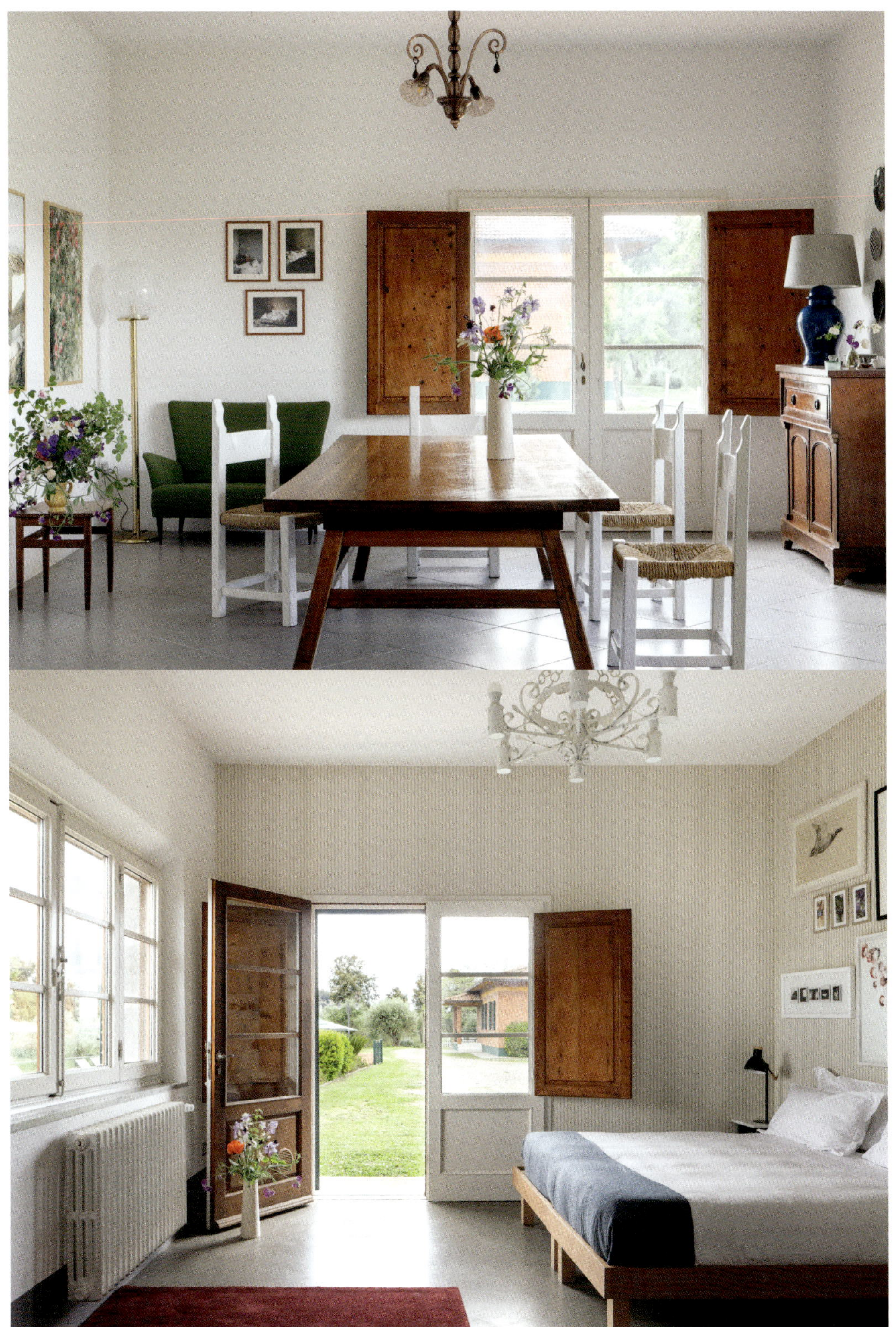

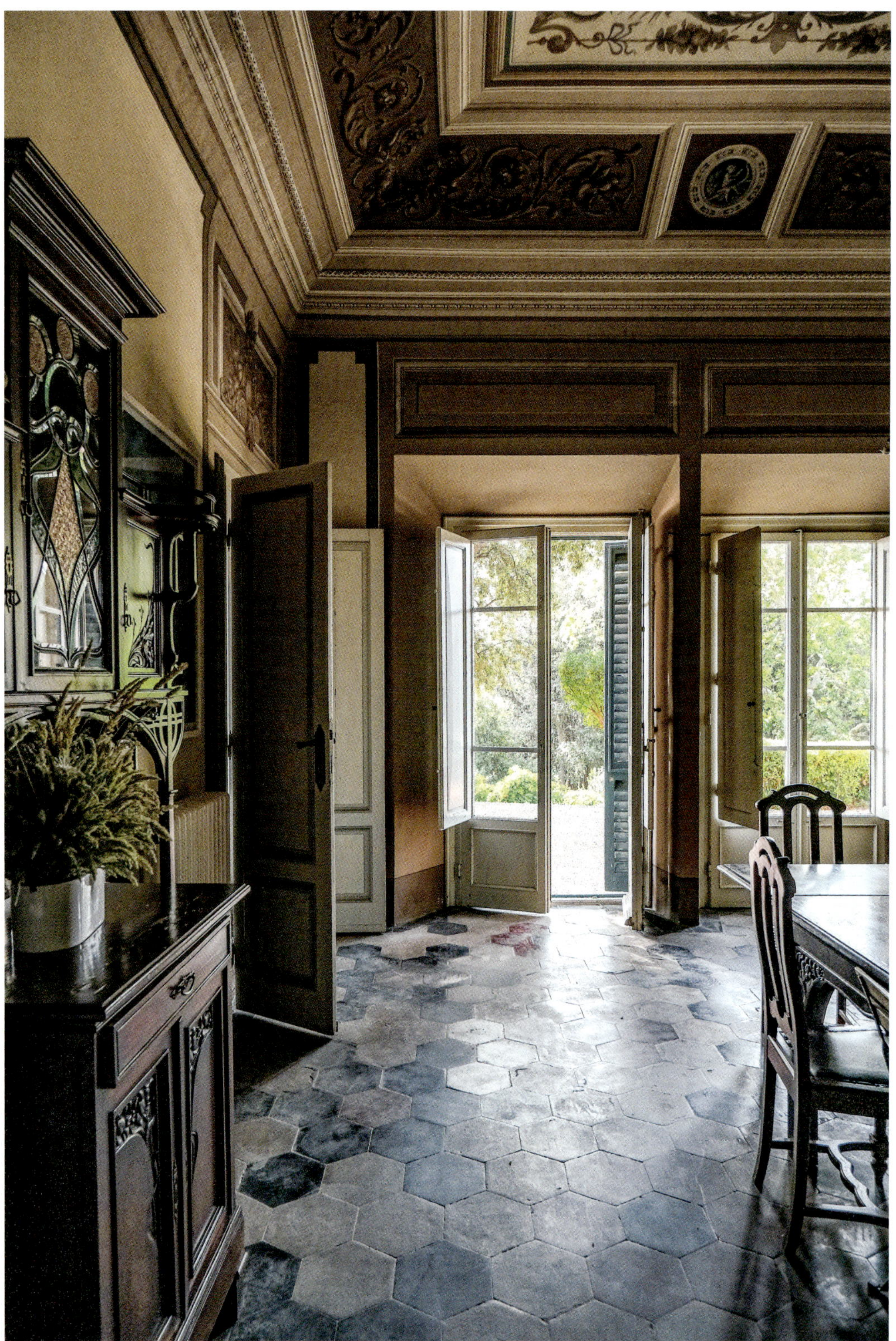

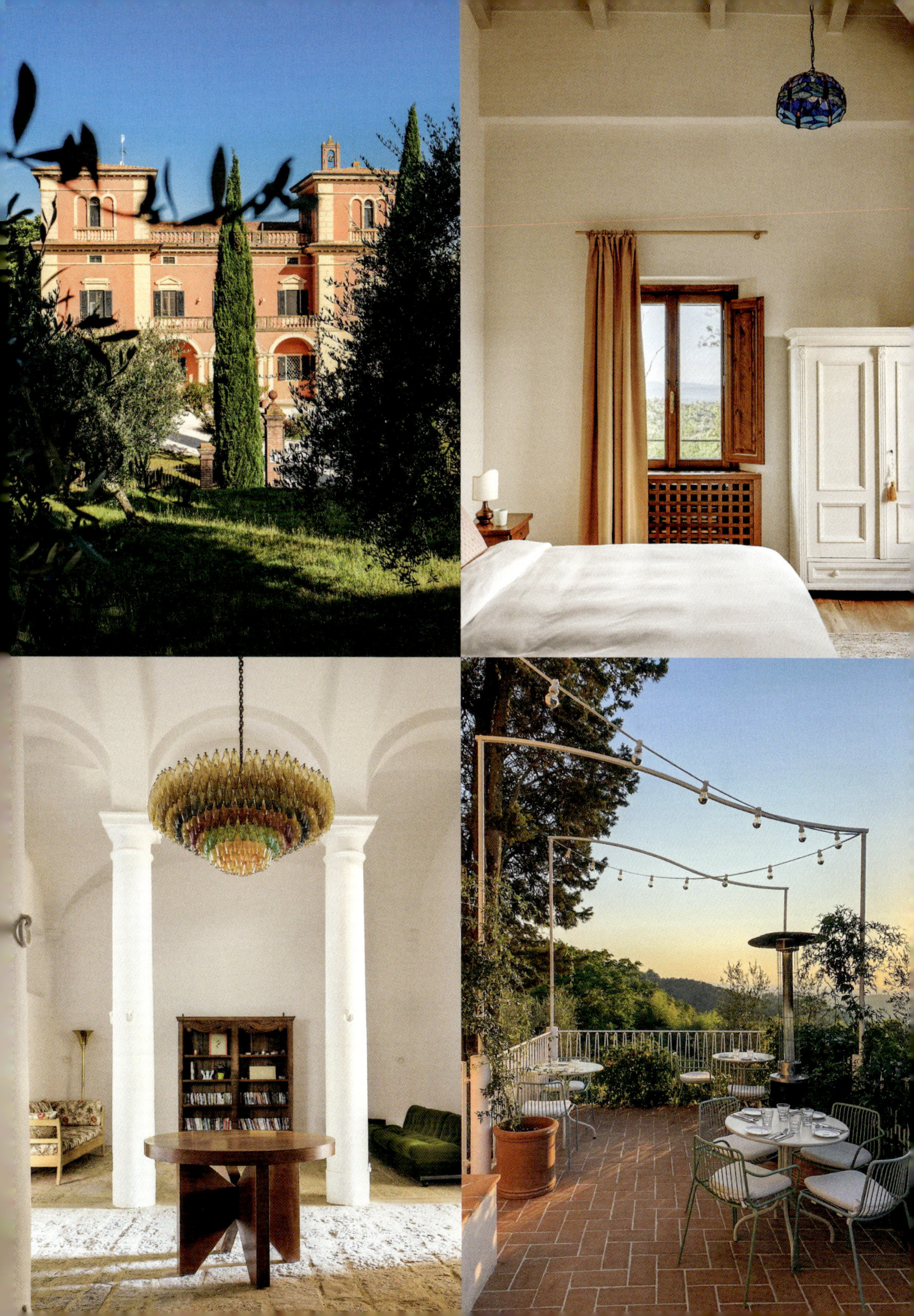

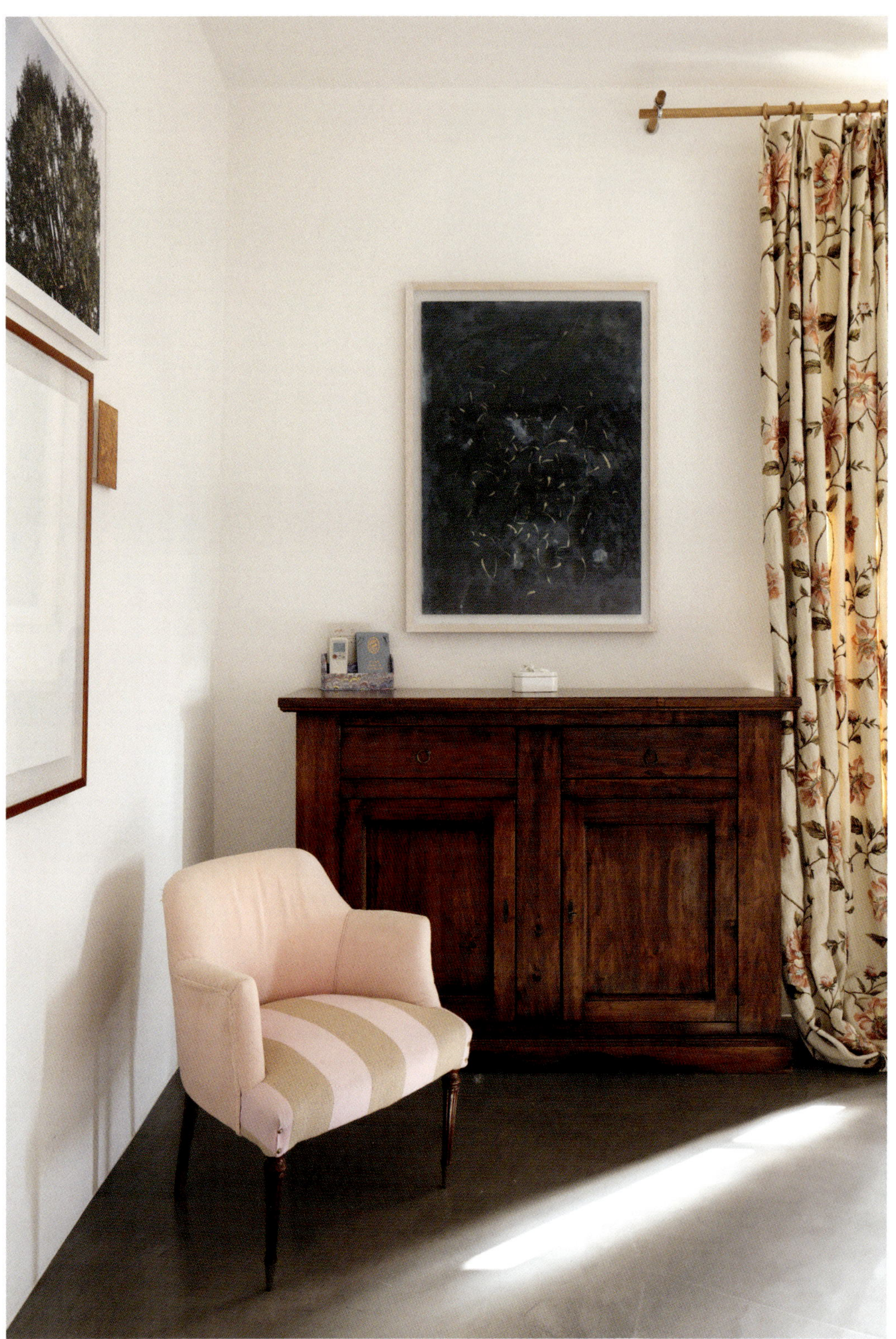

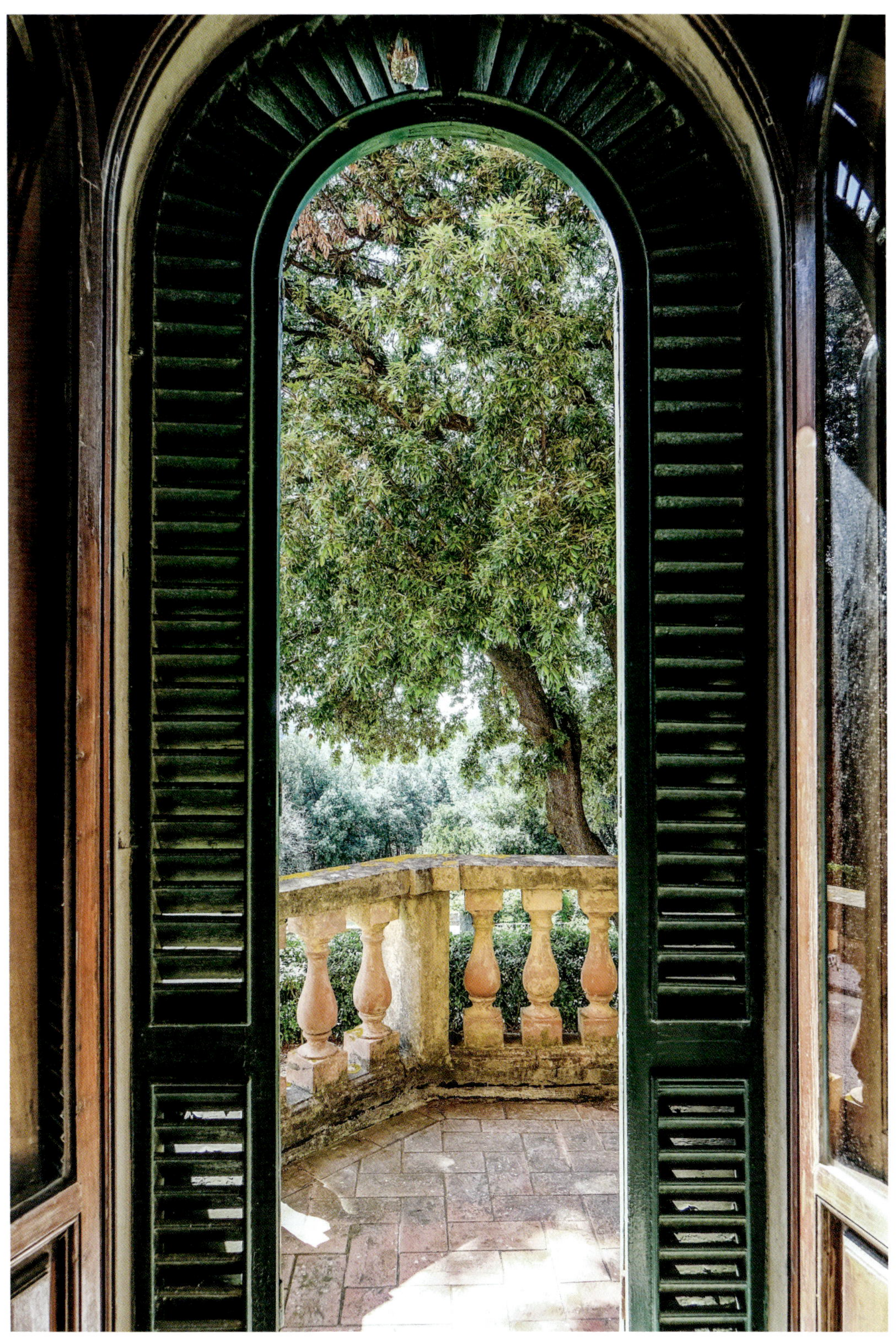

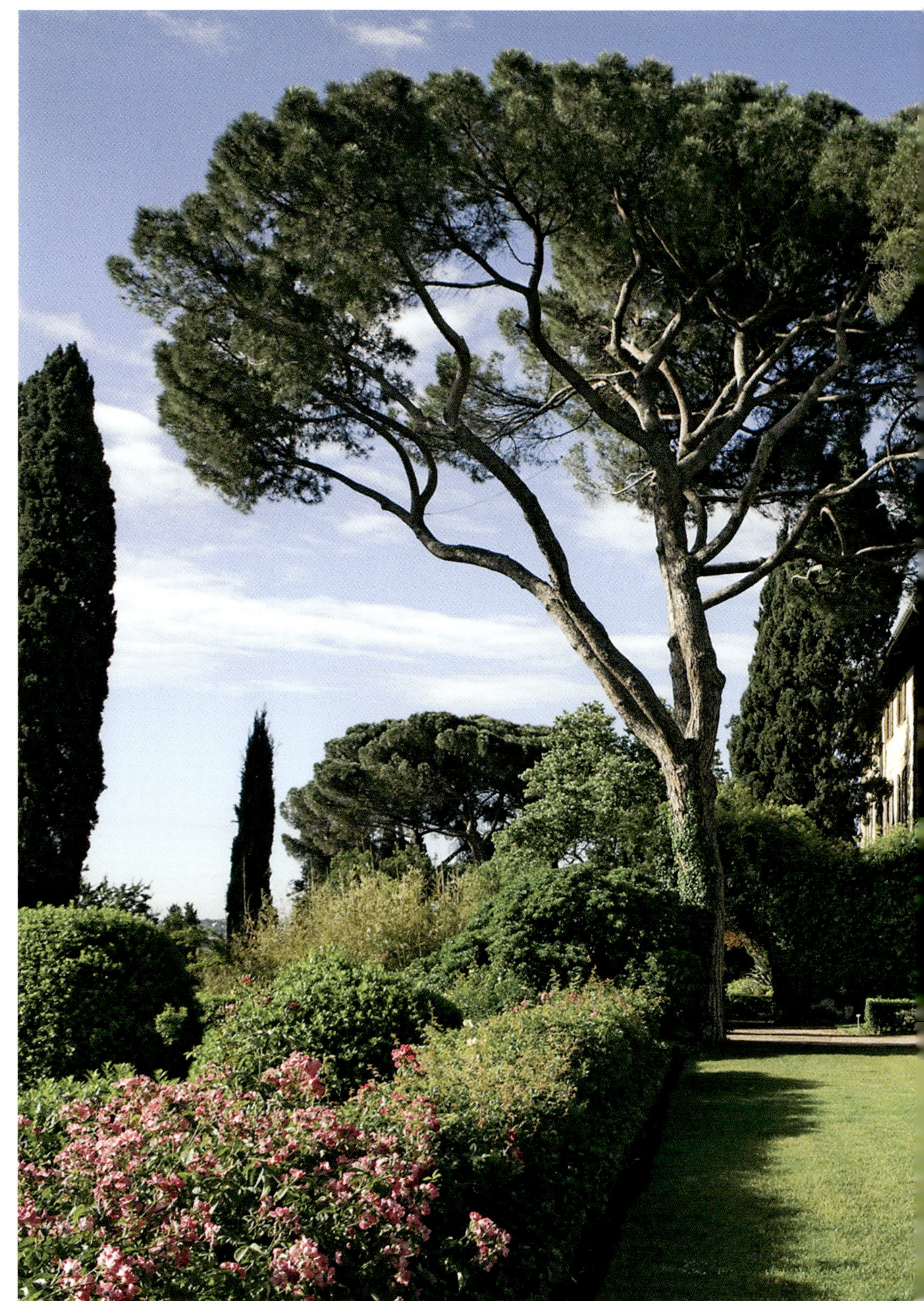

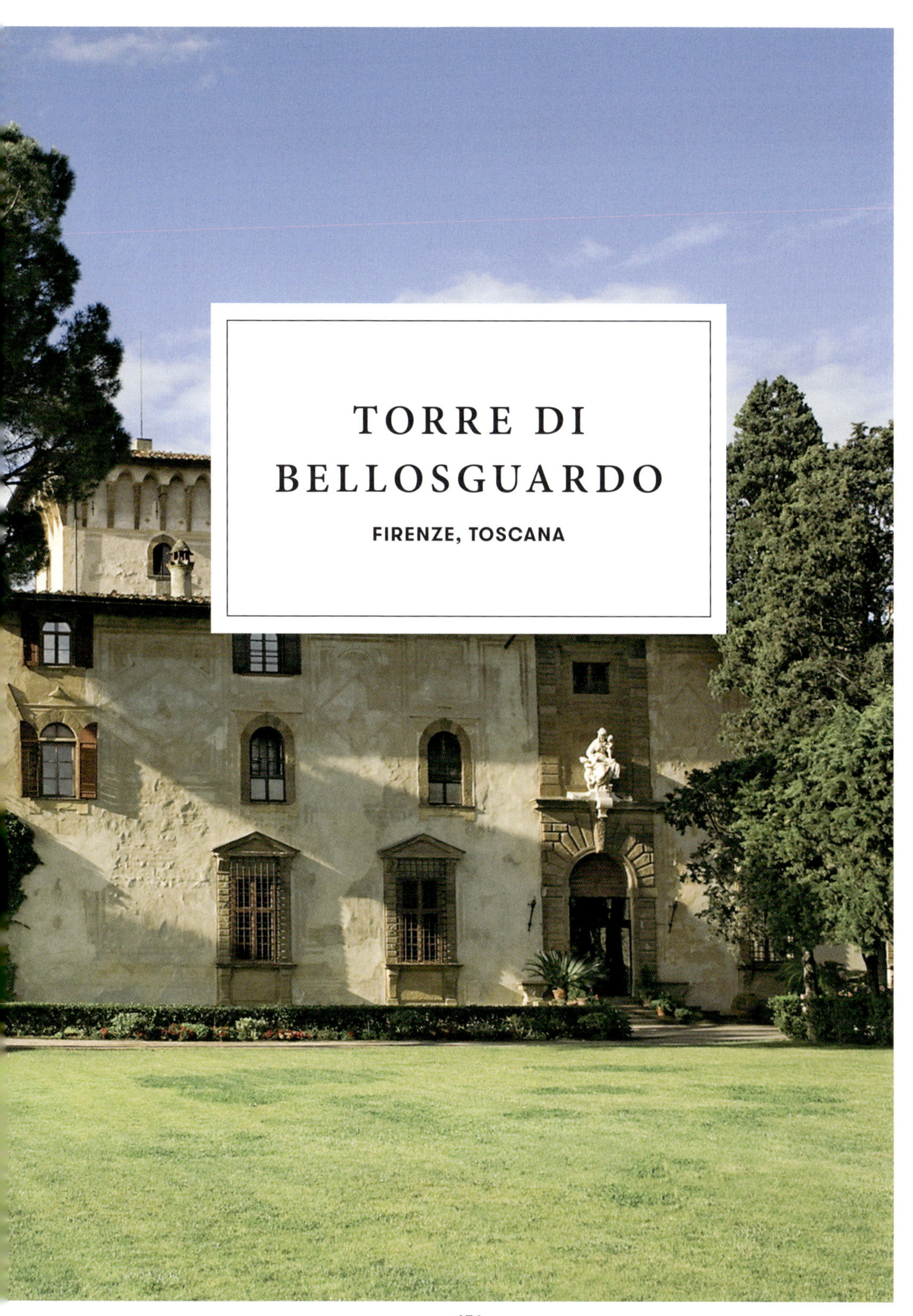

TORRE DI BELLOSGUARDO

FIRENZE, TOSCANA

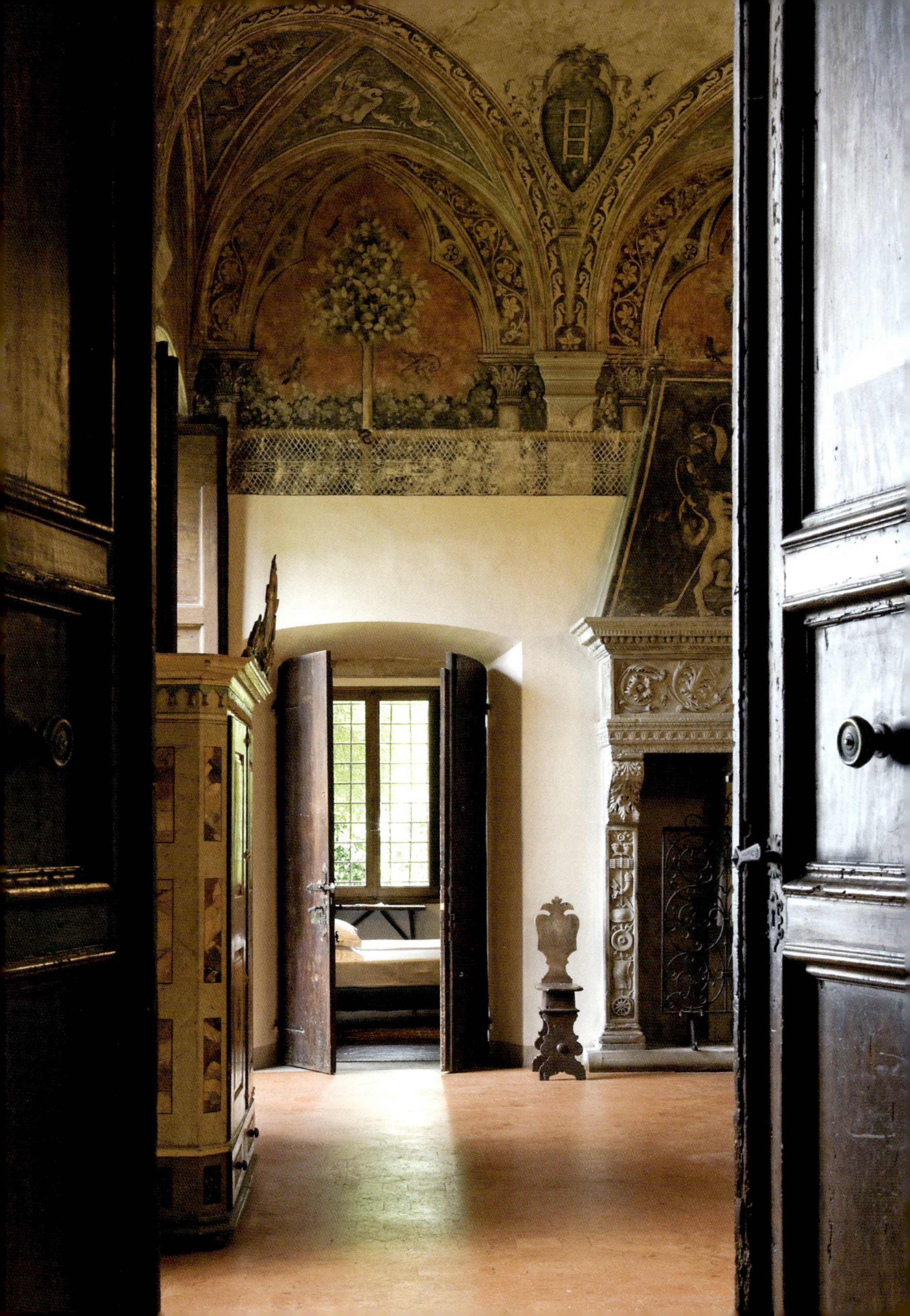

TORRE DI BELLOSGUARDO

Via Roti Michelozzi 2, 50124 Firenze
Tel. +39 055 229 8145 · info@torrebellosguardo.com
www.torrebellosguardo.com

A VIEW OF HISTORY There is only one way to get out of the tourist bustle of Florence while still enjoying all the beauty of the city: a trip into the hills that surround the historic center and afford a sensational prospect of the cathedral and roofs of the city. An elevation to the south of the Arno provides the best view, as the name says: Bellosguardo, a place where the loveliest postcard motifs have been photographed, where painters have captured the panorama in oil on canvas and thinkers have found inspiration – among them Galileo Galilei, who wrote his "Dialogue Concerning the Two Chief World Systems" on Bellosguardo. For a journey in time to Galileo's age and even further back, book a room in the Torre di Bellosguardo. A friend of Dante built the tower in the 13th century as a hunting lodge, and during the Renaissance the Marchesi Roti Michelozzi added a villa. Artists and aristocrats from all over Europe have always been guests here. Between 1920 and 1940 a German baroness even established an intellectual circle on the estate. To this day the Torre has an atmosphere of history, nobility and Bohemian life: a statue of Mercy by Pietro Francavilla still greets visitors, frescoes by Bernardino Poccetti adorn the lobby and the rooms are museums where almost all the furniture derives from the former owners. But don't get so carried away by the antique interior that you forget to look out through the windows of the tower to admire Florence lying at your feet. ◆ Book to pack: "Portrait of a Lady" by Henry James.

EIN BLICK AUF DIE GESCHICHTE Um dem Touristentrubel von Florenz zu entkommen, die Stadt aber dennoch in ihrer ganzen Schönheit zu genießen, gibt es nur ein Mittel: ein Ausflug auf die Hügel, die das Zentrum umgeben und eine sensationelle Sicht über Dom und Dächer eröffnen. Eine Anhöhe im Süden des Arno bietet den besten Blick – und trägt ihn sogar im Namen: Vom Bellosguardo aus wurden die schönsten Postkartenmotive fotografiert, Maler verewigten das Panorama in Öl, Denker fanden hier Inspiration – unter ihnen Galileo Galilei, der auf dem Bellosguardo seinen „Dialog über die beiden hauptsächlichsten Weltsysteme" verfasste. Wer in die Epoche Galileis und noch weiter zurück in die Geschichte reisen möchte, sollte im Torre di Bellosguardo reservieren. Ein Freund Dantes ließ den Turm im 13. Jahrhundert als Jagdschloss errichten, die Marchesi Roti Michelozzi fügten in der Renaissance eine Villa hinzu. Stets waren hier Künstler und Adlige aus ganz Europa zu Gast – zwischen 1920 und 1940 machte eine deutsche Baronin das Anwesen sogar zu einem Intellektuellenzirkel. Bis heute besitzt der Torre ein Flair von Historie, Noblesse und Boheme: So heißt noch immer eine Statue der Barmherzigkeit von Pietro Francavilla Besucher willkommen, die Lobby schmücken Fresken von Bernardino Poccetti, und die Zimmer sind Museen, in denen nahezu alle Möbel von den einstigen Eigentümern stammen. Vor lauter Begeisterung fürs antike Interieur sollte man aber nicht vergessen, aus den Turmfenstern hinauszuschauen und Florenz zu bewundern, das einem zu Füßen liegt. ◆ Buchtipp: „Bildnis einer Dame" von Henry James.

AU FIL DES SIÈCLES Pour admirer la beauté de Florence en échappant aux légions de touristes, il suffit de faire une excursion sur les collines qui l'entourent et offrent une vue sensationnelle sur le dôme et les toits. Une hauteur située au sud de l'Arno, le Bellosguardo, propose le meilleur panorama. C'est d'ici que les plus beaux motifs de cartes postales ont été photographiés, des peintres ont immortalisé la vue sur la toile, des penseurs y ont trouvé l'inspiration – c'est le cas de Galilée qui a rédigé sur le Bellosguardo son « Dialogue concernant les deux principaux systèmes du monde ». Celui qui veut faire un voyage dans le temps, jusqu'à l'époque de Galilée et plus loin encore, devrait réserver une chambre au Torre di Bellosguardo. Au XIIIe siècle, un ami de Dante fit ériger la tour qui servait de pavillon de chasse, les marquis Roti Michelozzi y ajoutèrent une villa à la Renaissance. Des aristocrates et des artistes venus de toute l'Europe ont toujours été les bienvenus ici – entre 1920 et 1940, une baronne allemande fit même de la propriété un cénacle d'intellectuels. Jusqu'à ce jour, la Tour a conservé son atmosphère historique et aristocratique ainsi que son esprit bohème : ainsi, les visiteurs sont toujours accueillis par une statue de la Charité de Pietro Francavilla, le hall est agrémenté de fresques de Bernardino Poccetti et les chambres, dont presque tous les meubles proviennent des anciens propriétaires, sont de véritables musées. Mais notre admiration pour les antiquités ne devrait pas nous faire oublier de jeter un coup d'œil par la fenêtre et de contempler Florence qui s'étend à nos pieds. ◆ À lire : « Un portrait de femme » de Henry James.

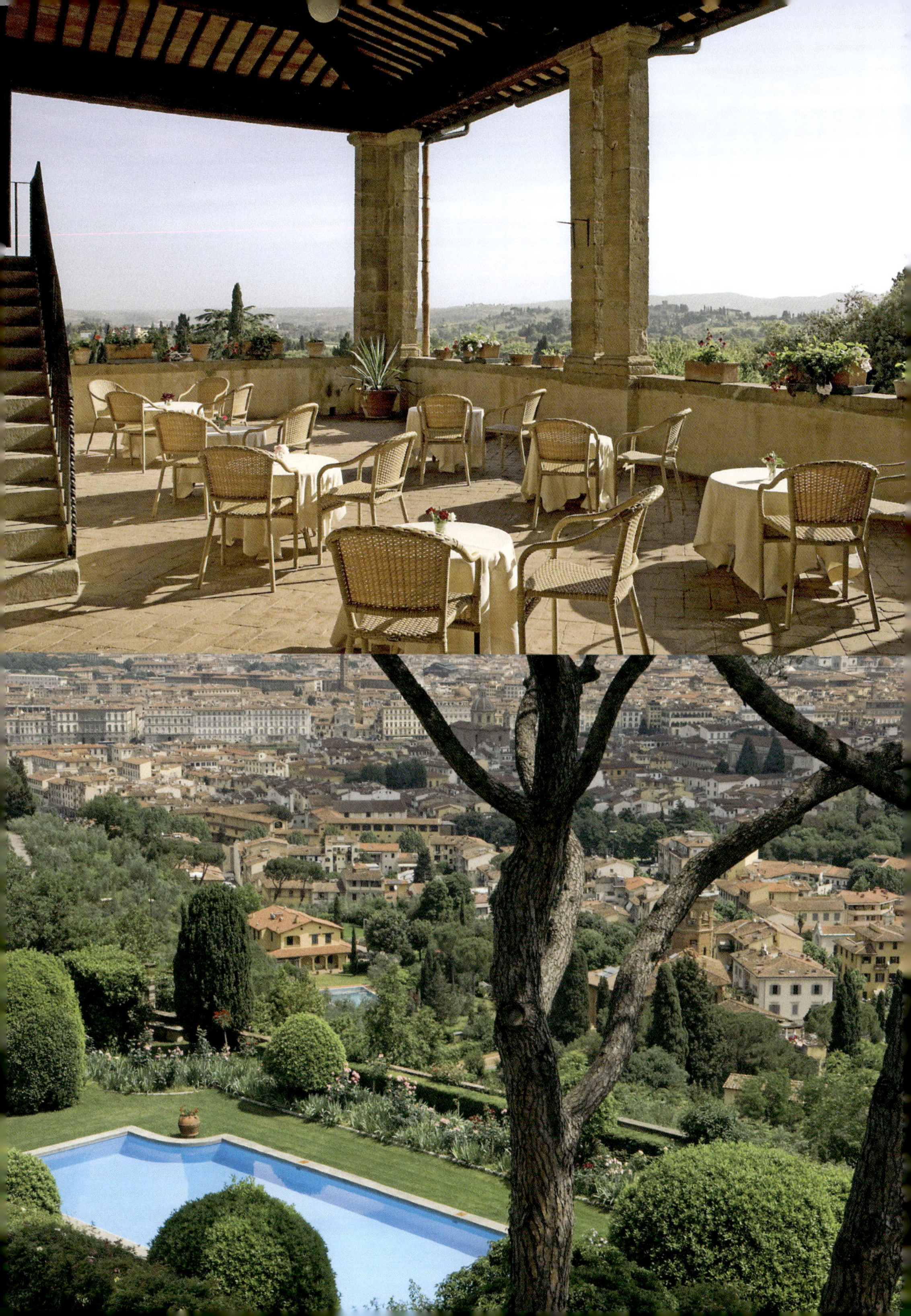

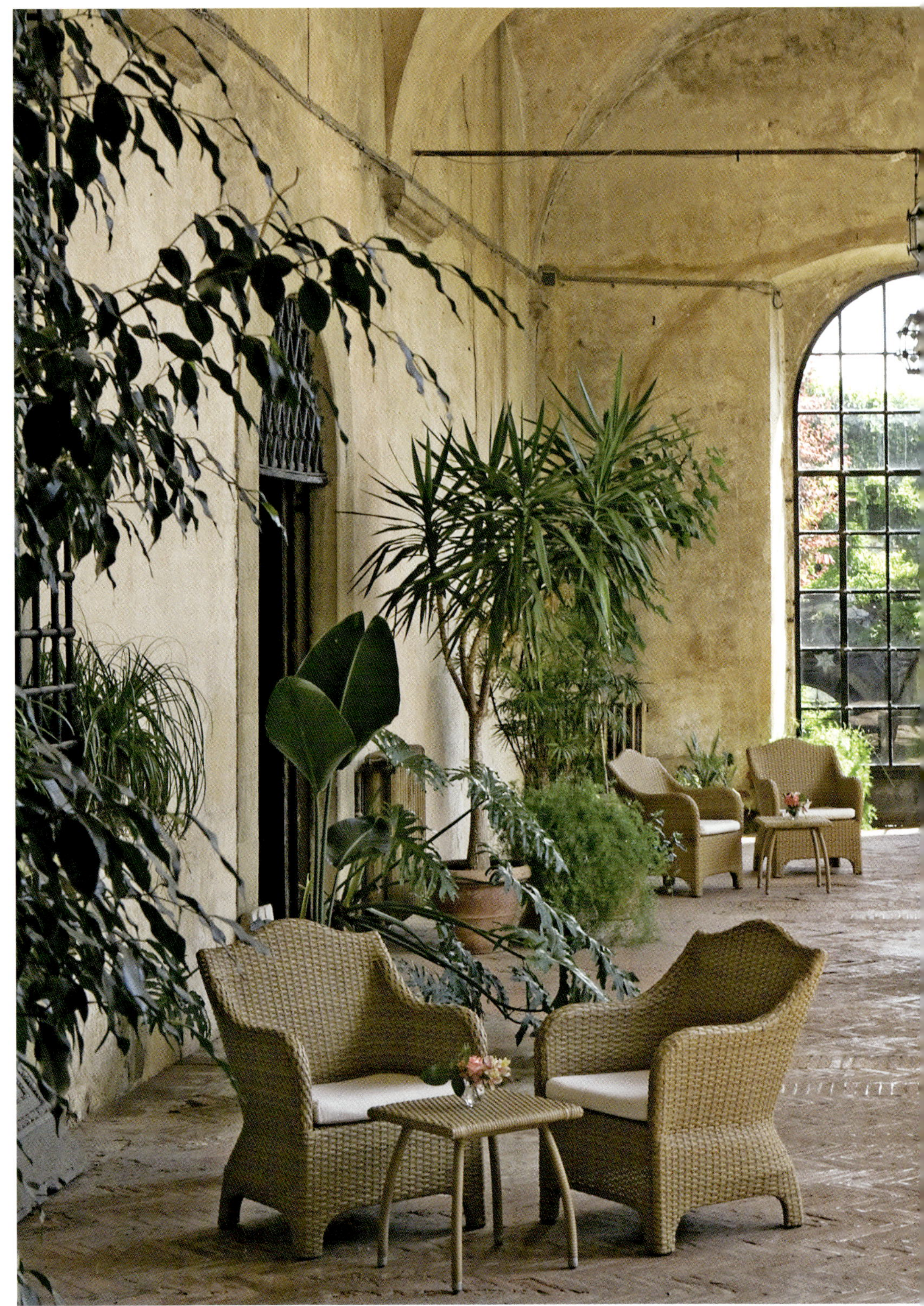

TOSCANA

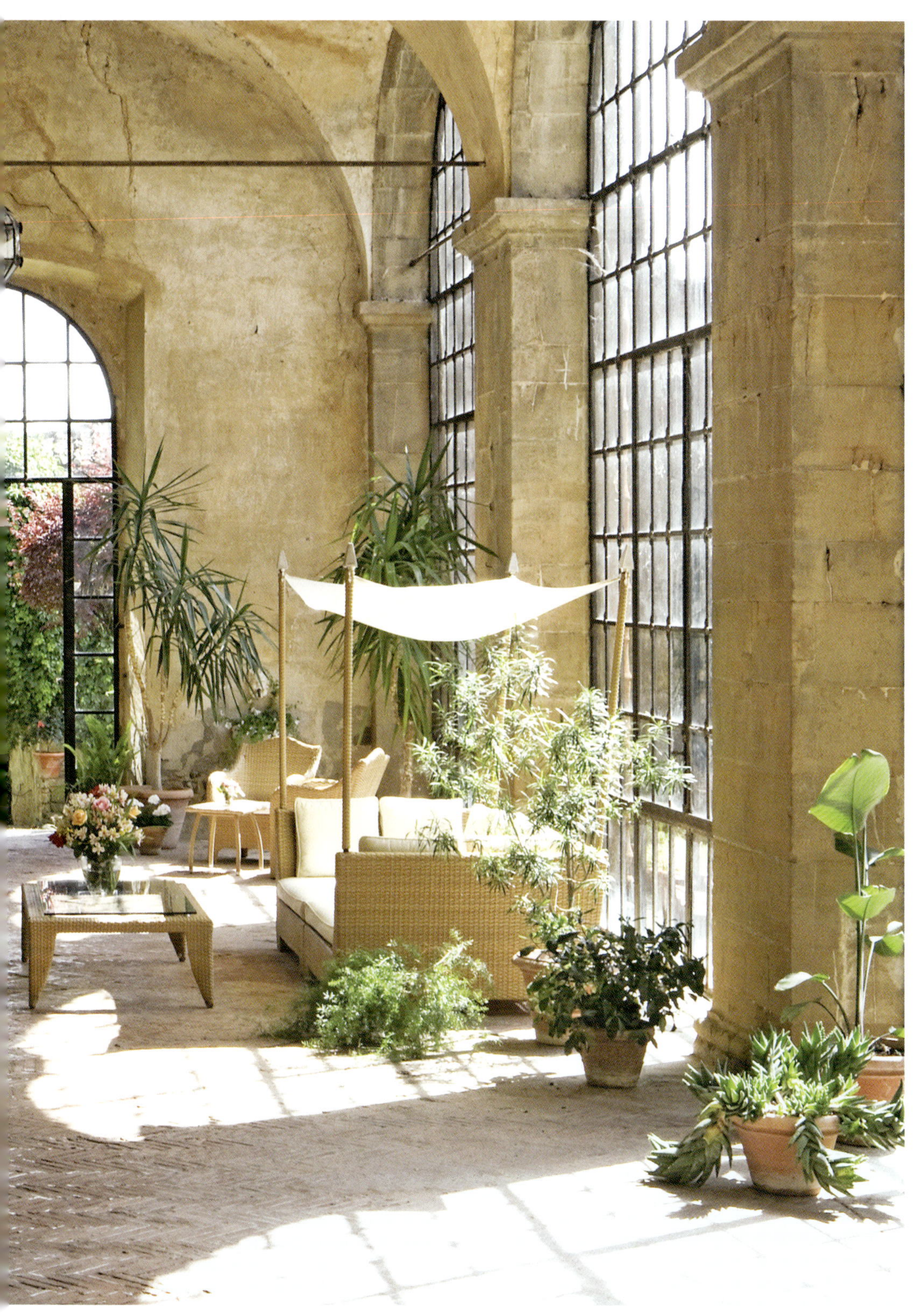

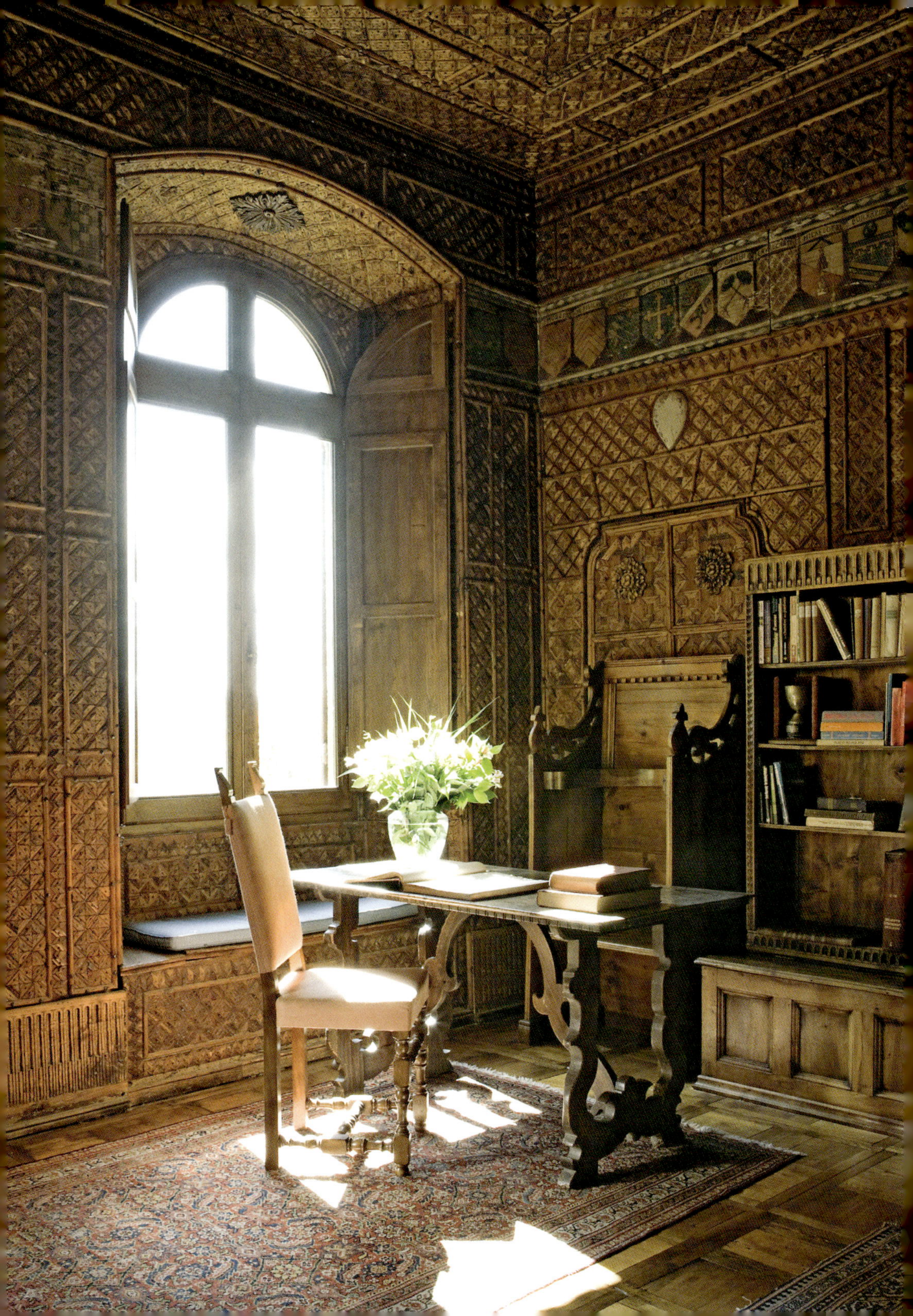

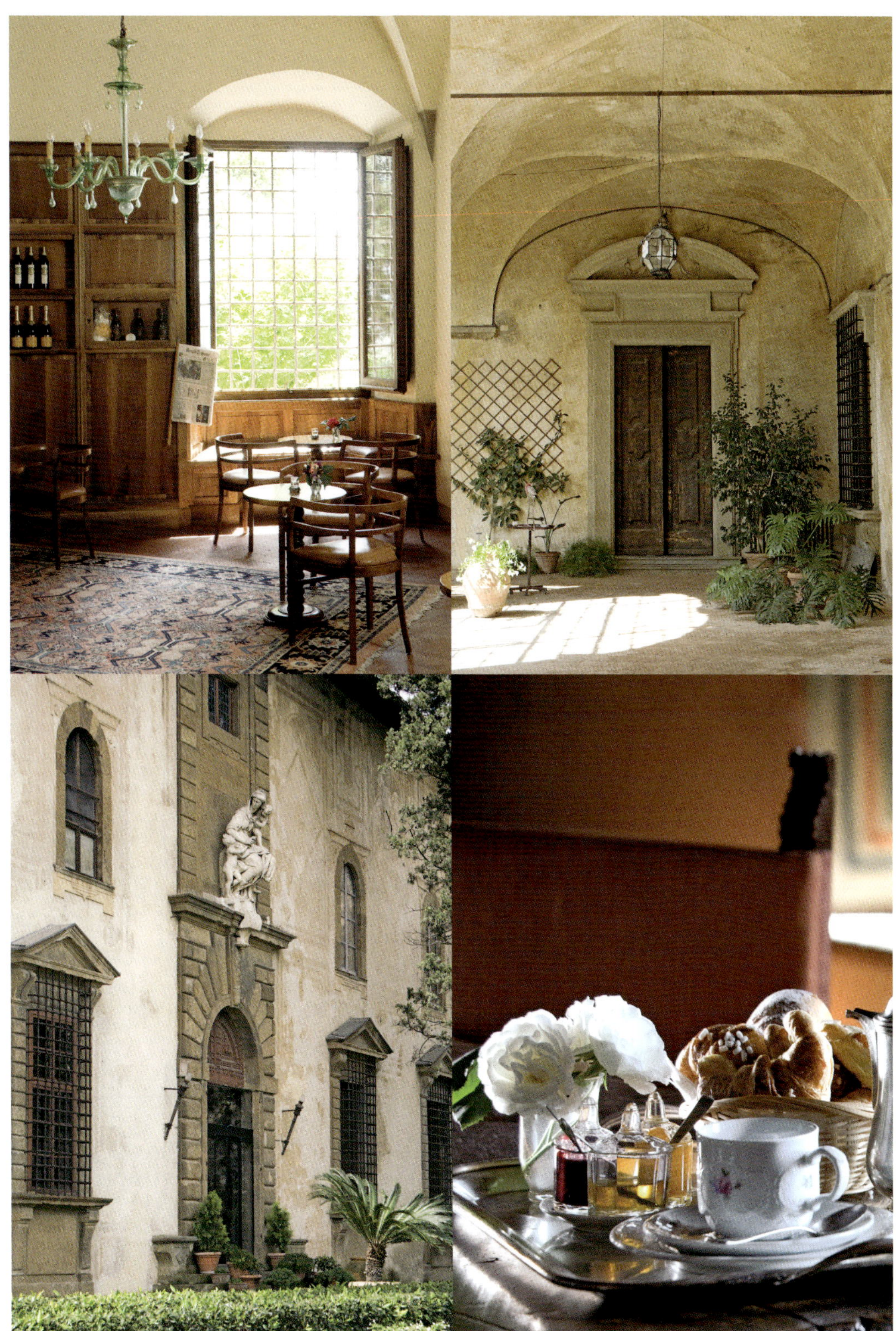

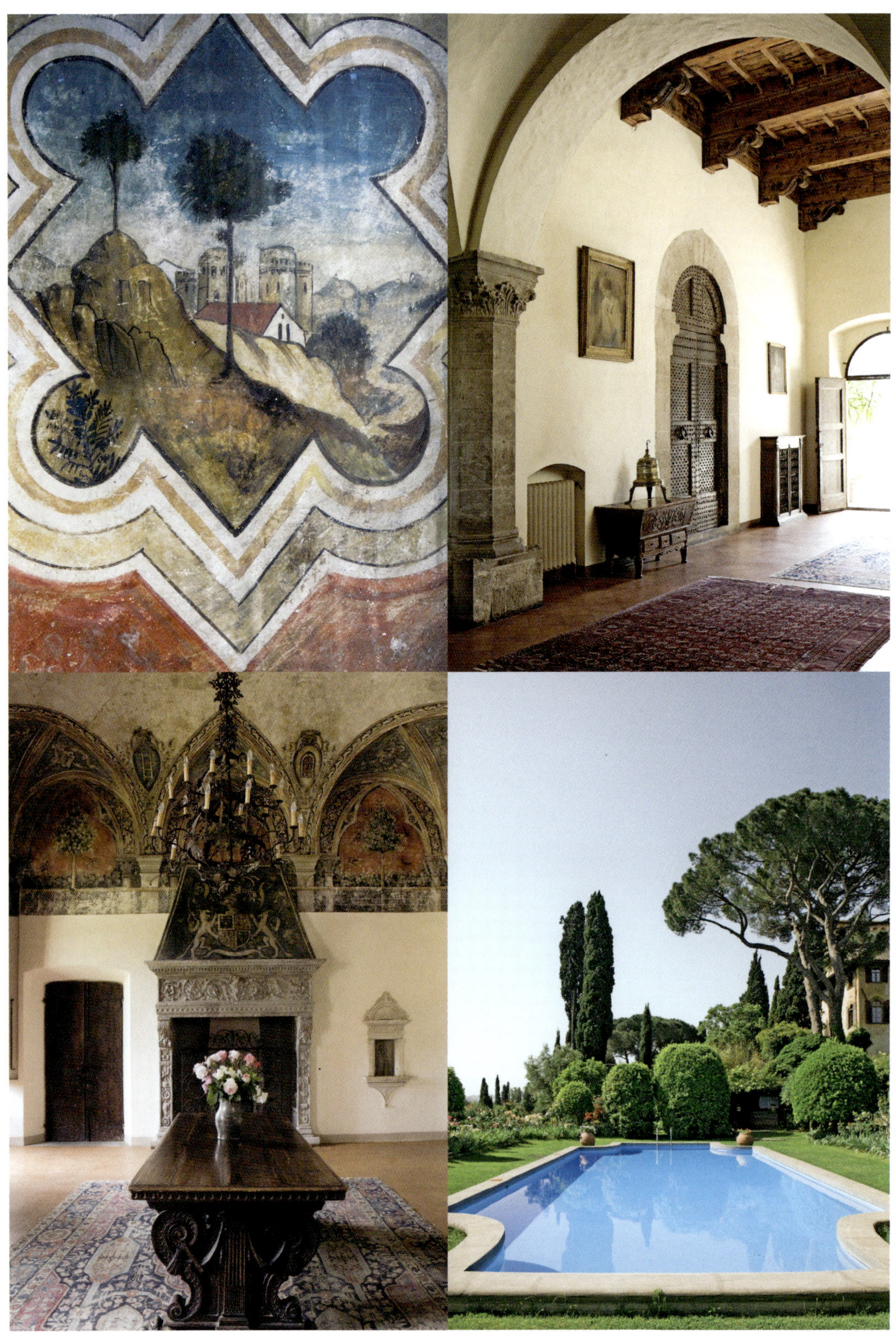

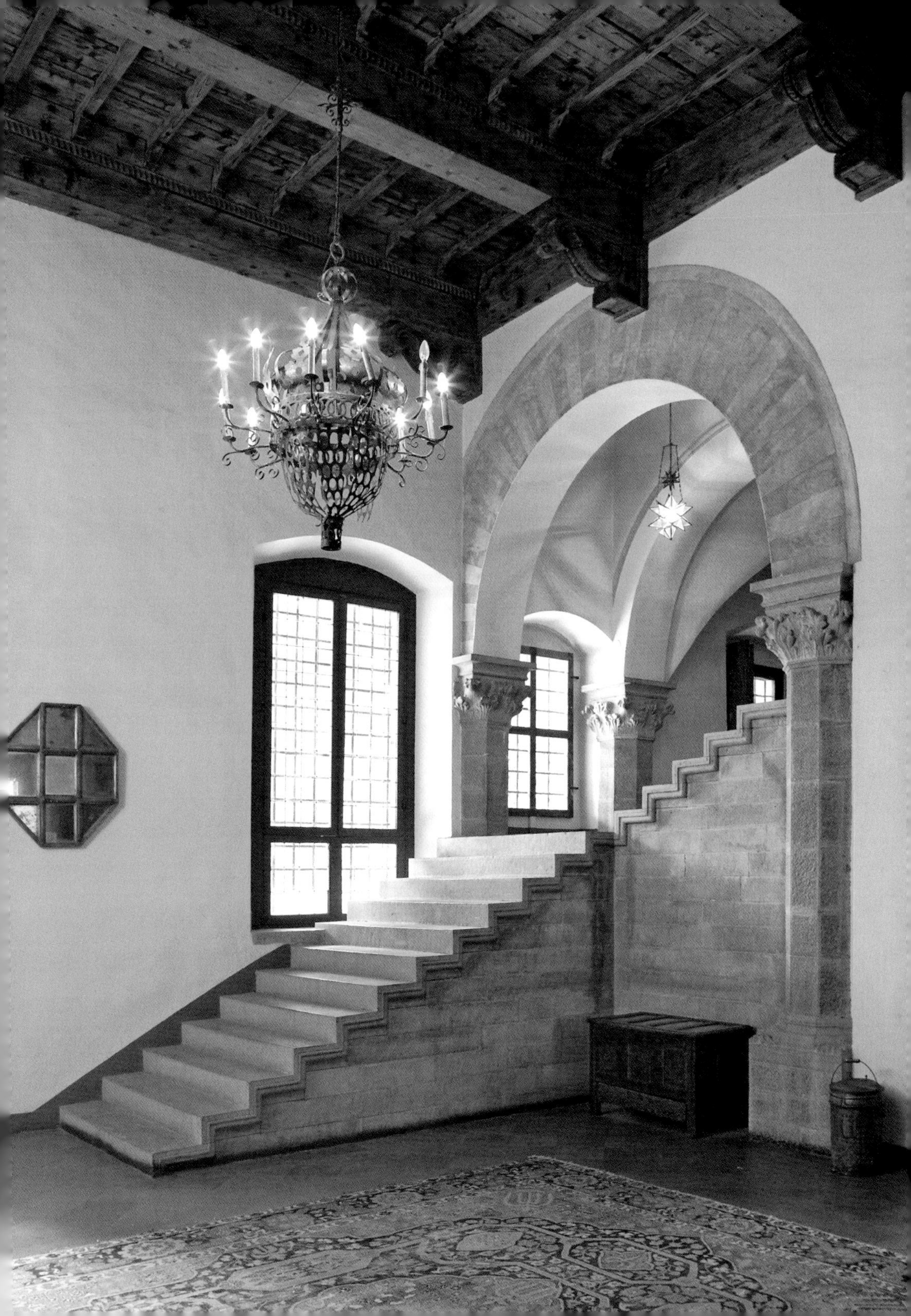

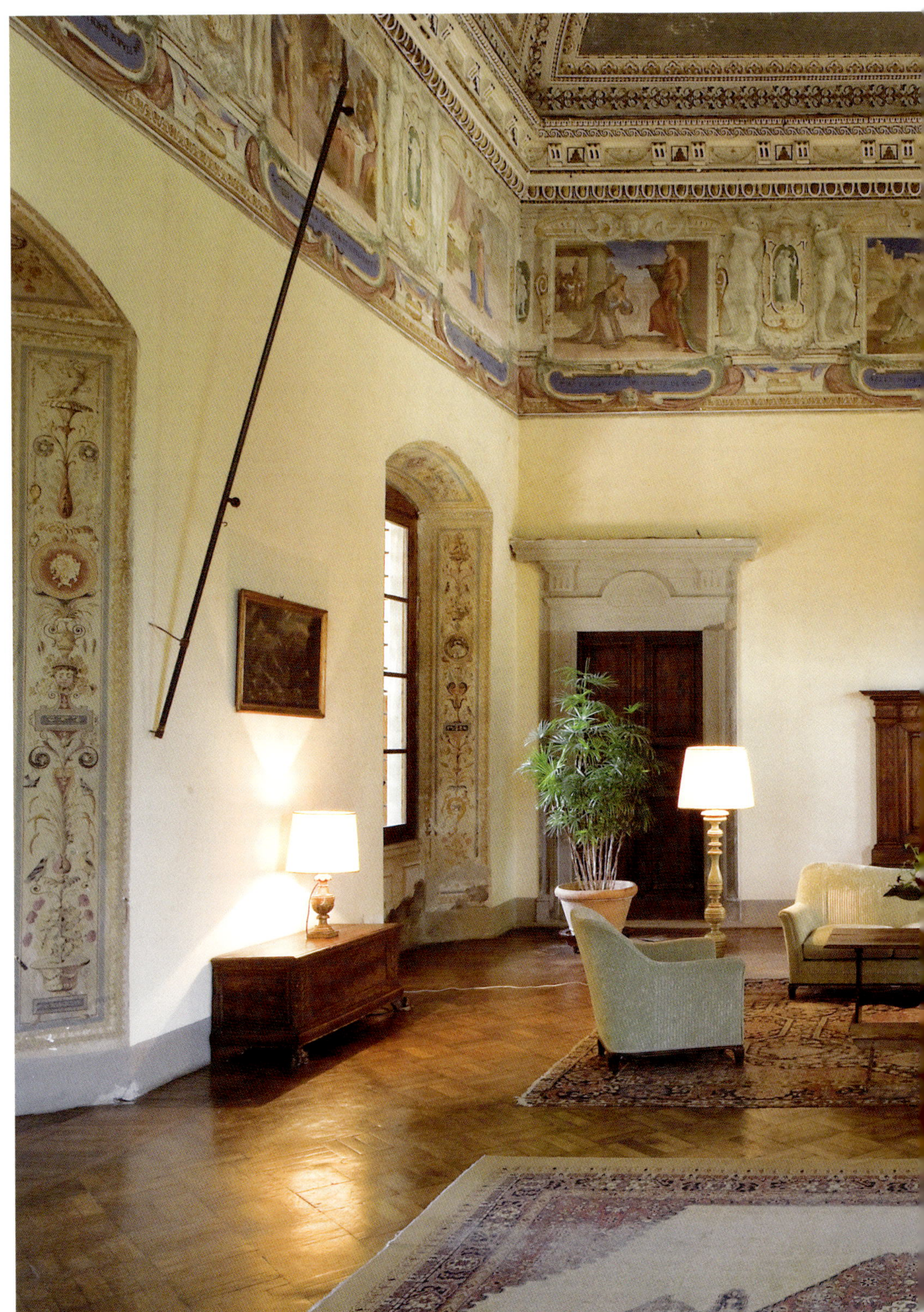

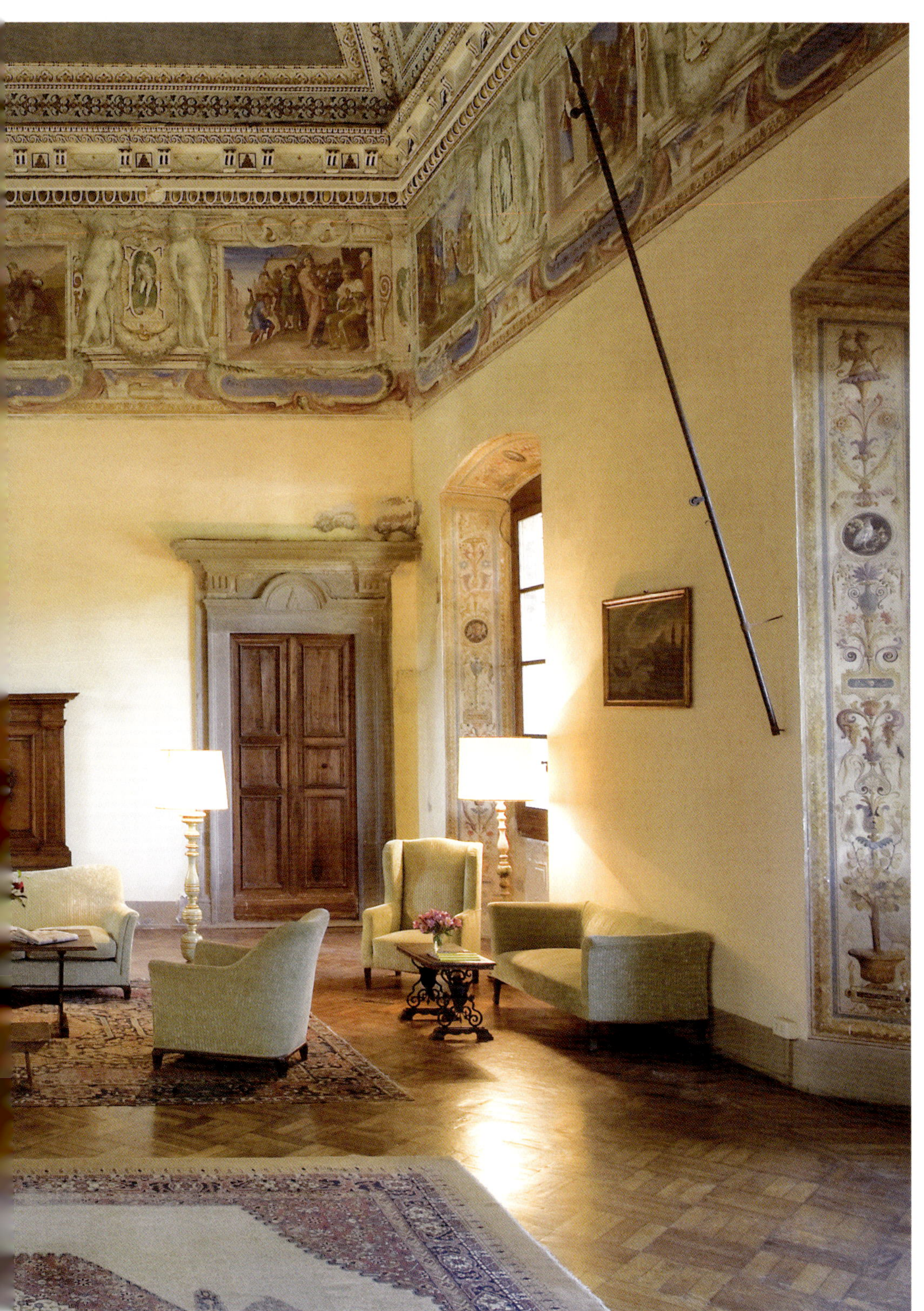

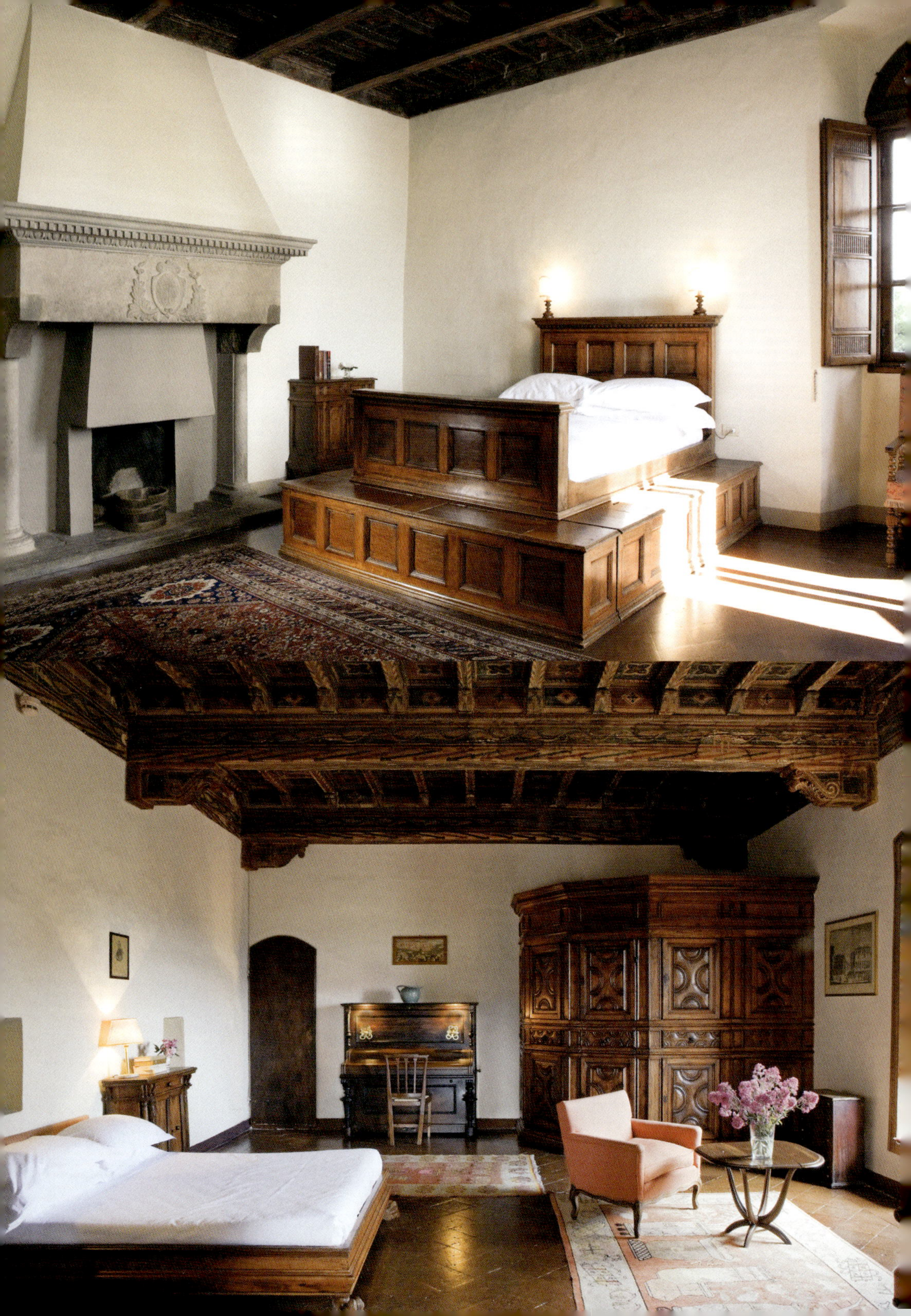

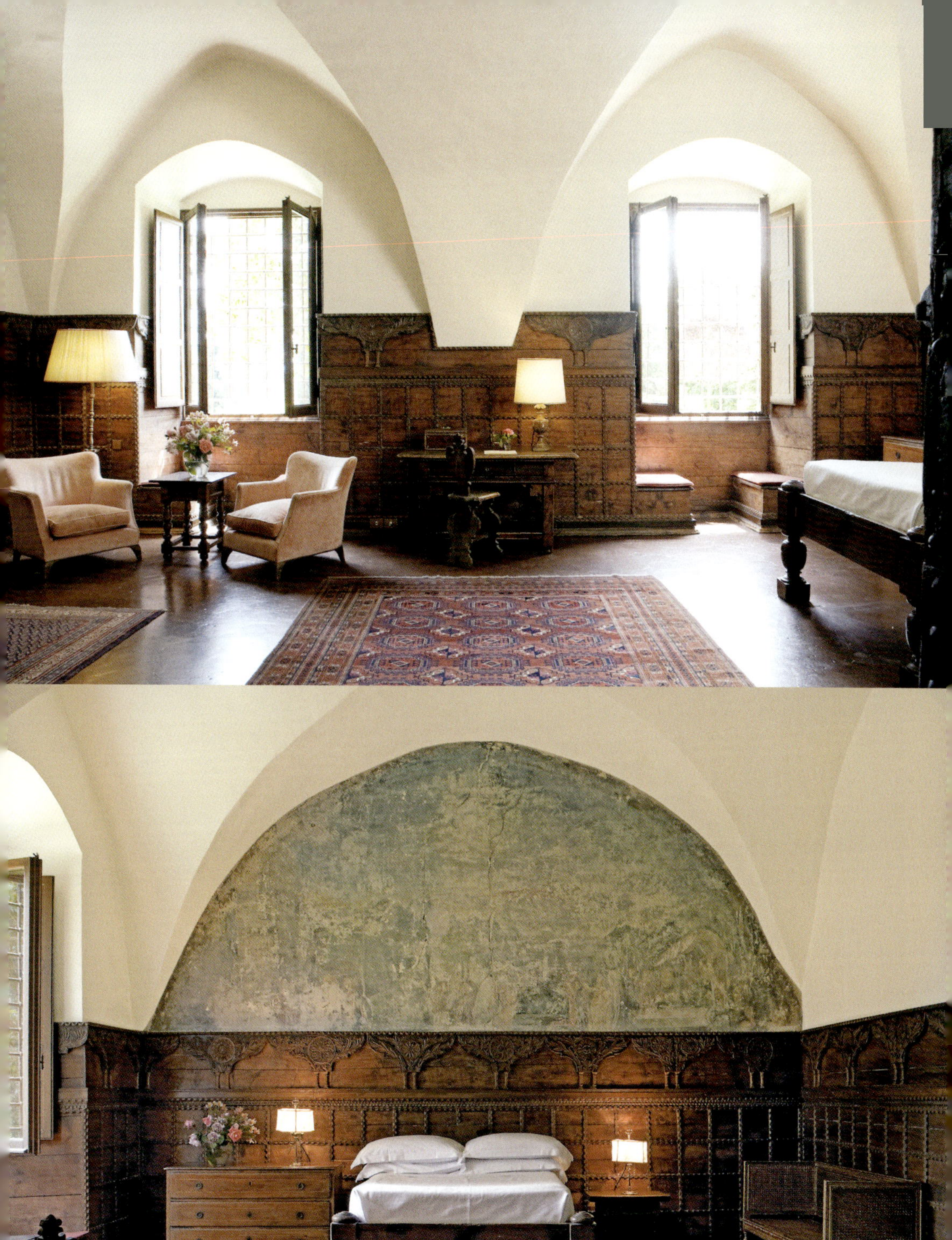

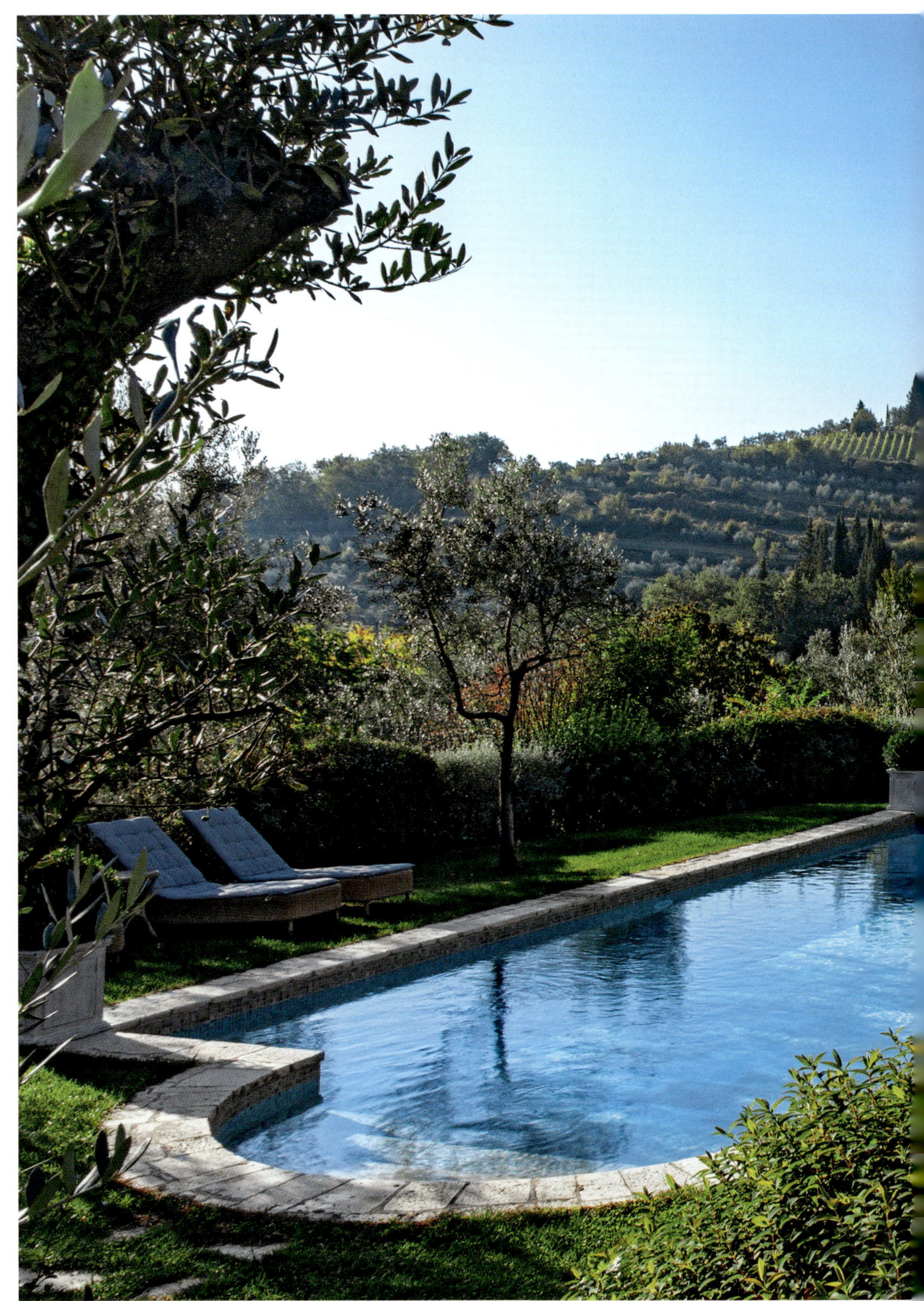

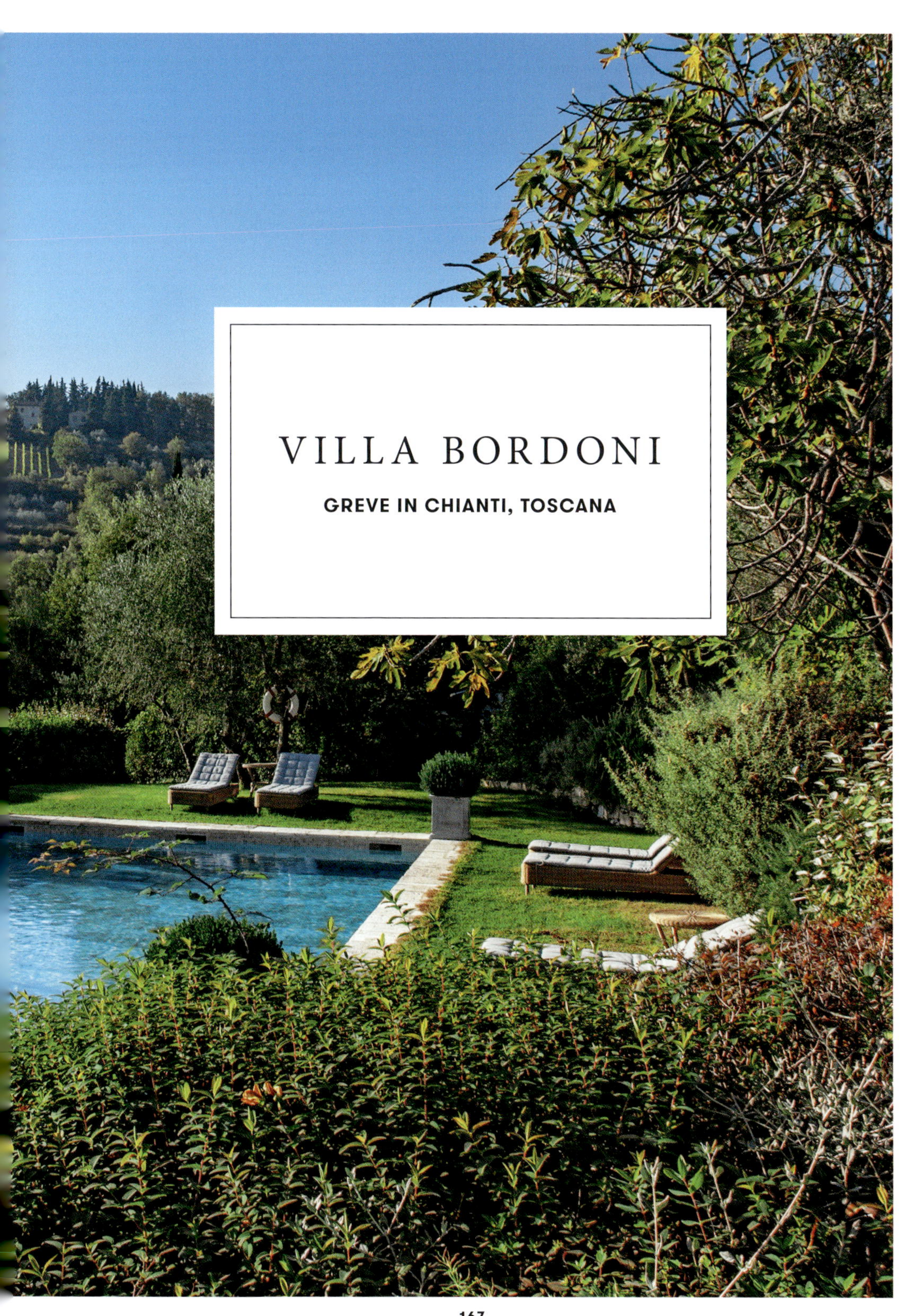

VILLA BORDONI

GREVE IN CHIANTI, TOSCANA

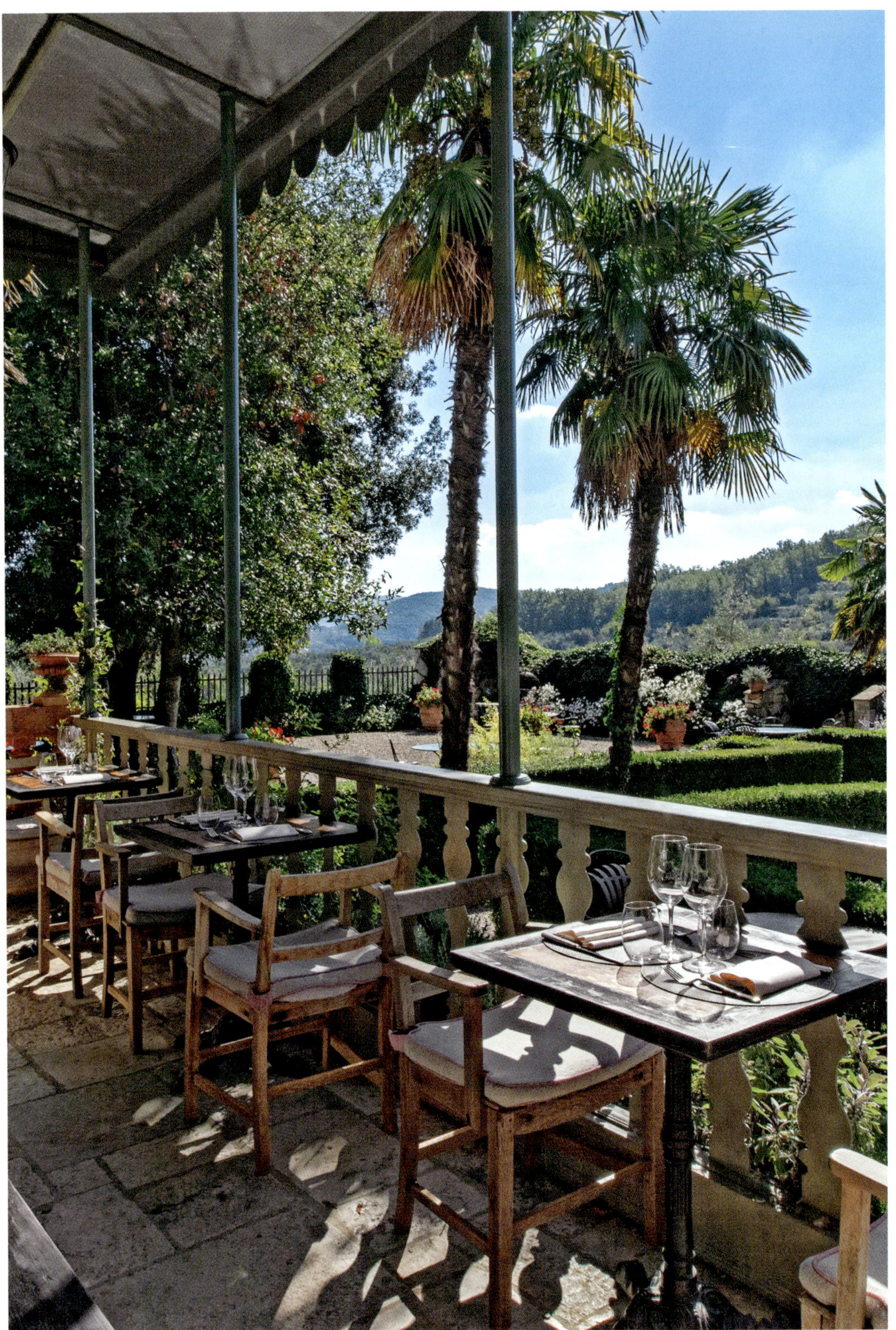

VILLA BORDONI

Via San Cresci 31/32, 50022 Greve in Chianti
Tel. +39 055 854 6230 · info@villabordoni.com
www.villabordoni.com
Open early March to early January

SCOTTISH-ITALIAN FRIENDSHIP They exchanged the Scottish highlands for the Tuscan hills, thick tweeds for light cotton and dishes like haggis that lie heavy in the stomach for fine Mediterranean cooking: when Catherine and David Gardner left Scotland for Italy in the mid-1990s, they opened two restaurants in Florence, where the Mediterranean food on the menu was both creative and delicious, and even affordable, too. The Gardners' success with tourists and locals alike encouraged them to branch out from the restaurant business to a hotel: in the vineyards of Chianti they converted a 16th-century country house into the Villa Bordoni. With the help of the architect André Benaim and the designer Riccardo Barthel, the run-down estate was transformed into a guest house that lends a touch of elegance and extravagance to the Tuscan rustic style. The colors of each room take up the hues of the original Vietri tiles in the bathroom, rustic objects such as iron baskets or the doors of hen coops morph into lampshades or wall ornaments and curtains dyed by hand frame the windows (in order to enjoy the wonderful view, don't fail to book a room on the first floor!). The restaurant, too, is a gem, its walls adorned with a harlequin pattern of Italian vine leaves and Scottish thistles. And the Gardners' outstanding cookery courses prove to guests that not just the Scots but also travellers from all countries can master the art of Mediterranean cooking – buon appetito! ◆ Book to pack: "A Room with a View" by E. M. Forster.

SCHOTTISCH-ITALIENISCHE FREUNDSCHAFT Sie tauschten die schottischen Highlands gegen die Hügel der Toskana, dicke Tweedstoffe gegen leichte Baumwolle und etwas schwer im Magen liegende Gerichte wie Haggis gegen feine Mittelmeerküche: Als Catherine und David Gardner Mitte der 1990er aus Schottland nach Italien kamen, eröffneten sie in Florenz zwei Lokale, in denen mediterrane Spezialitäten auf der Karte standen, die so kreativ wie köstlich und noch dazu erschwinglich waren. Der Erfolg, den die Gardners bei Touristen und Einheimischen hatten, gab ihnen den Mut, ihre Gastronomie durch ein Hotel zu ergänzen. In den Weinbergen des Chianti verwandelten sie einen Landsitz aus dem 16. Jahrhundert in die Villa Bordoni. Mithilfe des Architekten André Benaim und des Designers Riccardo Barthel wurde aus dem verfallenen Anwesen ein Gästehaus, das dem rustikalen Stil der Toskana einen Hauch Eleganz und Extravaganz verleiht. So greifen die Farben jedes Zimmers die Töne der originalen Vietri-Fliesen im Bad auf, ländliche Objekte wie Eisenkörbe oder ausrangierte Hühnerstalltüren fungieren als Lampenschirme oder Wandornamente, und die Fenster rahmen von Hand gefärbte Vorhänge (um die wunderbare Aussicht zu genießen, unbedingt einen Raum im ersten Stock buchen!). Ein Schmuckstück ist auch das Restaurant, dessen Wände ein Harlekinmuster aus italienischen Weinblättern sowie schottischen Disteln ziert. Und dass nicht nur Schotten, sondern Reisende aller Nationen die mediterrane Küche beherrschen können, beweisen die Gardners ihren Gästen bei hervorragenden Kochkursen – buon appetito! ◆ Buchtipp: „Zimmer mit Aussicht“ von E. M. Forster.

VIVE L'AMITIÉ ITALIANO-ÉCOSSAISE Ils ont échangé les hauts plateaux écossais contre les collines de la Toscane, le tweed épais contre les cotonnades légères et des plats traditionnels comme le haggis contre la cuisine raffinée du Midi : arrivés en Italie au milieu des années 1990, Catherine et David Gardner ont ouvert à Florence deux restaurants proposant des spécialités méditerranéennes aussi originales que délicieuses – et, en plus, abordables. Le succès rencontré auprès des touristes et des gens du pays leur a donné des ailes et ils se sont lancés dans un projet hôtelier, transformant une propriété du XVIe siècle située dans les vignobles du Chianti en Villa Bordoni. L'architecte André Benaim et le designer Riccardo Barthel les ont aidés à faire du bâtiment délabré un hôtel qui apporte au style rustique de la Toscane un zeste d'élégance et d'extravagance. Ainsi, les couleurs de chaque chambre reprennent les teintes des carreaux de Vietri originaux de la salle de bains, des objets campagnards comme des corbeilles en fer forgé ou d'anciennes portes de poulailler servent d'abat-jours ou de décoration murale, et des rideaux teints à la main encadrent les fenêtres (pour bien profiter de la vue, il faut absolument prendre une chambre au premier !). Un autre petit bijou : le restaurant aux murs décorés d'un motif à carreaux associant feuilles de vignes italiennes et chardons écossais. Et, avec leurs remarquables cours de cuisine, les Gardner apportent la preuve que les Écossais ne sont pas les seuls à maîtriser la cuisine méditerranéenne – les voyageurs de tous les pays en sont capables aussi. Buon appetito ! ◆ À lire : « Une chambre avec vue » d'E. M. Forster.

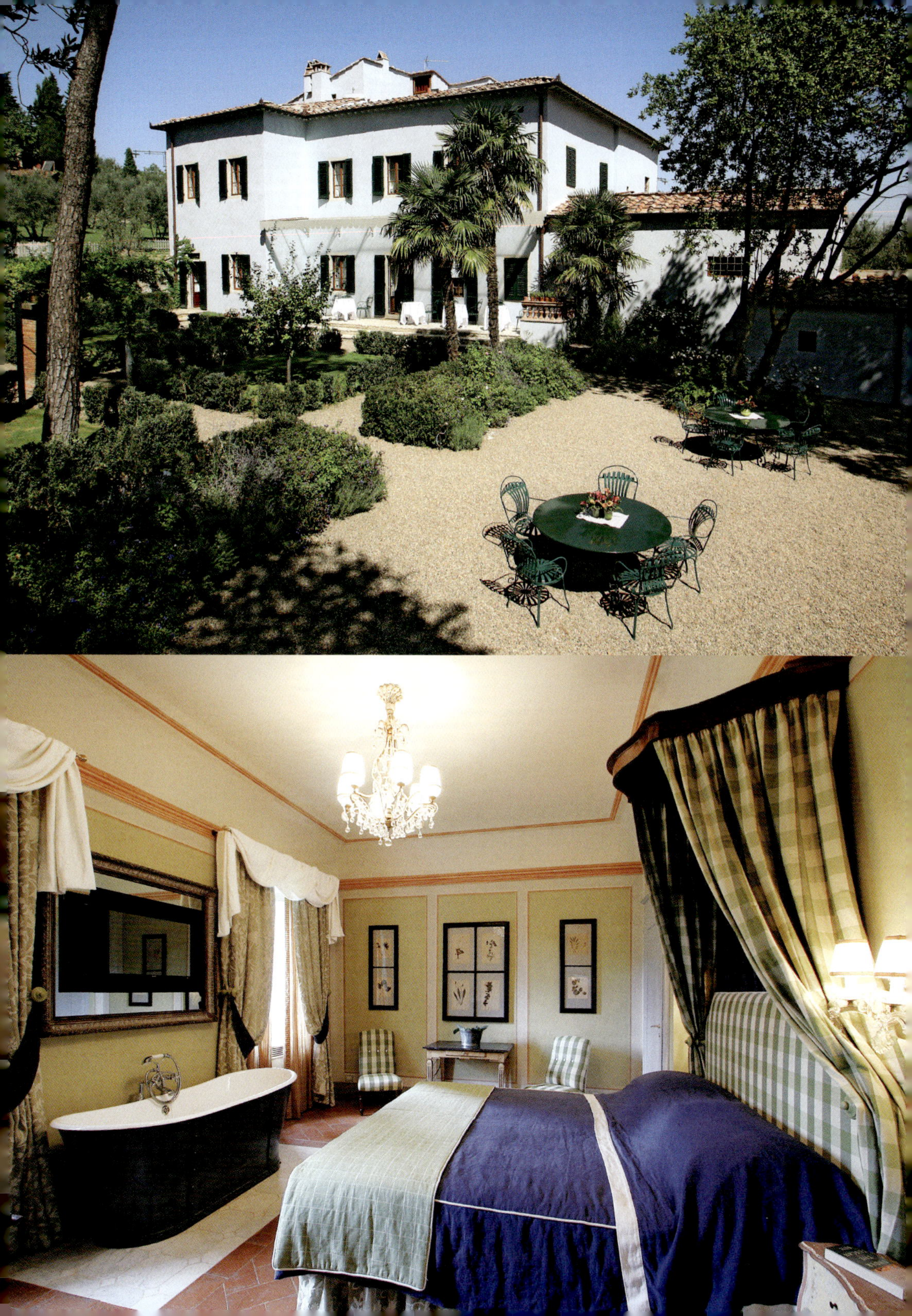

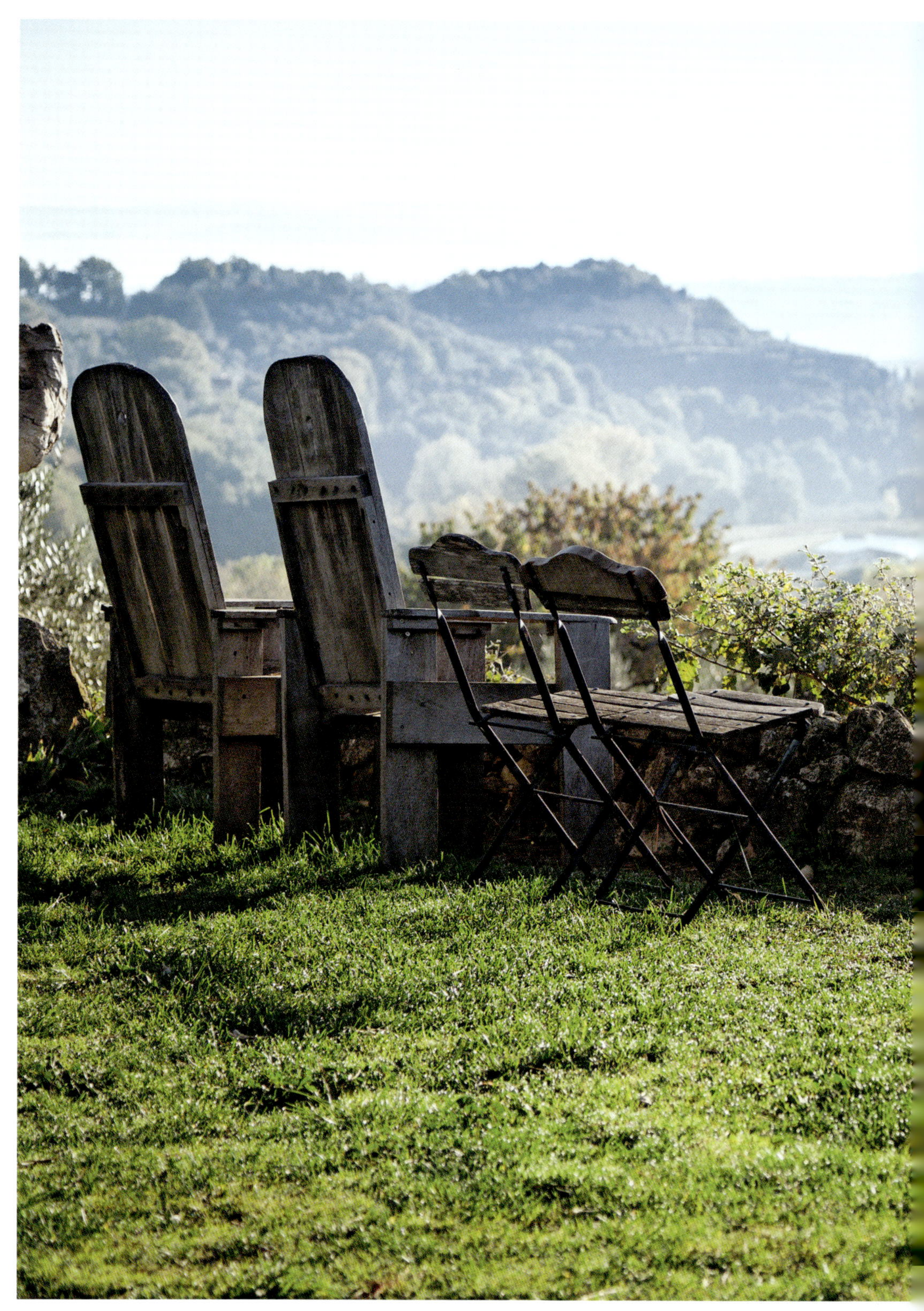

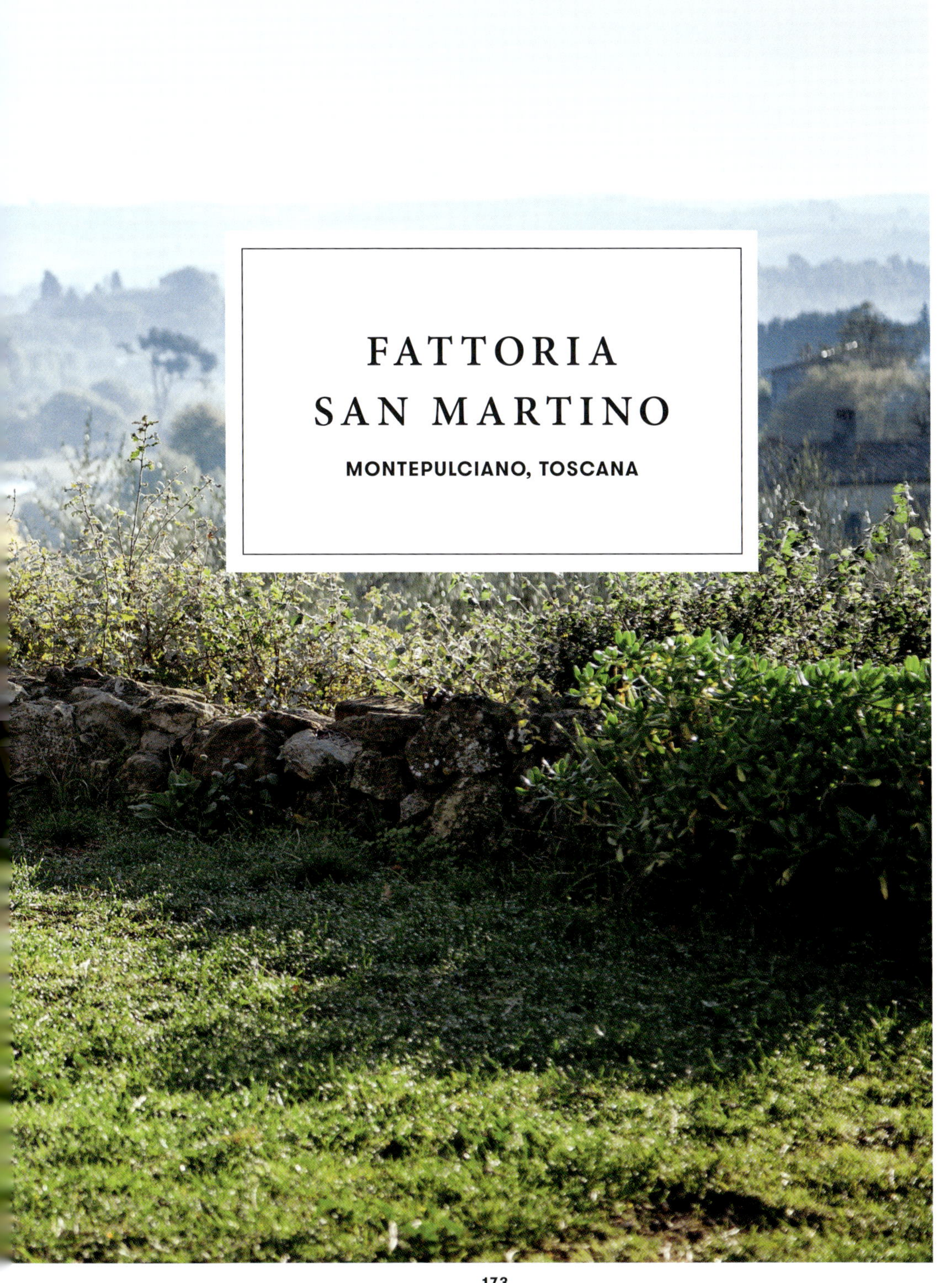

FATTORIA SAN MARTINO

MONTEPULCIANO, TOSCANA

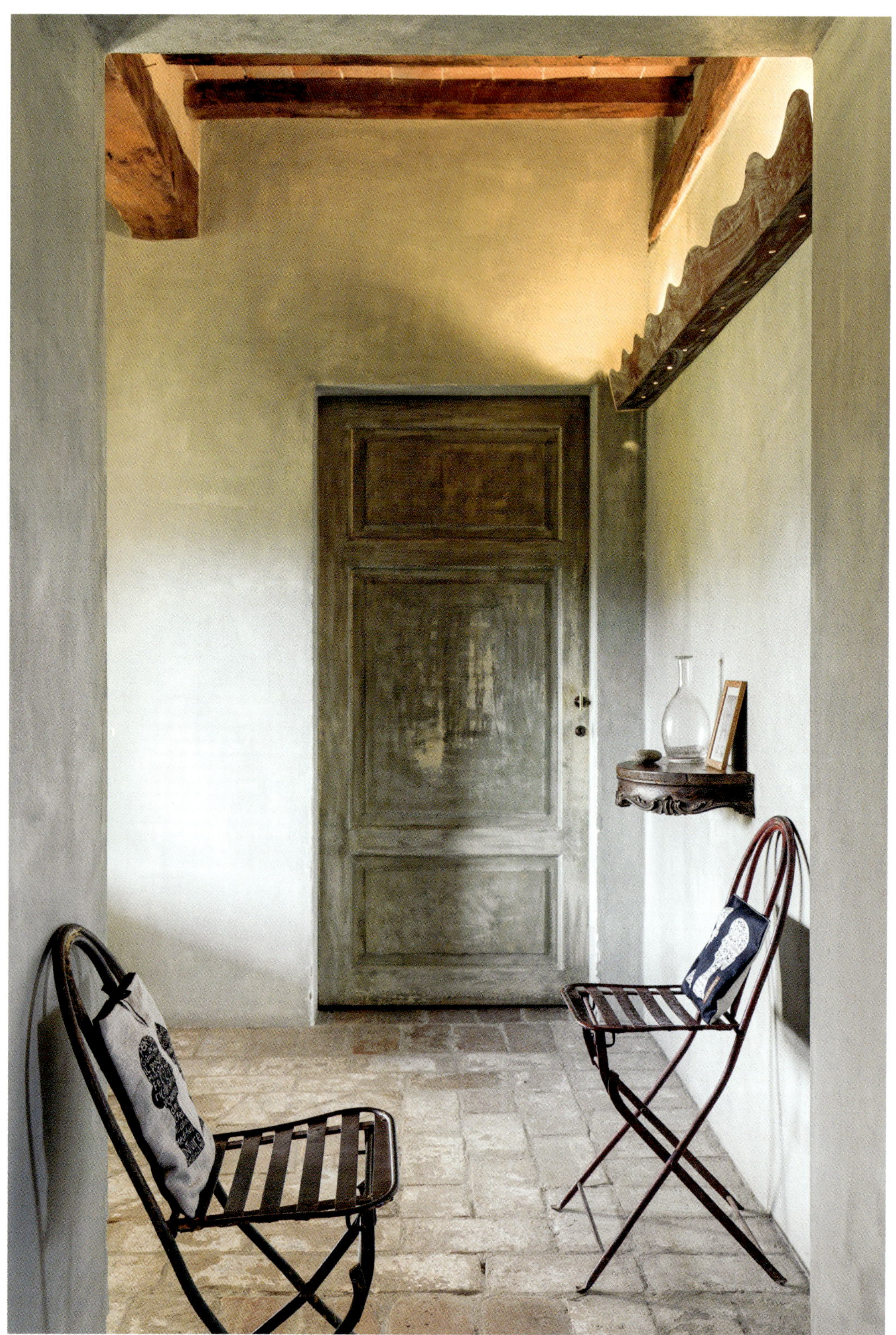

TOSCANA

FATTORIA SAN MARTINO

Via Martiena, 3, 53045 Montepulciano
Tel. +39 0578 717 463 · info@fattoriasanmartino.it
www.fattoriasanmartino.it
Open from late March to early November

EVERYTHING IN HARMONY In the 1980s, Karin Lijftogt and Antonio Giorgini's world was the fashion business in Milan. She worked as a designer, while he was in finance – a hip, fast-paced life that they both enjoyed. But when Antonio's mother died, they paused for thought and came to the conclusion that both of them longed for something simpler; for more time, more peace, more balance. They found all of this near Montepulciano, where Tuscany is almost too beautiful to be true. Here they transformed a villa dating from the 18th century into an organic B&B, a place where guests can get back to nature and find themselves. The suites have wonderful wooden floors polished with beeswax, are furnished with natural or recycled materials in a creative, rustic style, and get along without extras such as a television or minibar. In the restaurant Karin serves vegetarian and vegan dishes for which most of the ingredients are grown organically by themselves under Antonio's careful direction. The pond in the garden is balm for all the senses, a sequestered spot where you can simply sit for hours admiring the flowers, watching the play of colors and listening to the calls of animals. For those who do want to leave this little cosmos of the fattoria, the hosts are pleased to provide tips for herb walks or tastings of wine and olive oil. ◆ Book to pack: "Diary of a Journey to Italy" by Michel de Montaigne.

ALLES IM EINKLANG In den 1980er-Jahren war das Mailänder Modebusiness die Welt von Karin Lijftogt und Antonio Giorgini. Sie arbeitete als Designerin, er im Finanzwesen – ein schickes und schnelles Leben, das beiden Spaß machte. Doch als Antonios Mutter starb, hielten sie inne und stellten fest, dass sie sich nach etwas Einfacherem sehnten, nach mehr Zeit, mehr Ruhe, mehr Balance. All das fanden sie in der Nähe von Montepulciano, wo die Toskana fast zu schön ist, um wahr zu sein. Hier wandelten sie eine Villa aus dem 18. Jahrhundert in ein Bio-Bed & Breakfast um, dessen Besucher zurück zur Natur und zu sich selbst finden sollen. Die Suiten haben herrliche, mit Bienenwachs polierte Holzböden, sind mit natürlichen oder recycelten Materialien rustikal-kreativ ausgestattet und verzichten konsequent auf Extras wie Fernseher oder Minibar. Im Restaurant serviert Karin vegetarische und vegane Gerichte, für die die meisten Zutaten aus eigenem, organischem Anbau unter Antonios sorgsamer Leitung stammen. Balsam für alle Sinne ist der verwunschene Teich im Garten, an dem man stundenlang einfach nur dasitzen, Blumen bewundern, Farbspiele verfolgen und Tierstimmen lauschen kann. Wen es doch einmal aus dem kleinen Universum der Fattoria hinauszieht, den versorgen die Gastgeber gerne mit Tipps zu Kräuterwanderungen, Wein- und Olivenölverkostungen. ◆ Buchtipp: „Tagebuch einer Reise nach Italien" von Michel de Montaigne.

TOUT EST BIEN Au cours des années 1980, l'univers milanais de la mode était l'affaire de Karin Lijftogt et Antonio Giorgini. Elle travaillait comme designer, lui dans la finance – une vie chic et rapide qui les amusait beaucoup. Et puis la mère d'Antonio est morte, ils se sont alors arrêtés et ont réalisé qu'ils désiraient quelque chose de plus simple : plus de temps, plus de calme, plus d'équilibre. Ils ont trouvé tout cela près de Montepulciano, là où la Toscane est presque trop belle pour être vraie. Ici, ils ont transformé une villa du XVIIIe siècle en bed & breakfast bio, où les visiteurs ont la possibilité de redécouvrir la nature et se ressourcer. Les suites ont de magnifiques planchers en bois poli à la cire d'abeille, sont meublées avec des matériaux naturels ou recyclés de manière rustique et créative, et renoncent radicalement aux extras comme les télévisions ou les minibars. Au restaurant, Karin sert des plats végétariens et végétaliens à base de produits issus pour la plupart de sa propre culture biologique que supervise attentivement Antonio. L'étang enchanté du jardin apaise tous les sens : vous pouvez simplement vous y asseoir pendant des heures, admirer des fleurs, observer des jeux de couleurs et écouter les animaux. Mais si vous voulez sortir du petit univers de la Fattoria, les hôtes se feront un plaisir de vous donner des conseils sur les randonnées-découvertes de plantes sauvages, les dégustations de vin et d'huile d'olive. ◆ À lire : « Journal de voyage en Italie » de Michel de Montaigne.

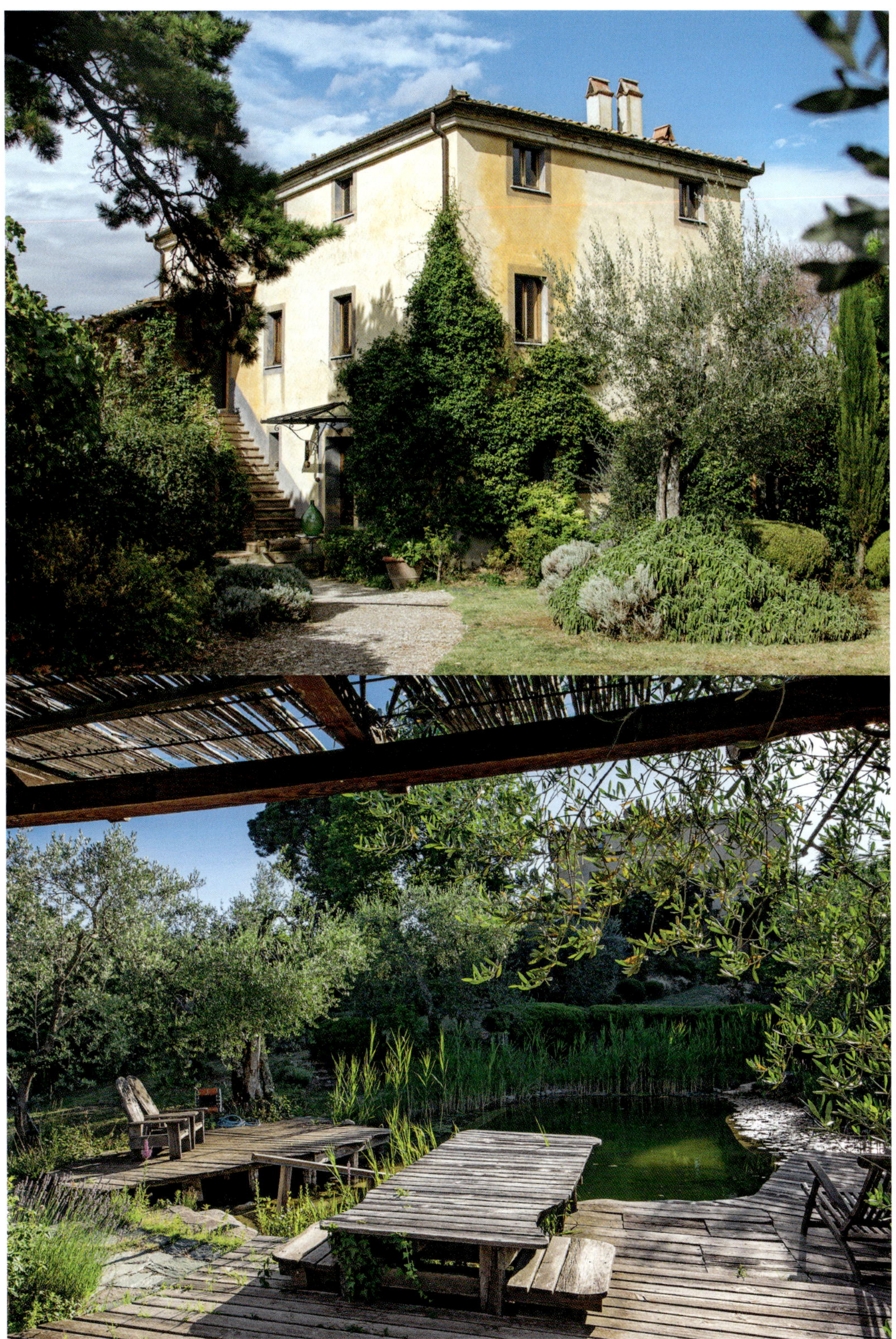

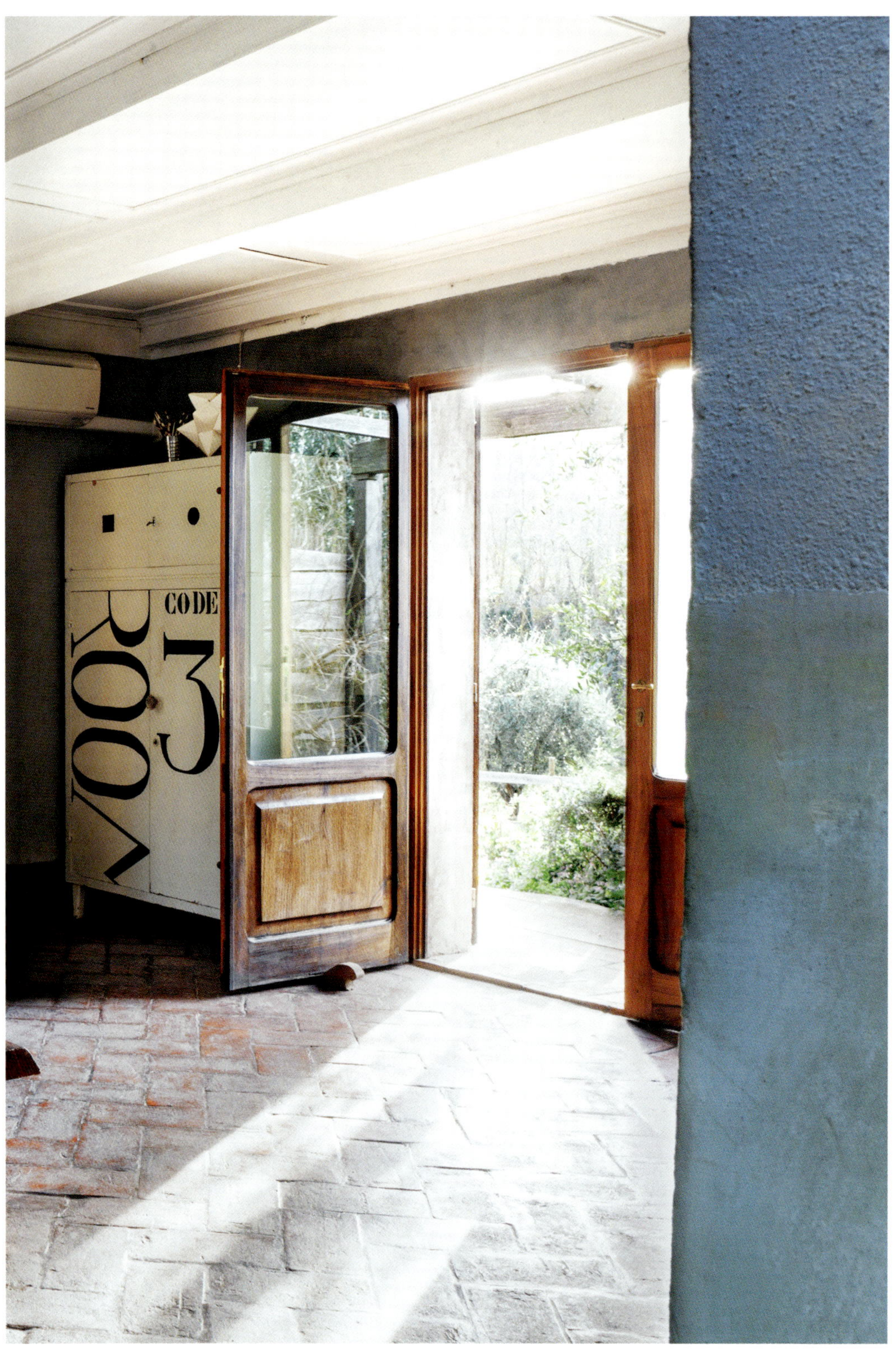
CODE
3

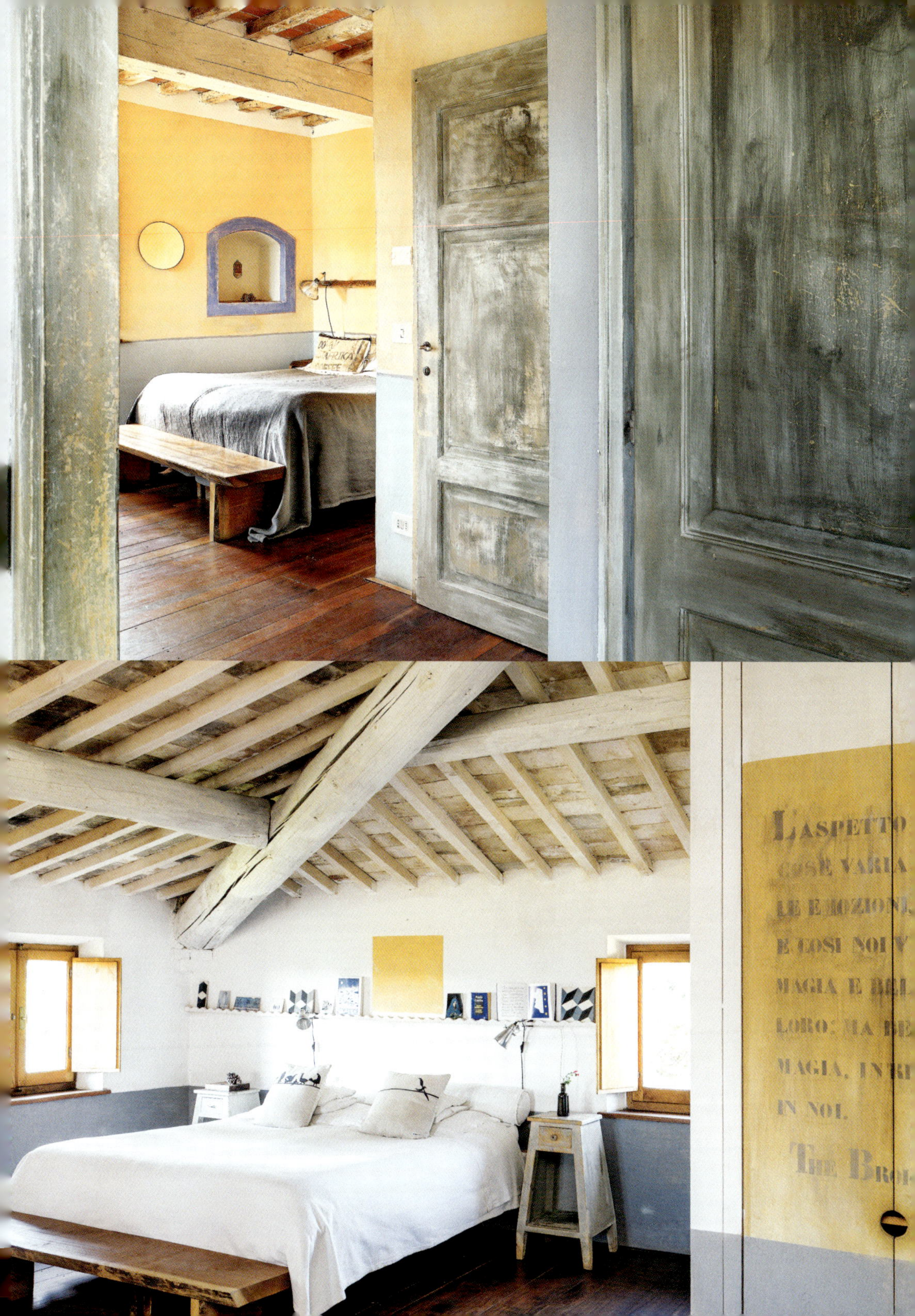
LASPETTO
COSE VARIA
LE EMOZIONI
E COSI NOI V
MAGIA E BEL
LORO: MA BE
MAGIA, IN RI
IN NOI.
THE BRO

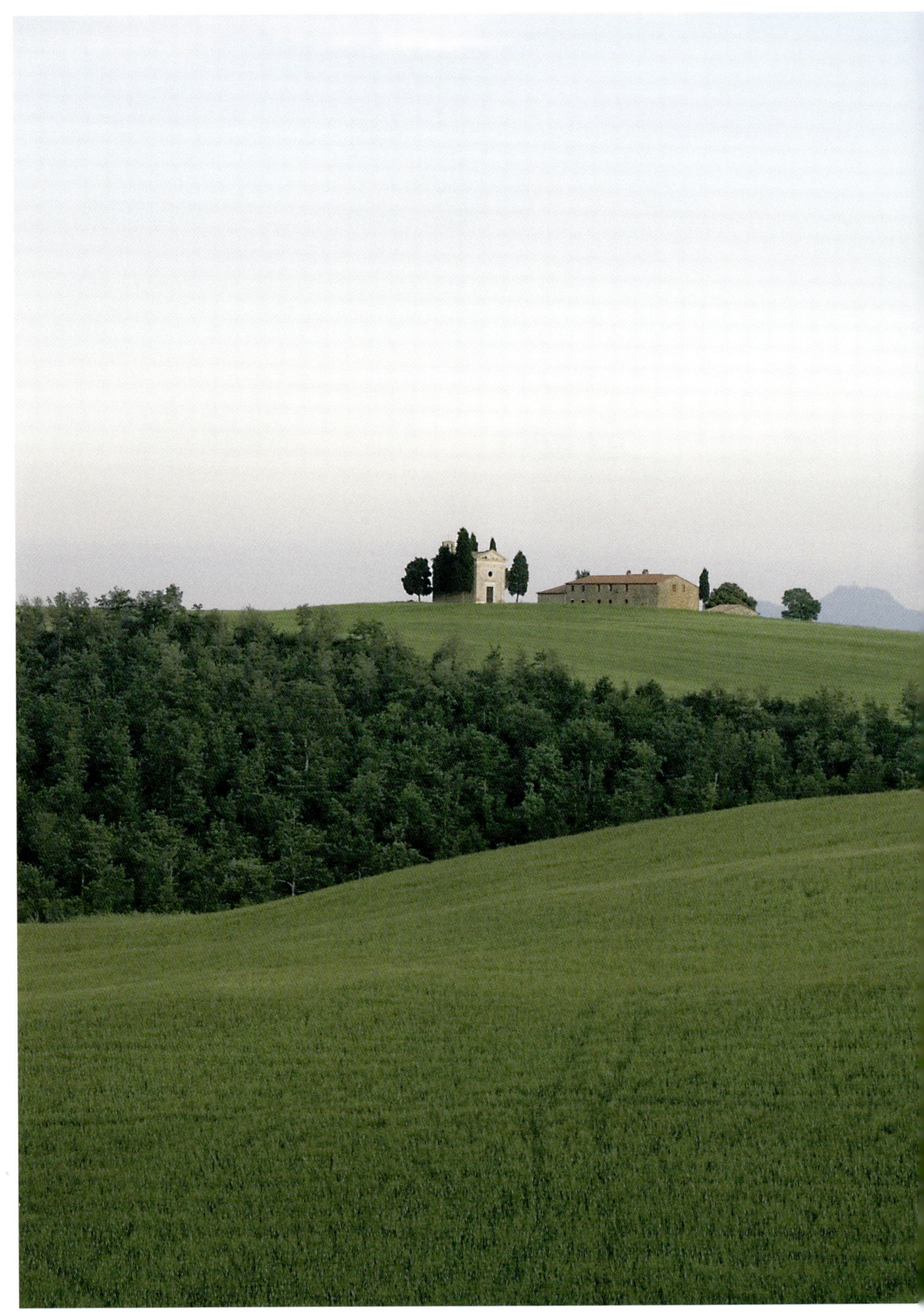

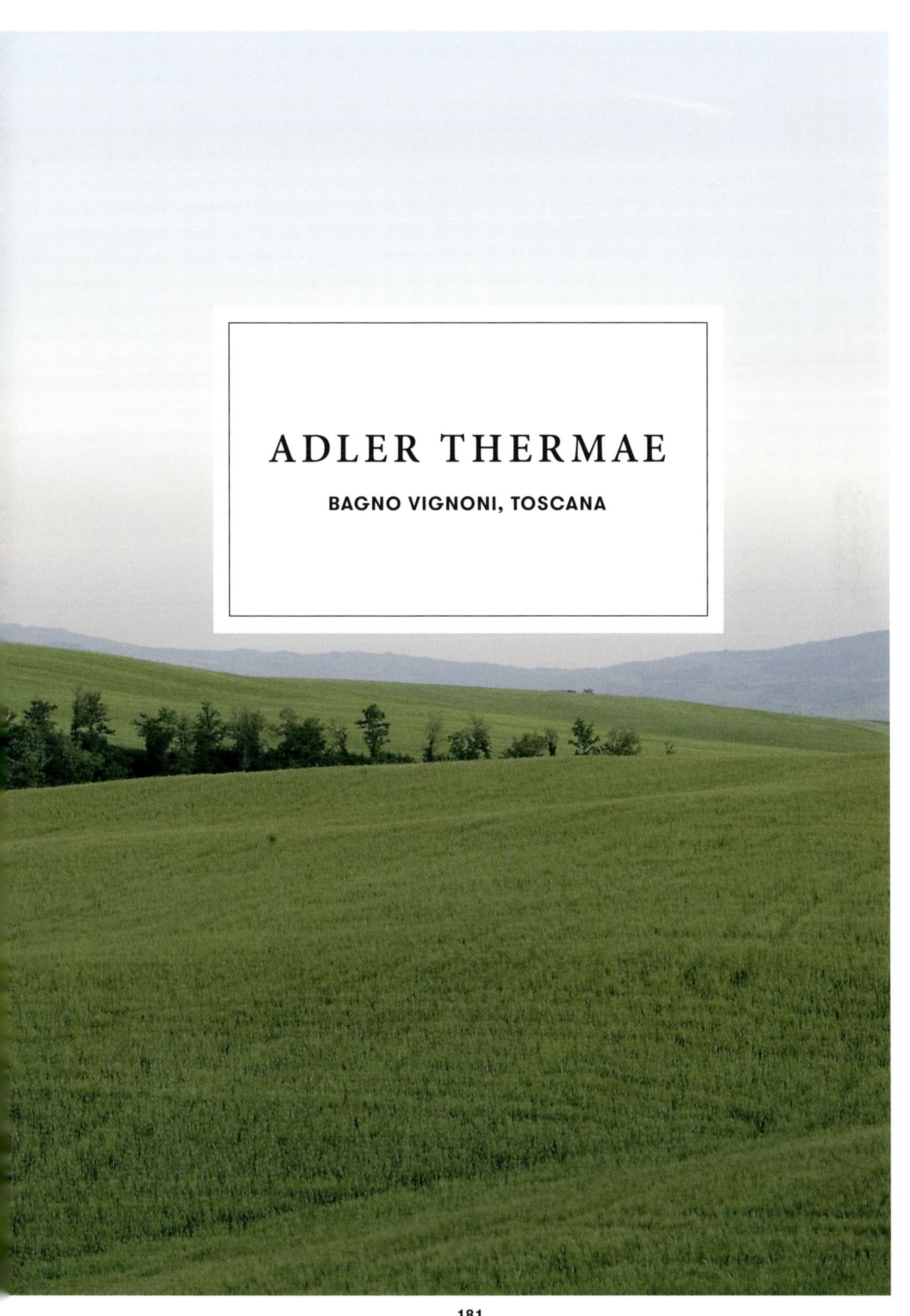

ADLER THERMAE

BAGNO VIGNONI, TOSCANA

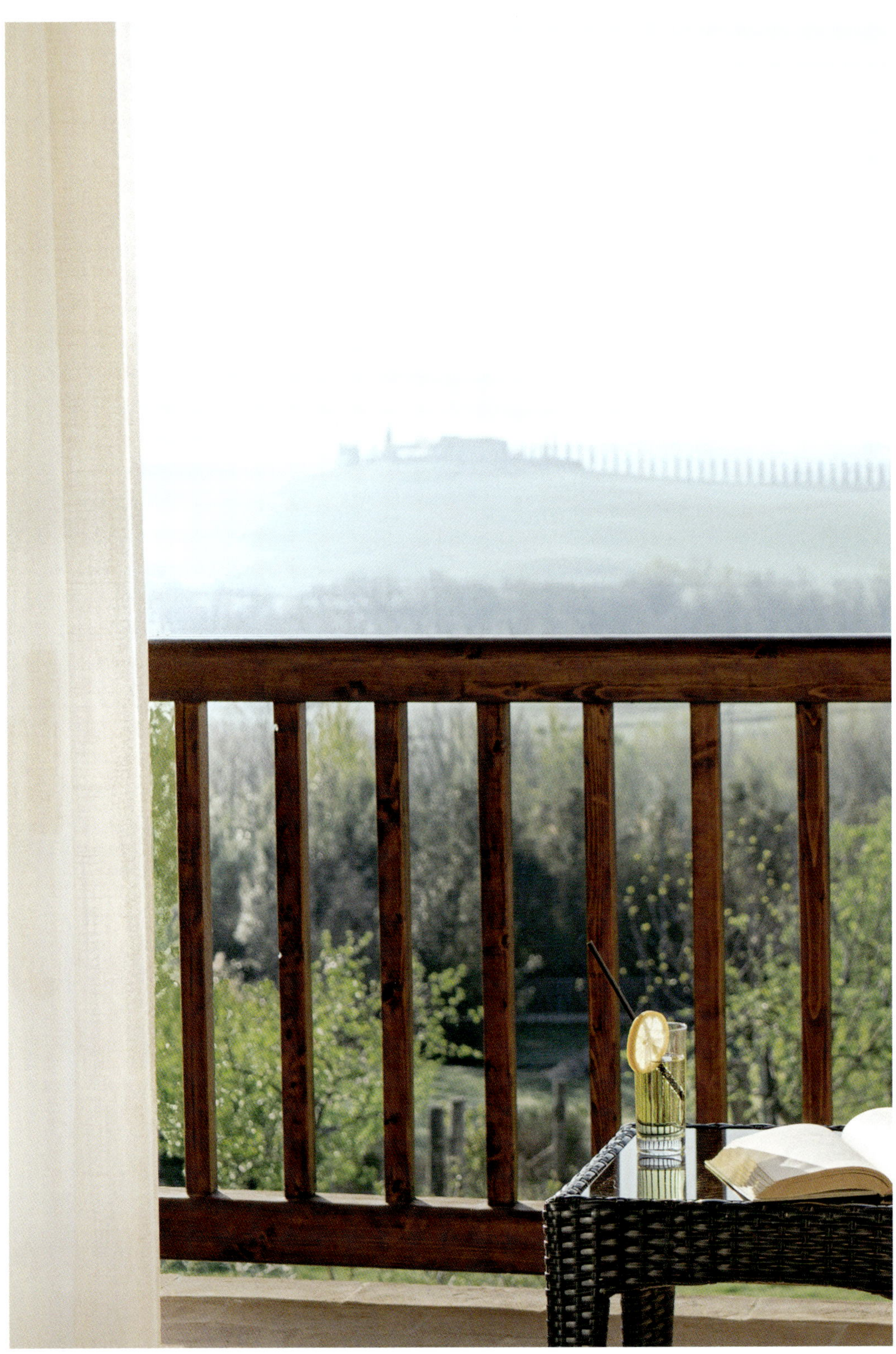

TOSCANA

ADLER THERMAE

Strada di Bagno Vignoni 1, 53027 San Quirico d'Orcia
Tel. +39 0577 889 000 · info@adler-thermae.com
www.adler-thermae.com

RELAXATION FOR ALL THE SENSES 3,300 feet below the earth it is warmed to 50 degrees Celsius by hot volcanic rock; it has an intense smell, as it contains not only bicarbonate but also sulphur, and it works wonders for skin irritations, painful joints and chronic bronchitis: the water of the springs at Bagno Vignoni, a tiny village south of Siena. The Etruscans and Romans knew about its healing powers, and in the 14th and 15th centuries it eased the pains of Lorenzo de' Medici, Pope Pius II and St Catherine of Siena. The pilgrimage church on the outskirts of the thermal baths, with its ancient stone pool, which seems a substitute for a piazza, is also named after her. Health cures are no longer possible in the historic buildings – but are in the modern Adler Spa Resort Thermae close by. Constructed in what was a quarry for travertine stone, the resort has a view of the picture-postcard scenery of Bagno Vignoni and supplements the old healing rituals of the region with modern treatments: in the in-house spa, guests relax with massages from Tuscany and the whole world or train with a personal coach. The hotel also provides the treatments of aesthetic medicine.
◆ Book to pack: "Selected Poems" by Giosuè Carducci.

MIT ALLEN SINNEN ENTSPANNEN Es wird tausend Meter unter der Erde von heißem Vulkangestein auf 50 Grad Celsius erwärmt, riecht etwas intensiver, da es neben Bikarbonat auch Schwefel enthält, und wirkt Wunder bei gereizter Haut, schmerzenden Gelenken sowie chronischer Bronchitis: das Quellwasser von Bagno Vignoni, einem winzigen Dorf südlich von Siena. Schon die Etrusker und Römer kannten seine wohltuende Kraft, und im 14. und 15. Jahrhundert linderte es die Leiden von Lorenzo de' Medici, Papst Pius II. und der Heiligen Katharina von Siena. Nach ihr ist auch die Wallfahrtskirche am Rande des Thermalbades mit seinem antiken Steinbecken benannt, das einst mitten im Ort erbaut wurde und die Piazza zu ersetzen schien. Kuren kann man in den historischen Bauten heute nicht mehr – dafür aber im modernen Adler Spa Resort Thermae ganz in der Nähe. In einem ehemaligen Travertinsteinbruch errichtet, blickt es auf die Bilderbuchlandschaft von Bagno Vignoni und ergänzt die alten Heilrituale der Region um moderne Anwendungen: Im Spa des Hauses entspannen die Gäste aus der Toskana und aller Welt bei Massagen oder trainieren mit einem persönlichen Coach. Zudem bietet das Hotel Anwendungen der ästhetischen Medizin an. ◆ Buchtipp: „Ça ira. Zwölf Sonette“ von Giosuè Carducci.

DÉTENTE ET BIEN-ÊTRE L'eau de la source de Bagno Vignoni, un minuscule village au sud de Sienne, est réchauffée mille mètres sous terre par la pierre volcanique chaude. Elle atteint une température de 50 degrés Celsius, contient du bicarbonate et du soufre, ce qui lui donne une certaine odeur. Ses effets sont merveilleux en cas d'irritation cutanée, d'articulations douloureuses et de bronchite chronique. Les Étrusques et les Romains connaissaient déjà ses propriétés bienfaisantes et, au XIVe et au XVe siècle, elle soulageait les douleurs de Laurent de Médicis, du pape Pie II et de sainte Catherine de Sienne. L'église de pèlerinage édifiée au bord du bain thermal, avec son bassin de pierre construit autrefois au milieu du village et qui semble remplacer la piazza, lui doit aussi son nom. Les cures ne se font plus aujourd'hui dans les bâtiments historiques, mais dans l'Adler Spa Resort Thermae moderne tout proche. Dans le spa de la maison, la détente est assurée par des massages basés sur des produits toscans ou du monde entier, ou de l'entraînement avec un coach personnel. L'hôtel propose en outre des applications de la médecine esthétique. ◆ À lire : « Ça ira » de Giosuè Carducci.

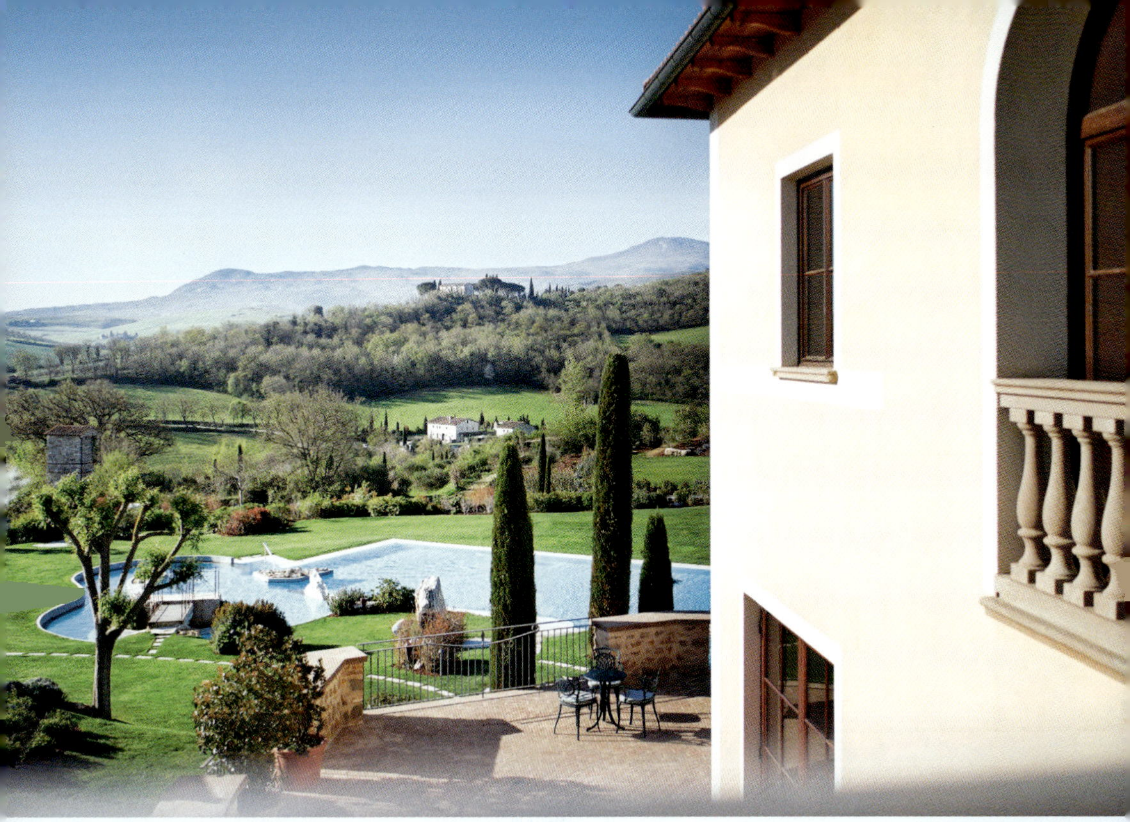

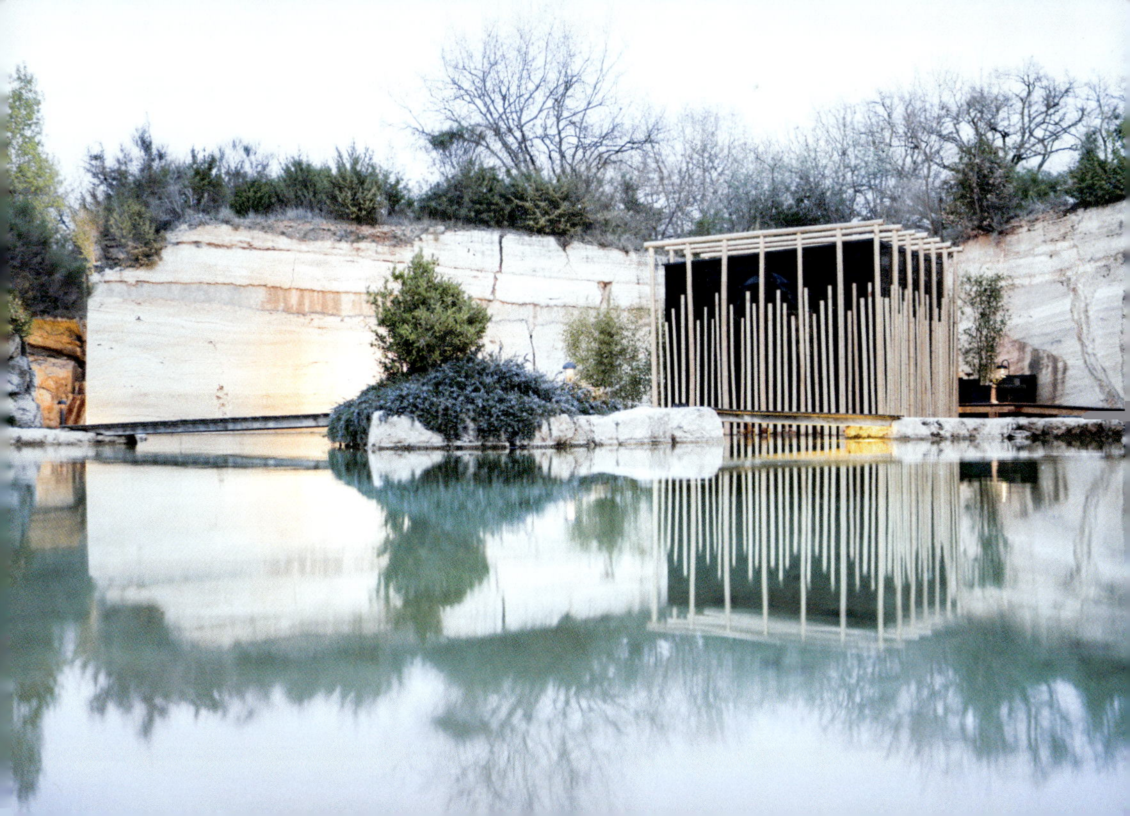

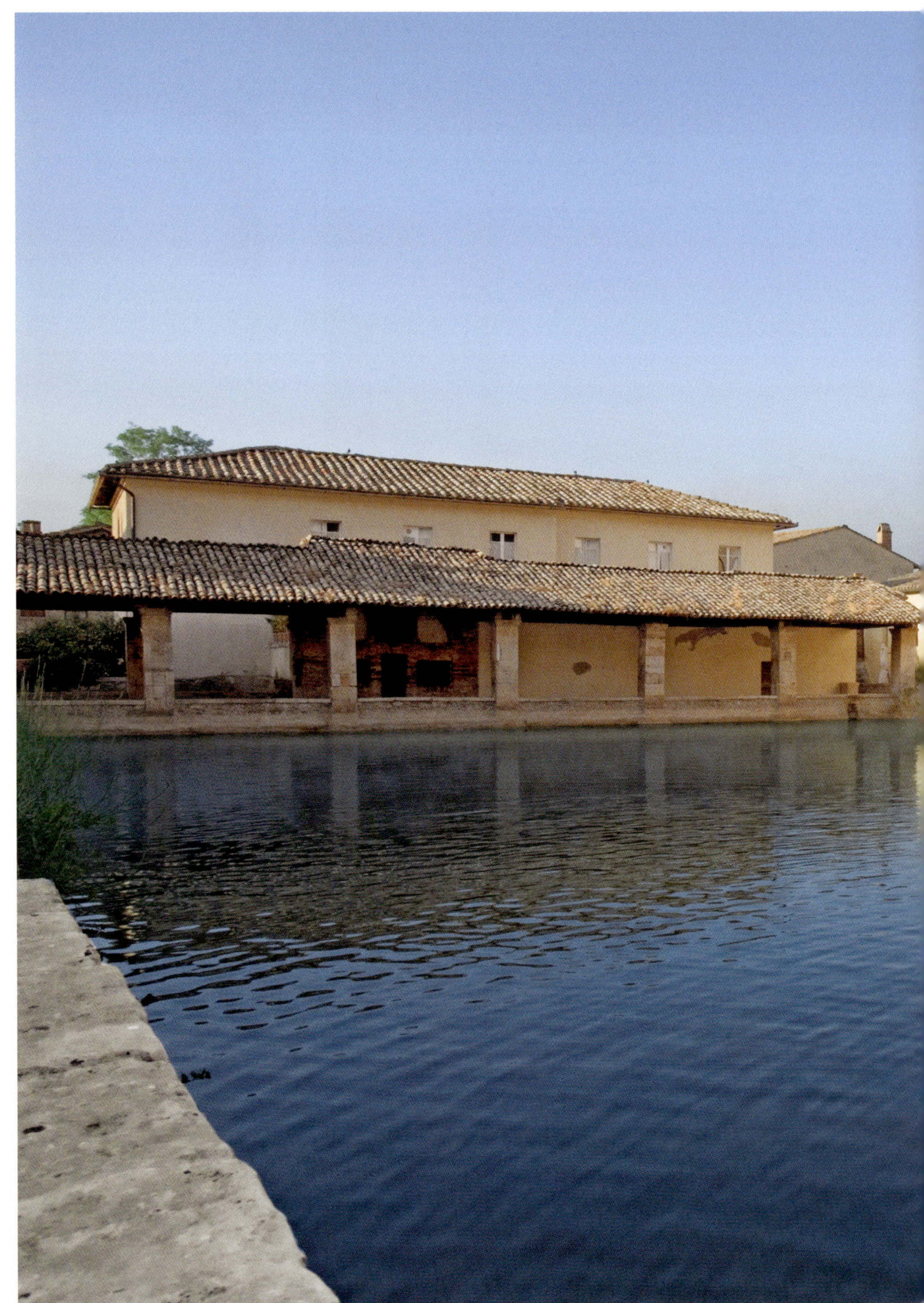

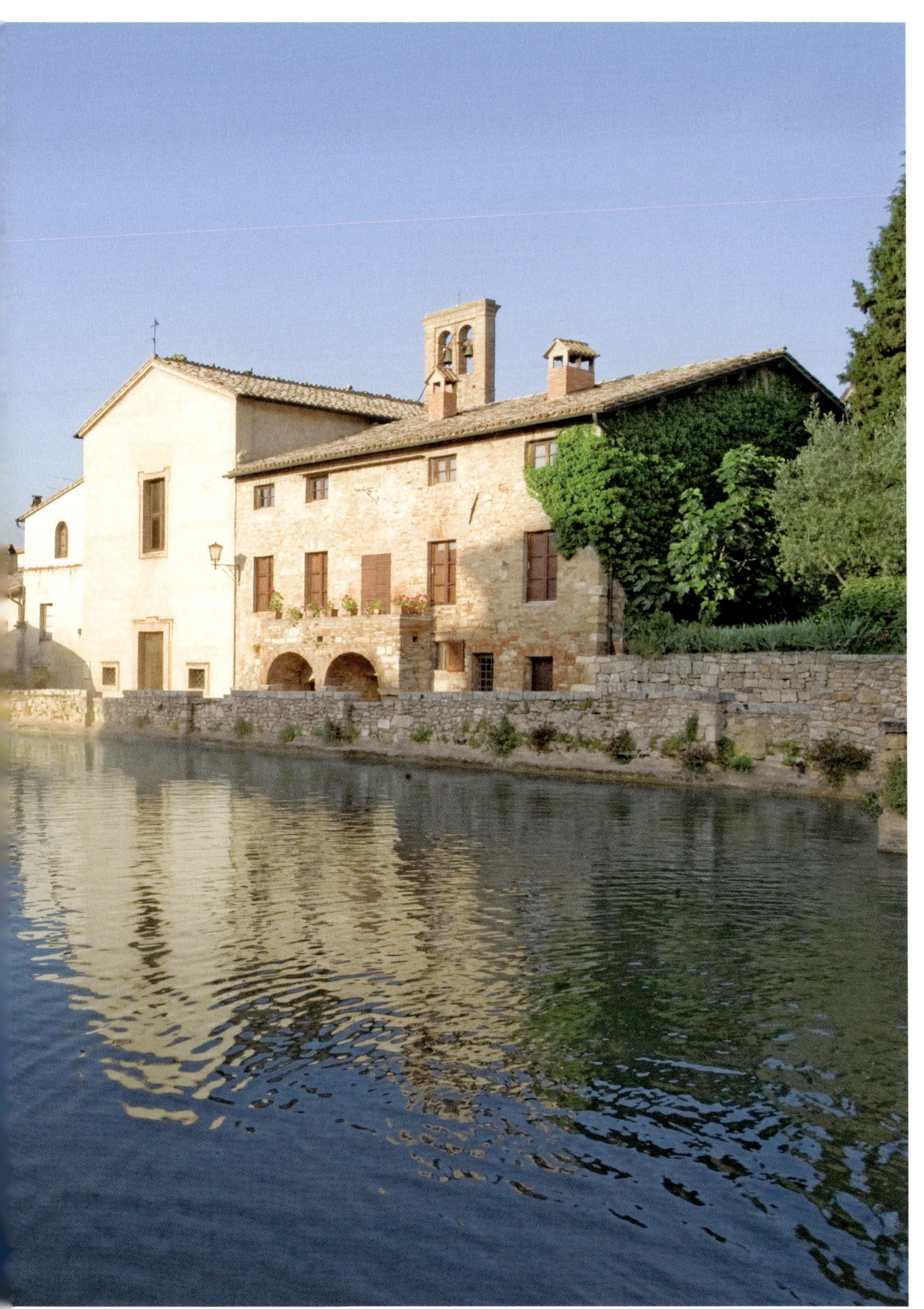

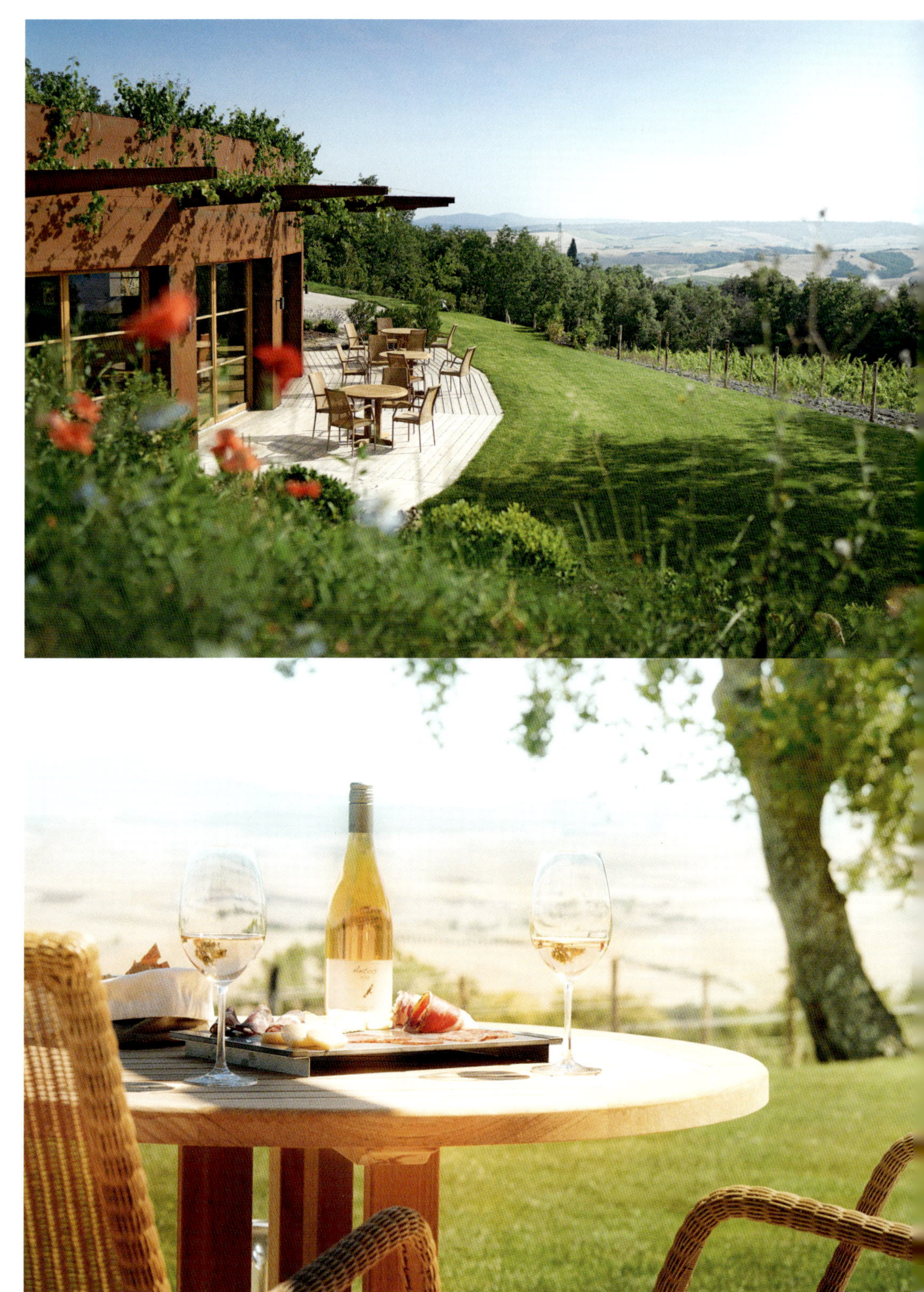

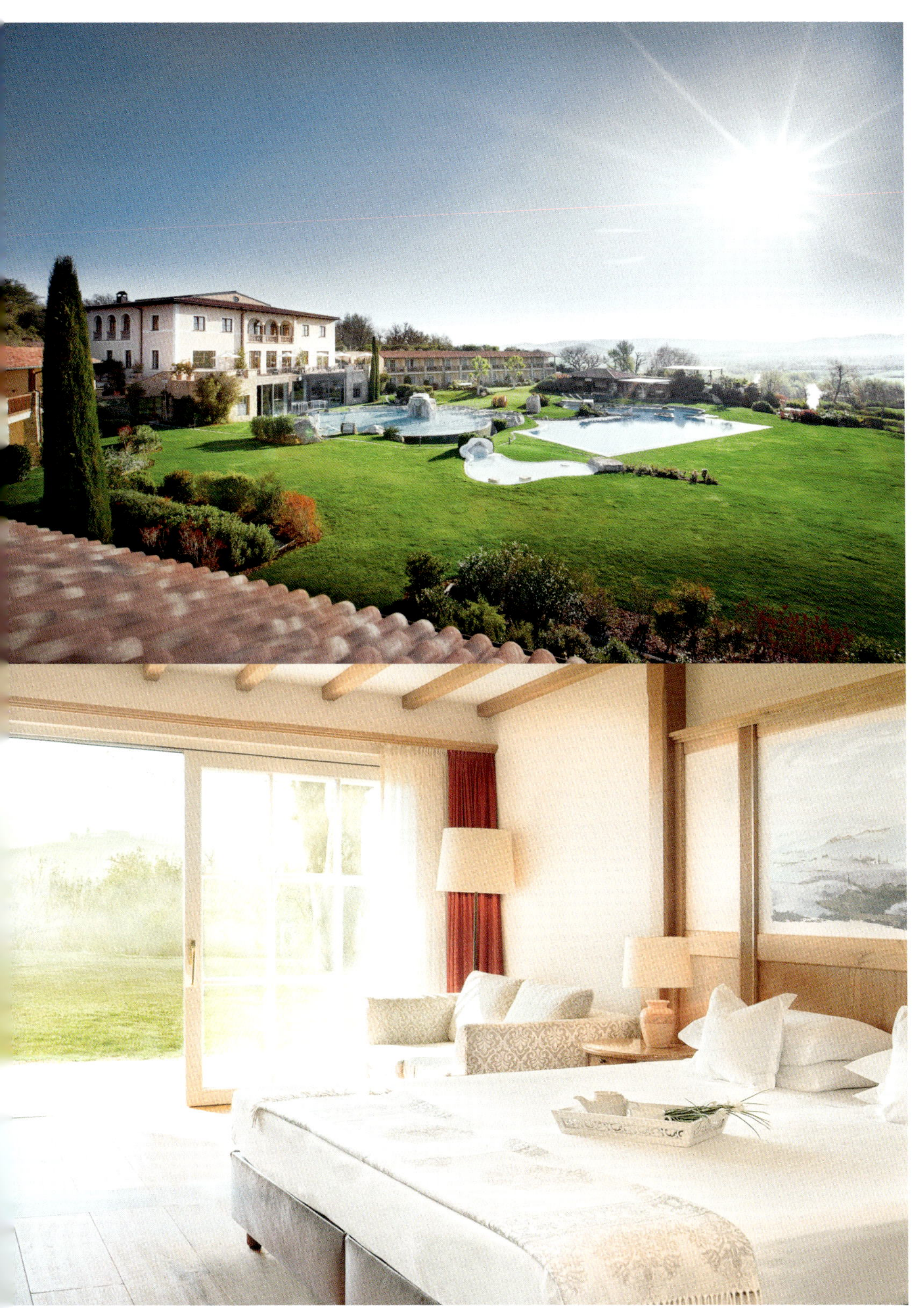

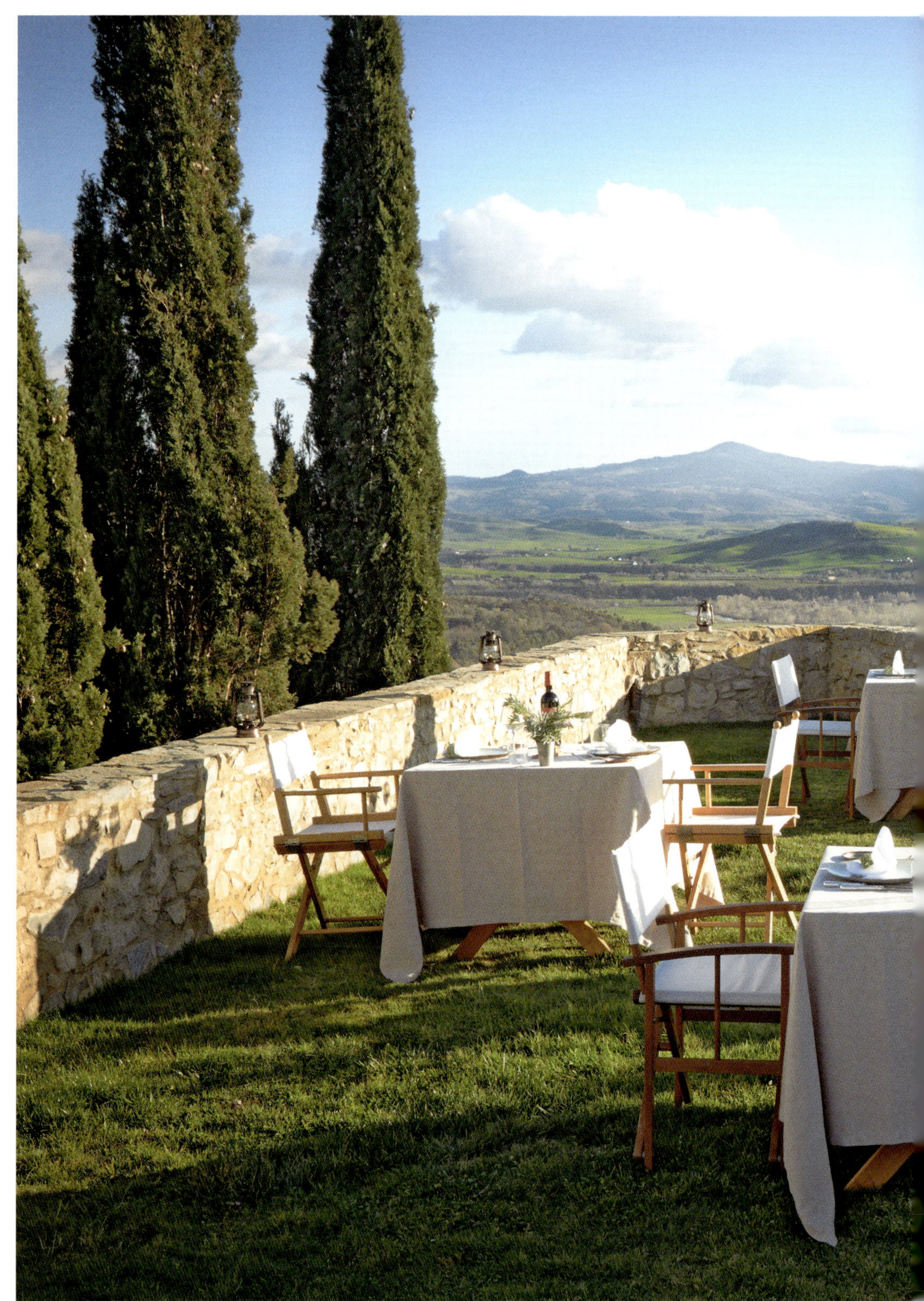

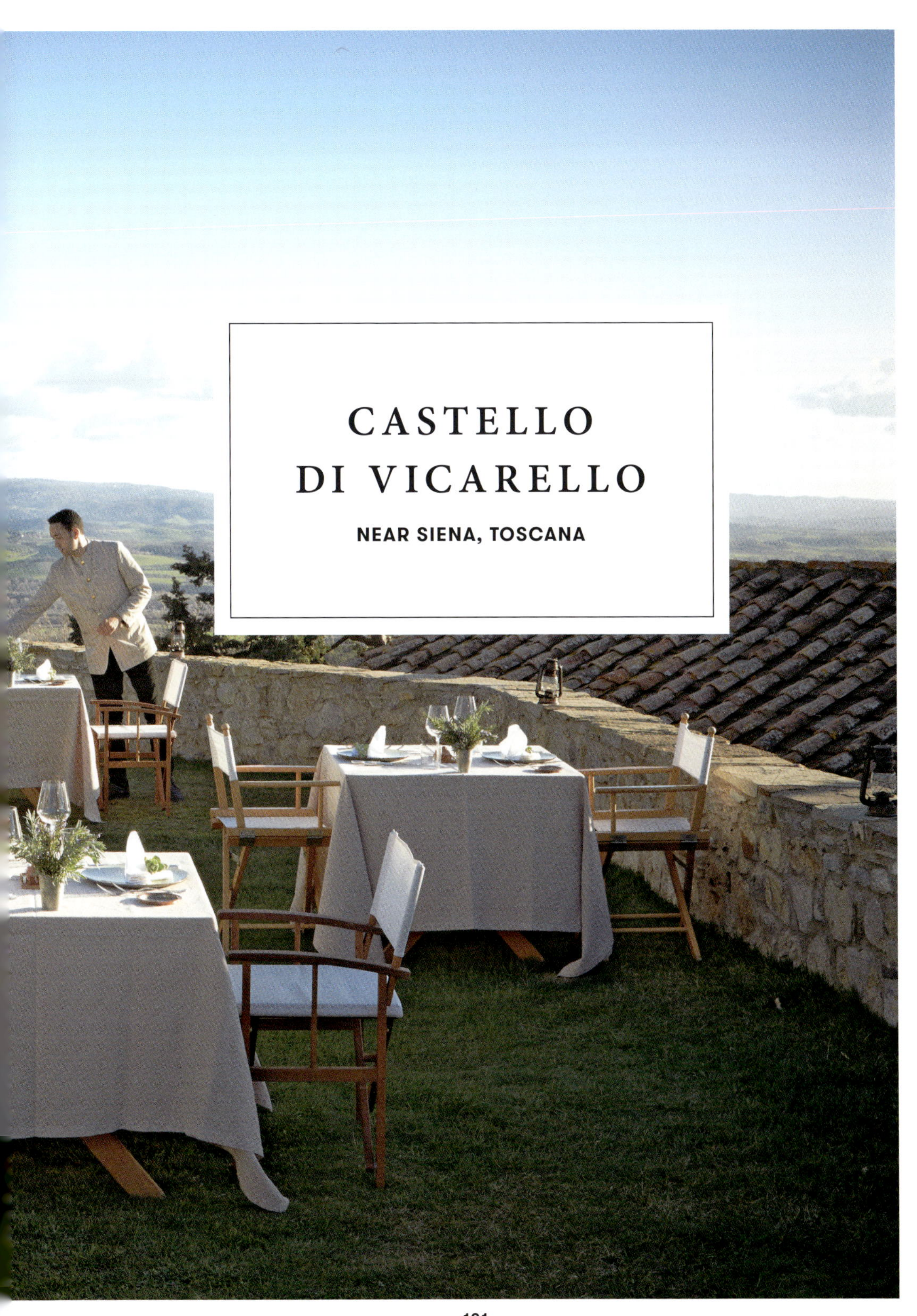

CASTELLO DI VICARELLO

NEAR SIENA, TOSCANA

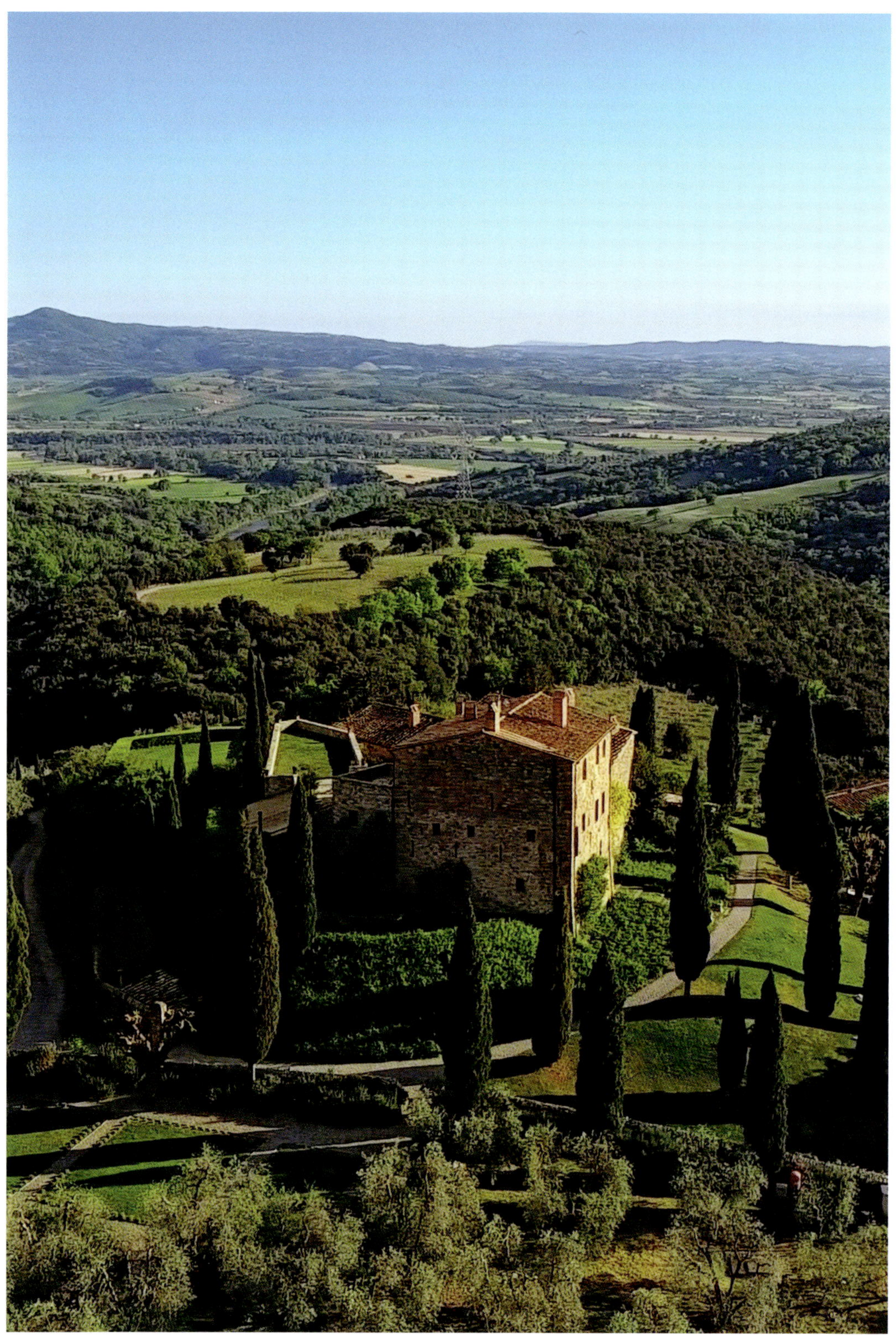

TOSCANA

CASTELLO DI VICARELLO

Via Vicarello 1, 58044 Poggi del Sasso
Tel. +39 0564 990 718 · info@vicarello.it
www.castellodivicarello.com
Open from March to November

A PRIVATE STAY IN TUSCANY The Maremma is the other face of Tuscany: away from the rolling hills, picturesque villages and cities of art, Tuscany is less spectacular and more authentic, with a raw beauty that visitors passing through often fail to notice. But those who do take note sense something wild and romantic, perhaps familiar from the Camargue, or something melancholy, as on the Peloponnese out of season – and they fall in love with it. This is what happened to Carlo and Aurora Baccheschi Berti. They had seen the world and worked for many years on Bali as textile designers before discovering a tumbledown castle in the Maremma – and the magic of the place. They restored Castello di Vicarello energetically and stylishly, and turned it into a hotel that exudes the rustic charm of the region and at the same time lends it a touch of Bohemian atmosphere, a hotel that is run like a private home and, wonderfully, attracts just the right clientele: people who travel often and in style, and are as happy to talk about this as they are to hear the stories of like-minded guests. The best part of a stay is dinner, sitting at a long table, or relaxing together by the pools. For the necessary bit of privacy there are eight suites and a villa furnished with antiques, art books and some open fireplaces. Hotel guests have to do without extras such as television – but who needs a screen with pictures from round the world when the natural images of the Maremma are right outside? ◆ Book to pack: "Under the Tuscan Sun" by Frances Mayes.

DIE TOSKANA GANZ PRIVAT In der Maremma zeigt die Toskana ihr zweites Gesicht: Abseits der sanften Hügel, der pittoresken Dörfer und berühmten Kunststädte gibt sie sich hier unspektakulärer und ursprünglicher, von einer rauen Schönheit, an der manche Besucher achtlos vorüberfahren. Doch wer sie bemerkt, spürt etwas Wildromantisches, das er vielleicht aus der Camargue kennt, etwas Melancholisches, wie es der Peloponnes außerhalb der Saison besitzt – und er verliebt sich in sie. So ging es auch Carlo und Aurora Baccheschi Berti. Sie hatten die Welt gesehen und lange Jahre auf Bali als Textildesigner gearbeitet, ehe sie in der Maremma eine verfallene Burg entdeckten – und ihre Magie. Sie restaurierten das Castello di Vicarello mit so viel Energie wie Stil und verwandelten es in ein Hotel, das den rustikalen Charme der Region verströmt und ihm zugleich einen Hauch Boheme verleiht, das wie ein Privathaus geführt wird und wunderbarerweise die exakt passende Klientel anzieht: Menschen, die oft und gepflegt reisen und gerne davon erzählen, genauso wie sie neugierig auf die Geschichten Gleichgesinnter sind. Am schönsten sitzt man beim Dinner an der langen Tafel zusammen oder entspannt gemeinsam an den Pools. Für das nötige Quäntchen Privatsphäre sorgen die Suiten sowie eine Villa, die mit Antiquitäten, Kunstbüchern und zum Teil offenen Kaminen ausgestattet sind. Auf Extras wie einen Fernseher muss man verzichten – doch wer braucht schon flimmernde Bilder aus aller Welt, wenn er die natürlichen der Maremma direkt vor der Tür hat? ◆ Buchtipp: „Unter der Sonne der Toskana“ von Frances Mayes.

LA TOSCANE EN PRIVÉ C'est dans la Maremme que la Toscane montre son autre visage : à l'écart des collines aux formes douces, des villages pittoresques et des villes au riche patrimoine artistique, elle est moins spectaculaire et plus authentique, d'une beauté rude que l'on peut méconnaître. Mais celui qui la remarque y discerne un romantisme sauvage qu'il a peut-être déjà rencontré en Camargue, quelque chose de mélancolique que possède aussi le Péloponnèse hors-saison – et il en tombe amoureux. C'est ce qui est arrivé à Carlo et Aurora Baccheschi Berti. Ils avaient vu le monde et travaillé de longues années à Bali comme designers textiles, lorsqu'ils découvrirent un château fort en ruine dans la Maremme et la magie des lieux. Ils ont restauré le Castello di Vicarello avec autant d'énergie que d'élégance et l'ont transformé en un hôtel qui possède le charme rustique de la région, mais avec un accent bohème. Il est dirigé comme une maison particulière et attire miraculeusement la clientèle adéquate : des gens qui voyagent souvent, recherchent le raffinement, et aiment autant raconter leurs passions qu'écouter les récits de ceux qui partagent leurs idées. Le soir, pour dîner, la longue table accueille tous les hôtes, et il est bon aussi de se détendre ensemble au bord de la piscine. L'intimité nécessaire est assurée par les suites et la villa, en partie dotées de cheminées et décorées d'antiquités et de livres d'art. Il faut renoncer à la télévision – mais qui a besoin de voir des images du monde sur un écran quand le paysage de la Maremme est devant sa porte ? ◆ À lire : « Sous le soleil de Toscane » de Frances Mayes.

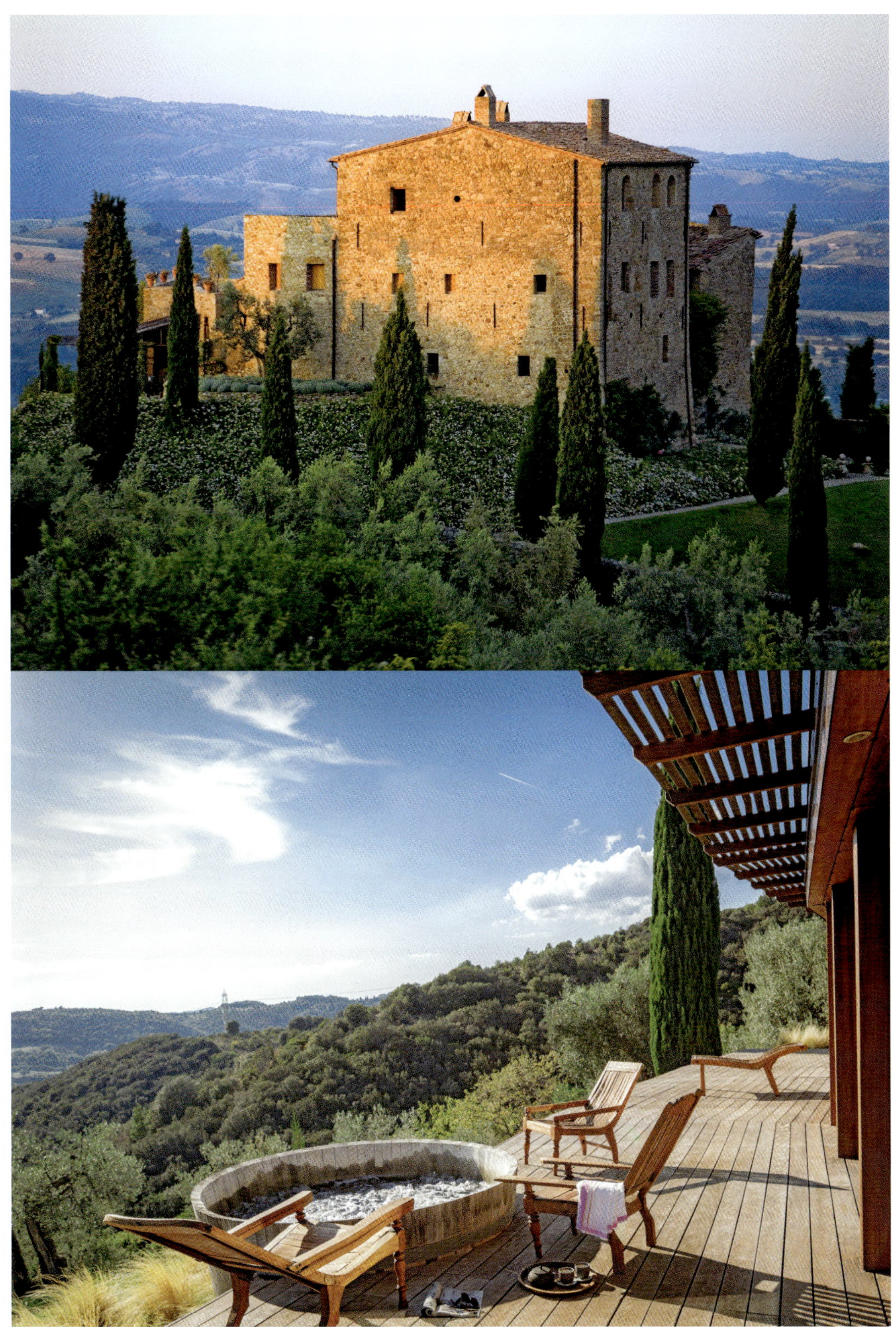

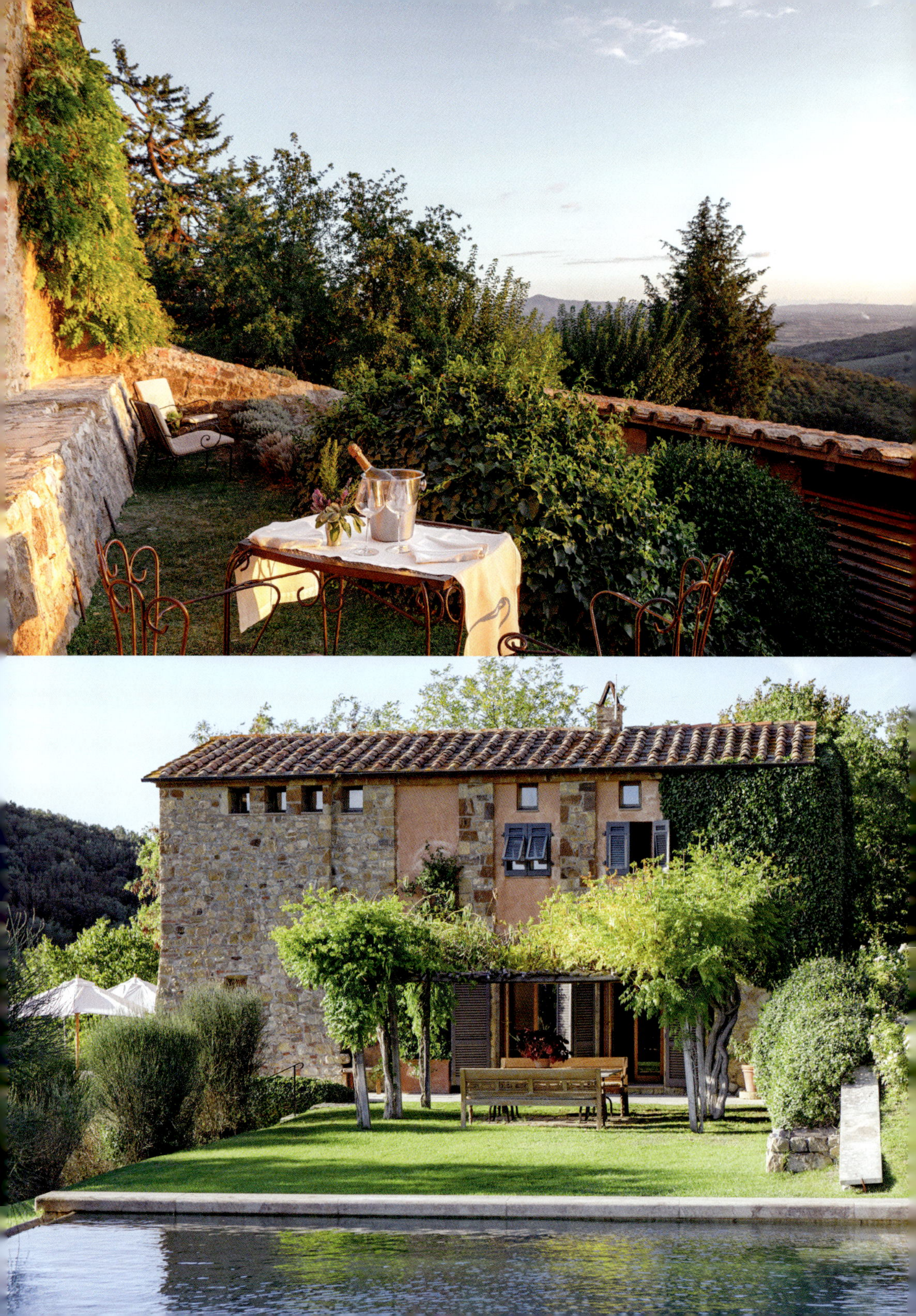

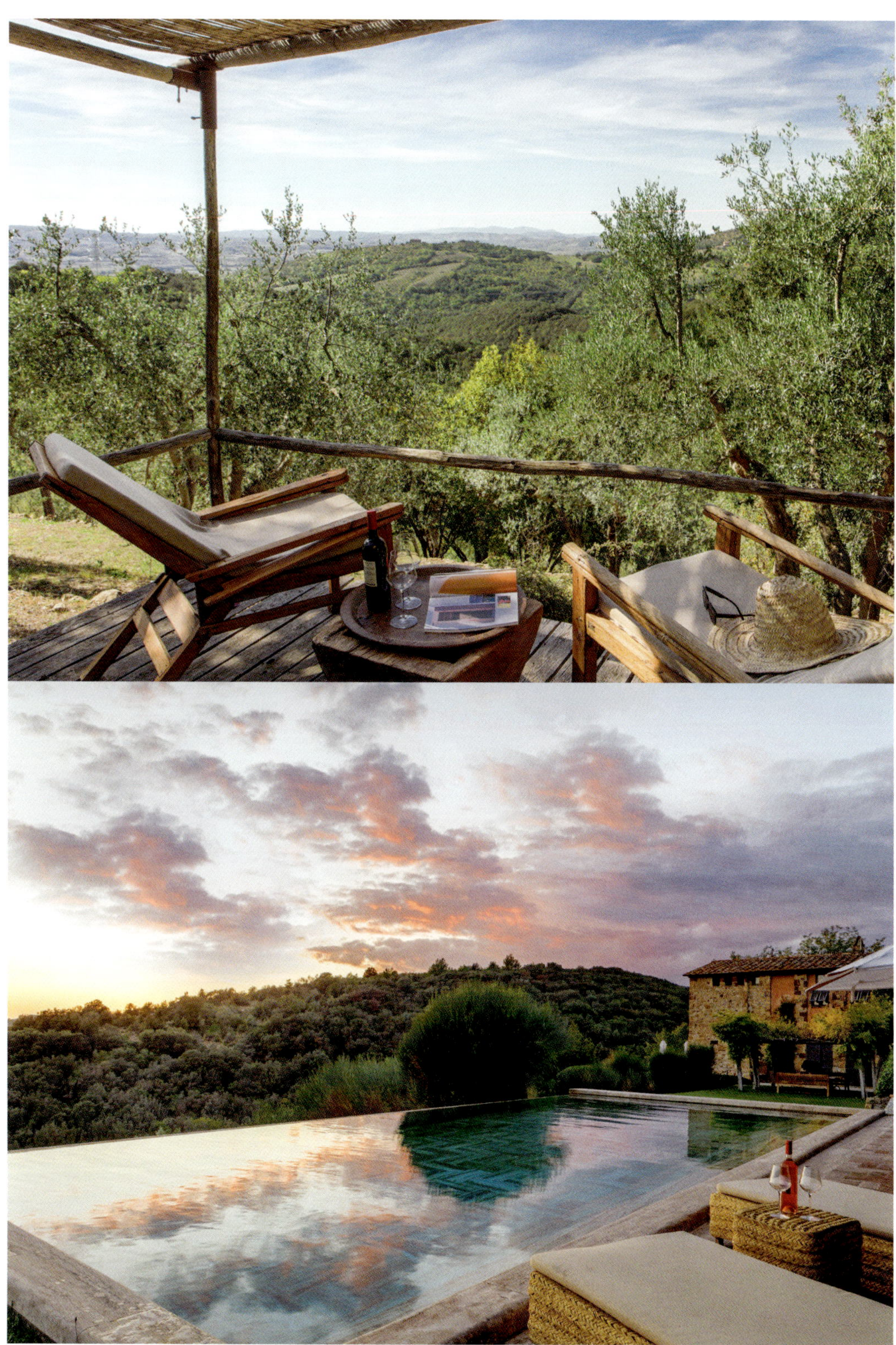

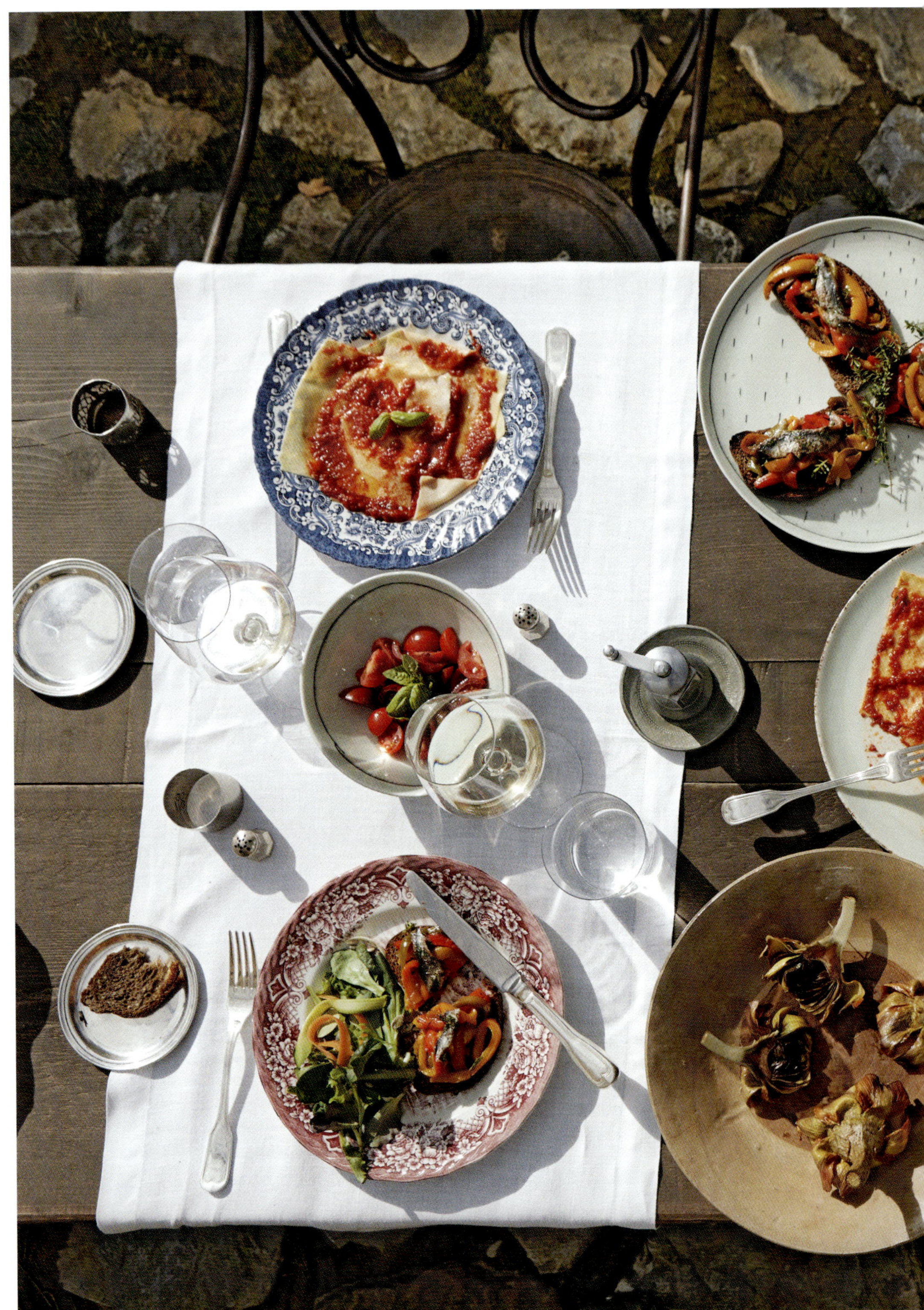

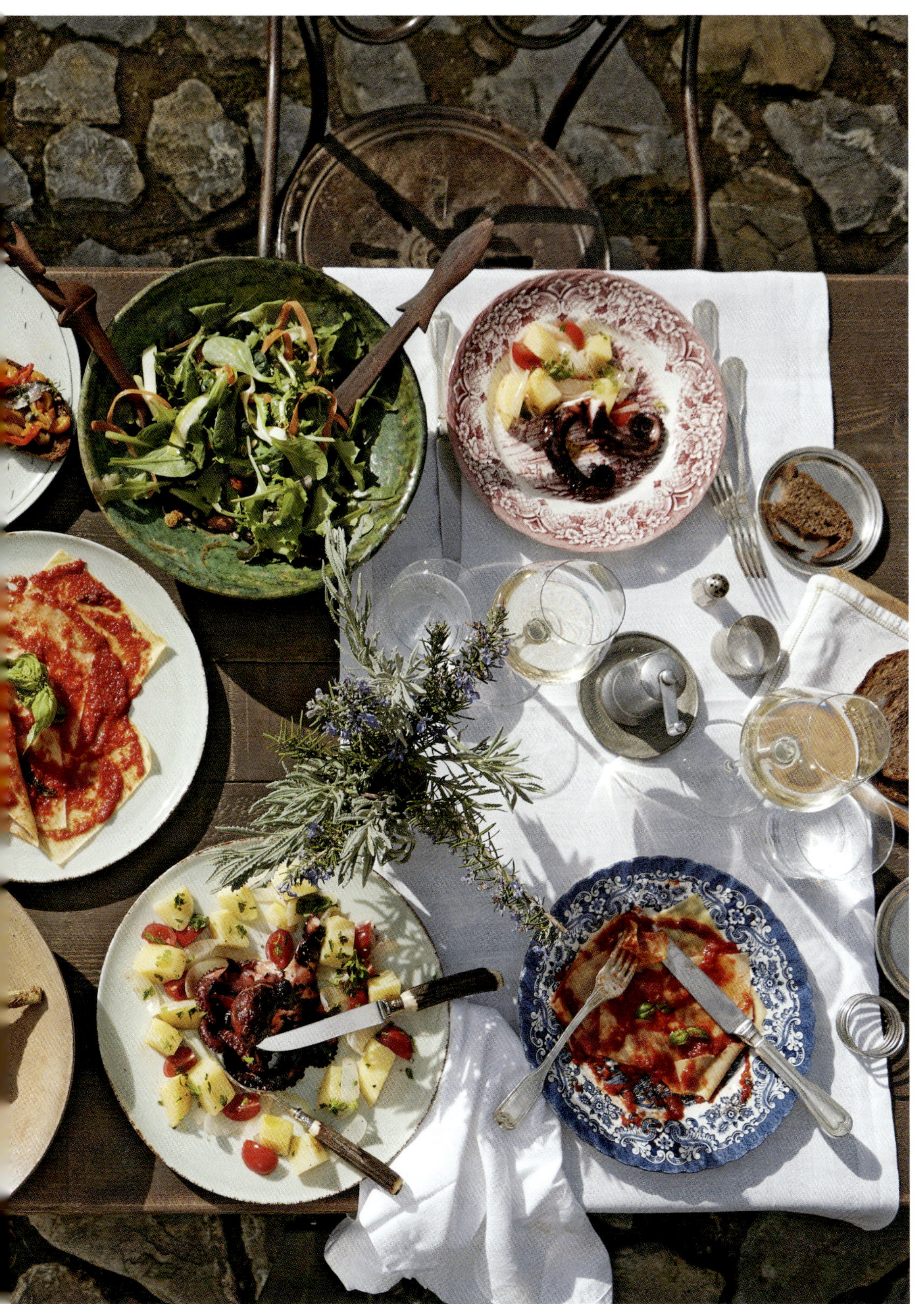

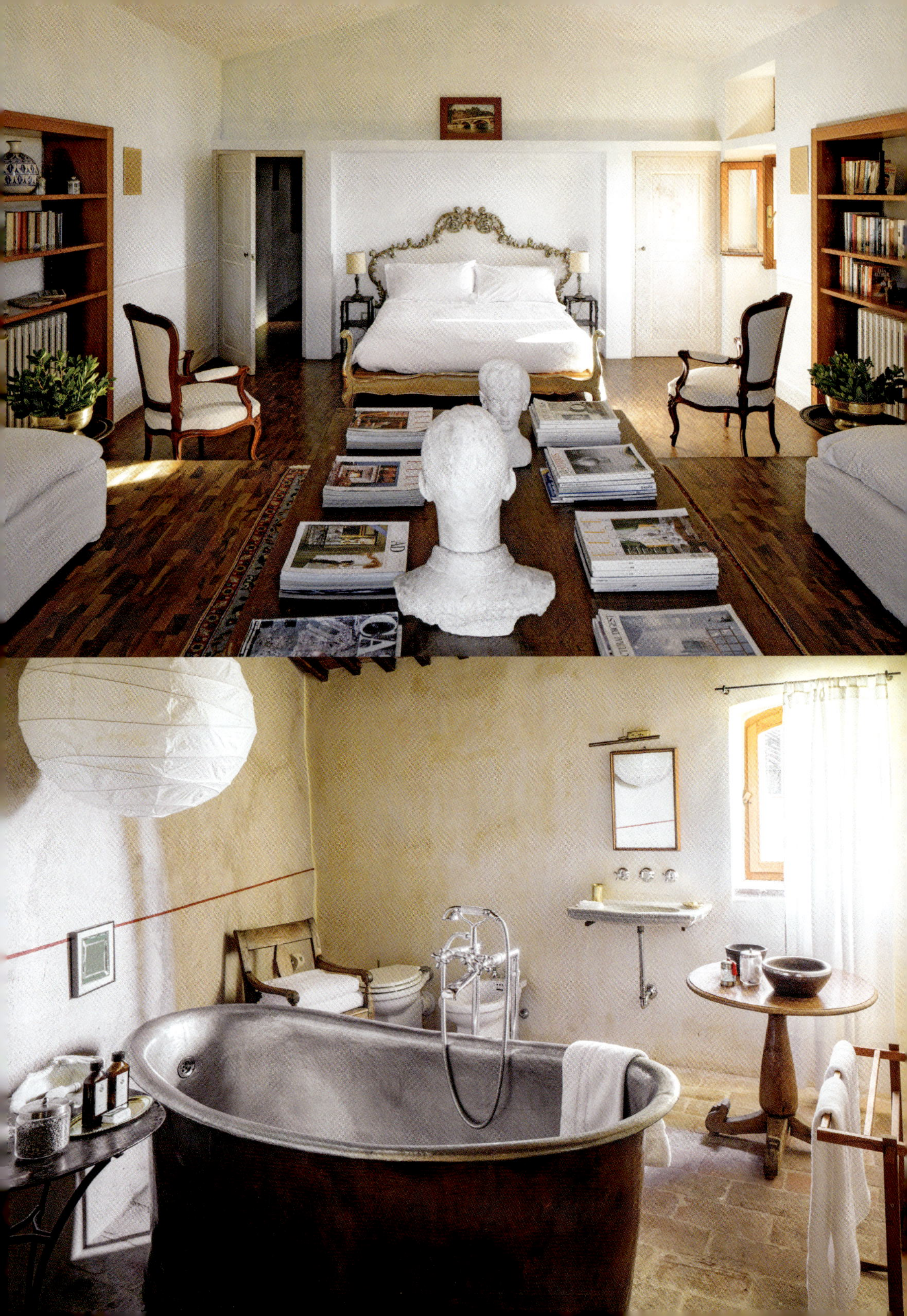
AD

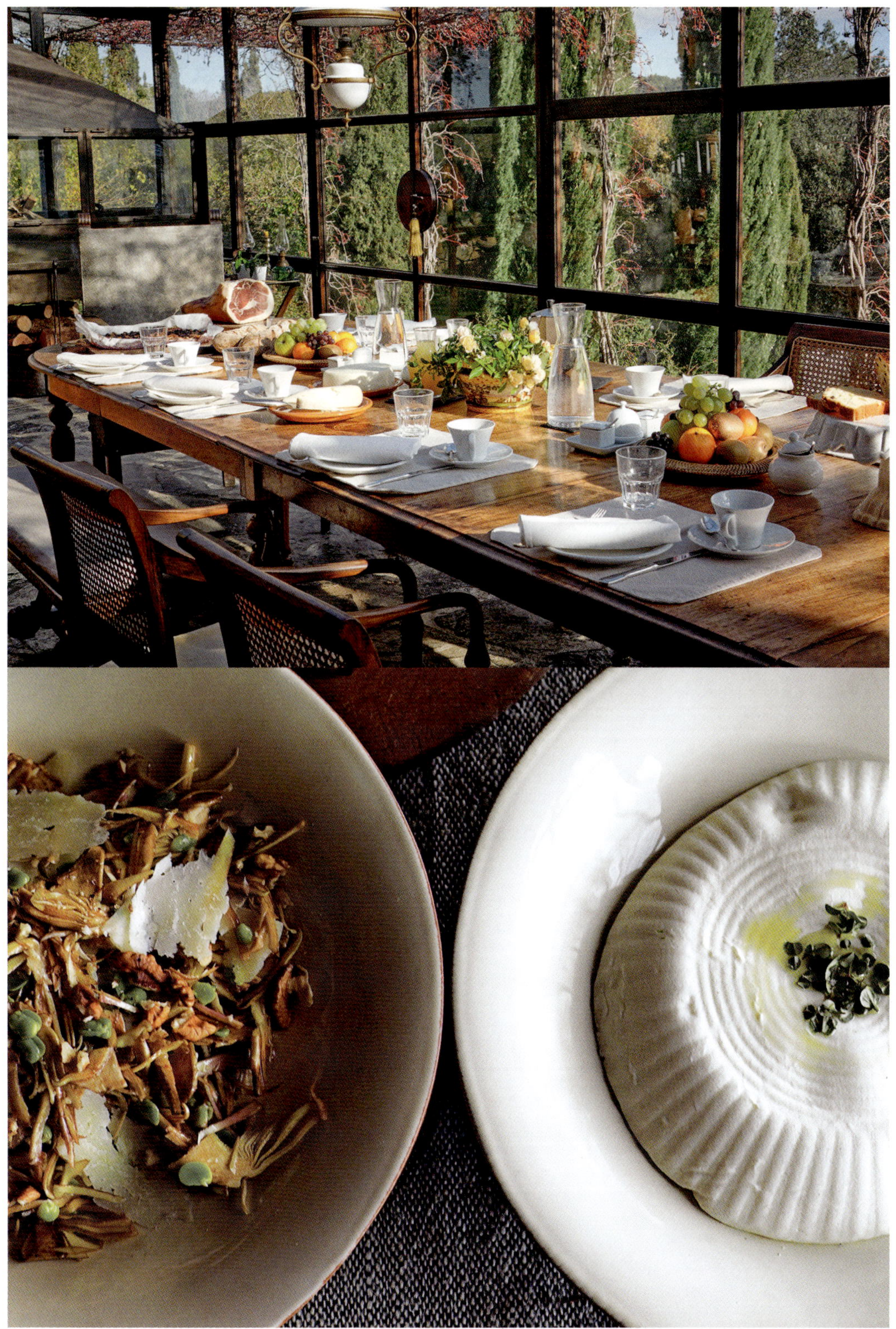

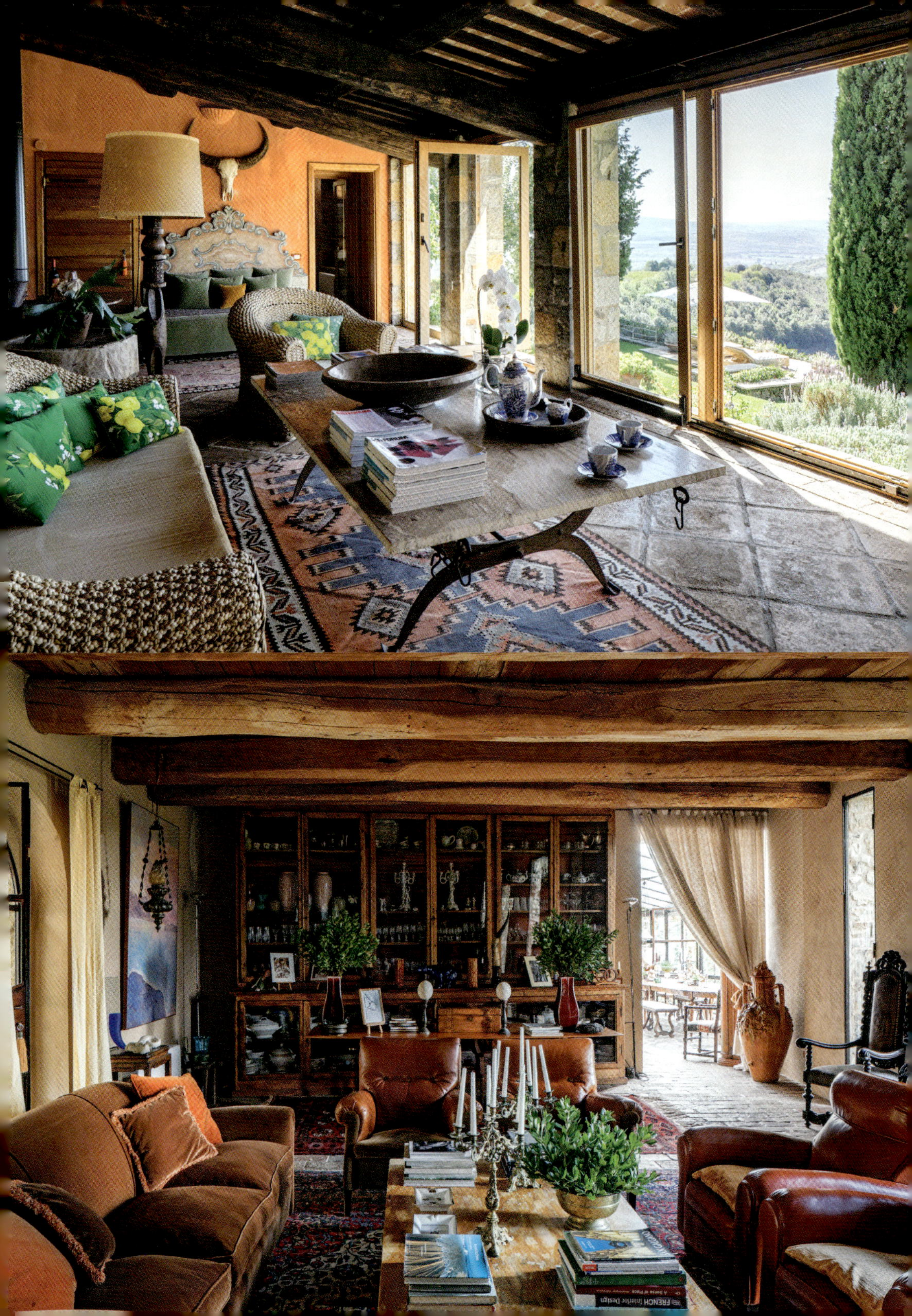
A Sense of Place
FRENCH Interior Design

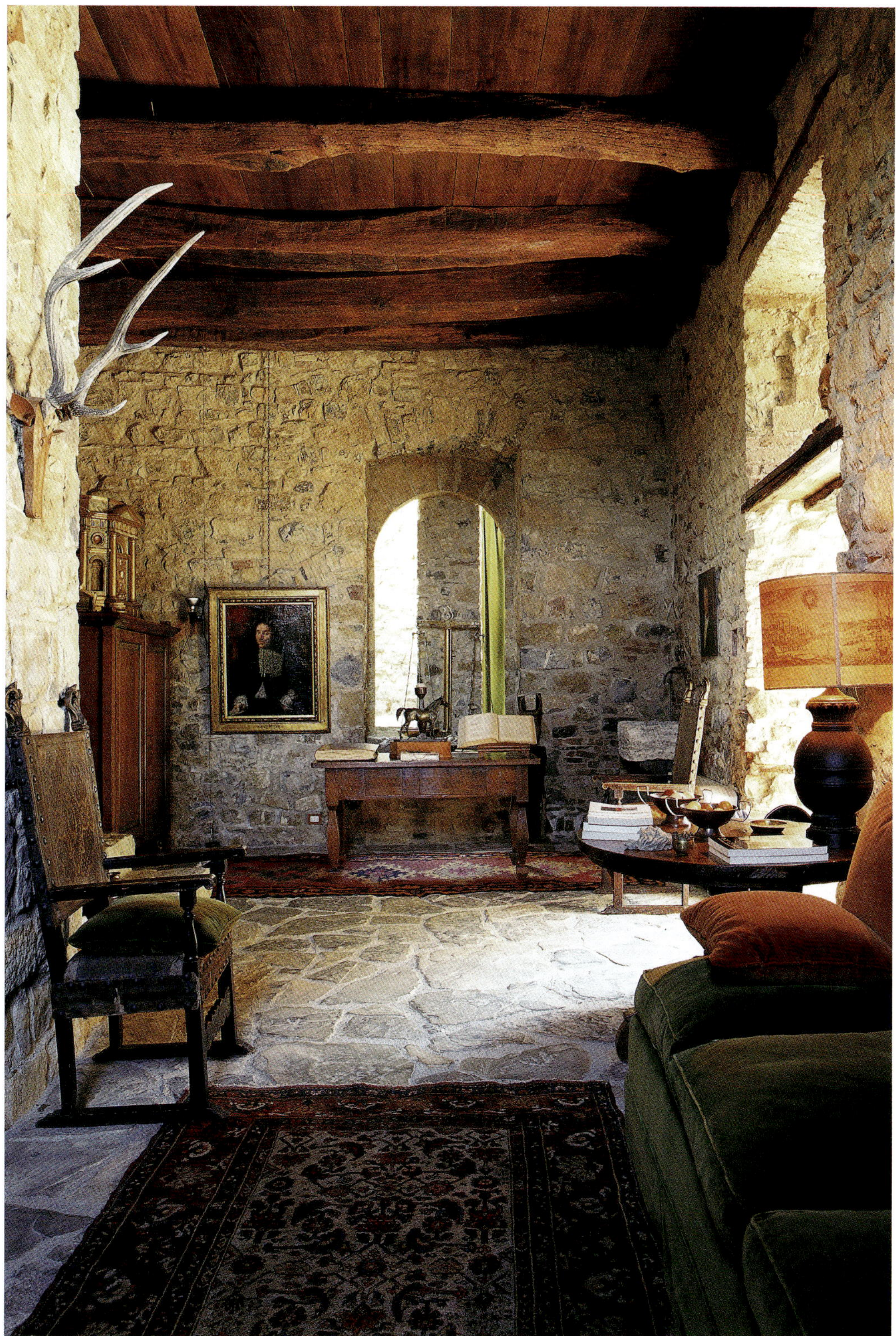

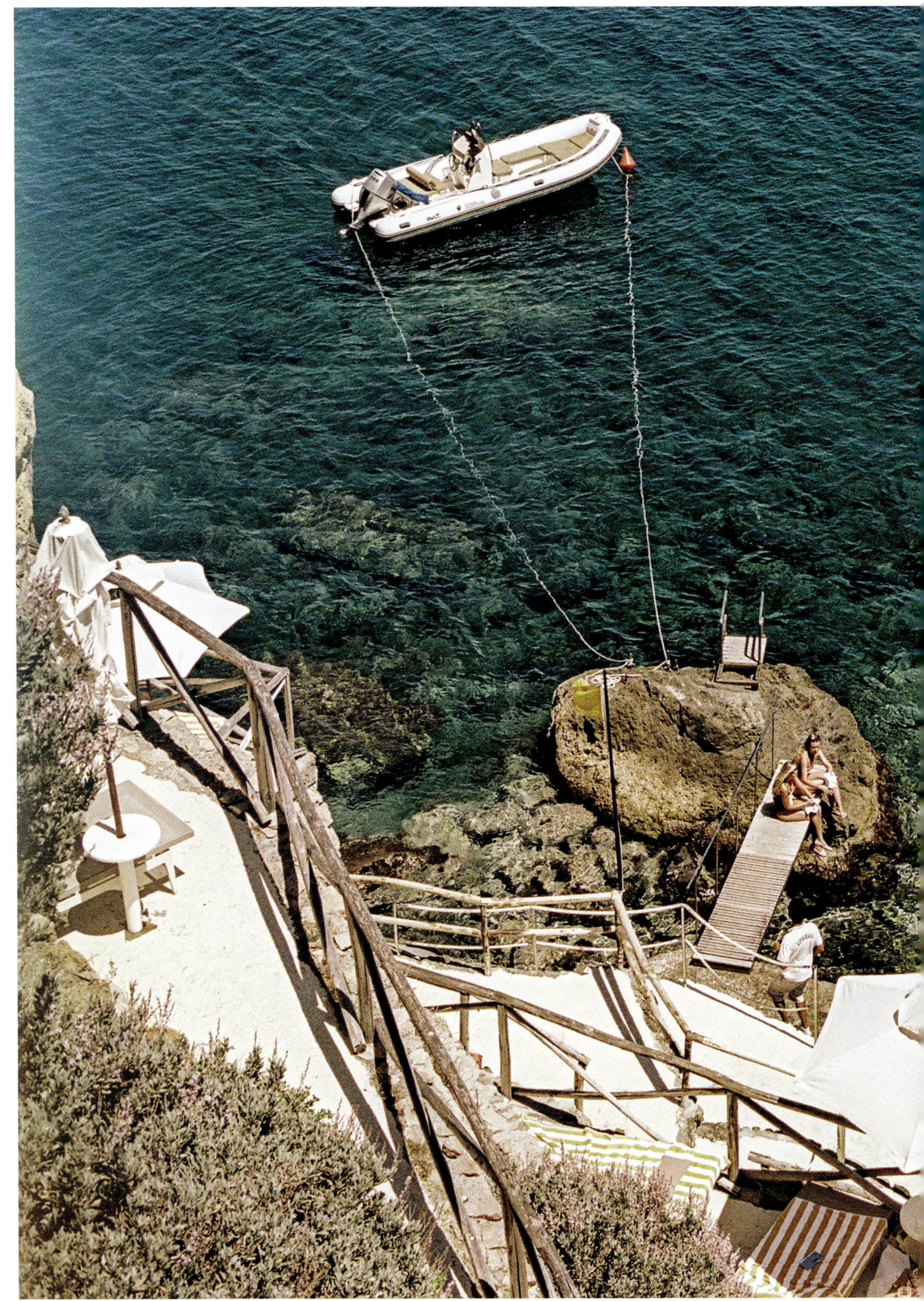

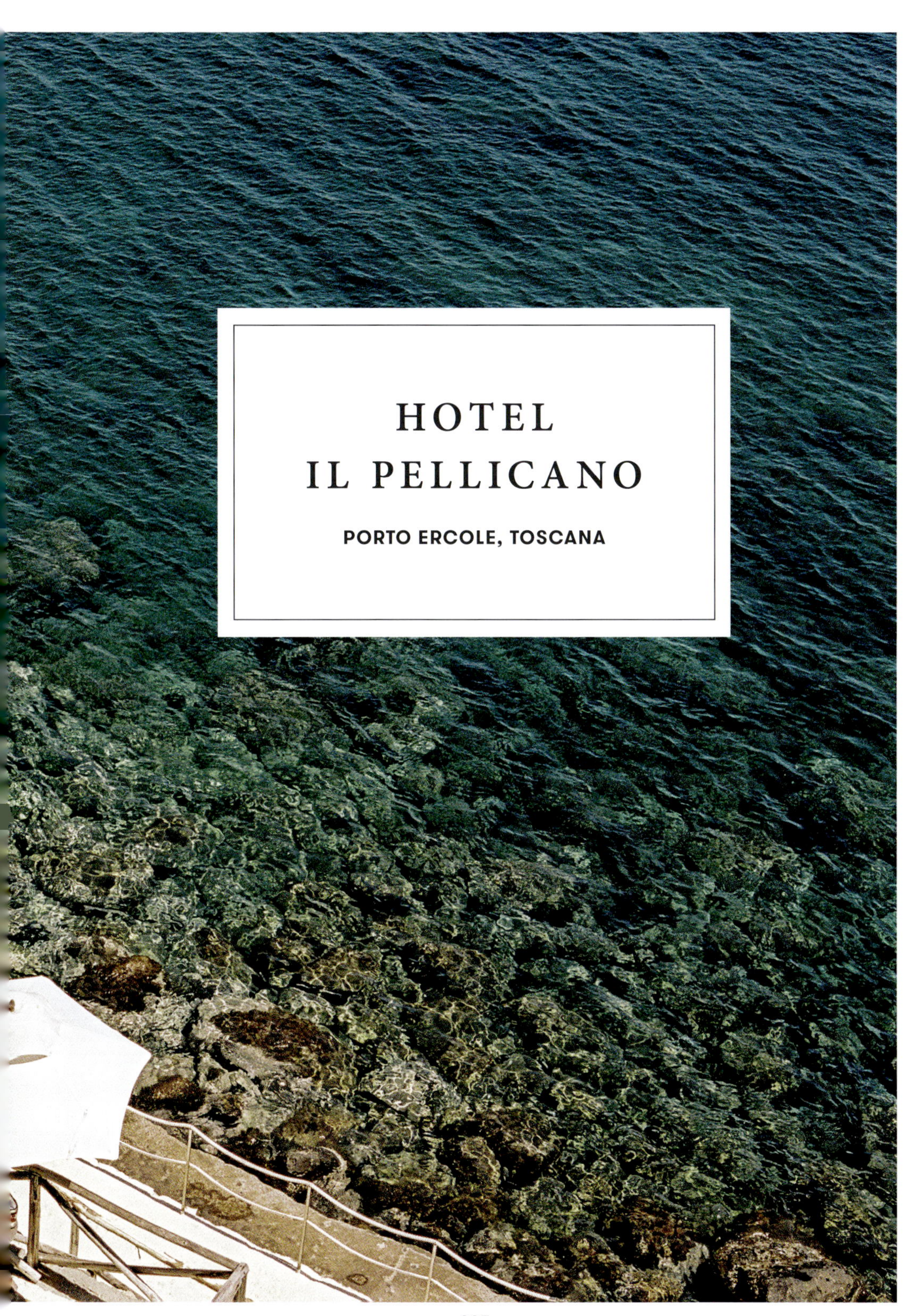

HOTEL IL PELLICANO

PORTO ERCOLE, TOSCANA

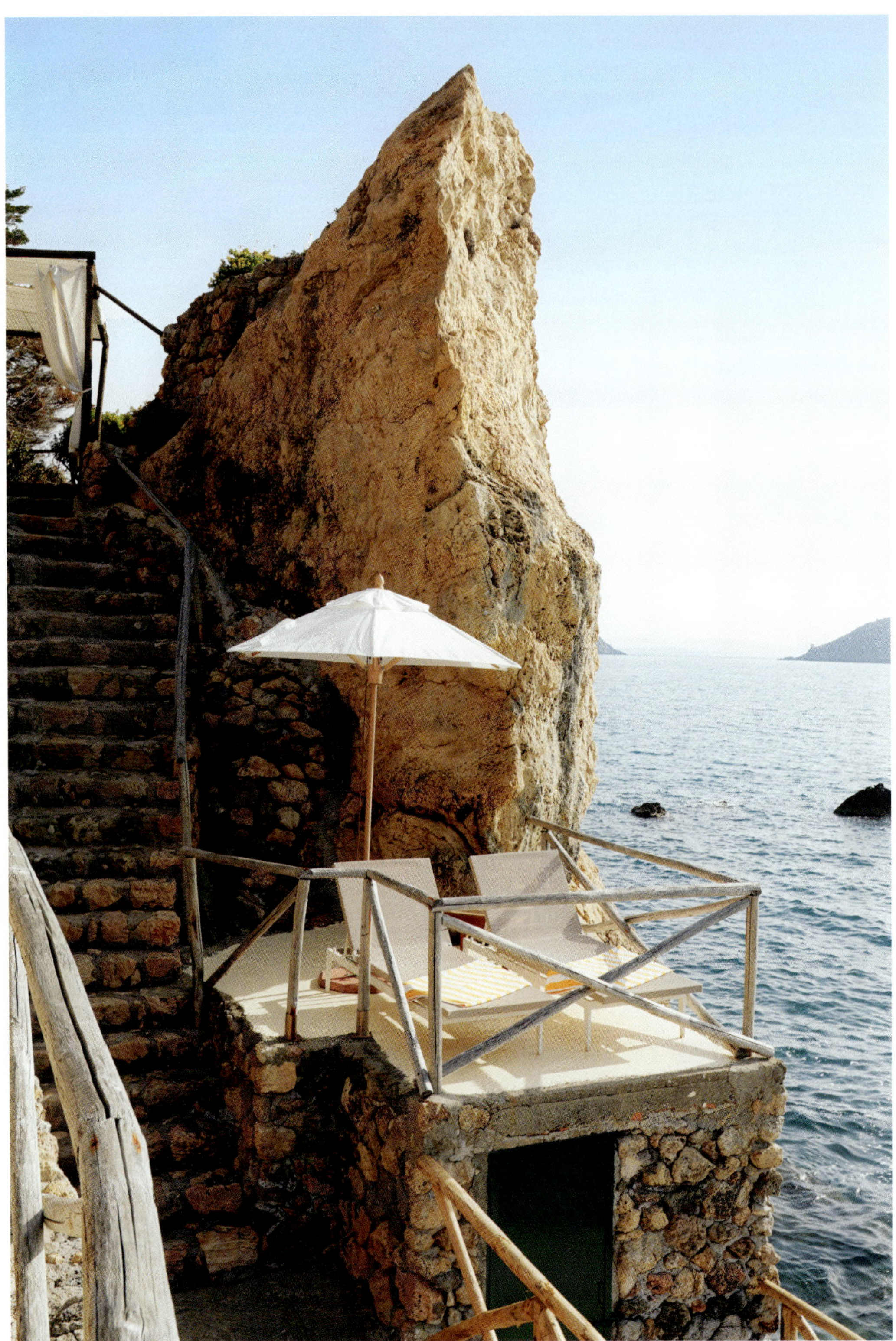

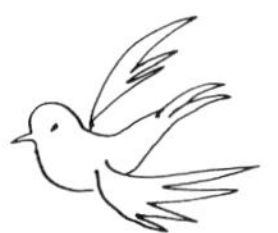

HOTEL IL PELLICANO

Località Sbarcatello, 58018 Porto Ercole
Tel. +39 0564 858 111 · reservations@pellicanohotels.com
www.pellicanohotel.com
Open from early April to late October

A DECLARATION OF LOVE He was a British pilot who came to fame when he jumped out of his crashing plane without a parachute and survived. She was an American socialite who looked a little like Grace Kelly and had an affair with Clark Gable. When Michael Graham and Patsy Daszel met at Pelican Point in California, it was love at first sight. Together the couple moved to Italy and fell in love all over again – with a plot of land on the rocky coast of Monte Argentario, which was once an island and is now connected to the mainland of the Maremma. They built themselves a home there high above the Mediterranean in 1965 and named it "Il Pellicano" after the place where they met. Their private paradise quickly became a destination for the jet set – the Grahams invited Ted Kennedy to stay, lay in the sun with Charlie Chaplin and clinked glasses with Gianni Agnelli. When they returned to America they sold the estate to a friend, who converted it into a public hotel. Since then guests have been able to enjoy a holiday as stylish and sophisticated as the first glamorous residents. The best accommodation is in the cottages that are situated highest up (don't fail to book a room with a sea view). By day guests swim in the seawater pool and in the evening enjoy Michelin-starred dishes. The spa, newly renovated in the style of a beach house, is truly wonderful. What a pity Michael Graham and Patsy Daszel never saw it – it would have been love at first sight once more. ◆ Book to pack: "The Divine Comedy" by Dante Alighieri.

EINE LIEBESERKLÄRUNG Er war ein britischer Pilot, der berühmt wurde, als er bei einem Absturz seiner Maschine ohne Fallschirm aus dem Flugzeug sprang und überlebte. Sie war eine amerikanische Salonlöwin, die ein bisschen an Grace Kelly erinnerte und eine Liaison mit Clark Gable hatte: Als sich Michael Graham und Patsy Daszel am Pelican Point in Kalifornien trafen, war es „love at first sight". Gemeinsam zog das Paar nach Italien und verliebte sich dort erneut – in ein Grundstück an der Felsenküste des Monte Argentario, einer ehemaligen Insel, die heute mit dem Festland der Maremma verbunden ist. Hoch über dem Mittelmeer bauten sie dort 1965 ihre Residenz und tauften sie nach dem Ort ihres Kennenlernens „Il Pellicano". Aus dem persönlichen Paradies wurde schnell ein Lieblingsziel des Jetsets – die Grahams hatten Ted Kennedy zu Gast, lagen mit Charlie Chaplin in der Sonne und stießen mit Gianni Agnelli aufs Leben an. Als sie nach Amerika zurückkehrten, verkauften sie das Anwesen an einen Freund, der es in ein öffentliches Hotel verwandelte – seitdem kann man hier so stilvoll und elegant urlauben wie einst die glamourösen Bewohner. Am besten wohnt man in den höchstgelegenen Cottages (unbedingt Zimmer mit Meerblick buchen!), genießt tagsüber den Salzwasserpool und abends Menüs, die mit einem Michelin-Stern gekrönt sind. Fabelhaft ist das im Stil eines Strandhauses renovierte Spa; fast schade, dass Michael Graham und Patsy Daszel es nicht mehr erlebt haben – es wäre ein weiteres Mal Liebe auf den ersten Blick gewesen. ◆ Buchtipp: „Die Göttliche Komödie" von Dante Alighieri.

LE JOYAU DU LAC Il était une fois un pilote britannique rescapé d'un crash – il avait sauté sans parachute, ce qui le rendit célèbre. Elle était une héritière américaine, ressemblait un peu à Grace Kelly et avait eu une liaison avec Clark Gable : le jour où Michael Graham et Patsy Daszel firent connaissance à Pelican Point en Californie, ce fut le coup de foudre. Partis s'installer en Italie, ils tomberont à nouveau amoureux, cette fois d'un terrain sur la falaise escarpée du Monte Argentario, une ancienne île reliée aujourd'hui à la Maremme. Ils y construiront en 1965 leur résidence qui surplombe la Méditerranée et la baptiseront « Il Pellicano », en souvenir de leur première rencontre. Ils accueillirent bientôt leurs amis de la jet-set dans leur paradis personnel – invitant Ted Kennedy, se reposant au soleil avec Charlie Chaplin et trinquant avec Gianni Agnelli. Lorsqu'ils retournèrent aux États-Unis, les Graham vendirent la propriété à un ami qui la transforma en hôtel. Depuis, on peut passer ici des vacances aussi élégantes et sophistiquées que les hôtes glamour d'autrefois. Pour vivre des moments parfaits, il faut séjourner dans l'un des cottages situés en hauteur (réserver absolument une chambre avec vue sur la mer), se détendre pendant la journée dans la piscine d'eau salée et savourer, le soir, les menus du restaurant pourvu d'une étoile au Michelin. Le spa rénové dans le style d'une maison de plage est fabuleux ; dommage que Michael Graham et Patsy Daszel ne l'aient pas connu, ils auraient craqué une fois de plus, c'est sûr. ◆ À lire : « La Divine Comédie » de Dante Alighieri.

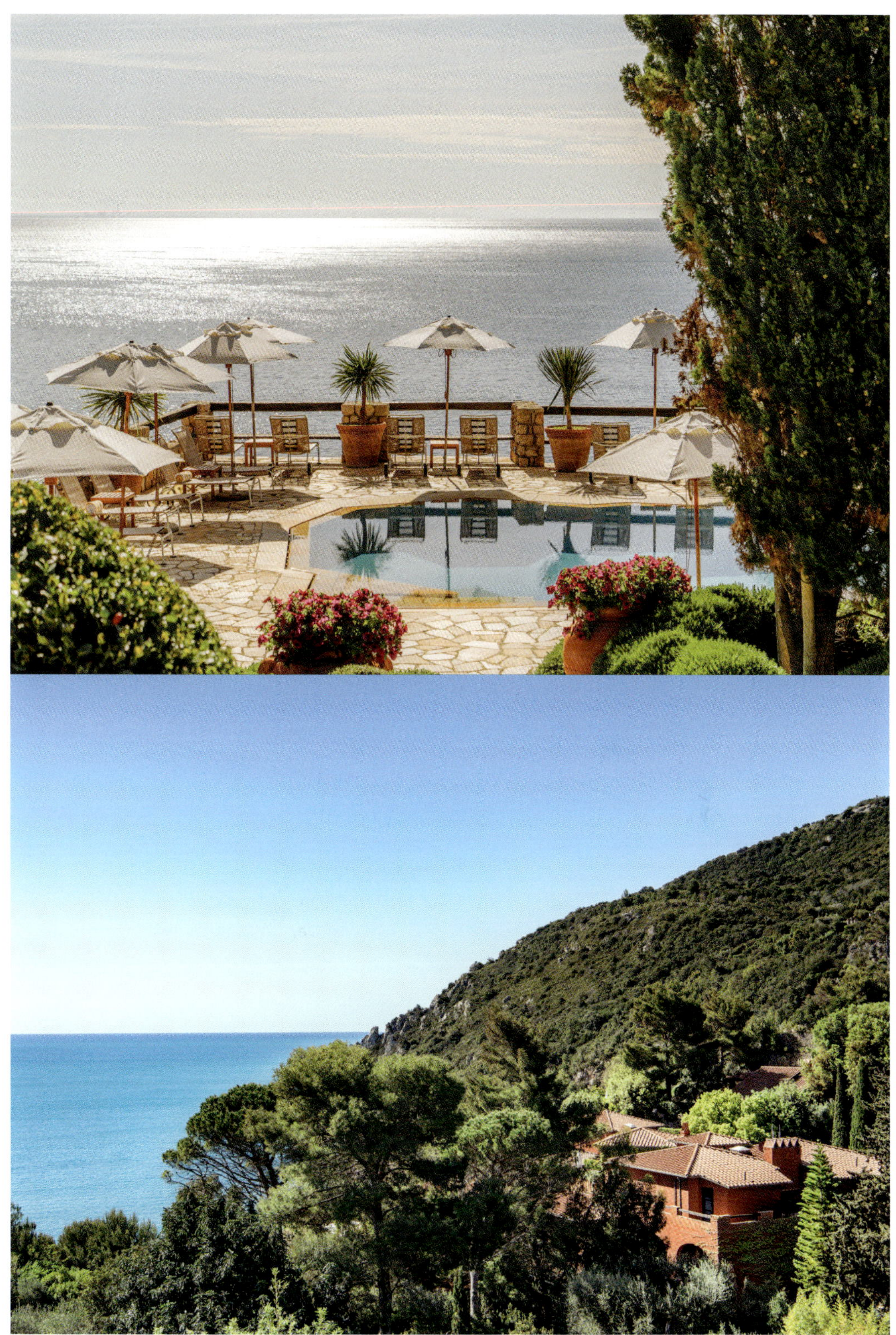

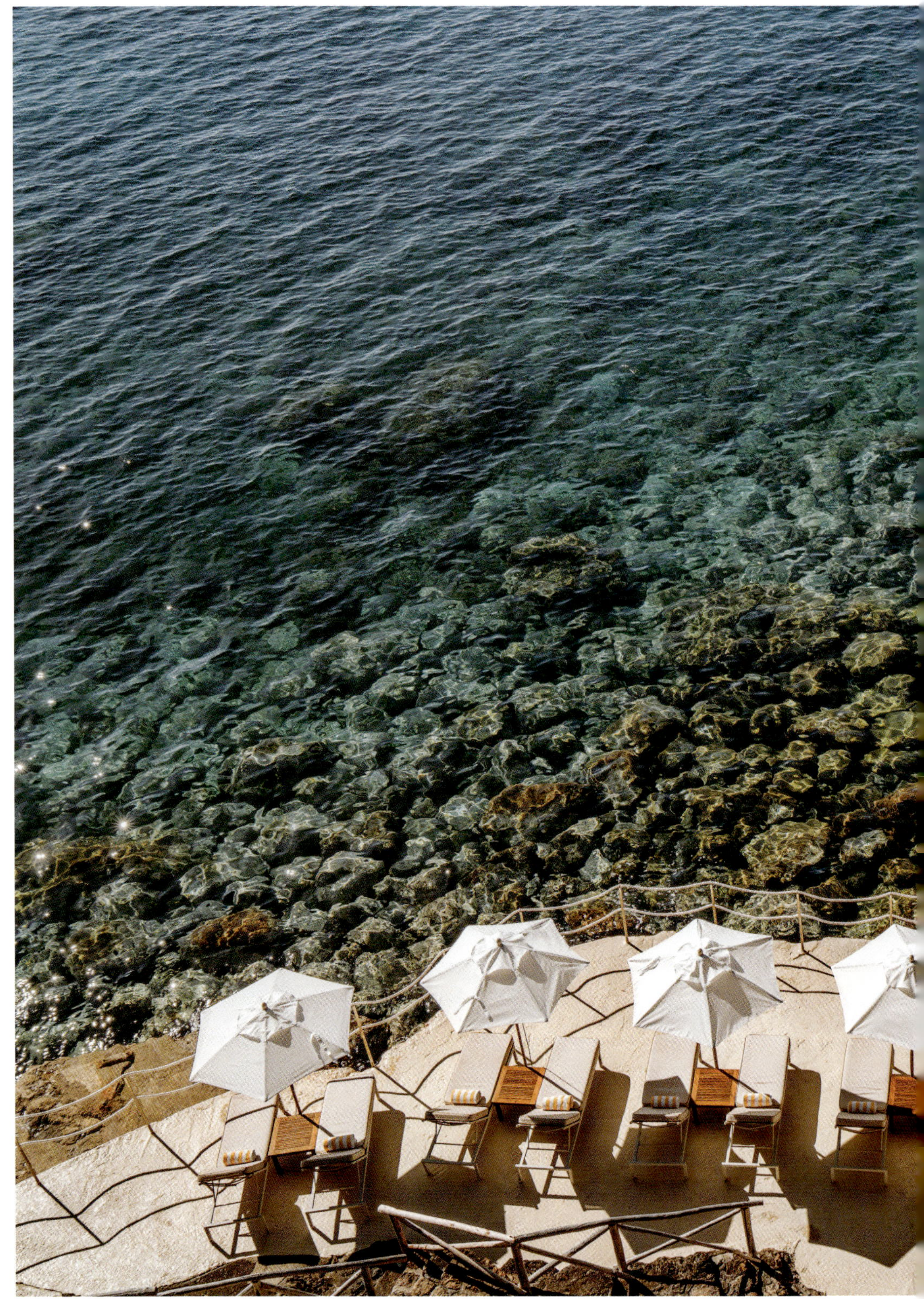

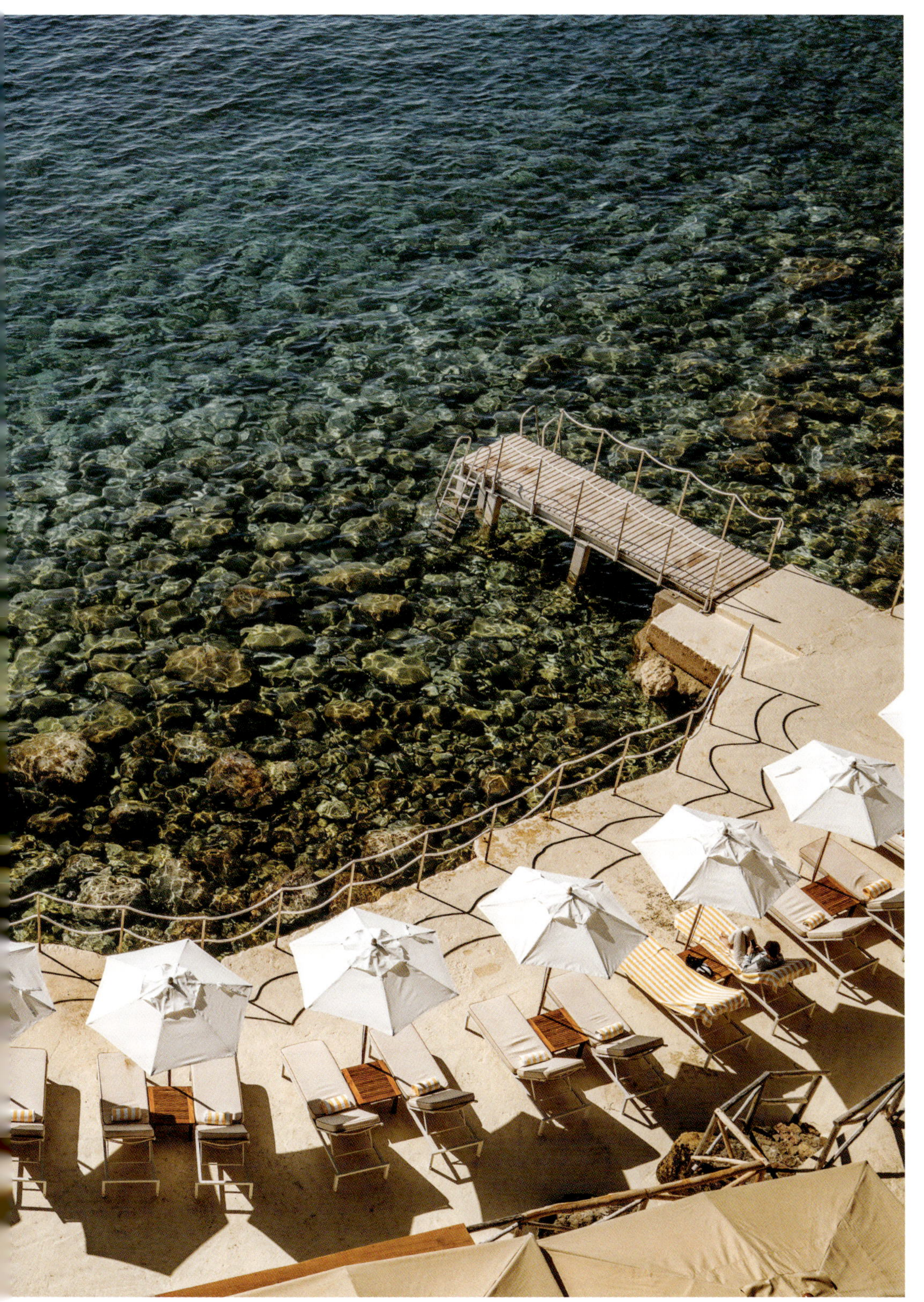

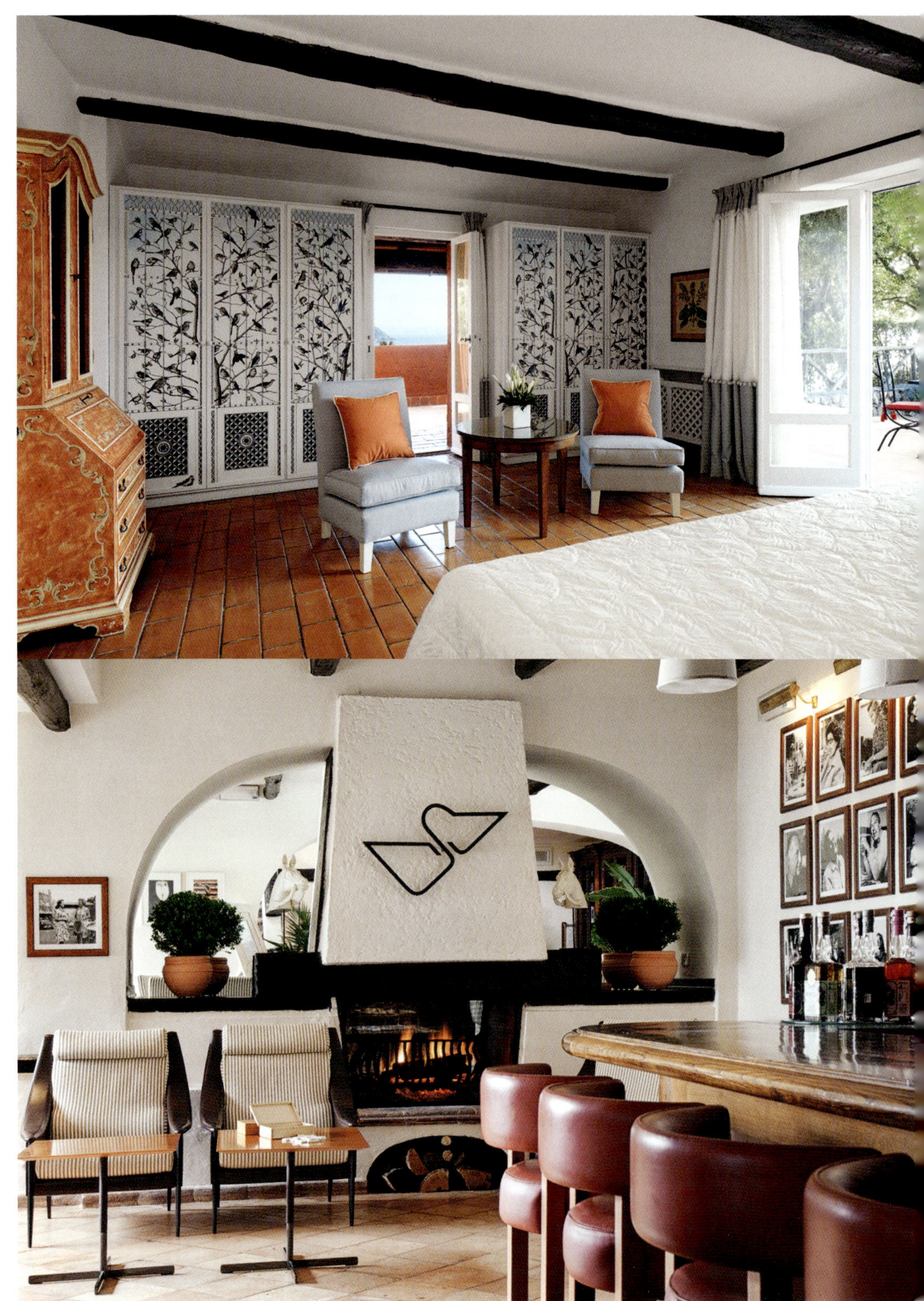

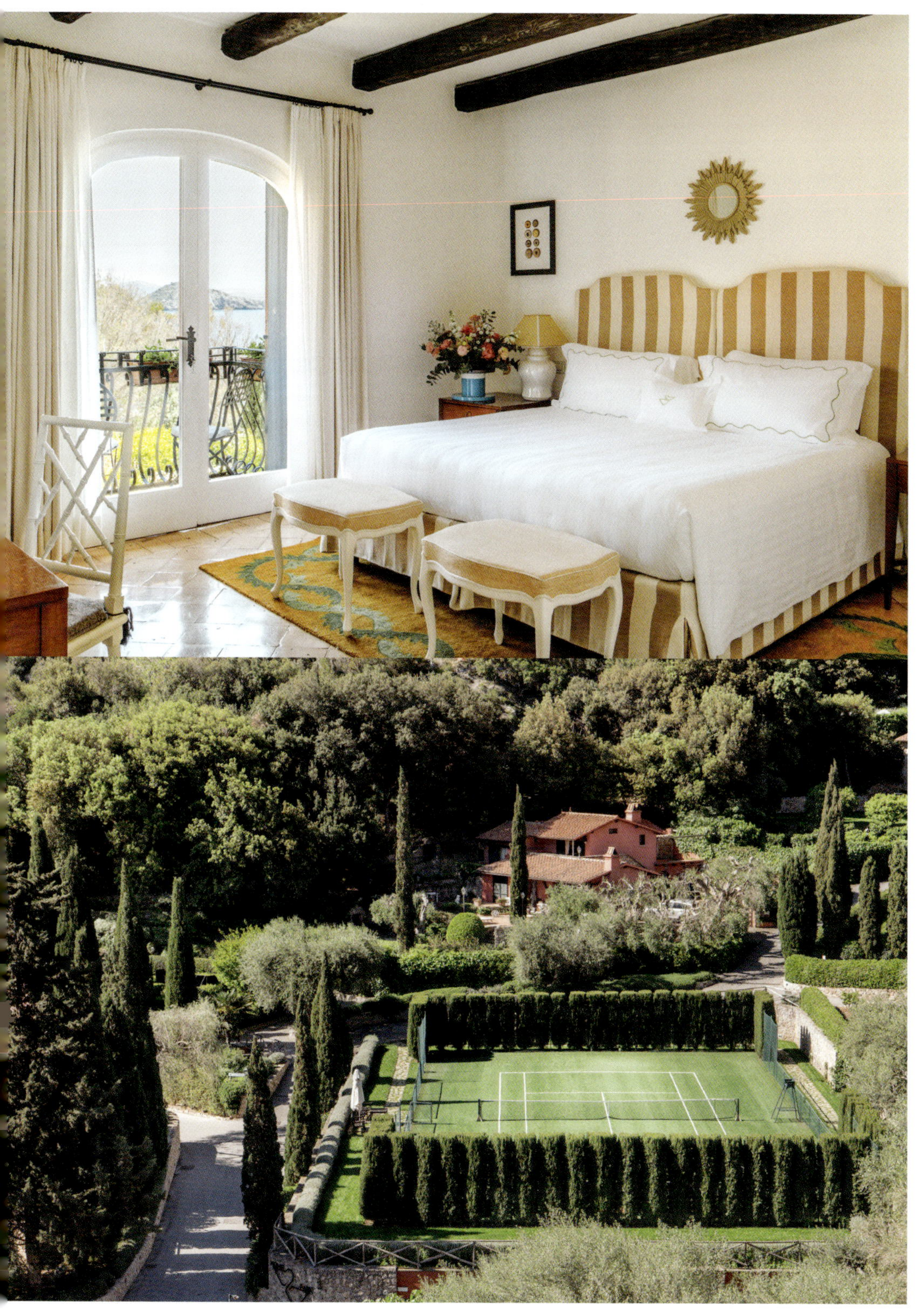

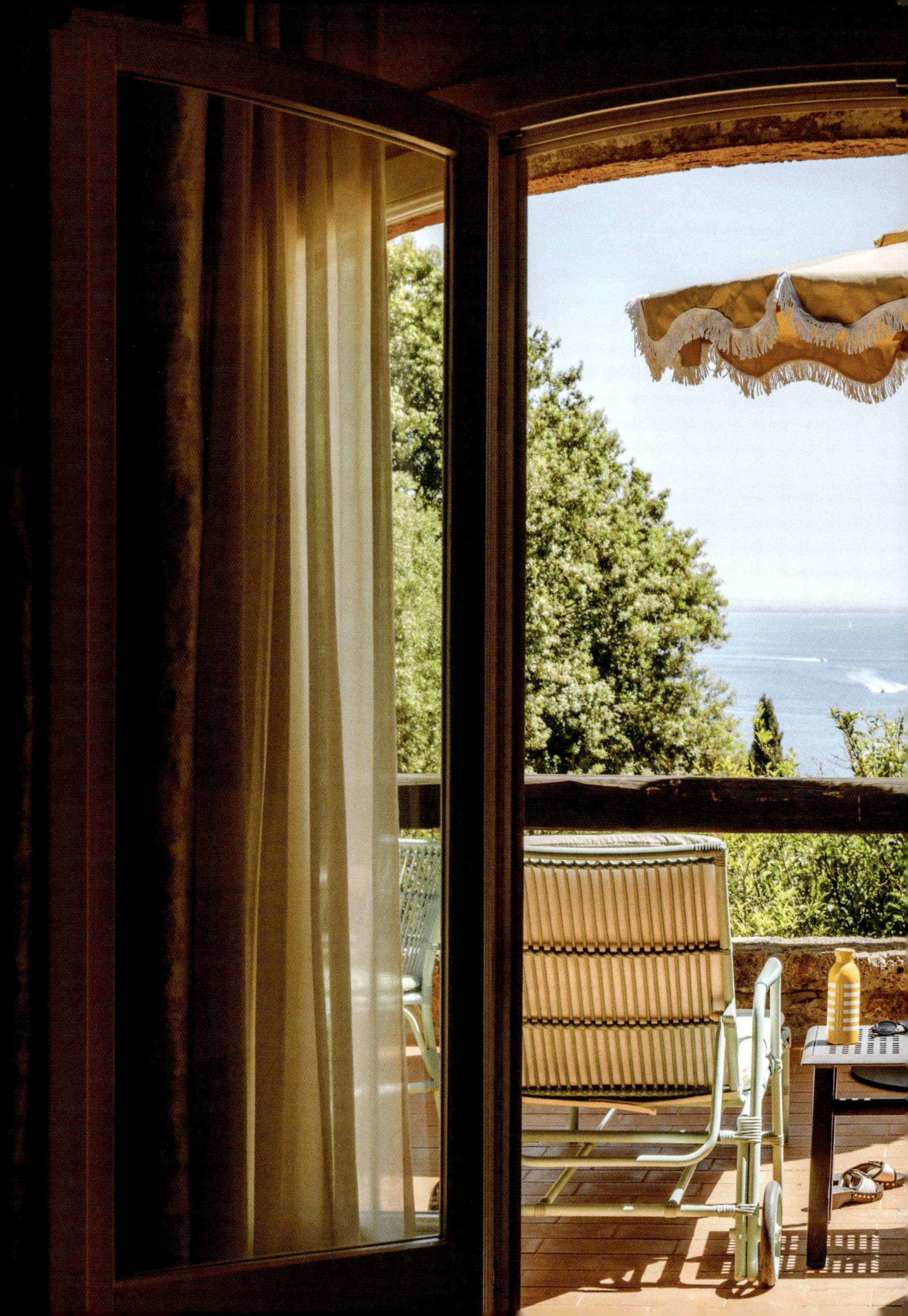

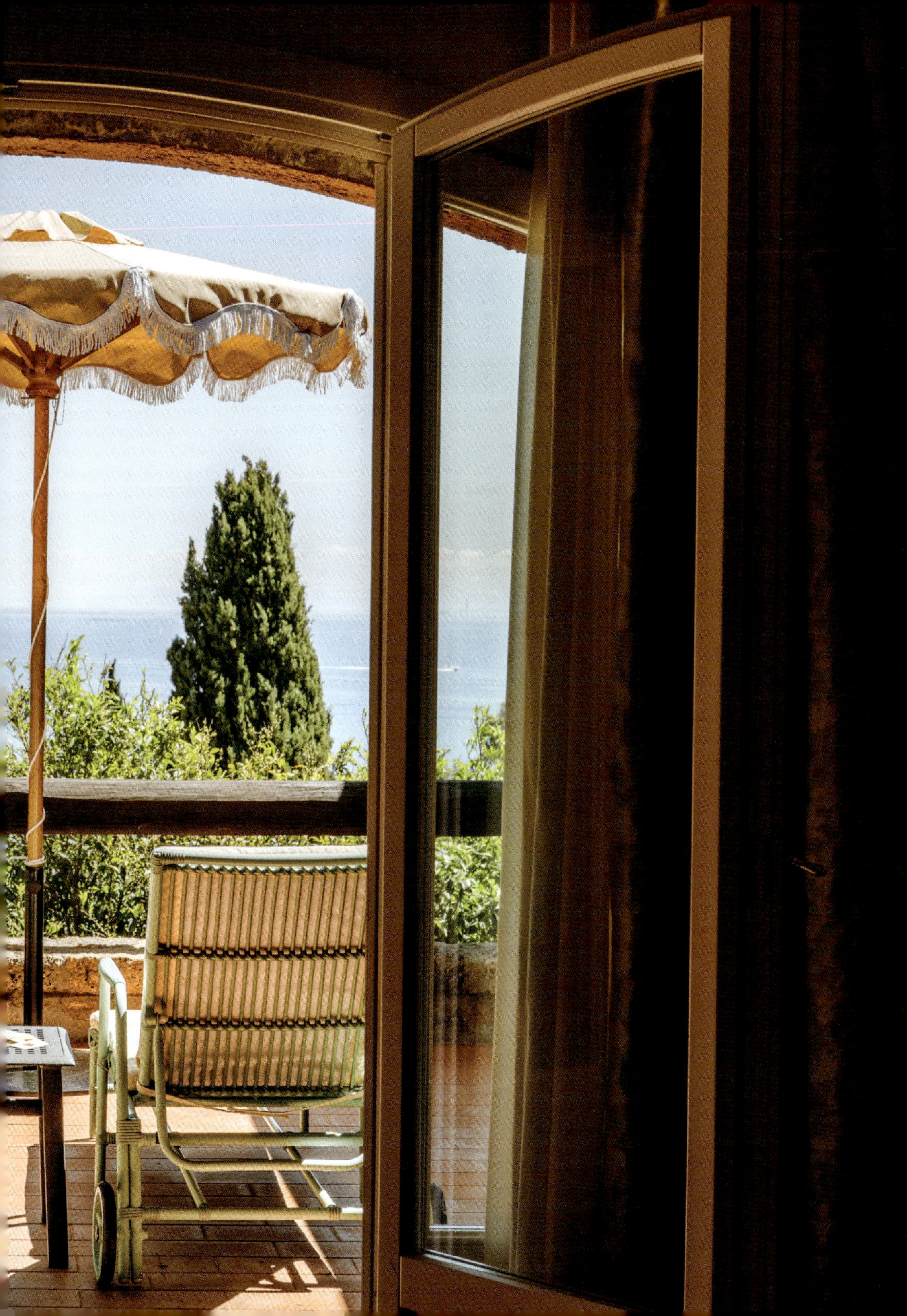

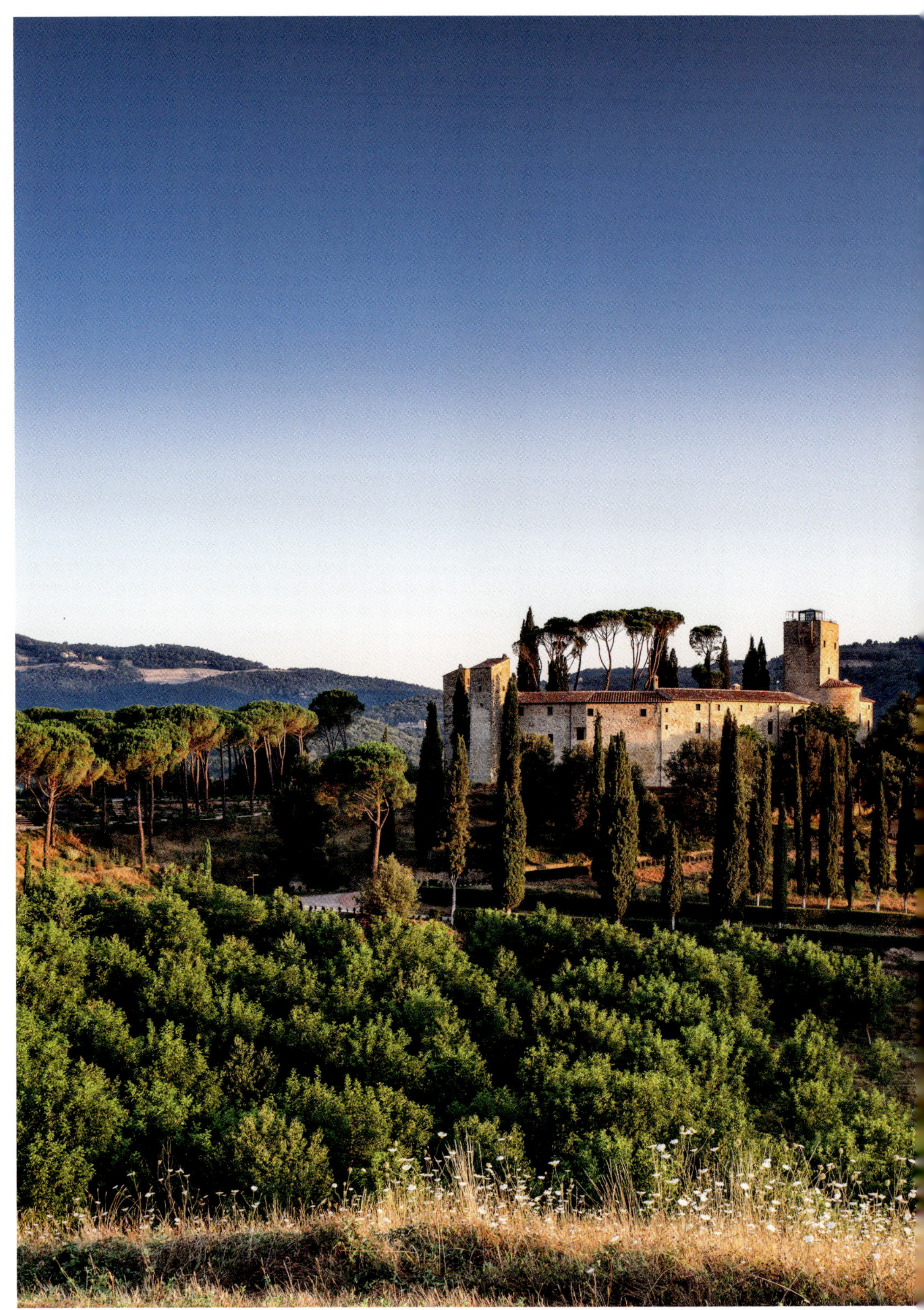

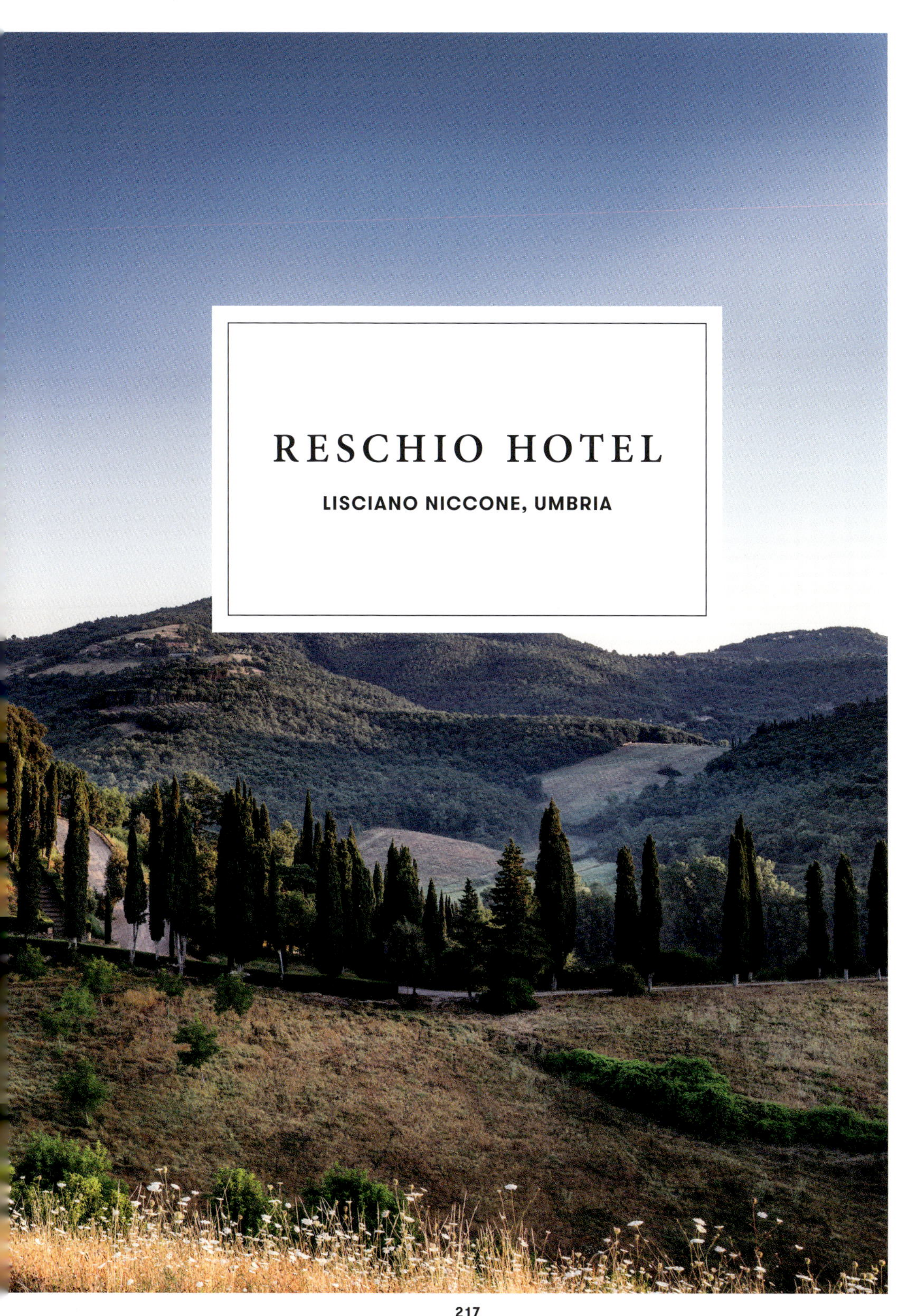

RESCHIO HOTEL

LISCIANO NICCONE, UMBRIA

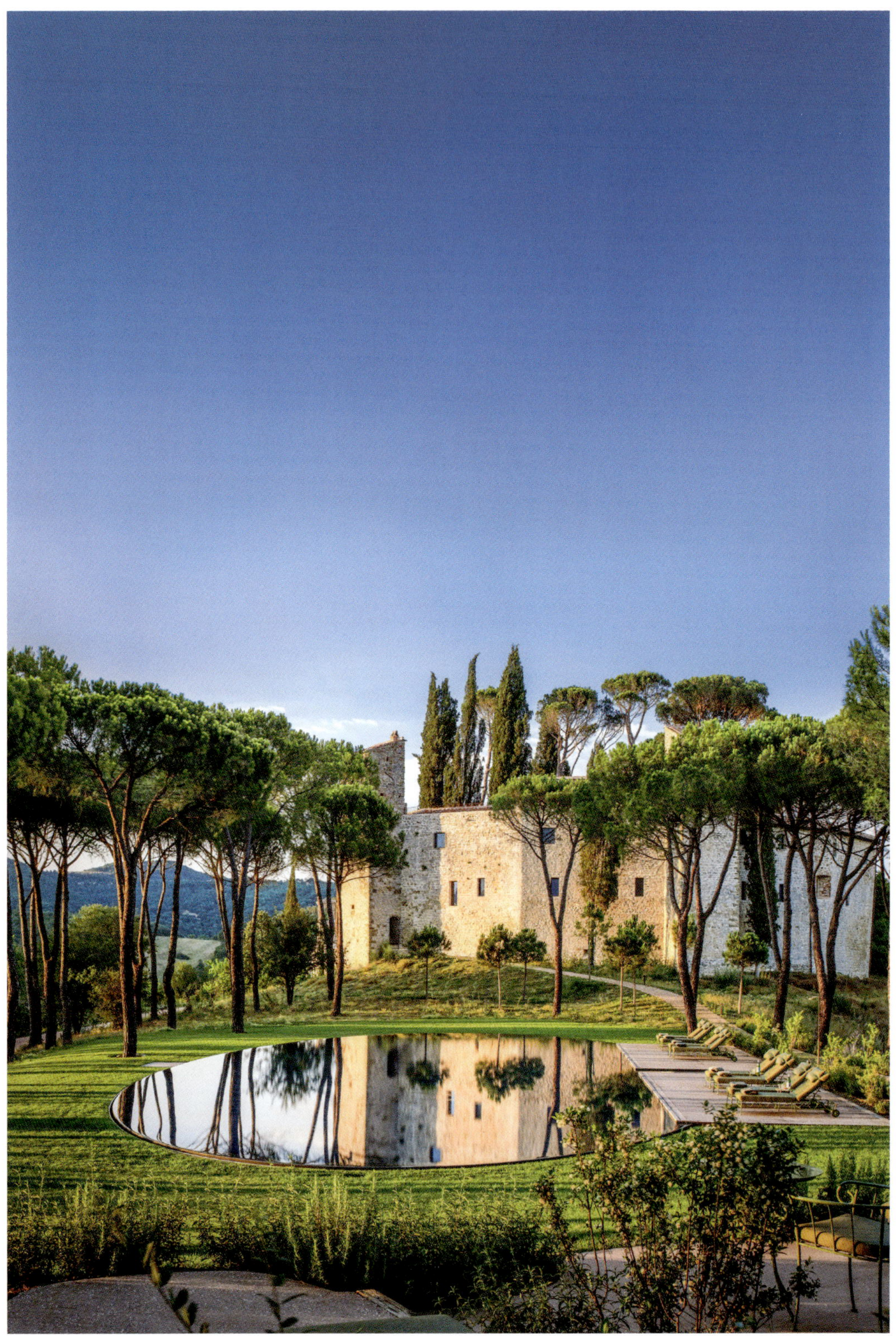

UMBRIA

RESCHIO HOTEL

Tabaccaia di Reschio, 06060 Lisciano Niccone, Perugia
Tel. +39 075 844 362 · reservations@reschio.com
www.reschio.com

MY HOME IS MY CASTLE When Count Antonio Bolza bought this estate in Umbria in the mid-1990s, it consisted of 4,000 acres of wilderness, 50 abandoned rustic houses and a castle about 1,000 years old with a roof so leaky that you got almost as wet inside as outside when it rained. However, since then the family has devoted a lot of money and even more passion to renovating it, and turned Reschio into one of the most adorable country hotels in Italy. Antonio's son Benedikt, who studied architecture in London, and his wife Nencia, a talented fresco painter, personally attended to every detail of the design. They created an exotic palm court with a fin-de-siècle atmosphere, complete with bar and piano, and they installed a five-story suite with a roof terrace in the castle tower. They also converted two dovecotes into romantic retreats and the old wine cellar into a bathhouse. Every item of furniture and accessory in the luxurious rooms is hand-picked, and either tells a story or lends a modern touch. Where the ramparts once stood, there is now a restaurant with a view, and the outdoor pool glitters against the backdrop of the mighty castle walls. By the way, Reschio is especially popular with equestrians: Antonio, who was a great fan of the Spanish Riding School in Vienna even as a child, has established one of the leading stud farms in the country here, where he breeds and trains horses and runs a riding school. ◆ Book to pack: "My Poems Won't Change the World" by Patrizia Cavalli.

MY HOME IS MY CASTLE Als Graf Antonio Bolza dieses Anwesen in Umbrien Mitte der 1990er kaufte, bestand es aus 1500 Hektar überwuchertem Land, 50 verlassenen Bauernhäusern und einem etwa tausend Jahre alten Schloss mit derart undichtem Dach, dass man bei Regen drinnen beinahe so nass wurde wie draußen. Doch inzwischen hat die Familie viel Geld und noch mehr Herzblut in die Sanierung gesteckt und Reschio zu einem der schönsten Landhotels Italiens gemacht. Antonios Sohn Benedikt, der in London Architektur studierte, und dessen Frau Nencia, eine talentierte Freskenmalerin, kümmerten sich persönlich um jedes Designdetail. So schufen sie einen exotischen Palmenhof mit Fin-de-Siècle-Atmosphäre samt Bar und Piano, richteten im Schlossturm eine fünfstöckige Suite mit Dachterrasse ein und verwandelten zwei ehemalige Taubenhäuser in romantische Refugien sowie den alten Weinkeller in ein Badehaus. In den luxuriösen Zimmern ist jedes Möbelstück oder Accessoire handverlesen und erzählt entweder eine Geschichte oder sorgt für einen modernen Touch. Wo sich einst die Burgwälle entlangzogen, liegt jetzt ein Restaurant mit Aussicht, und vor den mächtigen Schlossmauern schimmert der Außenpool. Besonders beliebt ist Reschio übrigens bei Reitern: Antonio, der schon als Kind von der Spanischen Hofreitschule begeistert war, hat hier eines der renommiertesten Gestüte des Landes aufgebaut, züchtet und dressiert Pferde und führt eine Reitschule. ◆ Buchtipp: „Diese schönen Tage“ von Patrizia Cavalli.

MY HOME IS MY CASTLE Lorsque le comte Antonio Bolza a acheté ce domaine en Ombrie au milieu des années 1990, il s'est trouvé face à 1 500 hectares de terrain envahis par la végétation, 50 fermes abandonnées et un château millénaire dont le toit fuyait tellement qu'on était presque aussi mouillé à l'intérieur qu'à l'extérieur lorsqu'il pleuvait. La famille a investi beaucoup d'argent et encore plus de cœur dans la rénovation, faisant de Reschio l'un des plus beaux hôtels de campagne d'Italie. Le fils d'Antonio, Benedikt, qui a étudié l'architecture à Londres, et sa femme Nencia, une fresquiste de grand talent, se sont personnellement occupés de chaque détail du design. Ils ont ainsi créé une cour exotique de palmiers à l'atmosphère fin-de-siècle avec bar et piano, aménagé dans la tour du château une suite de cinq étages avec terrasse sur le toit et transformé deux anciens pigeonniers en refuges romantiques ; l'ancienne cave à vin est devenue un spa. Dans les chambres luxueuses, chaque meuble et accessoire est soigneusement choisi et raconte une histoire ou apporte une touche de modernité. Là où se dressaient autrefois les remparts du château se trouve désormais un restaurant avec vue, et la piscine extérieure scintille au pied des murailles imposantes. Reschio est particulièrement apprécié des cavaliers : Antonio, déjà passionné par l'École espagnole d'équitation quand il était enfant, a créé ici l'un des haras les plus réputés du pays ; il élève et dresse des chevaux et dirige une école d'équitation. ◆ À lire : « Toujours ouvert théâtre » de Patrizia Cavalli.

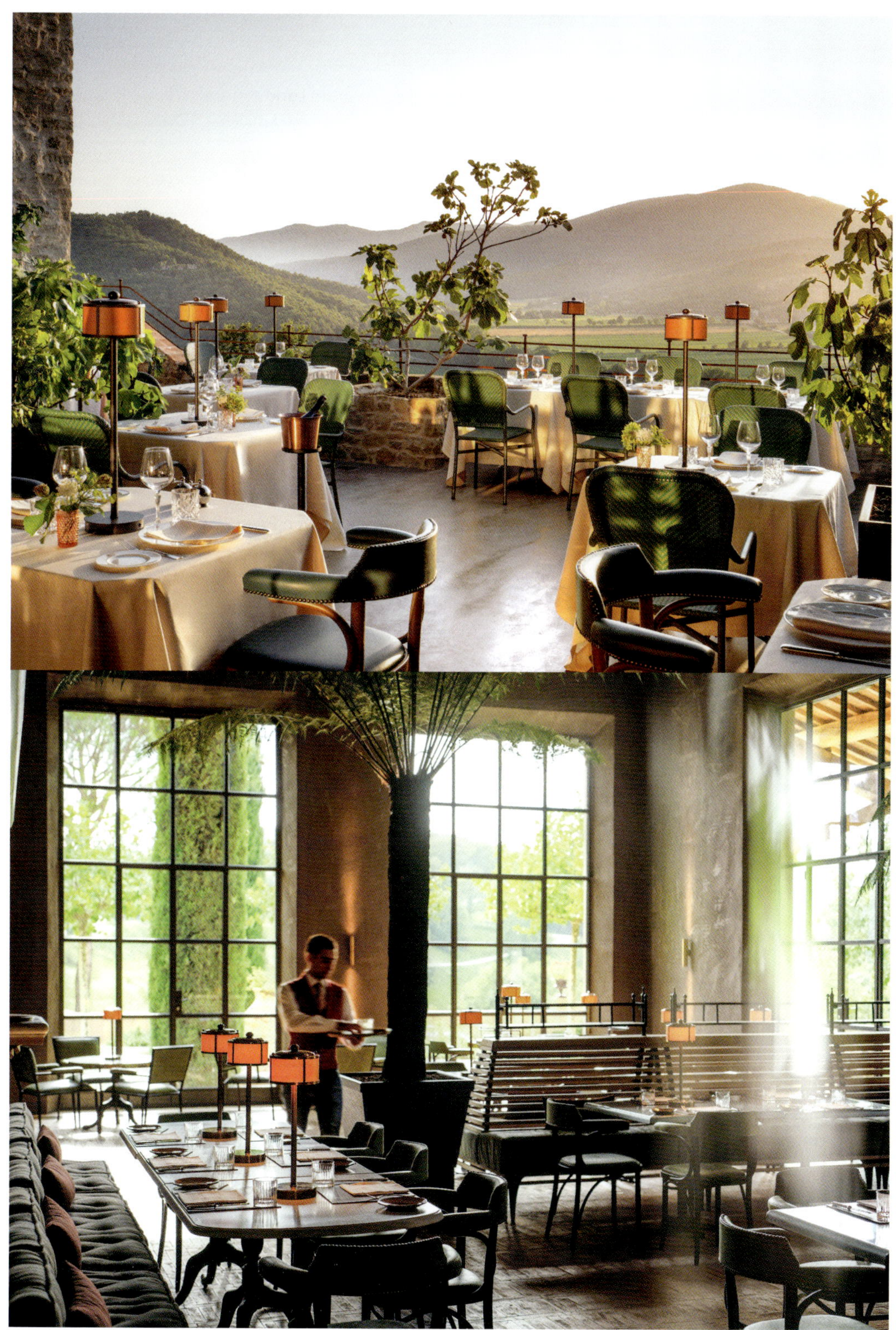

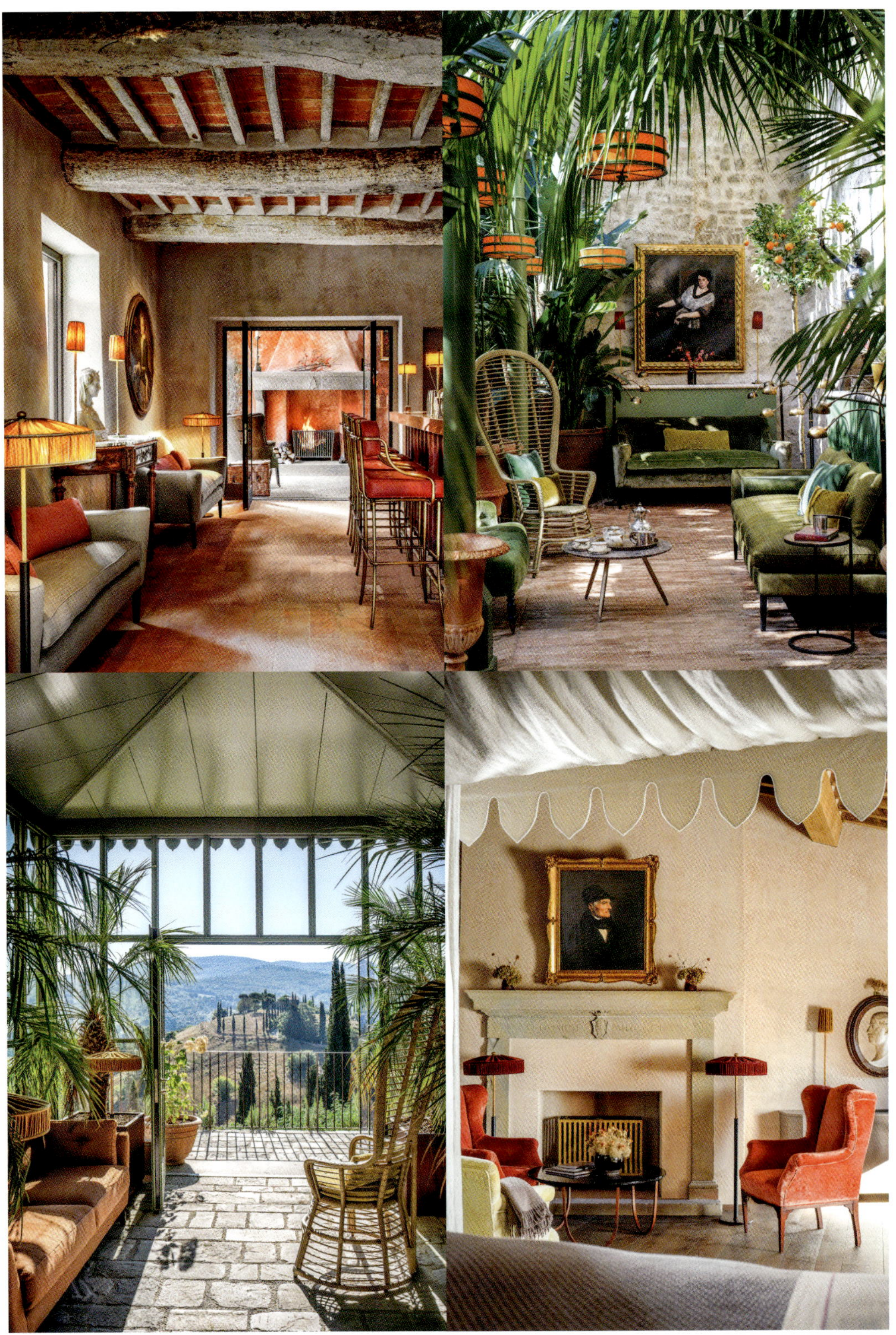

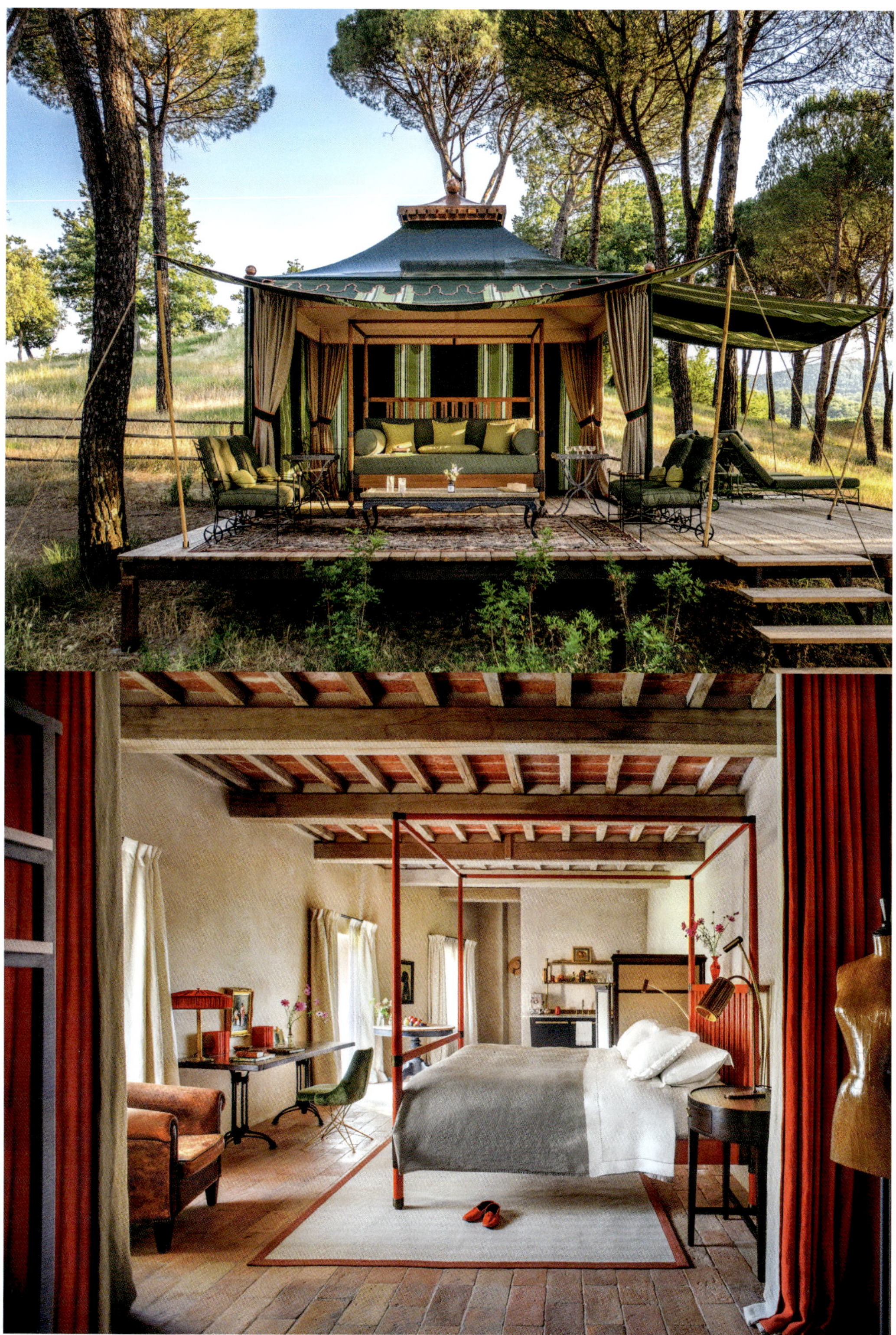

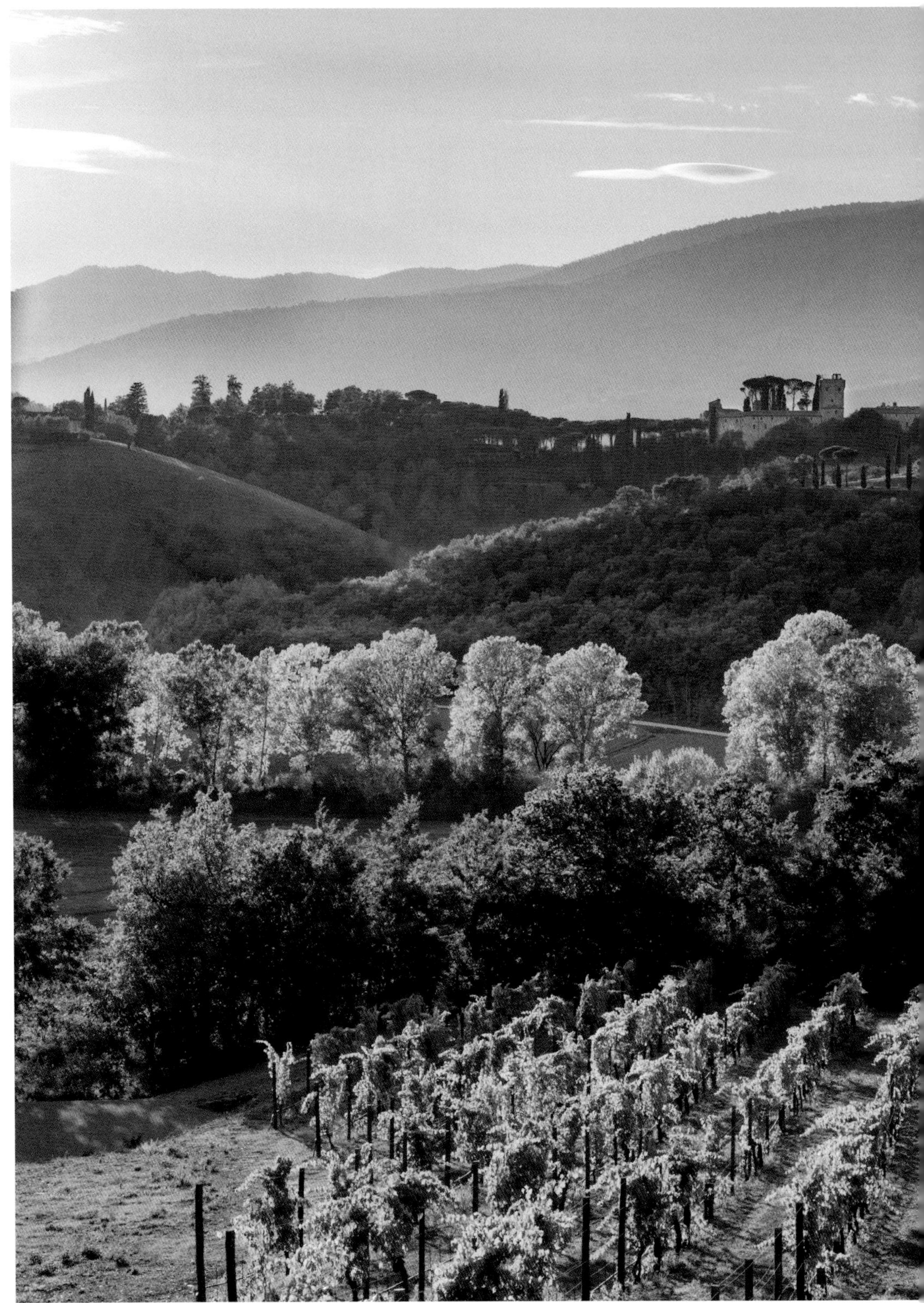

UMBRIA

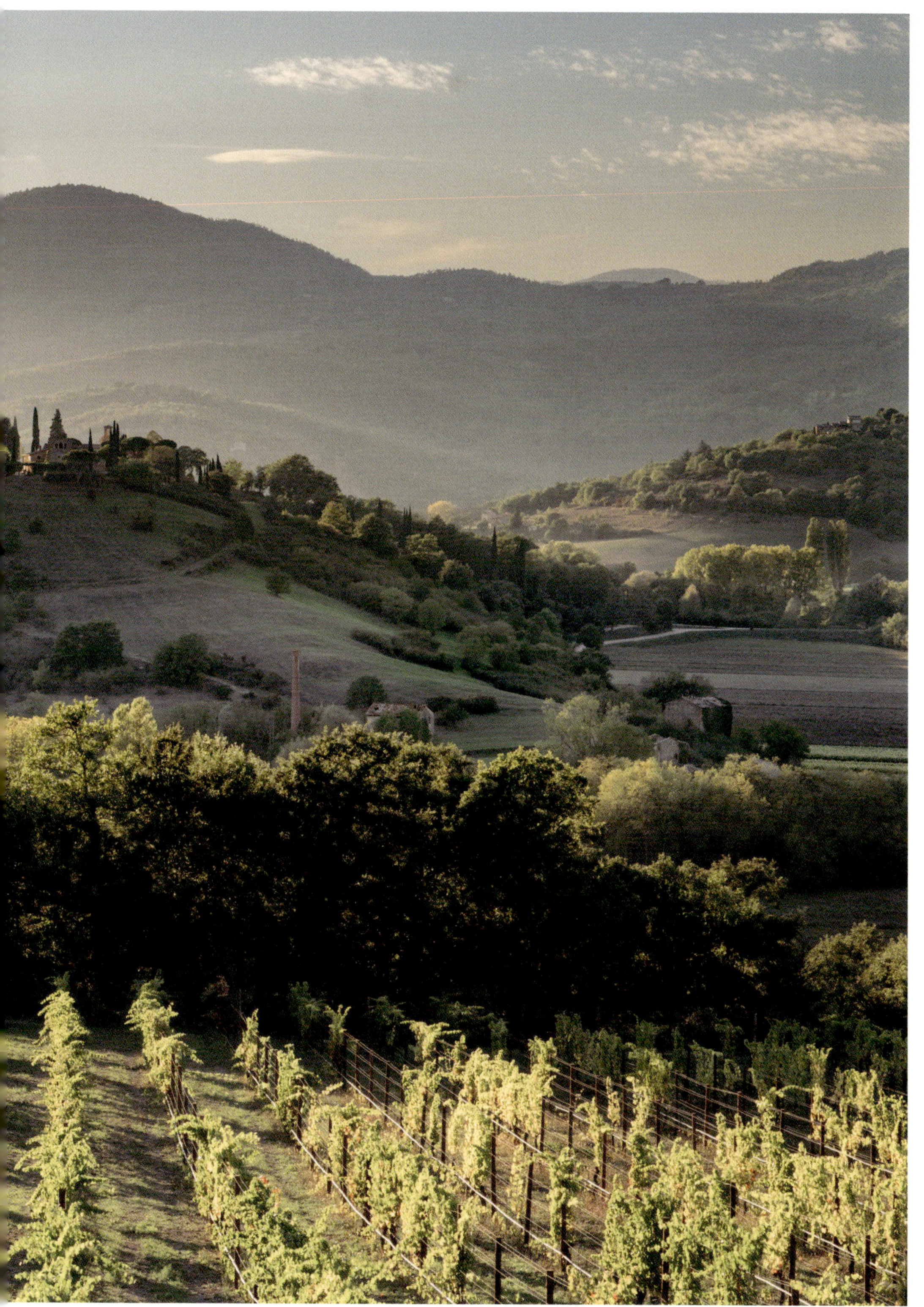

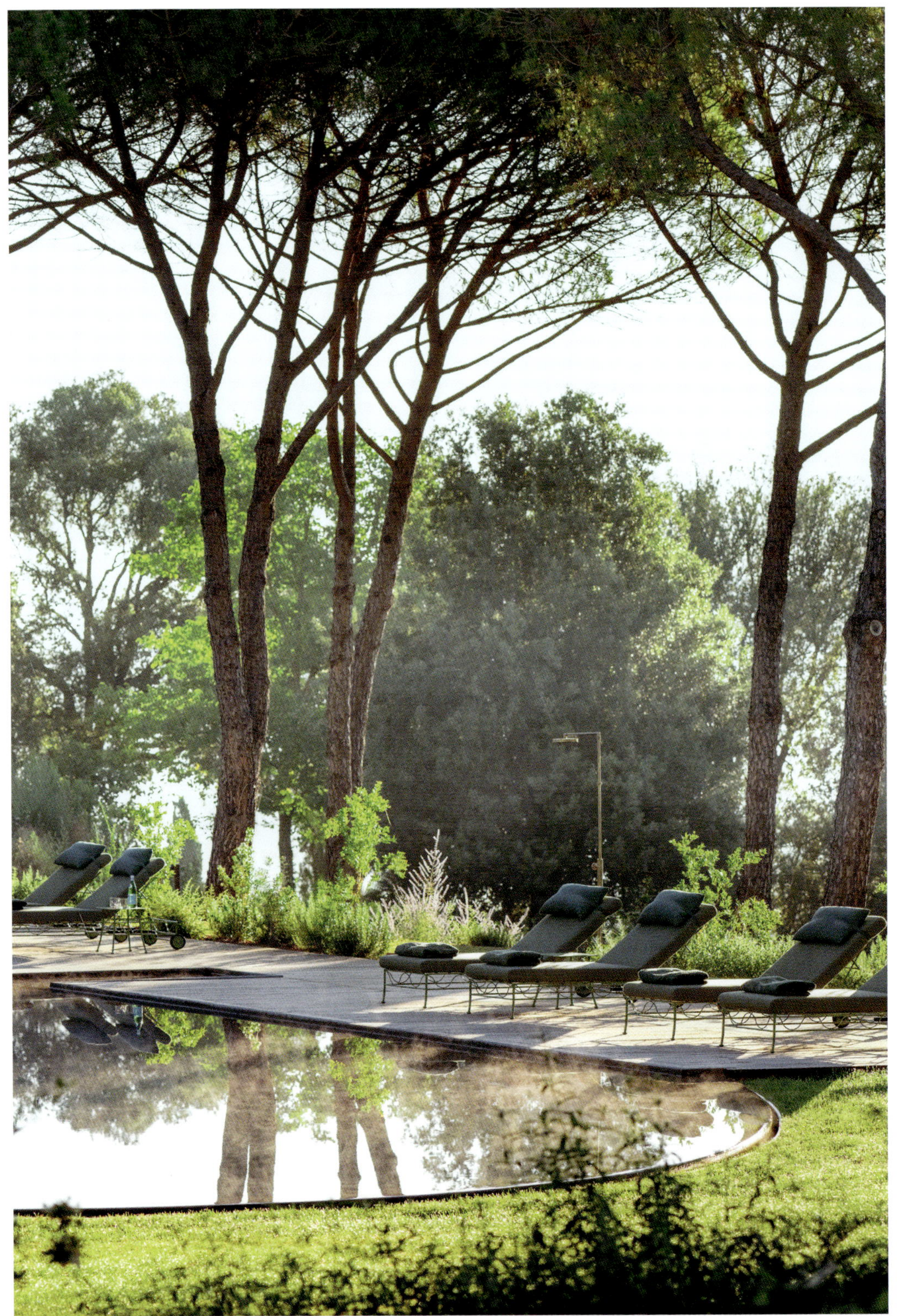

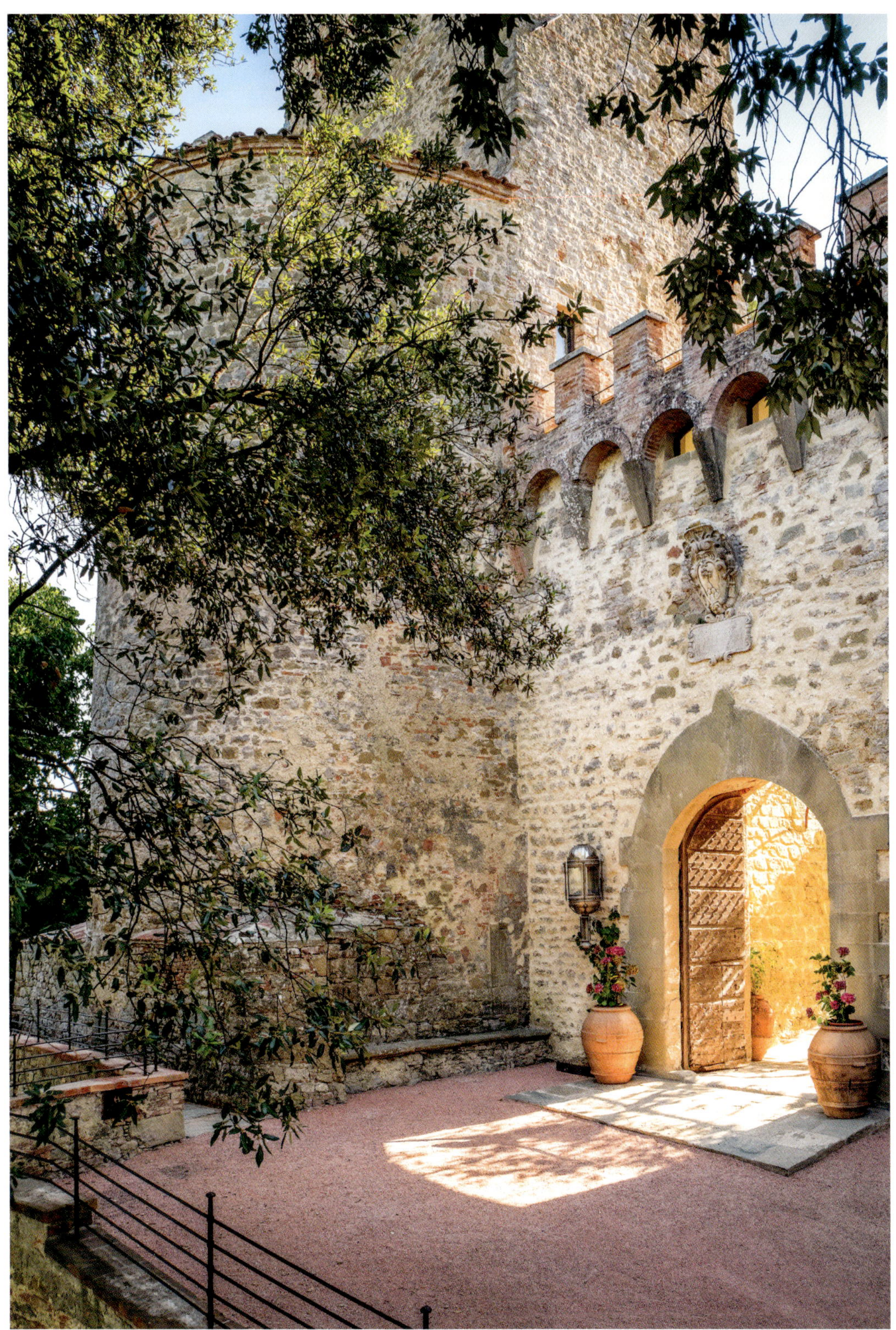

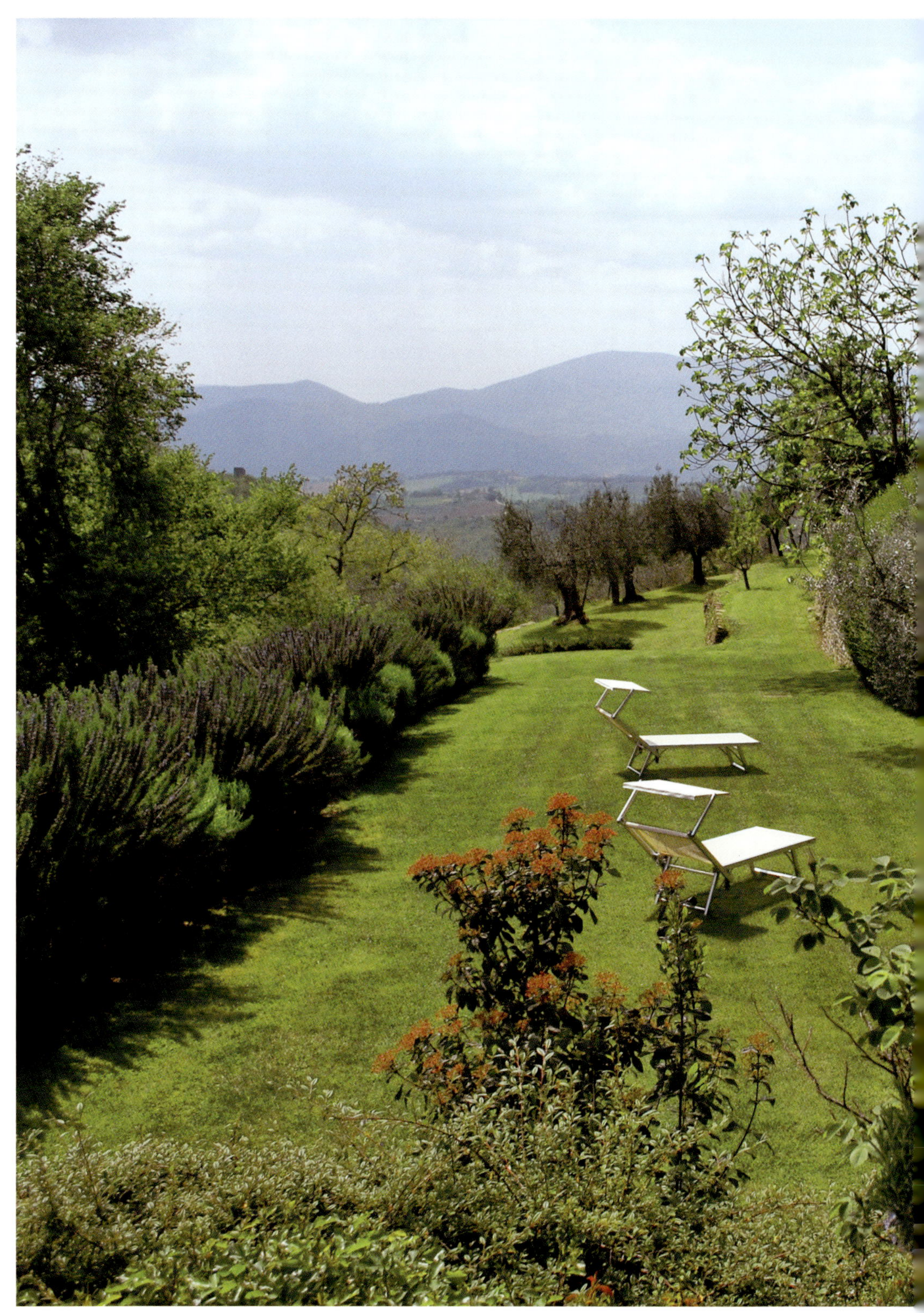

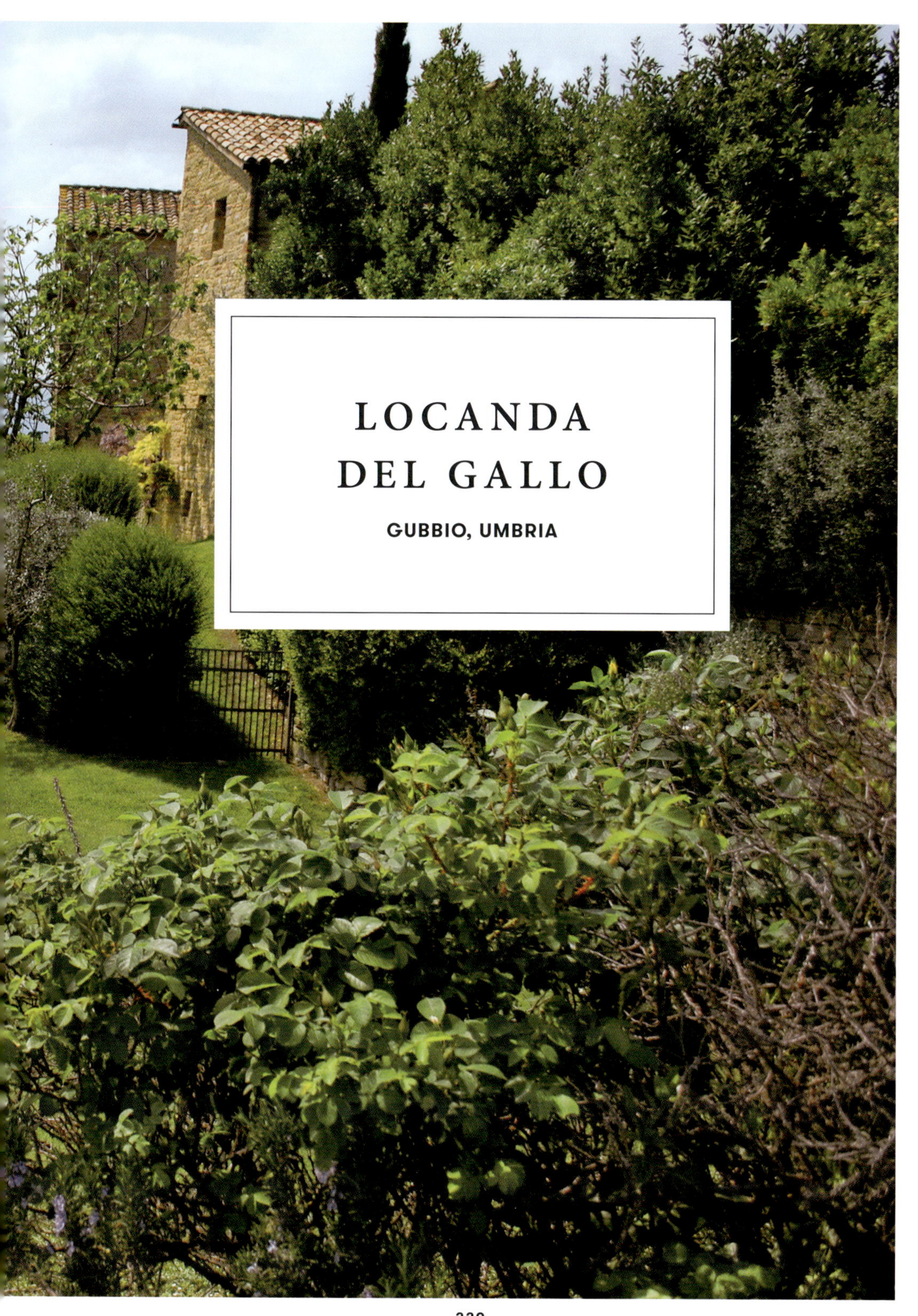

LOCANDA DEL GALLO

GUBBIO, UMBRIA

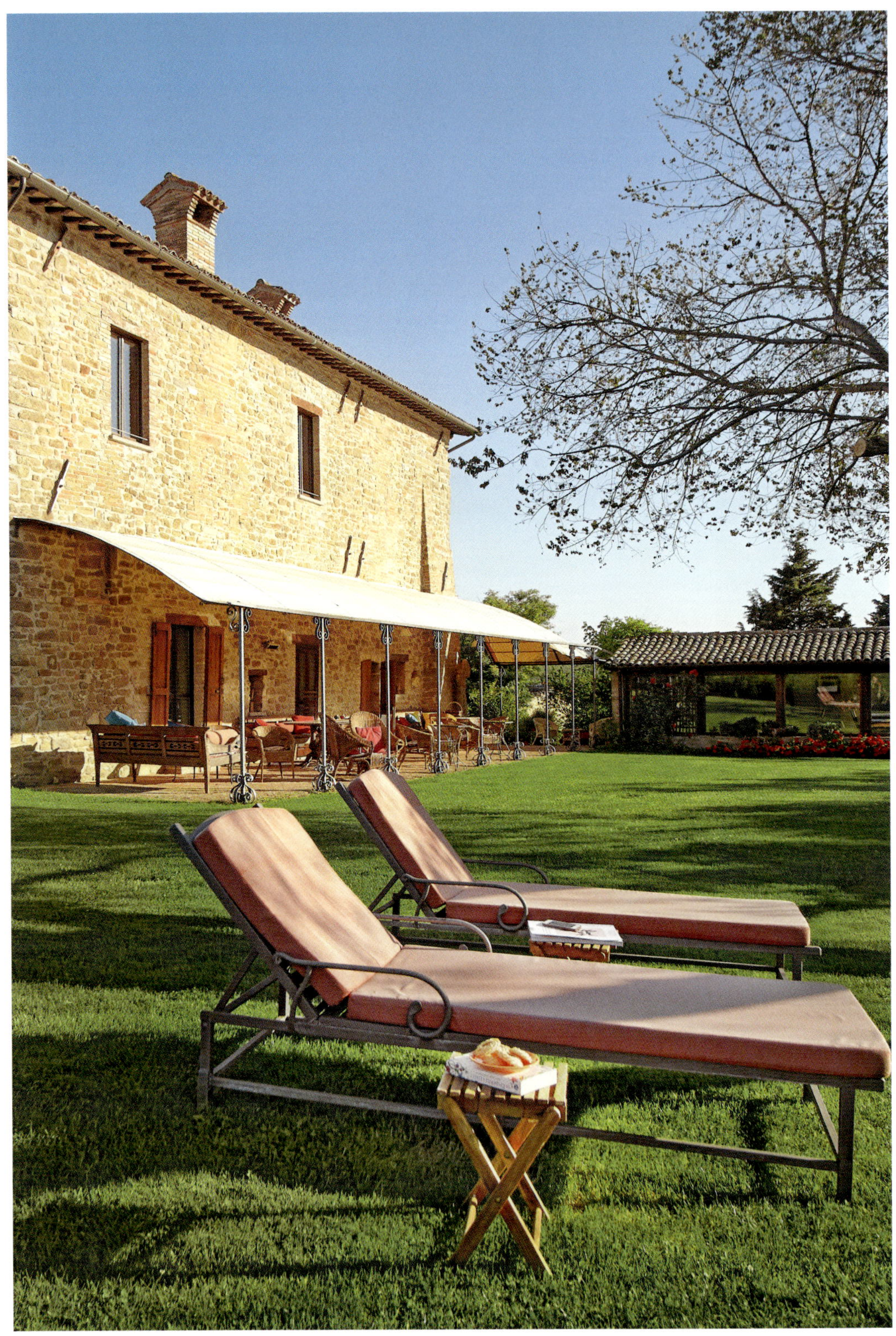

LOCANDA DEL GALLO

Località Santa Cristina, 06020 Gubbio
Tel. +39 075 922 9912 · info@locandadelgallo.it
www.locandadelgallo.it

LOVE AT SECOND SIGHT No, Umbria is not a great beauty, no star in the spotlight. This relatively bleak and thinly populated region in the heart of Italy, the only region in the country that has neither a coast nor a border to a neighbouring country, has always kept a low profile. Pilgrims and conquerors on the way to Rome used simply to pass through, and for many tourists today Umbria is just a place to stop over. However, it is possible to make history even in the shadow of the Eternal City and Tuscany, to be influential even from behind the scenes. To learn that Umbria has produced great men such as the Renaissance painter Raphael, possesses one of Europe's most important places of pilgrimage, in Assisi, and produces exquisite ceramics and wonderfully soft cashmere wool in Deruta and Solomeo comes as a surprise to many travellers – and is a good reason to spend more time here. Locanda del Gallo is a wonderful base for making excursions. Like the landscape itself, it has an unassuming appearance and reveals unexpected details only at a second glance. The simple rooms are equipped with furniture from the Far East that the owners brought back from many journeys, and in the restaurant oriental spices add refinement to the Mediterranean food. Those who like to take a look behind the scenes should ask Paola and Irish for their advice on sightseeing, and complement a trip to the cities of art with a course in weaving or cookery to round off a journey of discovery in Italy. ◆ Book to pack: "Wind Shift" by Andrea De Carlo.

LIEBE AUF DEN ZWEITEN BLICK Nein, eine Schönheit, ein Star im Rampenlicht ist Umbrien nicht. Die vergleichsweise raue und dünn besiedelte Region im Herzen Italiens (übrigens die einzige des Landes, die weder eine Meeresküste noch eine Grenze zum Ausland besitzt) wirkt seit jeher ein bisschen unscheinbar – für Pilger und Eroberer auf dem Weg nach Rom war sie früher nur Durchgangsstation, für viele Touristen ist sie heute lediglich Zwischenstopp. Doch selbst im Schatten der Ewigen Stadt und der Toskana lässt sich Geschichte schreiben, selbst aus der zweiten Reihe lassen sich Fäden ziehen: Dass Umbrien große Söhne wie den Renaissance-Meister Raffael hervorgebracht hat, mit Assisi eine der wichtigsten Wallfahrtsstätten Europas besitzt, in Deruta und Solomeo die edelste Keramikware und die weichste Kaschmirwolle produziert werden, ist für so manchen Reisenden eine Überraschung – und Grund, sich hier mehr Zeit zu nehmen. Ein wunderbarer Ausgangspunkt für Ausflüge ist die Locanda del Gallo, die sich ganz wie das Land zunächst unaufgeregt zeigt und erst auf den zweiten Blick unerwartete Details freigibt. So stehen in den schlichten Zimmern Möbelstücke aus dem Fernen Osten, welche die Besitzer von zahlreichen Reisen mitgebracht haben, und im Restaurant werden mediterrane Menüs mit orientalischen Gewürzen verfeinert. Wer am Blick hinter die Kulissen Gefallen findet, sollte sich von Paola und Irish auch beim Sightseeing beraten lassen und neben den Kunststädten einen Weberei- oder Kochkurs aufs Programm setzen, der die italienische Entdeckungsreise komplett macht. ◆ Buchtipp: „Wenn der Wind dreht“ von Andrea De Carlo.

LE SECOND REGARD Non, l’Ombrie n’est pas une beauté, une star sous le feu des projecteurs. Rude et peu habitée, cette région située au cœur de la péninsule italienne – elle est la seule à ne pas être baignée par la mer et à ne pas avoir de frontière avec un autre pays – a toujours semblé plutôt insignifiante. Autrefois, les pèlerins et les conquérants en route vers Rome n’y restaient que le temps d’une brève station, de nombreux touristes aujourd’hui se contentent d’y faire étape. Pourtant, la Ville éternelle et la Toscane n’ont pas la prérogative de l’Histoire – il ne fallait pas être aux premières loges pour tirer les ficelles – et bien des voyageurs sont surpris d’apprendre que Raphaël, maître de la Renaissance, était un enfant du pays, qu’Assise, un des lieux de pèlerinage majeurs en Europe, est située en Ombrie, que la céramique la plus fine et le cachemire le plus soyeux sont produits à Deruta et Solomeo – raison de plus pour prendre son temps ici. Un merveilleux point de départ pour apprendre à connaître la région est la Locanda del Gallo qui, à l’instar du paysage, semble discrète et ne montre qu’au second coup d’œil des détails inattendus. Ainsi, les chambres sobres abritent des meubles originaires d’Extrême-Orient que les propriétaires ont rapportés de leurs nombreux voyages et, au restaurant, la cuisine méditerranéenne est enrichie d’épices orientales. Celui qui s’intéresse à l’envers du décor devrait chercher conseil auprès de Paola et Irish et mettre au programme, à côté de la visite des villes d’art, un cours de tissage ou de cuisine qui complète la découverte de l’Italie. ◆ À lire : « Week-end à Moulin-Vent » d’Andrea De Carlo.

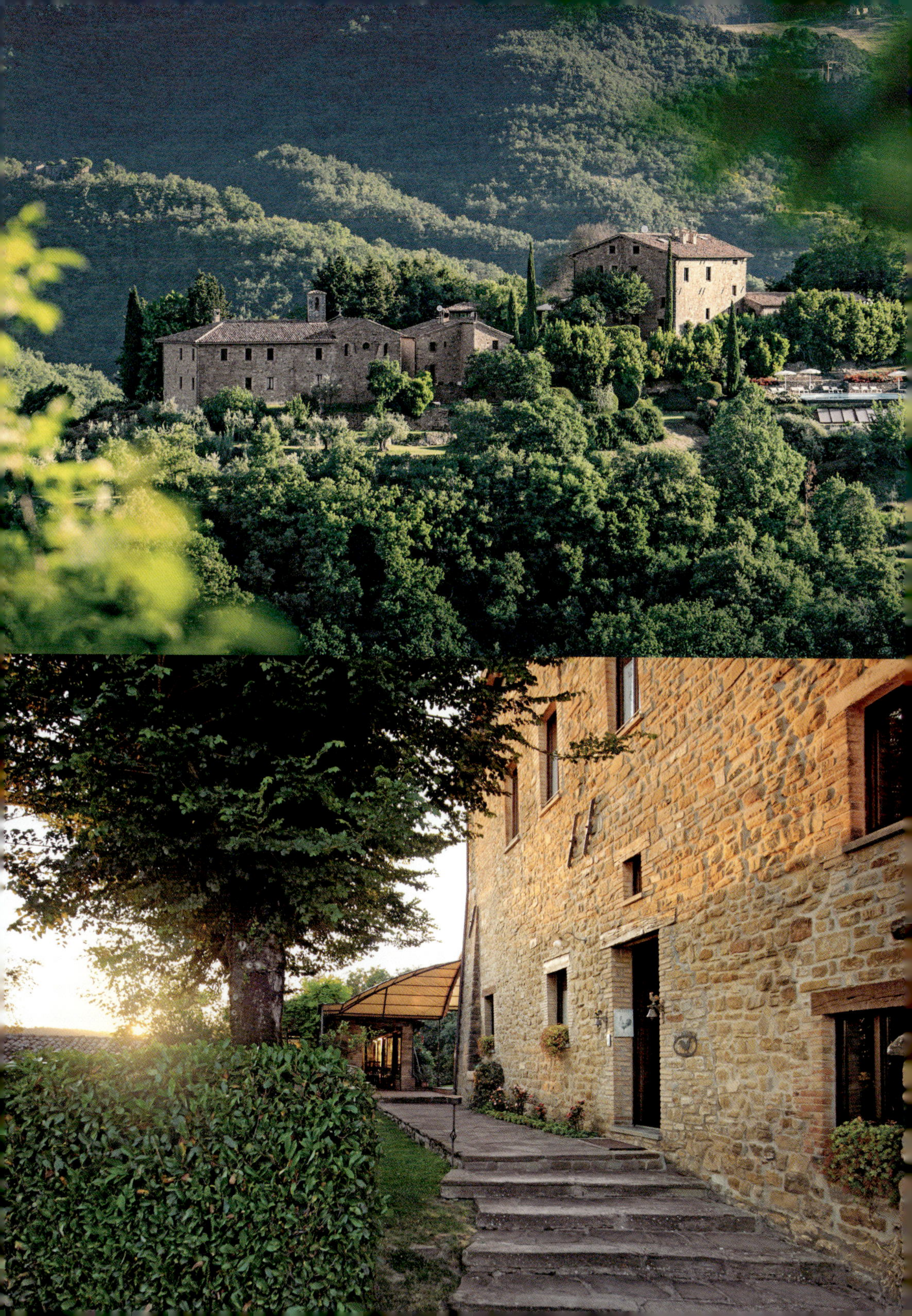

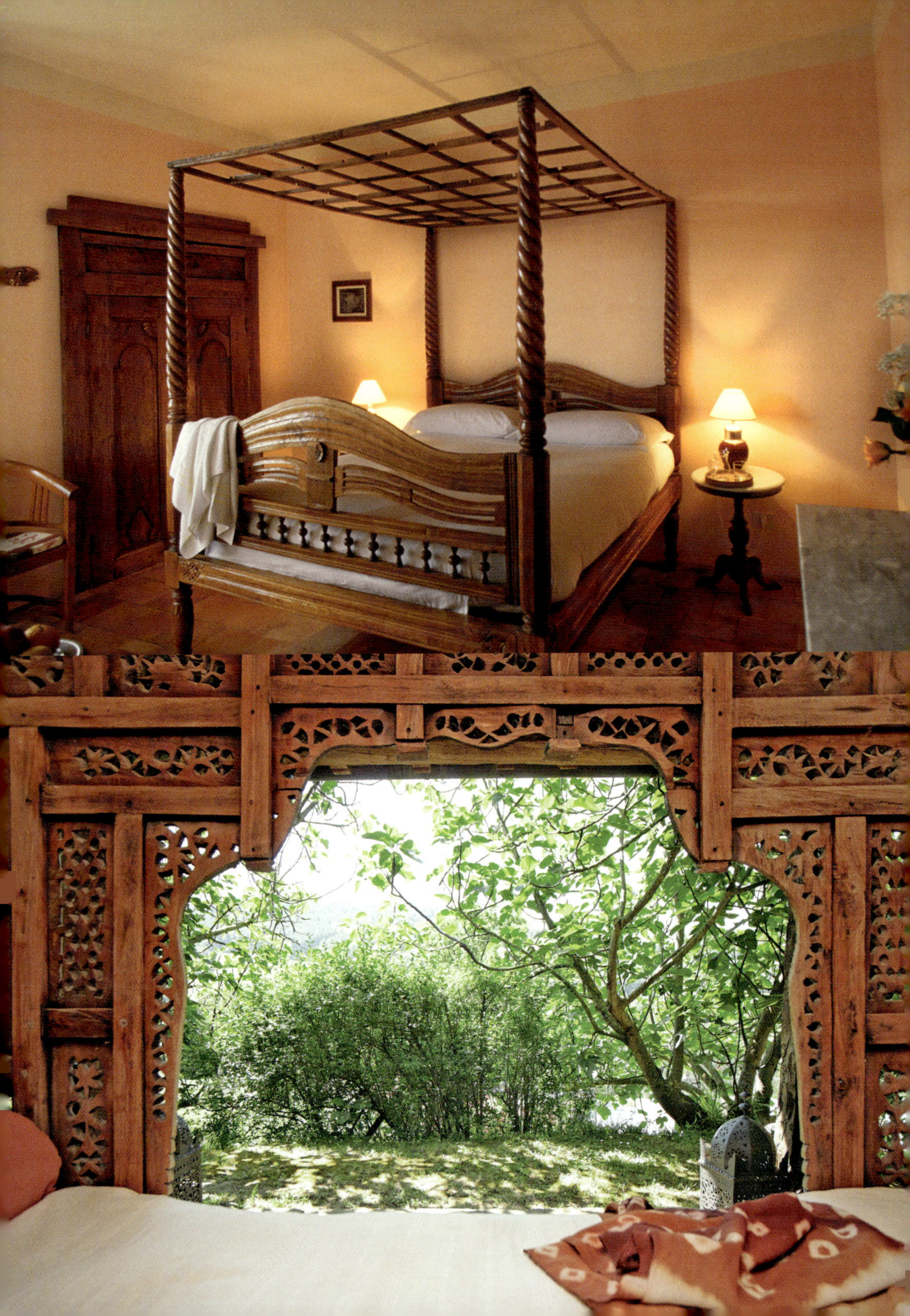

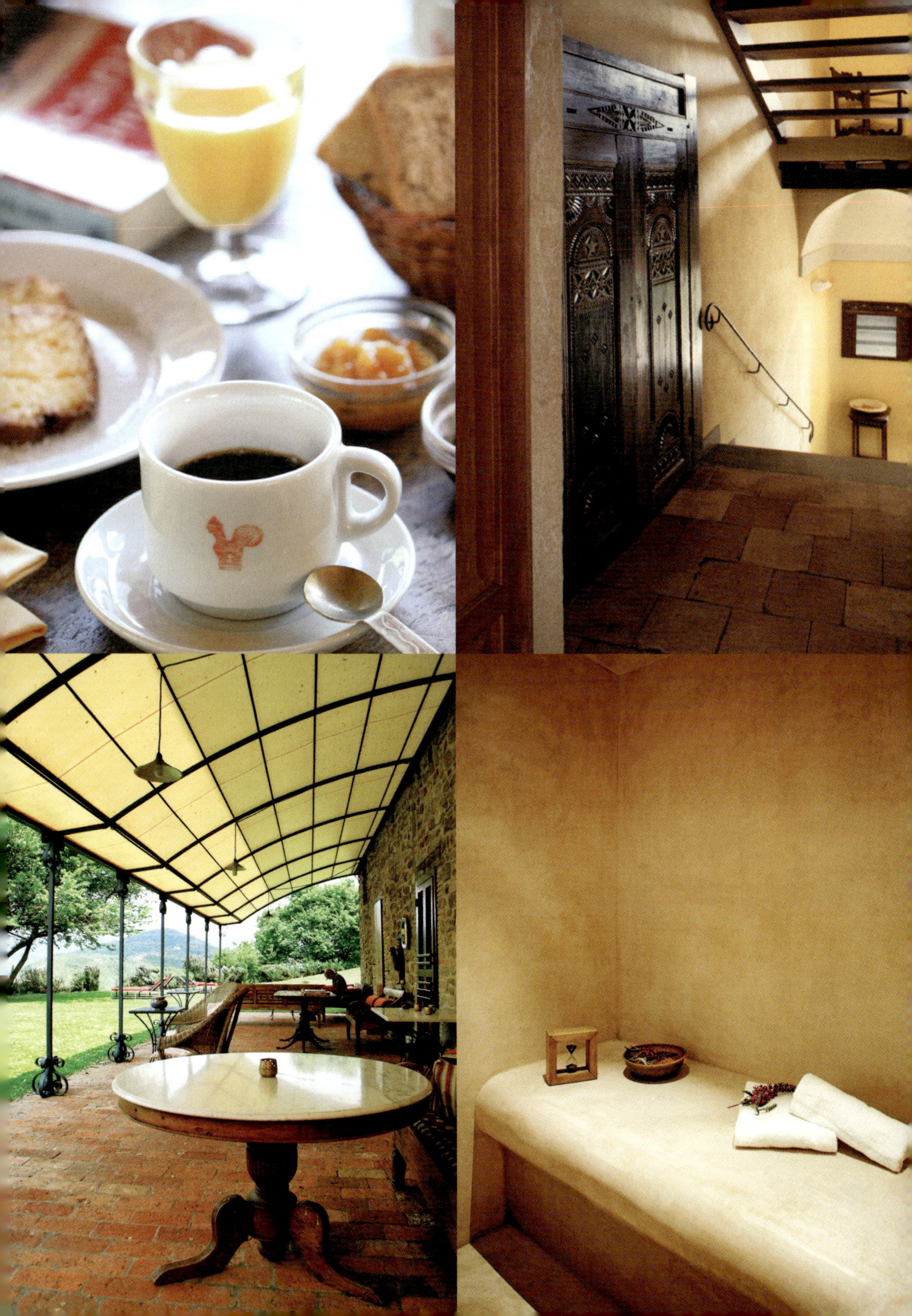

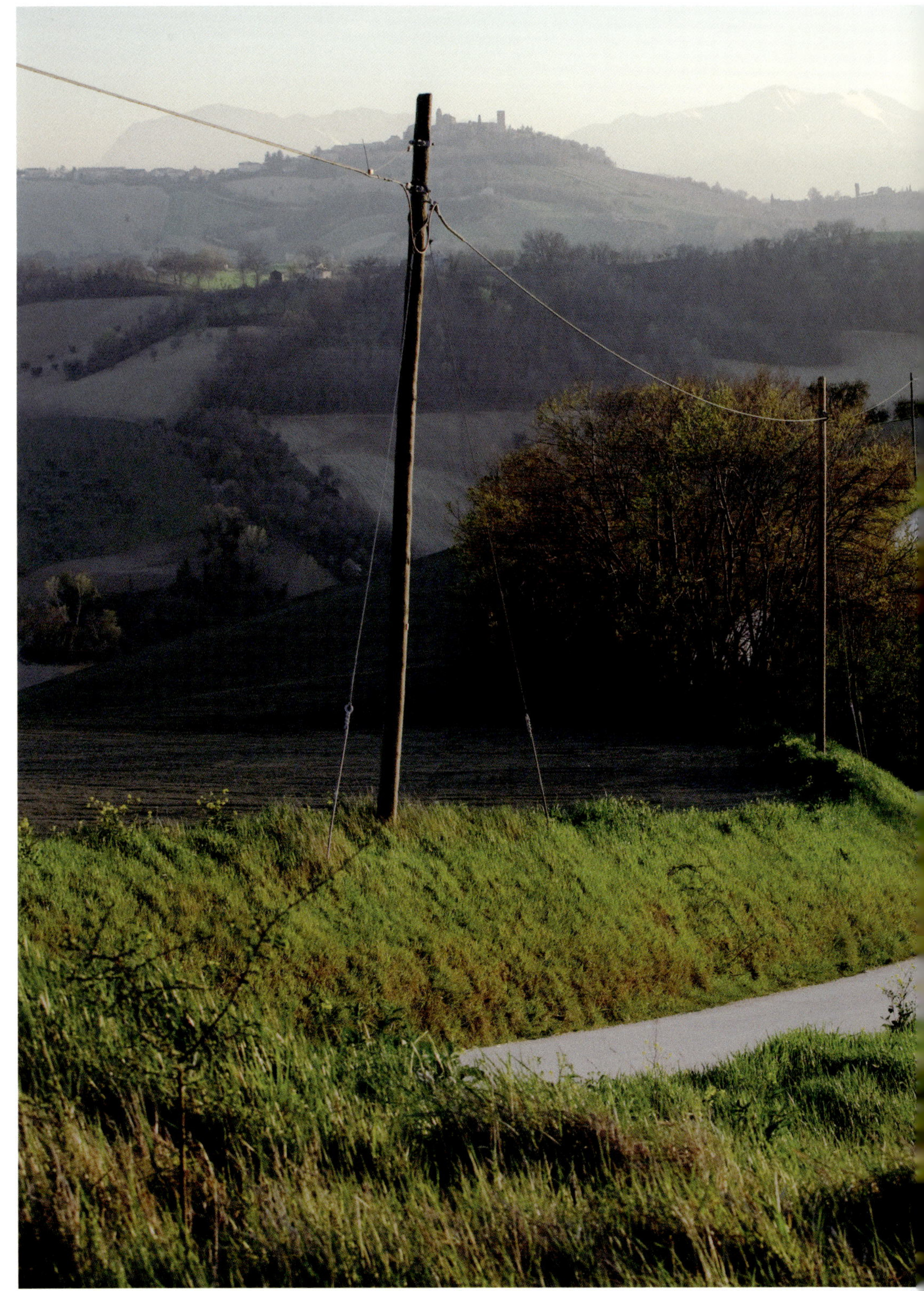

MARCHE

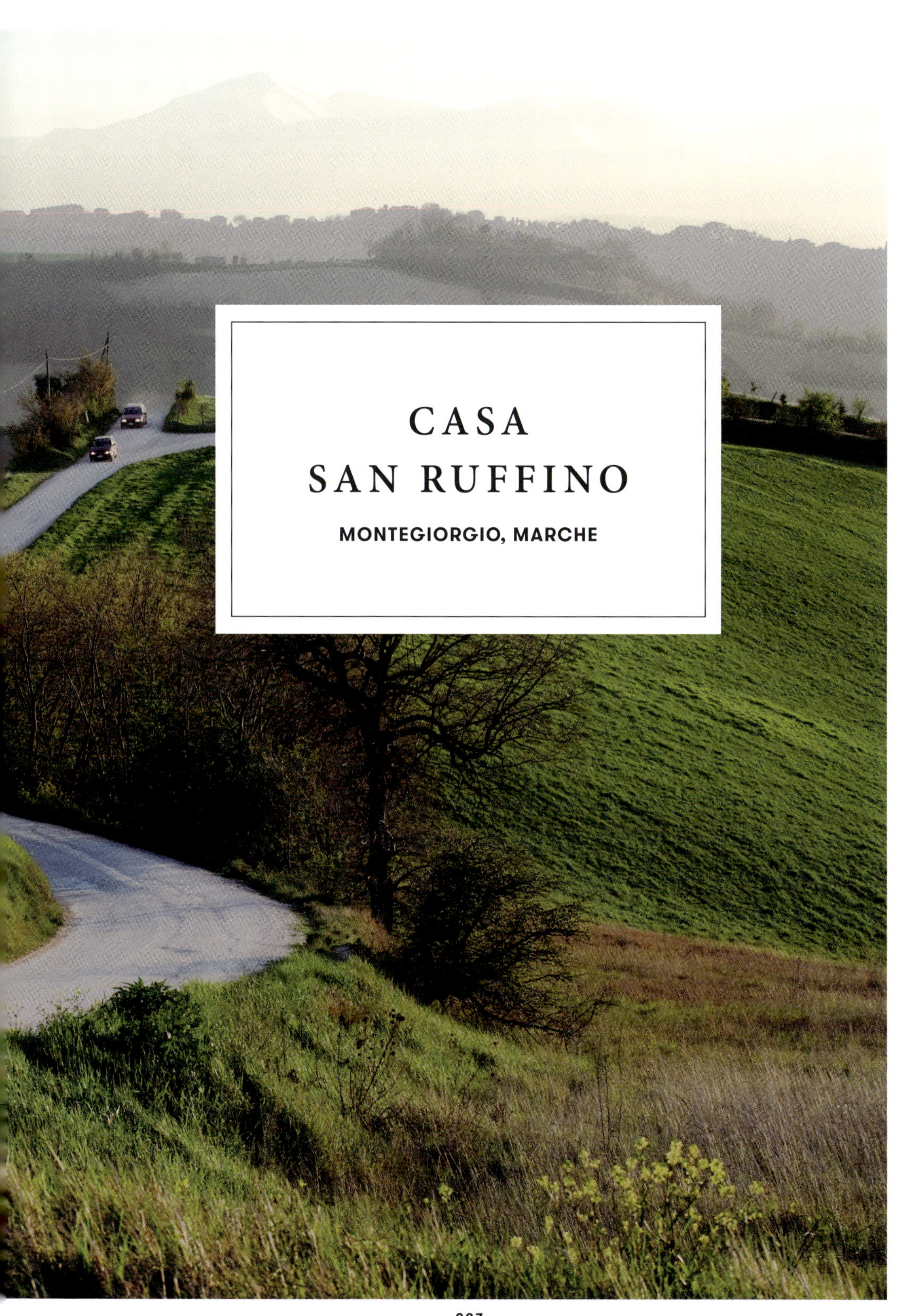

CASA SAN RUFFINO

MONTEGIORGIO, MARCHE

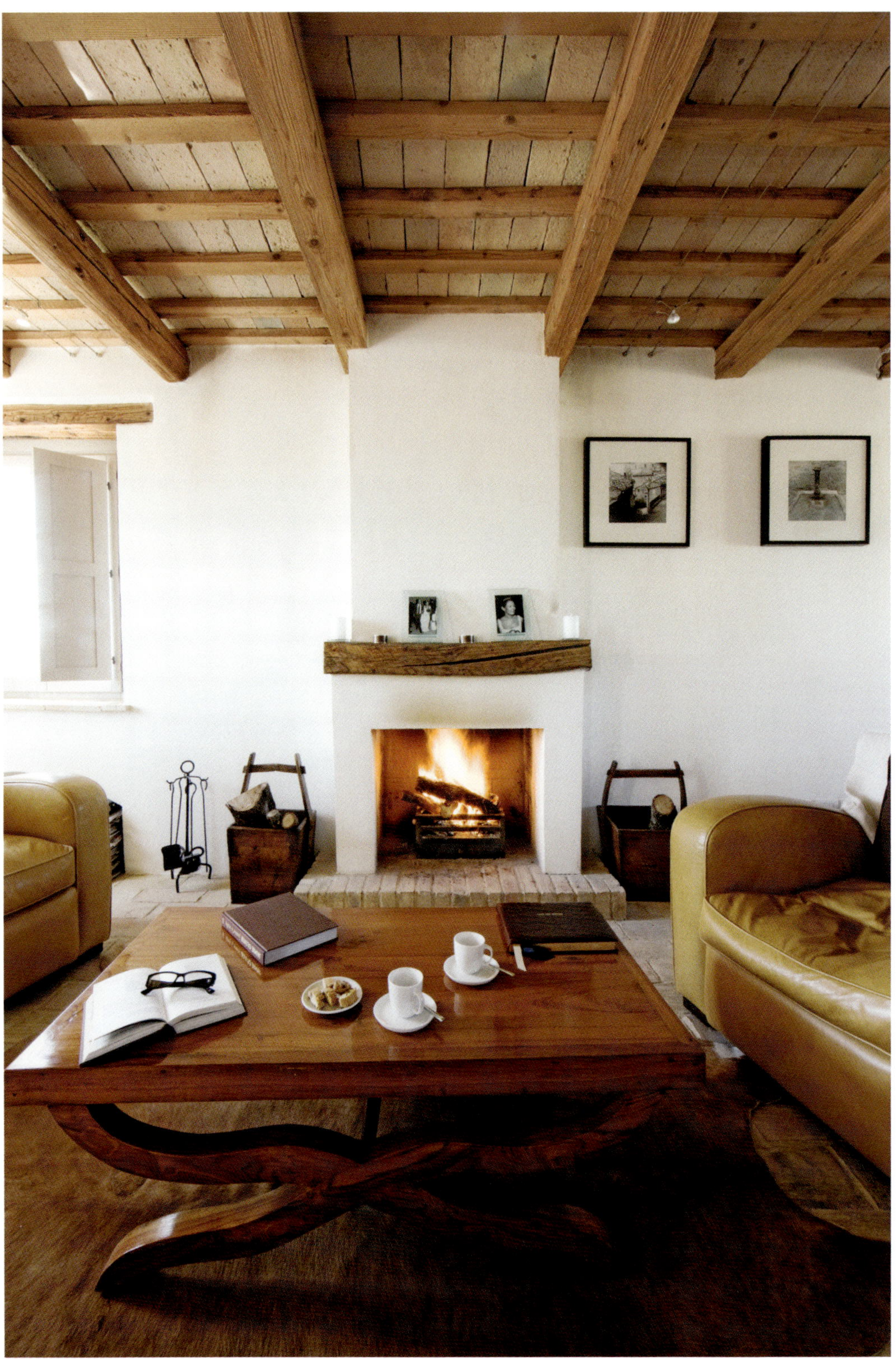

CASA SAN RUFFINO

Contrada Montese 13, 63833 Montegiorgio
Tel. +46 70 201 09 17 · peternordin@me.com
www.casasanruffino.com

IN THE HILLS OF THE MARCHE In one respect the Italians who live in the Marche are wholly un-Italian: they are not proponents of the "dolce far niente", the life of sweet idleness for which their compatriots are renowned. A lazy morning, an extended lunch break or a late dinner is not their way of doing things. They are hardworking and punctual, and were once regarded as the strictest tax-collectors for the papacy. In the rest of Italy they still hold on to the saying that it is better to have a corpse in your bed than a Marchigiano at the door. Perhaps the locals' passion for financial affairs was the reason why a British couple made Marche their home and transformed an abandoned farm into a highly atmospheric B&B. Since 2017 the property has belonged to Peter and Carina Nordini – two award-winning Swedish restaurateurs who moved south after 35 years in Stockholm. The five rooms with old ceiling beams are furnished with dark wood, bright fabrics, photographic art and some knick-knacks. During the day guests at Casa San Ruffino can discover the Adriatic or the Apennines, the dripstone caves at Frasassi, the harbor of Ancona or the Renaissance architecture of Urbino. The pool and the open fireplace provide relaxation after a day out – because even when staying in the businesslike Marche, you have to practice a little bit of "dolce far niente". ◆ Book to pack: "The Worldwide Machine" by Paolo Volponi.

IN DEN HÜGELN DER MARKEN In einem Punkt sind die Italiener, die in den Marken leben, gänzlich unitalienisch: Sie sind keine Anhänger des Dolcefarniente, des süßen Nichtstuns, für das ihre Landsleute so berühmt sind. Ein vertrödelter Morgen, eine verlängerte Pause oder ein verspätetes Dinner passen nicht in ihr Konzept. Sie sind so fleißig wie pünktlich und galten einst als die strengsten Steuereintreiber des Papstes – noch heute kursiert im übrigen Italien der Spruch, es sei besser, einen Toten im Bett zu haben als einen Marchigiano vor der Tür. Vielleicht war diese Leidenschaft der Einheimischen für finanzielle Angelegenheiten der Grund dafür, dass einst ein britisches Ehepaar die Marken zu seiner Wahlheimat machte und einen verlassenen Bauernhof in ein sehr atmosphärisches Bed & Breakfast verwandelte. Seit Februar 2017 gehört das Haus Peter und Carina Nordini – zwei preisgekrönten schwedischen Gastronomen, die es nach 35 Jahren in Stockholm gen Süden zog. Die fünf Zimmer unter alten Deckenbalken sind mit dunklem Holz, hellen Stoffen, Fotokunst und etwas Nippes eingerichtet. Tagsüber erkunden die Gäste der Casa San Ruffino die Adria oder die Apenninen, die Tropfsteinhöhlen von Frasassi, den Hafen von Ancona oder die Renaissance-Bauten von Urbino. Entspannung nach den Exkursionen bieten Pool und Kamin – denn selbst wenn man sich in den geschäftigen Marken befindet: Ein bisschen Dolcefarniente muss sein. ◆ Buchtipp: „Die Weltmaschine" von Paolo Volponi.

DANS LES COLLINES DES MARCHES Il y a un point sur lequel les habitants des Marches se différencient des autres Italiens : ils ne sont pas fervents du « dolce farniente », cette douce oisiveté qui fait la célébrité de leurs compatriotes. Une matinée passée à musarder, une pause un peu trop longue ou un dîner en retard les contrarient. Aussi travailleurs que ponctuels, ils étaient autrefois considérés comme les plus sévères collecteurs d'impôts du pape – aujourd'hui encore, on entend dire dans les autres régions d'Italie qu'il vaut mieux avoir un mort dans son lit qu'un Marchigiano à sa porte. Mais cette passion des habitants de la région pour la finance est peut-être la raison pour laquelle un couple britannique a fait autrefois des Marches son foyer d'adoption et a transformé une ferme abandonnée en un bed & breakfast plein de charme. Depuis février 2017, la maison appartient à Peter et Carina Nordini – deux gastronomes suédois primés qui se sont installés dans le sud après avoir vécu 35 ans à Stockholm. Les cinq chambres sous les vieilles poutres du plafond abritent des meubles de bois foncé, des tissus clairs, des photos d'art et quelques bibelots. Pendant la journée, les hôtes de la Casa San Ruffino explorent la mer Adriatique ou les Apennins, les grottes de Frasassi, le port d'Ancône ou les constructions Renaissance d'Urbin. Après les excursions, la piscine et un bon feu dans la cheminée invitent à la détente : un peu de farniente, même ici dans les Marches. ◆ À lire : « Le Système d'Anteo Crocioni » de Paolo Volponi.

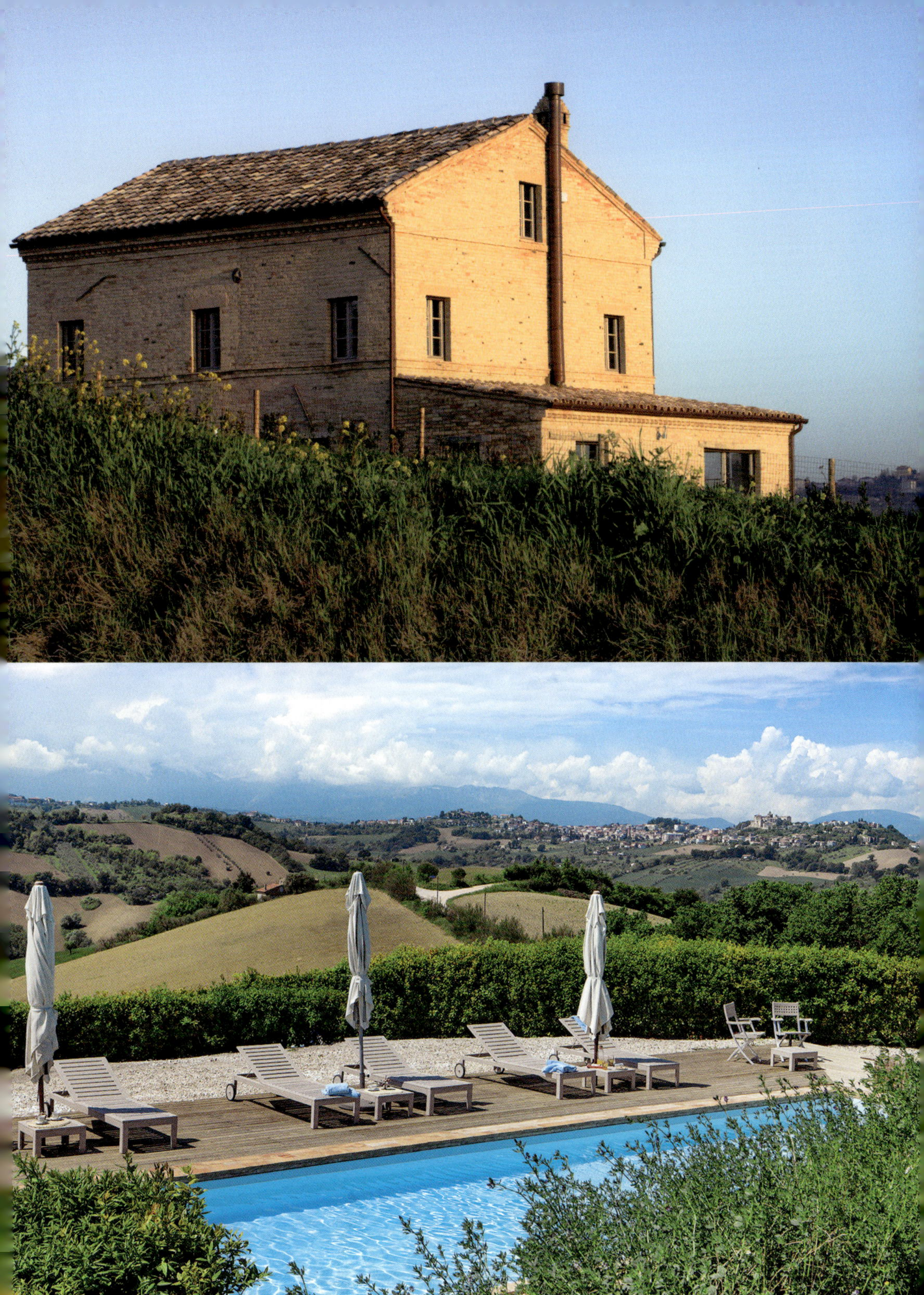

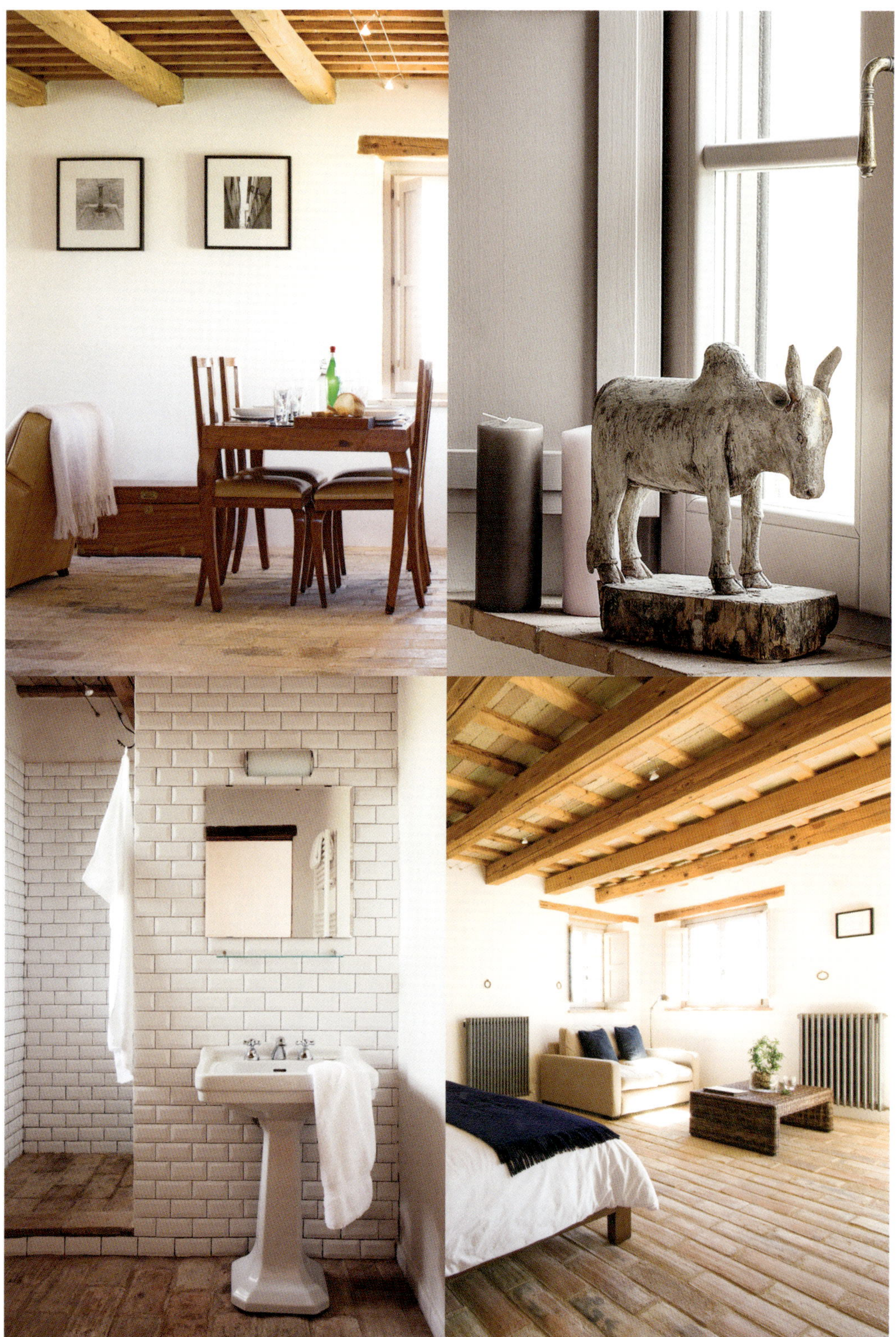

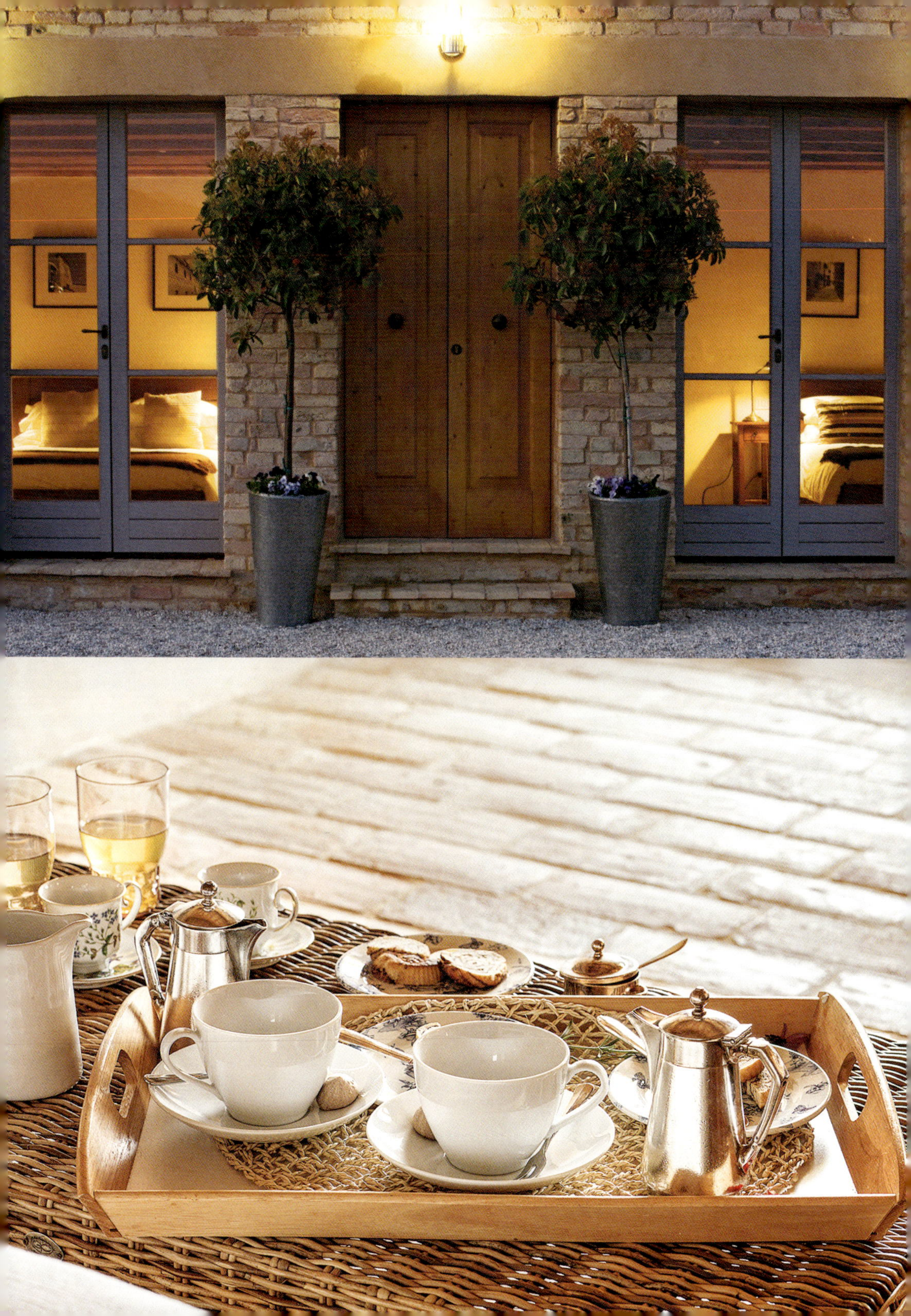

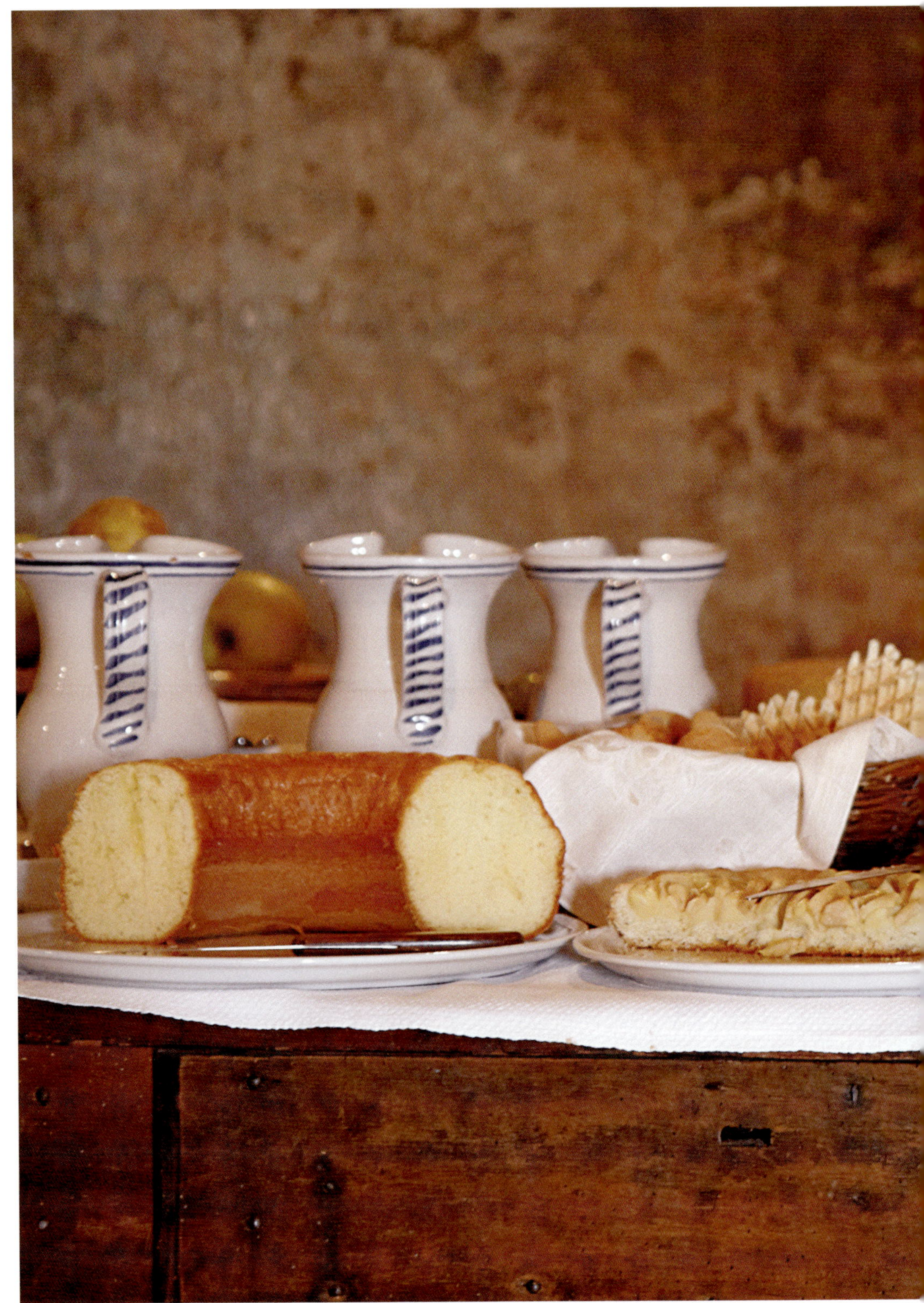

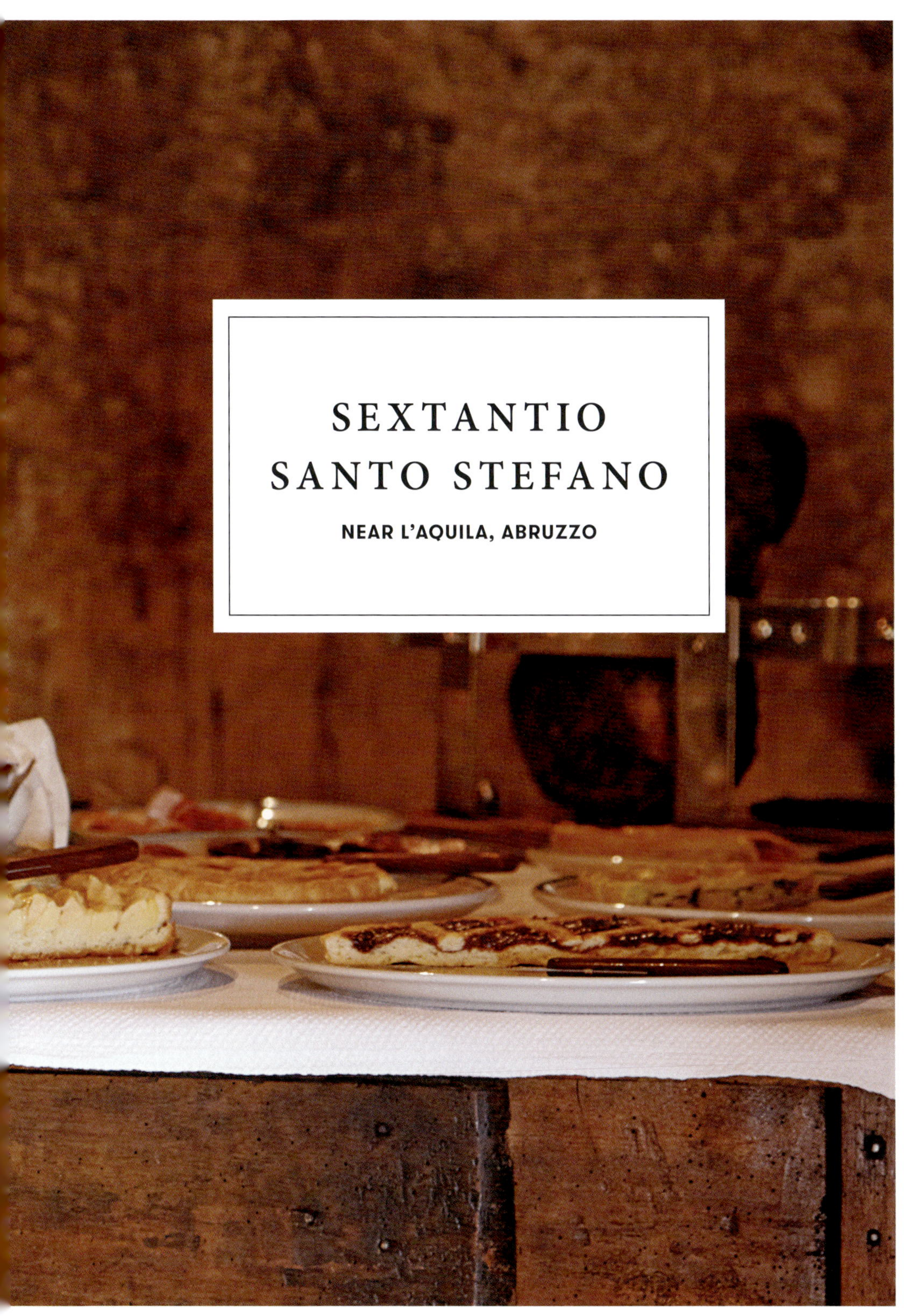

SEXTANTIO SANTO STEFANO

NEAR L'AQUILA, ABRUZZO

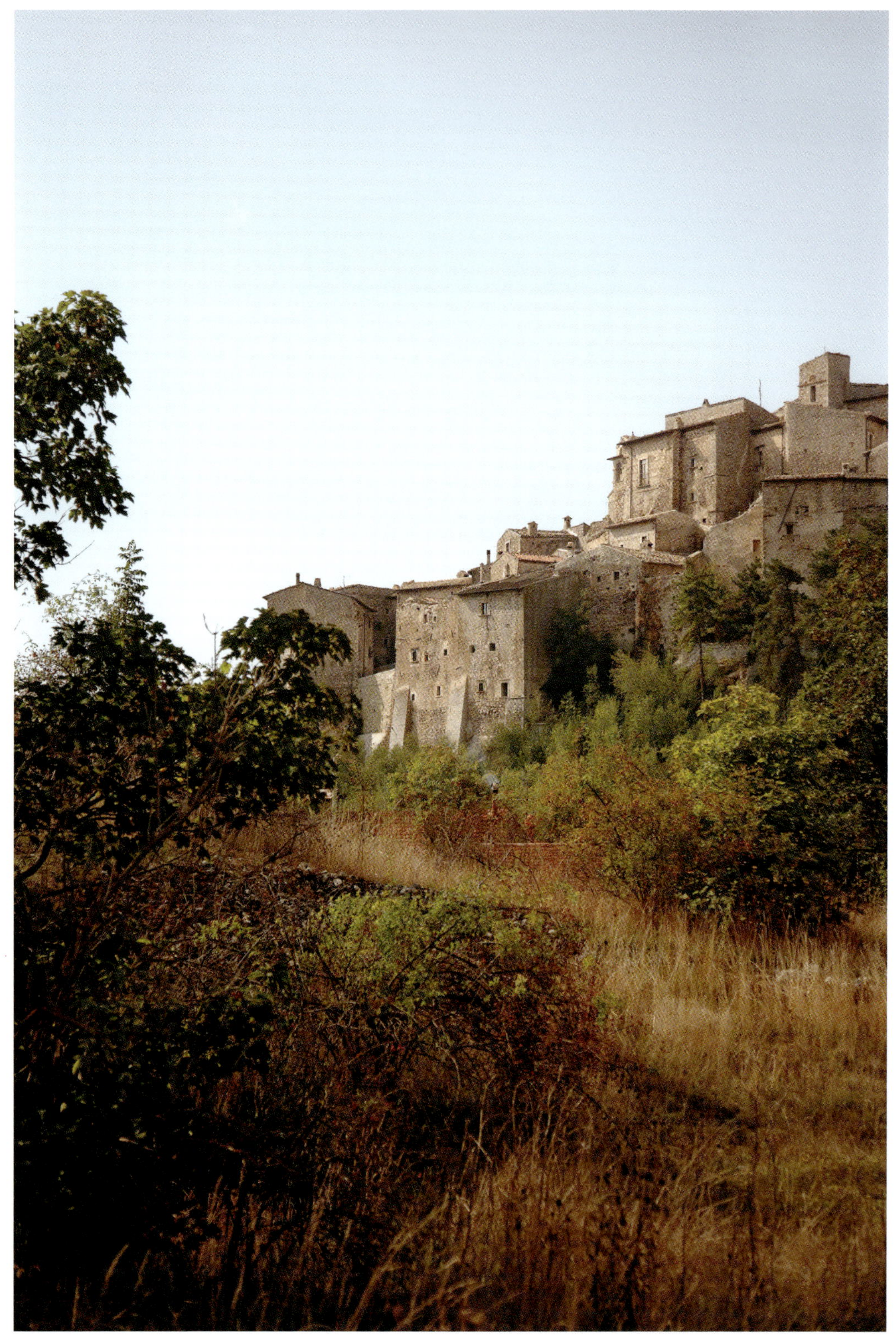

SEXTANTIO SANTO STEFANO

Via Principe Umberto, 67020 Santo Stefano di Sessanio
Tel. +39 0862 899 112 · santostefano@sextantio.it
www.sextantio.it

A VILLAGE MAKES HISTORY Daniele Kihlgren discovered the village purely by chance: the son of an industrialist from Milan, he got lost on his motorbike in the Abruzzi mountains and made a stop near Santo Stefano di Sessanio – a break that was to lead to the project of a lifetime. He was so fascinated by this medieval shepherds' settlement, although it had fallen into ruin and was almost deserted, that he revived it, investing his inheritance in the village, buying part of it and transforming it into one of Italy's most unusual hotels. His "albergo diffuso" (scattered hotel) comprises 27 rooms in several different houses, which were restored authentically in the archaic Arte Povera style with the advice of archaeologists, archivists and locals. From the soot-blackened walls to the wooden beds with sheep's-wool mattresses and the heavy roof beams, everything is original or true to the original. If the interiors were not equipped with underfloor heating, electric lighting and bathrooms by Philippe Starck, guests would think they were living in the depths of the Middle Ages. In order to present as genuine a picture as possible of the culture of the Abruzzi, Kihlgren undertook research into old regional recipes, fitted out ateliers where the work was done using historic methods and founded his own music ensemble. His energy even extends beyond the boundaries of the village: on his motorbike he now roams throughout southern Italy in search of further villages where the Sextantio group that he founded can continue to use the past to create a future. ◆ Book to pack: "The Last World" by Christoph Ransmayr.

EIN DORF SCHREIBT GESCHICHTE Daniele Kihlgren entdeckte das Dorf ganz zufällig: Der Industriellensohn aus Mailand hatte sich mit seinem Motorrad in den Bergen der Abruzzen verfahren, legte in der Nähe von Santo Stefano di Sessanio einen Stopp ein – und aus der kurzen Pause wurde das Projekt seines Lebens. Er war von der mittelalterlichen Hirtensiedlung, obgleich sie zur Ruine verfallen und fast verlassen war, so fasziniert, dass er sie wiederbelebte. Er investierte sein Erbe in den Ort, kaufte einen Teil davon und verwandelte ihn in eine der ungewöhnlichsten Herbergen Italiens. Sein „albergo diffuso" (verstreutes Hotel) umfasst 27 Zimmer in mehreren Häusern, die authentisch und unter Beratung von Archäologen, Archivaren sowie Einheimischen im archaischen Stil der Arte Povera renoviert wurden. Von den rußgeschwärzten Mauern über die Holzbetten mit Schafswollmatratzen bis hin zu den schweren Deckenbalken ist alles original oder originalgetreu. Wäre das Interieur nicht mit Fußbodenheizung, elektrischem Licht und Philippe-Starck-Bädern ausgestattet, könnte man meinen, im tiefsten Mittelalter zu Gast zu sein. Um so unverfälscht wie möglich von der Kultur der Abruzzen zu erzählen, ließ Kihlgren auch nach alten Rezepten der Region forschen, richtete Werkstätten ein, in denen mit historischen Techniken gearbeitet wird, und gründete ein eigenes Musikensemble. Seine Energie reicht sogar über die Dorfgrenzen hinaus: Er rollt auf seinem Motorrad inzwischen durch ganz Süditalien und sucht nach weiteren Orten, denen die von ihm gegründete Sextantio-Gruppe mithilfe der Vergangenheit eine Zukunft geben kann. ◆ Buchtipp: „Die letzte Welt" von Christoph Ransmayr.

RETOUR AUX SOURCES Daniele Kihlgren a découvert le village tout à fait par hasard : ce fils d'industriels de Milan s'était perdu en faisant une virée en moto dans les Abruzzes ; il s'arrêta à proximité de Santo Stefano di Sessanio, et de cette petite pause naquit le projet de sa vie. Le petit bourg médiéval n'était plus que ruines et pratiquement abandonné, mais il le fascina tellement qu'il lui rendit la vie – il investit son héritage dans le village, en acheta une partie et le transforma en l'une des auberges les plus insolites d'Italie. Son « albergo diffuso » (auberge éparpillée) comprend 27 chambres réparties dans plusieurs maisons, restaurées de manière authentique dans le style archaïque de l'Arte Povera grâce aux conseils des archéologues, des archivistes et des gens du pays. Des murs noircis de suie aux lourdes poutres de plafond en passant par les lits en bois garnis de matelas pure laine, tout est original ou fidèlement reproduit. Et on pourrait se croire au plus profond du Moyen Âge si ces intérieurs ne disposaient pas de chauffage au sol, de lumière électrique et de salles de bains Philippe Starck. Pour transmettre le plus authentiquement possible la culture des Abruzzes, Kihlgren a aussi fait rechercher de vieilles recettes régionales, il a créé des ateliers travaillant avec des techniques historiques et fondé un ensemble musical. Mais il lui reste beaucoup d'énergie : sillonnant l'Italie du Sud sur sa moto, il est à la recherche d'autres lieux à qui le groupe Sextantio, qu'il a fondé, peut donner un avenir grâce à l'histoire. ◆ À lire : « Le Dernier des mondes » de Christoph Ransmayr.

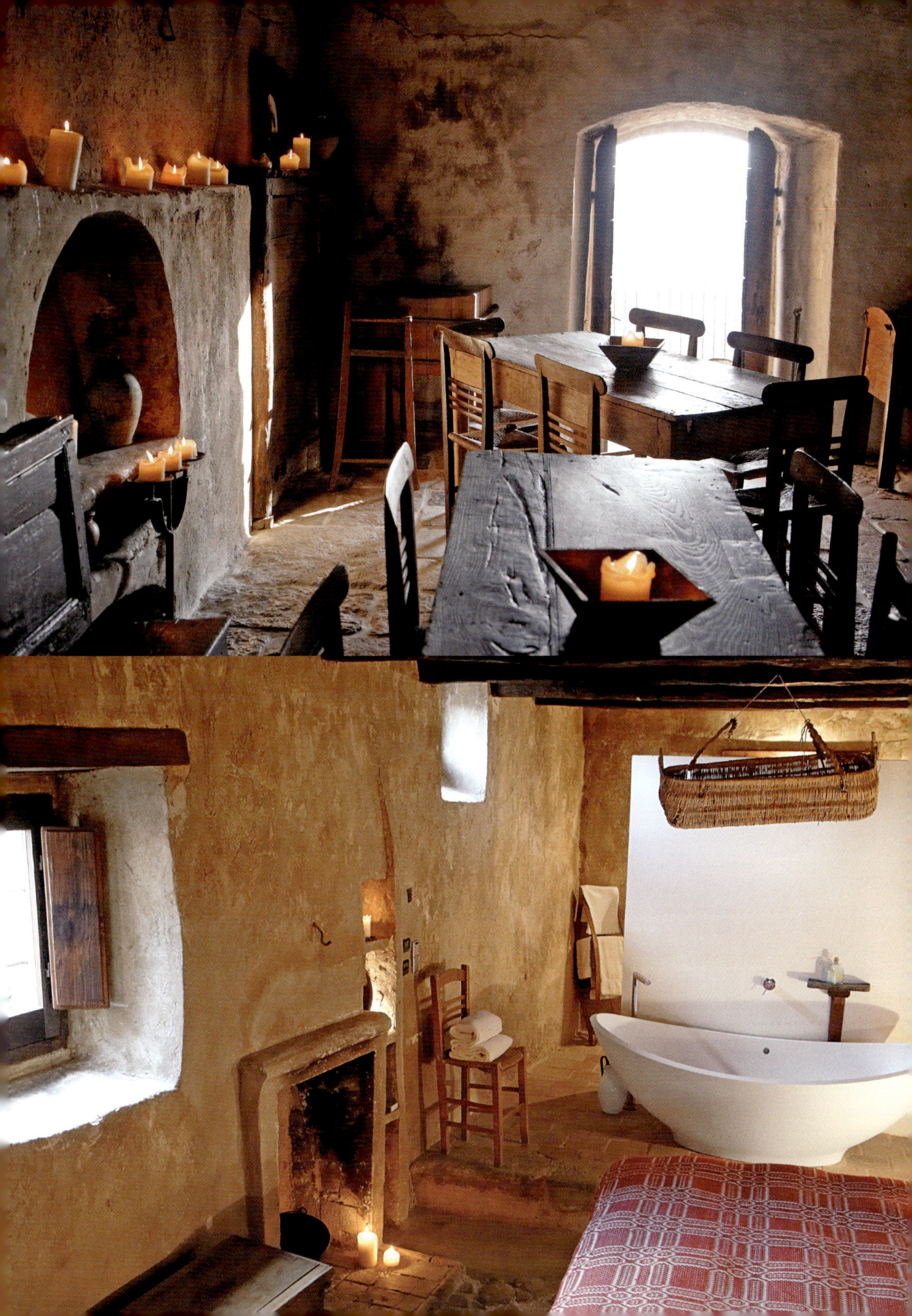

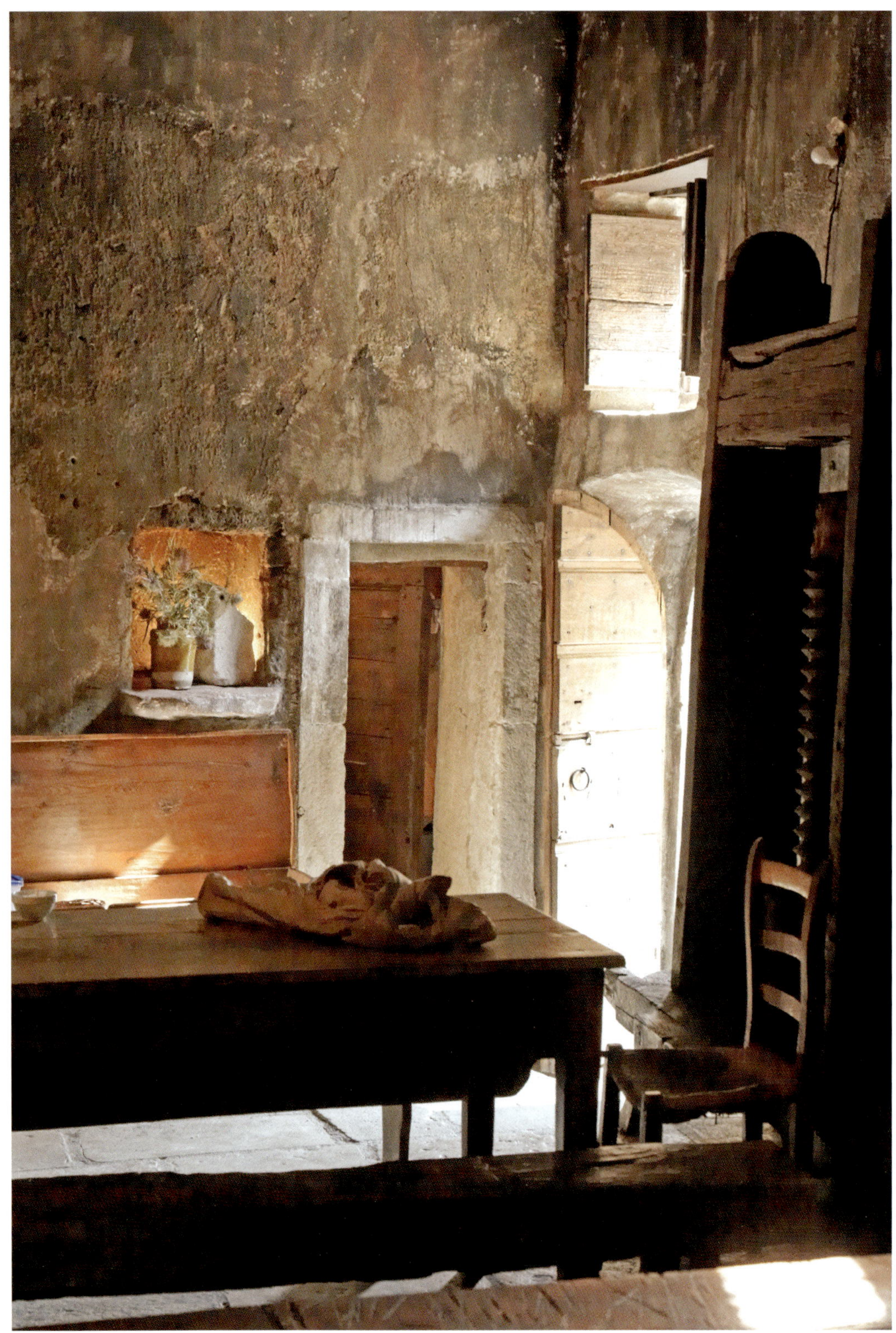

ABRUZZO

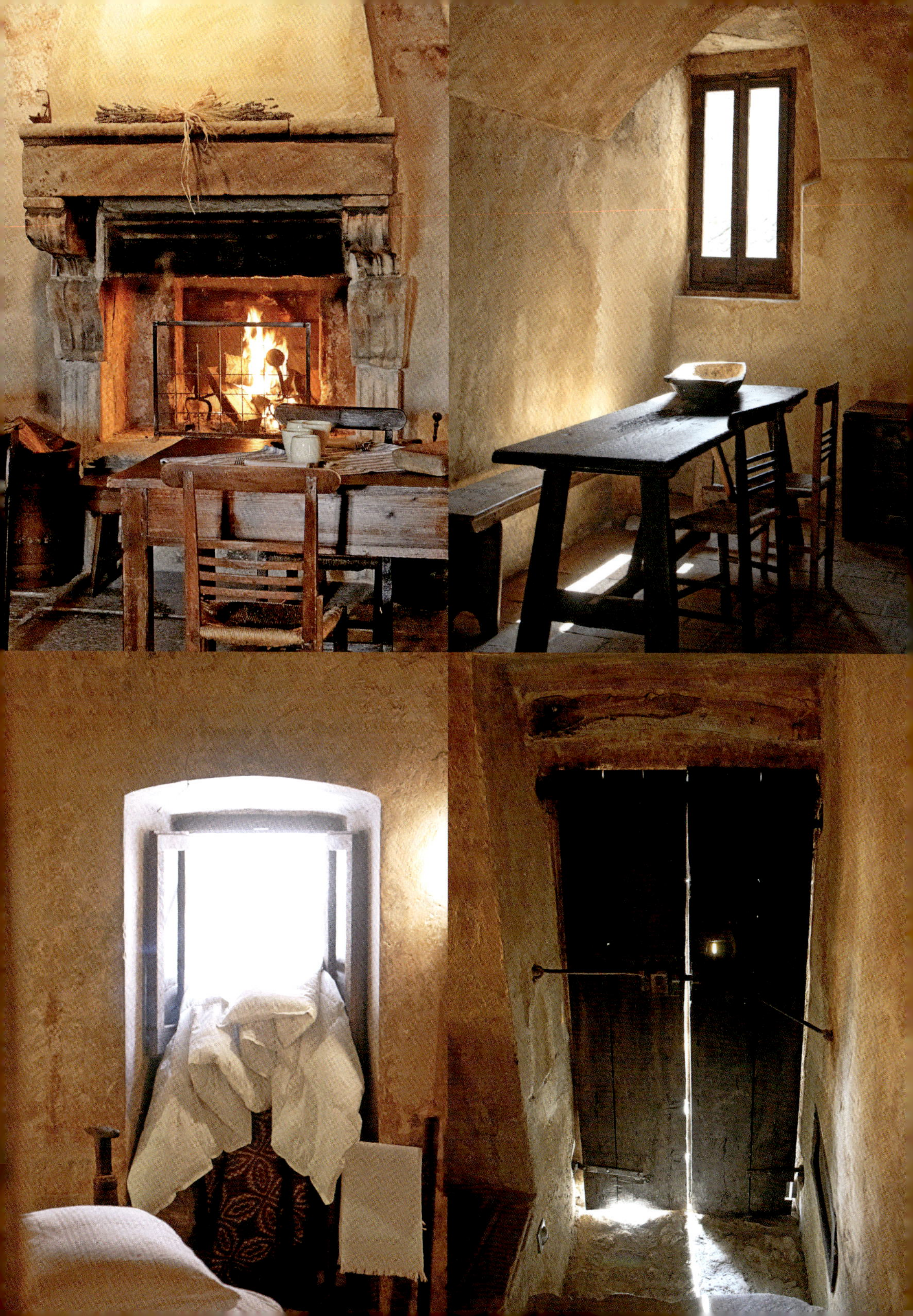

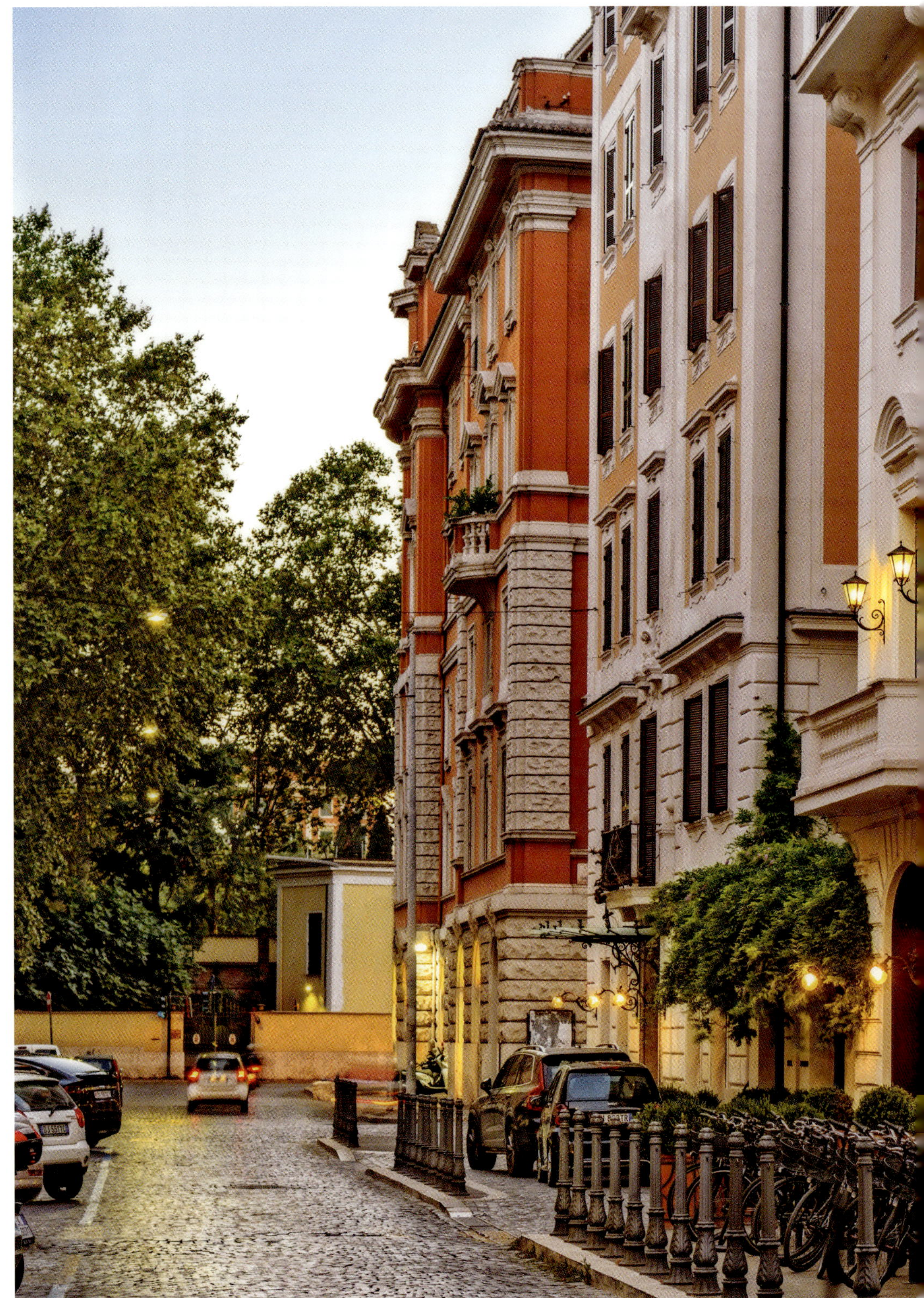

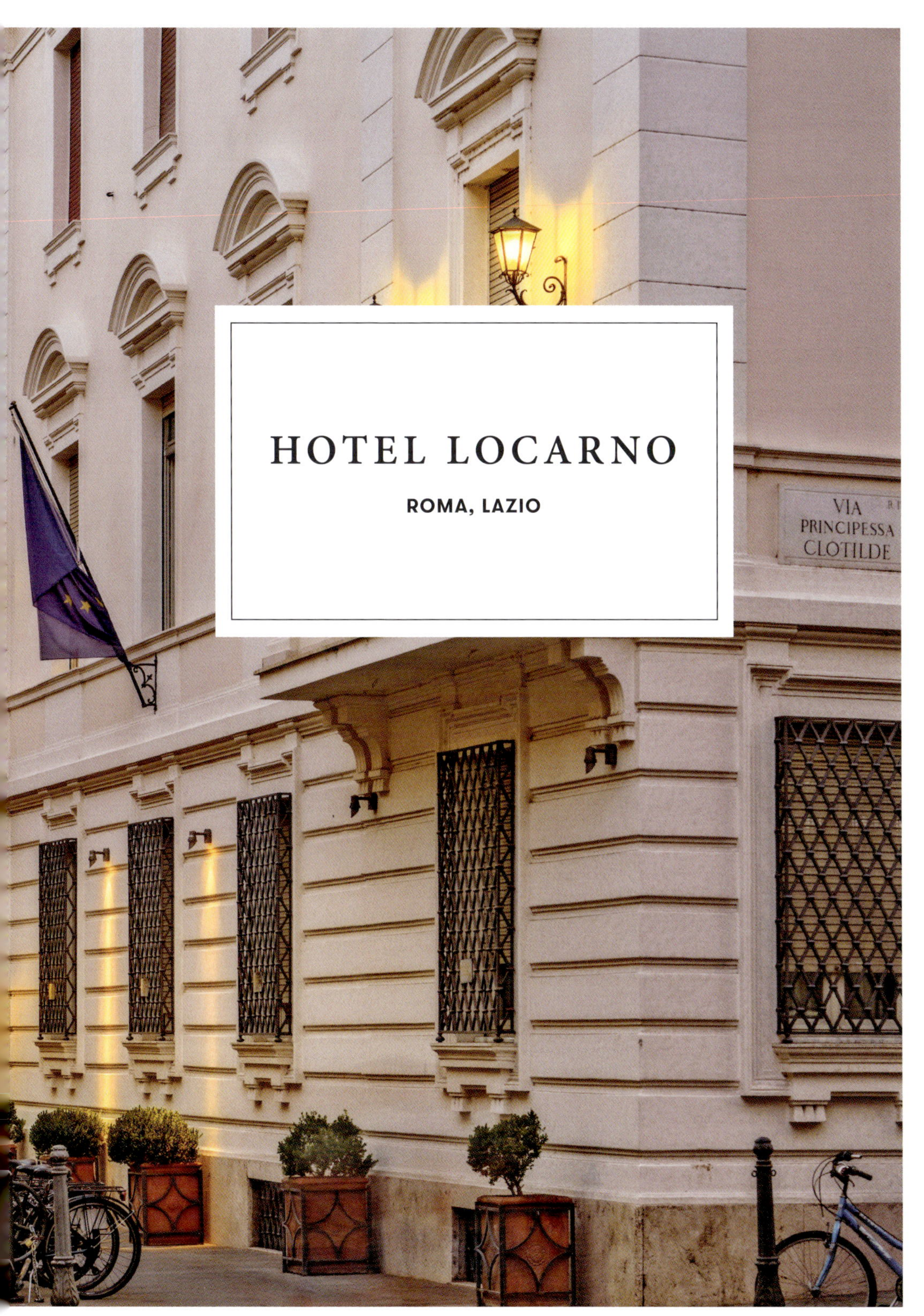

HOTEL LOCARNO

ROMA, LAZIO

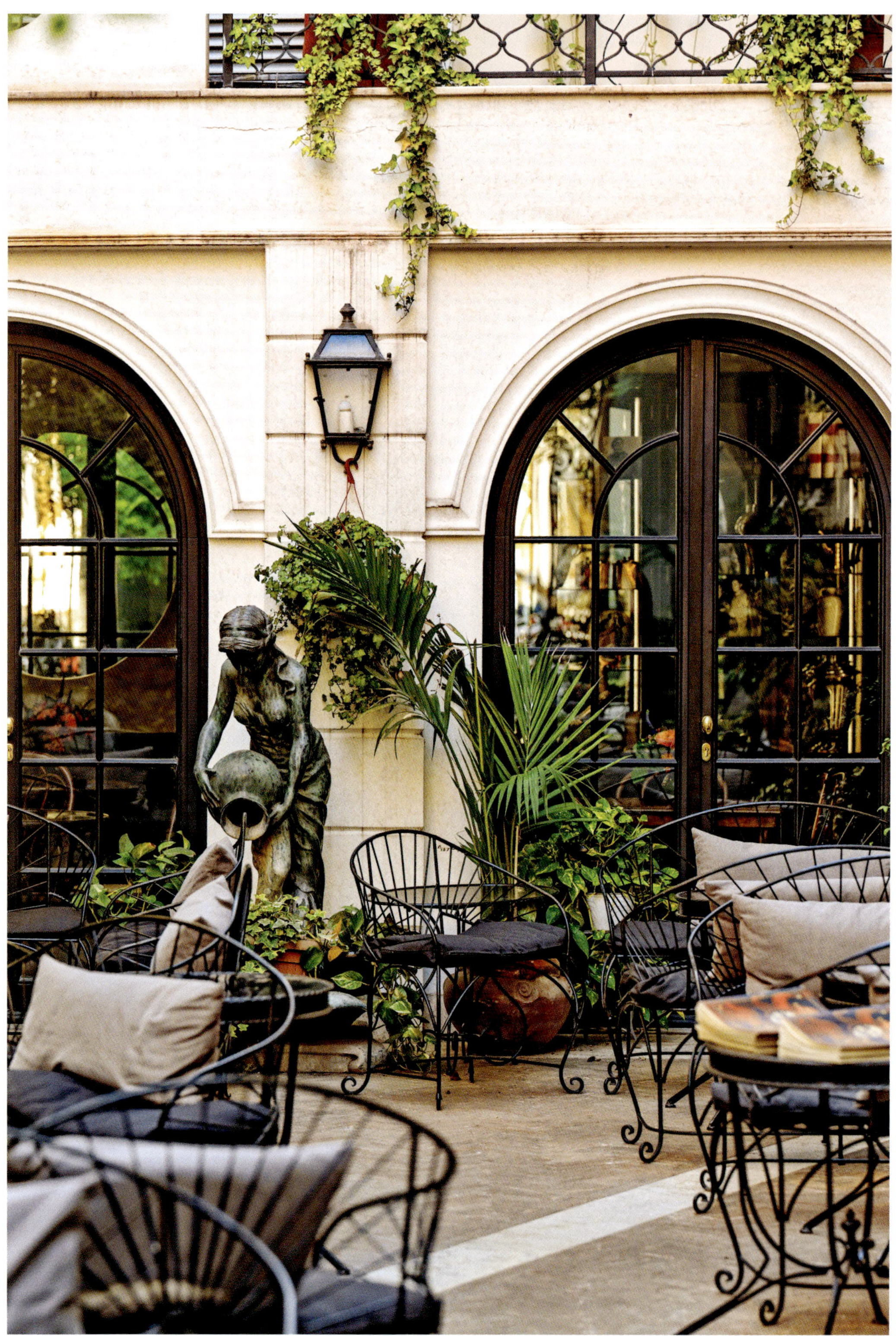

HOTEL LOCARNO

Via della Penna 22, 00186 Roma
Tel. +39 06 36 10 841 · booking@hotellocarno.com
www.hotellocarno.com

ROME, RETRO-STYLE If one hotel exists in Rome that is so Roman even the Romans love it – then it is the Hotel Locarno. Situated just behind Piazza del Popolo, it is so cool and charming, so sexy and stylist, so casual and passionate that it could be nothing other than a genuine Italian institution. Only the name derives from the first owners, who came from Switzerland and founded it in 1925 under the name Albergo Locarno – the poster for the opening by Anselmo Ballester, the legendary designer of film posters, still hangs in the lobby. When Maria Teresa Celli took over the hotel in the 1960s, she fitted out every room in a different design with antiques that partly came from her own collection – yet she designed every room in elegant Art Nouveau style. This retro ambience with splendid furniture, exquisite fabrics and beautiful lamps is a sight for sore eyes. The Locarno became famous for its bar on the ground floor, whose guest list reads like a who's who of the Italian creative scene. From Federico Fellini and his wife Giulietta Masina to Umberto Eco and Isabella Rossellini, everyone who mattered in Italy came here for a drink and a talk. Don't miss the roof terrace, which is reached in a rickety old lift. The view of the roofs and domes of Rome is pure cinema.
◆ Book to pack: "Hotel Locarno" by Alain Elkann.

ROM IM RETRO-STIL Wenn es in Rom ein Hotel gibt, das so römisch ist, dass sogar die Römer es lieben, dann ist es das Hotel Locarno. Gleich hinter der Piazza del Popolo gelegen, ist es so cool und charmant, so sexy und stilsicher, so lässig und leidenschaftlich, wie es nur eine echte italienische Institution sein kann. Lediglich den Namen hat es von seinen ersten Besitzern, die aus der Schweiz stammten und es 1925 als „Albergo Locarno" gründeten – das Eröffnungsplakat des legendären Filmplakatgestalters Anselmo Ballester hängt noch heute in der Lobby. Als die Italienerin Maria Teresa Celli das Hotel in den 1960er-Jahren übernahm, gestaltete sie jedes Zimmer unterschiedlich und mit Antiquitäten teils aus ihrem eigenen Besitz – doch sie hielt alle Räume im eleganten Art-nouveau-Stil: Das Retro-Ambiente mit prachtvollen Möbeln, feinsten Stoffen und formschönen Lampen ist ein Augenschmaus. Berühmt wurde das Locarno dank seiner Bar im Erdgeschoss, deren Gästeliste sich wie das Who's who der italienischen Künstlerszene liest. Von Federico Fellini und seiner Gattin Giulietta Masina über Umberto Eco bis hin zu Isabella Rossellini trank und diskutierte hier schon jeder, der im Land Rang und Namen hat. Nicht verpassen sollte man aber auch die Dachterrasse, zu der ein alter Aufzug hinauf rumpelt. Der Blick über die Dächer und Kuppeln Roms ist filmreif. ◆ Buchtipp: „Hotel Locarno" von Alain Elkann.

ROME, STYLE RÉTRO S'il y a bien à Rome un hôtel si romain que même les Romains l'adorent, c'est l'hôtel Locarno. Situé juste derrière la Piazza del Popolo, il est aussi cool et charmant, sexy et élégant, décontracté et passionné que peut l'être une véritable institution italienne. Seul le nom lui vient de ses premiers propriétaires, originaires de Suisse, et qui l'ont fondé en 1925 sous le nom d'« Albergo Locarno » – l'affiche d'inauguration du légendaire dessinateur d'affiches de cinéma Anselmo Ballester est aujourd'hui encore accrochée dans le hall. Lorsque l'Italienne Maria Teresa Celli a repris l'hôtel dans les années 1960, elle a conçu chaque chambre différemment avec des antiquités tirées en partie de sa propre collection, mais optant dans toutes les pièces pour le style Art nouveau élégant : l'ambiance rétro avec des meubles magnifiques, les tissus les plus raffinés et des lampes décoratives est un plaisir pour les yeux. Le Locarno est devenu célèbre grâce à son bar au rez-de-chaussée, dont la liste d'invités se lit comme le Who's Who de la scène artistique italienne. De Federico Fellini et son épouse Giulietta Masina à Umberto Eco et Isabella Rossellini, tous ceux qui ont un nom dans le pays ont bu et discuté ici. Mais ne manquez pas la terrasse sur le toit, où vous mènera un vieil ascenseur cahotant. La vue sur les toits et les coupoles de Rome est digne d'un film. ◆ À lire : « Hôtel Locarno » d'Alain Elkann.

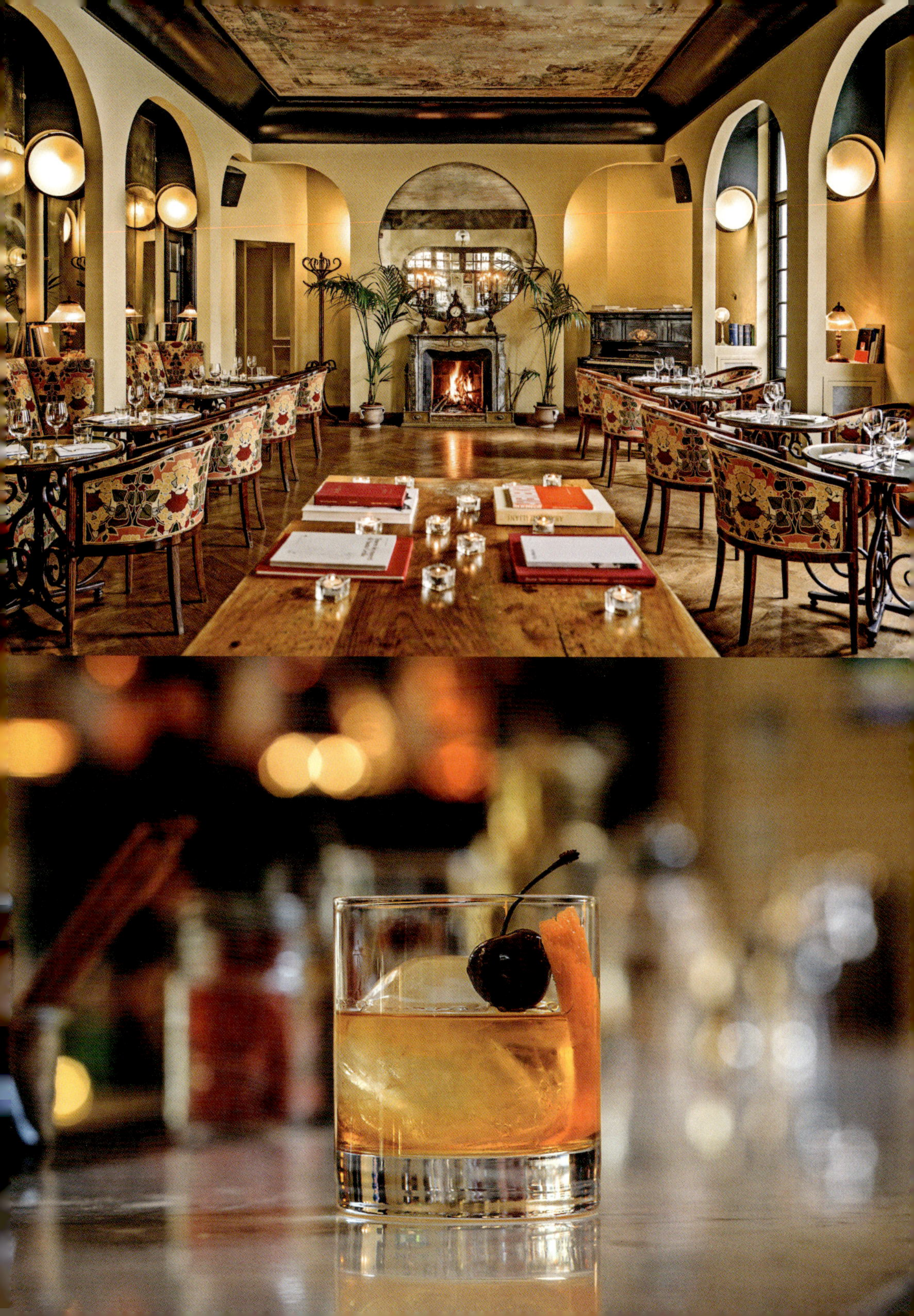

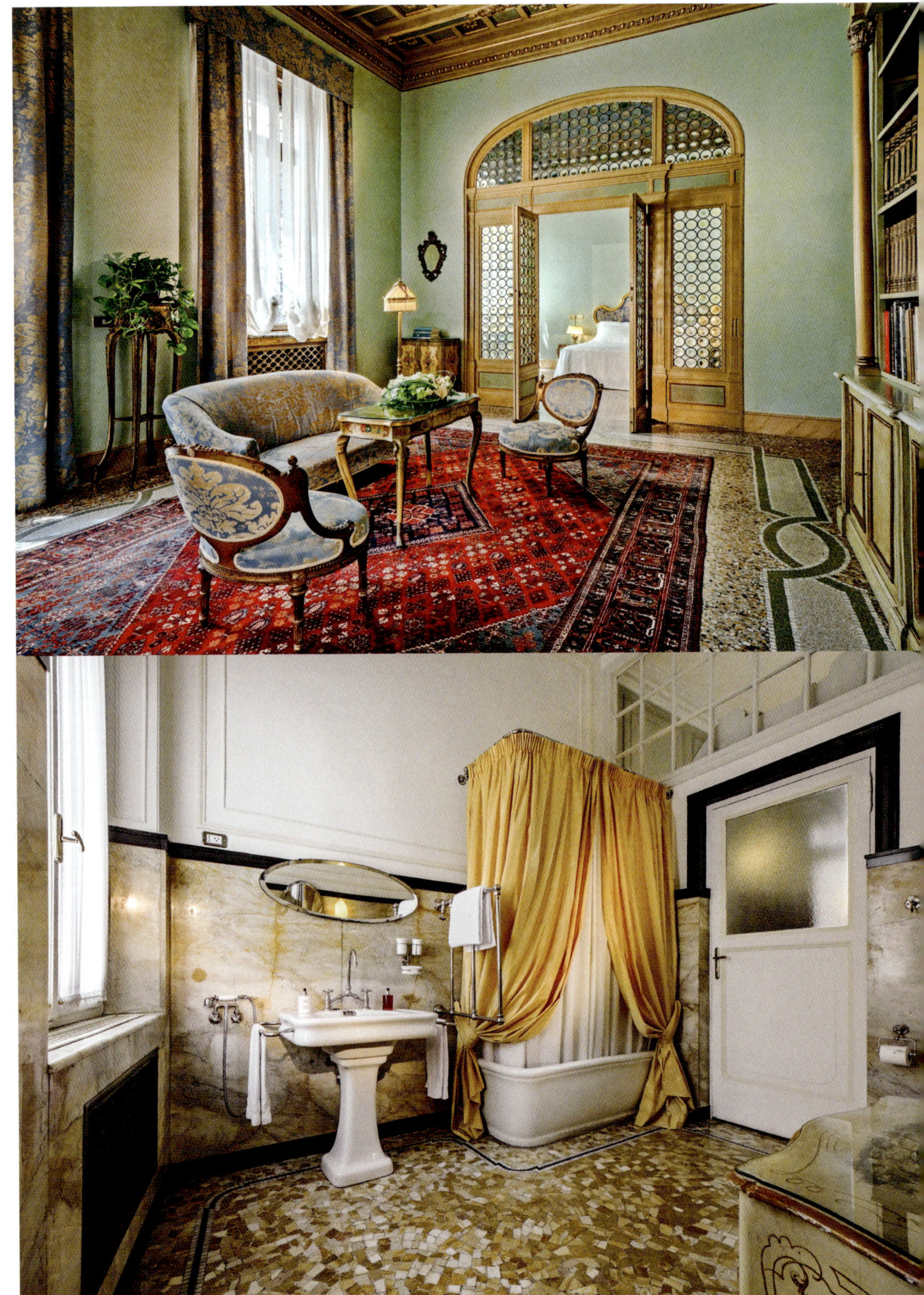

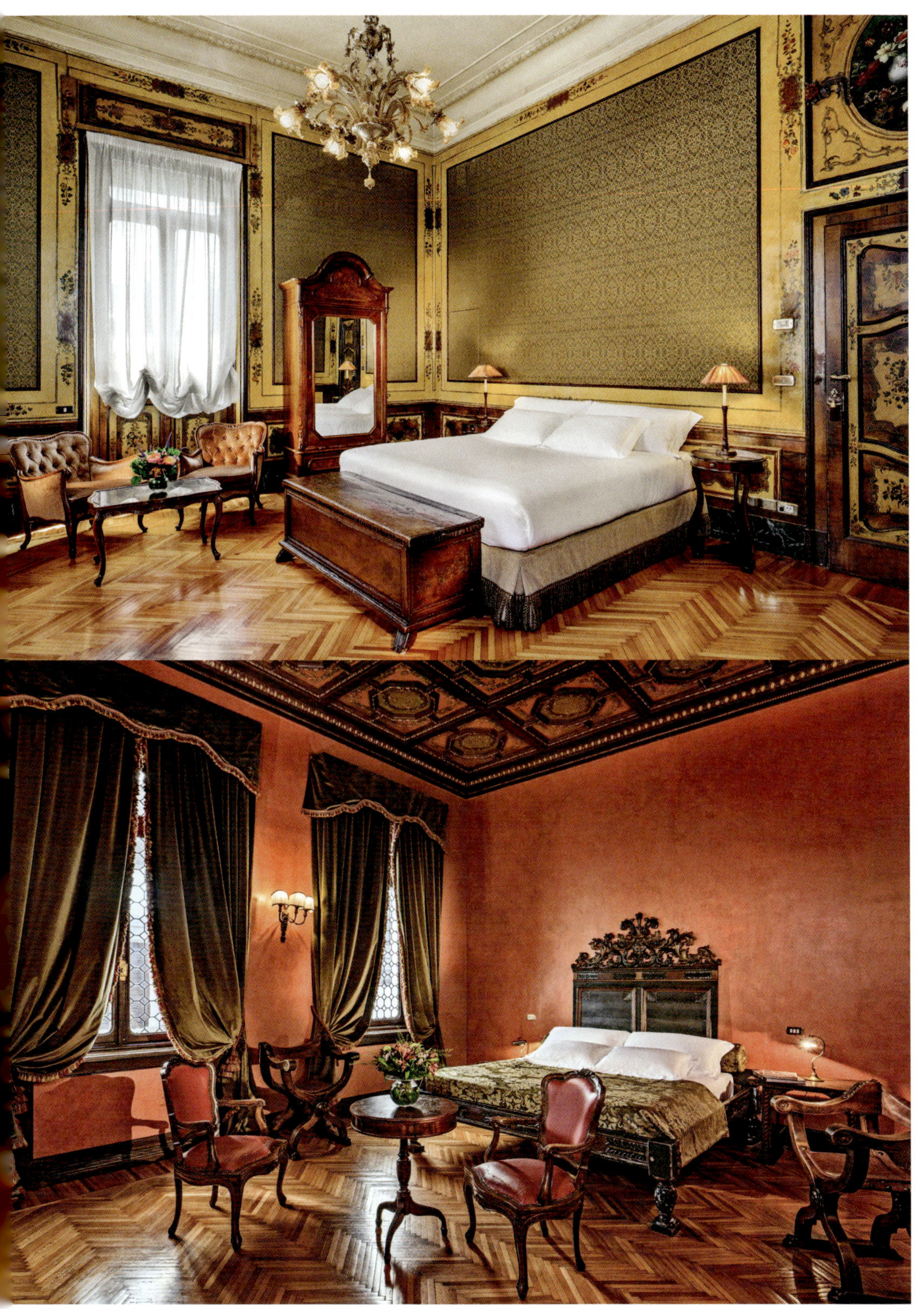

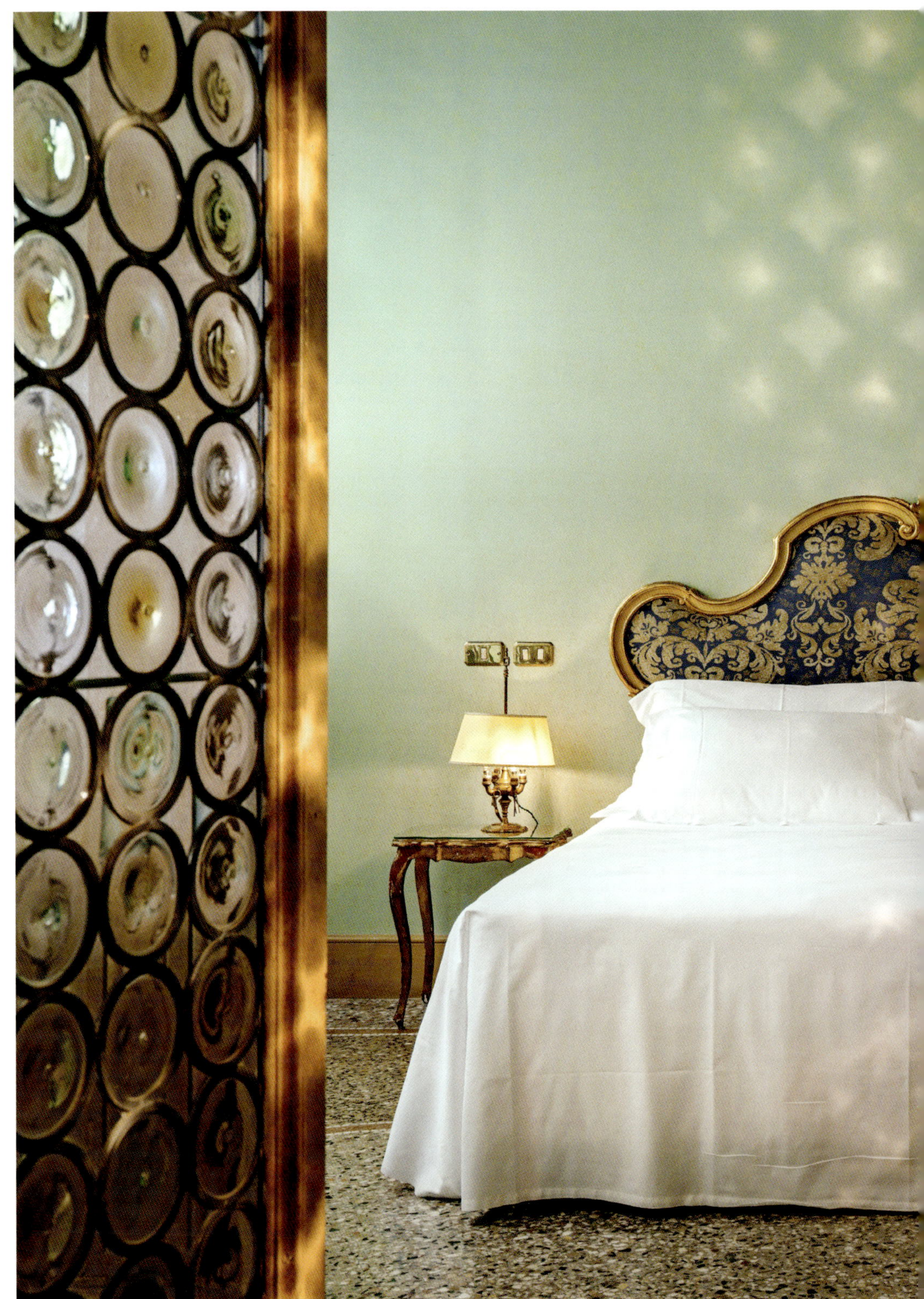

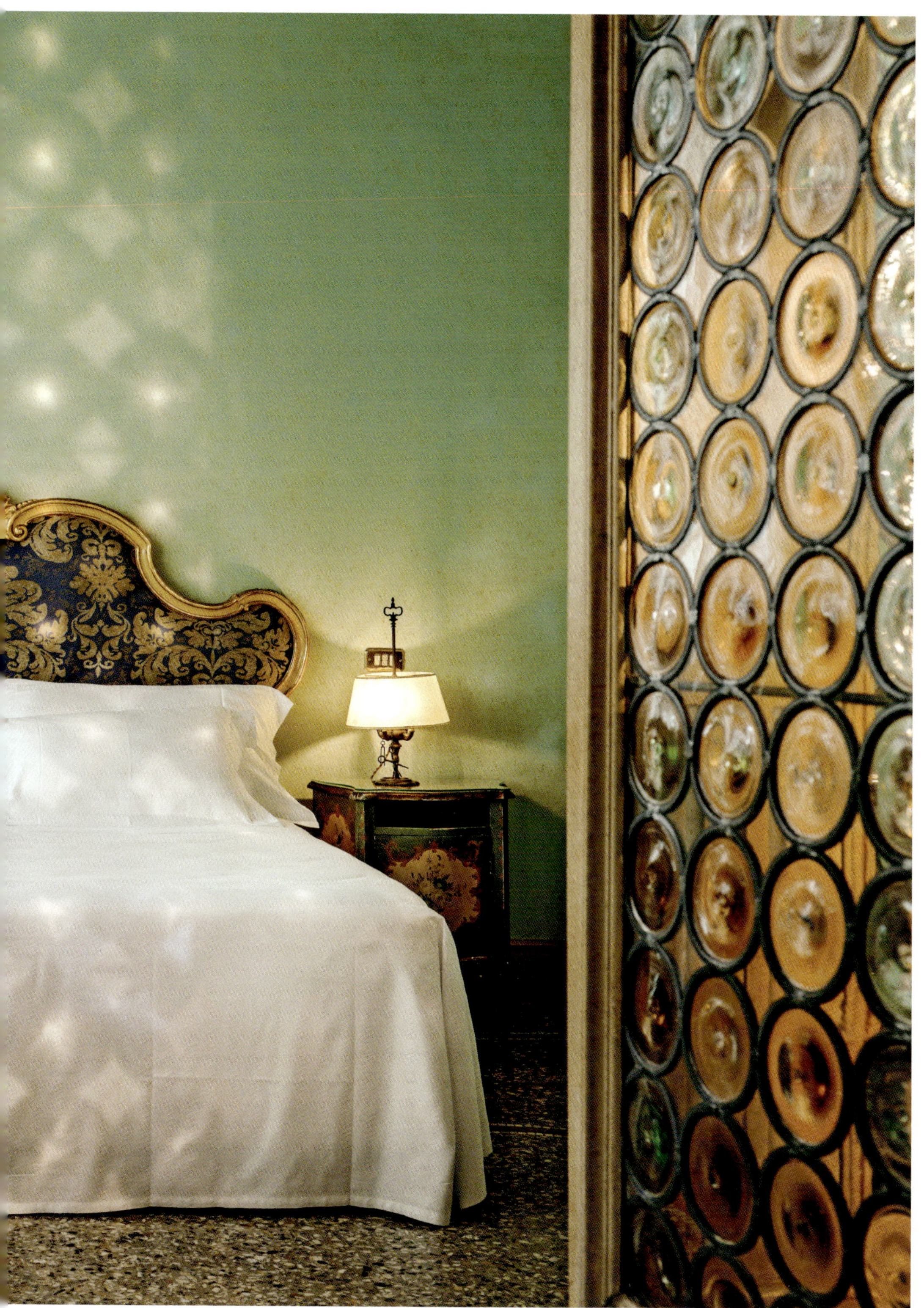

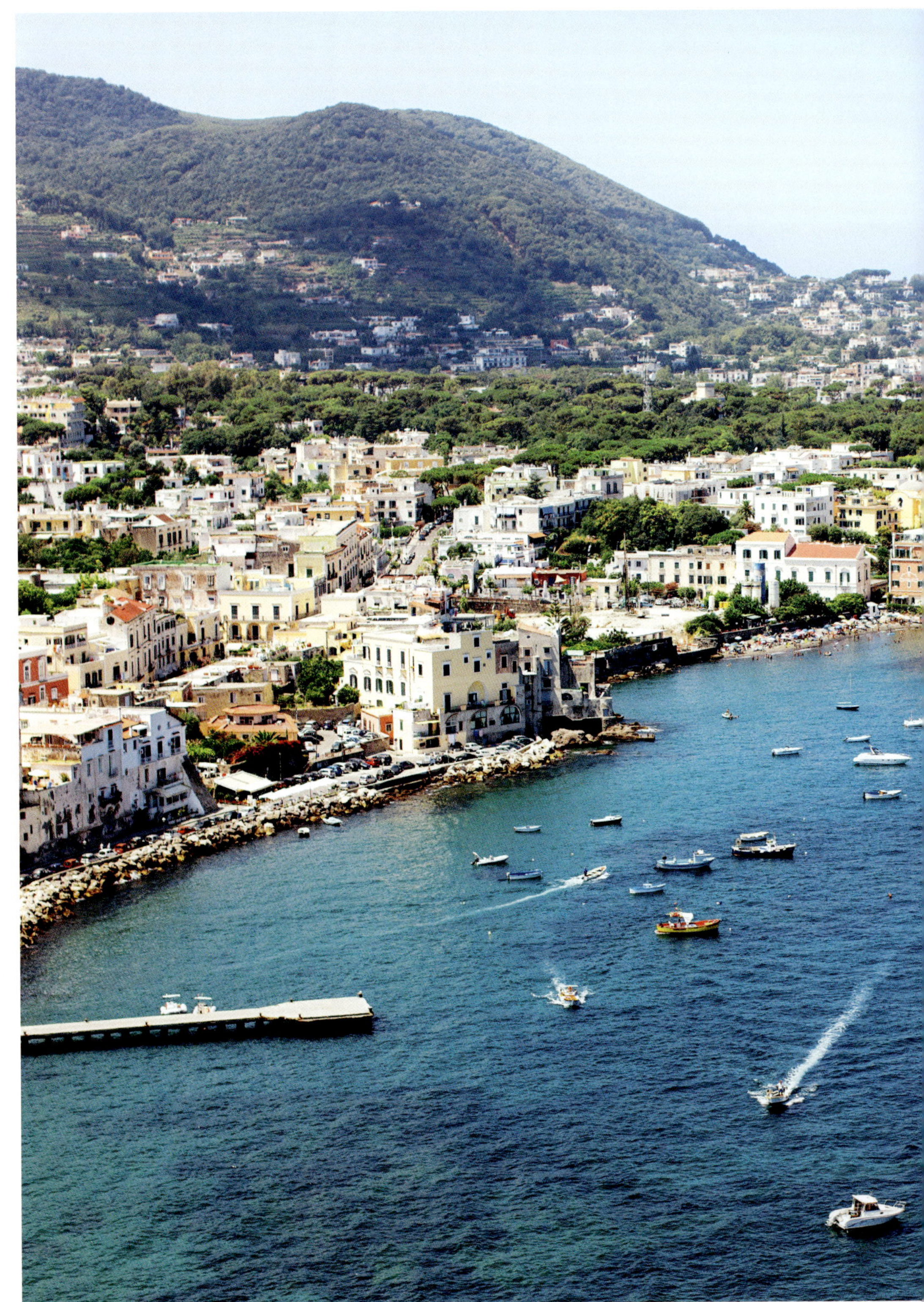

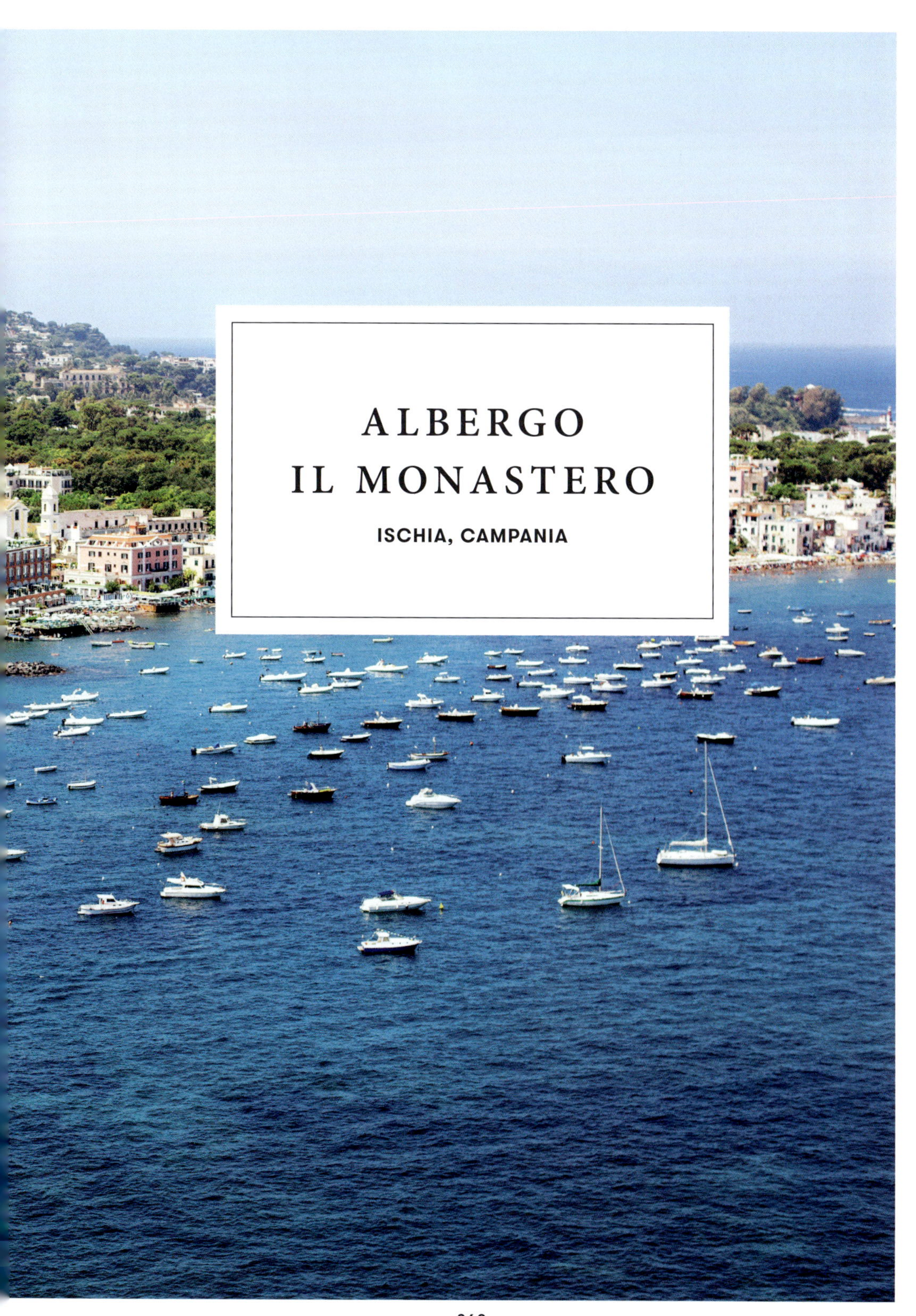

ALBERGO IL MONASTERO

ISCHIA, CAMPANIA

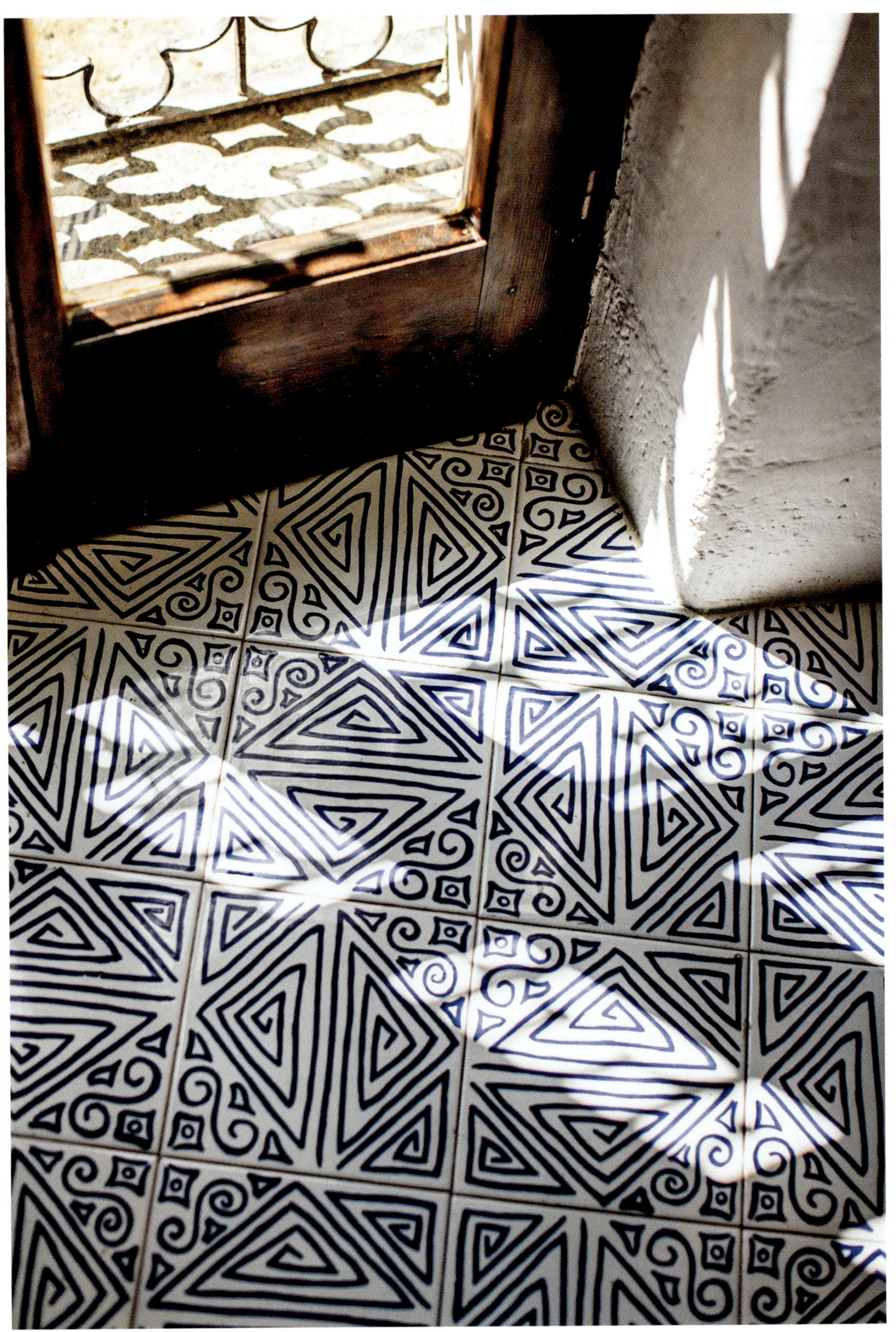

ALBERGO IL MONASTERO

Castello Aragonese, 80070 Ischia
Tel. +39 081 992 435 · info@ilmonasteroischia.com
www.albergoilmonastero.it
Open from mid-April to late October

SIMPLY BEAUTIFUL It came to the island with Greek settlers as long ago as the eighth century BC, and in the Middle Ages, above all, brought sweetness to residents' lives in the evenings: the biancolella grape, which grows on volcanic soil next to olive trees and wild herbs. Its juice produces an aromatic white wine with hints of spice. When the Mattera family revived the almost forgotten vineyard of the Aragonese castle on Ischia about 30 years ago, they planted biancolella vines – and since then have been serving an authentic (and delicious!) wine to their visitors. The Albergo Il Monastero itself is closely linked to the history and character of the island: the building was once a monastery dedicated to Santa Maria della Consolazione. Behind strong walls and beneath barrel vaults and cross vaults lie simple rooms that stick to the essentials with whitewashed walls, dark wooden furnishings and cotto tiles. As a result of their monastic past, they only have small windows – but the terrace and garden reveal a wonderful panorama from Campagnano across the fishing village of Ischia Ponte to the beach of Cartaromana and the inland hills. An ideal day of vacation here starts with Ischia's citrus marmalades and home-baked cake for breakfast, and ends with a Campanian dinner – including a view of the starry sky and a glass of Castello wine. ◆ Book to pack: "Vittoria Colonna" by Maria Musiol.

EINFACH SCHÖN Sie kam mit griechischen Siedlern schon im 8. Jahrhundert vor Christus auf die Insel und versüßte vor allem den Menschen im Mittelalter so manchen Abend: die Biancolella-Traube, die auf vulkanischem Boden dicht an Olivenbäumen und Wildkräutern wächst und aus der ein aromatischer Weißwein mit Gewürznoten gekeltert wird. Als die Familie Mattera vor rund 30 Jahren den fast vergessenen Weinberg der Aragoner Burg auf Ischia wiederbelebte, pflanzte sie Biancolella-Rebstöcke an – und serviert seither ihren Besuchern einen authentischen (und köstlichen!) Wein. Auch das Albergo Il Monastero selbst ist eng mit Geschichte und Charakter der Insel verbunden: Einst war das Gebäude ein der Santa Maria della Consolazione geweihtes Kloster. Hinter trutzigen Mauern und unter Tonnen- und Kreuzgewölben liegen einfache Zimmer, die sich aufs Wesentliche beschränken und mit weiß getünchten Wänden, dunklen Holzmöbeln sowie Cotto-Fliesen eingerichtet sind. Aufgrund der klösterlichen Vergangenheit haben sie nur kleine Fenster – doch Terrasse und Garten eröffnen wunderbare Ausblicke von Campagnano über den Fischerort Ischia Ponte bis zum Strand von Cartaromana und den Hügeln des Hinterlands. Ein idealer Urlaubstag beginnt mit einem Frühstück mit Zitruskonfitüren aus Ischia und selbst gebackenen Kuchen und endet bei einem kampanischen Dinner – Sicht in den Sternenhimmel und ein Glas Castello-Wein inbegriffen. ◆ Buchtipp: „Vittoria Colonna“ von Maria Musiol.

BEAU, TOUT SIMPLEMENT Arrivé sur l’île avec des colons grecs dès le VIIIe siècle av. J.-C., le Biancolella, un cépage qui pousse sur un sol volcanique à proximité des oliviers et des herbes sauvages, et qui donne un vin blanc aromatique aux notes épicées, a souvent rendu les soirées plus douces, surtout pour les gens du Moyen Âge. Il y a une trentaine d’années, lorsque la famille Mattera a fait revivre le vignoble presque oublié du Château Aragonais à Ischia, elle a planté des vignes de Biancolella – et depuis, elle sert à ses visiteurs un vin authentique (et délicieux !). Le Monastère d’Albergo Il est également étroitement lié à l’histoire et au caractère de l’île : il était autrefois dédié à sainte Marie de la Consolation. Derrière les murailles fortifiées et sous les voûtes en berceau et à croisées d’ogives, on découvre des pièces simples, limitées à l’essentiel, avec des murs blanchis à la chaux, un carrelage en terre cuite, et des meubles en bois foncé. Les fenêtres sont petites – passé monastique oblige –, mais la terrasse et le jardin offrent une vue magnifique de Campagnano à la plage de Cartaromana et les collines de l’arrière-pays, en passant par le village de pêcheurs Ischia Ponte. Une journée de vacances idéale commence par un petit déjeuner agrémenté de confitures aux agrumes d’Ischia et de gâteaux maison, et se termine par un dîner campanien – avec vue sur le ciel étoilé et un verre de vin du Castello. ◆ À lire : « Vittoria Colonna » de Maria Musiol.

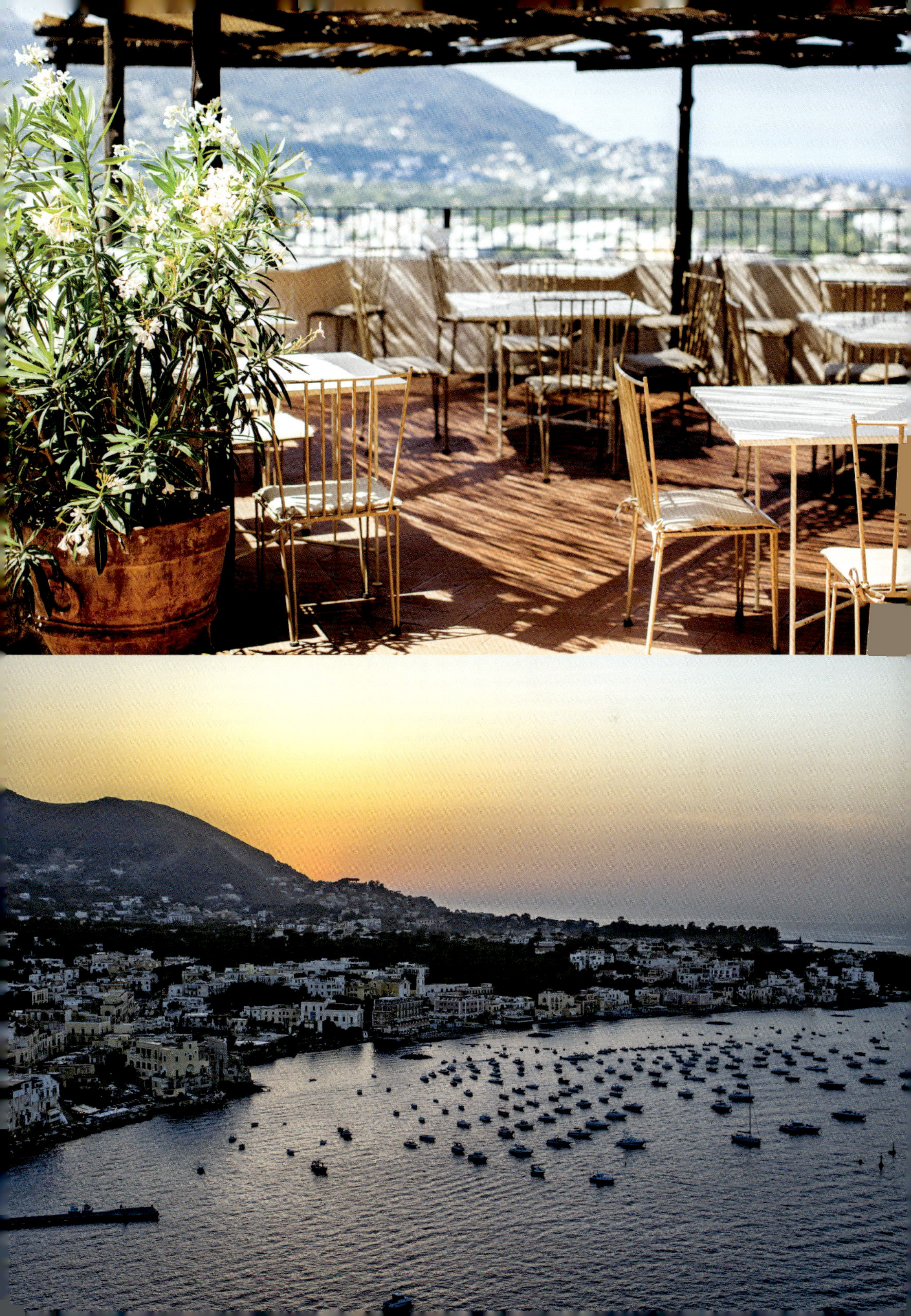

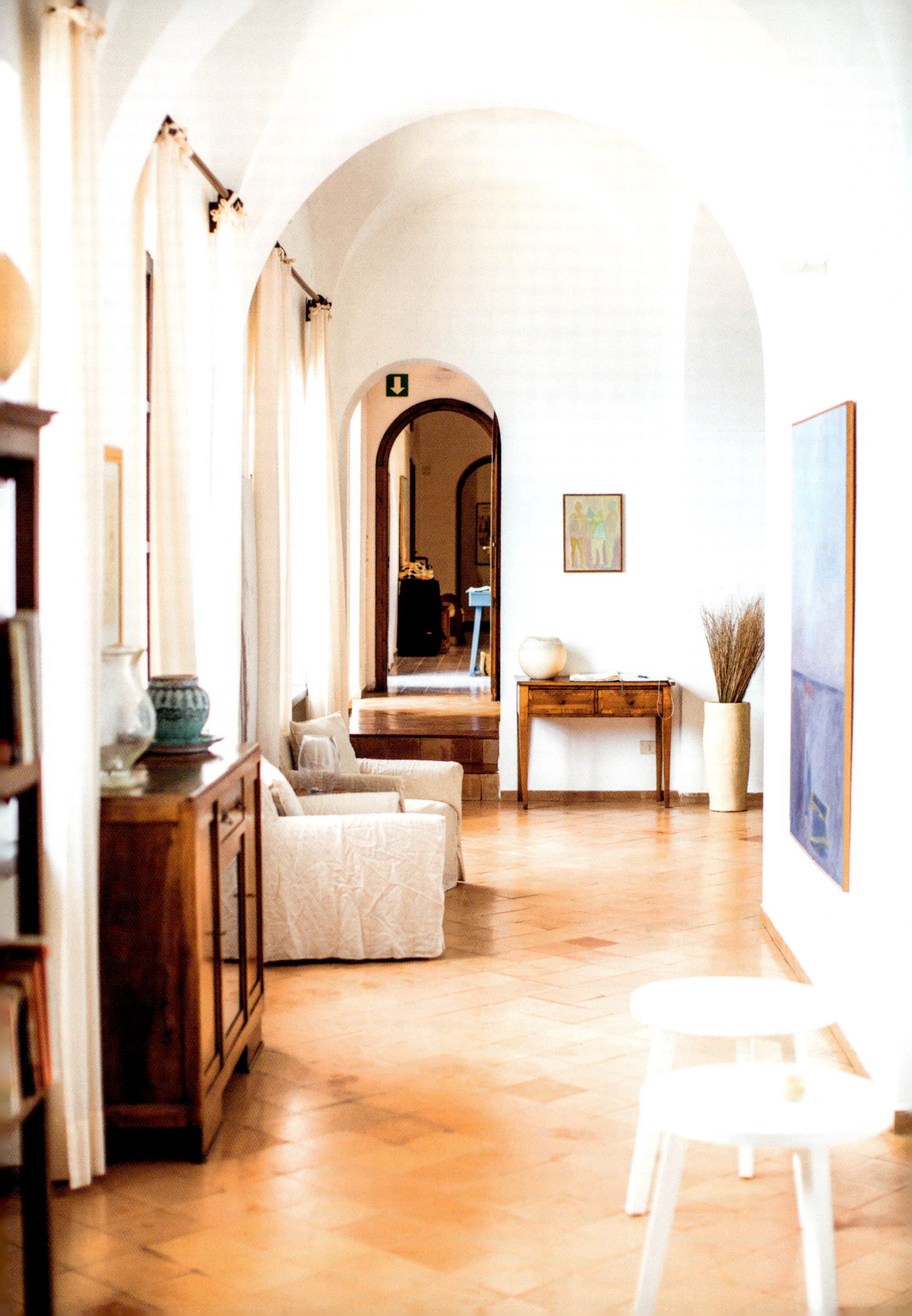

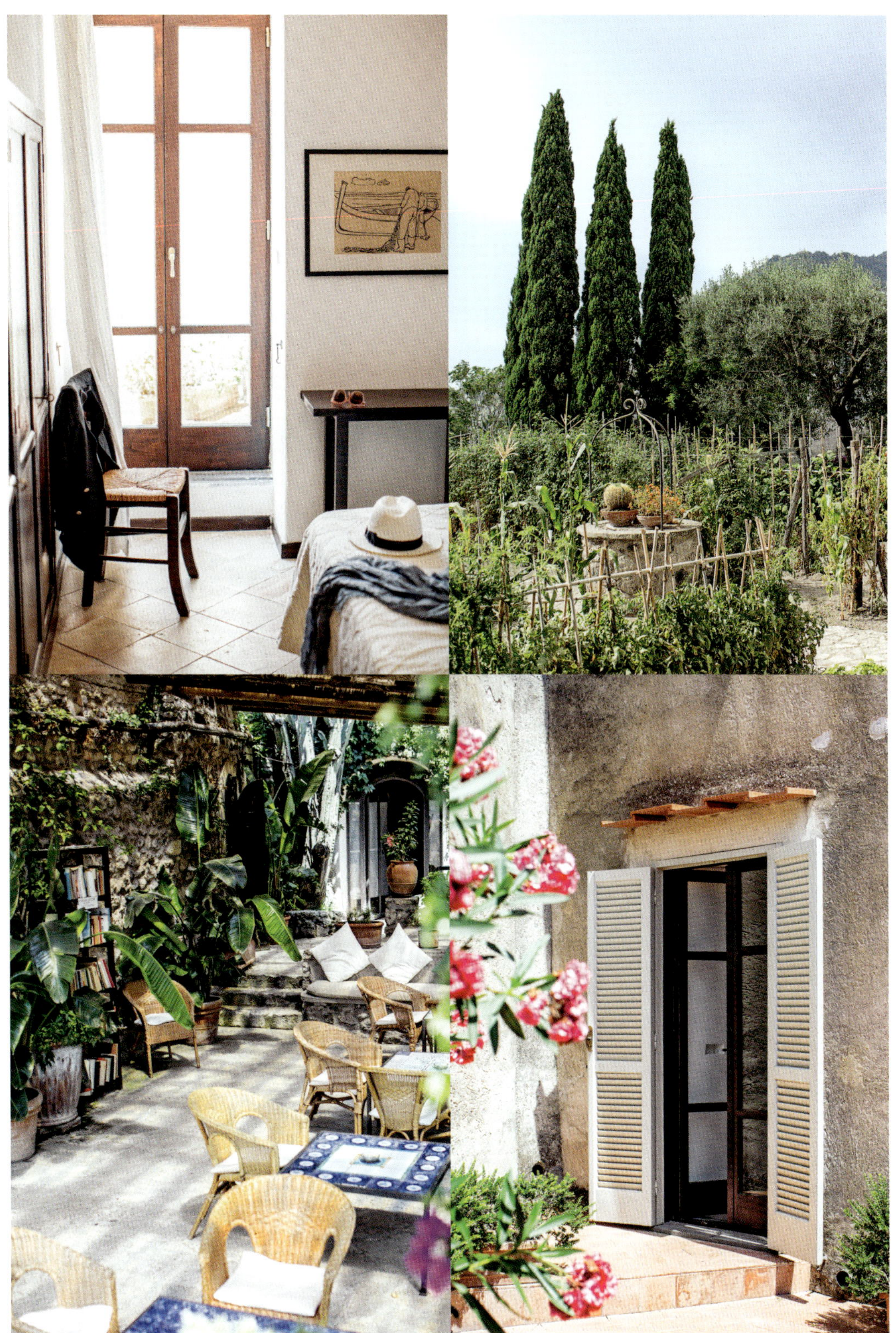

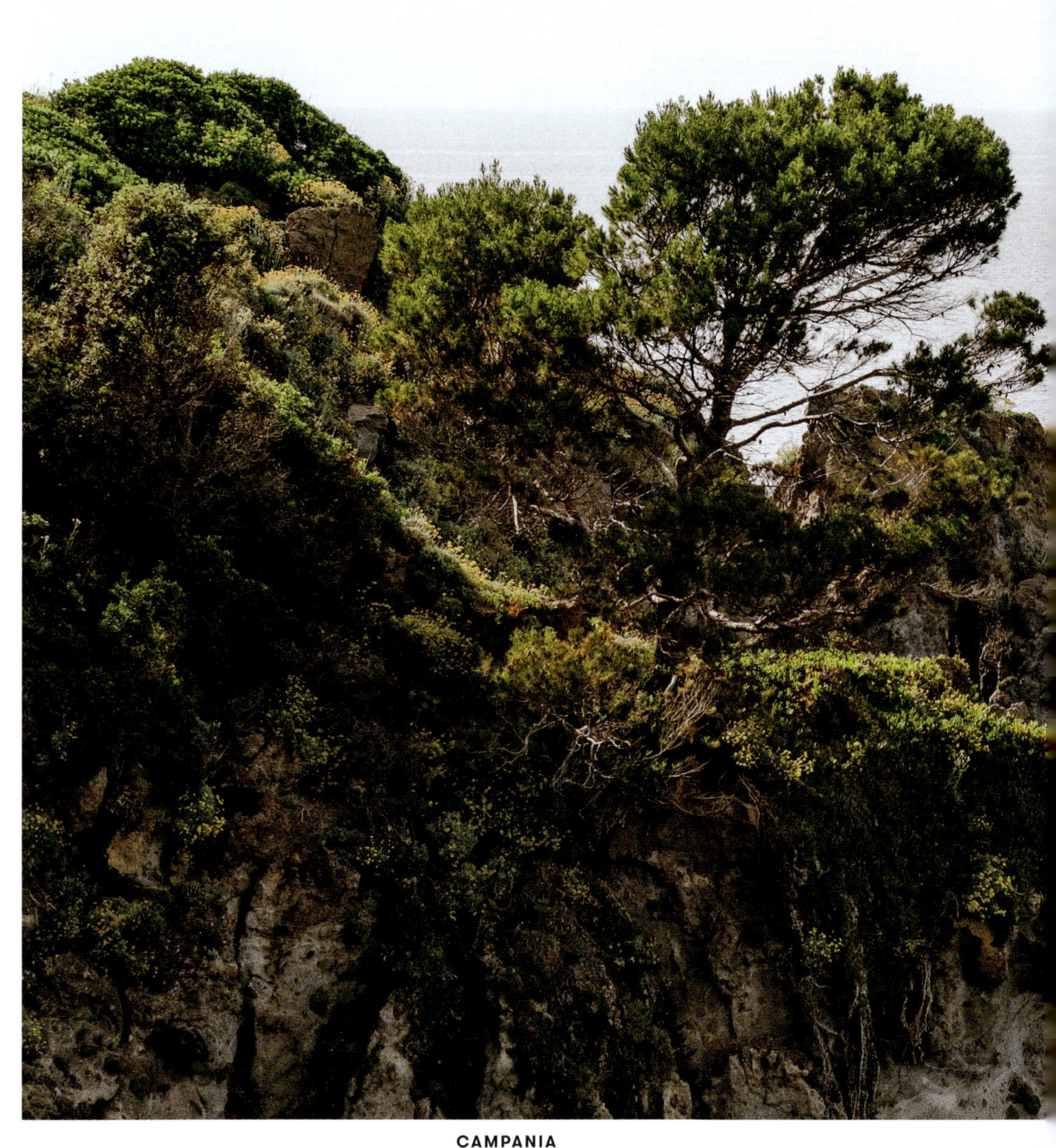

MEZZATORRE

ISCHIA, CAMPANIA

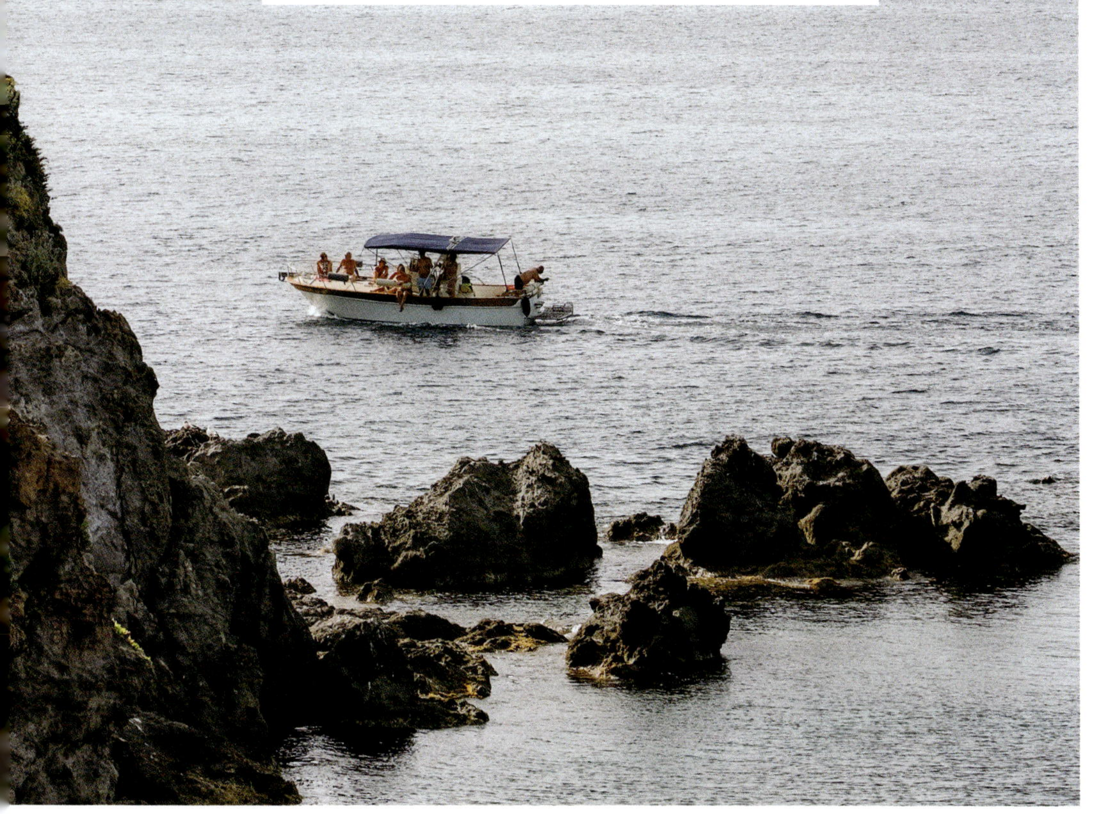

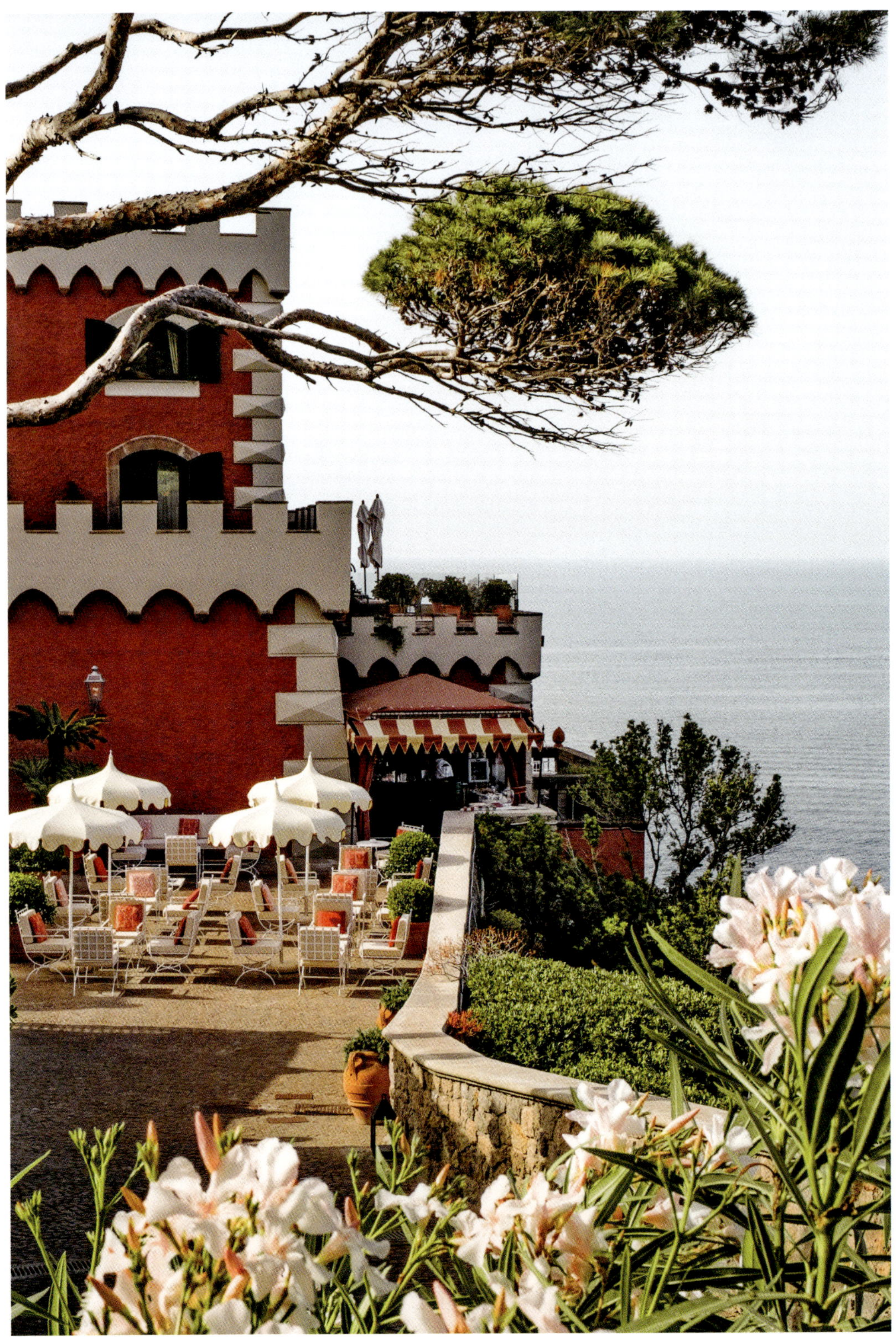

CAMPANIA

MEZZATORRE

Hotel & Thermal SPA
Via Mezzatorre 23, 80075 Forio d'Ischia, Italy
Tel: +39 08 1986 111 · reservations@pellicanohotels.com
www.mezzatorre.com

A MUCH-LOVED DESTINATION As a child she played hide-and-seek in the corridors and rooms of the famous hotel La Posta Vecchia near Rome, and with her brother she released lobsters into the pool of Il Pellicano in Tuscany to save them from being eaten. Marie-Louise Sciò, daughter of the founder of the Pellicano Hotel and now in charge of the family company, has always mastered the balance between luxury and lightness, glamour and casualness. And she has a sure Italian sense of beauty and style: in the space of only four months she turned the hotel Mezzatorre at the north-western tip of Ischia, which she bought in December 2018, into a gem, a destination that is popular with the international jet set. She renovated the rooms in bright colors with superb beds, Italian bathroom tiles and a touch of retro charm. For the restaurant "La Torre" she hired a high-caliber kitchen team and made the dining area a delight for the eyes thanks to a sophisticated wall covering by Pierre Frey. The spa, which used to have the atmosphere of a clinic, was transformed with a wave of her wand into an oasis for wellness with thermal waters from the hotel's own spring. Even the parasols around the outdoor pools are the work of designers. The only aspect of the hotel that required no makeover was its backdrop. This was already as good as a film set: guests can look out into infinity across the sea, stroll in an aromatic pine wood and get a glimpse of Villa Colombaia, which was once the home of the star director Luchino Visconti. ◆ Film to watch: "Rocco and His Brothers" (1960) by Luchino Visconti.

EIN LIEBLINGSZIEL Als Kind spielte sie Verstecken in den Gängen und Zimmern des berühmten Hotels La Posta Vecchia in der Nähe von Rom und ließ gemeinsam mit ihrem Bruder im Pool des toskanischen Il Pellicano Hummer frei, um sie vor dem Verzehr zu retten: Marie-Louise Sciò, Tochter des Gründers der Pellicano Hotels und inzwischen Chefin des Familienunternehmens, beherrscht seit jeher die Balance zwischen Luxus und Leichtigkeit, Glamour und Gelassenheit. Und sie besitzt einen sicheren italienischen Sinn für Schönheit und Stil: Aus dem Hotel Mezzatorre an der Nordwestspitze Ischias, das sie im Dezember 2018 kaufte, machte sie in nur vier Monaten ein Schmuckstück und ein Lieblingsziel des internationalen Jetsets. Sie renovierte die Zimmer in hellen Tönen, mit traumhaften Betten, italienischen Badfliesen und ein bisschen Retro-Charme. Für das Restaurant „Torre“ engagierte sie eine Küchenbrigade mit Klasse und verwandelte das Lokal dank einer raffinierten Tapete von Pierre Frey auch in einen Augenschmaus. Aus dem ehemals klinisch anmutenden Spa wurde wie von Zauberhand eine Wellnessoase mit Thermalwasser aus hauseigener Quelle, und selbst die Sonnenschirme rund um die Außenpools sind Designerentwürfe. Lediglich die Kulisse, vor der das Hotel steht, bedurfte keiner Überarbeitung – sie war bereits kinotauglich: Man kann fast unendlich weit übers Meer schauen, durch einen duftenden Kiefernwald spazieren und einen Blick in die Villa Colombaia werfen, in der Starregisseur Luchino Visconti einst lebte. ◆ Filmtipp: „Rocco und seine Brüder“ (1960) von Luchino Visconti.

UNE DESTINATION PRIVILÉGIÉE Quand elle était petite, elle jouait à cache-cache dans les couloirs et les chambres du célèbre hôtel La Posta Vecchia près de Rome, et lâchait, avec son frère, des homards dans la piscine du Pellicano toscan pour qu'ils échappent à la cuisson. Marie-Louise Sciò, fille du fondateur des hôtels Pellicano et aujourd'hui à la tête de l'entreprise familiale, a toujours su trouver l'équilibre entre luxe et légèreté, glamour et sérénité. Et elle a un sens italien inné de la beauté et du style : en quatre mois seulement, sous ses doigts experts, l'hôtel Mezzatorre, situé à la pointe nord-ouest d'Ischia et qu'elle a acheté en décembre 2018, est devenu un vrai bijou et une destination favorite de la jet-set internationale. Elle a rénové les chambres dans des tons clairs, les a dotées de lits magnifiques, de carreaux de salle de bains italiens, le tout agrémenté d'un zeste de charme rétro. Pour le restaurant « La Torre », elle a engagé une brigade de cuisine talentueuse et a fait de l'endroit un festin pour les yeux grâce à un papier peint raffiné de Pierre Frey. L'ancien spa aux airs de clinique s'est transformé comme par magie en une oasis de bien-être disposant des eaux thermales de l'hôtel, et même les parasols autour des piscines extérieures sont des créations de designers. Seule la toile de fond n'avait pas besoin d'être retravaillée – elle était déjà faite pour le cinéma : on peut regarder infiniment loin de l'autre côté de la mer, se promener dans une forêt de pins odorants et jeter un coup d'œil à la Villa Colombaia, où a vécu le réalisateur vedette Luchino Visconti. ◆ À voir : « Rocco et ses frères » (1960) de Luchino Visconti.

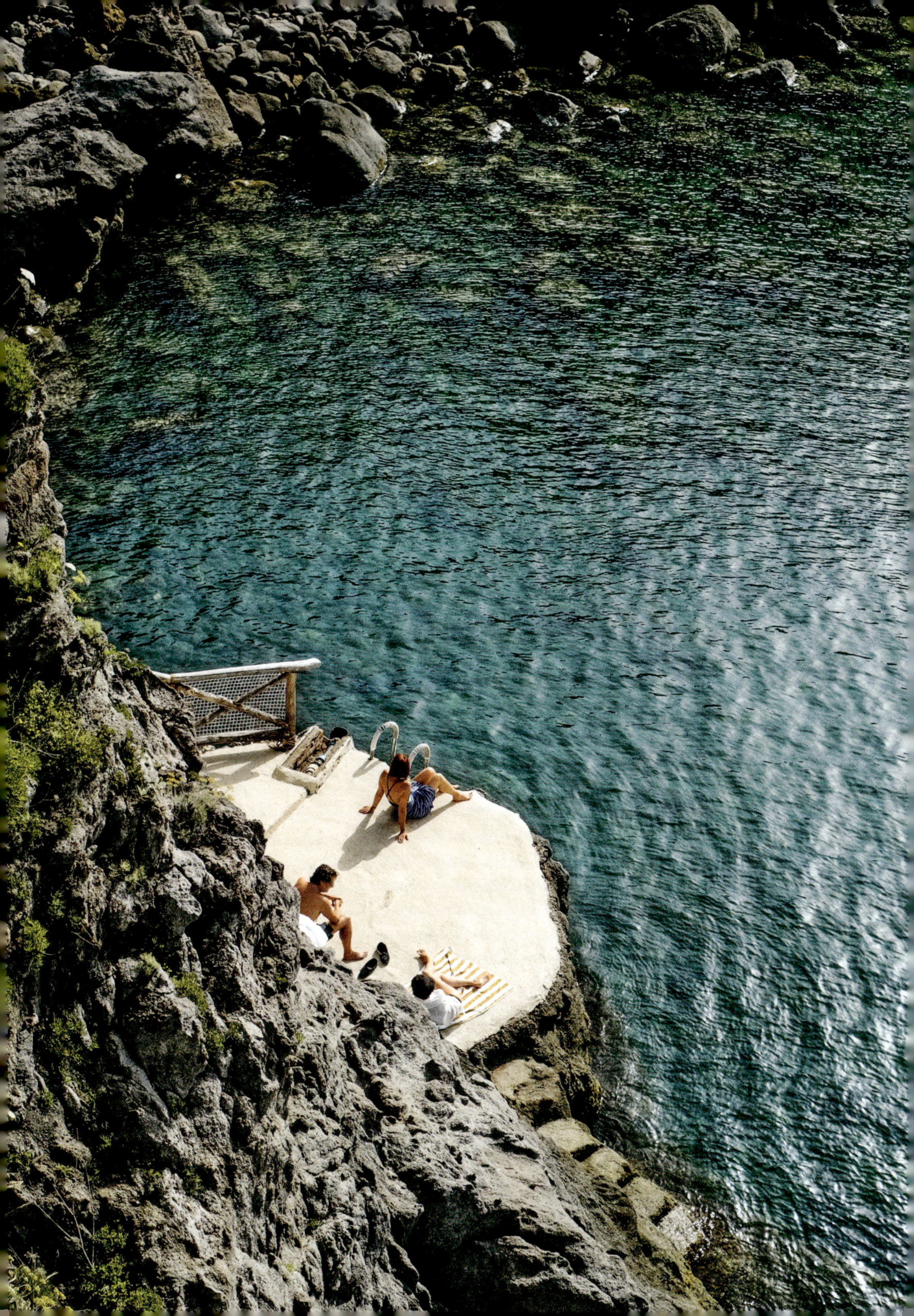

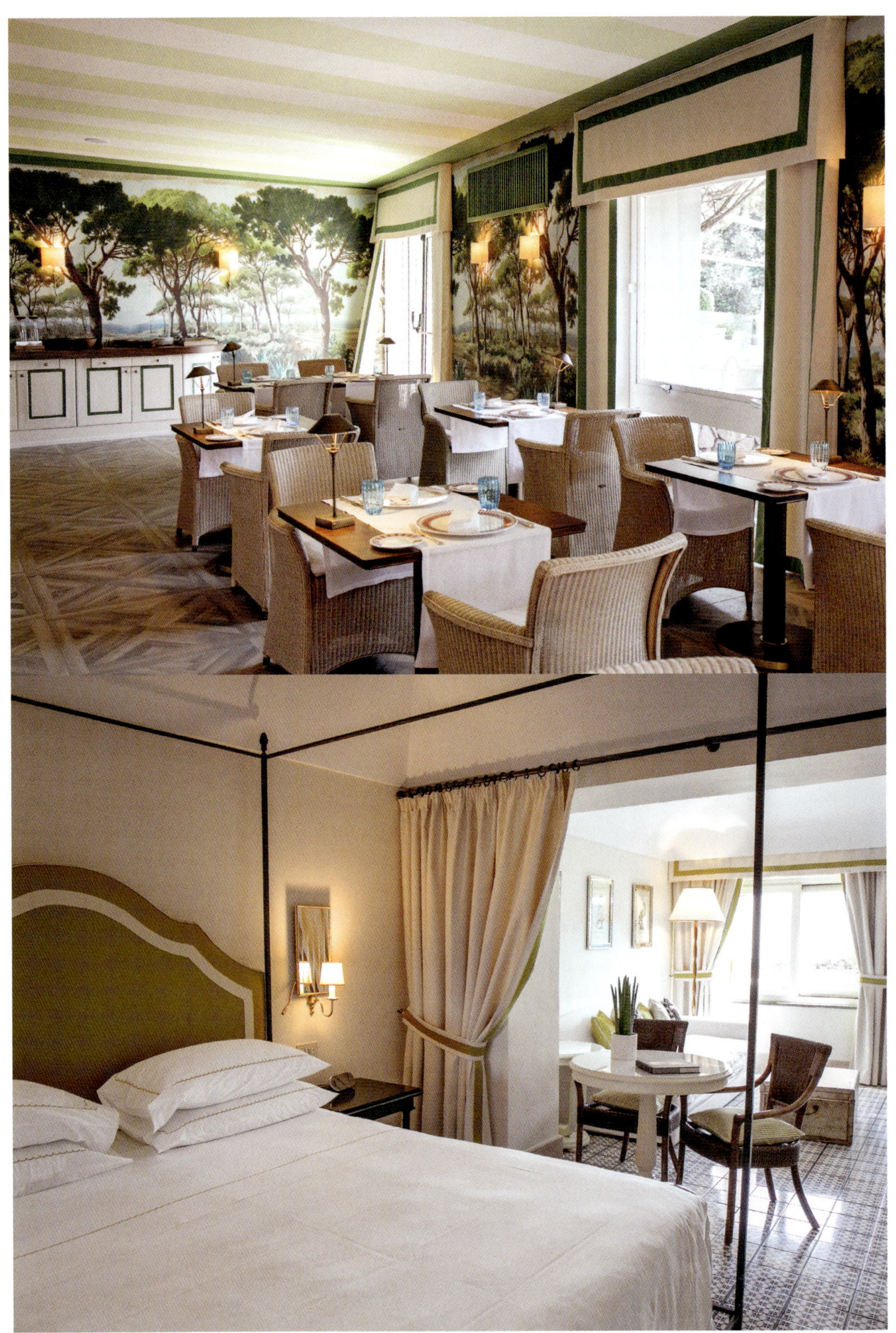

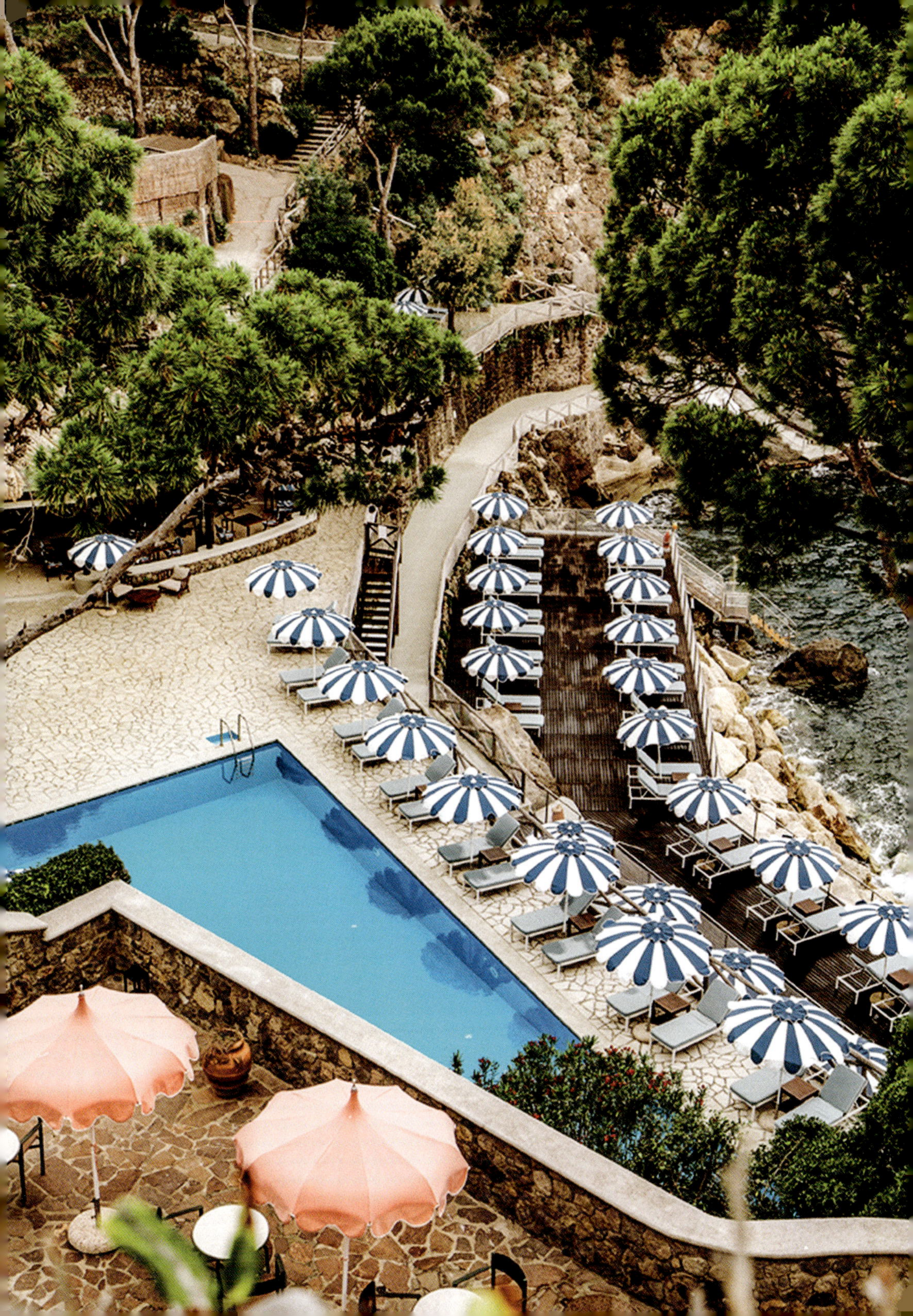

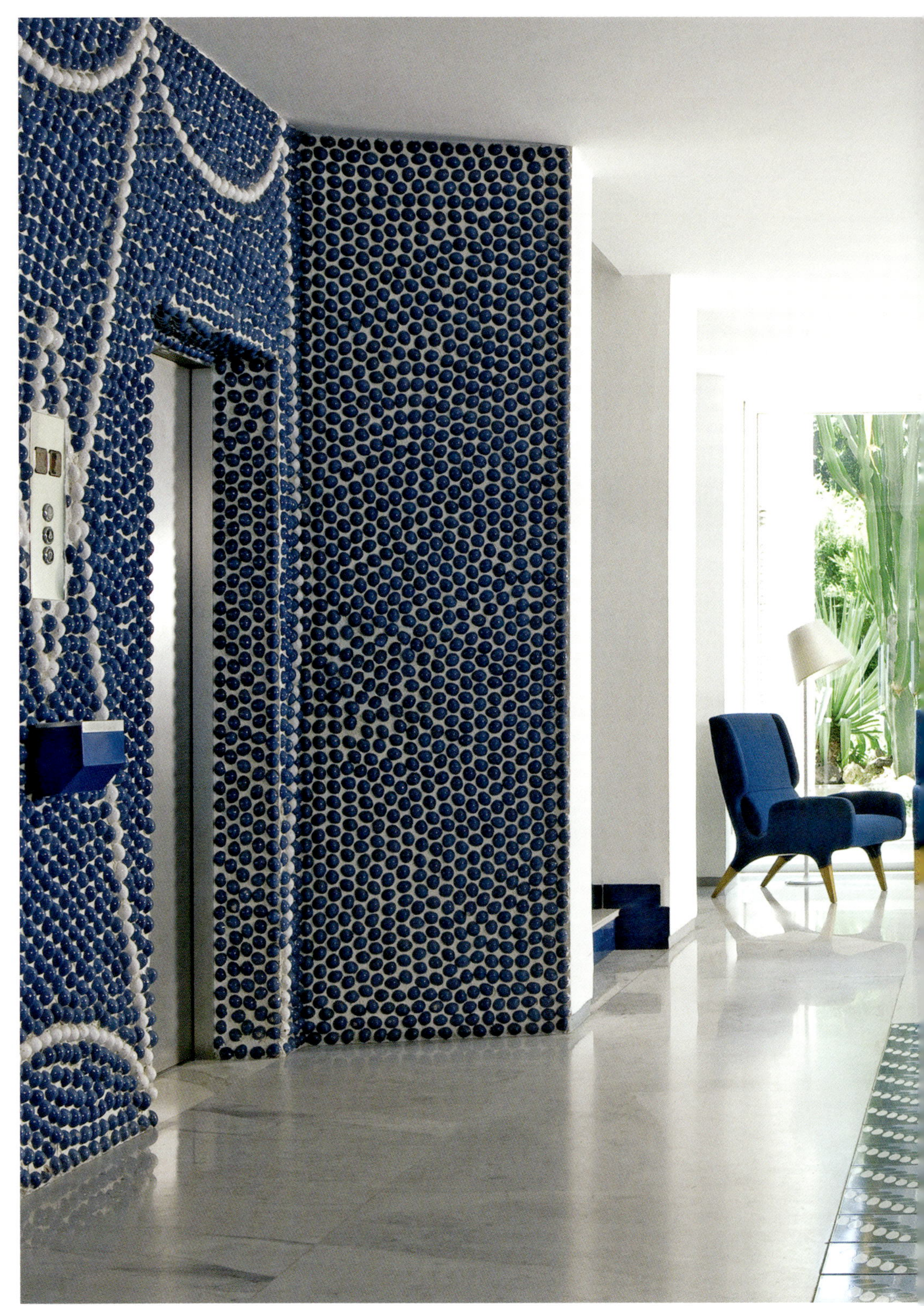

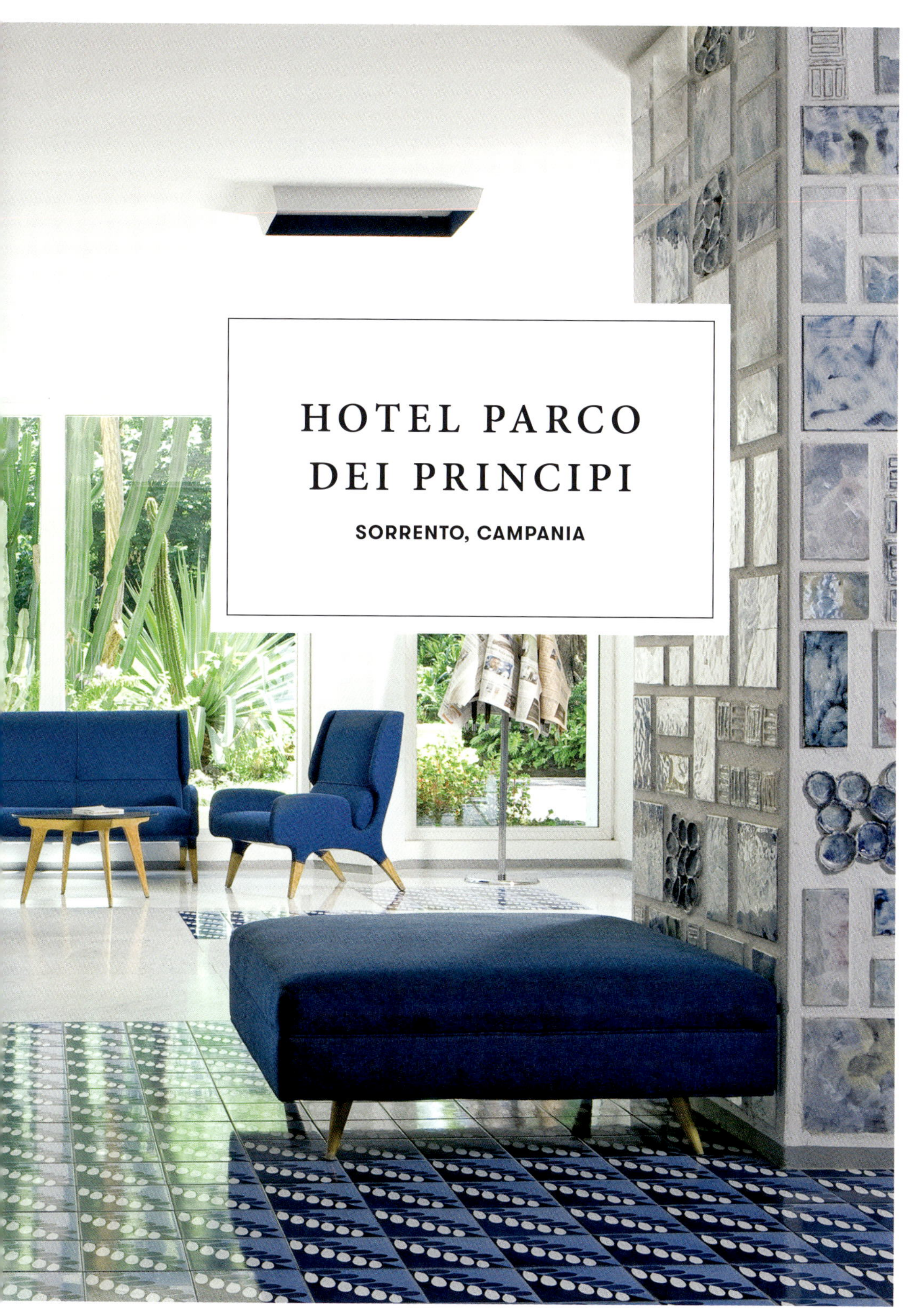

HOTEL PARCO DEI PRINCIPI

SORRENTO, CAMPANIA

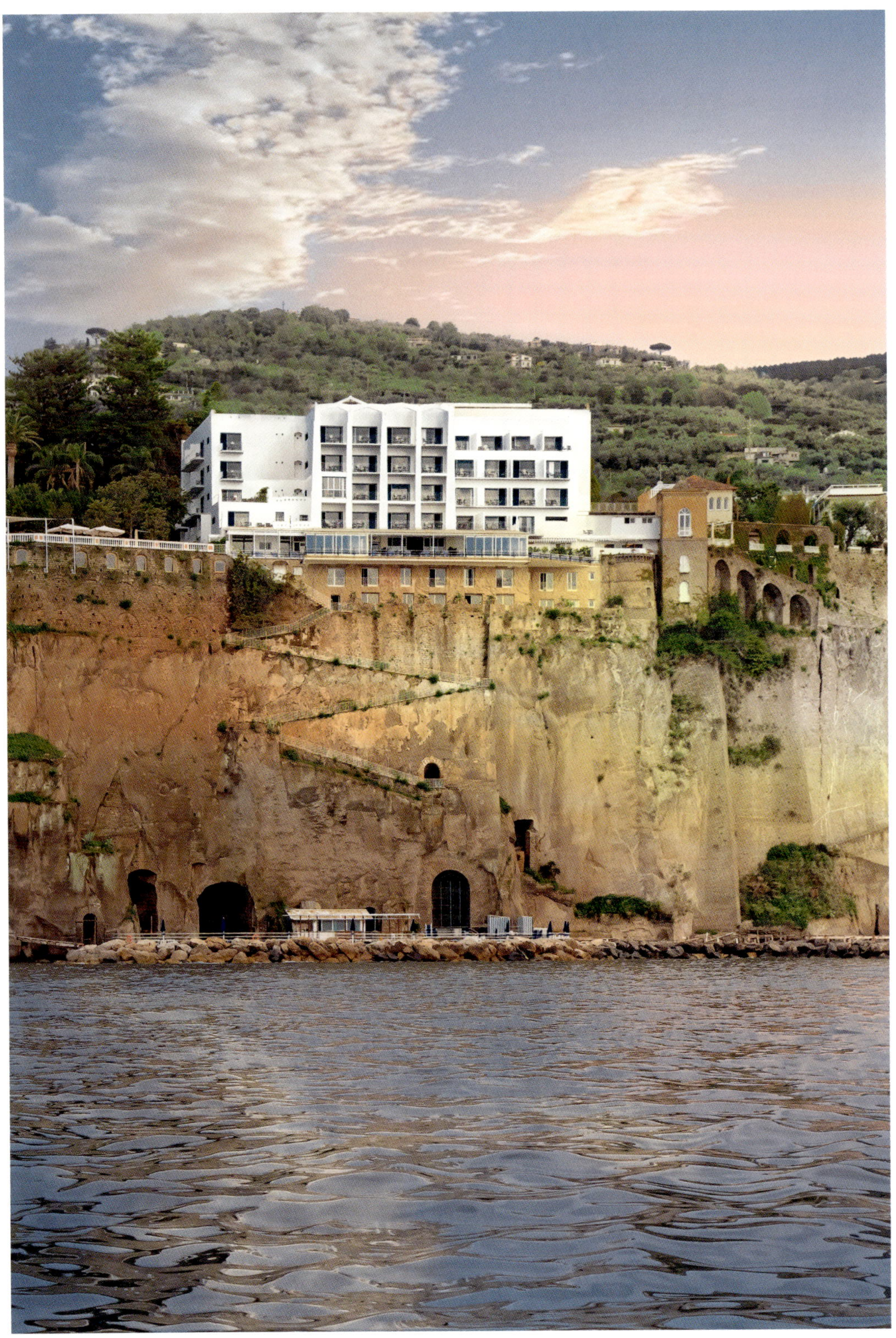

CAMPANIA

HOTEL PARCO DEI PRINCIPI

Via Rota 44, 80067 Sorrento
Tel: + 39 0818 784 644 · info@hotelparcoprincipi.com
www.royalgroup.it/parcodeiprincipi

IN A BLUE MOOD According to the legend, the sirens who tempted Ulysses with their enchanting songs lived in the Sorrentine Sea. In the real world, the charms of the Hotel Parco dei Principi have lured other travellers to that same coastline. Built on a cliff in one of the most famous gardens in Italy, the hotel's clean lines and cool blue and white decor seem to reflect the color of the sea below. Master architect Gio Ponti created the hotel in the 1960s, applying his one-color theory of interior design to striking effect, from the tiled floors to the window blinds. The spacious terraces offer a dazzling view of the blue Bay of Naples and the volcano of Mount Vesuvius. An elevator or stairway built into an ancient cave takes the guests down to the hotel's private jetty and beach. Or bathers may prefer the swimming pool, secluded in the historic park that was once the property of various noble families. Nearby is the picturesque town of Sorrento that crowns the rocky cliffs close to the end of the peninsula. In the cafés you can taste delicious cakes, ice cream, and a glass of the local liqueur "Limoncello", just some of the many attractions of this much-celebrated place.
◆ Books to pack: "The Island of the Day Before" by Umberto Eco and "Thus Spake Bellavista: Naples, Love and Liberty" by Luciano De Crescenzo.

BLAUE STUNDE Der Legende zufolge war es vor Sorrent, wo Odysseus und seine Gefährten von den Gesängen der Sirenen betört wurden. In der realen Welt werden indes andere Reisende vom Zauber des Hotels Parco dei Principi an diese Küste gelockt. Die klaren Linien und das kühle Blau und Weiß dieses auf einer Steilküste aus Tuffstein erbauten Hotels, welches inmitten eines der berühmtesten Gärten Italiens liegt, scheinen das Farbenspiel des Meeres widerzuspiegeln. Der Meisterarchitekt Gio Ponti, der das Hotel in den 1960er-Jahren entwarf, hat hier seine Philosophie von einer monochromen Innenraumgestaltung mit spektakulärem Erfolg umgesetzt: von den gekachelten Fußböden bis hin zu den Jalousien. Die großzügigen Terrassen bieten fantastische Ausblicke auf die blaue Bucht von Neapel und den Vesuv. Über einen Aufzug oder eine Treppe, die durch das Innere der Tuffsteinfelsen führt, gelangen Gäste zu dem Privatstrand des Hotels, der auch über einen eigenen Steg verfügt. Wassernixen können sich ebenso im Pool tummeln. Dieser liegt versteckt in dem historischen Park, der sich früher im Besitz verschiedener Adelsfamilien befand. In der Nähe liegt die malerische Stadt Sorrent auf den Felsklippen am Ende der Halbinsel. Hier kann man sich in den Cafés an köstlichem Kuchen, Eis-Spezialitäten und einem Glas Limoncello, dem in der Region produzierten Zitronenlikör, erbauen, um dann eine der zahlreichen Sehenswürdigkeiten dieses viel gepriesenen Ortes zu erkunden. ◆ Buchtipps: „Die Insel des vorigen Tages“ von Umberto Eco und „Also sprach Bellavista. Neapel, Liebe und Freiheit“ von Luciano De Crescenzo.

CONTE BLEU Selon la légende, les sirènes qui séduisirent Ulysse et ses compagnons par leur chant trompeur vivaient dans la mer de Sorrente. Dans le monde réel, les charmes de l'hôtel Parco dei Principi ont attiré d'autres voyageurs vers ce littoral. Les lignes pures et le décor bleu et blanc de l'hôtel, construit sur une falaise dans l'un des jardins les plus célèbres d'Italie, semblent refléter les couleurs de la mer qui danse à ses pieds. Du carrelage aux stores, le célèbre architecte Gio Ponti, qui a créé l'hôtel dans les années 1960, a appliqué avec bonheur sa théorie selon laquelle la décoration d'intérieur se doit d'être monochrome. Depuis les terrasses spacieuses, on découvre une vue éblouissante sur la mer bleue de la baie de Naples et sur le Vésuve. Les clients de l'hôtel descendent à la jetée et à la plage privées par un ascenseur ou un escalier qui traverse une grotte ancienne. On peut aussi se baigner dans la piscine, cachée dans le parc historique qui a appartenu autrefois à diverses familles nobles. Tout près, la ville pittoresque de Sorrente couronne les falaises rocheuses proches de l'extrémité de la péninsule. Dans les salons de thé, on peut goûter aux gâteaux délicieux, aux glaces ou au limoncello, la liqueur de citron locale, quelques-uns seulement des nombreux attraits de cet endroit si célèbre. ◆ À lire : « L'Île du jour d'avant » d'Umberto Eco et « Ainsi parlait Bellavista » de Luciano De Crescenzo.

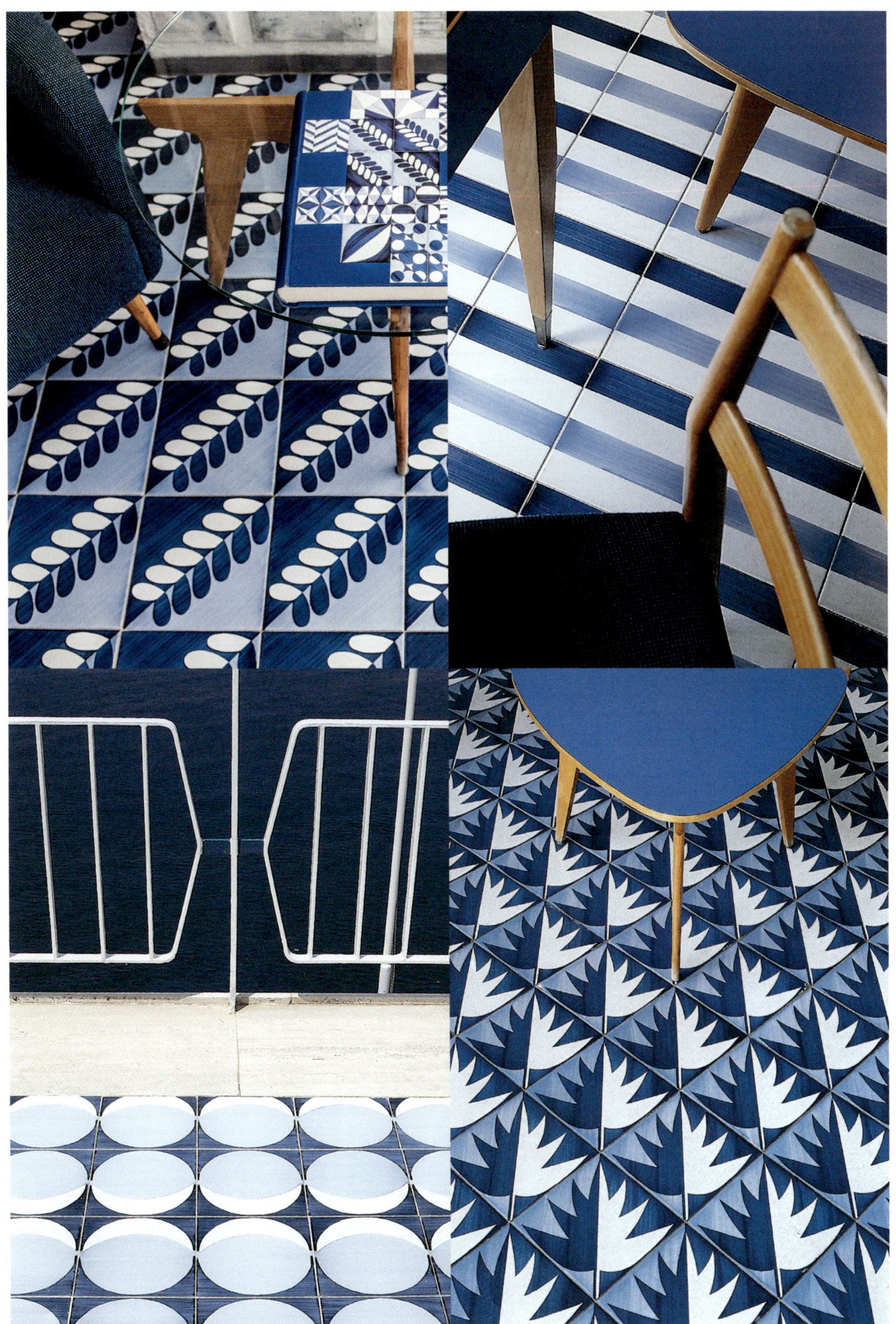

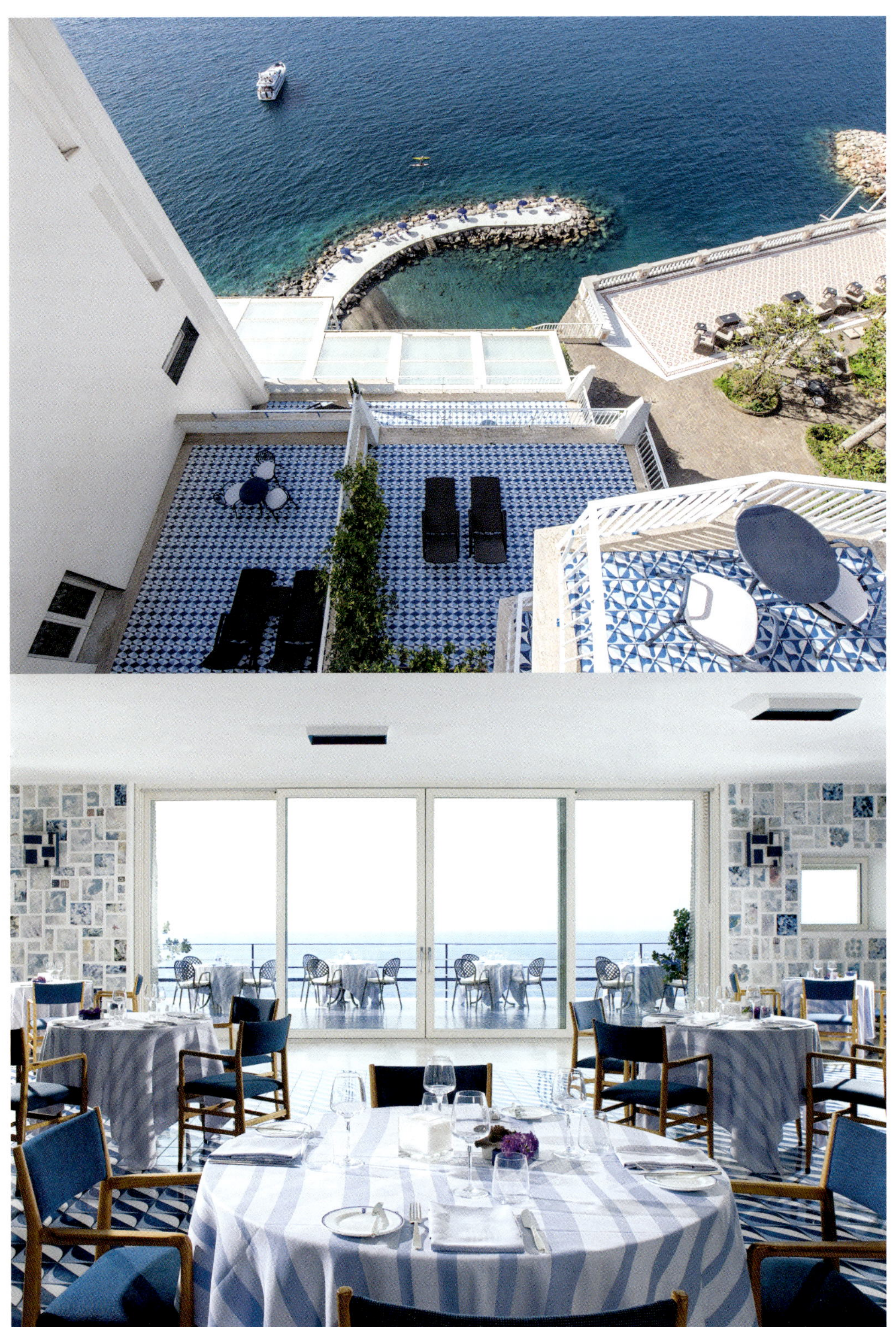

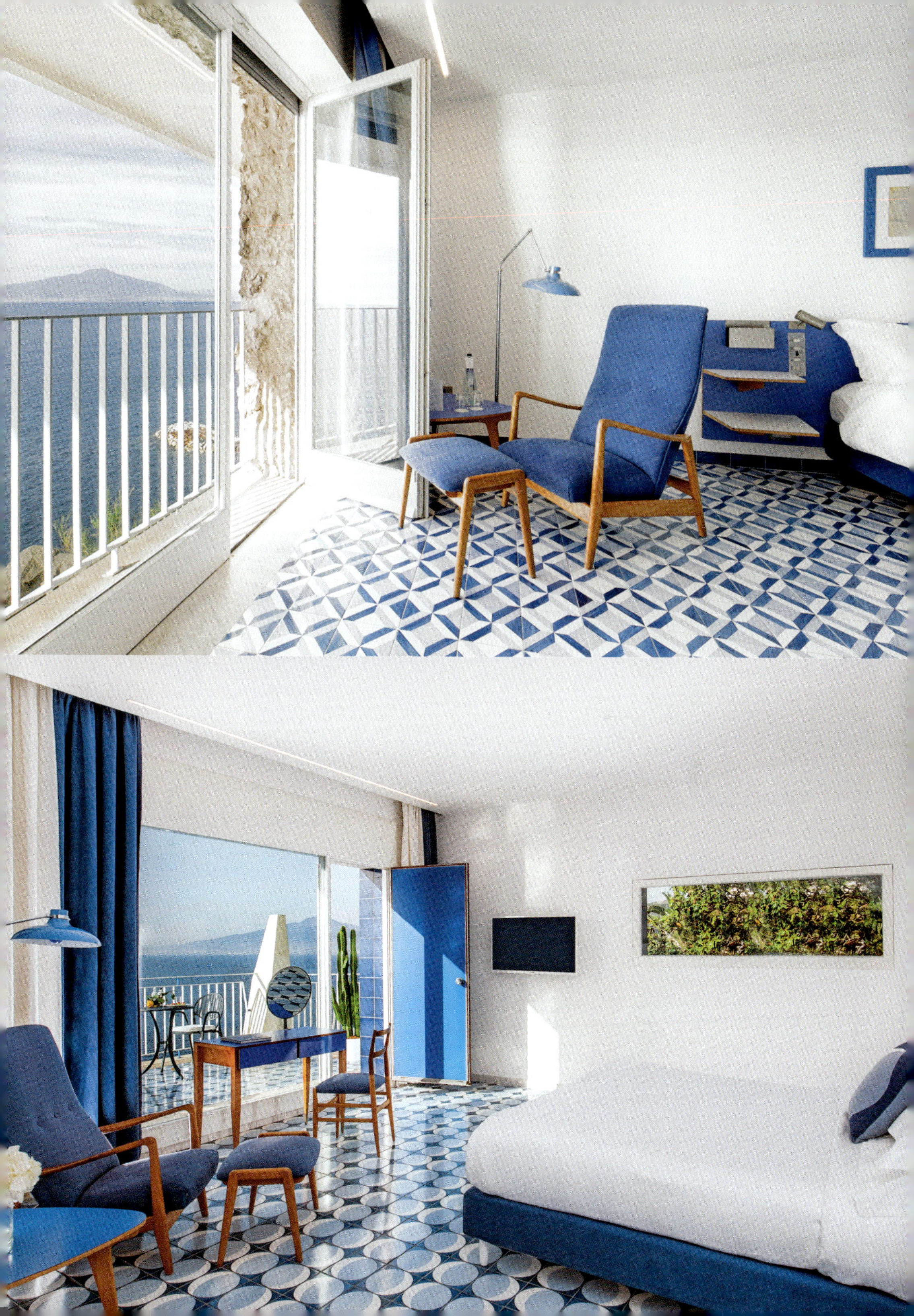

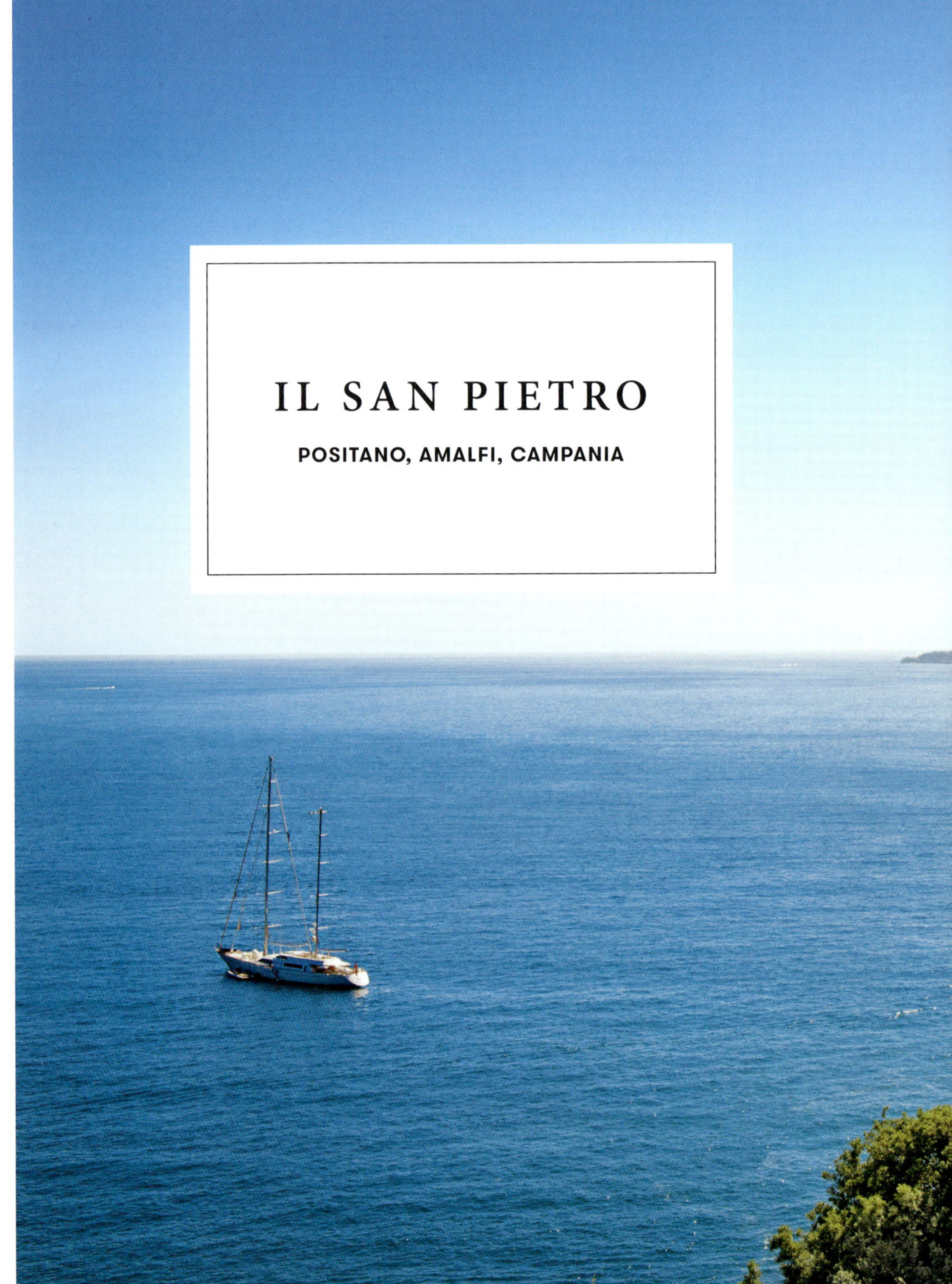

IL SAN PIETRO

POSITANO, AMALFI, CAMPANIA

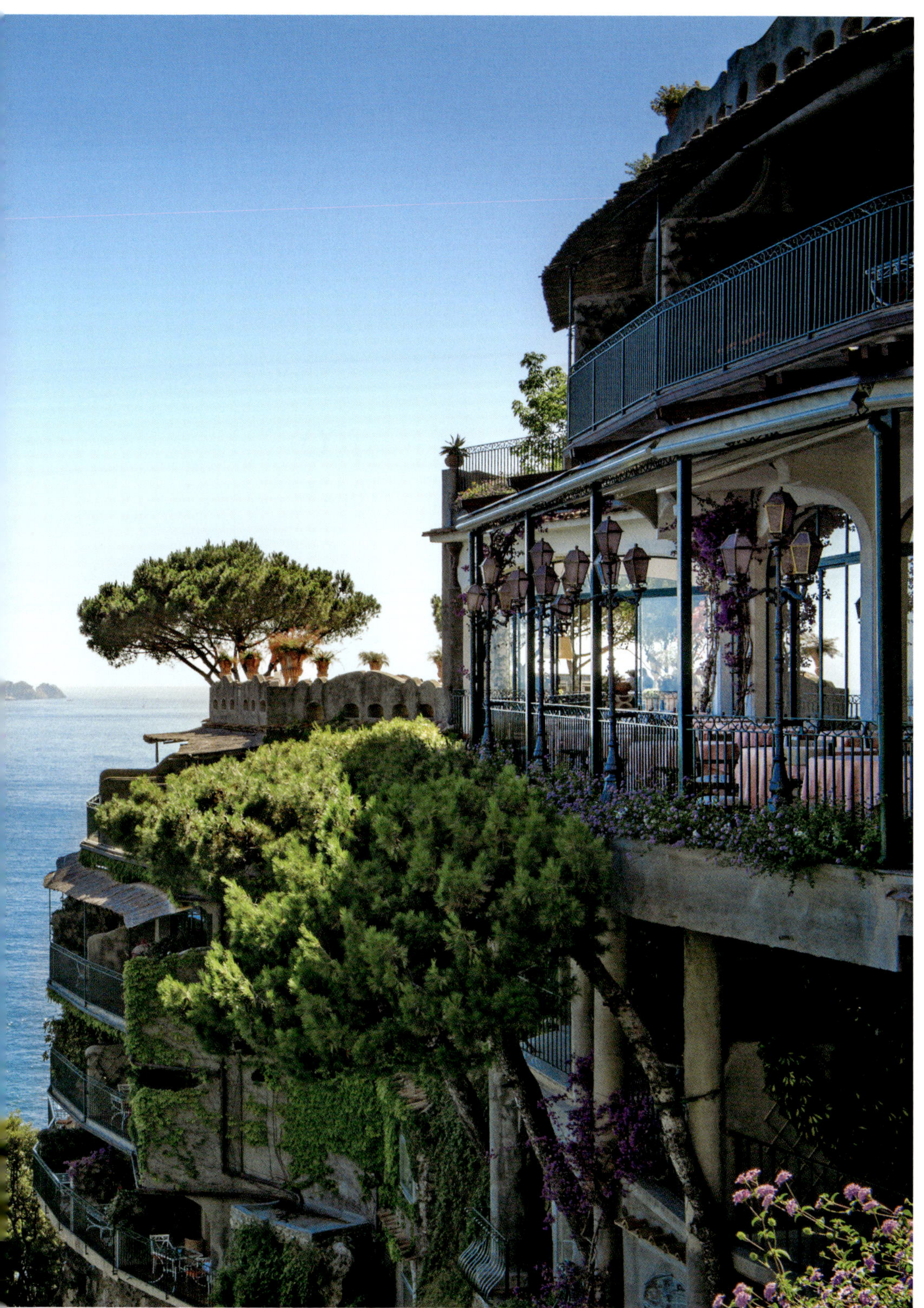

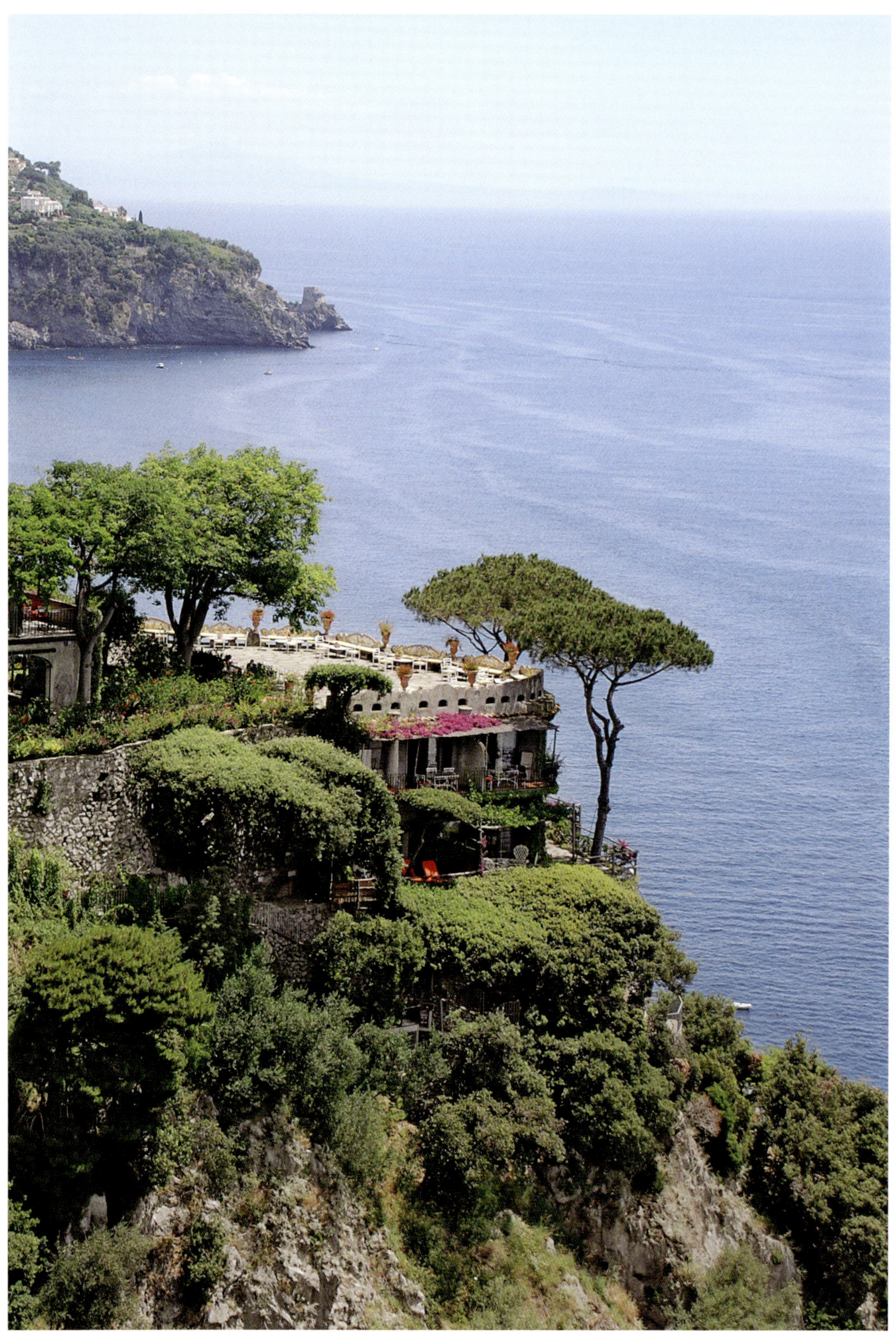

CAMPANIA

IL SAN PIETRO

Via Laurito 2, 84017 Positano
Tel. +39 089 812 080 · reservations@ilsanpietro.it
www.ilsanpietro.it
Open from the beginning of April to the end of October

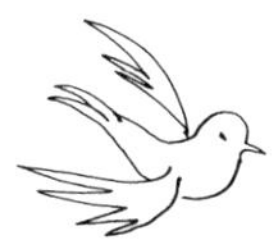

THE VIEW IS EVERYTHING His trademark was a wide-brimmed straw hat. He was so stylish that he still looked irresistible in shorts and sandals, and even Hollywood stars described his parties as legendary: Carlo Cinque, a self-made man and visionary who gave Positano its finest hotel and most spectacular look-out point, Il San Pietro. He had the hotel built in the 1960s on terraces on a rock projecting far into the sea on the Amalfi coast, and took advice for the work solely from an electrical engineer – he himself carried out the tasks of architect, construction engineer, site supervisor and interior designer. And decades before the profession of "guest relations manager" was invented, Carlo Cinque was a master of the art of caring for his hotel guests. Today his niece Virginia and her sons display the same talent in running Il San Pietro, and they are achieving the feat of discreetly updating the estate without destroying its stylish ambience. They have decorated the panorama terrace with ceramic tiles that depict marine scenes in 17th-century style, established an excellent spa beneath lemon trees and have been so successful at refining traditional cooking that they have been awarded a Michelin star. Right next to their private beach they have opened a second restaurant and named it "Carlino" in honour of their great role model. To travel the 288 feet in height between the reception and the restaurant, guests take a lift. The lift shaft was once hewn straight from the rock – by Carlo Cinque personally, of course. ◆ Book to pack: "Lady Windermere's Fan" by Oscar Wilde – filmed on the Amalfi coast with the title "A Good Woman".

AUSSICHT IST ALLES Ein Strohhut mit breiter Krempe war sein Markenzeichen. Er hatte so viel Stil, dass er sogar in Shorts und Sandalen umwerfend aussah, und seine Partys bezeichneten selbst Stars aus Hollywood als legendär: Carlo Cinque, der Selfmademan und Visionär, der Positano mit Il San Pietro sein schönstes Hotel und seinen spektakulärsten Aussichtspunkt gab. Terrassenartig ließ er das Haus in den 1960ern an einen weit vorspringenden Felsen der Amalfiküste bauen und holte sich dabei lediglich den Rat eines Elektroingenieurs – als Architekt, Statiker, Bauleiter und Ausstatter fungierte er höchstpersönlich, ebenso als Gästebetreuer in seinem Hotel – Jahrzehnte, ehe man den Beruf des „Guest Relation Manager" erfand, war Carlo Cinque bereits Meister dieses Fachs. Heute führen seine Nichte Virginia und ihre Söhne Il San Pietro mit demselben Talent und bringen das Kunststück fertig, das Anwesen dezent aufzufrischen, ohne sein stilvolles Ambiente zu zerstören. Sie ließen die Panoramaterrasse mit Keramikfliesen schmücken, die maritime Szenen im Stil des 17. Jahrhunderts zeigen, richteten unter Zitronenbäumen ein exzellentes Spa ein und verfeinerten die traditionelle Küche so gelungen, dass sie einen Michelin-Stern erhielt. Direkt am Privatstrand eröffneten sie ein zweites Lokal und benannten es zu Ehren ihres großen Vorbilds „Carlino". Die 88 Meter Höhenunterschied zwischen Rezeption und Restaurant überwindet man im Lift, dessen Schacht einst direkt in den Fels geschlagen wurde – natürlich von Carlo Cinque persönlich. ◆ Buchtipp: „Lady Windermeres Fächer" von Oscar Wilde – wurde an der Amalfiküste verfilmt („Good Woman – Ein Sommer in Amalfi").

LA MER ET LE CIEL Carlo Cinque ne quittait jamais son chapeau de paille à large bord ; même en shorts et nu-pieds, il avait une allure folle ; quant à ses fêtes, les stars hollywoodiennes les trouvaient légendaires. Le self-made-man visionnaire qui a donné à Positano son plus bel hôtel et son point de vue le plus spectaculaire fit bâtir la maison en terrasse sur un promontoire de la côte amalfitaine au cours des années 1960. Il n'écouta que les conseils d'un électro-ingénieur, faisant lui-même office d'architecte, d'ingénieur, de chef de chantier et de décorateur. Il continua sur sa lancée avec ses hôtes – des décennies avant que l'on ait inventé le métier de « guest relation manager », Carlo Cinque était déjà passé maître dans cet art. Aujourd'hui, sa nièce Virginia et ses fils dirigent le Il San Pietro avec la même virtuosité et ont réussi à moderniser discrètement les lieux sans détruire leur ambiance élégante. La terrasse panoramique a été pavée de carreaux de céramique montrant des scènes maritimes dans le style du XVIIe siècle, un spa a été aménagé sous les citronniers et la cuisine traditionnelle perfectionnée de telle manière que le restaurant a obtenu une étoile au Michelin. Les propriétaires ont ouvert un second établissement sur la plage privée et l'ont baptisé « Carlino » en hommage à leur modèle. Un ascenseur relie la réception au restaurant situé 88 mètres plus haut. Il a été directement creusé dans le rocher – par Carlo Cinque, évidemment. ◆ À lire : « L'Éventail de Lady Windermere » d'Oscar Wilde (son adaptation cinématographique « La Séductrice » a été tournée sur la côte d'Amalfi).

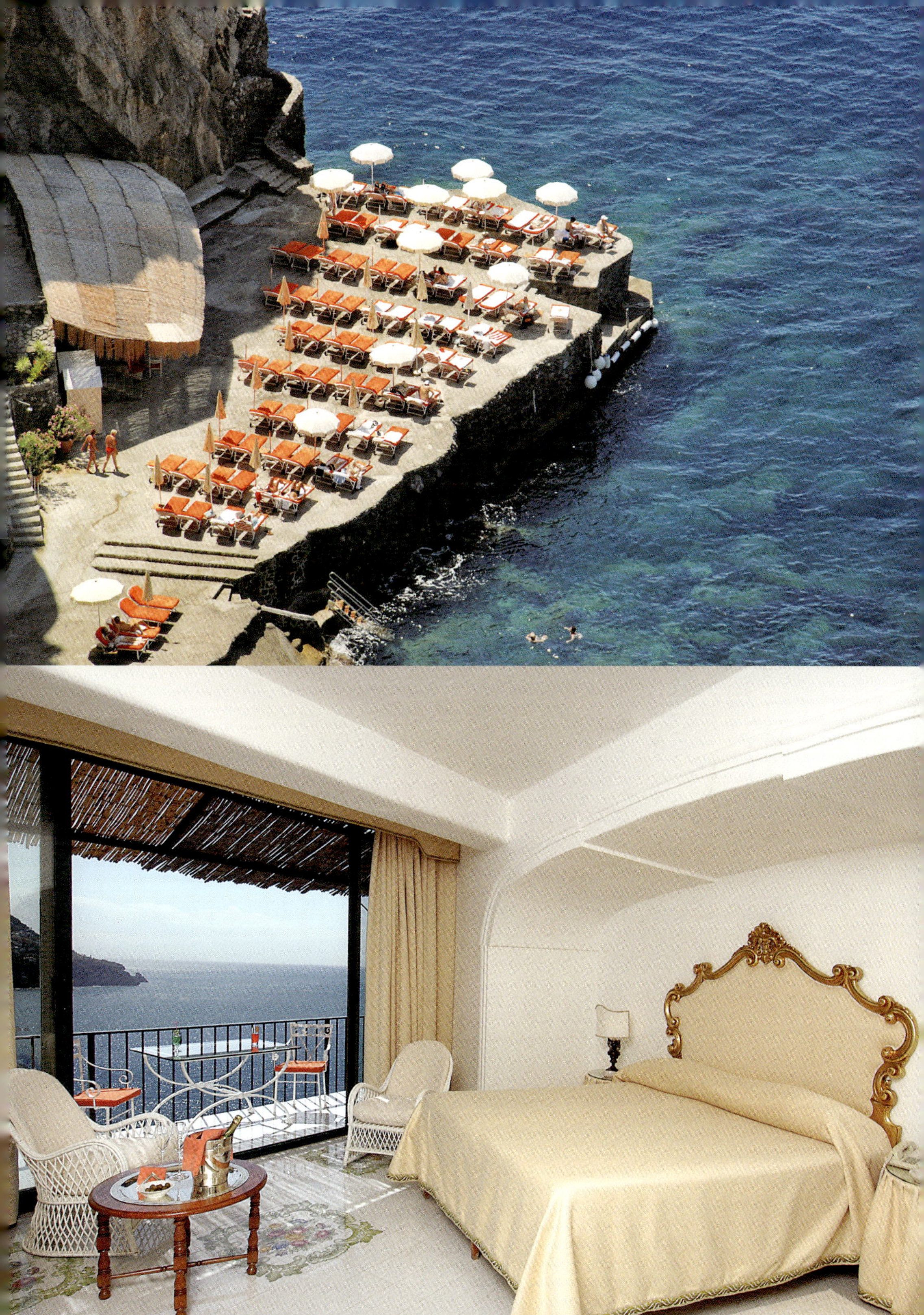

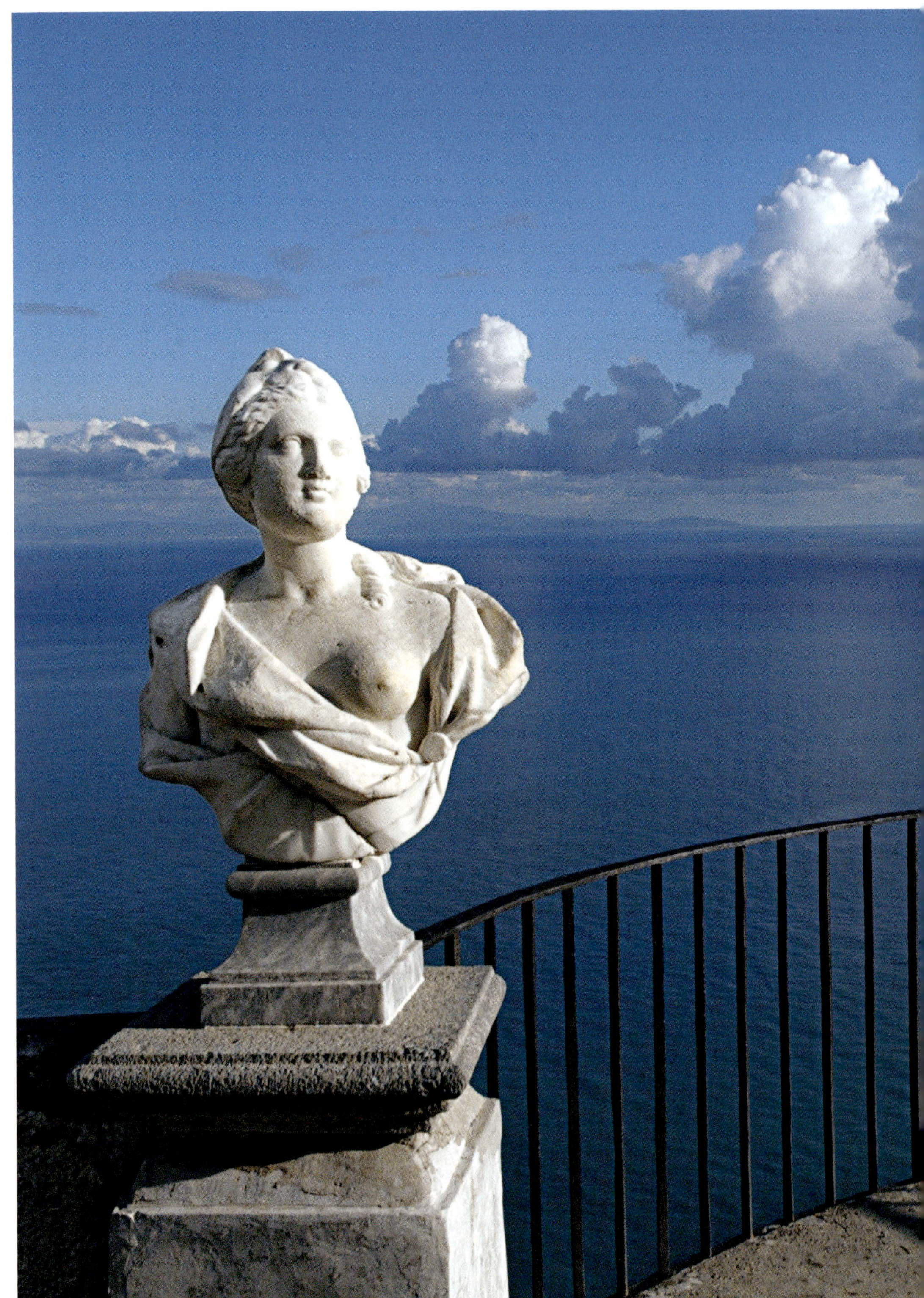

CAMPANIA

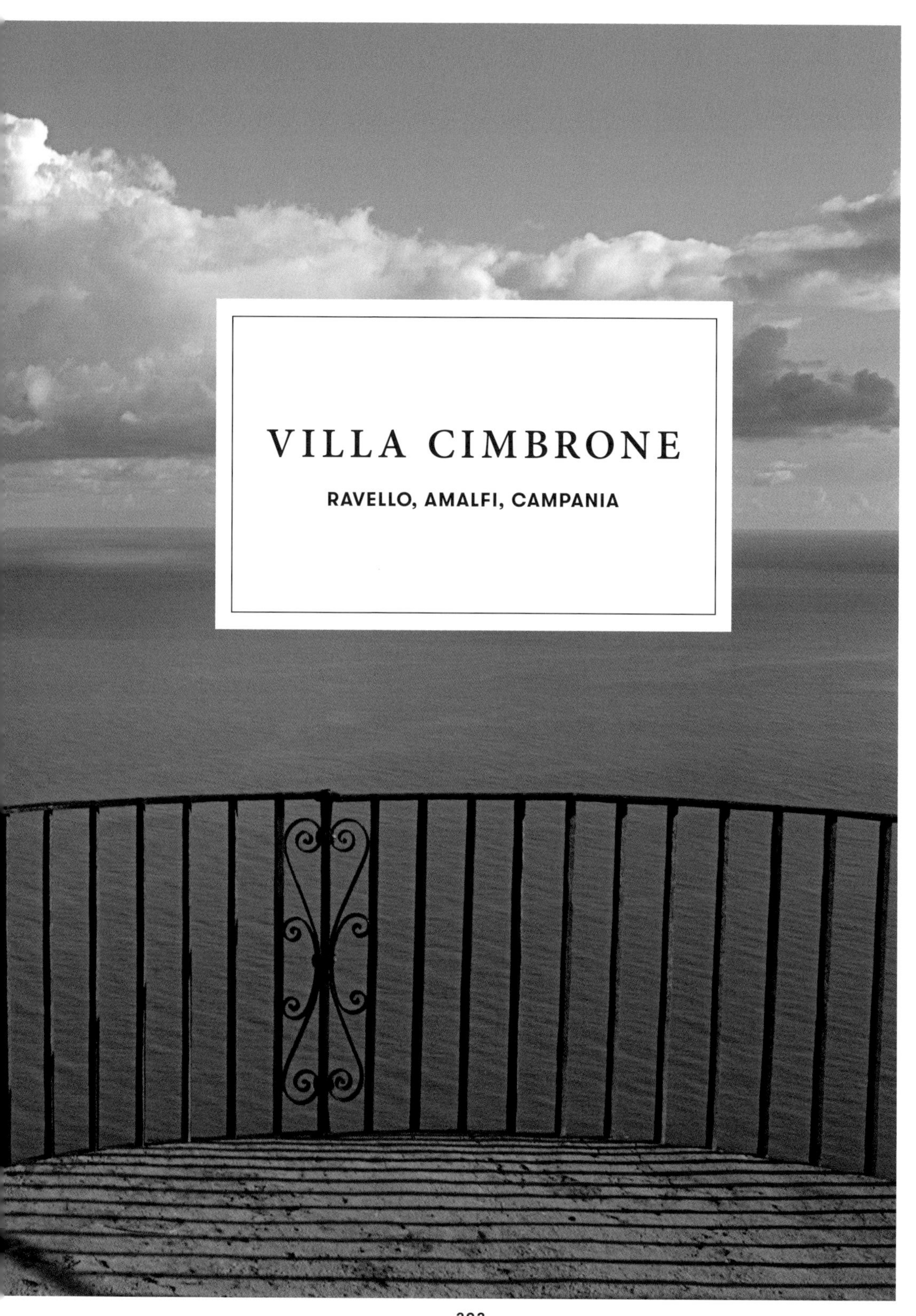

VILLA CIMBRONE

RAVELLO, AMALFI, CAMPANIA

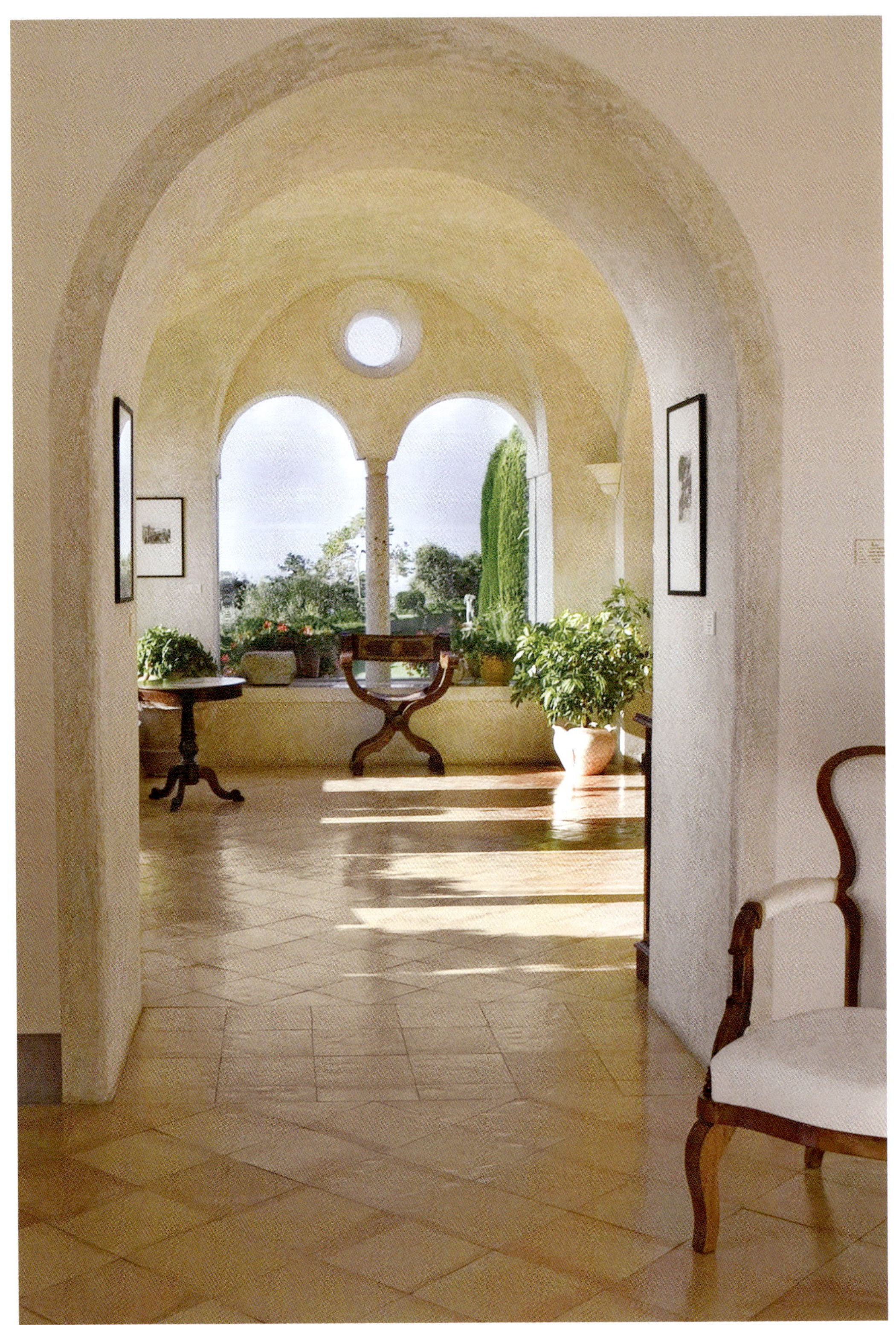

VILLA CIMBRONE

Via Santa Chiara 26, 84010 Ravello
Tel. +39 089 857 459 · info@villacimbrone.com
www.villacimbrone.com
Open from early April to late December

ALMOST LIKE BEING IN HEAVEN When the writer Ferdinand Gregorovius reached Ravello, he found the most beautiful park that he had ever seen around Villa Cimbrone: "In the prettily kept garden the most magnificent show of flowers from countless southern plants blazed all around, in all the glory of the month of July", he enthused in 1861 in his "Siciliana". Today visitors can still stroll around cloisters and beneath bowers, between cypresses, palms and pines, discover hidden wells, temples and grottoes and breathe in the scent of roses. This oasis was created on a spectacular mountain ridge in the early 20th century by Ernest William Beckett, a British dandy later known as Lord Grimthorpe, who had fallen head over heels in love with Villa Cimbrone and transformed it into his private paradise. In accordance with his somewhat eccentric way of life he used a carefree mix of styles. In the house and garden he combined Greek, Roman, Moorish and Venetian elements into a curious but enormously charming work of art. The main building has now become a hotel, provided with every luxury but at the same time fitted out as creatively as in Beckett's day: the best rooms have floors of Vietri tiles, frescoes and open fireplaces. The two large suites have a terrace with a sea view – only the outlook from the belvedere in the park is more beautiful. This was also the opinion of Ferdinand Gregorovius, who wrote: "When looking out from this garden to the siren sea (…), one has a yearning to fly". ◆ Book to pack: "Siciliana: Wanderings in Naples and Sicily" by Ferdinand Gregorovius.

FAST WIE IM HIMMEL Als der Schriftsteller Ferdinand Gregorovius nach Ravello kam, fand er rings um die Villa Cimbrone den schönsten Park, den er je gesehen hatte: „In dem zierlich gehaltenen Garten flammte ringsum die köstlichste Blütenpracht ungezählter Gewächse des Südens, in der vollen Glorie des Julimonats", schwärmte er 1861 in seiner „Siciliana". Noch heute kann man hier in Kreuzgängen und unter Lauben wandeln, zwischen Zypressen, Palmen und Pinien spazieren gehen, versteckte Brunnen, Tempel und Grotten entdecken und den Duft von Rosen einatmen. Angelegt wurde diese Oase auf einem spektakulären Berggrat Anfang des 20. Jahrhunderts von Ernest William Beckett. Der britische Dandy, der später als Lord Grimthorpe berühmt wurde, hatte sich damals unsterblich in die Villa Cimbrone verliebt und sie in sein privates Paradies verwandelt. Seinem etwas exzentrischen Lebensstil entsprechend, mischte er dabei unbekümmert die Stile – in Haus und Garten verband er griechische, römische, maurische und venezianische Elemente zu einem kuriosen, aber ungeheuer charmanten Kunstwerk. Inzwischen ist aus dem Hauptgebäude ein Hotel geworden, das mit allem Luxus ausgestattet, aber zugleich so kreativ wie damals gehalten ist: Die besten Zimmer besitzen Vietri-Fliesenböden, Fresken und offene Kamine. Zu den zwei größten Suiten gehören Terrassen mit Meerblick – noch schöner ist die Sicht nur vom Belvedere im Park aus. Dieser Meinung war übrigens auch schon Ferdinand Gregorovius, der schrieb: „Schaut man aus diesem Garten in jenes sirenische Meer (...), dann sehnt man sich zu fliegen." ◆ Buchtipp: „Siciliana. Wanderungen in Neapel und Sicilien" von Ferdinand Gregorovius.

COMME AU CIEL Lorsque l'écrivain Ferdinand Gregorovius arriva à Ravello, il trouva autour de la Villa Cimbrone le parc le plus beau qu'il ait jamais vu : « Dans le plaisant jardin s'enflammait alentour le décor floral le plus exquis d'innombrables plantes du Sud dans la gloire du mois de juillet », s'extasie-t-il en 1861. On peut aujourd'hui encore déambuler dans les cloîtres et sous les tonnelles, se promener entre les cyprès, les palmiers et les pins, découvrir des fontaines cachées, des temples et des grottes et humer le parfum des roses. Ce lieu enchanteur a été aménagé au début du XXe siècle sur une arête spectaculaire par Ernest William Beckett. Le dandy britannique, devenu célèbre sous le nom de Lord Grimthorpe, était tombé amoureux fou de la Villa Cimbrone qu'il avait transformée en un paradis à son usage personnel. Fidèle à son mode de vie excentrique, il maria nonchalamment les styles, associant dans la maison et le jardin les éléments grecs, romains, maures et vénitiens pour créer une œuvre d'art singulière, mais ô combien charmante. Aujourd'hui, le bâtiment principal est devenu un hôtel doté de tout le luxe possible, mais qui a su conserver son originalité d'antan : les meilleures chambres abritent des carrelages de Vietri, des fresques murales et des cheminées. Les deux suites les plus vastes sont dotées de terrasses avec vue sur la mer – seule la perspective du belvédère, dans le parc, est plus belle. D'ailleurs, Ferdinand Gregorovius était bien de cet avis lorsqu'il écrivait : « Si l'on regarde la mer sirénique de ce jardin (...), on a envie de voler. » ◆ À lire : « Promenades en Italie et en Corse » de Ferdinand Gregorovius.

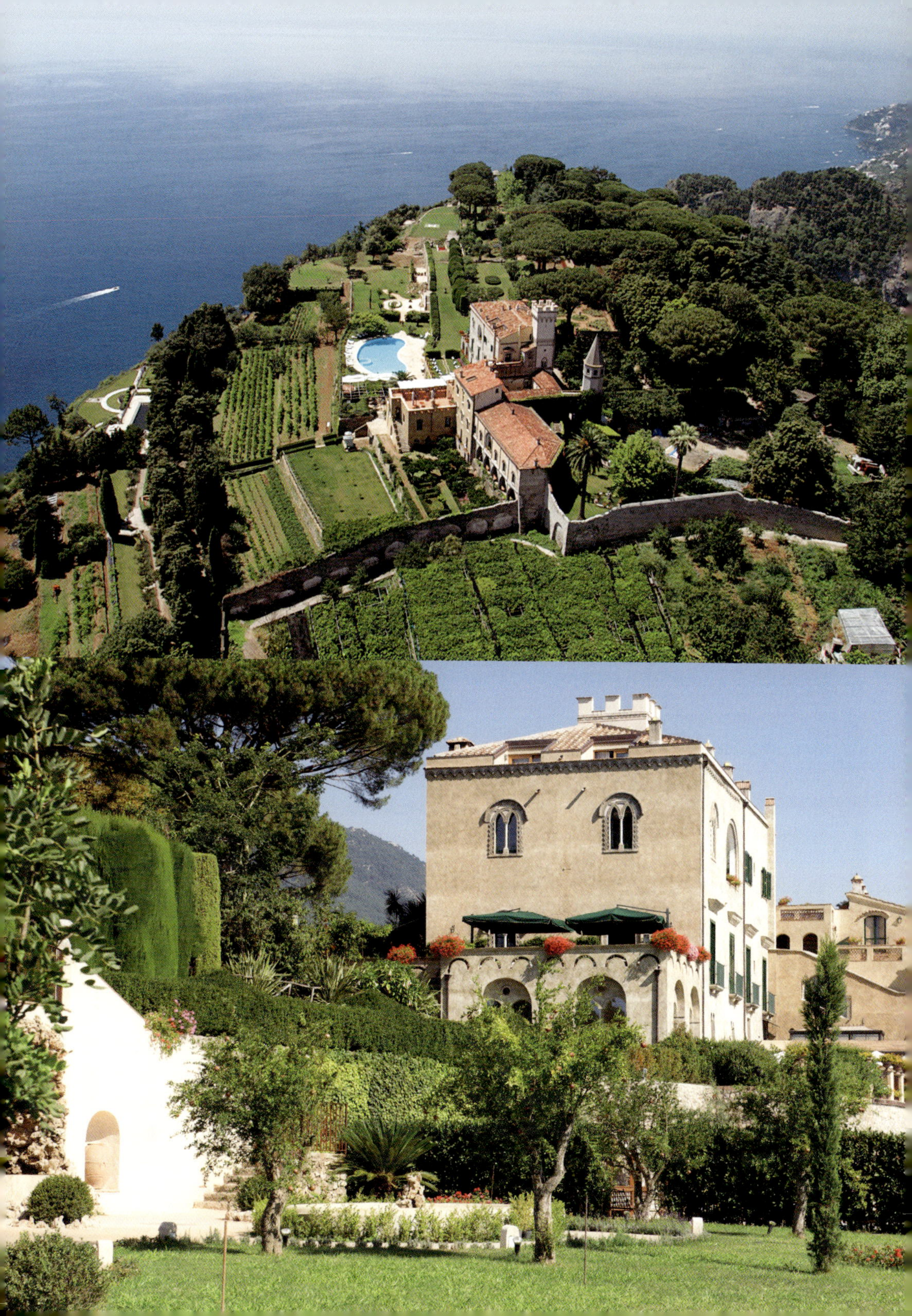

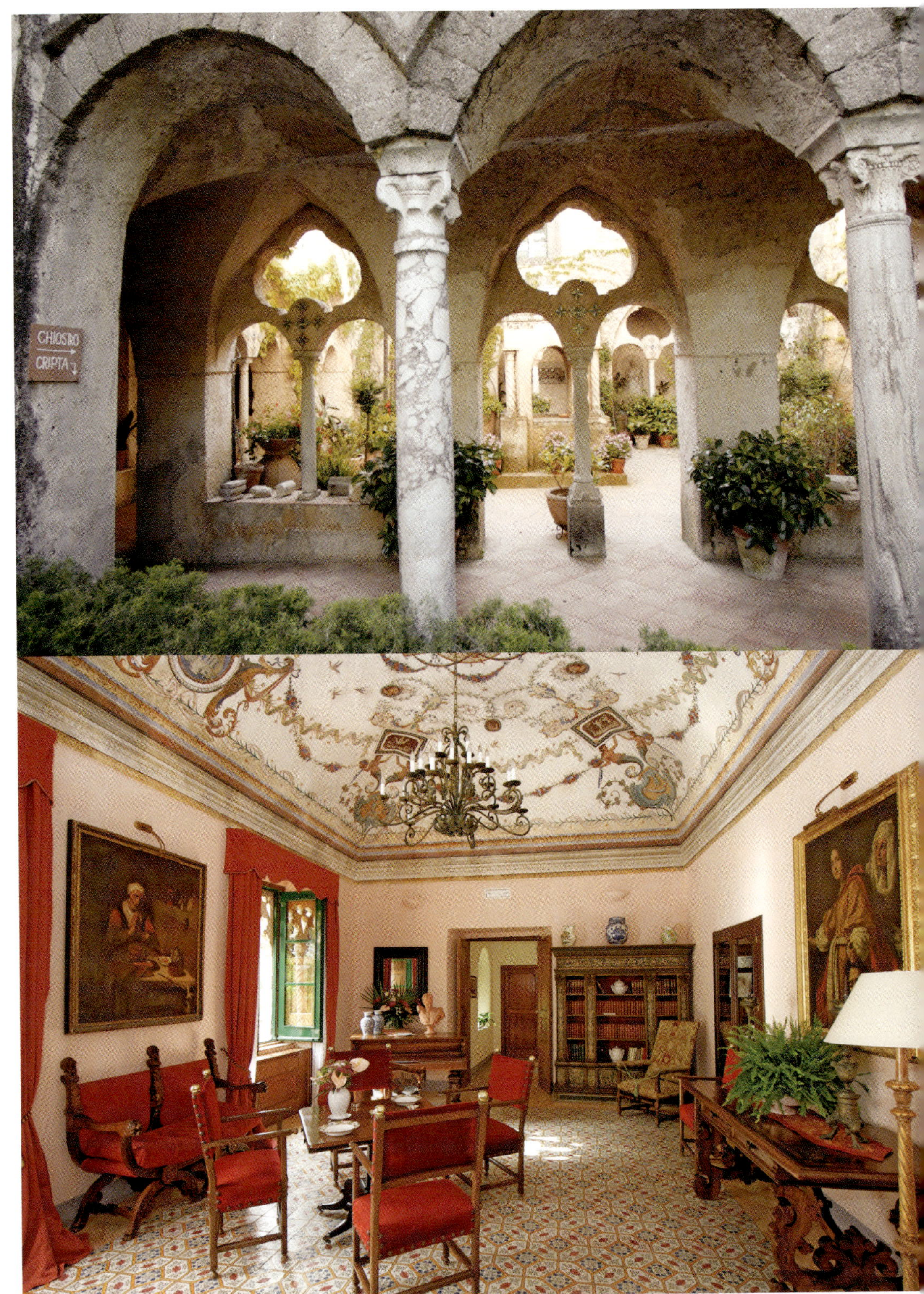
CHIOSTRO
CRIPTA

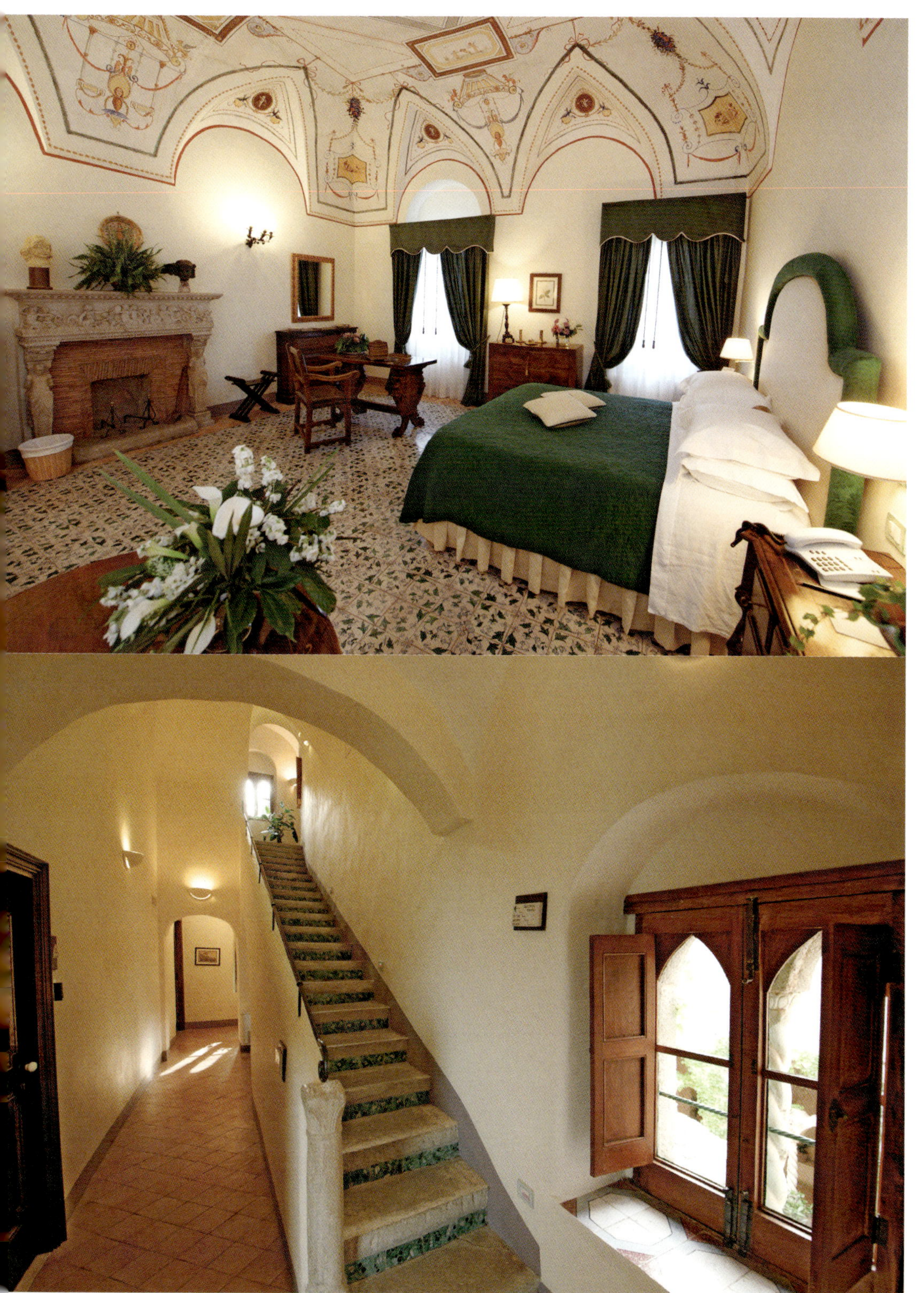

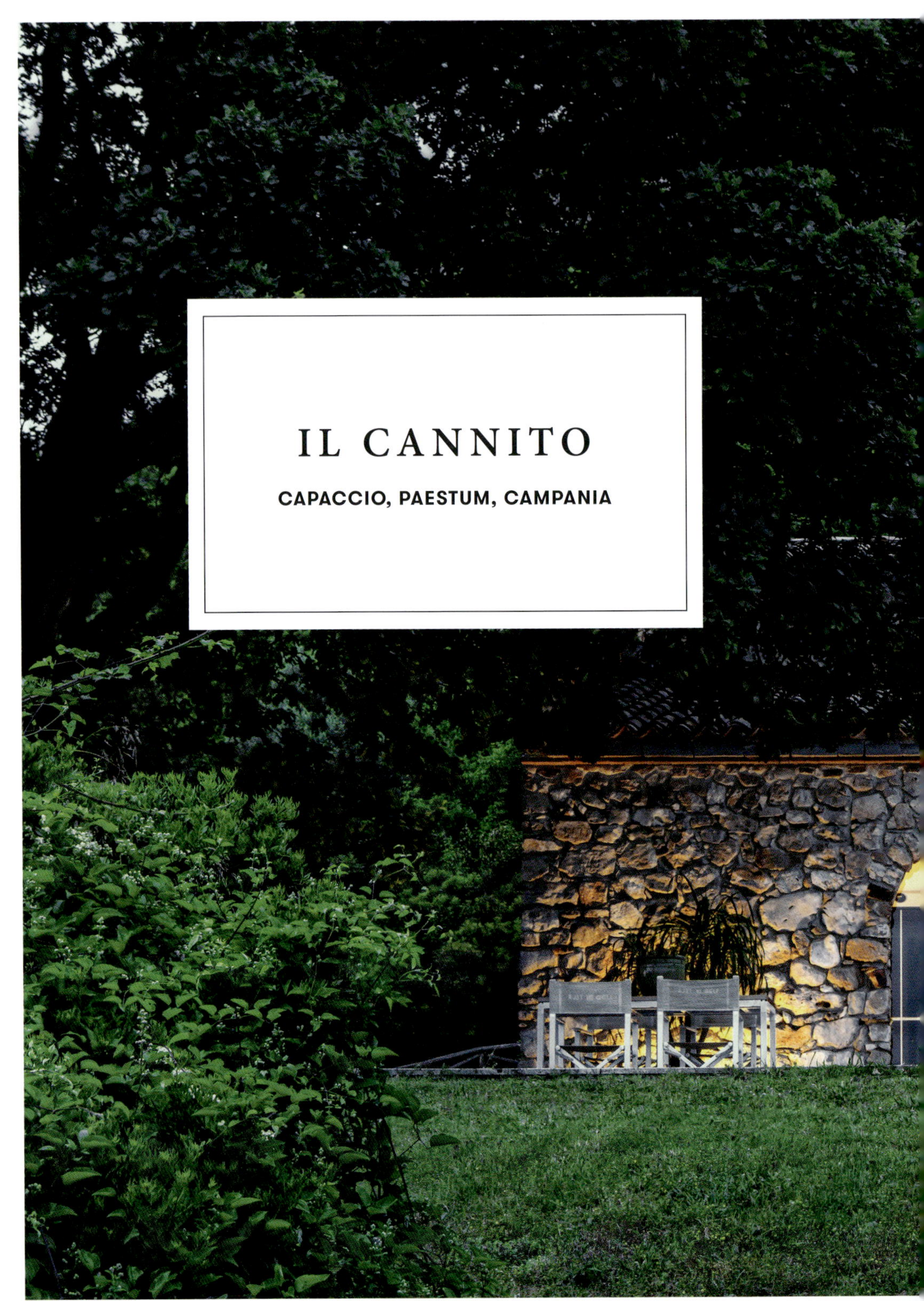

IL CANNITO

CAPACCIO, PAESTUM, CAMPANIA

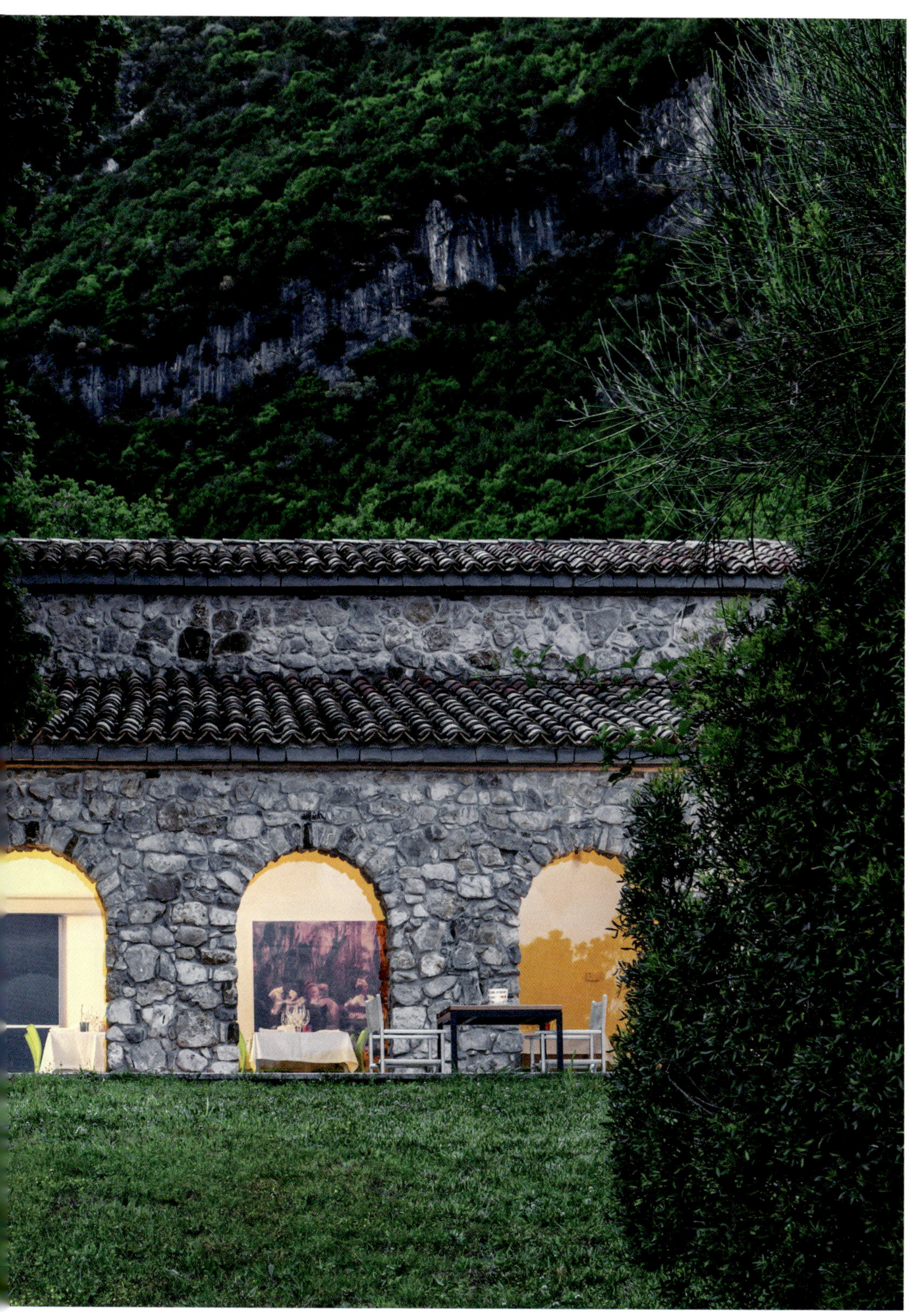

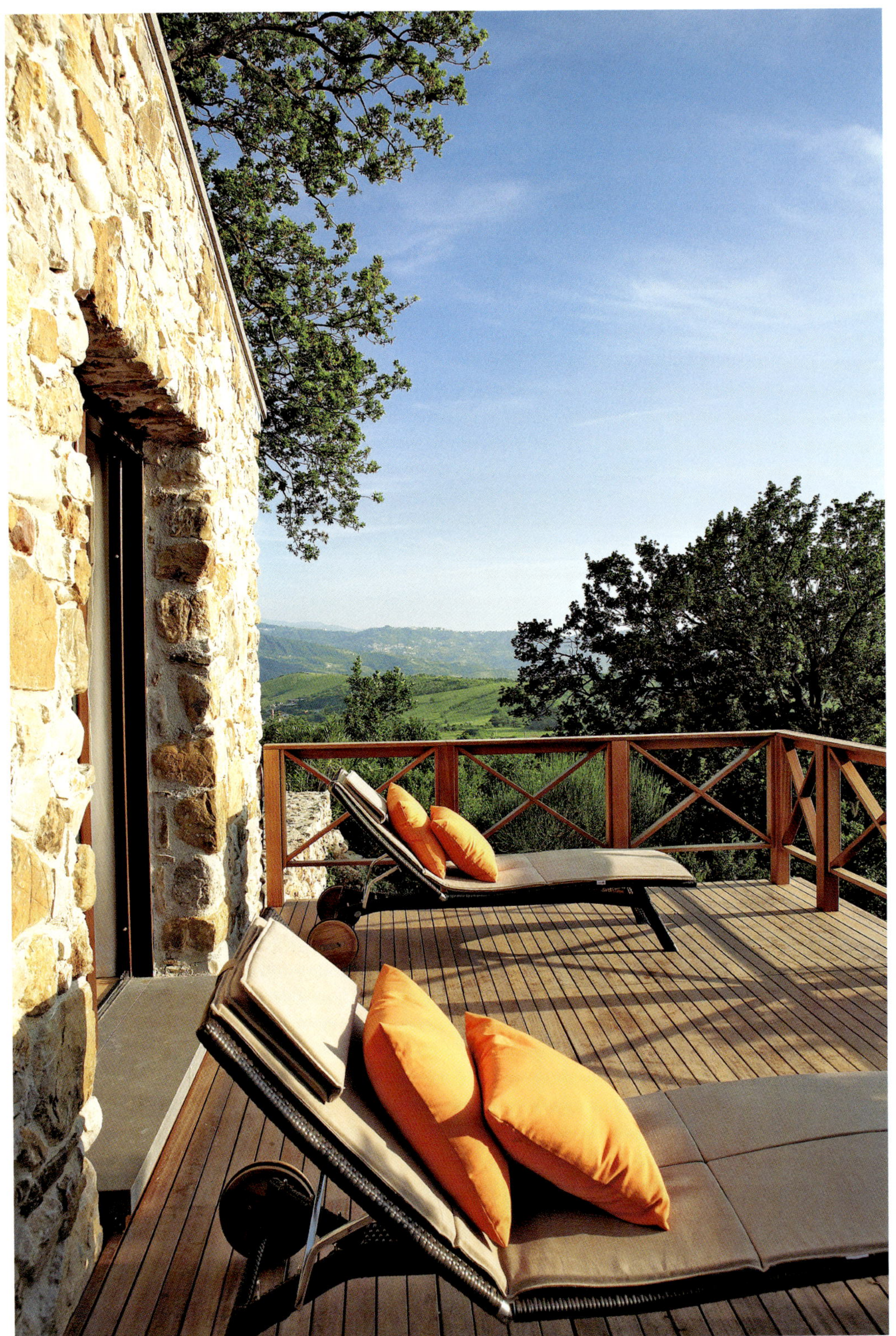

CAMPANIA

IL CANNITO

Via Cannito, 84047 Paestum
Tel. +39 0828 1962 277 · info@ilcannito.com
www.ilcannito.com
Open from early April to late October

IN THE COUNTRY "I arranged a tour of the buildings with a native of the land; a first impression could only cause astonishment. I found myself in a completely strange world," wrote Johann Wolfgang von Goethe on 23 March 1787, when his Italian journey took him to Paestum. This place near the coast of Campania had been rediscovered by archaeologists only a few years previously. In a nearly forgotten area of marshland they found temples from the Greek and Roman periods, an amphitheater and a city wall almost three miles long. To explore this UNESCO World Heritage site today in the company of a "native of the land", the best accommodation is Il Cannito, which the Gorga family run with a great deal of love and passion for their home country. On a 15-hectare site where a Franciscan monastery once stood and huge, centuries-old trees now grow, the Gorgas restored two old stone buildings, creating four guest rooms with resonant names – Sole, Terra, Mare and Luna (sun, earth, sea and moon) with a modern, minimalistic interior. From the pool guests have a sweeping view across Paestum and to the Amalfi coast, including Capri, and can discover the region on individual excursions. For lots of atmosphere, take a boat trip in a wooden barge, with lunch served on board. ◆ Book to pack: "Italian Journey" by Johann Wolfgang von Goethe.

AUF DEM LANDE „Von einem Landmanne ließ ich mich indessen in den Gebäuden herumführen; der erste Eindruck konnte nur Erstaunen erregen. Ich befand mich in einer völlig fremden Welt", schrieb Johann Wolfgang von Goethe am 23. März 1787, als ihn seine italienische Reise nach Paestum führte. Der Ort nahe der Küste Kampaniens war erst wenige Jahre zuvor von Archäologen wiederentdeckt worden – in einem beinahe vergessenen Sumpfgebiet fand man Tempel aus griechischer und römischer Zeit, ein Amphitheater sowie eine fast fünf Kilometer lange Stadtmauer. Wer das UNESCO-Weltkulturerbe heute in Begleitung von „Landmannen" entdecken möchte, quartiert sich am besten im Il Cannito ein, das die Familie Gorga mit viel Liebe und Leidenschaft für ihre Heimat führt. Auf einem 15 Hektar großen Grundstück, das einst ein Franziskanerkloster beherbergte und auf dem jahrhundertealte Baumriesen stehen, restaurierten die Gorgas zwei alte Steinhäuser und schufen vier Gästezimmer mit den klangvollen Namen „Sole", „Terra", „Mare" und „Luna" (Sonne, Erde, Meer und Mond) sowie modern-minimalistischem Interieur. Vom Pool aus blickt man weit über Paestum bis zur Amalfiküste samt Capri und kann die Region bei individuellen Ausflügen erkunden – sehr stimmungsvoll ist eine Bootsfahrt im Holzkahn, bei der Lunch an Bord serviert wird. ◆ Buchtipp: „Italienische Reise" von Johann Wolfgang von Goethe.

À LA CAMPAGNE « Pendant ce temps, je me fis guider dans ces bâtiments par un homme du pays ; la première impression ne pouvait susciter que l'étonnement. J'étais dans un monde tout à fait étranger », écrit Johann Wolfgang von Goethe le 23 mars 1787, lorsque son voyage en Italie l'emmène à Paestum. L'endroit situé près de la côte de Campanie n'avait été redécouvert que quelques années auparavant par des archéologues – dans une zone marécageuse presque oubliée, on avait découvert des temples de l'époque grecque et romaine, un amphithéâtre et un rempart de près de cinq kilomètres de long. Si vous souhaitez découvrir aujourd'hui le patrimoine mondial de l'UNESCO en compagnie de « gens du pays », le meilleur endroit pour séjourner est Il Cannito, que la famille Gorga dirige avec beaucoup d'amour et de passion pour sa terre natale. Sur un site de 15 hectares, qui abritait autrefois un monastère franciscain et sur lequel se dressent d'immenses arbres centenaires, les Gorga ont restauré deux vieilles maisons en pierre et créé quatre chambres d'hôtes aux noms évocateurs « Sole », « Terra », « Mare » et « Luna » (soleil, terre, mer et lune) et à la décoration moderne minimaliste. De la piscine, vous pouvez voir loin au-delà de Paestum et jusqu'à la côte amalfitaine et Capri, et des excursions individuelles permettent d'explorer la région – une promenade dans la péniche en bois, avec le déjeuner servi à bord est particulièrement romantique. ◆ À lire : « Voyage en Italie » de Johann Wolfgang von Goethe.

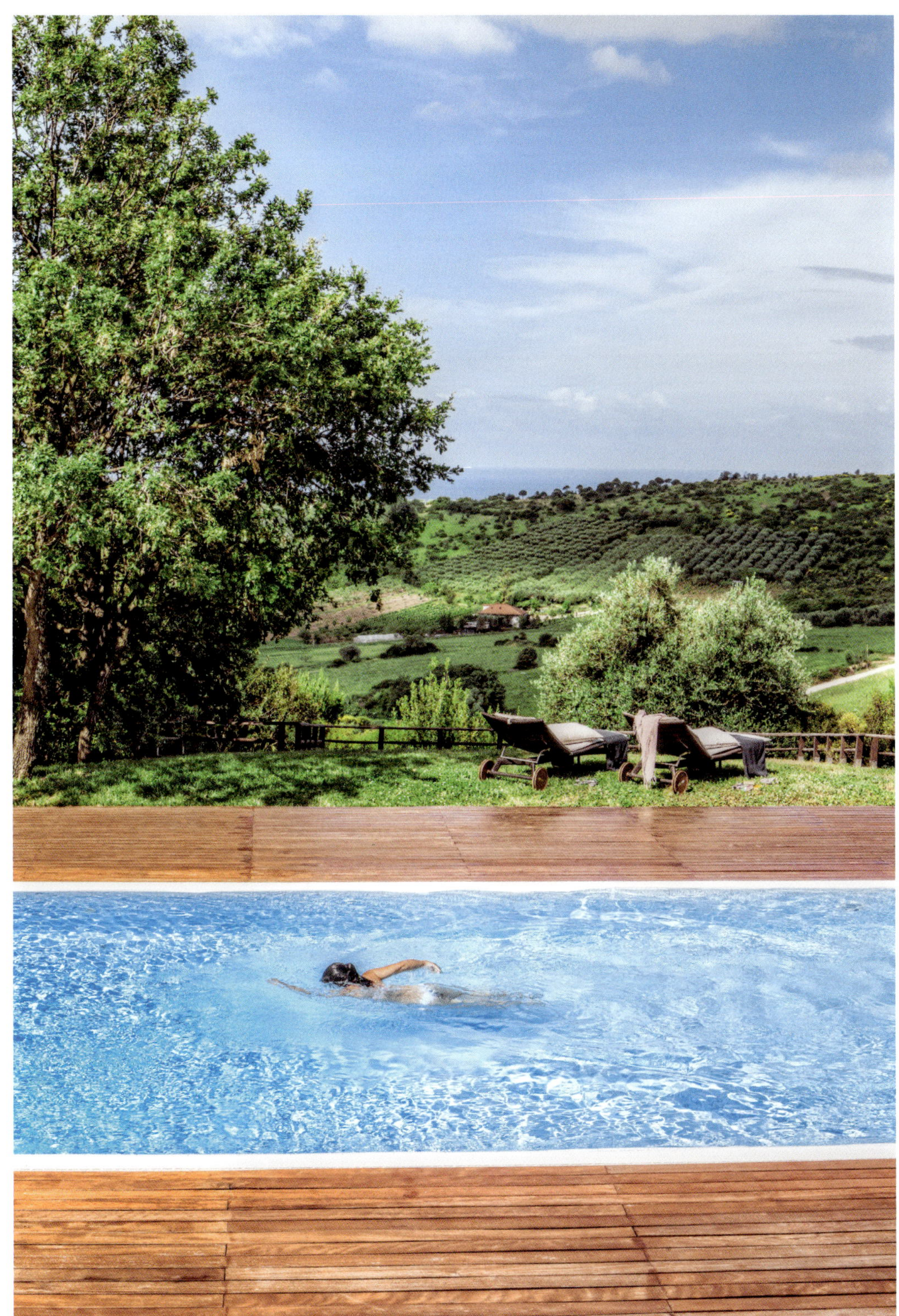

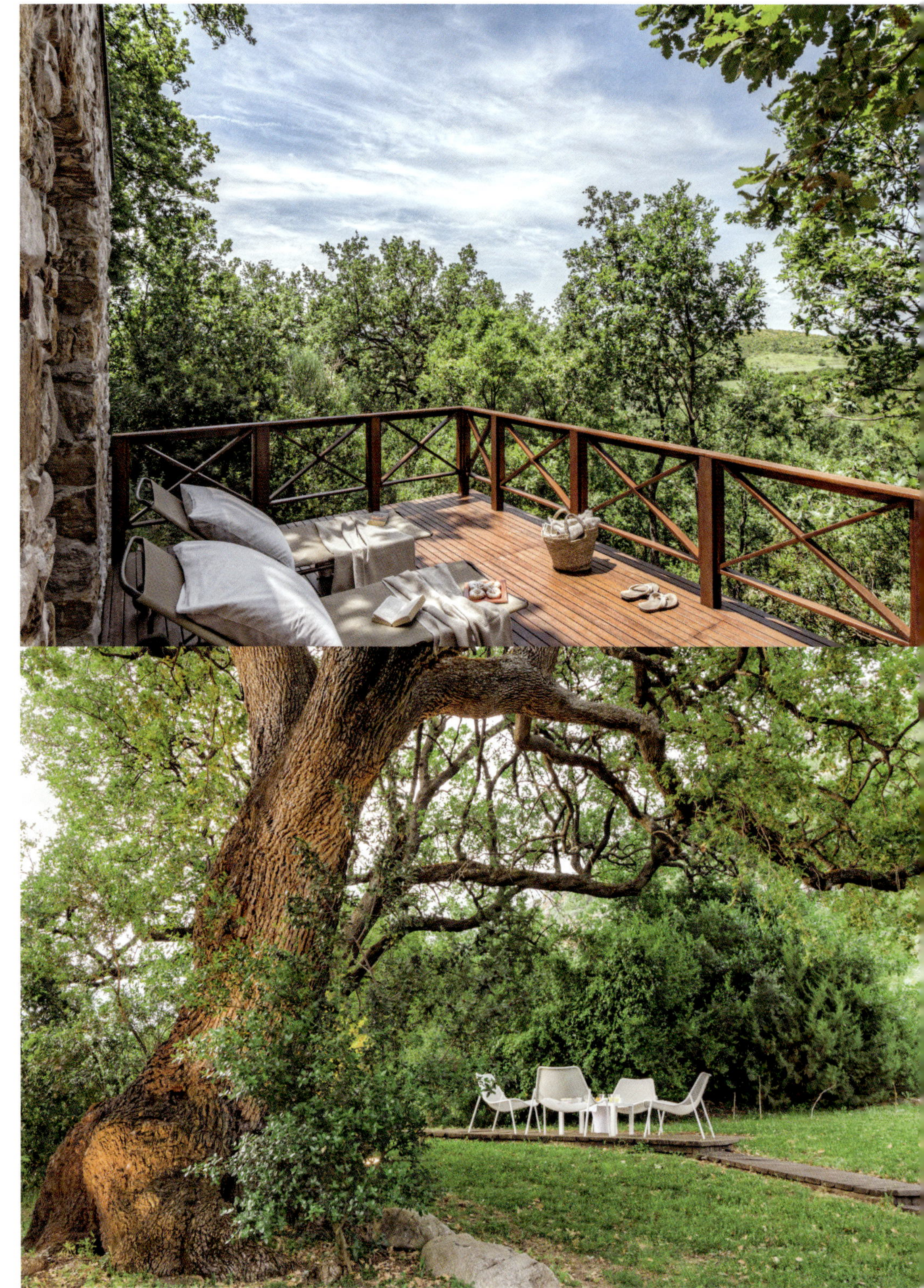

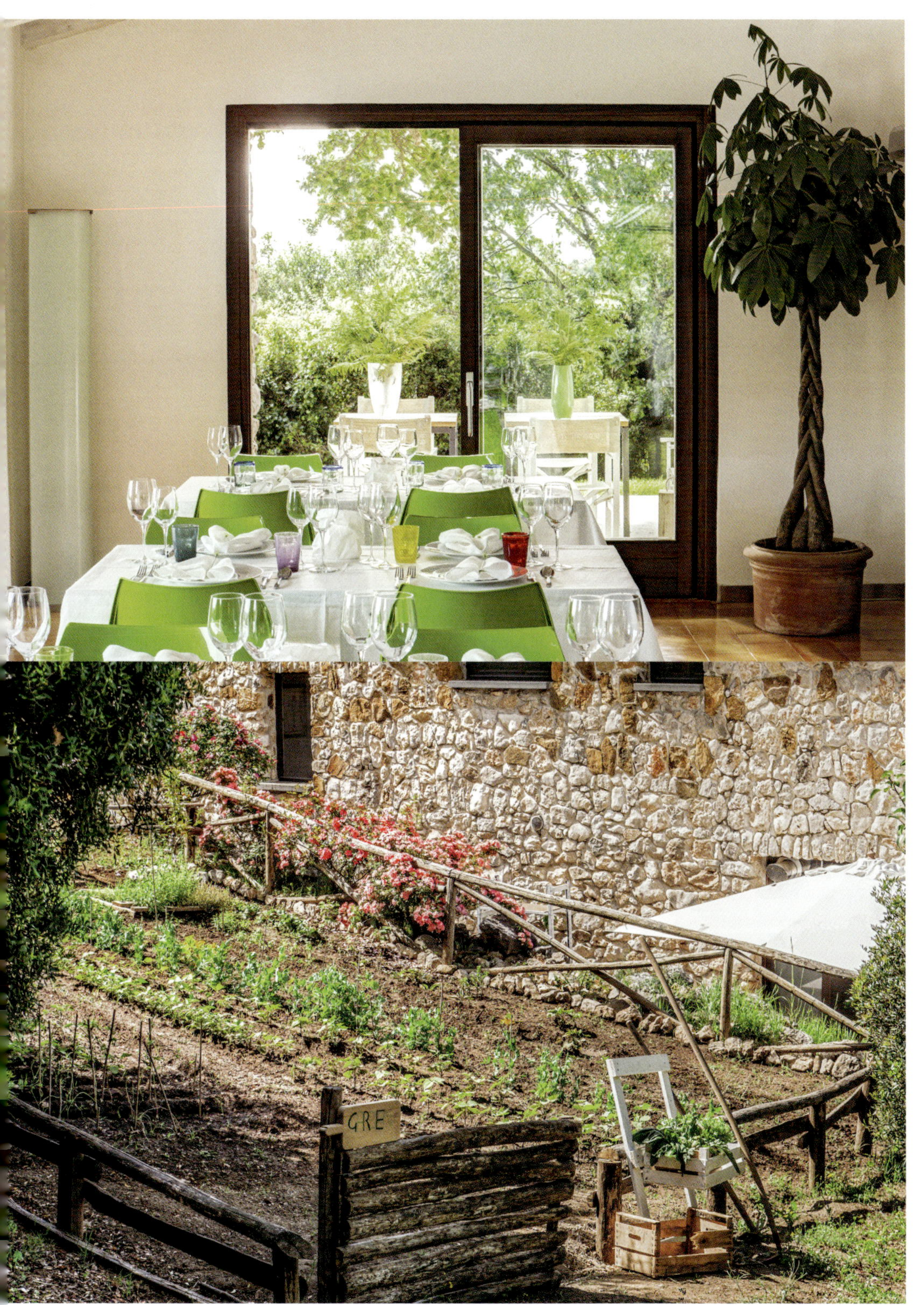
GRE

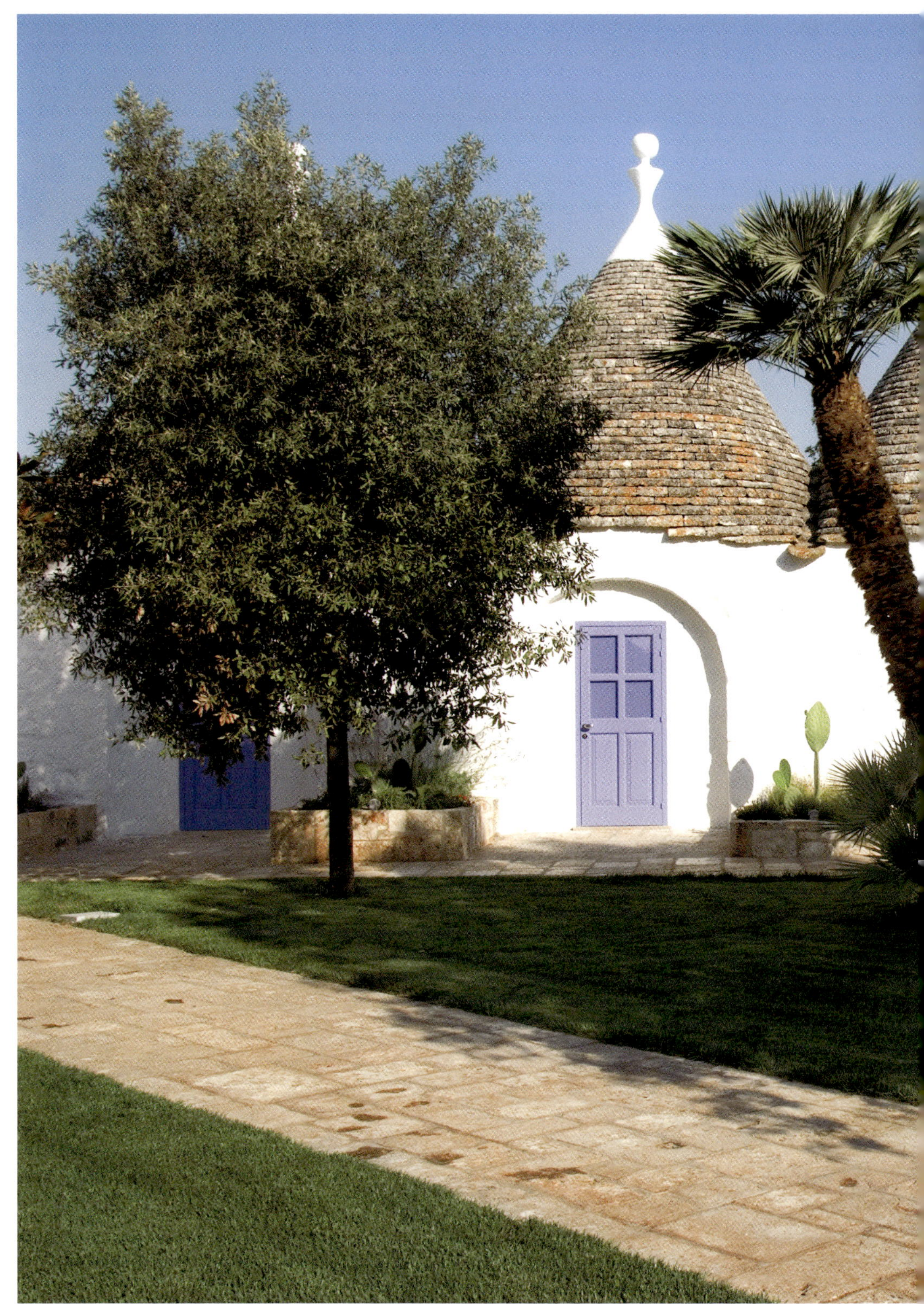

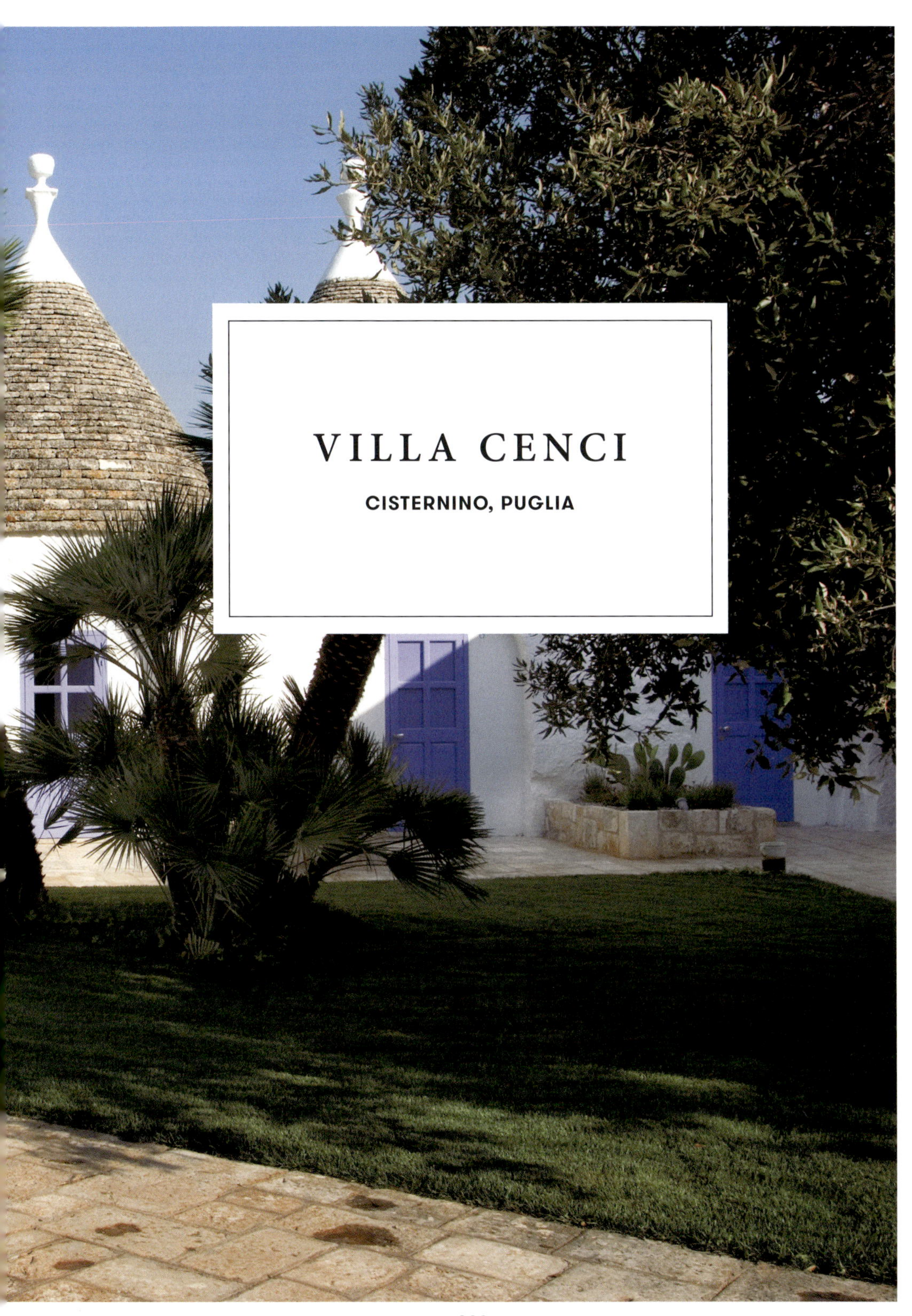

VILLA CENCI

CISTERNINO, PUGLIA

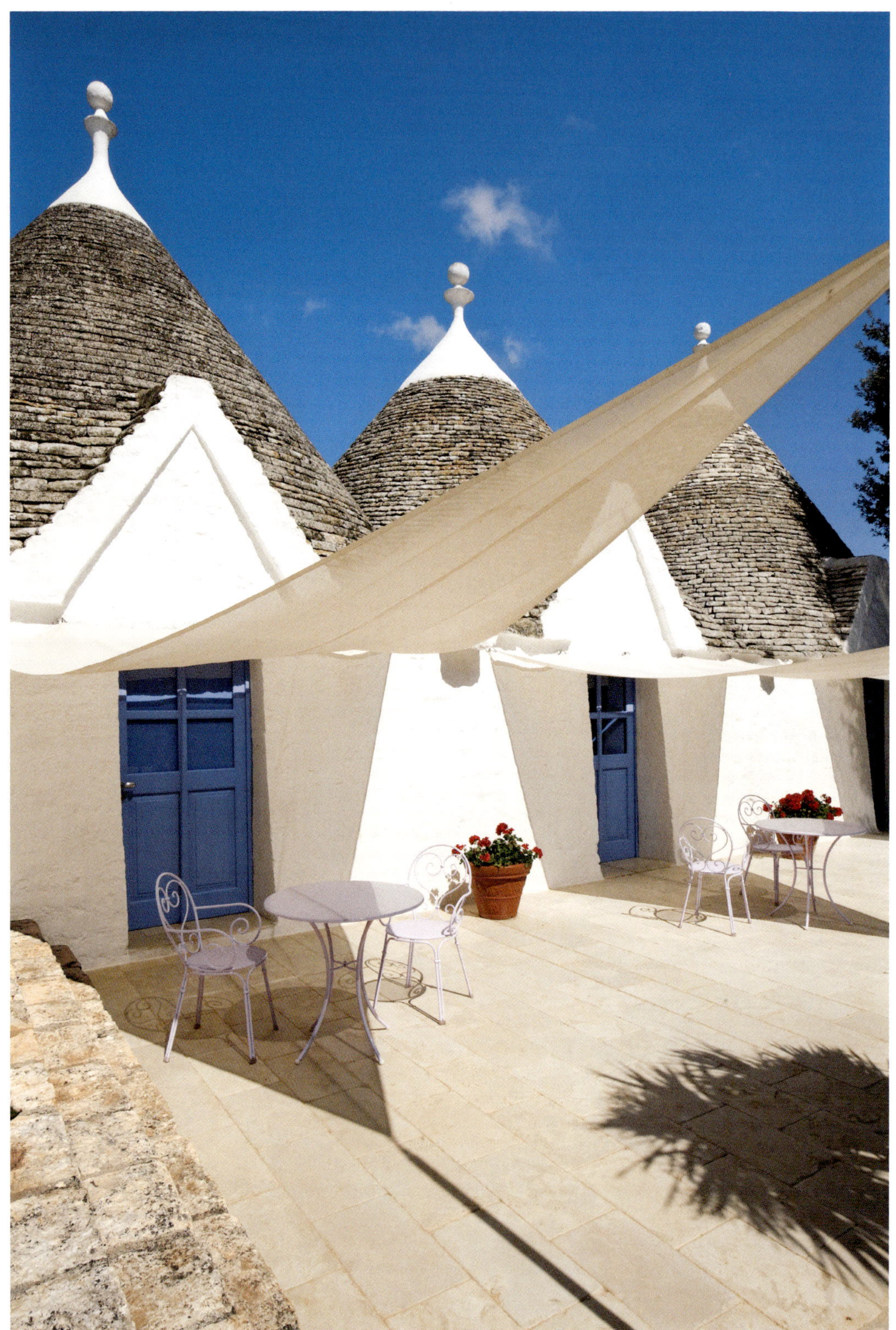

PUGLIA

VILLA CENCI

Strada Provinciale per Ceglie Messapica, 72014 Cisternino
Tel. +39 080 4448 208 · info@villacenci.it
www.villacenci.it
Open early March to late December

GOOD ALL ROUND They were too poor to own their own plot of land, but they knew a little trick that made it possible to be house owners all the same: the Apulian peasants of the 13th to 17th centuries built their trulli, simple round houses with a cone-shaped roof, solely from stones that lay in the fields and without any mortar at all. In this way their habitations could be dismantled in the twinkling of an eye if the authorities made checks, and reconstructed as soon as the danger was past. Once accommodation for times of need, today they are national monuments: the trulli are among the most coveted and famous buildings in Apulia, and the radiant whitewashed trulli of Alberobello have even been listed as UNESCO World Heritage since 1996. Just under 12 miles east of the town one of the loveliest trulli hotels welcomes its guests: Villa Cenci is an old country estate that has been restored both expertly and tastefully, and in addition to guest rooms in the main building possesses nine rooms in trulli – an indispensable feature, of course, in this place. The only reminder of past austerity is the shape of the houses; apart from that modern times have arrived, with sunshades, four-poster beds, TV and air conditioning. And the owners of Villa Cenci are not short of land: all around the buildings lie 32 acres of natural beauty, of which there is a wonderful view from the pool. The fruit and vegetables that grow on the land are the basis for the fine organic cuisine, which is served in the hotel restaurant or right in front of the trulli. ◆ Book to pack: "I'm not Scared" by Niccolò Ammaniti.

EINE RUNDE SACHE Sie waren zu arm, um ein eigenes Stück Land zu besitzen – doch dank eines kleinen Tricks konnten sie dennoch ein Haus ihr Eigen nennen: Die apulischen Bauern des 13. bis 17. Jahrhunderts bauten ihre Trulli, schlichte Rundhäuser mit kegelförmigem Dach, nur aus Steinen aufs Feld und verzichteten ganz auf Mörtel. So ließen sich die Behausungen im Fall einer behördlichen Kontrolle im Handumdrehen abbauen und wieder neu errichten, sobald die Gefahr vorüber war. Heute sind aus den einstigen Notunterkünften Nationaldenkmäler geworden: Die Trulli zählen zu den begehrtesten und berühmtesten Bauten Apuliens – die strahlend weiß getünchten Trulli von Alberobello stehen seit 1996 sogar auf der Weltkulturerbe-Liste der UNESCO. Knapp 20 Kilometer östlich der Stadt wartet eines der schönsten Trulli-Hotels auf Gäste: Die Villa Cenci ist ein altes Landgut, das mit ebenso viel Sachverstand wie Stil restauriert wurde und neben Gästezimmern im Hauptgebäude neun Räume in Trulli besitzt – diese sind hier natürlich ein Muss. An die karge Vergangenheit erinnert dabei nur noch die Form der Häuser; ansonsten sind mit Sonnensegel, Himmelbett, Fernseher sowie Klimaanlage moderne Zeiten eingezogen. Auch an Land mangelt es den Besitzern der Villa Cenci nicht: Rund um das Anwesen erstrecken sich 13 Hektar herrlichste Natur, über die man vom Pool aus einen wunderschönen Blick hat. Das Obst und Gemüse, das auf dem Grundstück gedeiht, ist Basis für die feine Bio-Küche des Hotels, die im Restaurant serviert wird – oder direkt vor der Tür der Trulli. ◆ Buchtipp: „Die Herren des Hügels“ von Niccolò Ammaniti.

TOUT BEAU, TOUT ROND Trop pauvres pour acheter un peu de terre, ils étaient assez malins pour avoir une maison bien à eux : du XIIIe au XVIIe siècle, les paysans des Pouilles bâtirent dans les champs des trulli, de sobres maisons rondes au toit conique construites sans mortier, à l'aide de galets. Si quelqu'un venait contrôler, ils pouvaient démonter leurs habitations en un rien de temps et les reconstruire dès que le danger était passé. Ces logements provisoires sont devenus des monuments nationaux et font aujourd'hui partie des constructions les plus convoitées et les plus célèbres des Pouilles – les trulli d'un blanc éclatant d'Alberobello sont même classés depuis 1996 au patrimoine mondial de l'UNESCO. L'un des plus beaux ensembles de trulli attend ses hôtes à une vingtaine de kilomètres à l'est de la ville : la villa Cenci est un ancien domaine rural restauré avec style par des experts en la matière. Á côté des chambres situées dans le bâtiment principal, elle possède neuf pièces dans des trulli – un must dans cette région. Seule la forme des maisons évoque encore le dénuement des habitants de jadis ; sinon, la modernité a fait son apparition, apportant des tauds de soleil, des lits à baldaquin, la télévision et la climatisation. Les propriétaires de la villa Cenci ne manquent pas de terrain non plus : 13 hectares de nature se déploient autour de la propriété, et la vue que l'on en a de la piscine est sublime. Les fruits et légumes cultivés sur place sont la base de la cuisine bio raffinée, proposée au restaurant de l'hôtel – ou directement à la porte des trulli. ◆ À lire : « Je n'ai pas peur » de Niccolò Ammaniti.

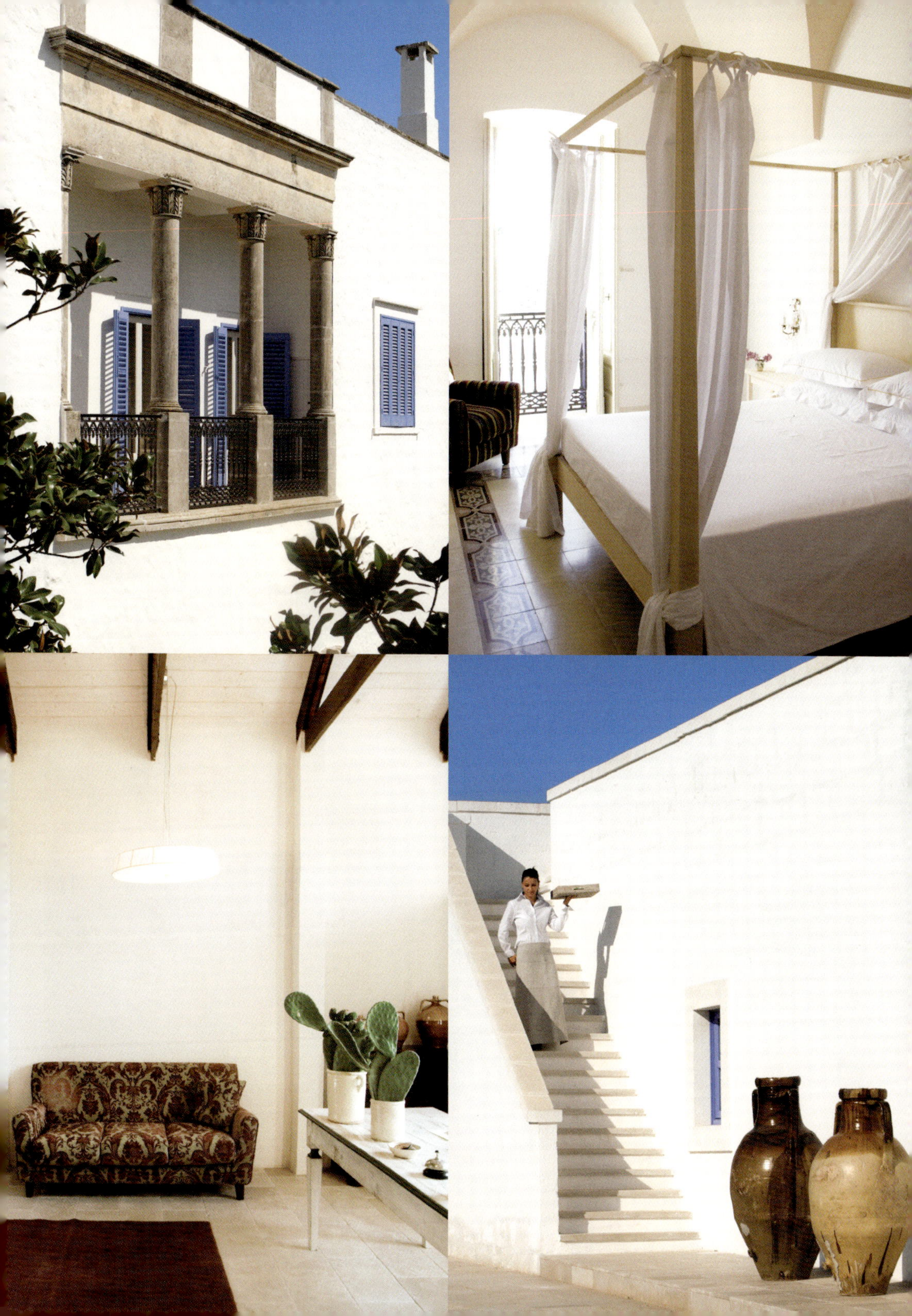

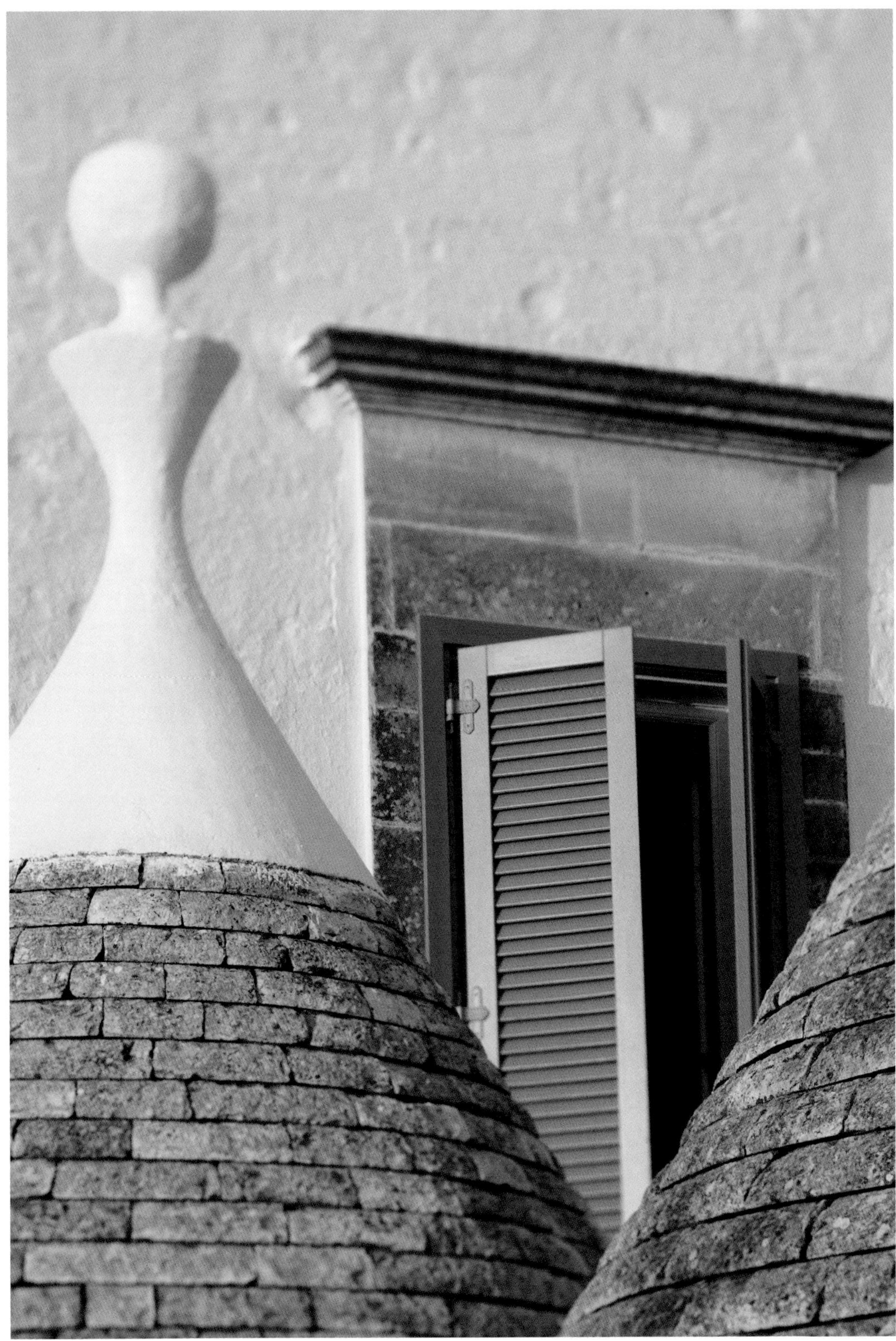

PUGLIA

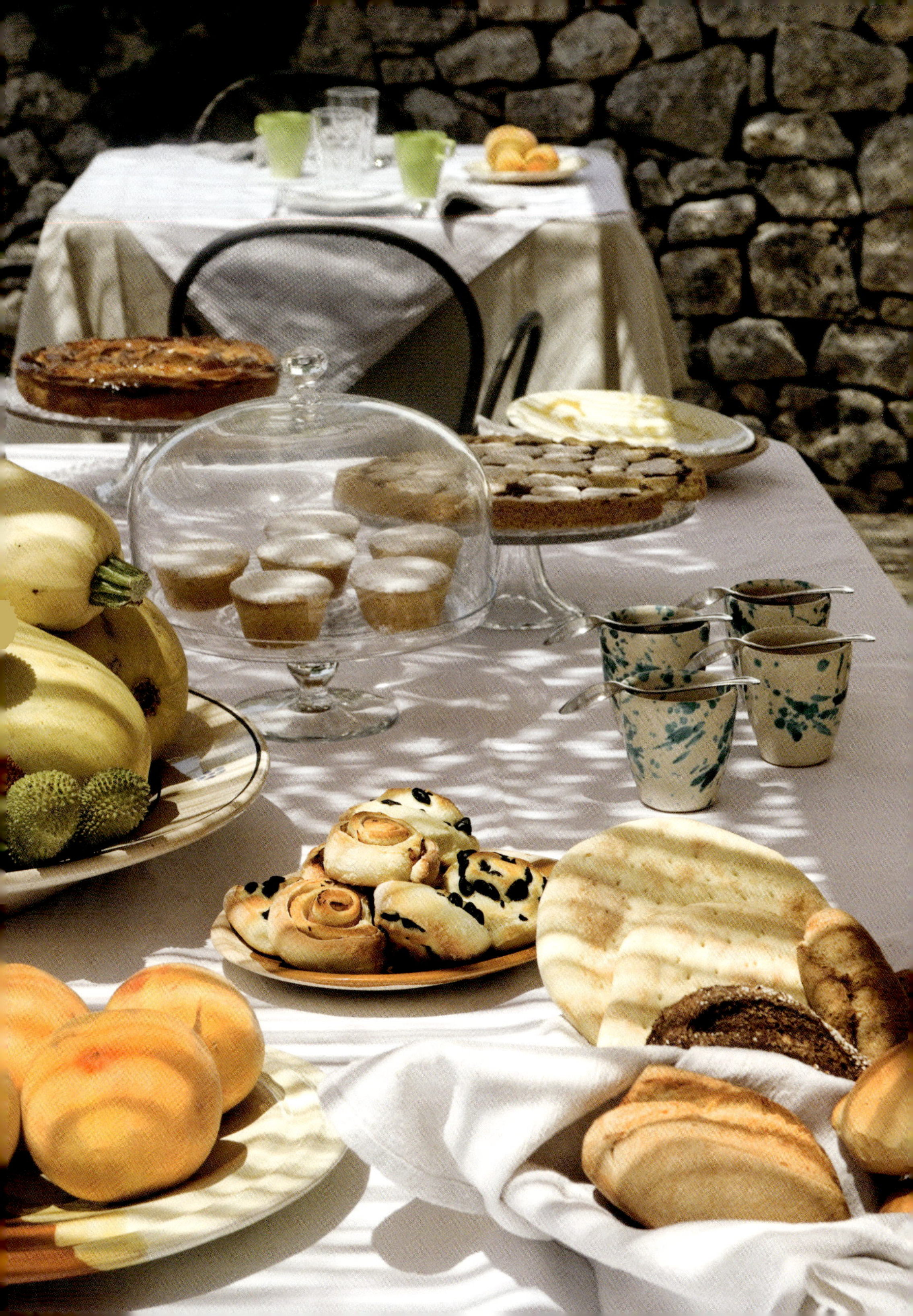

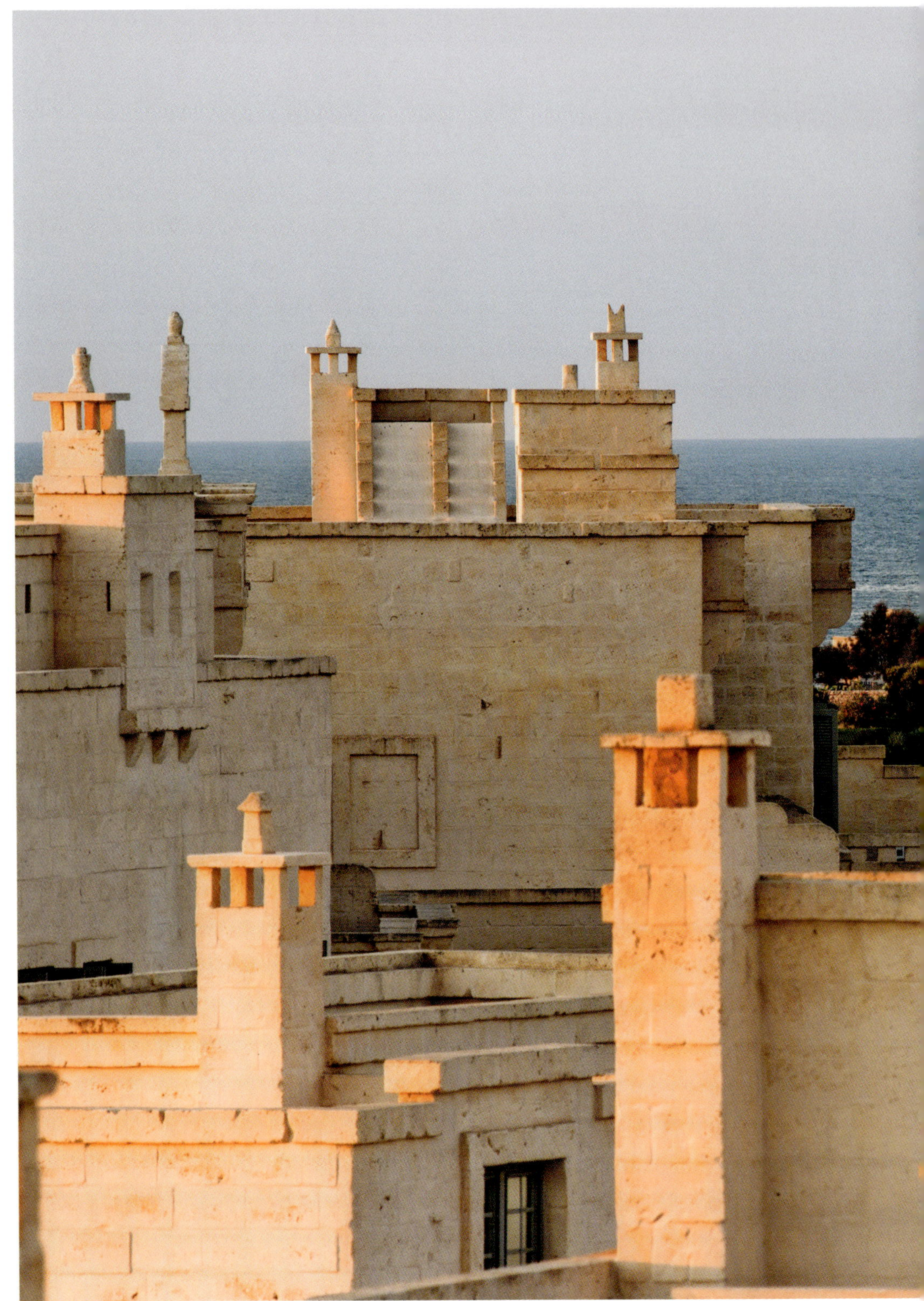

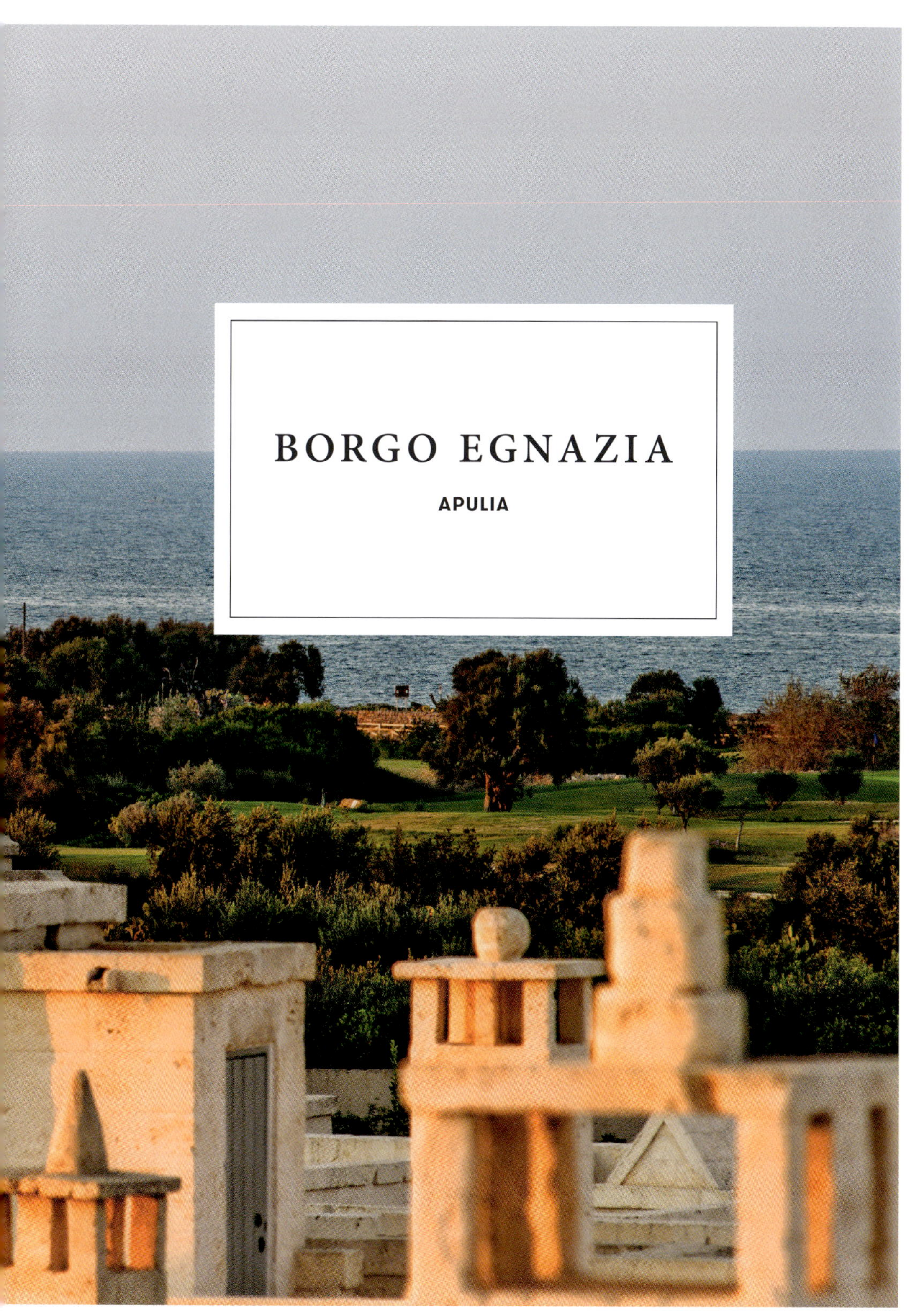

BORGO EGNAZIA

APULIA

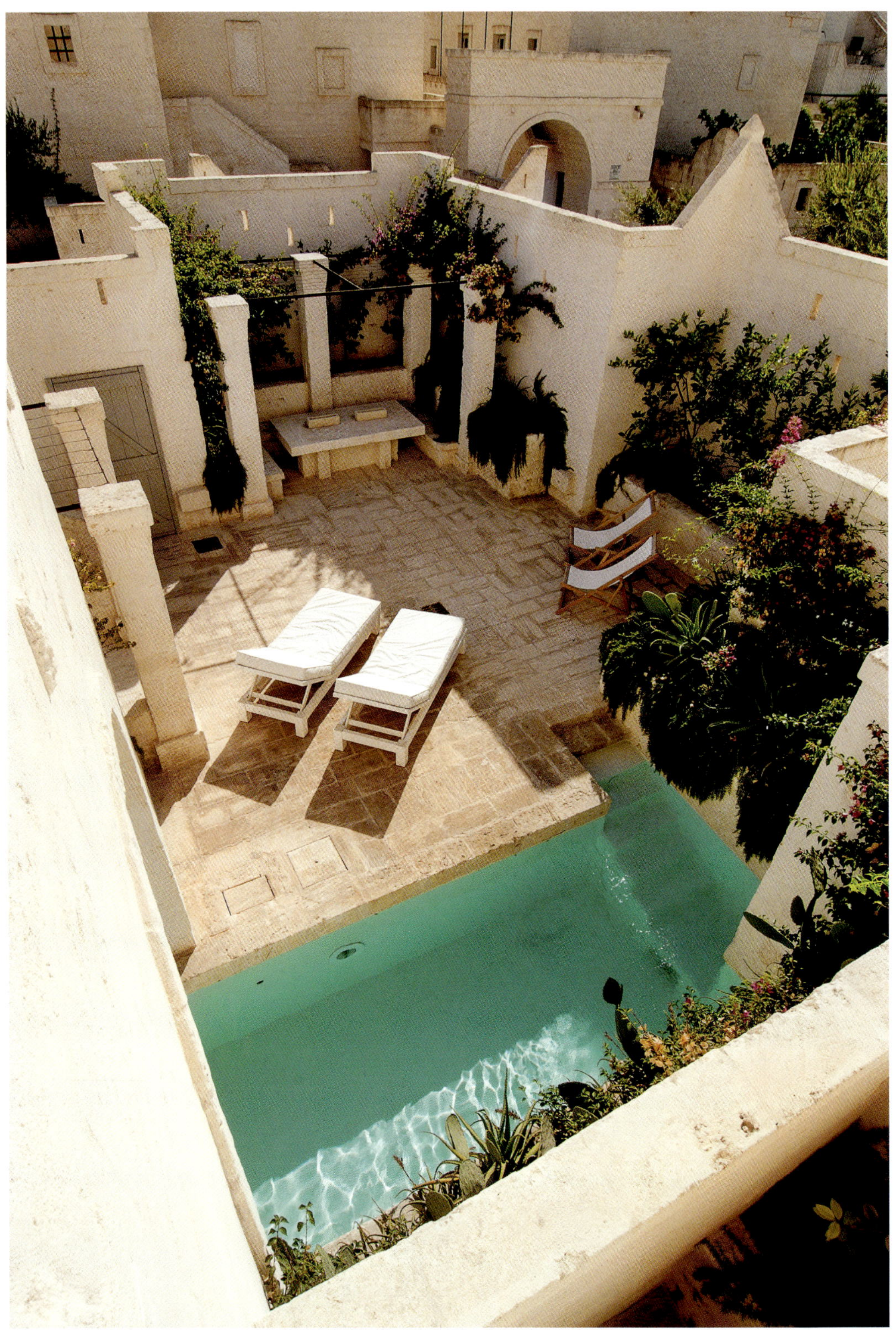

BORGO EGNAZIA

Savelletri di Fasano, 72015 Fasano/Brindisi, Italy
Tel: +39 080 225 5000 · info@borgoegnazia.com
www.borgoegnazia.com

A NEW OLD VILLAGE A village on the coast. With houses built from pale tufa stone that has gained a bit of a patina. With winding alleys that all lead sooner or later to a piazza with a bell tower. With olive and lemon trees, magenta-flowering bougainvillaea and aromatic rosemary. Typical. Apulian. Hundreds of years old. No! Borgo Egnazia was rebuilt and only opened in 2010 – as a world in miniature, a microcosm and modern interpretation of traditional rural Apulia. The fact that this really feels like an authentic Apulian village rather than a theater set is due to the owner, Aldo Melpignano. His roots are in Apulia, and he has close links to his homeland. In Ian Schrager's Morgans Hotel Group in New York he learned what guests from all over the world expect from a top hotel. And he has a nose for successful business models, having also worked as an investment banker. In cooperation with the designer Pino Brescia from nearby Fasano, he combined three elements to form a single architectural entity: "La Corte" is the entrance and hotel area of the village, complemented by the "Il Borgo" quarter with its pretty buildings, and by the area called "Le Ville," where magnificent country houses have private pools. Everywhere the interiors are decorated in shades of white, cream and beige, display natural materials and local crafts, and provide all the luxury of five-star accommodation. Original Apulian cuisine is celebrated in all of the village's six restaurants – and the 2,000-square-meter spa, too, avoids all international compromises, indulging its guests with the aromatic oils and healing plants of the region.
◆ Book to pack: "A Night in Bari" by Gianrico Carofiglio.

EIN NEUES ALTES DORF Ein Dorf an der Küste. Mit Häusern aus hellem Tuffstein, der schon ein bisschen Patina angesetzt hat. Mit verwinkelten Gassen, die alle irgendwann zu einer Piazza mit Glockenturm führen. Mit Oliven- und Zitronenbäumen, magentafarbenen Bougainvilleen und duftendem Rosmarin. Typisch. Apulisch. Jahrhundertealt. Nein! Borgo Egnazia ist ein Neubau, der erst 2010 eröffnet wurde – als Miniaturwelt, Mikrokosmos und moderne Interpretation des traditionellen ländlichen Apuliens. Dass man sich hier wirklich wie in einem authentischen apulischen Dorf und nicht wie in einer Theaterkulisse fühlt, ist dem Besitzer Aldo Melpignano zu verdanken. Er hat seine Wurzeln in Apulien und ist seiner Heimat eng verbunden. In Ian Schragers Morgans Hotel Group in New York lernte er, was Gäste aus aller Welt sich von einem Tophotel wünschen. Und er besitzt einen Sinn für erfolgreiche Geschäftsmodelle, denn Investmentbanker war er auch schon einmal. Gemeinsam mit dem Designer Pino Brescia aus dem nahen Fasano verband er drei Elemente zu einer architektonischen Einheit: „La Corte" ist der Eingangs- und Hotelbereich des Dorfes, der ergänzt wird durch das Viertel „Il Borgo" mit seinen hübschen Gebäuden sowie den Bereich „Le Ville" mit prachtvollen Landhäusern, die über private Pools verfügen. Überall zeigen sich die Innenräume in Weiß-, Creme- und Beigetönen, setzen auf Naturmaterialien und lokales Kunsthandwerk und bieten allen Luxus einer Fünf-Sterne-Herberge. Die unverfälschte Küche Apuliens wird in sämtlichen sechs Restaurants des Dorfes gefeiert – und auch das 2000 Quadratmeter große Spa macht keine internationalen Kompromisse, sondern verwöhnt mit Aromaölen und Heilpflanzen der Region. ◆ Buchtipp: „Eine Nacht in Bari" von Gianrico Carofiglio.

UN ANCIEN NOUVEAU VILLAGE Un village de la côte avec ses maisons en pierre de tuf légère, un peu patinée déjà, et dont les ruelles tortueuses mènent toutes, tôt ou tard, à une place où s'élève une église. Et puis des oliviers et des citronniers, des bougainvilliers magenta et du romarin odorant. Un village typique des Pouilles, vieux de plusieurs siècles ? Non ! Borgo Egnazia est un complexe nouveau qui n'a ouvert ses portes qu'en 2010 – un monde miniature, un microcosme et une interprétation moderne des Pouilles rurales traditionnelles. C'est grâce au propriétaire Aldo Melpignano que l'on se sent vraiment dans un authentique village des Pouilles et non dans un décor de théâtre. Il a ses racines ici, dans les Pouilles, et est étroitement lié à sa terre natale. Dans le Morgans Hotel Group de Ian Schrager à New York, il a appris ce que les clients du monde entier attendent d'un grand hôtel. Et il a le sens des modèles d'entreprise à succès, car il a également été banquier d'affaires. Avec le designer Pino Brescia, originaire de la ville voisine de Fasano, il a combiné trois éléments en une unité architecturale : « La Corte » est l'entrée et la zone hôtelière du village, complétée par le quartier « Il Borgo » avec ses jolis bâtiments et la zone « Le Ville » avec de magnifiques maisons de campagne disposant d'une piscine privée. Partout, les intérieurs sont dans les tons blancs, crème et beige, misent sur les matériaux naturels et les artisans locaux, et offrent tout le luxe d'un établissement cinq étoiles. La cuisine authentique des Pouilles est célébrée dans les six restaurants du village – et les 2 000 mètres carrés du centre balnéaire ne font pas non plus de compromis, en choyant les clients avec des huiles aromatiques et des plantes médicinales de la région. ◆ À lire : « Les raisons du doute » de Gianrico Carofiglio.

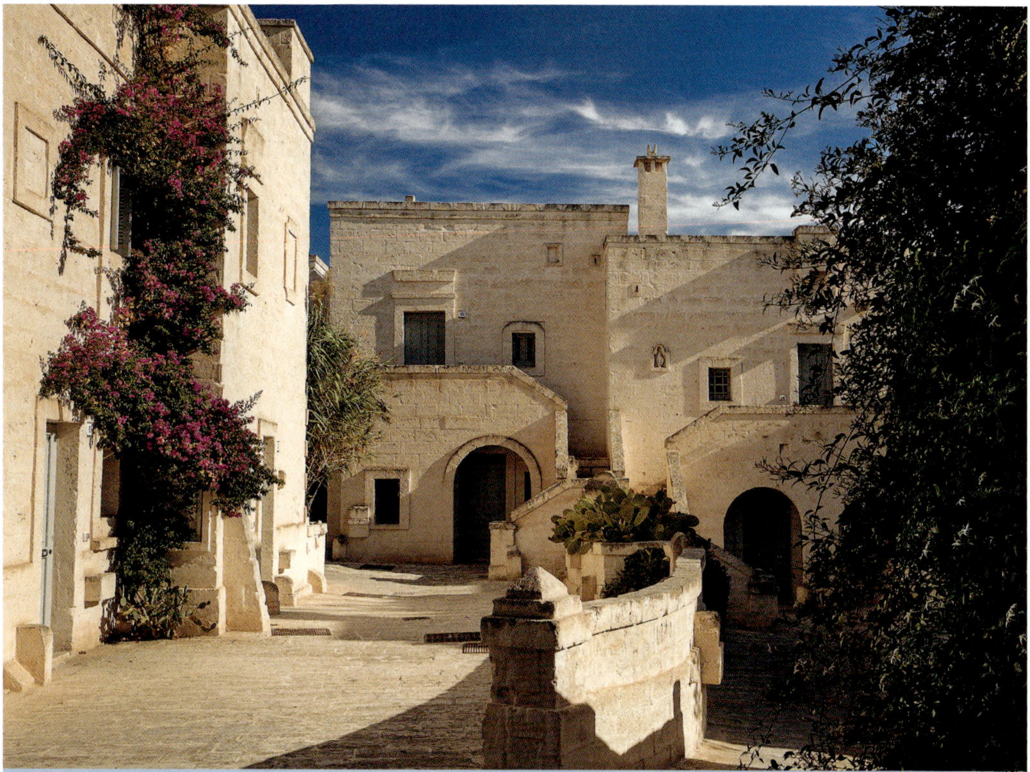

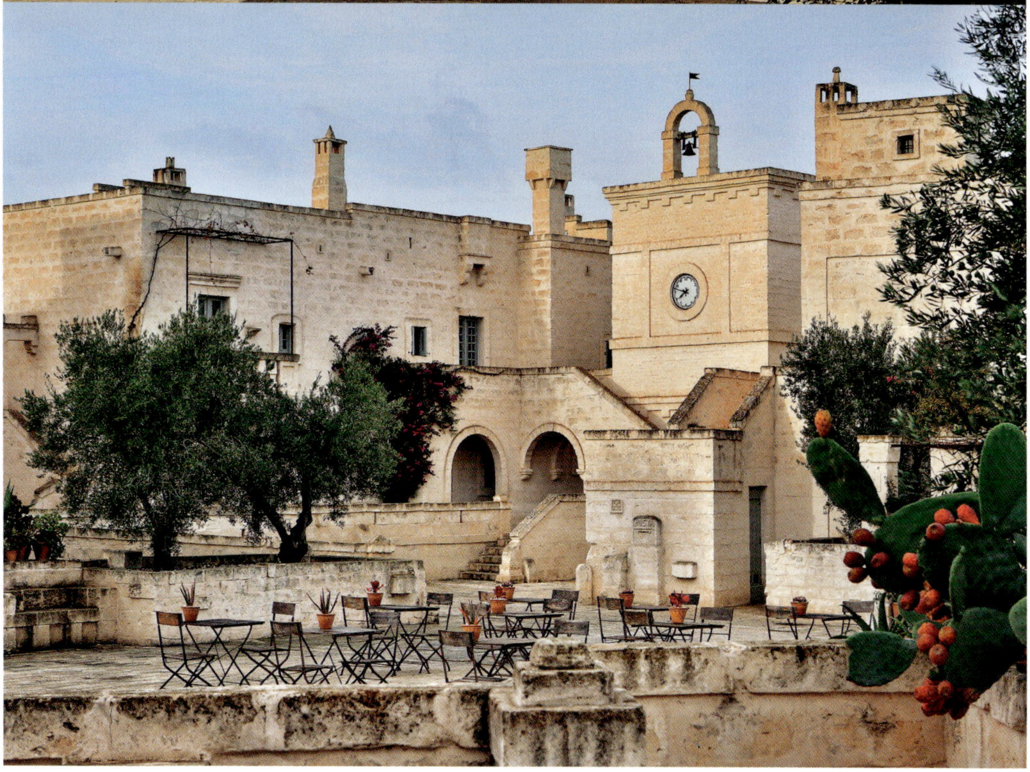

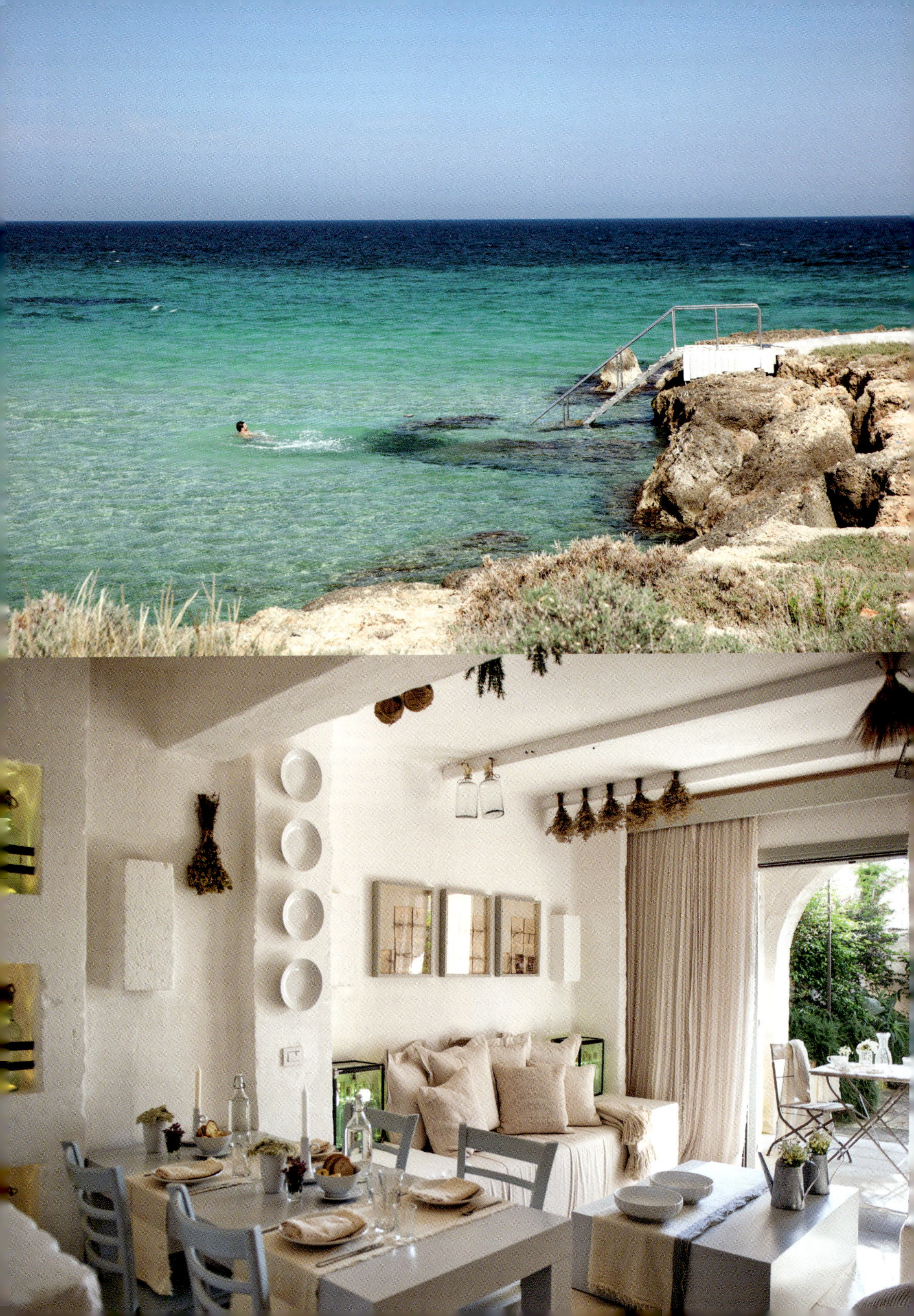

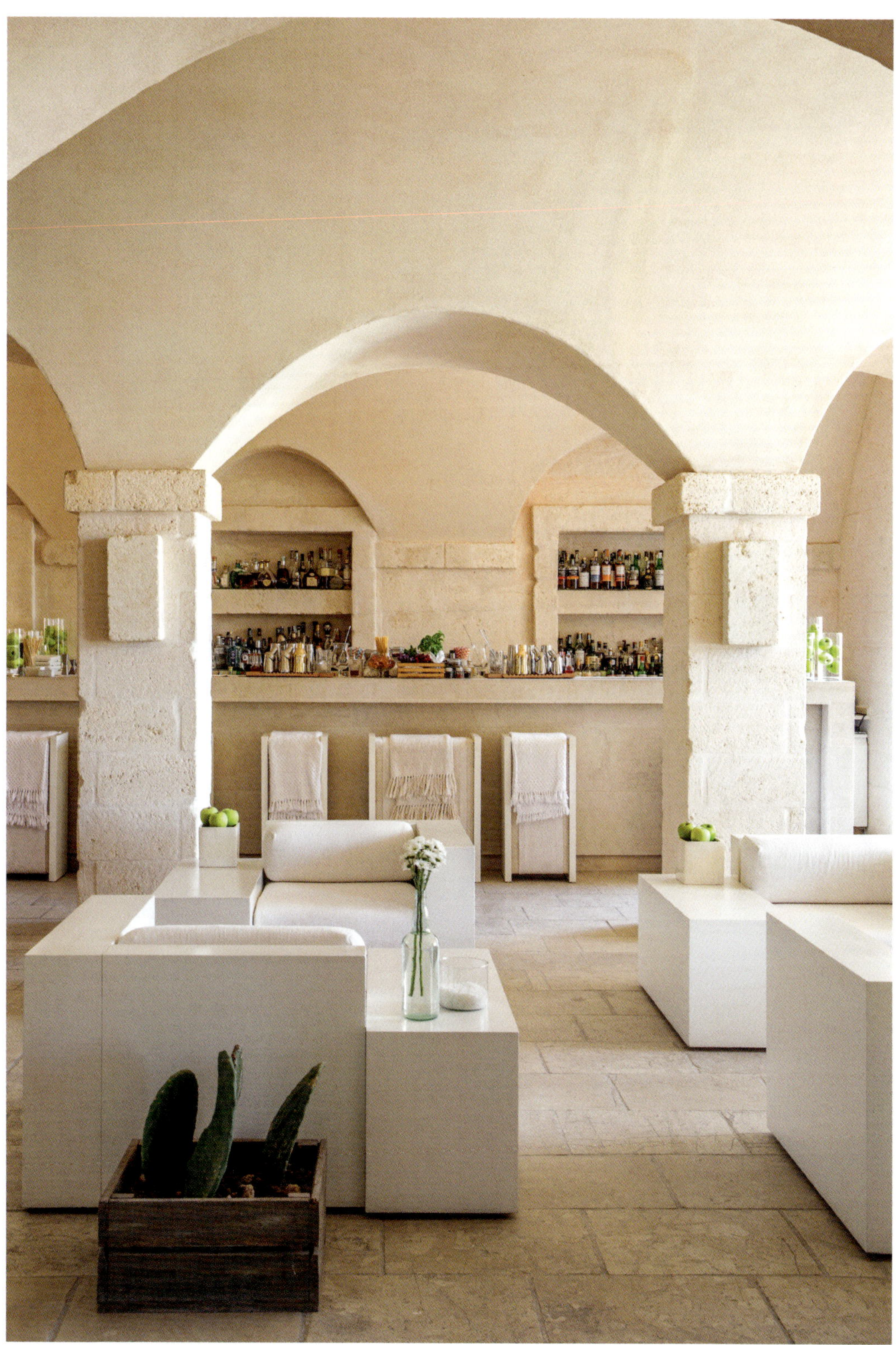

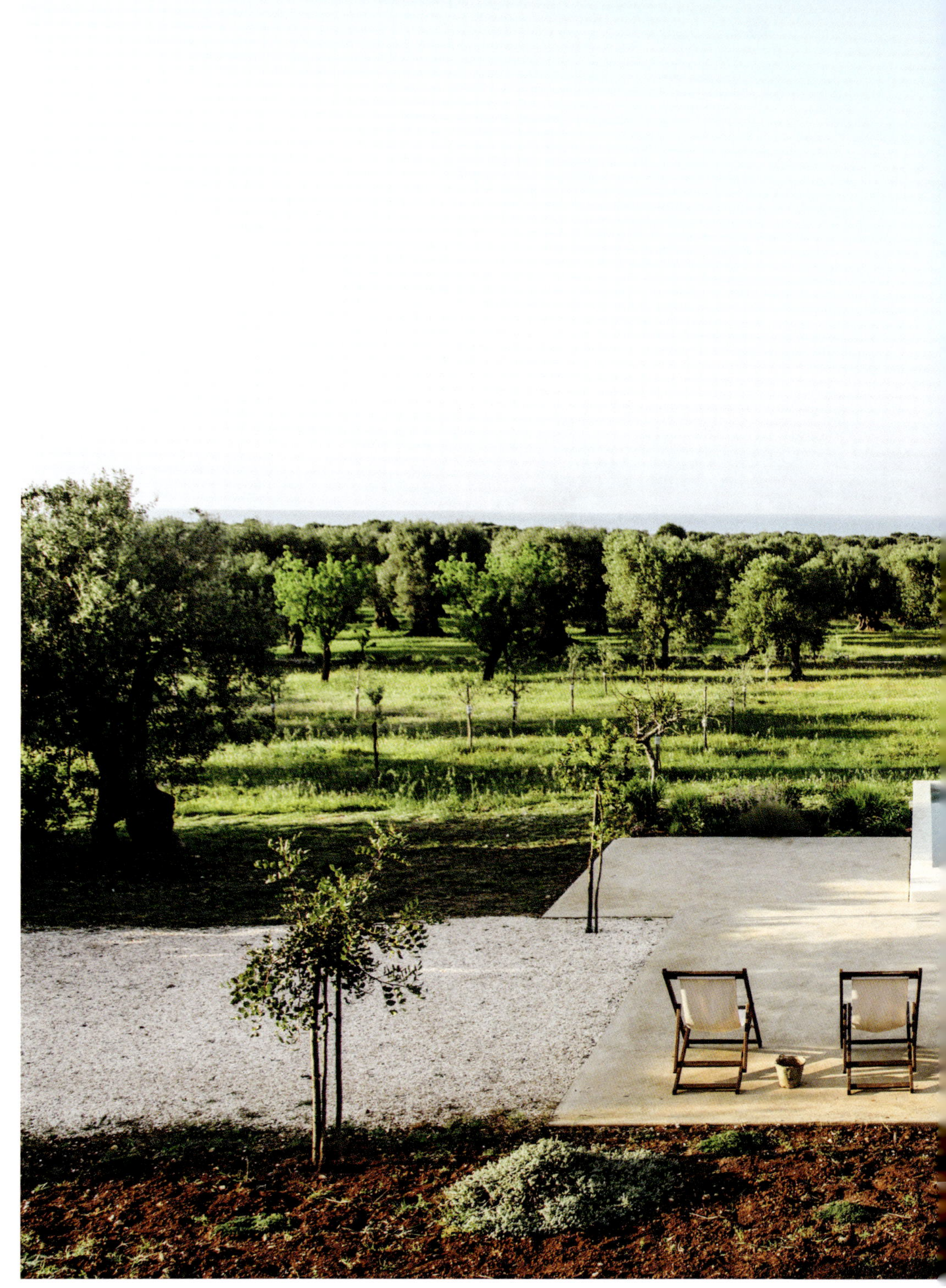

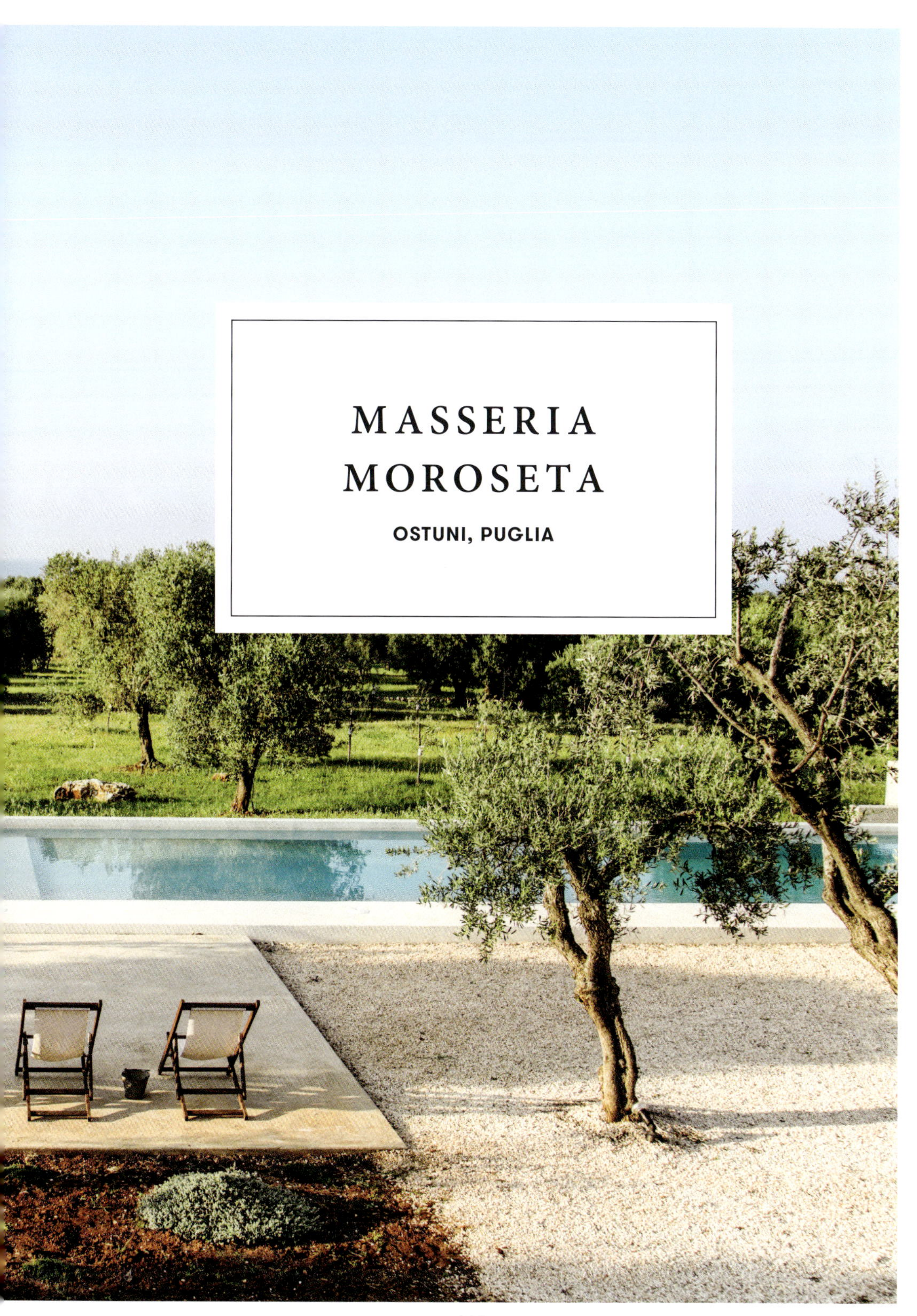

MASSERIA MOROSETA

OSTUNI, PUGLIA

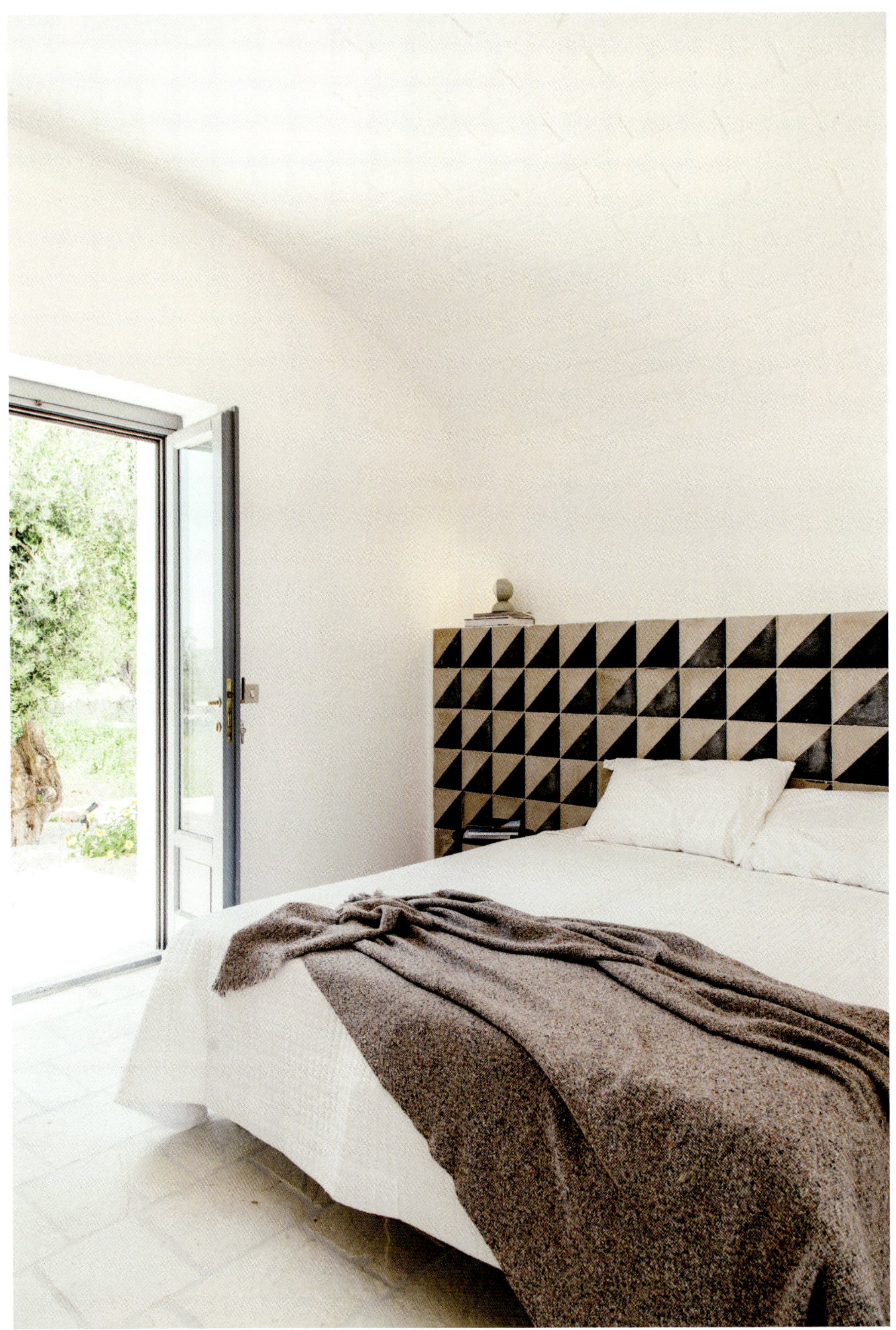

MASSERIA MOROSETA

Contrada Lamacavallo s.n, 72017 Ostuni
Tel. +39 376 0798 288 · info@masseriamoroseta.it
www.masseriamoroseta.it

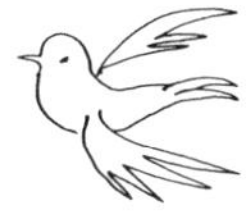

HERE'S TO FRIENDSHIP! The friendship between Carlo Lanzini and Andrew Trotter began in London, where Carlo was studying cinematography and Andrew was working as an interior designer, and their talk ranged far and wide as they ate Carlo's home-made pasta. When Carlo returned to Italy to build his dream home and fell in love with a plot of land near the "white town" of Ostuni in Apulia, Andrew designed Masseria Moroseta. It was his first architectural work – a minimalistic building with clear lines and geometric shapes, inspired by old Apulian farmhouses, built using traditional materials but at the same time equipped with modern technology: thanks in part to a solar power plant, Masseria Moroseta can generate 80 per cent of the energy it requires. The rooms and suites of the house are painted radiant white, individually furnished with vintage and flea-market items, and have their own verandas or gardens. From the distinctive pool, made from poured concrete, and from the roof terrace guests have a sweeping view over an estate with 600 ancient olive trees, which produce an aromatic oil that is pressed and sold on site. Regional delicacies are an important part of breakfast – and of dinner, which is sometimes cooked spontaneously for guests. ◆ Reading: "Openhouse", a lifestyle and arts magazine published twice a year by Andrew Trotter.

AUF DIE FREUNDSCHAFT Die Freundschaft zwischen Carlo Lanzini und Andrew Trotter begann in London, wo Carlo Kinematografie studierte und Andrew als Interiordesigner arbeitete und sie bei Carlos selbst gemachter Pasta über Gott und die Welt diskutierten. Als Carlo in seine Heimat Italien zurückkehrte, um dort sein Traumhaus zu bauen, und sich in ein Grundstück nahe der „weißen Stadt" Ostuni in Apulien verliebte, entwarf Andrew die Masseria Moroseta. Es war seine erste architektonische Arbeit – ein minimalistischer Bau mit klaren Linien und geometrischen Formen, inspiriert vom alten apulischen Bauernhaus, mit traditionellen Materialien errichtet und zugleich mit moderner Technik ausgestattet: Unter anderem dank einer Solaranlage kann die Masseria 80 Prozent ihrer benötigten Energie selbst herstellen. Die Zimmer und Suiten des Hauses sind in strahlendem Weiß gestrichen, individuell mit Vintage- und Flohmarktmöbeln ausgestattet und besitzen eigene Verandas oder Gärten. Vom Pool, der aus Beton gegossen wurde, und von der Dachterrasse sieht man weit über ein Grundstück mit 600 uralten Olivenbäumen. Aus den Früchten wird direkt vor Ort ein aromatisches Öl gepresst und verkauft. Regionale Köstlichkeiten bestimmen auch das Frühstück – und das Dinner, das an manchen Abenden spontan für die Gäste gezaubert wird. ◆ Lesetipp: „Openhouse" (das Lifestyle- und Kulturmagazin wird zweimal jährlich von Andrew Trotter herausgegeben).

À L'AMITIÉ Carlo Lanzini et Andrew Trotter se sont rencontré à Londres, où Carlo étudiait la cinématographie et Andrew travaillait comme décorateur d'intérieur. C'est ici que leur amitié est née, à refaire le monde devant un plat de pâtes faites par Carlo. Lorsque celui-ci est retourné dans son Italie natale pour y construire la maison de ses rêves et qu'il est tombé amoureux d'un terrain près d'Ostuni, la « ville blanche », dans les Pouilles, Andrew a dessiné la Masseria Moroseta. Il s'agissait de sa première architecture – un bâtiment minimaliste aux lignes claires et aux formes géométriques, inspiré de l'ancienne ferme des Pouilles, construit avec des matériaux traditionnels sans renier la technologie moderne : grâce en partie à un système photovoltaïque, la Masseria peut produire elle-même 80 % de l'énergie dont elle a besoin. Les chambres et suites de la maison sont peintes d'un blanc éclatant, aménagées individuellement avec des pièces vintage et des meubles trouvés sur les marchés aux puces, et possèdent leurs propres vérandas ou jardins. De l'impressionnante piscine en béton et de la terrasse sur le toit, on peut contempler une vaste propriété de 600 oliviers centenaires qui produisent une huile aromatique pressée et vendue localement. Les spécialités régionales déterminent également le petit déjeuner – et le dîner, qui est spontanément préparé pour les invités certains soirs. ◆ À lire : « Openhouse » (le magazine lifestyle et culture publié deux fois par an par Andrew Trotter).

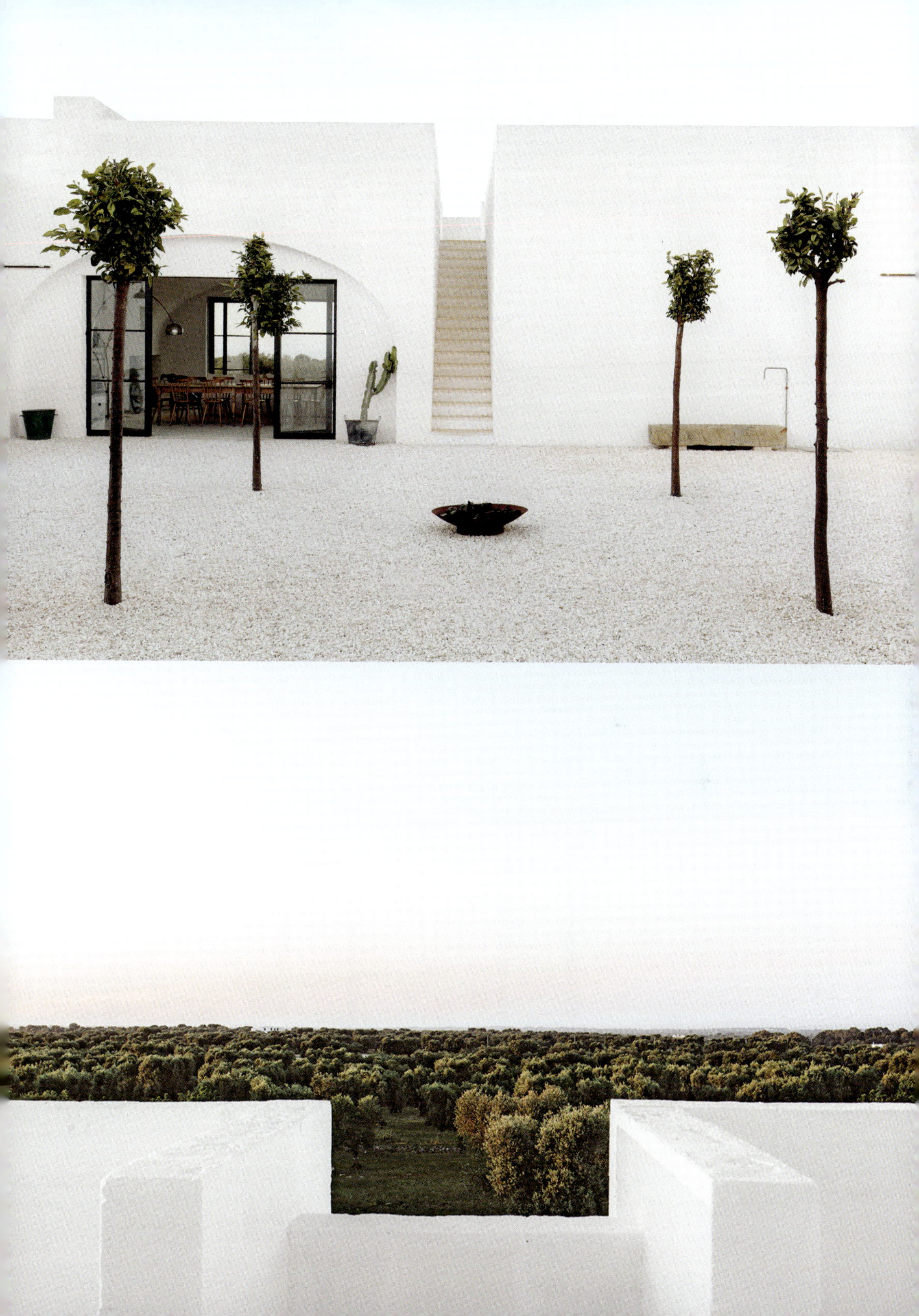

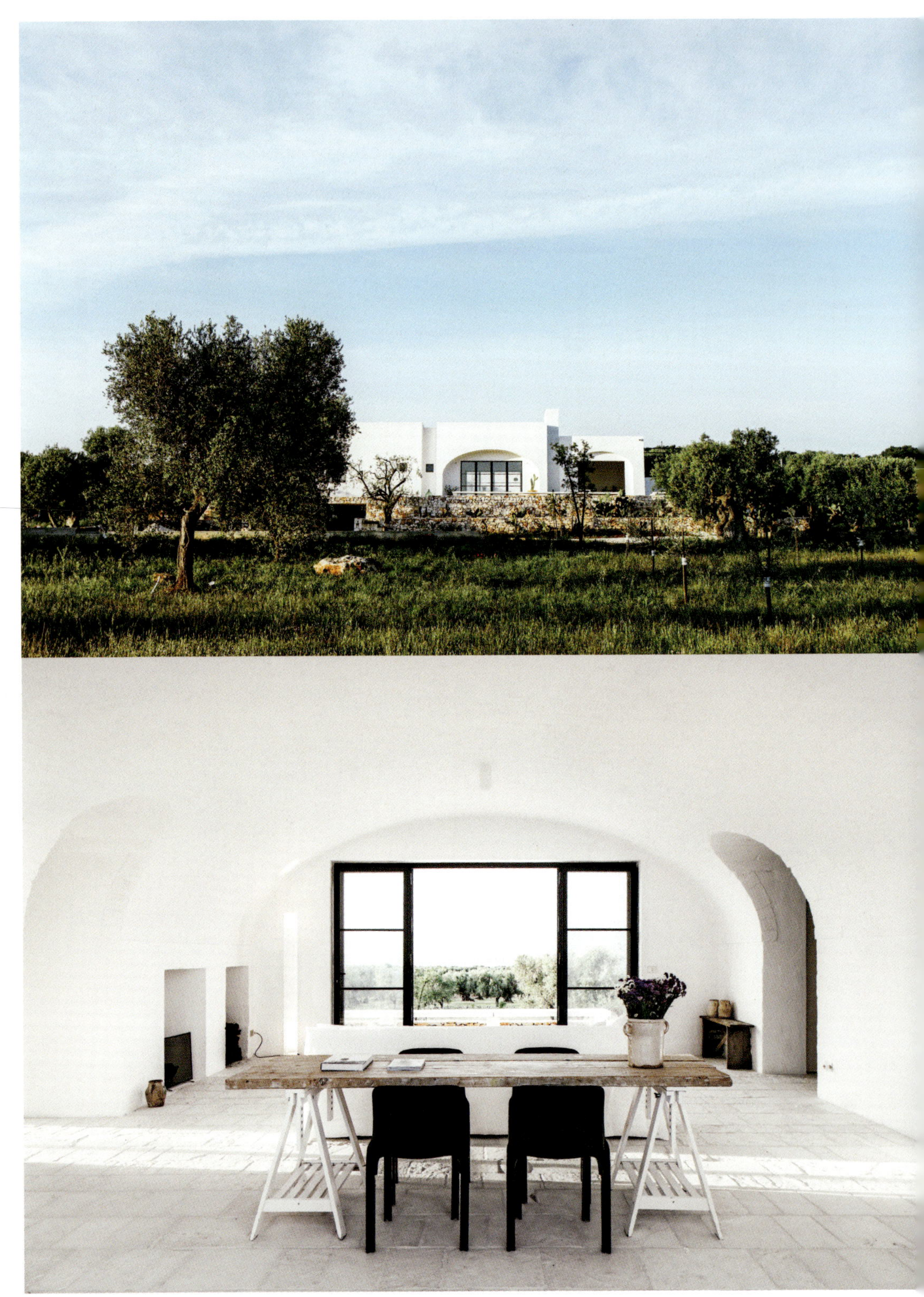

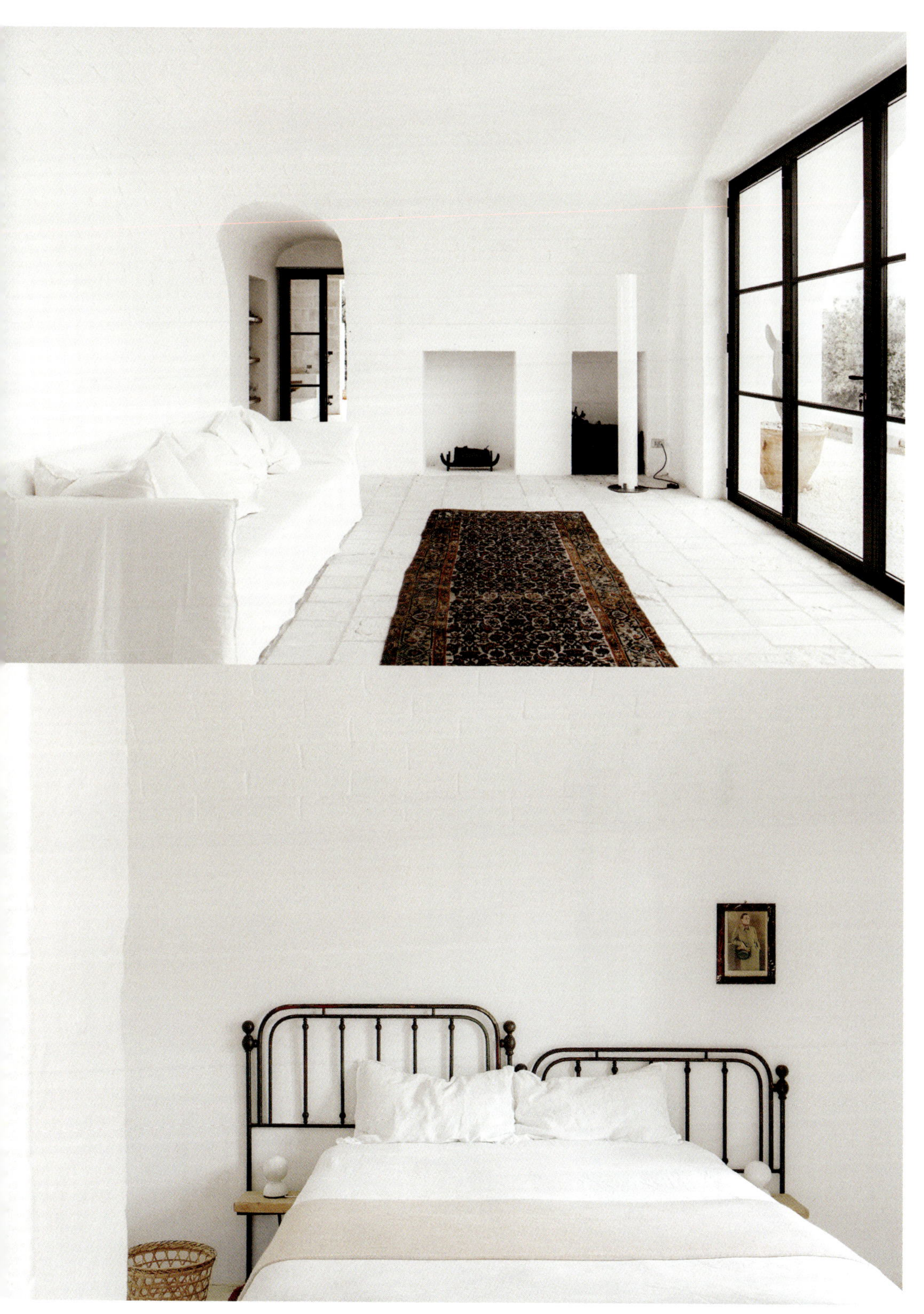

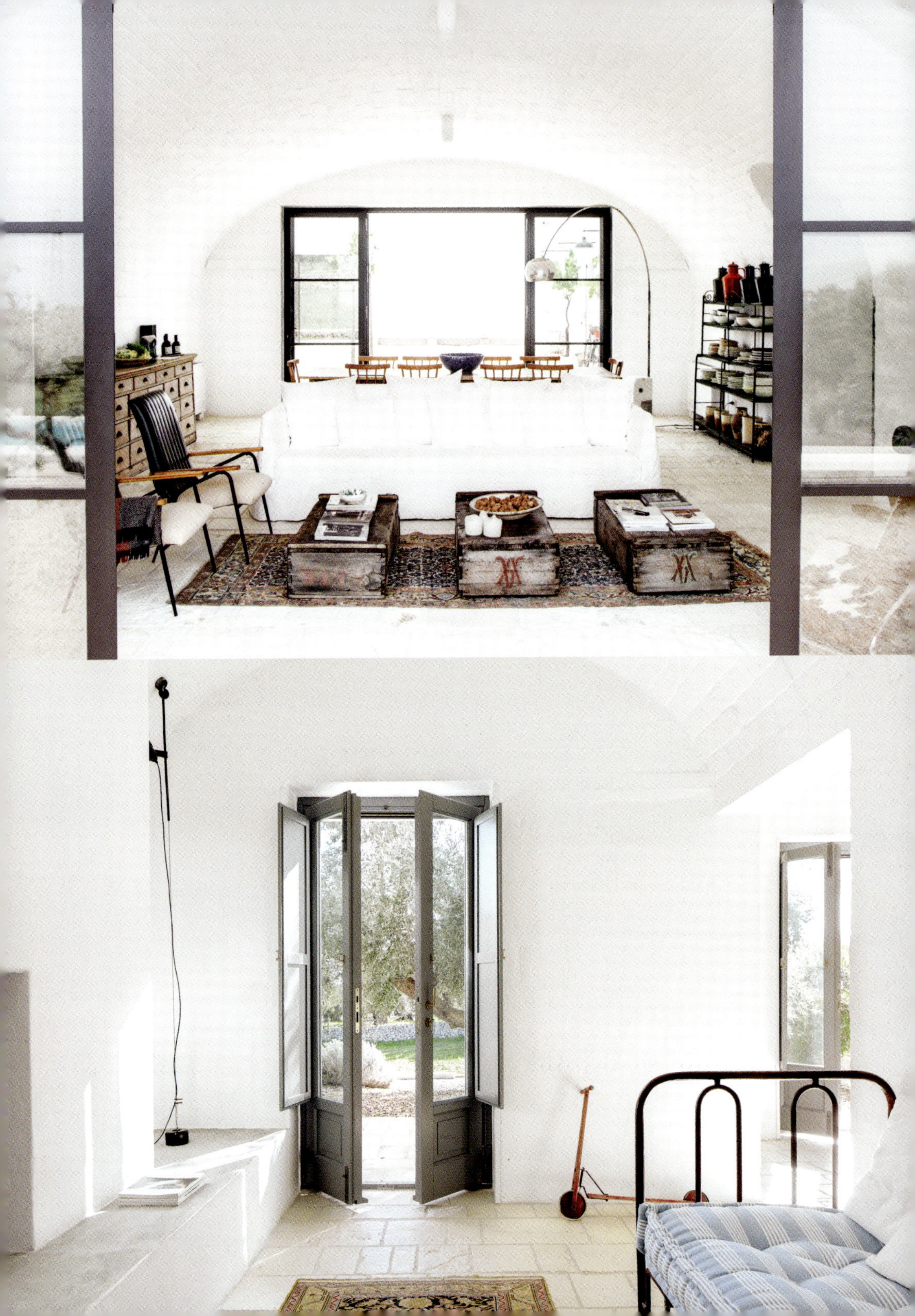

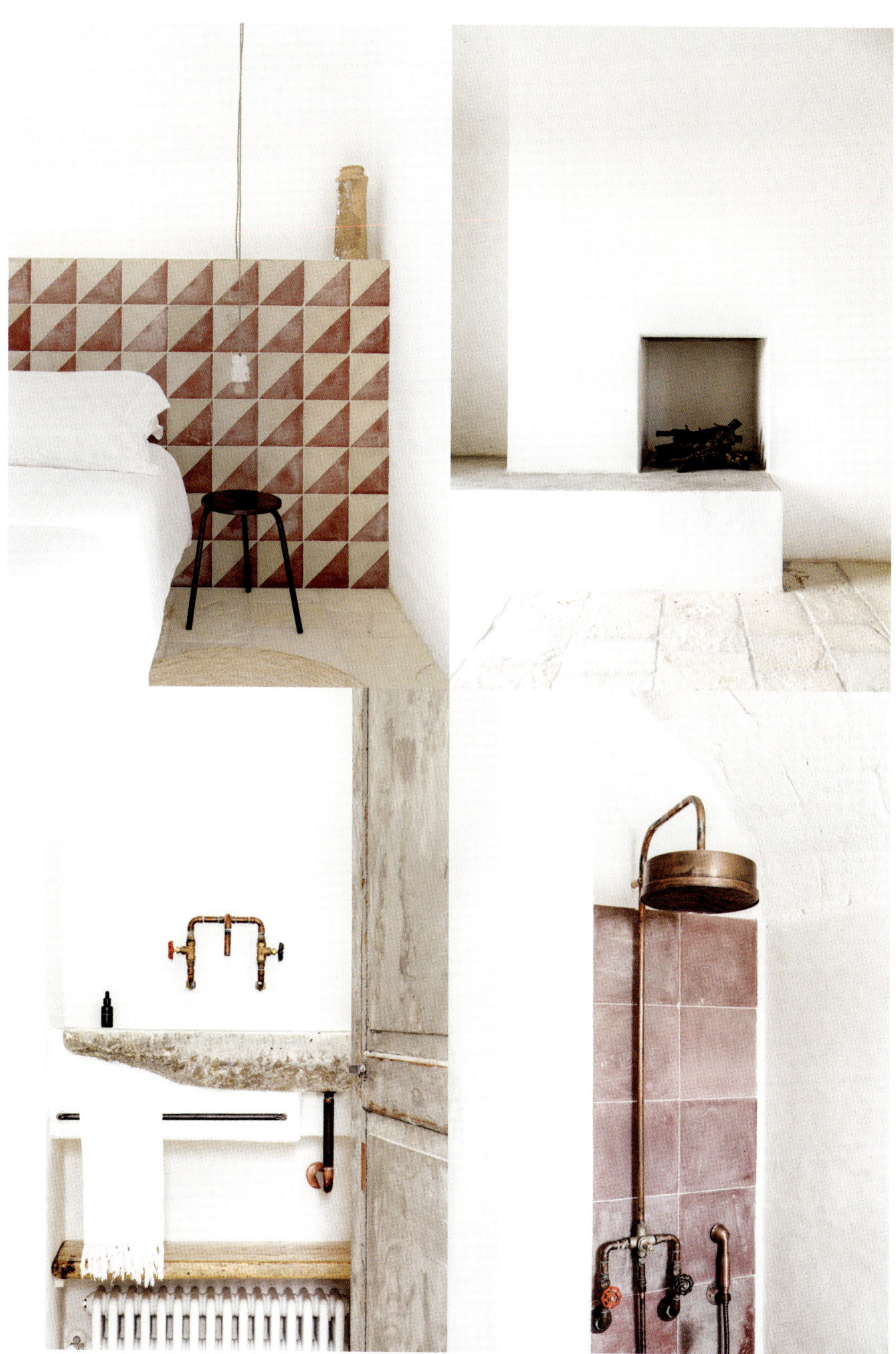

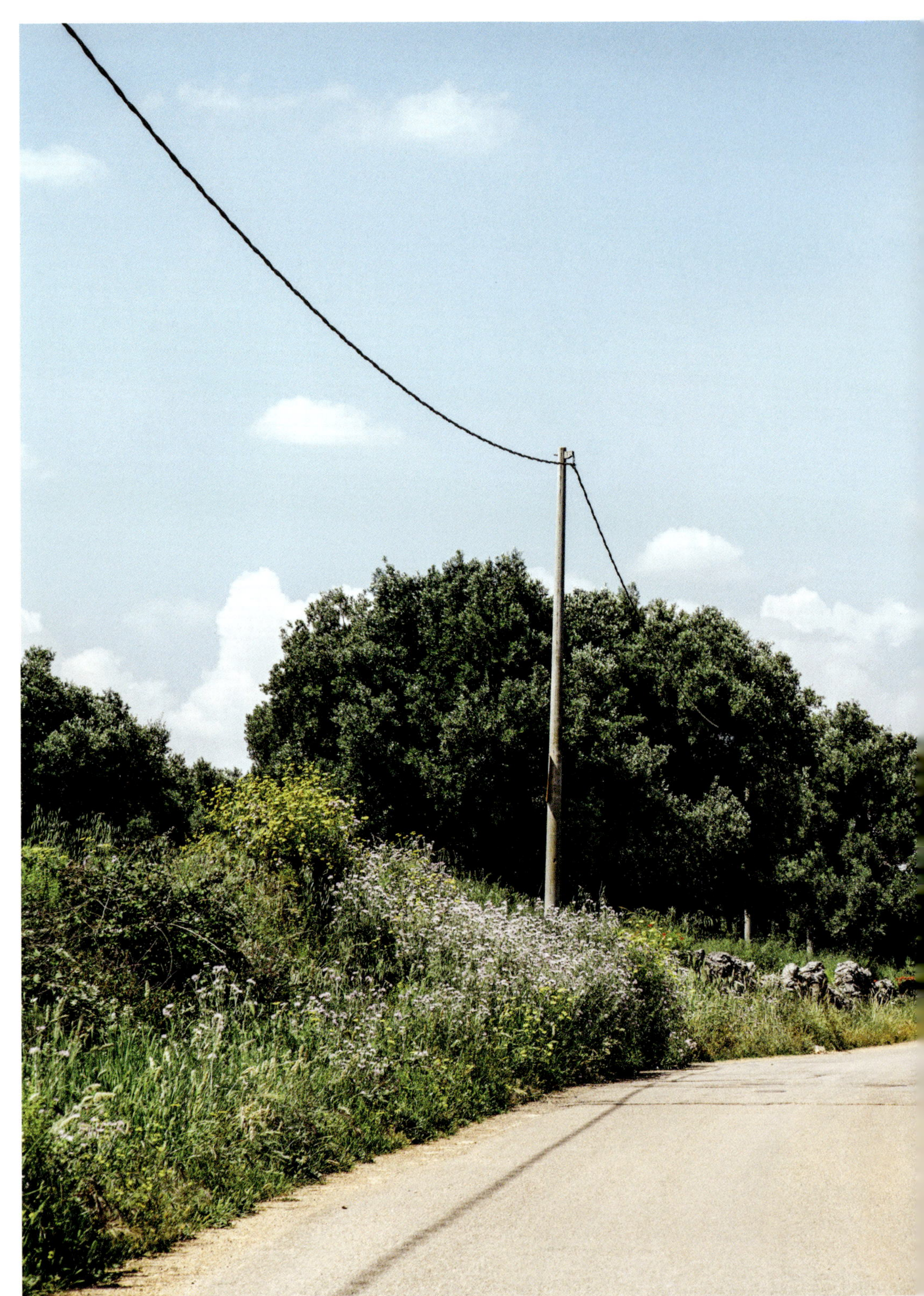

PUGLIA

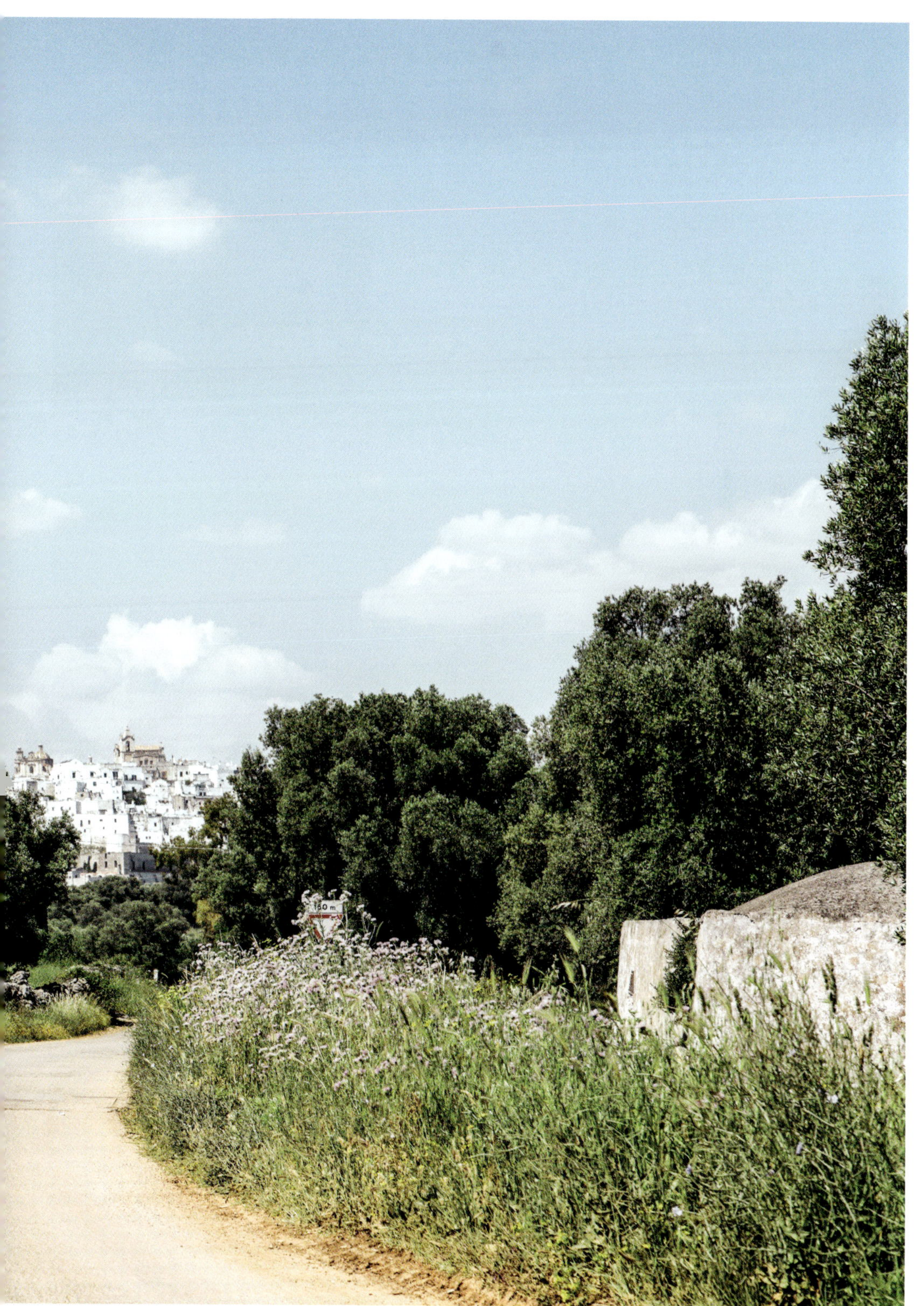
150 m

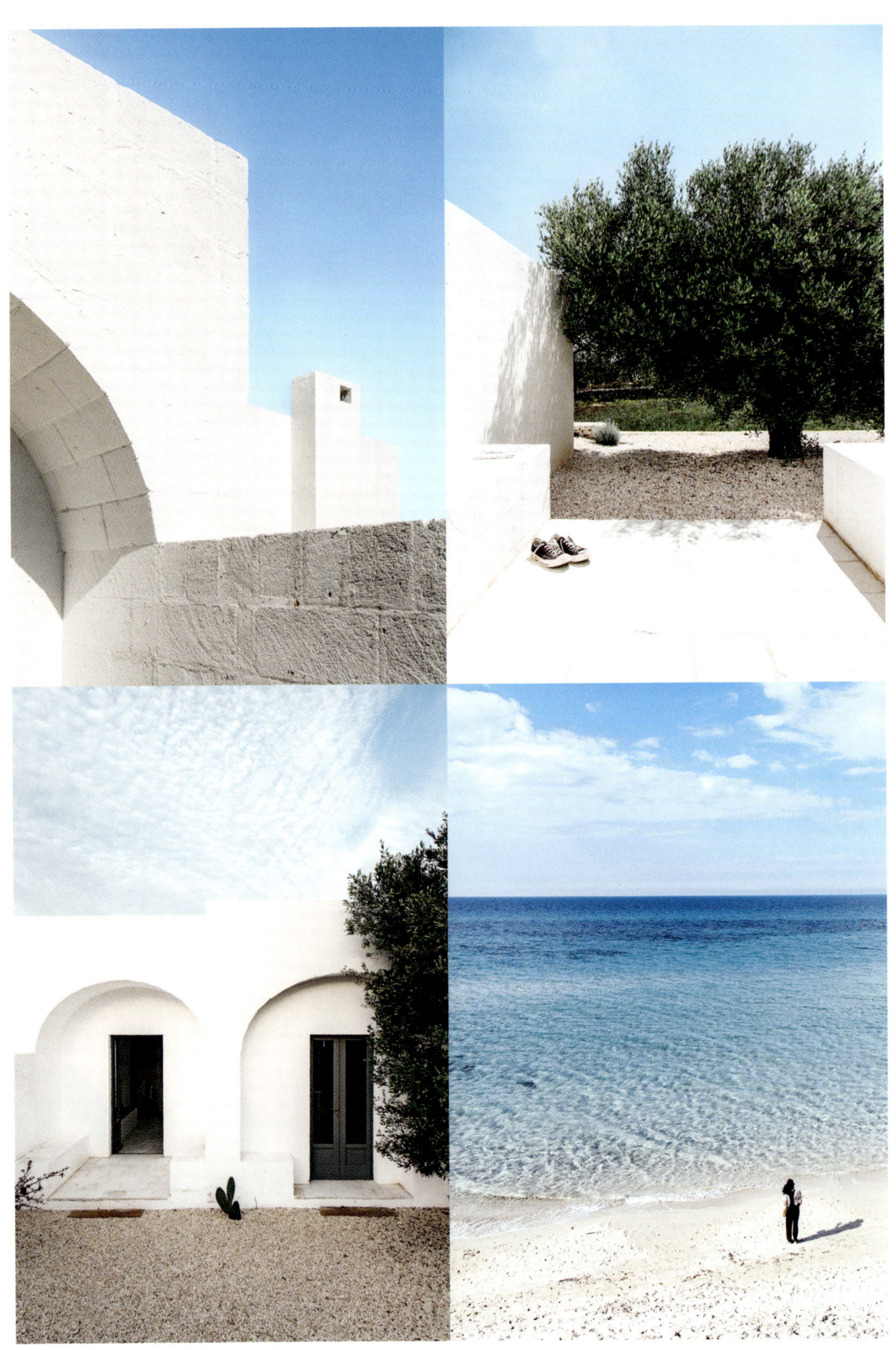

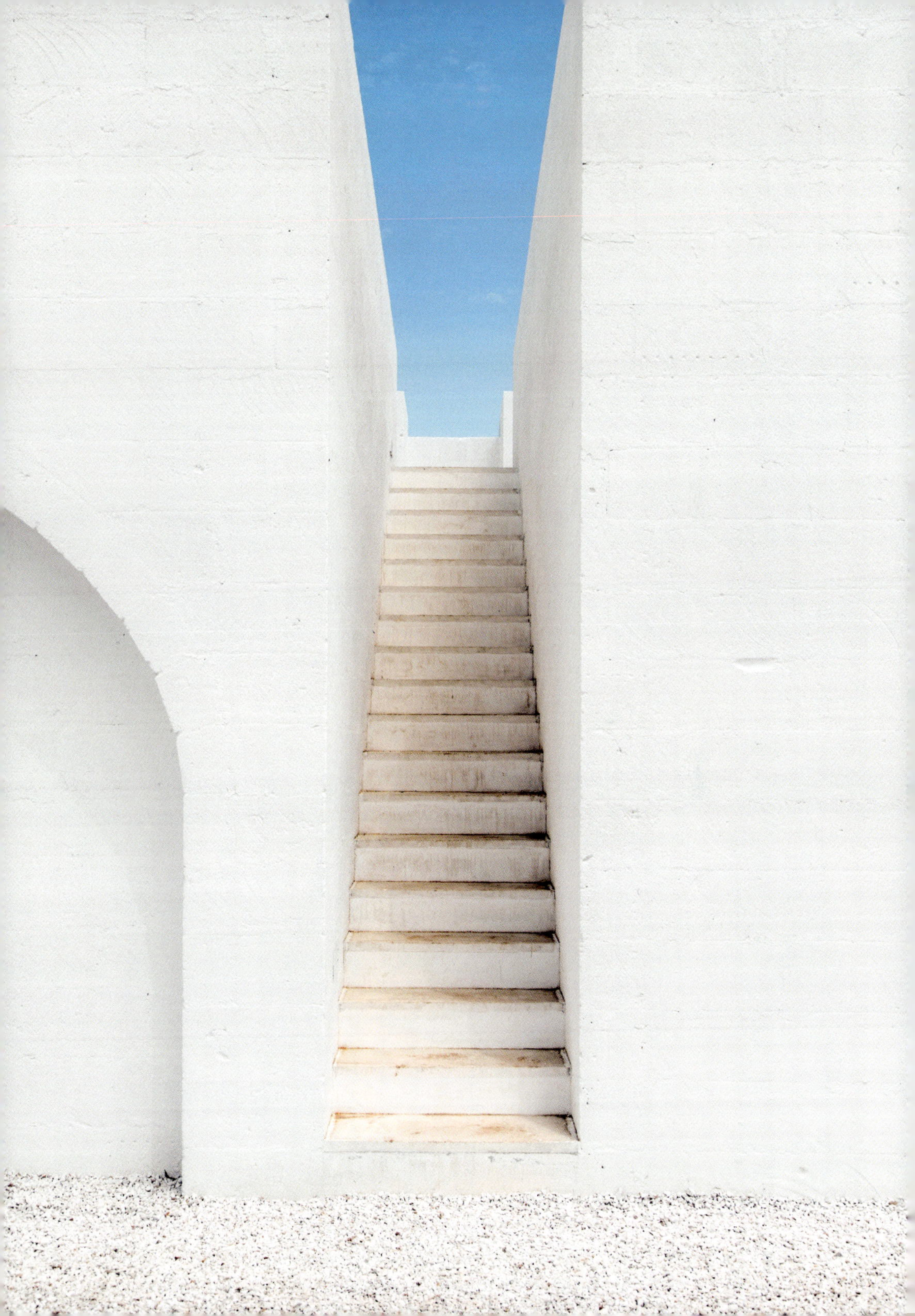

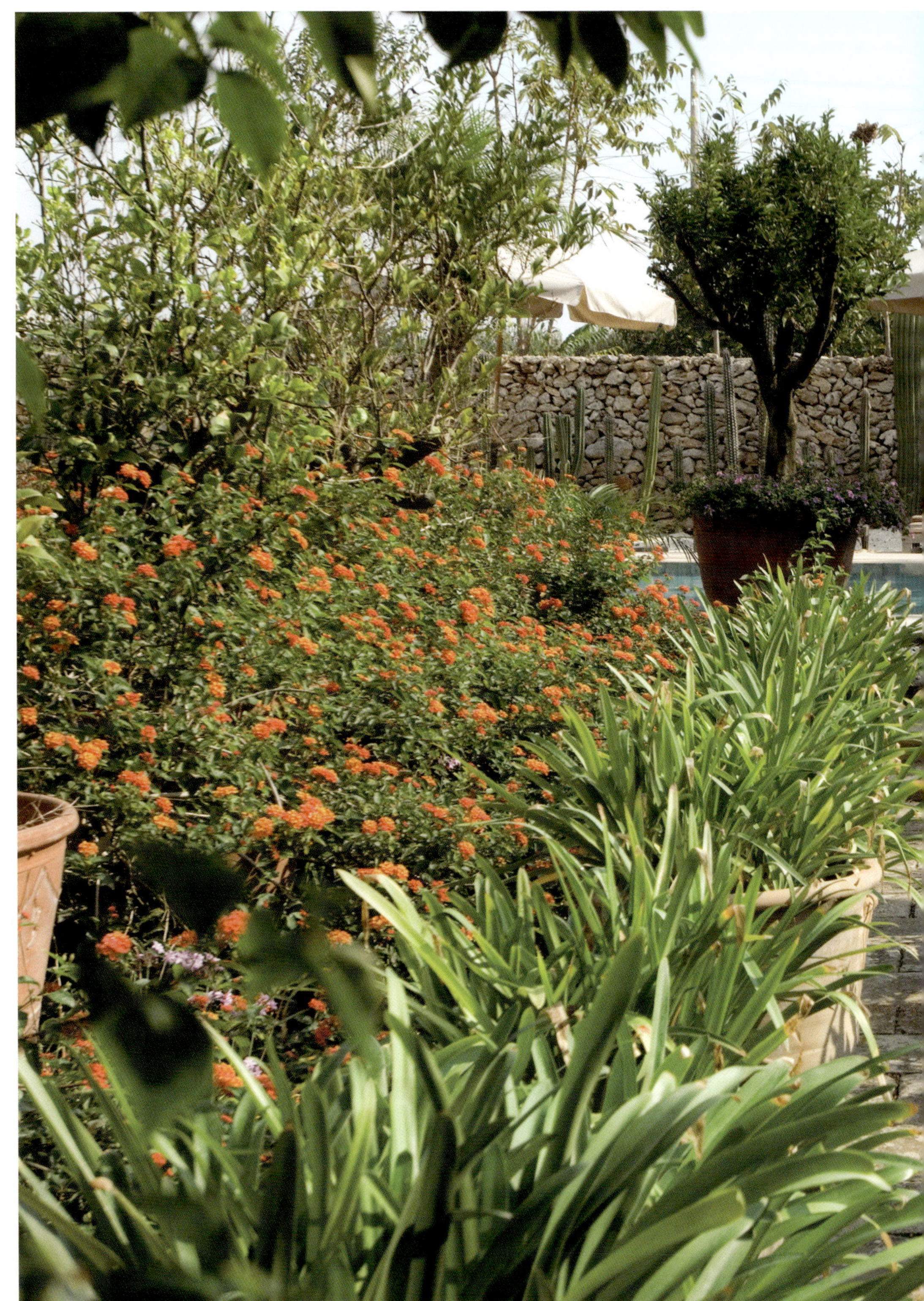

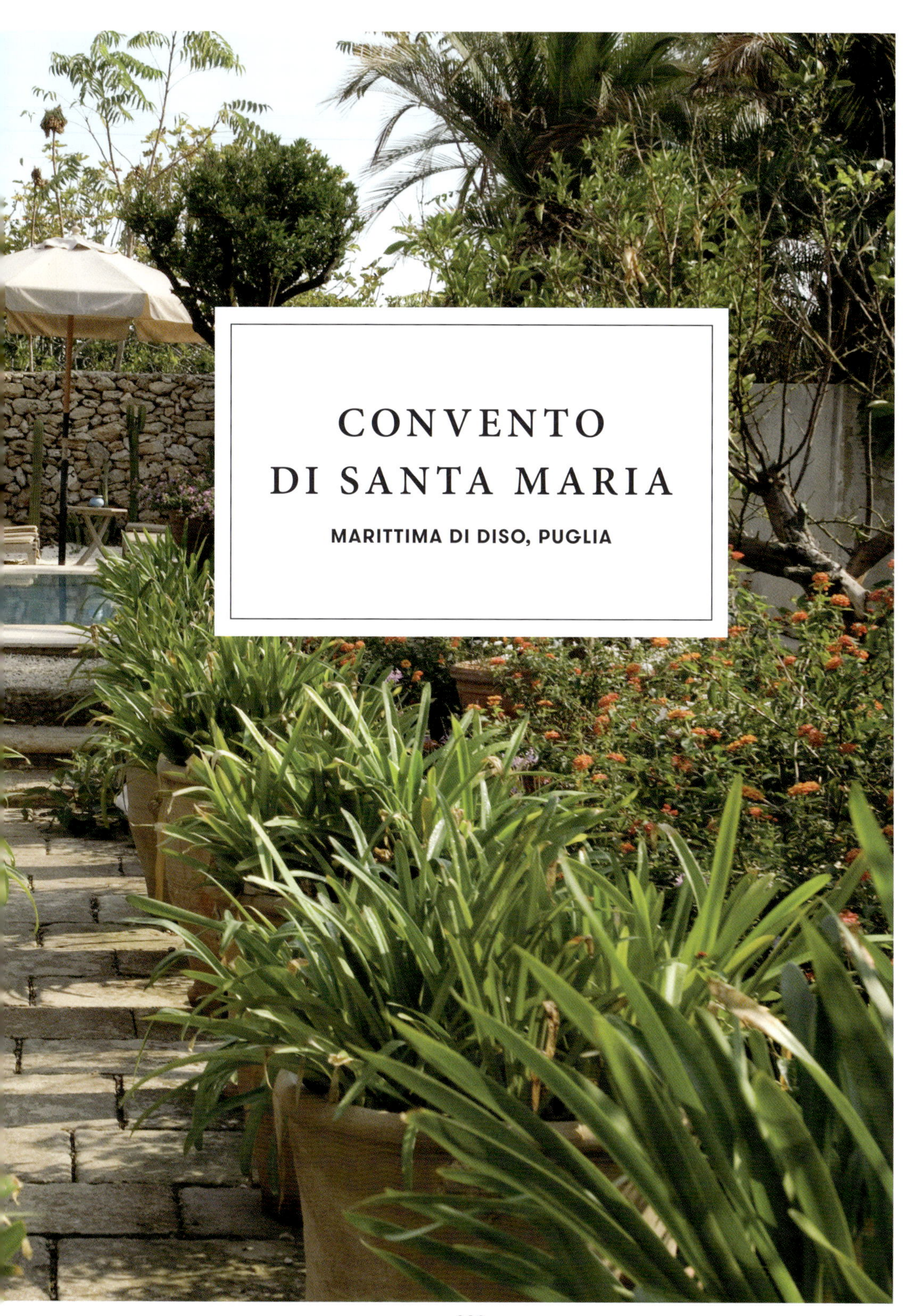

CONVENTO DI SANTA MARIA

MARITTIMA DI DISO, PUGLIA

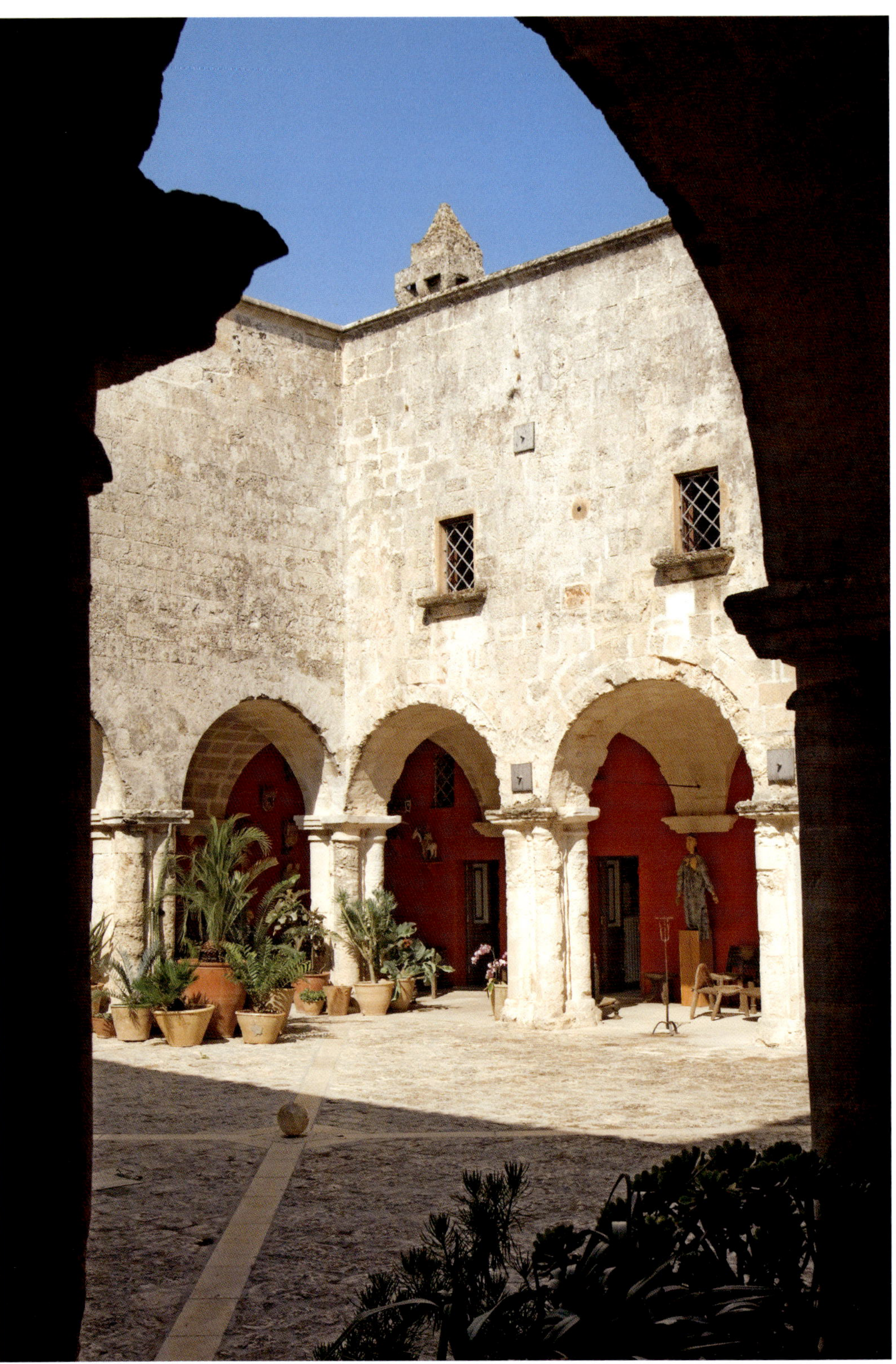

CONVENTO DI SANTA MARIA

Via Convento, 73030 Marittima di Diso
Tel. +44 1223 4601 003 · info@ilconventopuglia.com
www.ilconventopuglia.com
Open from March to October

A REMARKABLE COLLECTION When Alistair and Athena McAlpine moved to Apulia, British upper-class society was dumbfounded. What did this lord, once treasurer of Margaret Thatcher's Conservative Party, and his young wife, who had lived in such cosmopolitan cities as New York, see in this godforsaken area down on the heel of Italy? But the answer was simple: the couple had found a perfect and private spot there, a place that had been shaped by different cultures like their own lives and was filled with color and contrasts, a place whose raw beauty and magic aroused their urge to make discoveries. A former monastery became their home – and their treasure-house. Because Alistair had not just been politically active: a passionate collector, he had gathered over 14 tons of books and acquired thousands of examples of ethnic and folk art on his journeys round the world. With an unerring sense of style Athena shows fabrics from Morocco and Indonesia, works by Aborigines and Africans, painted glass from Kerala and parasols from Vietnam to best advantage and turns a diverse collection into a bohemian complete work of art. To be a guest here is to stay with friends and enjoy the relaxed Italian way of life at its very best. The food, too, matches the manners of the country: the Mediterranean meals have often been a reason for visitors to extend their stay. ◆ Book to pack: "Casa Rossa" by Francesca Marciano.

EINE AUSSERGEWÖHNLICHE SAMMLUNG Als Alistair und Athena McAlpine nach Apulien zogen, verstand man in besseren britischen Kreisen die Welt nicht mehr. Was wollten der Lord, einst Schatzmeister von Margaret Thatcher, und seine junge Frau, die in Metropolen wie New York gelebt hatte, in einer gottverlassenen Gegend am Absatz des italienischen Stiefels? Dabei war die Antwort so einfach – die beiden hatten dort einen perfekten und privaten Platz gefunden, einen Ort, der wie ihr eigenes Leben von verschiedenen Kulturen geprägt worden und voller Farben und Kontraste war, der mit seiner rauen Schönheit und seiner Magie ihren Entdeckersinn weckte. Ein ehemaliges Kloster wurde zu ihrem Heim – und zum Hort ihrer Schätze. Denn Alistair war nicht nur Politiker gewesen: Als leidenschaftlicher Leser hatte er über 14 Tonnen Bücher zusammengetragen und als Weltreisender Tausende Exponate von Stammes- und Volkskunst erstanden. Die Stoffe aus Marokko und Indonesien, die Arbeiten der Aborigines und Afrikaner, die Glasmalereien aus Kerala und die Schirme aus Vietnam setzt Athena absolut stilsicher in Szene und schafft aus dem Sammelsurium ein Gesamtkunstwerk der Boheme. Wer hier zu Gast ist, wohnt bei Freunden und genießt die italienische Lässigkeit in ihrer schönsten Form. Den guten Sitten des Landes entspricht auch das Essen: Die mediterranen Menüs waren schon mehrfach Grund dafür, dass Besucher ihren Aufenthalt verlängerten. ◆ Buchtipps: „Otranto" von Roberto Cotroneo und „Casa Rossa" von Francesca Marciano.

L'ART DE LA COLLECTION Lorsqu'Alistair et Athena McAlpine sont partis s'installer dans les Pouilles, la bonne société britannique n'en est pas revenue. Que cherchaient l'ancien trésorier de Margaret Thatcher et sa jeune femme dans un endroit perdu situé dans le talon de la botte italienne, eux qui avaient vécu dans des métropoles comme New York ? La réponse était simple pourtant – le couple a trouvé ici un paysage idéal et bien à lui, un endroit à son image marqué par différentes cultures et plein de couleurs et de contrastes, un lieu dont la beauté sauvage et la magie ont éveillé son instinct d'explorateur. Un ancien couvent est devenu leur foyer et l'écrin de leurs trésors. C'est que lord Alistair McAlpine ne s'est pas contenté de faire de la politique ; lecteur passionné, il a rassemblé plus de quatorze tonnes de livres et, voyageur infatigable, des milliers d'objets de l'art tribal et populaire. Avec une parfaite maîtrise stylistique, Athena met en scène des étoffes marocaines et indonésiennes, des travaux des Aborigènes et des Africains, des peintures sur verre du Kerala et des paravents du Vietnam, créant avec ces objets disparates une œuvre d'art totale tout à fait originale. Celui qui séjourne ici habite chez des amis et jouit de la nonchalance italienne sous sa forme la plus raffinée. La gastronomie est au rendez-vous : la cuisine méditerranéenne en a amené plus d'un à prolonger son séjour. ◆ À lire : « Le Soleil des Scorta » de Laurent Gaudé et « Casa Rossa » de Francesca Marciano.

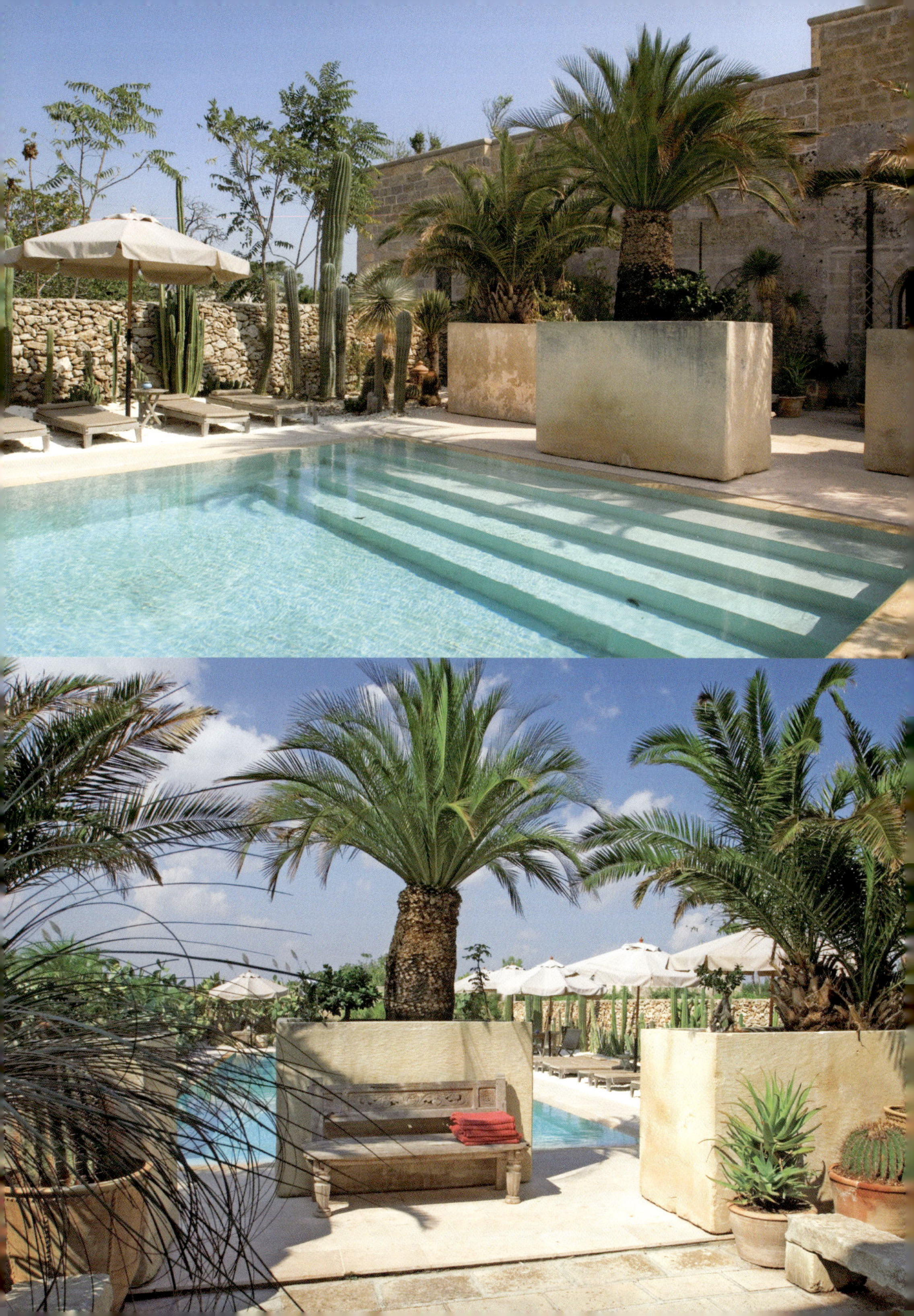

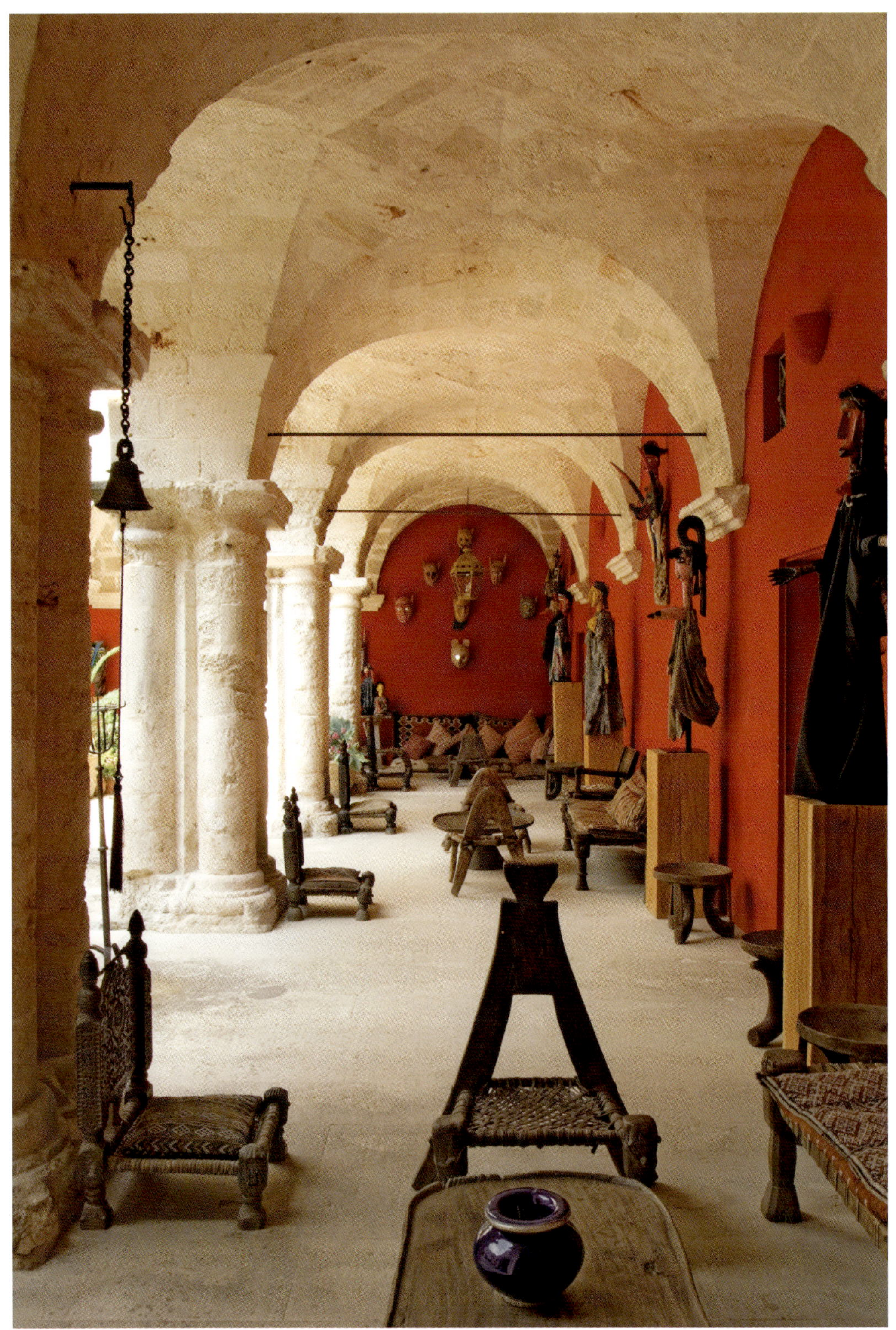

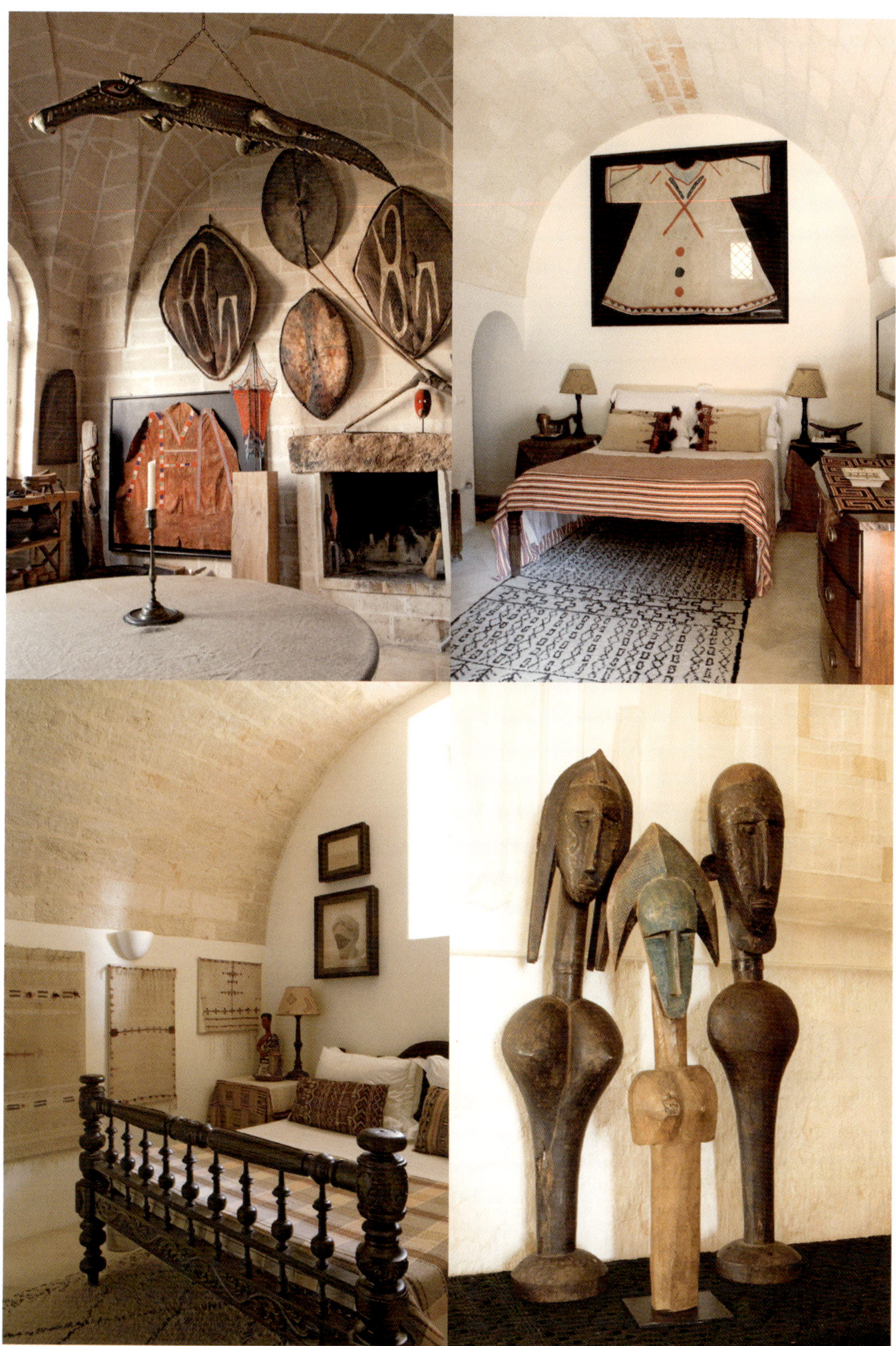

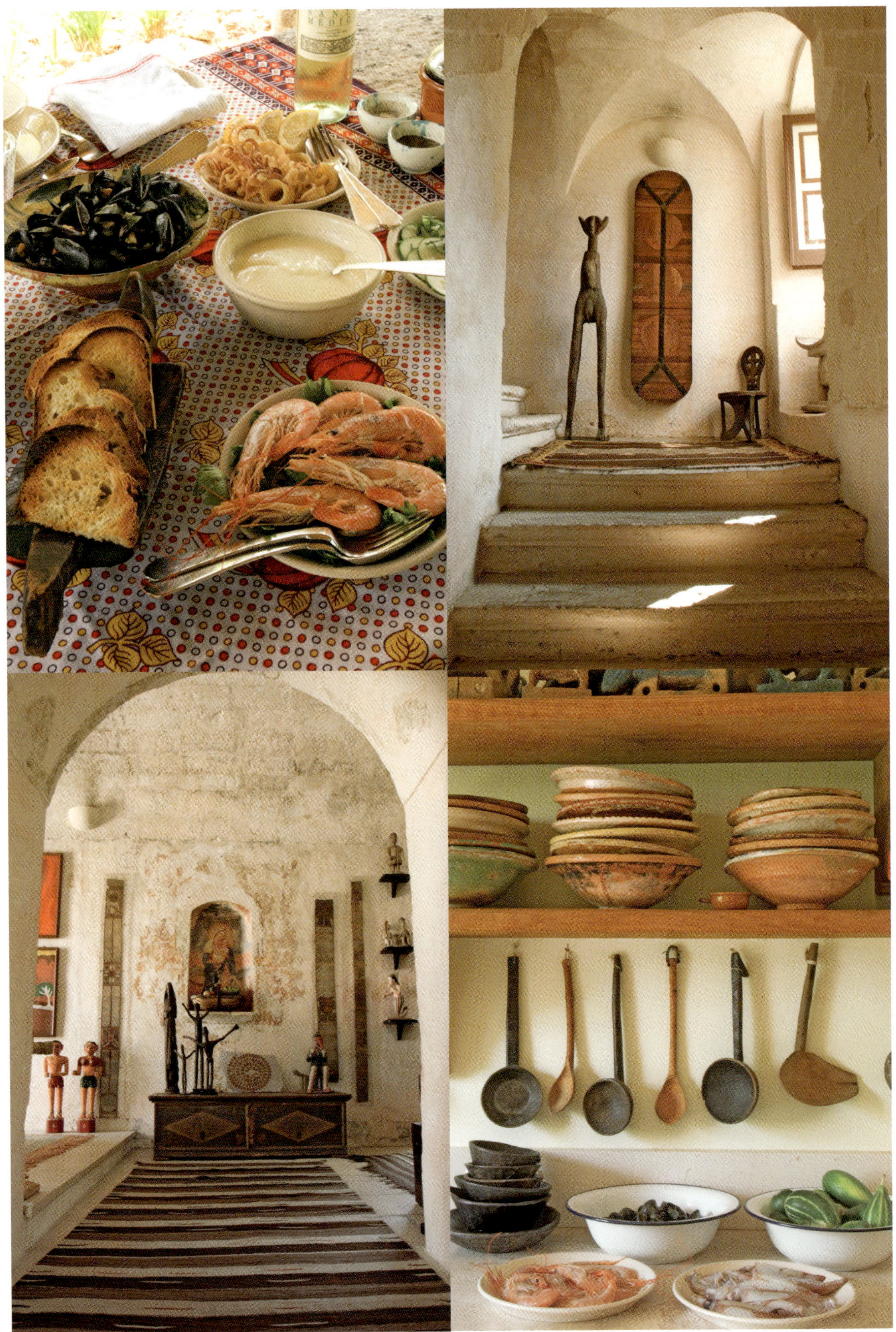

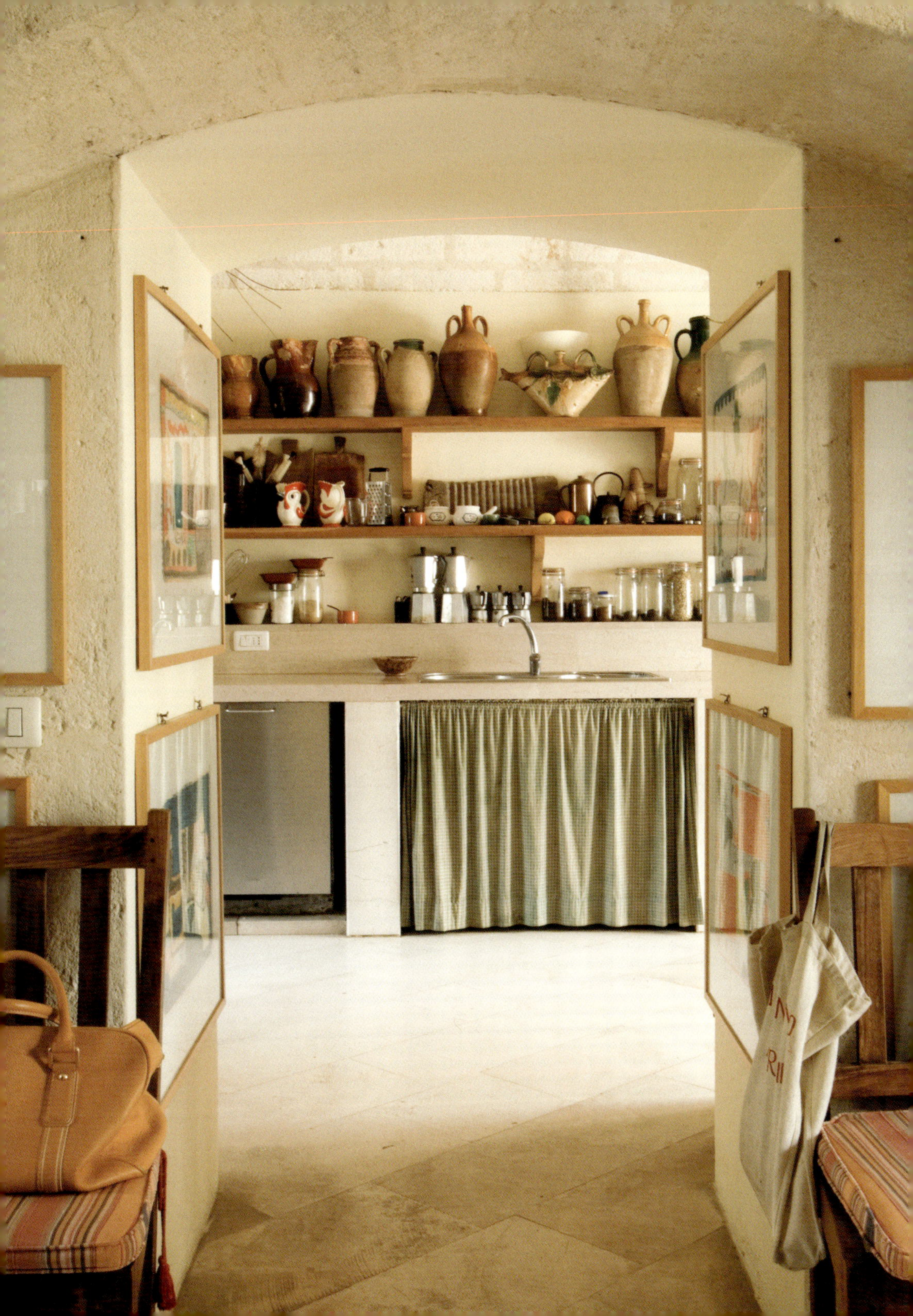

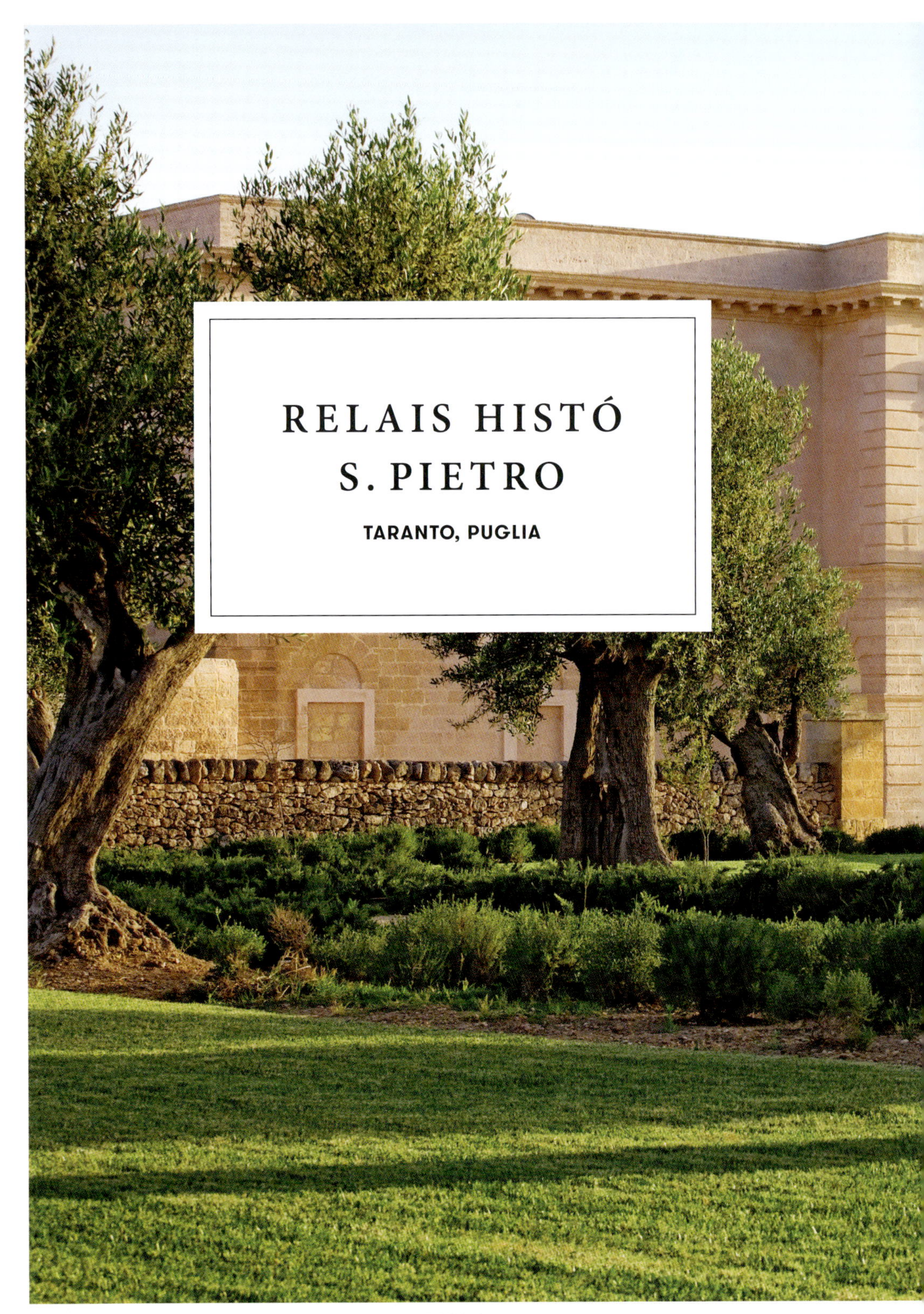

RELAIS HISTÓ S. PIETRO

TARANTO, PUGLIA

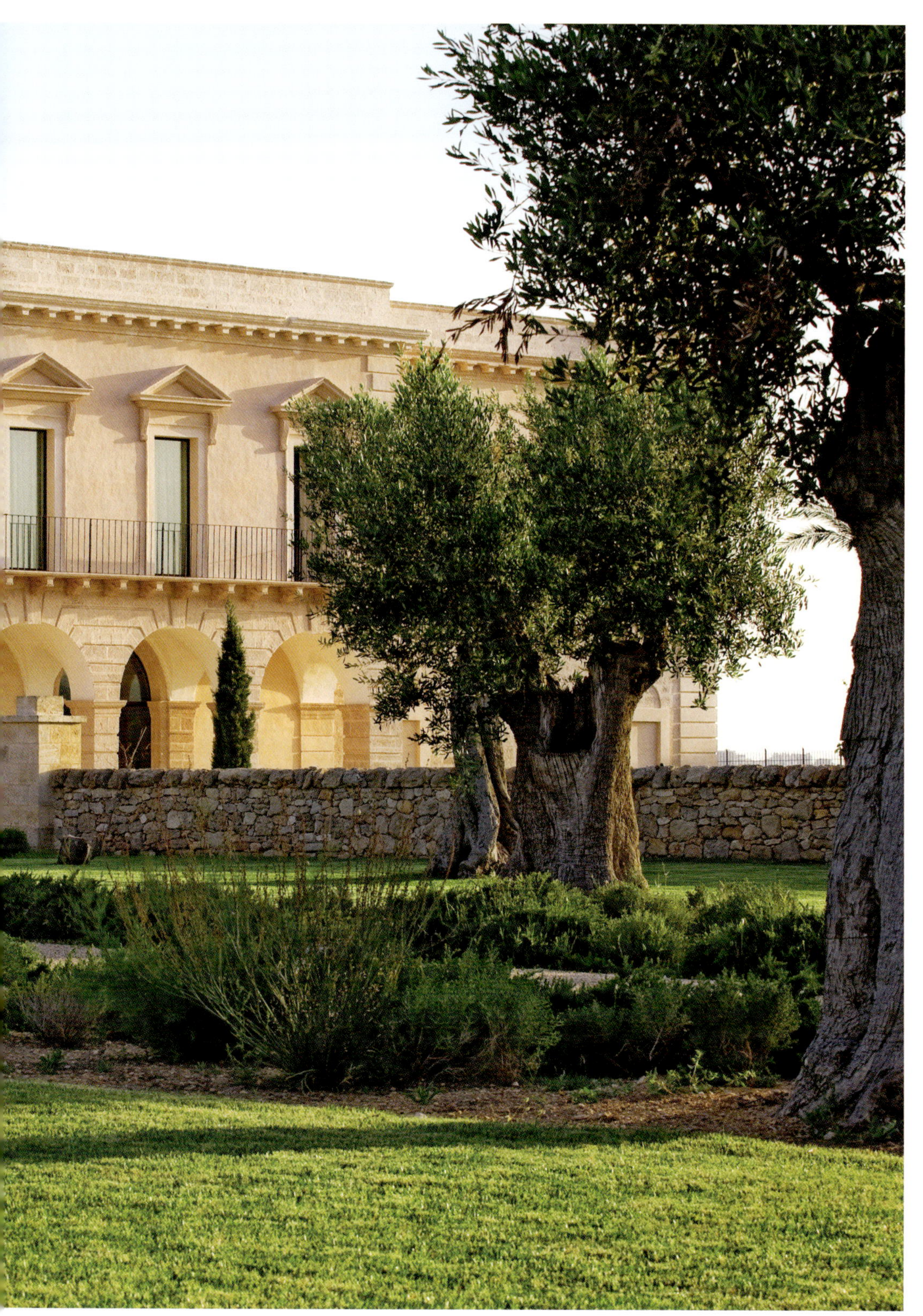

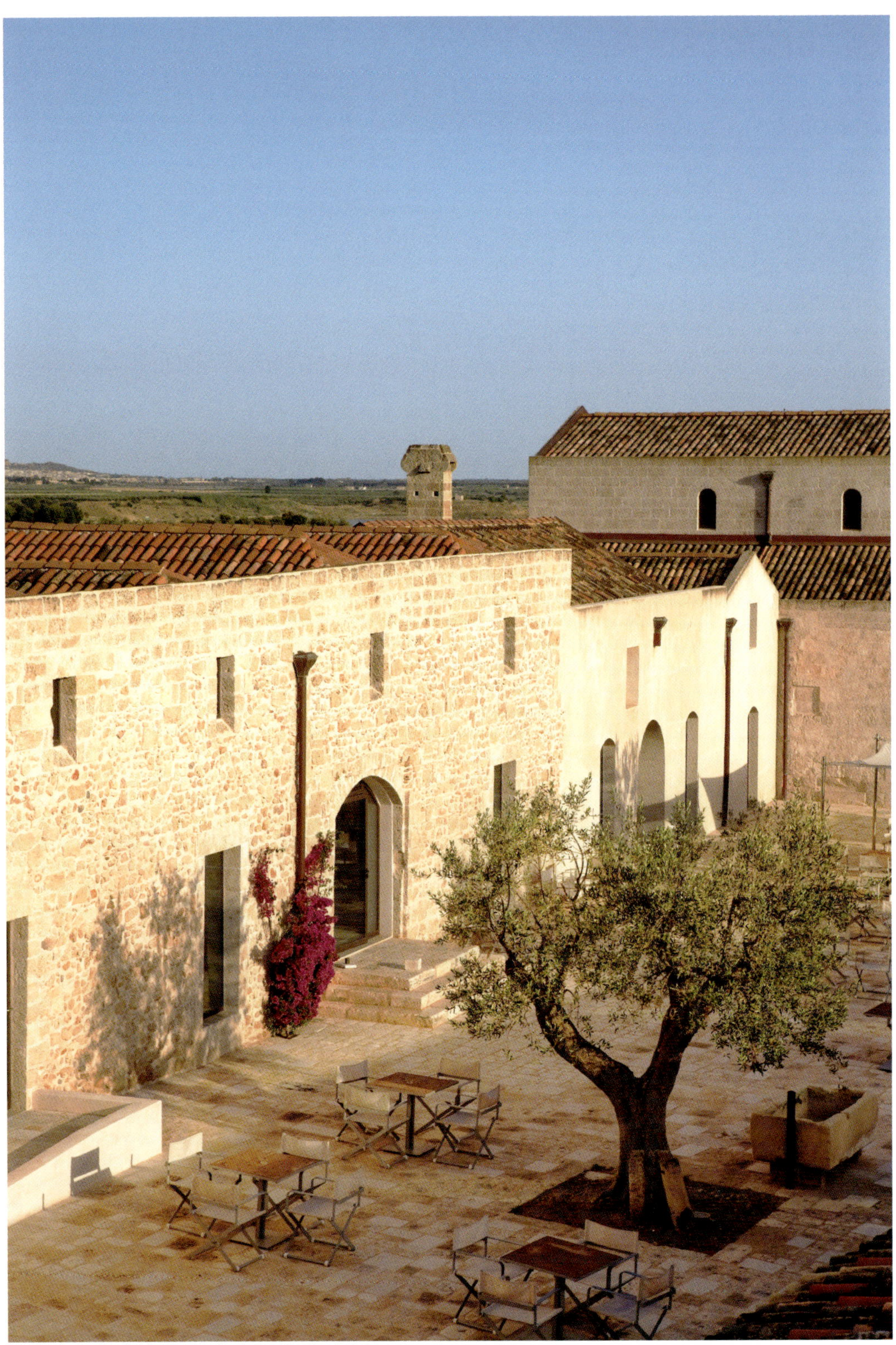

PUGLIA

RELAIS HISTÓ S. PIETRO

Via Santandrea Circummarpiccolo, 74123 Taranto
Tel. +39 099 472 1188 · info@relaishisto.it
www.relaishisto.it

TIMELESS BEAUTY There is no lack of legends about the origins of the city of Taranto. The pragmatic version quite simply attributes its foundation to Heracles. There is a more colorful story about Taras, a demi-god and son of Poseidon, who was saved by a dolphin after a storm at sea, rode to land on the dolphin's back and established the settlement. And the inhabitants' favourite tale is the myth of Phalanthus the Spartan, whom the oracle at Delphi prophesied would conquer a new place as soon as rain fell when all around was sunny. Phalanthus set out on a voyage, and one day when he saw his wife Ethra (the Greek word for "joyful") crying, had the solution to the riddle – he anchored and laid the foundation stone of Taranto on the nearest shore. Those who would like to immerse themselves in history more deeply and in surroundings to match should book a room in the Relais Histó, a medieval masseria that houses a stylish hotel today. Alessandro Agrati, who also designed Relais La Sommità, preserved the traditional structure and materials of the estate during restoration and combined it with modern Culti furniture in shades of cream, gray and brown – historic and contemporary elements in wonderful equilibrium. It is necessary to book early for a room with a sea view, but there is also much to be said for the ones that look out onto orange trees. The view and the ambience are just right in the restaurant and around the pool – the opening of this hotel has probably put an end once and for all to tears on a sunny day.
◆ Book to pack: "Myths and Legends of Ancient Greece and Rome" by E. M. Berens.

ZEITLOS SCHÖN An Legenden über ihre Entstehung mangelt es der Stadt Tarent nicht: Die pragmatische Version schreibt die Gründung schlicht und einfach Herakles zu. Etwas farbenprächtiger ist die Geschichte von Taras, Halbgott und Sohn Poseidons, der nach einem Seesturm von einem Delfin gerettet wurde, auf dessen Rücken an Land ritt und dort eine Siedlung errichtete. Und am liebsten erzählen die Bewohner die Sage von dem Spartaner Phalanto, dem das Orakel von Delphi vorhergesagt hatte, er werde einen neuen Ort erobern, sobald es aus heiterem Himmel regnen werde. Phalantus brach zu einer Schiffsreise auf, und als er eines Tages seine Frau Aithra (griechisch für „die Heitere") weinen sah, schien das Rätsel gelöst – er warf den Anker und legte am nächsten Ufer den Grundstein Tarents. Wer tiefer und in passendem Ambiente in die Historie eintauchen möchte, bucht am besten das Relais Histó – eine mittelalterliche Masseria, die heute ein stilvolles Hotel beherbergt. Alessandro Agrati, der auch das Relais La Sommità entwarf, hat bei der Renovierung des Anwesens dessen traditionelle Strukturen und Materialien erhalten und sie mit modernem Culti-Mobiliar in Creme-, Grau- und Braunnuancen kombiniert – eine wunderbare Balance zwischen Geschichte und Gegenwart. Die Zimmer mit Meerblick muss man rechtzeitig reservieren, doch auch der Blick über die Orangenbäume ist traumhaft. Aussicht und Ambiente stimmen im Restaurant ebenso wie am Pool – Tränen aus heiterem Himmel dürften in Tarent also spätestens seit der Eröffnung dieses Hotels passé sein. ◆ Buchtipp: „Sagen des klassischen Altertums" von Gustav Schwab.

D'HIER ET D'AUJOURD'HUI Les légendes décrivant la naissance de Tarente ne manquent pas, la version la plus pragmatique attribuant tout simplement sa fondation à Héraclès. Plus colorée est celle qui nous montre Tara, fils de Poséidon et d'une nymphe, pris dans une tempête en mer. Sauvé par un dauphin, il le chevauchera jusqu'à la terre ferme où il fondera une colonie. Mais la légende que les habitants racontent le plus volontiers est celle du Spartiate Phalantus, à qui l'oracle de Delphes avait prédit qu'il conquerrait un nouvel endroit dès qu'il verrait « pleuvoir par un temps serein ». Phalantus entreprit un voyage en Italie et comprit l'énigme le jour où il vit pleurer sa femme Ethra (en grec, la sereine) – il jeta l'ancre et posa sur la rive la plus proche la première pierre de Tarente. Les amateurs d'histoire appréciant le cadre adapté devraient réserver une chambre au Relais Histó – une masseria médiévale qui abrite aujourd'hui un hôtel élégant. Alessandro Agrati – il a aussi conçu le Relais La Sommità – a su conserver ses structures et matériaux traditionnels, les combinant à un mobilier moderne de Culti en tons crème, gris et bruns – un superbe équilibre entre le passé et le présent. Les chambres avec vue sur la mer doivent être réservées à temps, mais la vue de celles qui donnent sur les orangers n'est pas à dédaigner non plus. Que l'on se trouve au restaurant ou à la piscine, la vue et l'ambiance sont garanties. À Tarente, depuis l'ouverture de l'hôtel, les larmes ne devraient donc plus couler par un ciel serein. ◆ À lire : « Mythologie grecque et romaine » de Pierre Commelin.

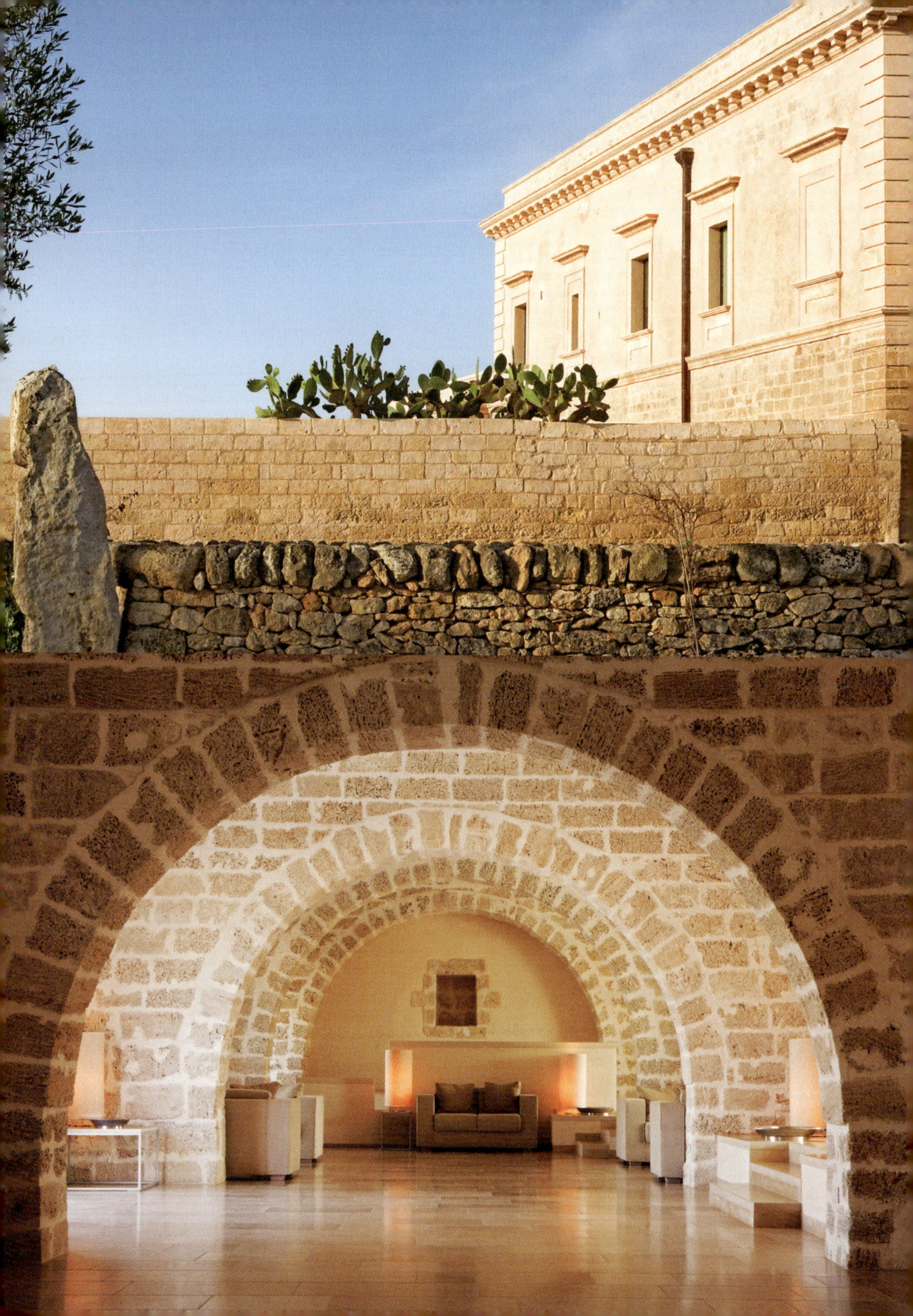

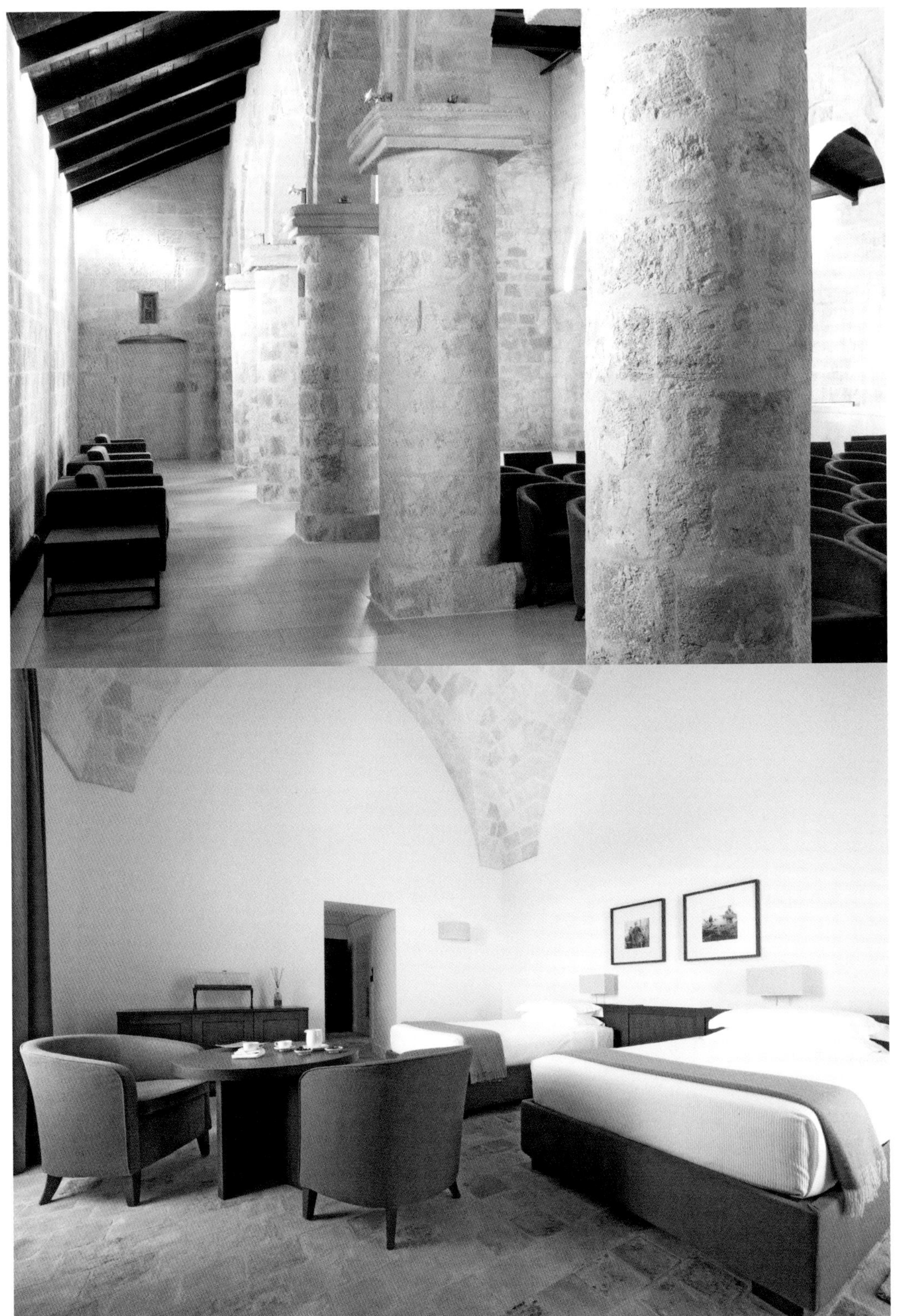

PUGLIA

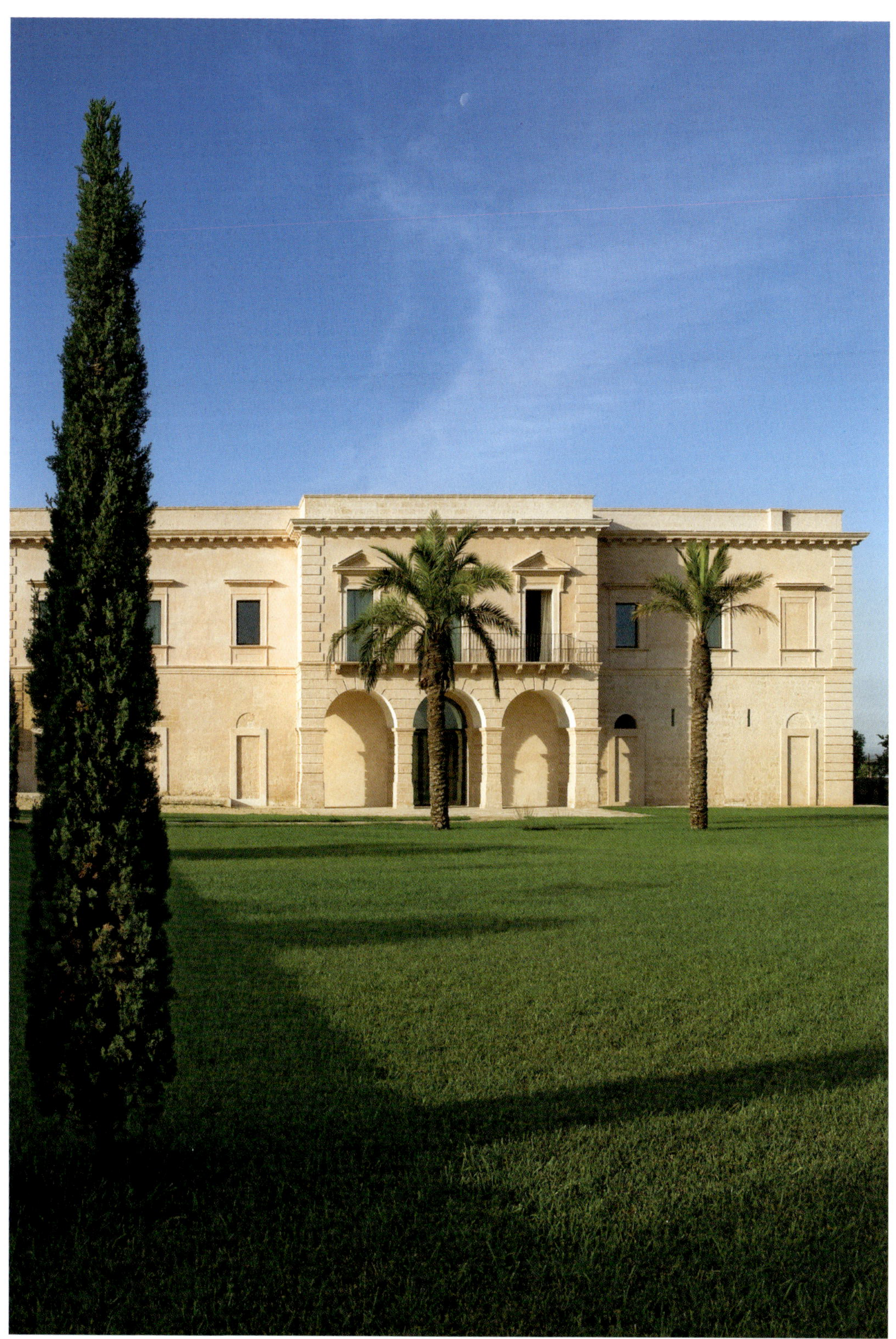

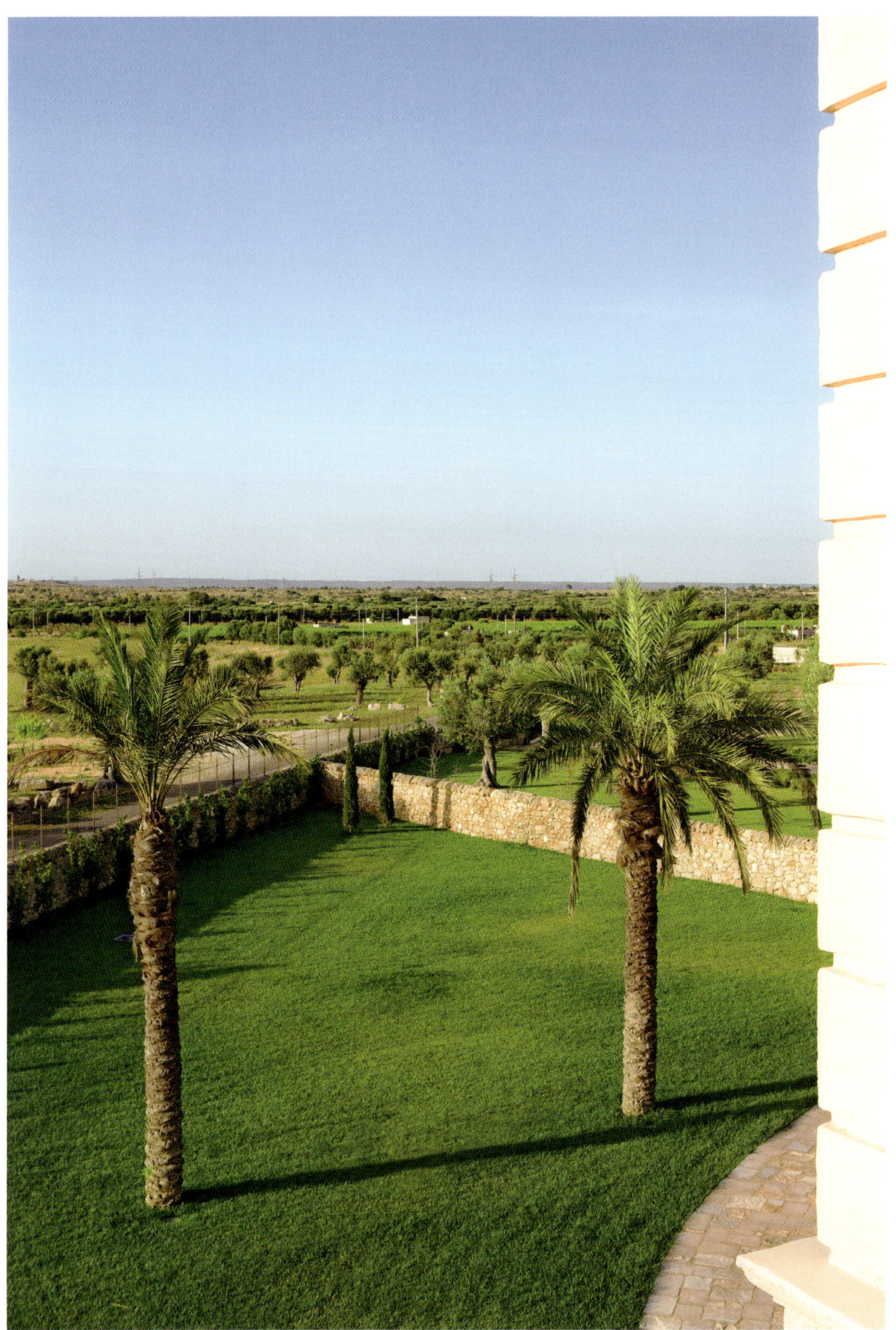

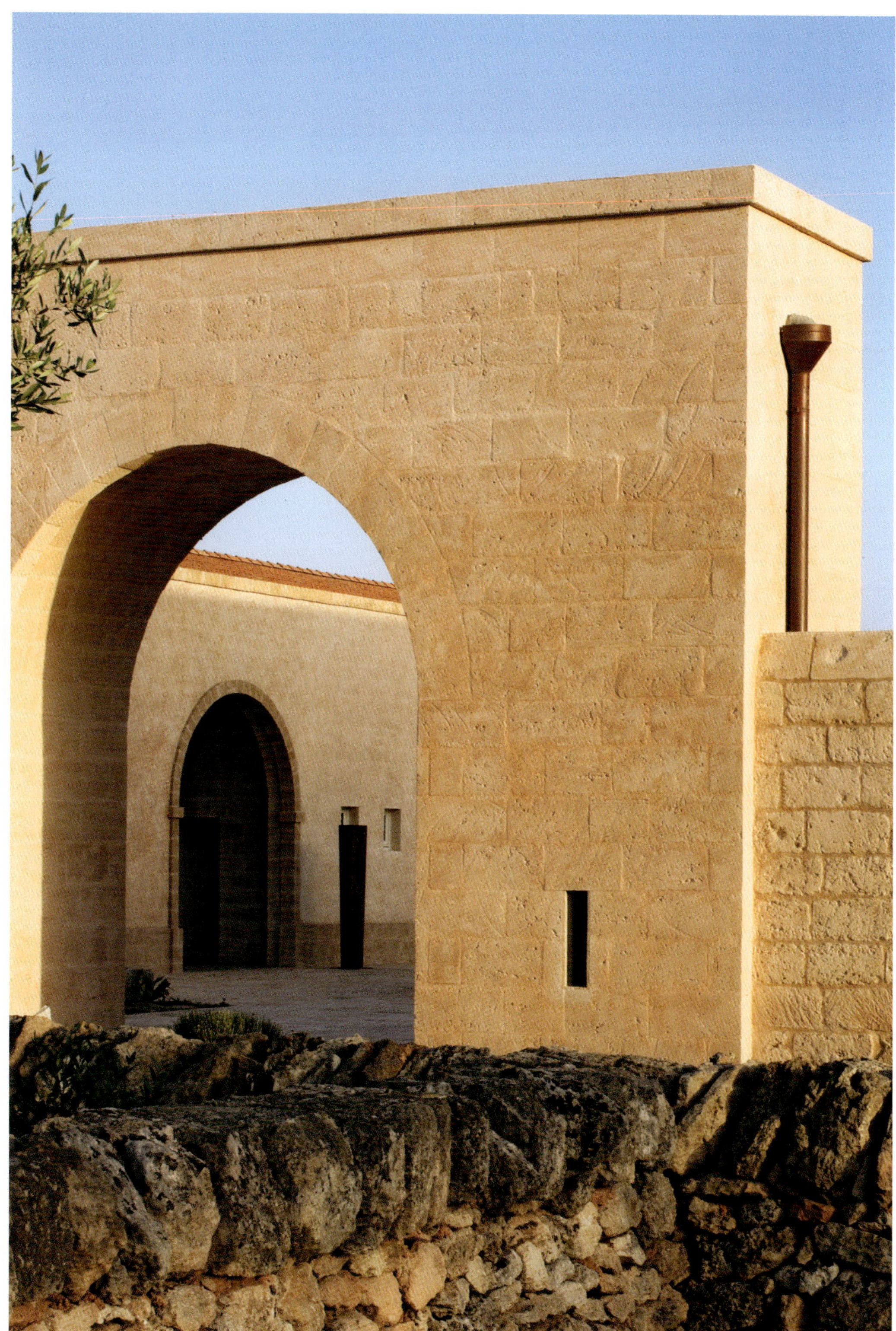

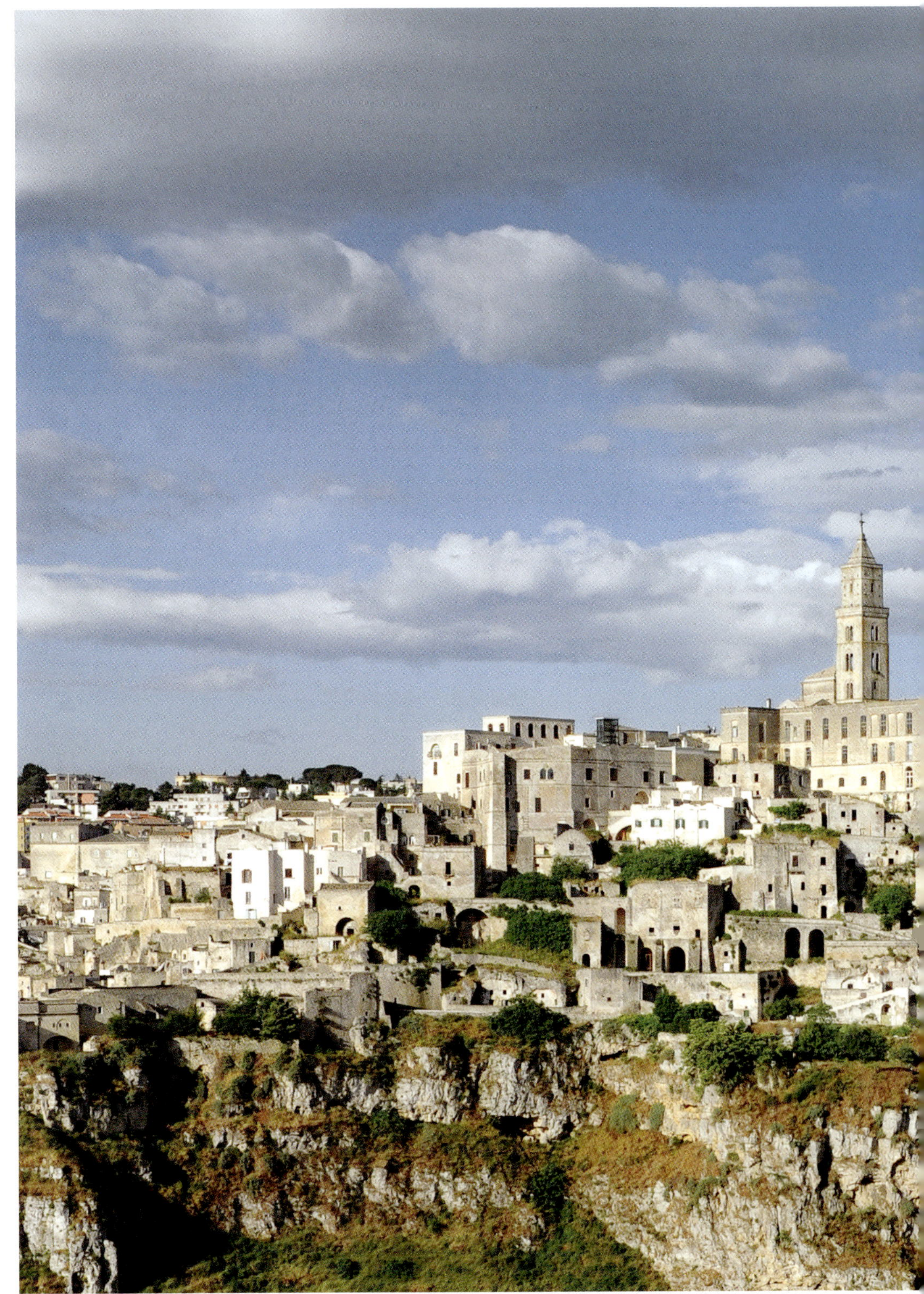

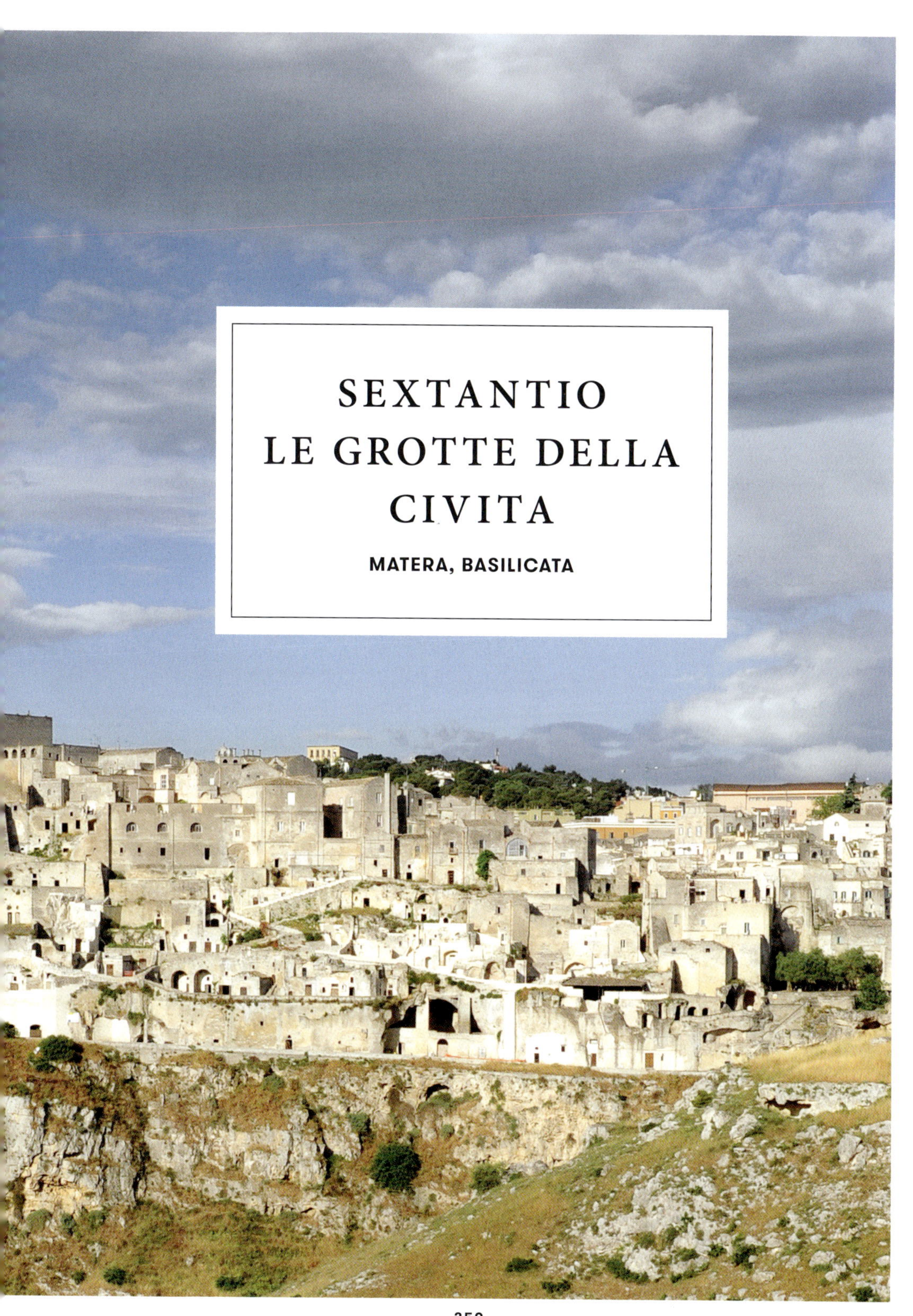

SEXTANTIO LE GROTTE DELLA CIVITA

MATERA, BASILICATA

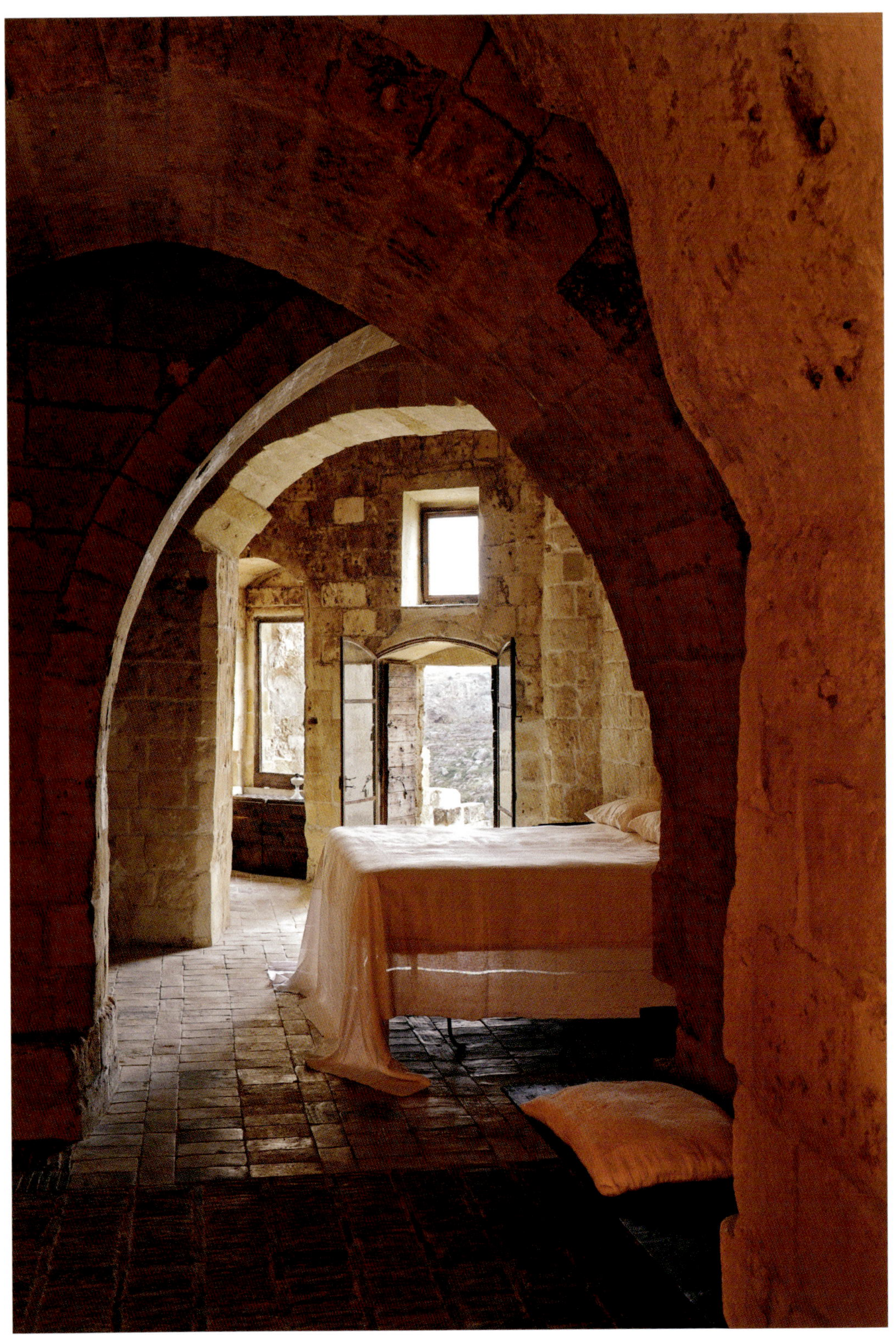

SEXTANTIO LE GROTTE DELLA CIVITA

Via Civita 28, 75100 Matera
Tel. +39 0835 332 744 · matera@sextantio.it
www.sextantio.it

ANCIENT HERITAGE REDISCOVERED It is hard to say where the rock stops and the town starts: on the steep slope where Matera lies, stone fuses with stone to form a surface that is glacier-gray under a cloudy sky and shimmers in pastel tones when the sun shines. Only on the crown of the hill can the outlines of individual houses be made out, with the silhouette of the tower rising above them. The reason for this seamless transition between architecture and nature is the element that binds them together – the legendary caves of tufa stone whose origins go back to the Bronze Age and thus make Matera one of the oldest towns in the world. Until the mid-20th century the "sassi" (rocks) were inhabited, but then were closed on hygienic grounds and decayed. It was not until the 1980s that Matera rediscovered its caves and began to restore them – with such success that they are now listed as a World Heritage Site. Recently a few caves became habitable once again – at least for guests at Sextantio's "albergo diffuso" Le Grotte della Civita. The Sextantio group brought to Matera its vision of conserving heritage that had almost been forgotten, of monuments authentically restored and at the same time incorporating a modern sensibility. Daniele Kihlgren has created a hotel of ultimate simplicity and almost unreal beauty, where you sometimes feel like an actor on a film set, sometimes like a researcher at a dig – and always in a state of suspension between past and present. Here, below the earth, the ages seem to fuse, as imperceptibly as the rock and the town outside. ◆ Book to pack: "Christ Stopped at Eboli" by Carlo Levi.

EIN ALTES ERBE, NEU ENTDECKT Es ist schwer zu sagen, wo der Fels aufhört und die Stadt anfängt: Unten am Steilhang von Matera verschmelzen sie zu einer Fläche, die bei bewölktem Himmel gletschergrau und im Sonnenschein pastellfarben schimmert. Erst auf der Kuppe des Hügels lassen sich die Umrisse einzelner Häuser ausmachen, gekrönt von der Silhouette des Turms. Dass Natur und Architektur so nahtlos ineinander übergehen, liegt an ihrem Bindeglied – den legendären Tuffsteinhöhlen, deren Ursprünge bis in die Bronzezeit zurückreichen und die Matera damit zu einer der ältesten Städte der Welt machen. Bis Mitte des 20. Jahrhunderts waren die „sassi“ (Felsen) bewohnt, ehe sie aus hygienischen Gründen geschlossen wurden und verfielen. Erst in den 1980ern besann sich Matera wieder auf seine Grotten und begann, sie zu sanieren – so erfolgreich, dass sie heute auf der Liste des Weltkulturerbes stehen. Seit Kurzem sind einige Höhlen auch wieder bewohnbar, zumindest für die Gäste von Sextantios „albergo diffuso“, Le Grotte della Civita. Die Sextantio-Gruppe hat ihre Vision vom Bewahren beinahe vergessenen Kulturguts, von originalgetreu restaurierten und zugleich modern wirkenden Denkmälern nach Matera gebracht, wo Daniele Kihlgren ein ultimativ schlichtes, fast unwirklich schönes Hotel geschaffen hat. Man fühlt sich manchmal wie ein Schauspieler am Filmset, manchmal wie ein Forscher am Ausgrabungsort – und immer wie im Schwebezustand zwischen Geschichte und Gegenwart. Die Zeiten scheinen hier unter der Erde zusammenzufließen – so unmerklich wie draußen der Fels und die Stadt.
◆ Buchtipp: „Christus kam nur bis Eboli“ von Carlo Levi.

LE PATRIMOINE REDÉCOUVERT Où s’arrête la falaise et où commence la ville ? C’est difficile à dire : en bas, sur la pente escarpée de Matera, la surface des pierres ressemble à un glacier gris lorsque le ciel est nuageux, et elle a des tons bleu pastel au soleil. On ne distingue les contours de quelques maisons que lorsqu’on a atteint le sommet de la colline sur lequel est posée une tour. Si la nature et l’architecture font si bon ménage, c’est grâce aux légendaires grottes de tuf, dont l’origine remonte à l’âge de bronze et qui font donc de Matera l’une des plus anciennes villes du monde. Les « sassi », les cavités naturelles du rocher, ont abrité des troglodytes jusqu’au milieu du XXe siècle ; elles ont ensuite été fermées pour des raisons de salubrité. Et puis, au cours des années 1980, Matera s’est souvenue de ses grottes et a commencé à les réhabiliter, et ce, avec tant de succès qu’elles sont aujourd’hui inscrites sur la liste du patrimoine mondial. Depuis peu, certaines grottes sont à nouveau habitables, du moins pour les hôtes de l’« albergo diffuso » de Sextantio, Le Grotte della Civita. Le groupe Sextantio a apporté à Matera sa vision de préservation d’un patrimoine presque oublié, de restauration fidèle à l’original mariée à une sensibilité moderne, et Daniele Kihlgren a créé ici un hôtel on ne peut plus sobre, d’une beauté presque irréelle. On se sent parfois comme un acteur sur le plateau de tournage, parfois comme un archéologue sur un lieu de fouilles, et toujours entre le passé et le présent qui semblent ici fusionner sous la terre, de manière aussi imperceptible que la roche et la ville au-dessus.
◆ À lire : « Le Christ s’est arrêté à Éboli » de Carlo Levi.

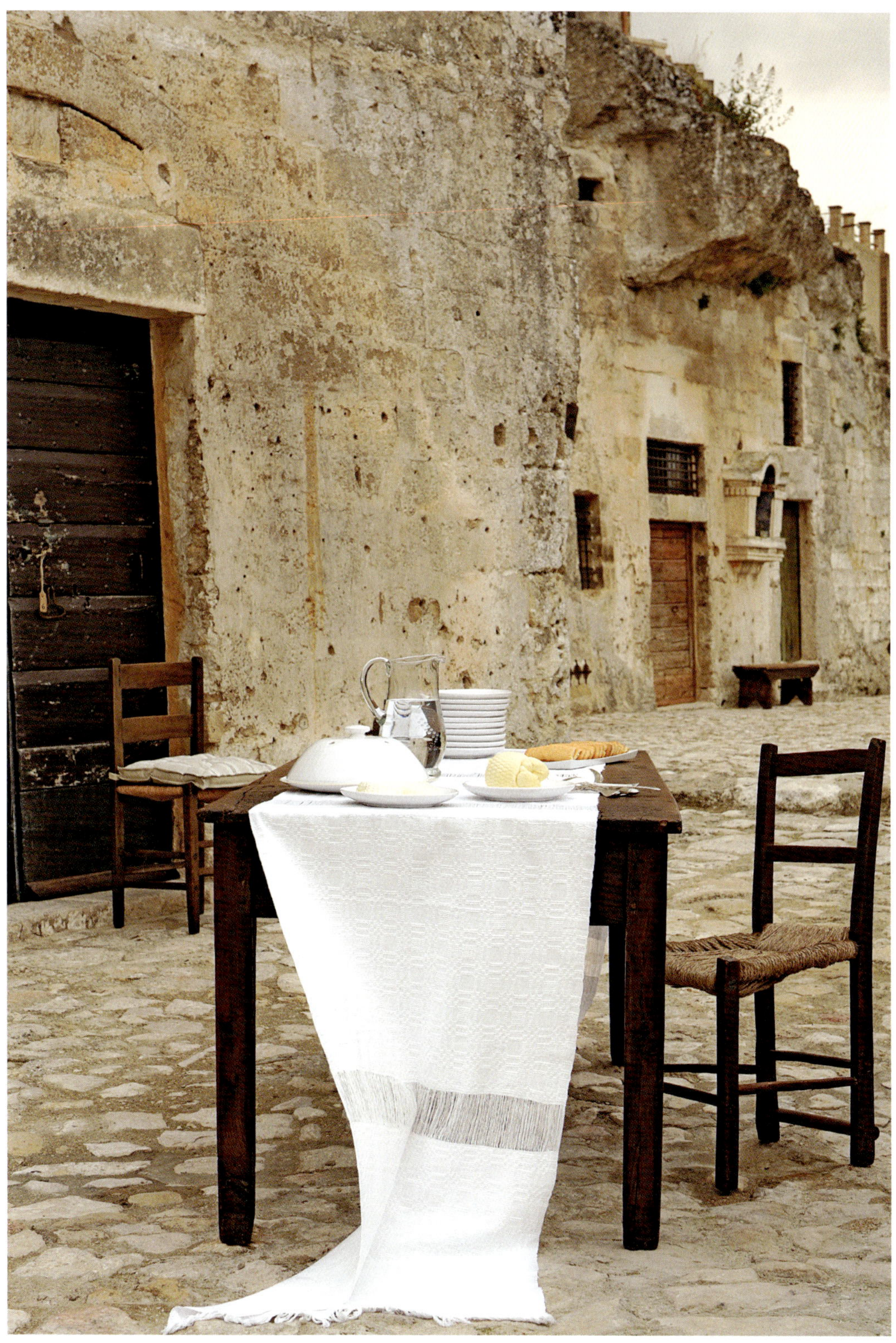

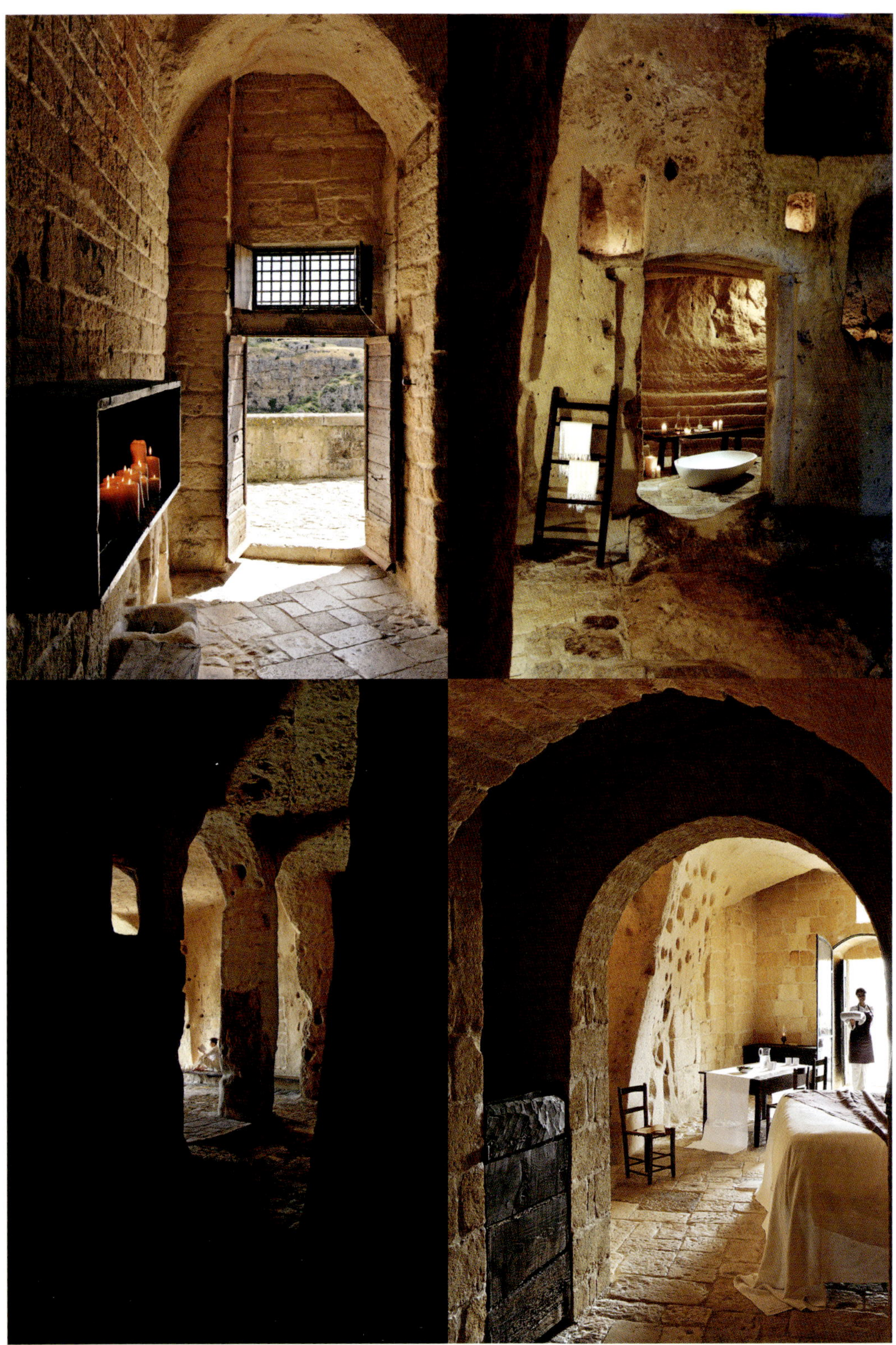

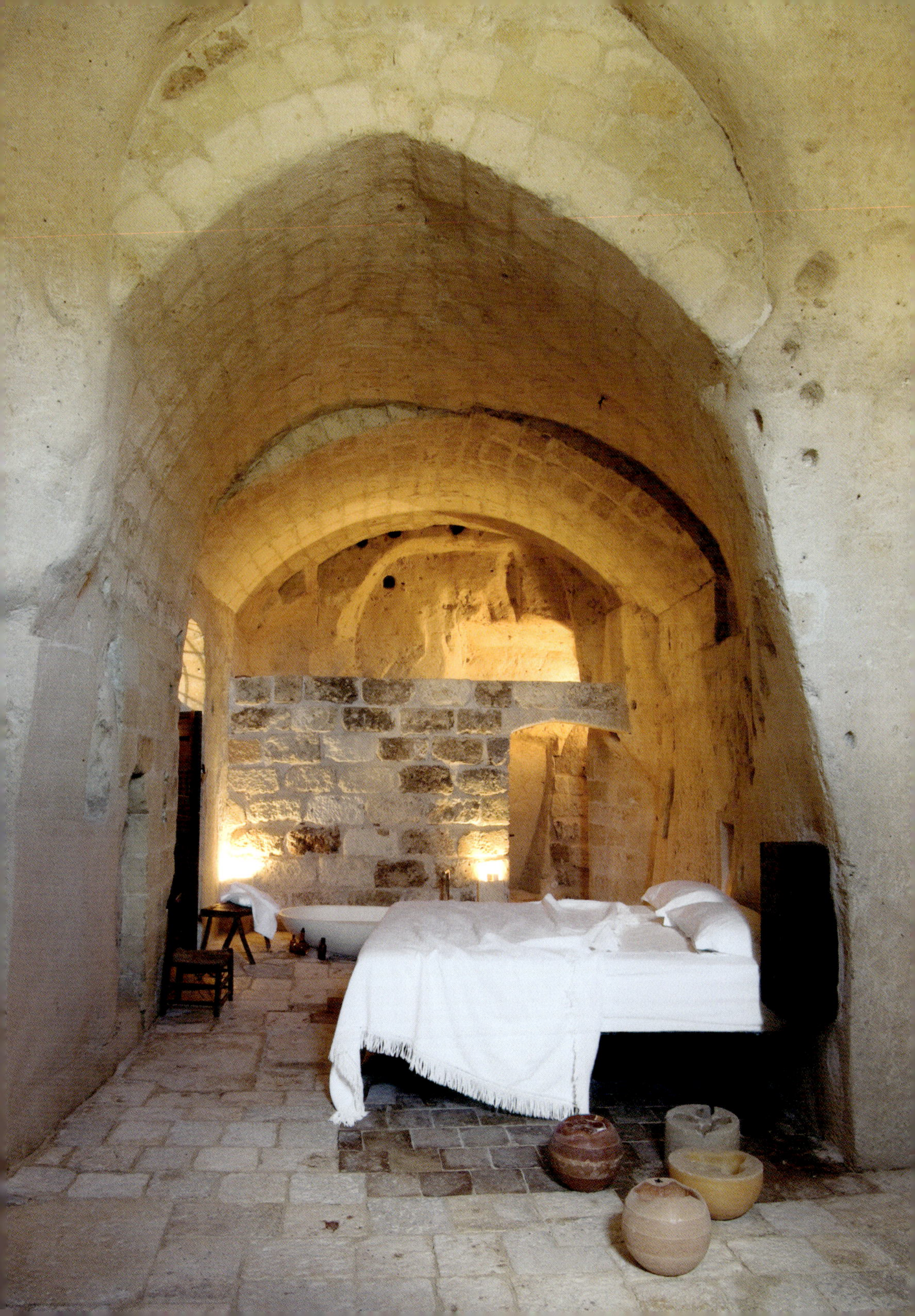

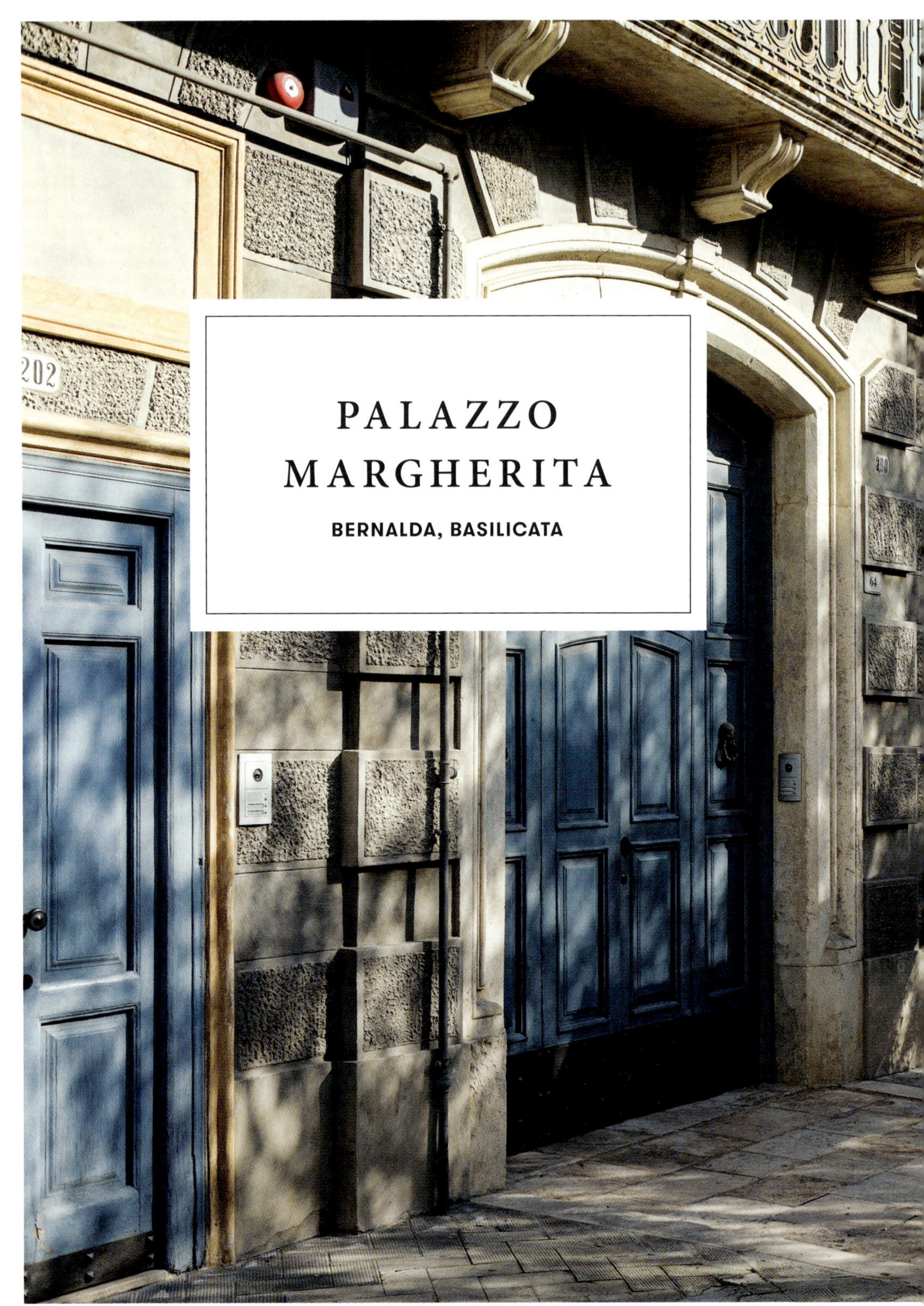

PALAZZO MARGHERITA

BERNALDA, BASILICATA

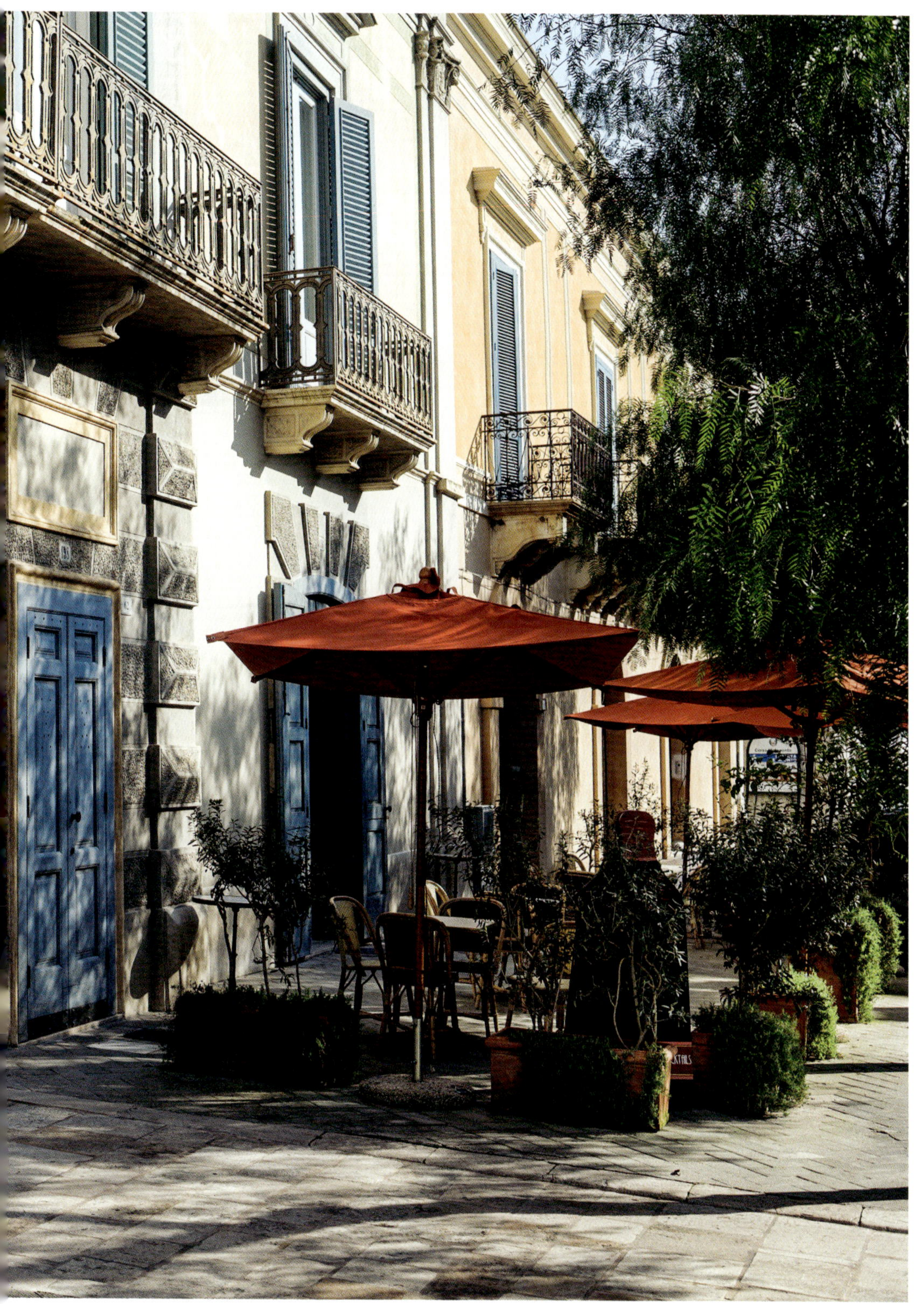

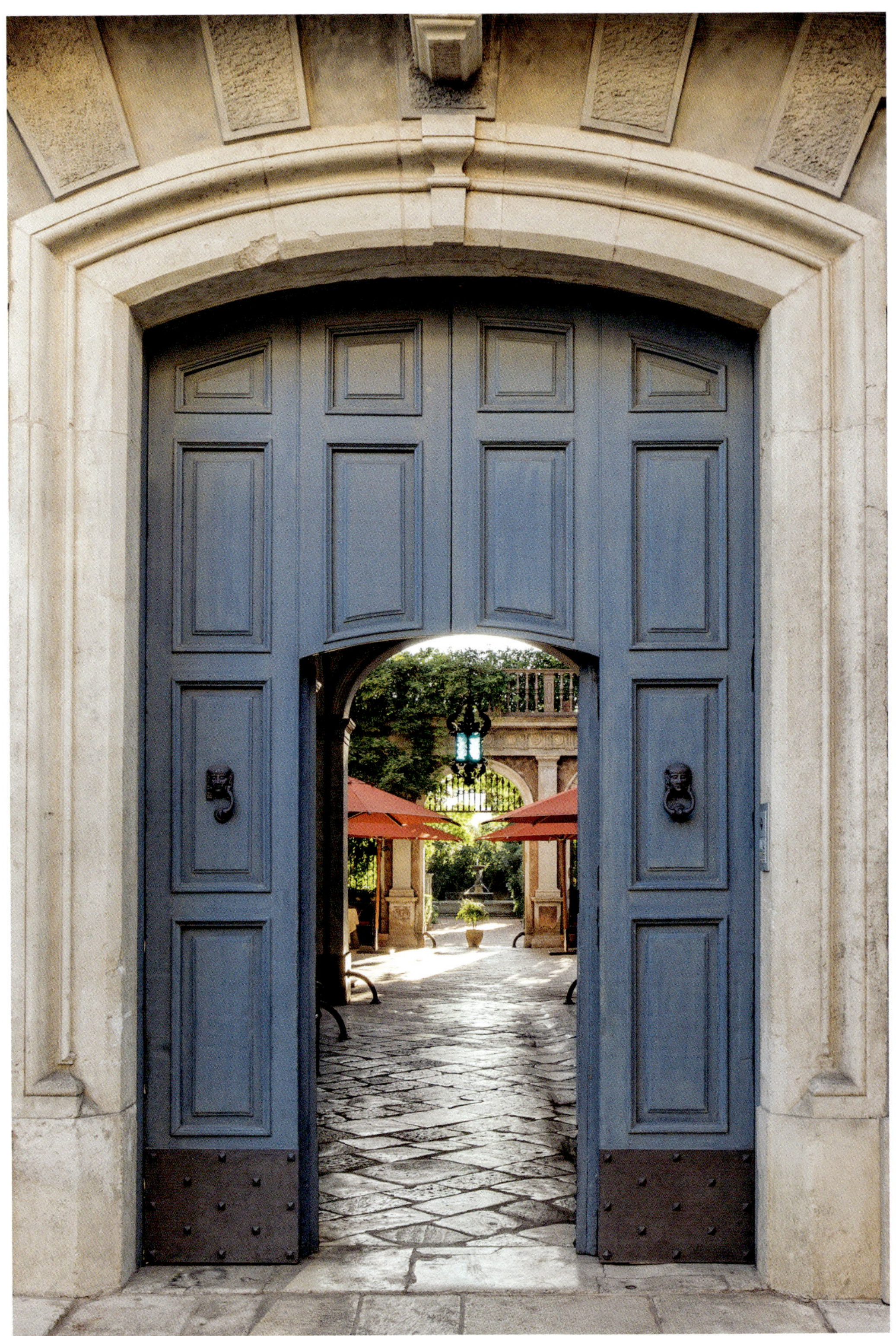

PALAZZO MARGHERITA

Corso Umberto I, 64, 75012 Bernalda
Tel. +39 0835 549 060 · info@palazzomargherita.com
www.thefamilycoppolahideaways.com/en/palazzo-margherita
Open from early April to late October

A FAMILY COMPANY "Running a hotel is like making a movie – it's all about putting on a show", Francis Ford Coppola once said, and with five luxurious houses he now proves that he is a showmaster as talented at managing hotels as in his role directing Hollywood movies. Palazzo Margherita, so far his only hotel in Europe, has a special place in his heart: it is situated in Bernalda, a small town in Basilicata where his grandfather Agostino was born and lived until he emigrated to America. The place where "la famiglia" originated is also the place where it should get back together, time and again – which is why, along with the interior designer Jacques Grange, Coppola involved the whole family in the design of the palazzo. He himself was responsible for a suite in North African style as homage to his grandmother Maria Zasa and her Tunisian roots, as well as presenting to his first granddaughter, Gia, a retreat with a romantic ceiling fresco in pink depicting Amor and Psyche. A further room was lent a touch of Art Deco by his son Roman, and the most beautiful suite bears the feminine signature of his daughter Sofia, who celebrated her second marriage here shortly before the hotel opened. The luxuriant garden was simply made for family get-togethers when days are passed by the pool and evenings at the barbecue – before a nightcap is served in the Family Bar. ◆ Book to pack: "The Godfather" by Mario Puzo.

EIN FAMILIENUNTERNEHMEN „Ein Hotel zu führen ist wie einen Film zu drehen – man muss eine Show auf die Beine stellen", sagte Francis Ford Coppola einmal und beweist mit mittlerweile fünf luxuriösen Häusern, dass er als Hotelbetreiber ebenso talentiert ist wie als Hollywood-Regisseur. Der Palazzo Margherita, sein bislang einziges Hotel in Europa, spielt eine ganz besondere Rolle für ihn: Es steht in Bernalda, einem Städtchen in der Basilikata, in dem sein Großvater Agostino geboren wurde und lebte, bis er nach Amerika auswanderte. Dort, wo „la famiglia" ursprünglich herkam, sollte sie auch immer wieder zusammenfinden – und so band Coppola neben Interior Designer Jacques Grange die gesamte Familie in die Gestaltung des Palazzos ein: Er selbst entwarf eine Suite im nordafrikanischen Stil als Hommage an seine Großmutter Maria Zasa und deren tunesische Wurzeln und schenkte seiner ersten Enkeltochter Gia ein Refugium mit einem romantischen Deckenfresko in Rosé, das Amor und Psyche zeigt. Einem weiteren Raum verlieh Sohn Roman einen Hauch Art déco, und die schönste Suite trägt die feminine Handschrift von Tochter Sofia, die kurz vor der Eröffnung des Hotels hier ihre zweite Hochzeit feierte. Wie geschaffen für Familientreffen ist der üppige Garten, in dem die Tage am Pool und die Abende am Grillfeuer vorbeiziehen – ehe ein Schlummertrunk drinnen in der „Family Bar" serviert wird.
◆ Buchtipp: „Der Pate" von Mario Puzo.

UNE ENTREPRISE FAMILIALE « Diriger un hôtel, c'est comme faire un film – il s'agit de monter un spectacle », a dit Francis Ford Coppola, et avec cinq hôtels de luxe, il prouve entre-temps que le show-master a autant de talent que le réalisateur hollywoodien. Le Palazzo Margherita, son seul hôtel en Europe à ce jour, joue un rôle très spécial pour lui : il est situé à Bernalda, une petite ville de la Basilicate où son grand-père Agostino est né et a vécu jusqu'à son émigration en Amérique. Il va de soi que la « famiglia » doit se retrouver dans les lieux dont elle est originaire, et Coppola, avec l'architecte d'intérieur Jacques Grange, a impliqué toute la famille dans la conception du palais : lui-même a dessiné une suite de style nord-africain en hommage à sa grand-mère Maria Zasa et ses racines tunisiennes, et offert à sa première petite-fille Gia un refuge au plafond orné d'une fresque romantique rose qui montre Amour et Psyché. Une autre pièce a reçu une touche d'Art Déco de son fils Roman, et la plus belle suite porte la signature féminine de sa fille Sofia, qui a célébré ici son second mariage peu avant l'ouverture de l'hôtel. Le jardin luxuriant est parfait pour les réunions de famille, les jours passent au bord de la piscine et les soirées à côté du coin barbecue – avant qu'un dernier verre ne soit servi à l'intérieur dans le « Family Bar ». ◆ À lire : « Le Parrain » de Mario Puzo.

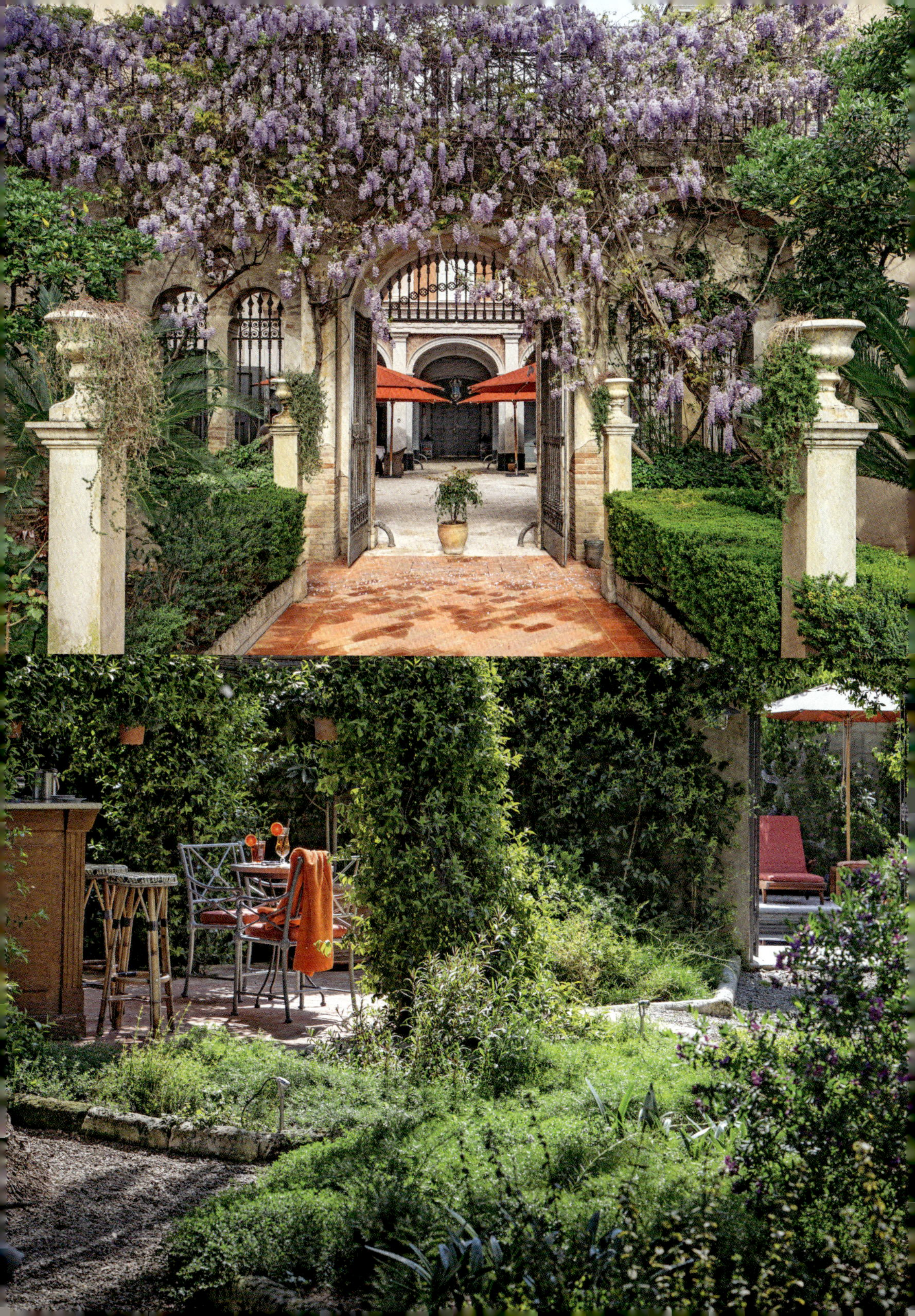

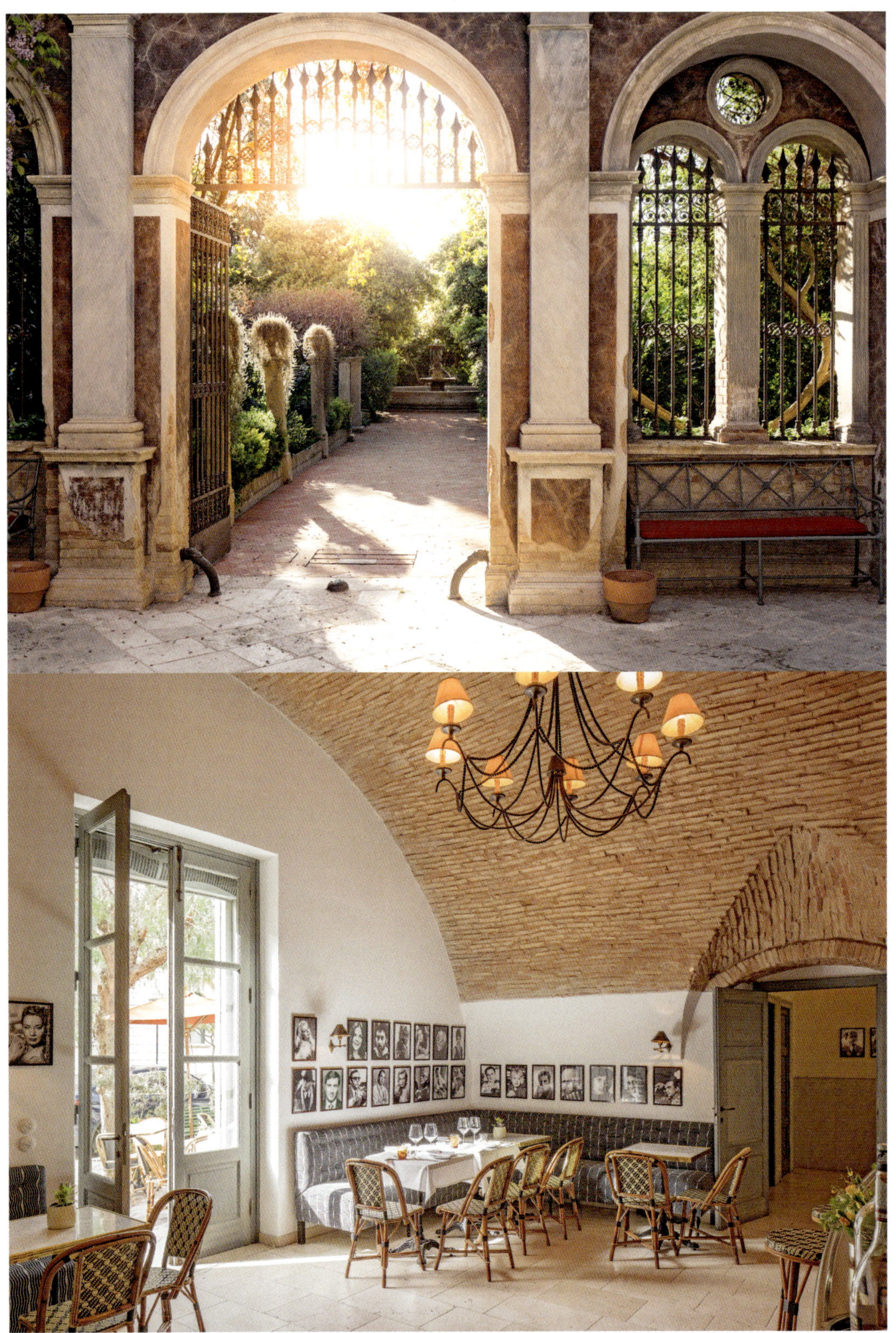

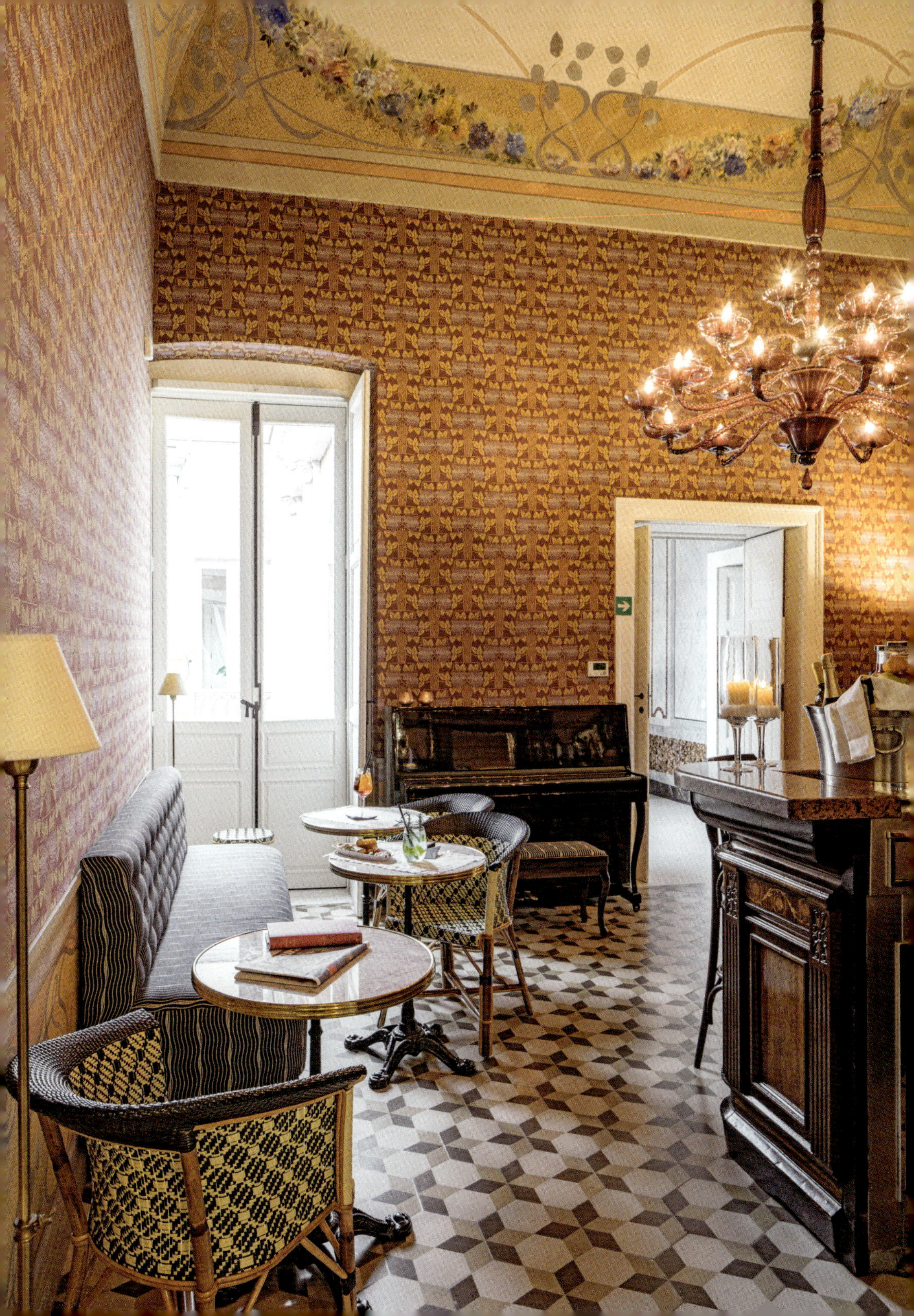

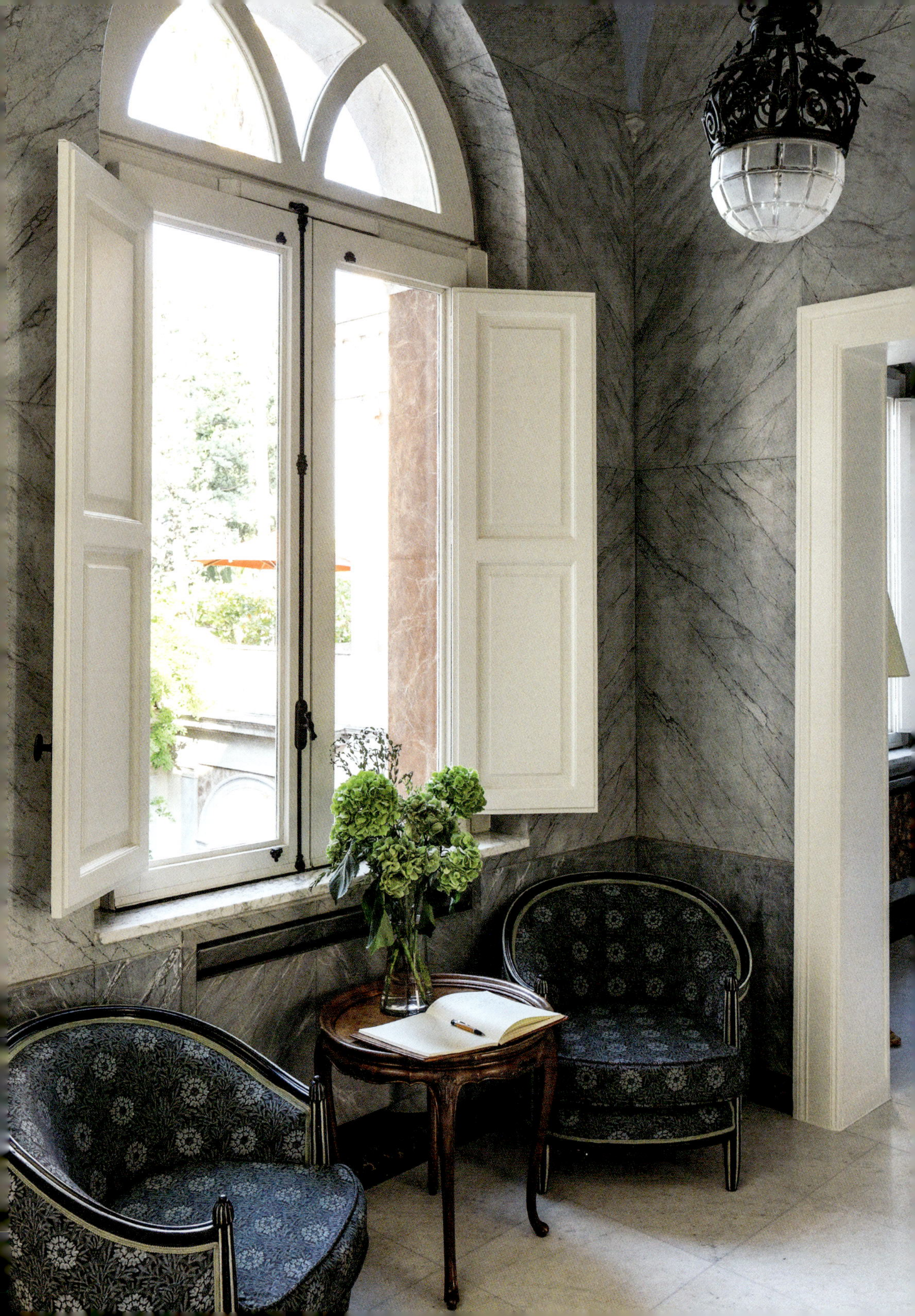

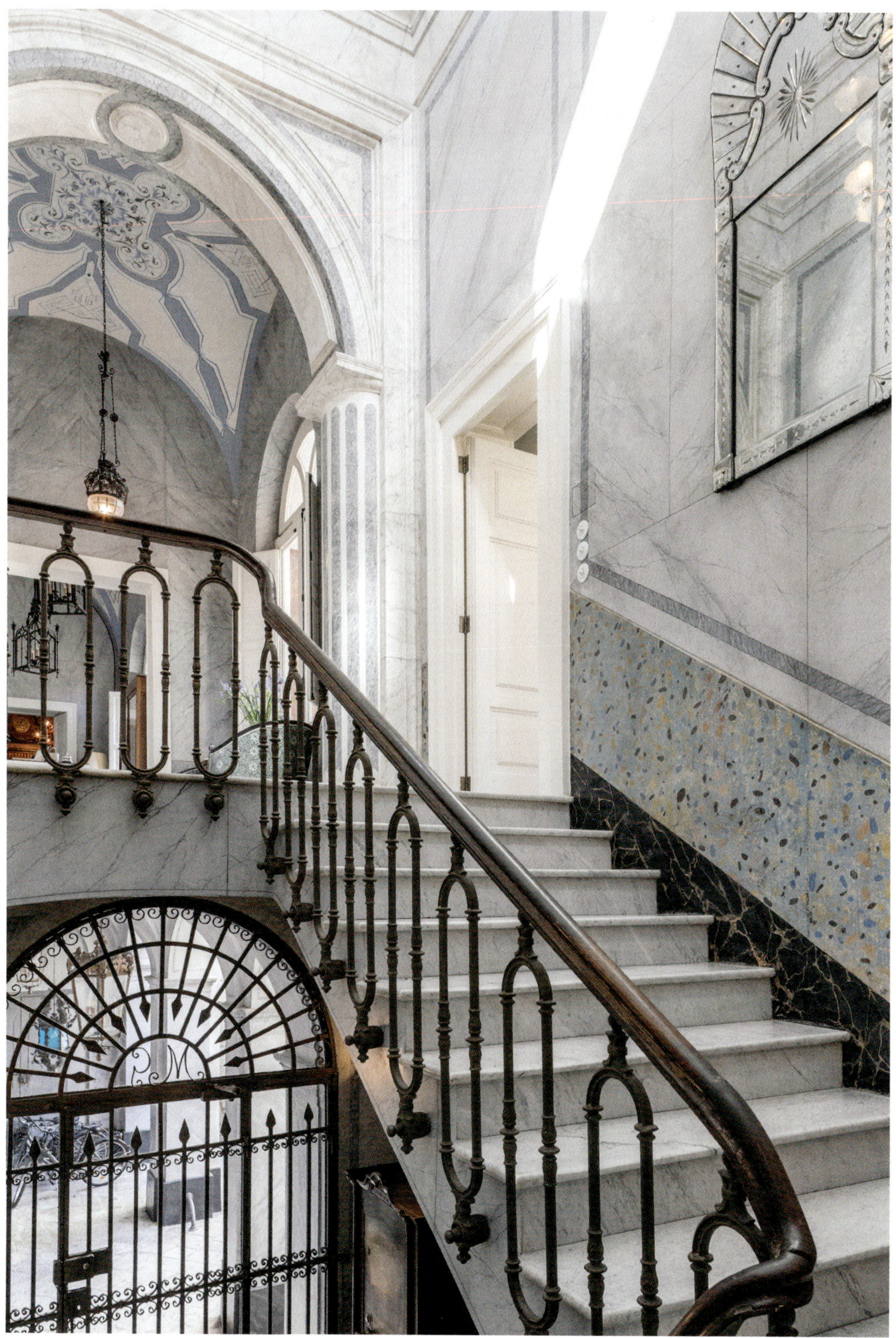

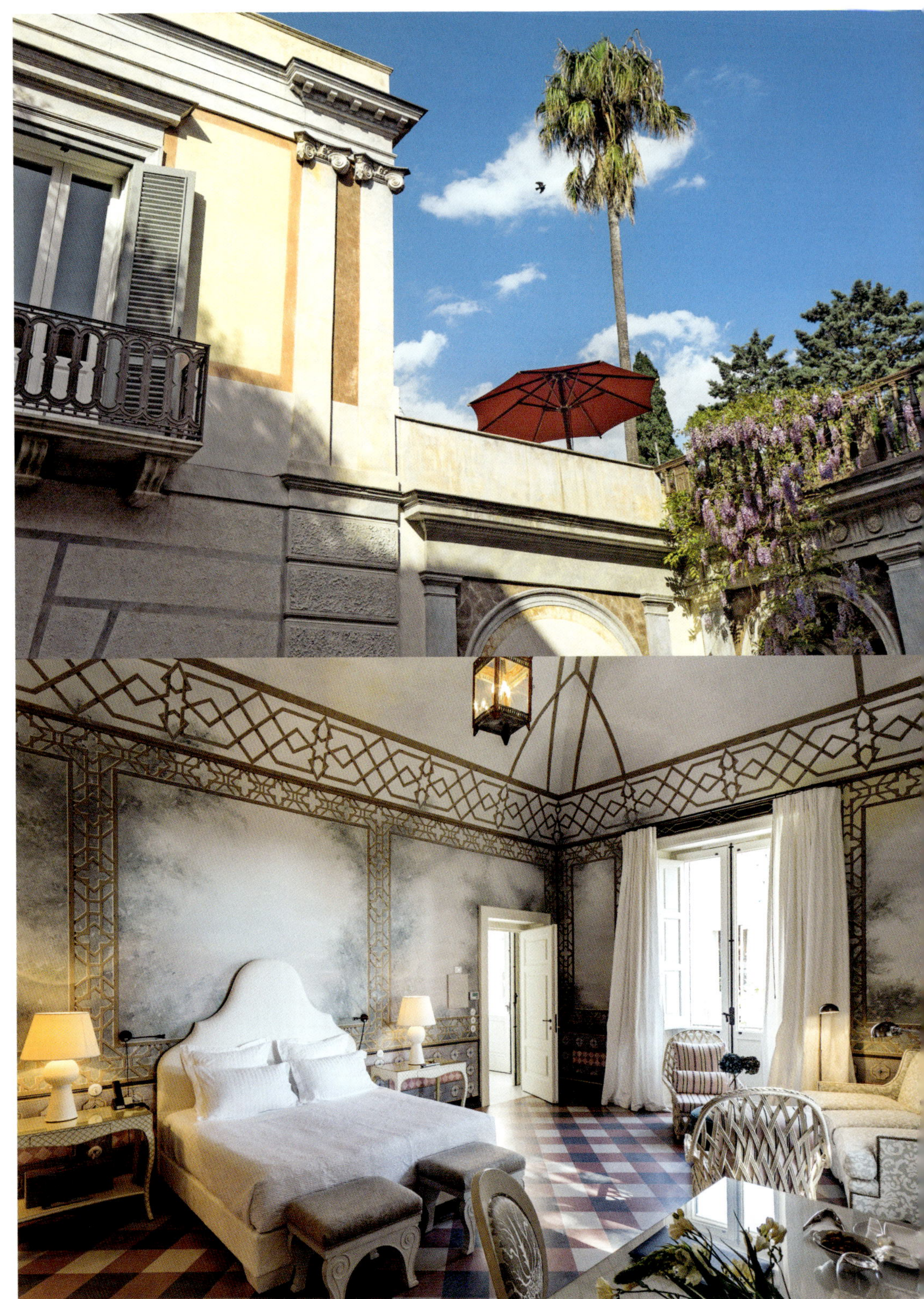

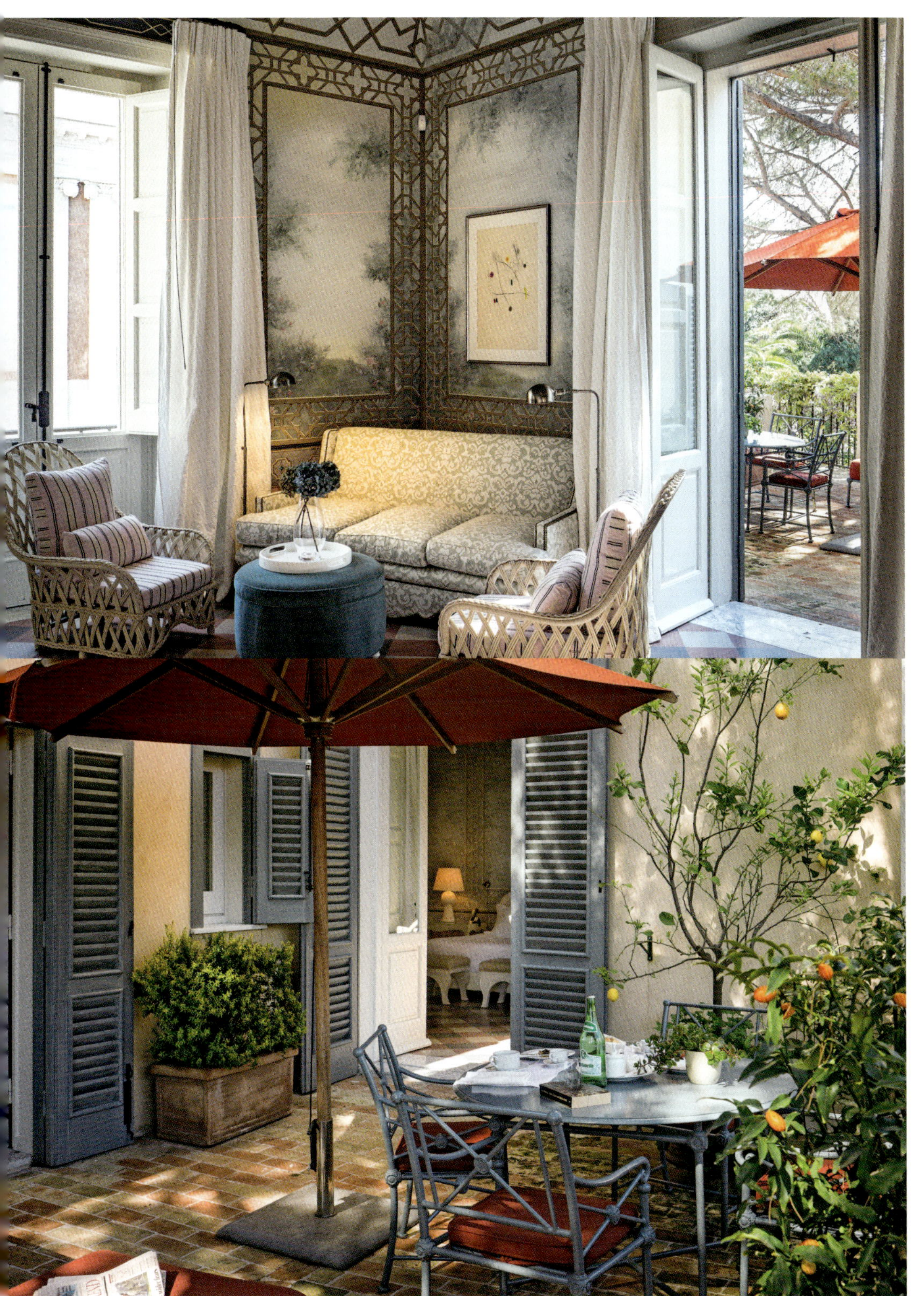

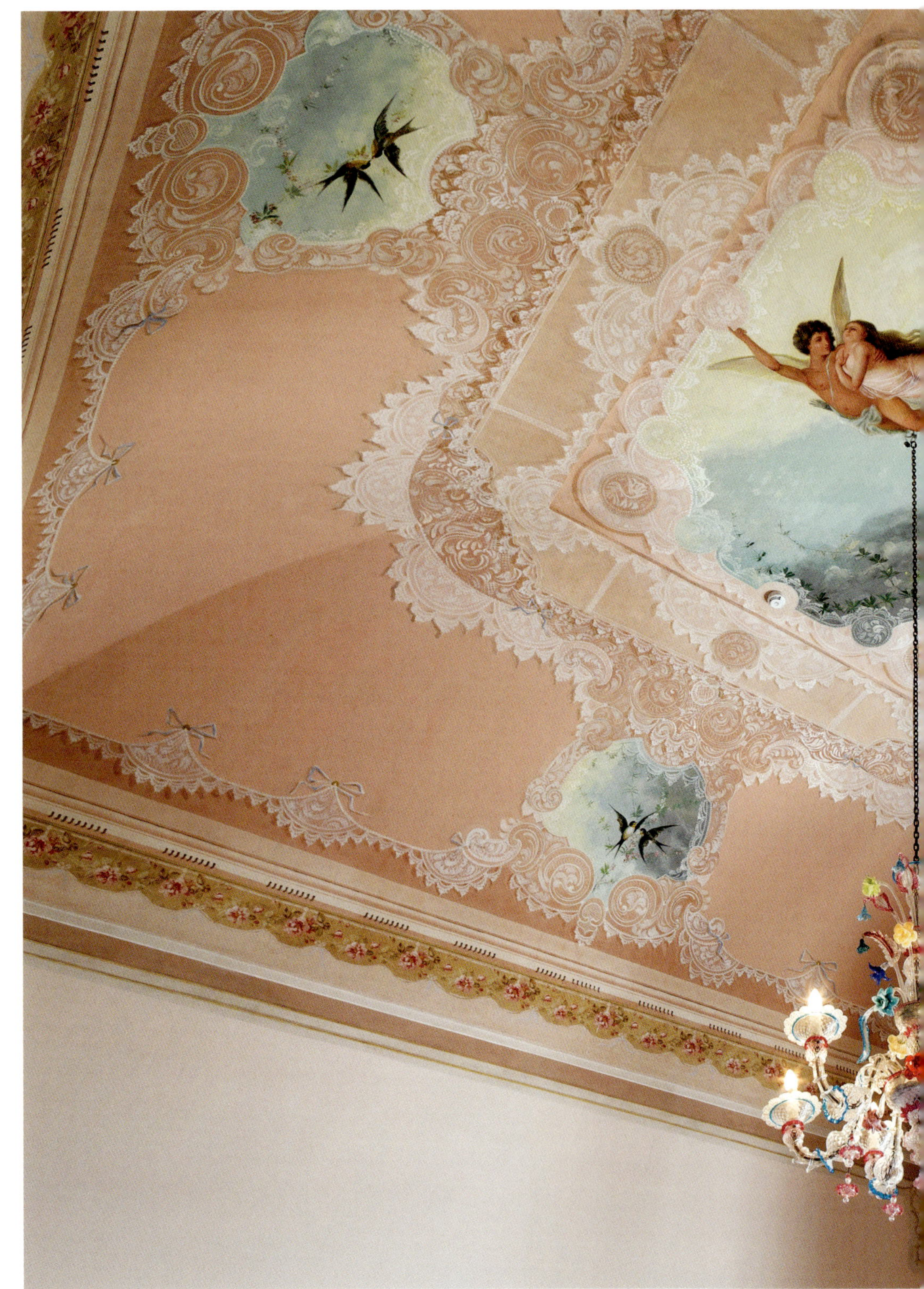

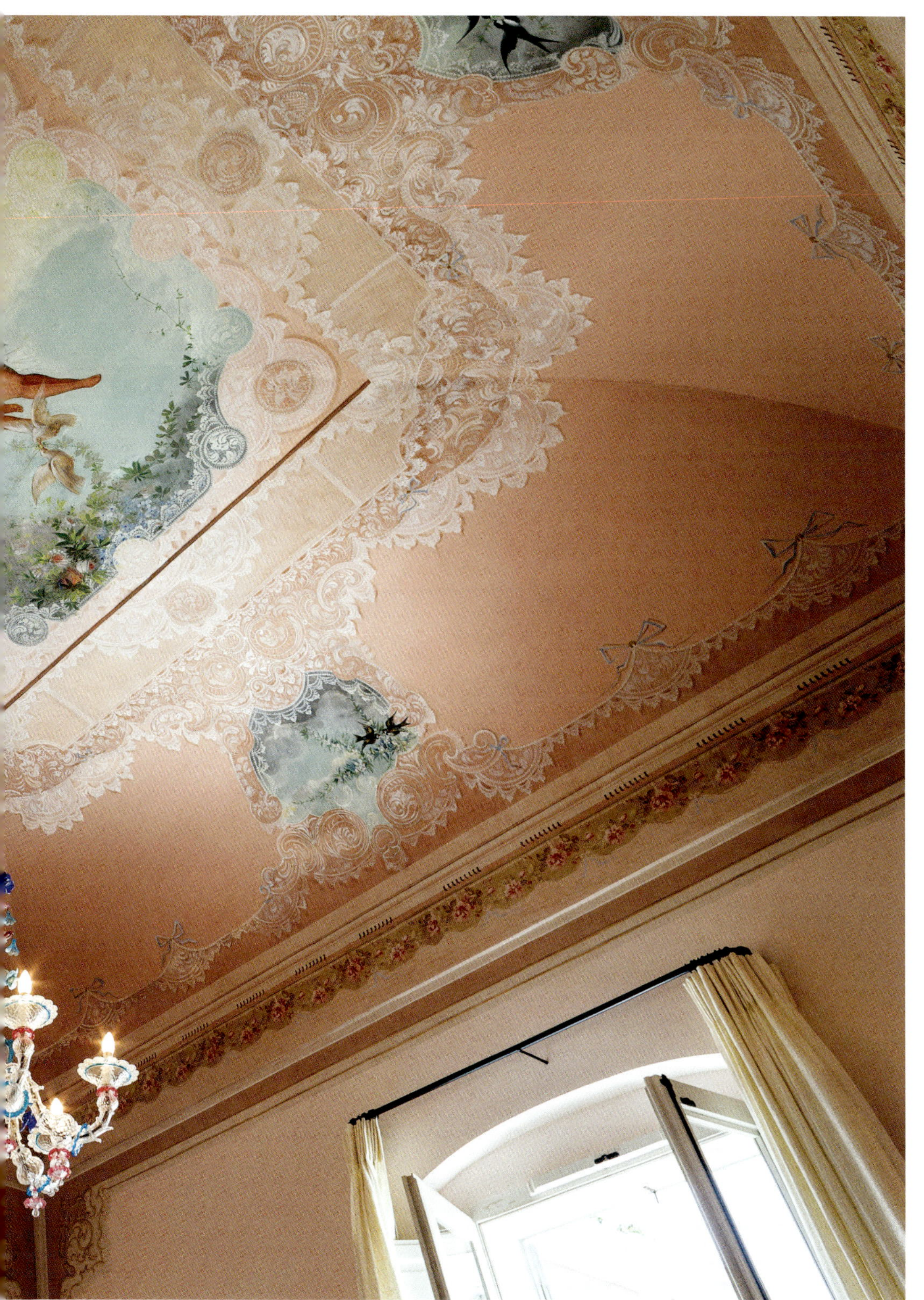

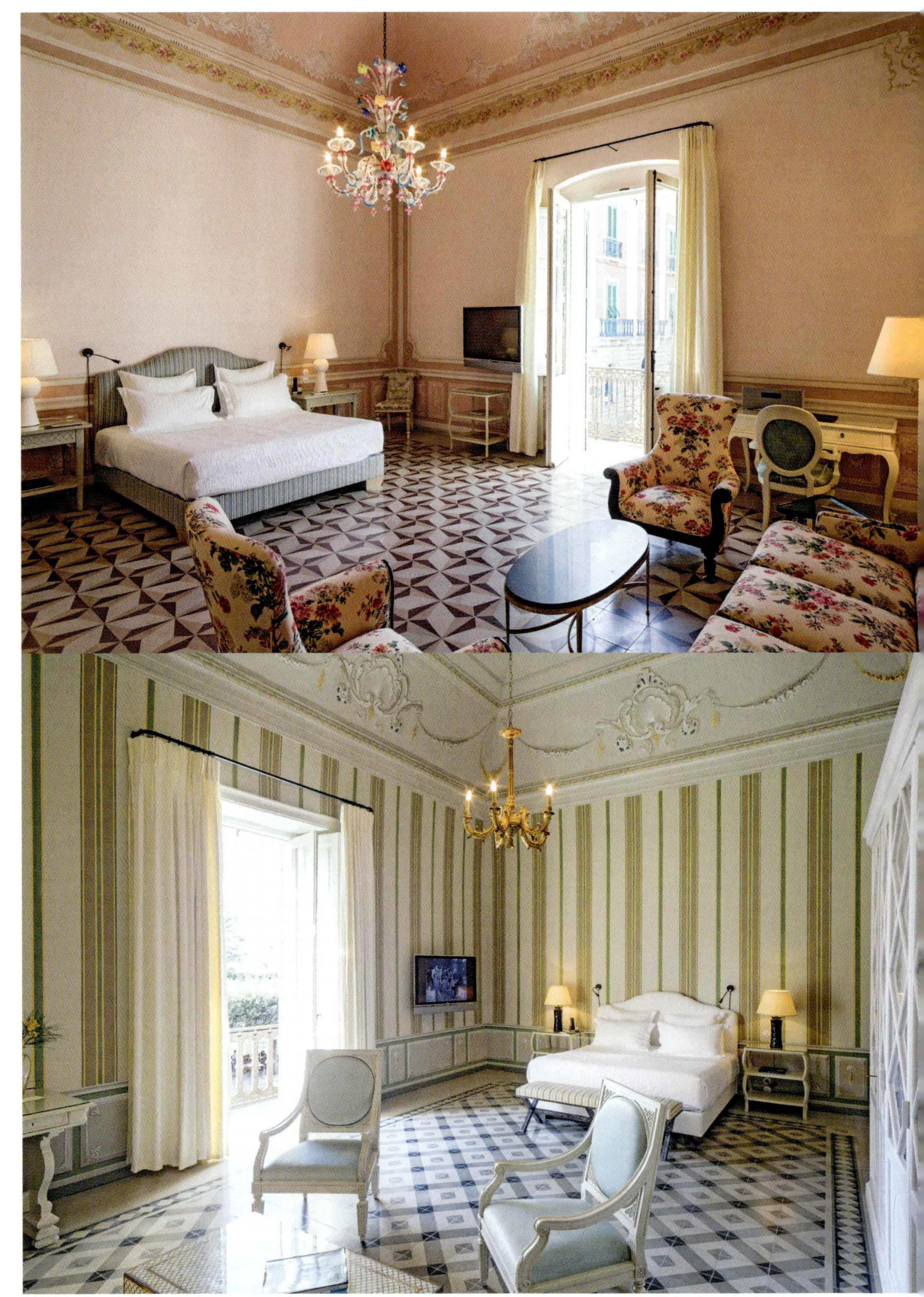

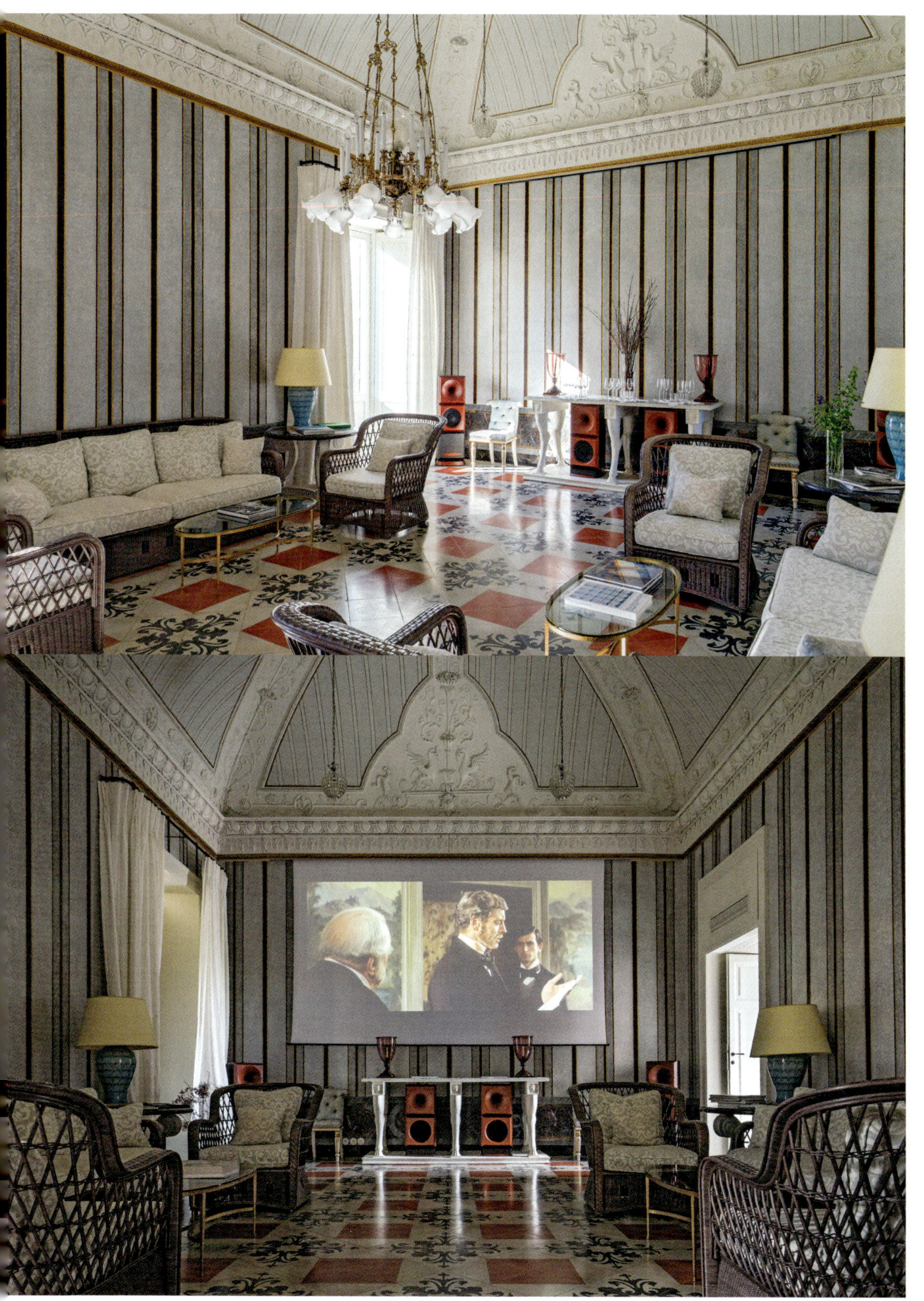

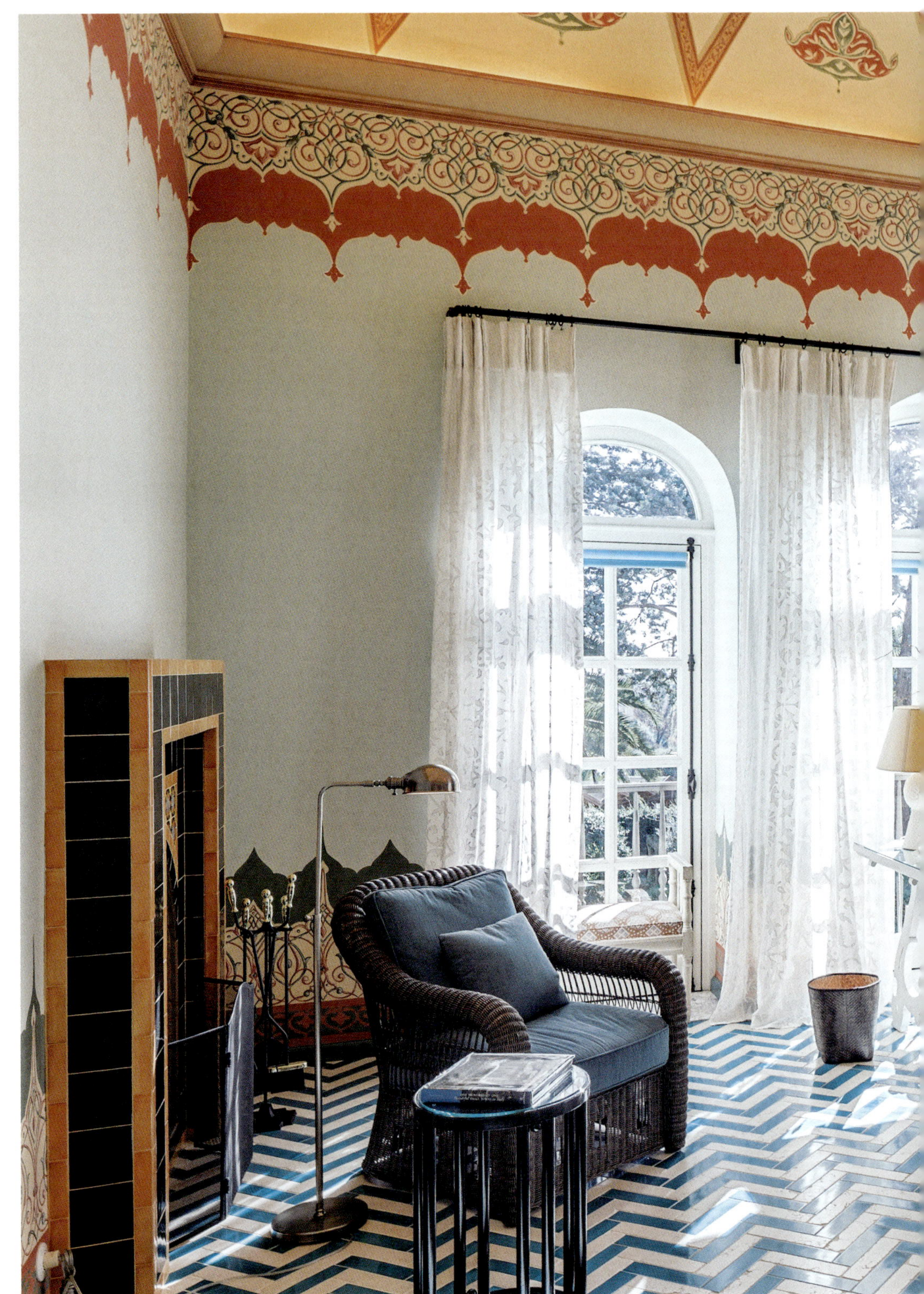

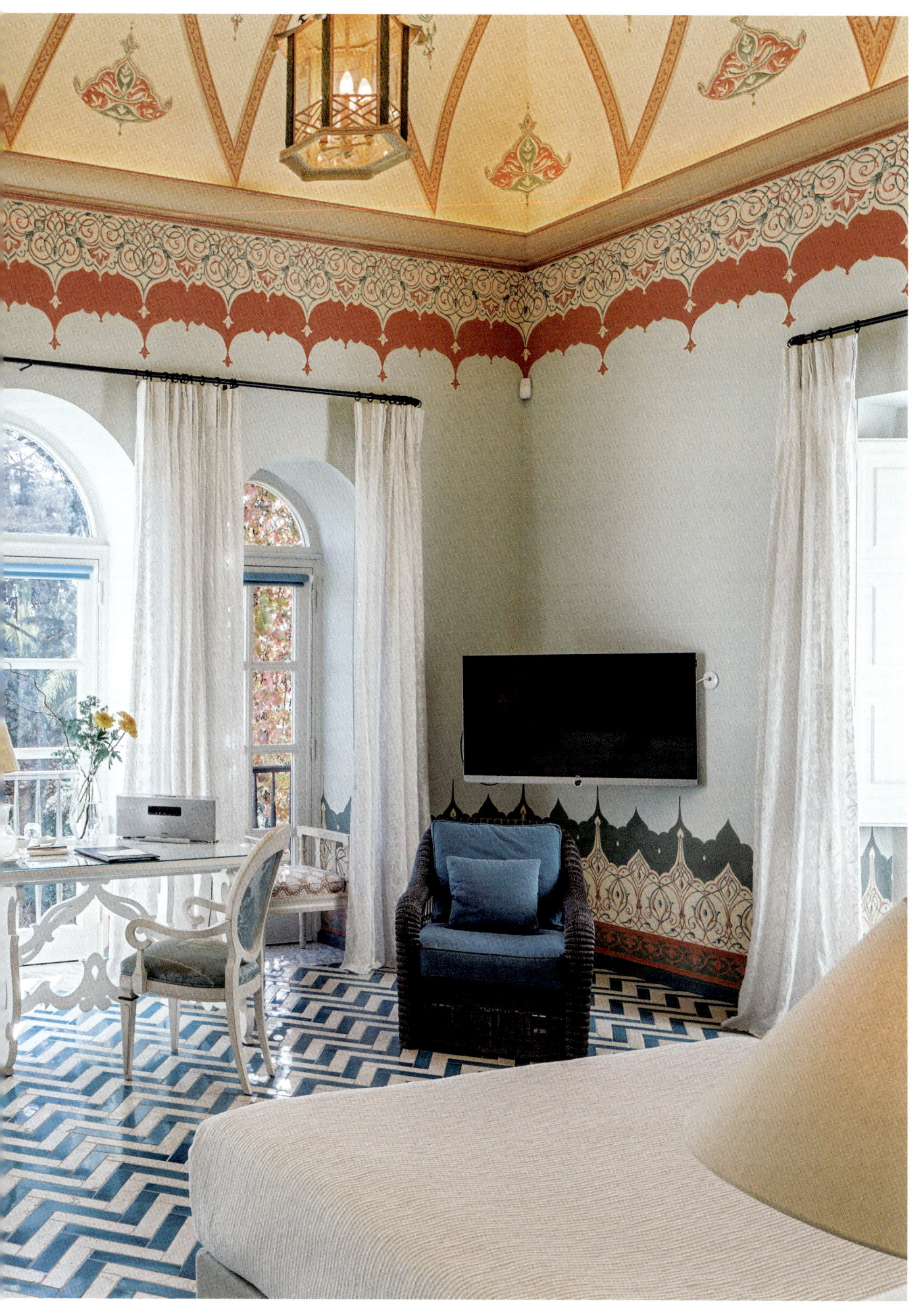

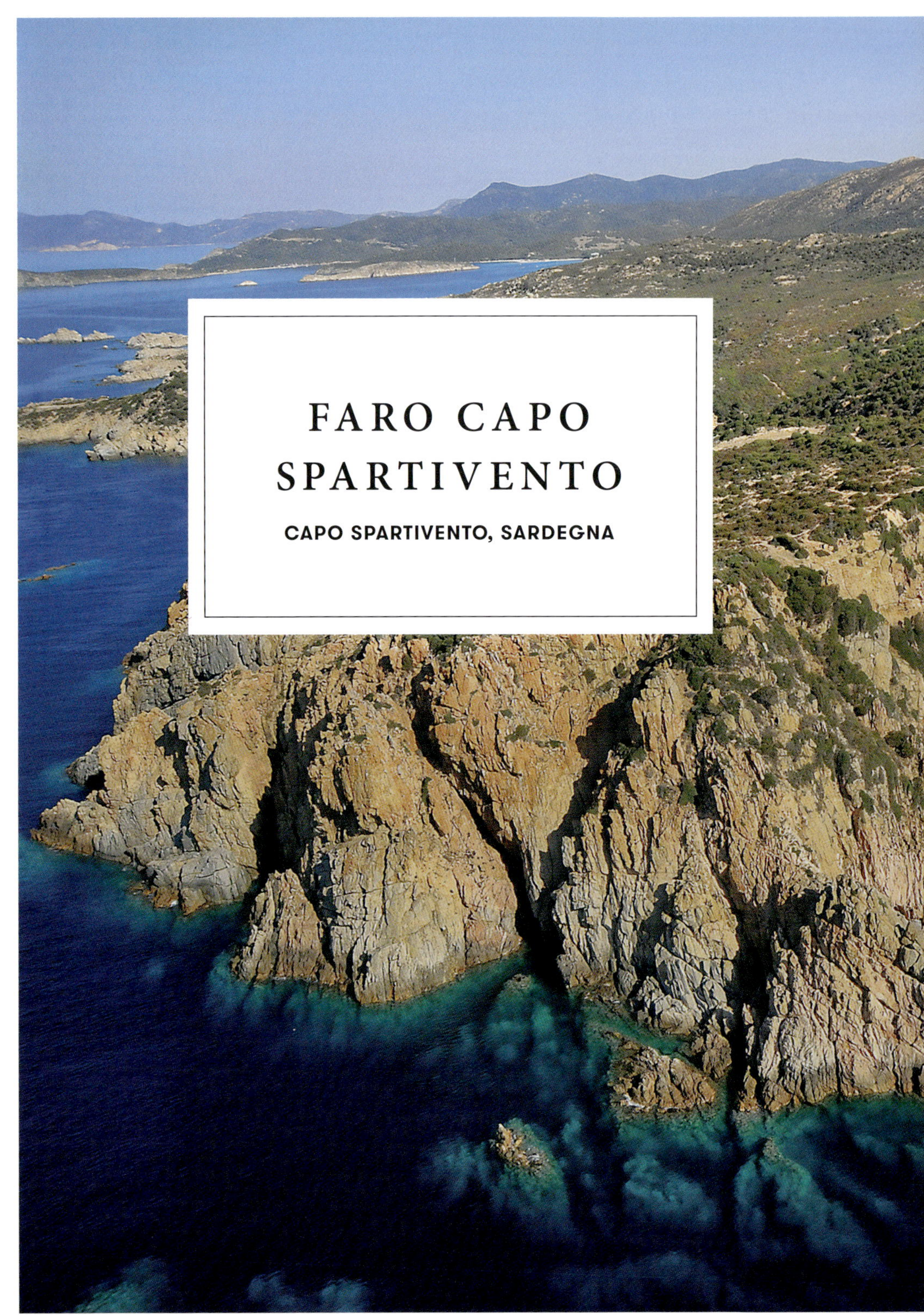

FARO CAPO SPARTIVENTO

CAPO SPARTIVENTO, SARDEGNA

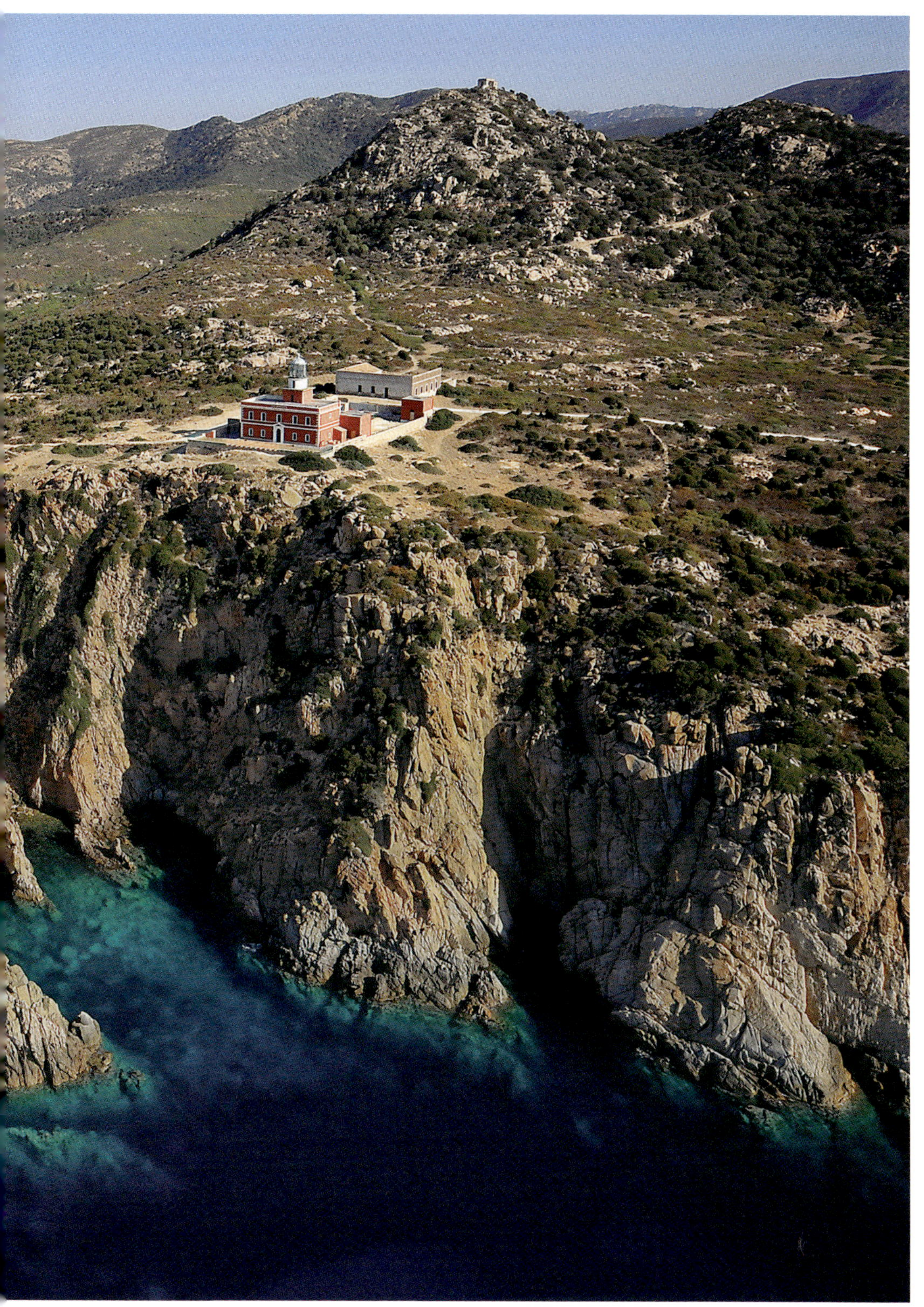

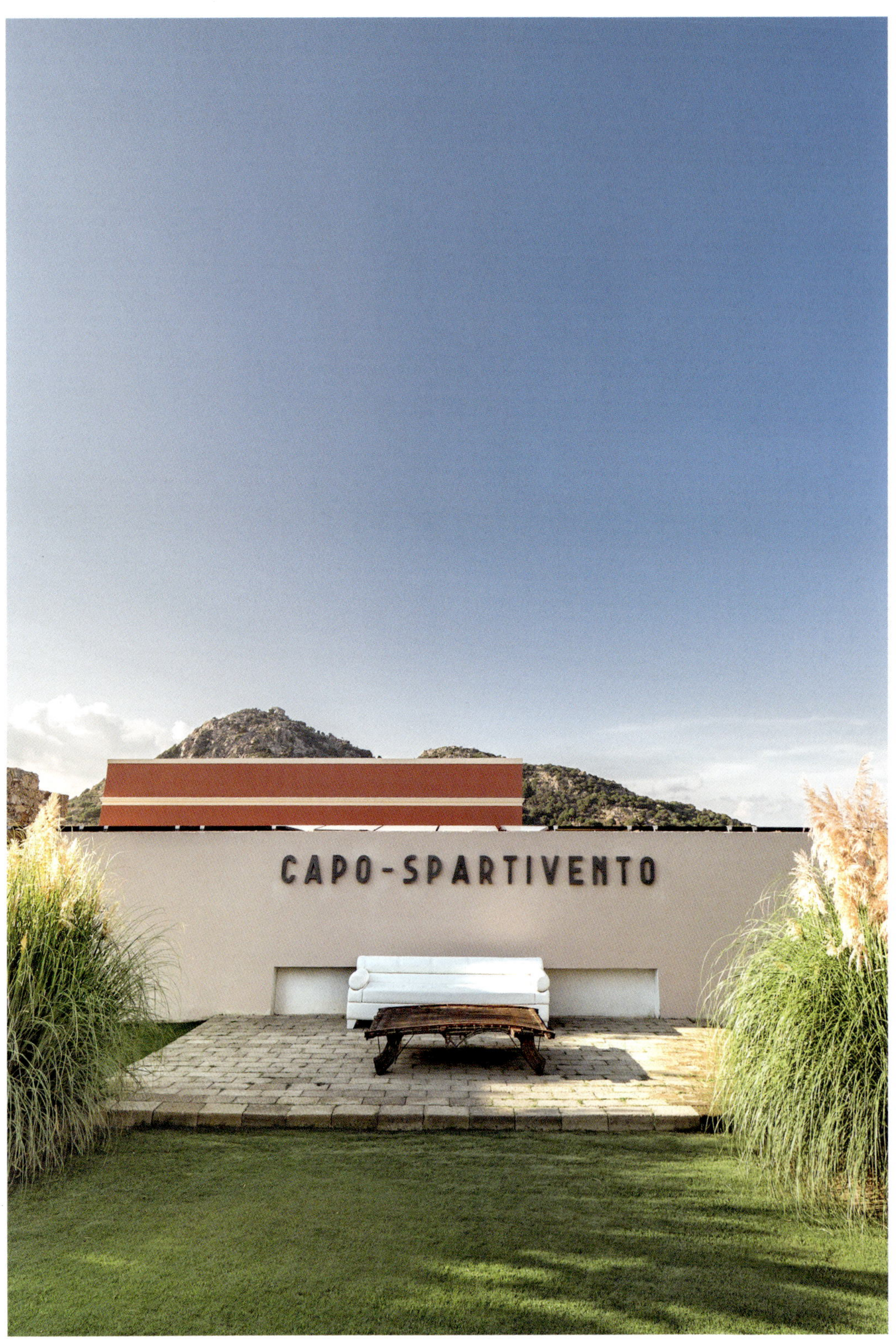
CAPO-SPARTIVENTO

FARO CAPO SPARTIVENTO

Viale Spartivento, 09010 Domus De Maria
Tel. +39 393 827 6800 · info@farocapospartivento.com
www.farocapospartivento.com

A BEACON OF STYLE Travellers with a taste for adventure but also for the avant-garde and aesthetics should put Faro Capo Spartivento right at the top of their list of places to be visited. High above the southernmost point of Sardinia, the lighthouse is the only building on the "cape that divides the wind". It looks down on a landscape with an eventful history of Saracen raids and naval battles, and breathtaking natural beauty: the cobalt-blue sea and the jagged rocks look so primeval and untouched that it is hard to believe that this is the jet set's favourite Italian island in the third millennium. King Vittorio Emanuele had the lighthouse built in 1856, and to this day a historic ornament with the royal initials crowns the entrance. The king would surely have appreciated the new interior designed by the owner, Alessio Raggio. He combines modern white sofas with vintage furniture from all over the world – highly eclectic and inventive, as shown by the Turkish carts that have been made into beds and the Mongolian quern that supports a washbasin. Since 2016 accommodation has also been available in the annexe. It must be the only former military building in Italy that has been converted to an inn. In the evening, don't fail to find time for a stroll outside the tower and residence to admire the starry sky and the beam of the lighthouse: Faro Capo Spartivento is still in operation. ◆ Book to pack: "Reeds in the Wind" by Grazia Deledda.

MIT SIGNALWIRKUNG Wer einen Sinn fürs Abenteuer hat und zugleich für Avantgarde und Ästhetik, der sollte den Faro Capo Spartivento weit oben auf seine Wunschliste künftiger Reiseziele setzen. Hoch über dem südlichsten Punkt Sardiniens gelegen, ist der Leuchtturm das einzige Gebäude auf dem „Kap, das den Wind teilt“ und blickt über eine Landschaft mit einer spannenden Geschichte voller Sarazenen-Angriffe und Seeschlachten sowie einer atemberaubenden Natur. Das kobaltblaue Meer und die zerklüfteten Felsen wirken so ursprünglich und unberührt, dass man kaum glauben kann, im dritten Jahrtausend und auf der italienischen Lieblingsinsel des Jetsets zu sein. Errichtet wurde der Leuchtturm 1856 im Auftrag Vittorio Emanueles – noch heute krönt ein antikes Ornament mit den Initialen des Königs den Eingang, und der Regent hätte sicherlich auch am neuen Interieur Gefallen gefunden, das Besitzer Alessio Raggio gestaltet hat. Er mischt moderne weiße Sofas mit Vintage-Mobiliar aus aller Welt – sehr eklektisch und erfinderisch, wie die türkischen Karren beweisen, aus denen Tagesbetten wurden, oder der Mörser aus der Mongolei, der ein Waschbecken stützt. Seit 2016 kann man auch im Nebenhaus wohnen. Es ist das wohl einzige ehemalige Militärgebäude Italiens, das zu einem Gasthof umgebaut wurde. Abends sollte man einen Moment vor die Türe von Turm und Residenz gehen, den Sternenhimmel bewundern und den Lichtkegel des Leuchtturms verfolgen – denn der Faro Capo Spartivento ist noch immer in Betrieb. ◆ Buchtipp: „Schilf im Wind“ von Grazia Deledda.

UN SIGNAL LUMINEUX Ceux qui aiment l'aventure, mais prisent aussi l'avant-garde et l'esthétique, devraient inscrire Faro Capo Spartivento tout en haut de la liste de leurs futurs voyages. Ce phare qui surplombe l'extrémité sud de la Sardaigne, le seul édifice sur le « cap qui divise le vent », pose ses regards sur un paysage d'une beauté à couper le souffle, dont le passé captivant est rempli d'attaques sarrasines et de batailles navales. La mer bleu cobalt et les falaises déchiquetées ont l'air si primitives et si sauvages que l'on a peine à croire que l'on se trouve, au XXIe siècle, sur l'île italienne préférée de la jet-set. Le phare a été construit en 1856 sur l'ordre de Victor-Emmanuel II de Savoie – ses initiales sont gravées sur un ornement ancien au-dessus de l'entrée –, qui aurait sans doute apprécié les nouveaux aménagements du propriétaire, Alessio Raggio. Celui-ci marie des canapés blancs modernes à des meubles vintage venus de partout, de manière très éclectique et créative ainsi qu'en témoignent les charrettes turques transformées en lit ou le mortier mongol qui soutient un lavabo. Depuis 2016, il est également possible d'habiter dans la maison attenante. C'est probablement le seul ancien bâtiment militaire en Italie qui a été converti en auberge. Le soir, il faut passer un moment à la porte de la tour et de la résidence, admirer le ciel étoilé et suivre le cône de lumière du phare – car le Faro Capo Spartivento est toujours en activité. ◆ À lire : « Des roseaux sous le vent » de Grazia Deledda.

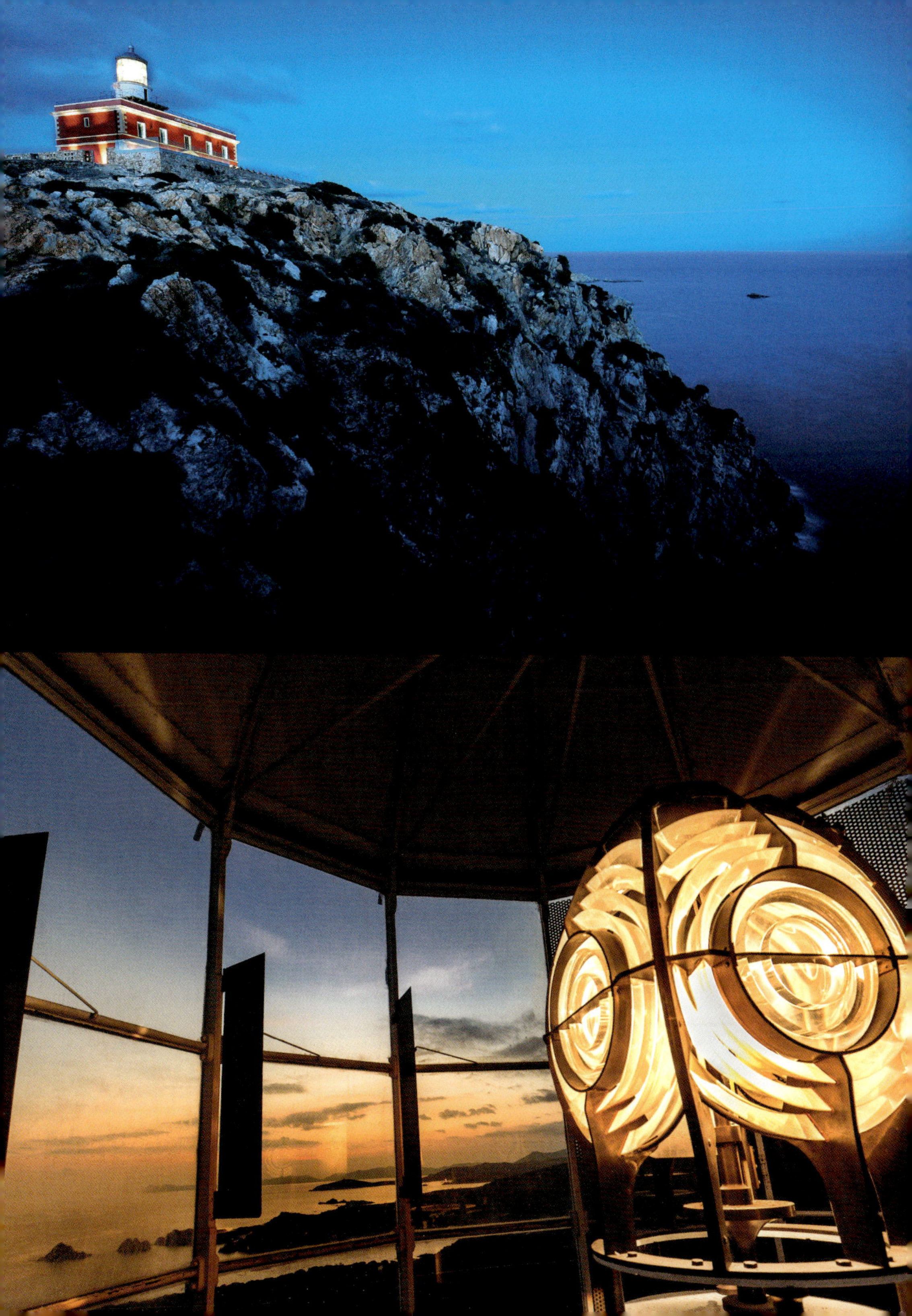

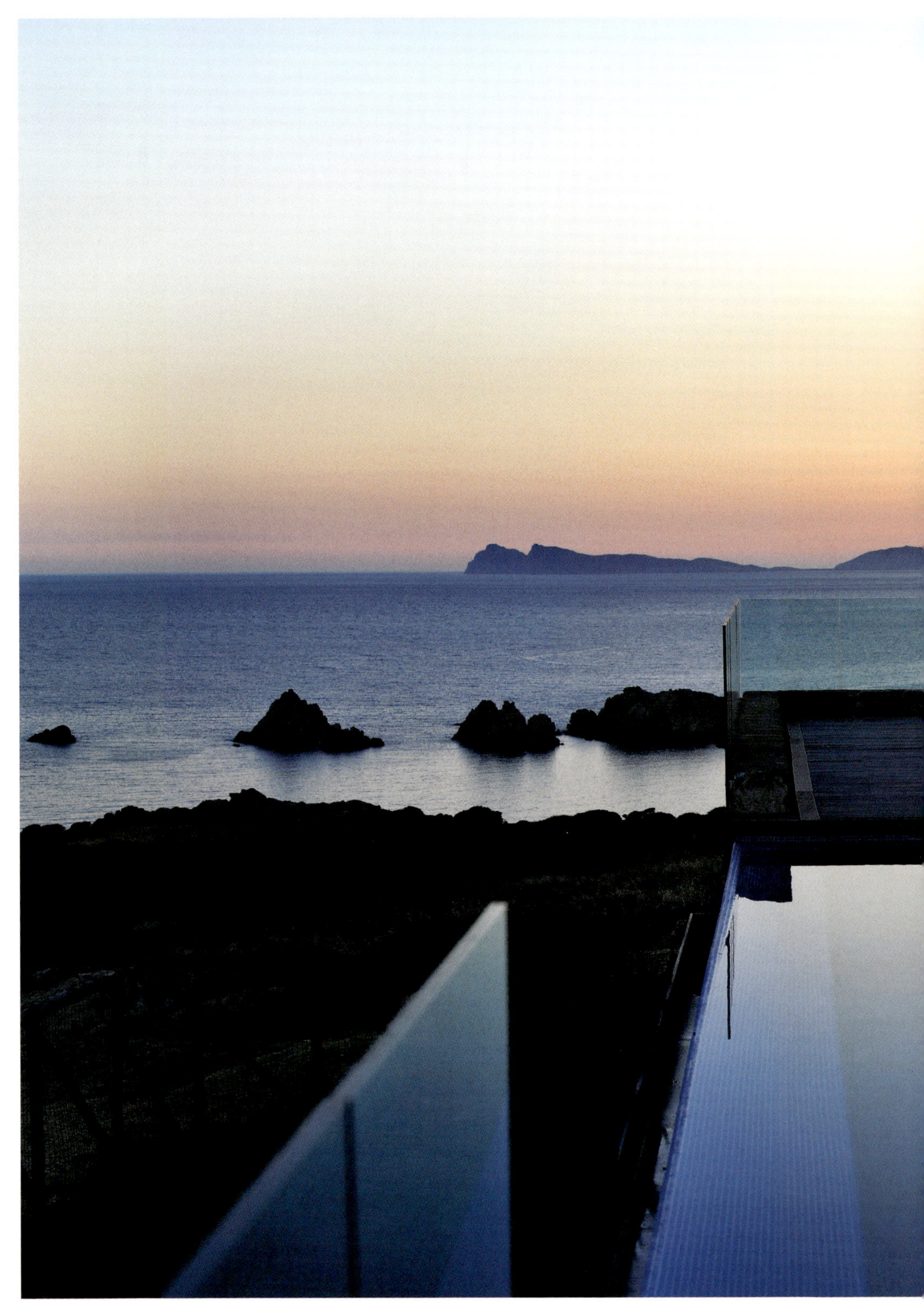

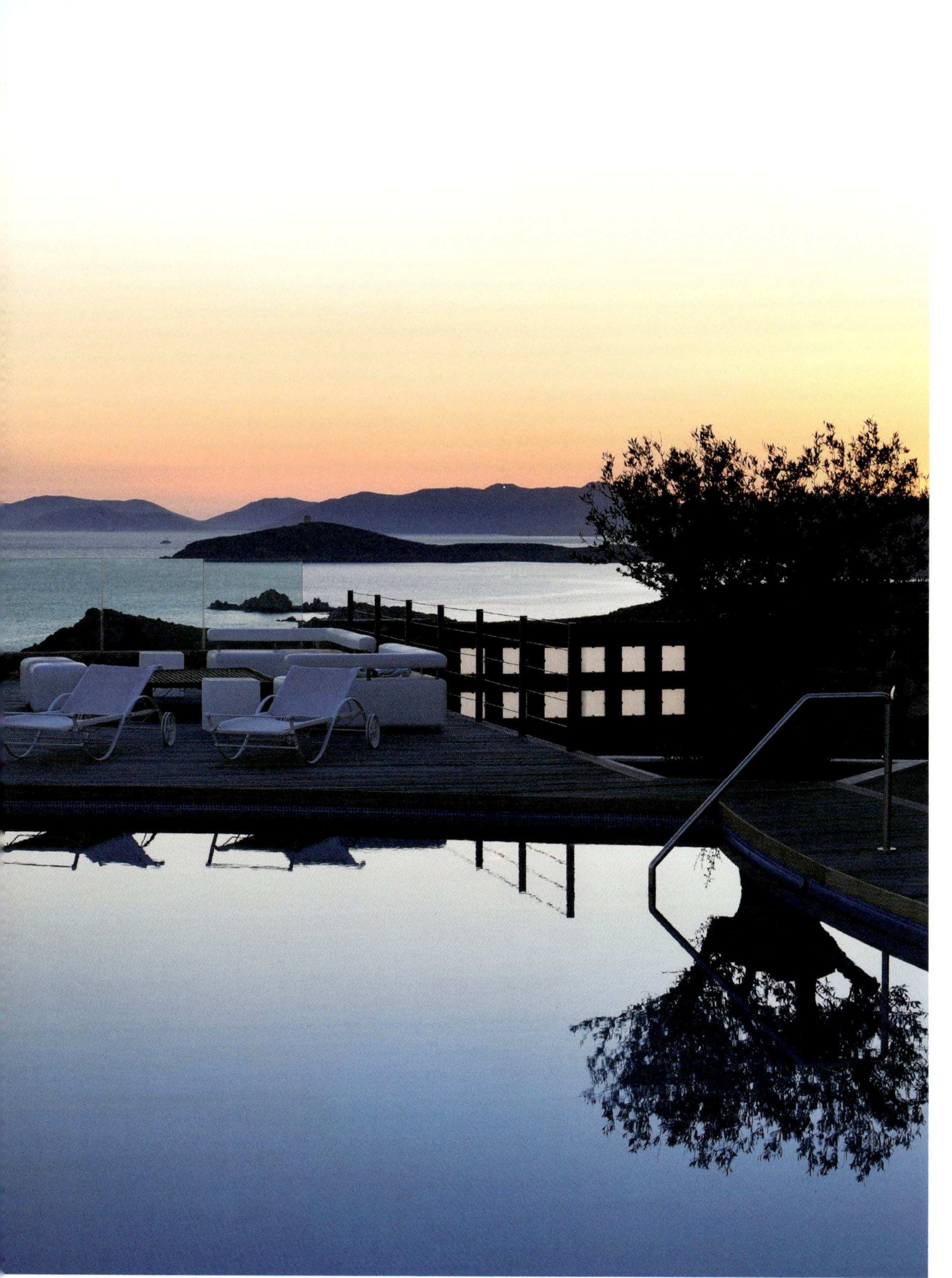

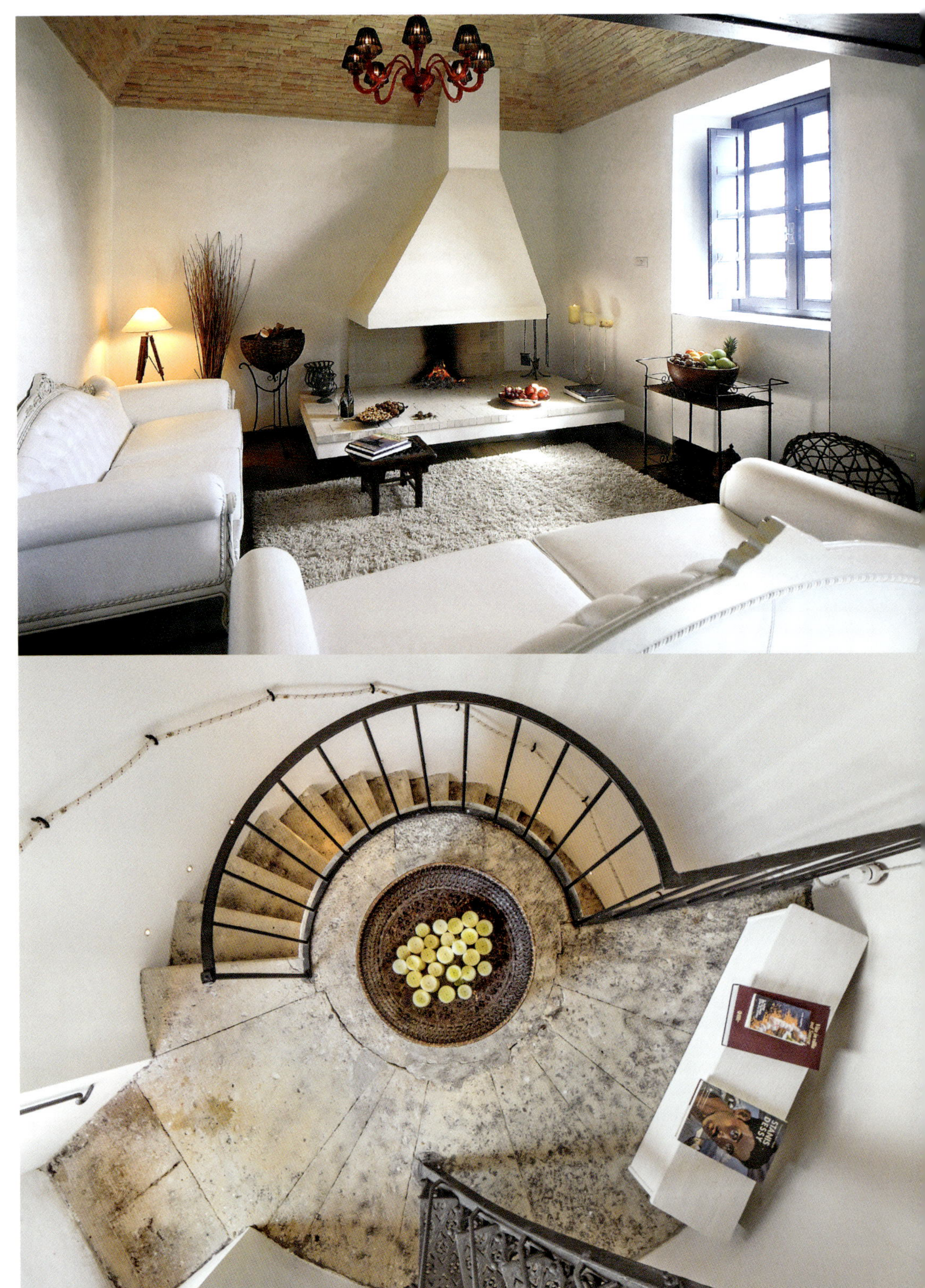

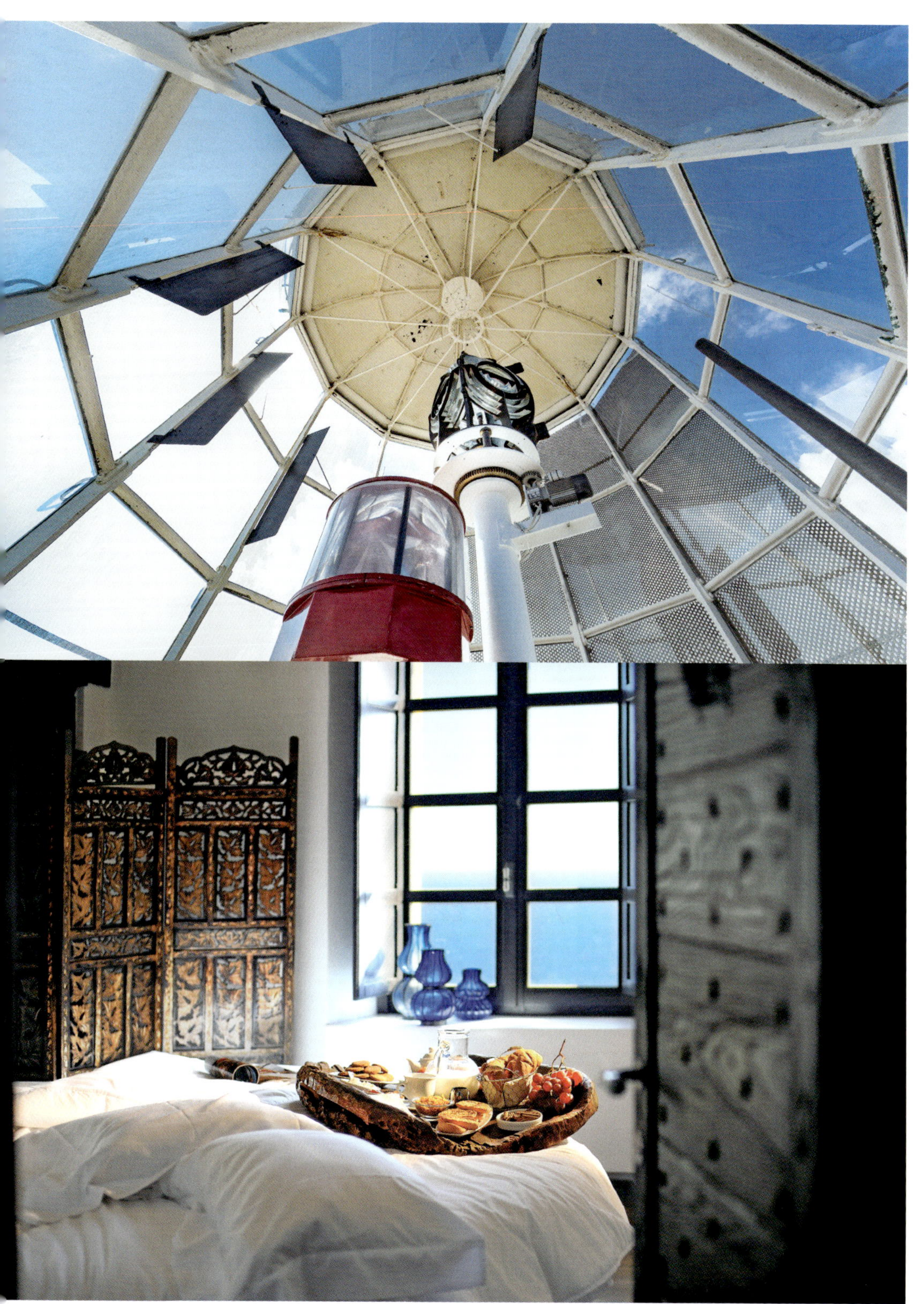

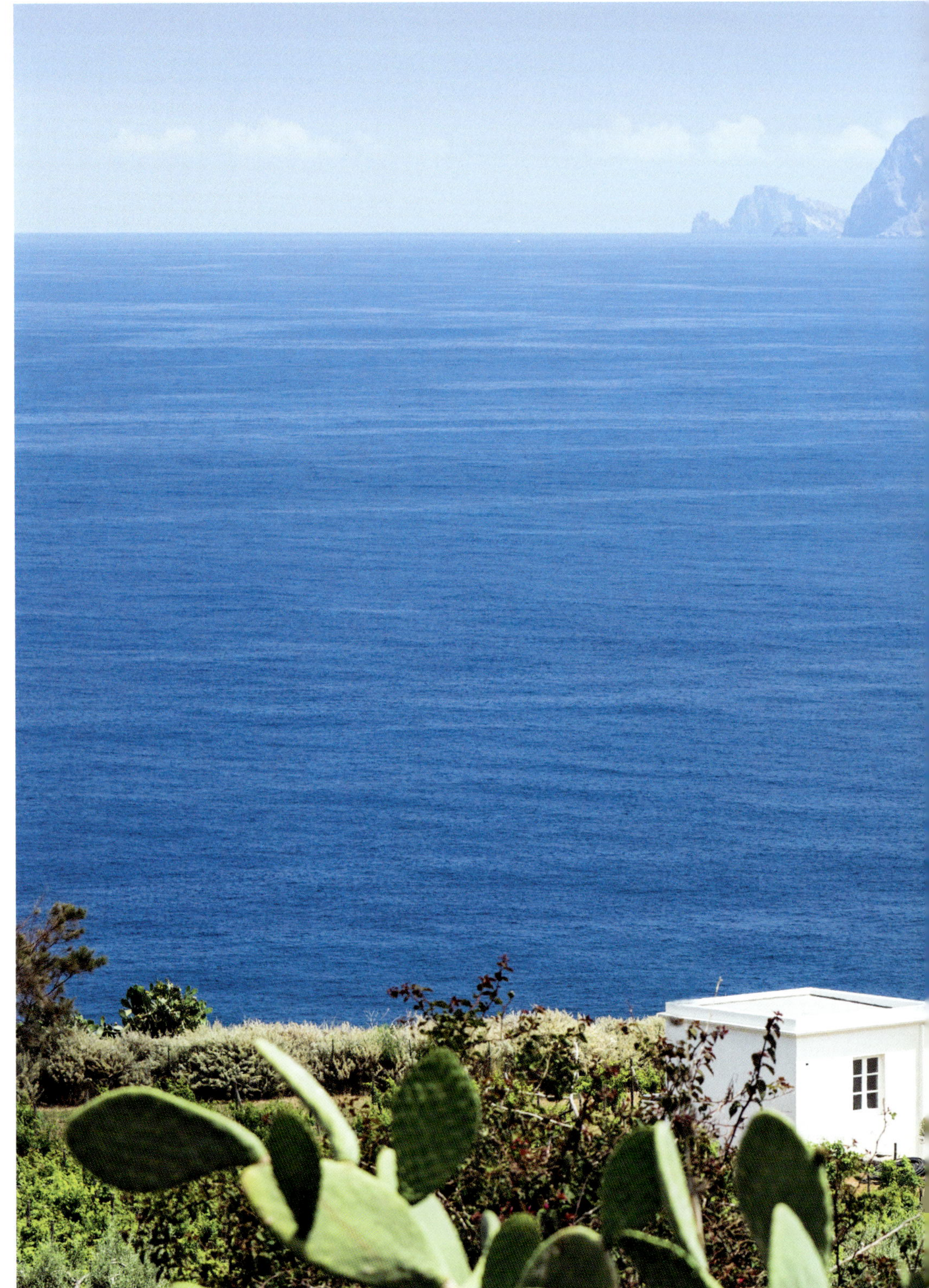

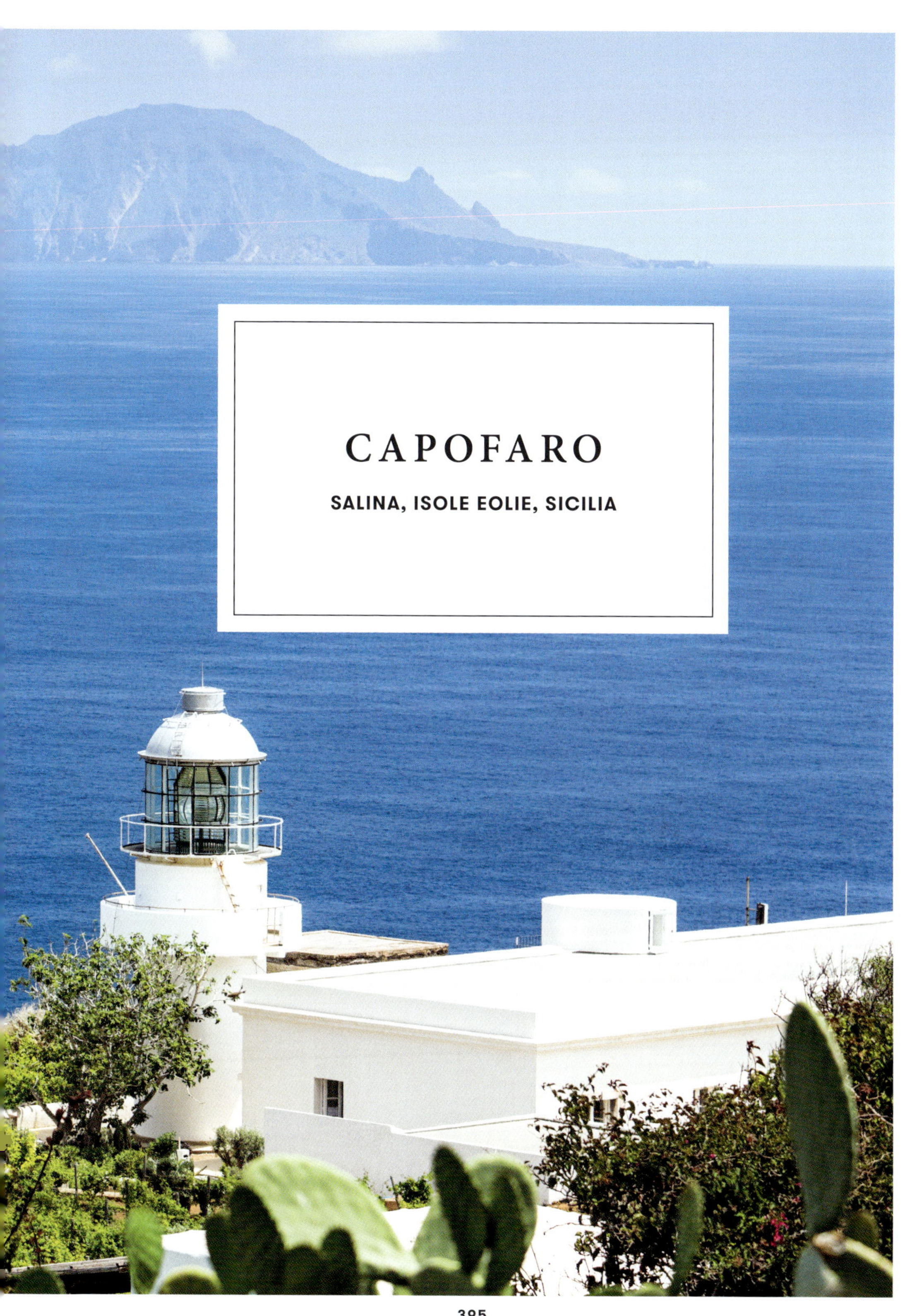

CAPOFARO

SALINA, ISOLE EOLIE, SICILIA

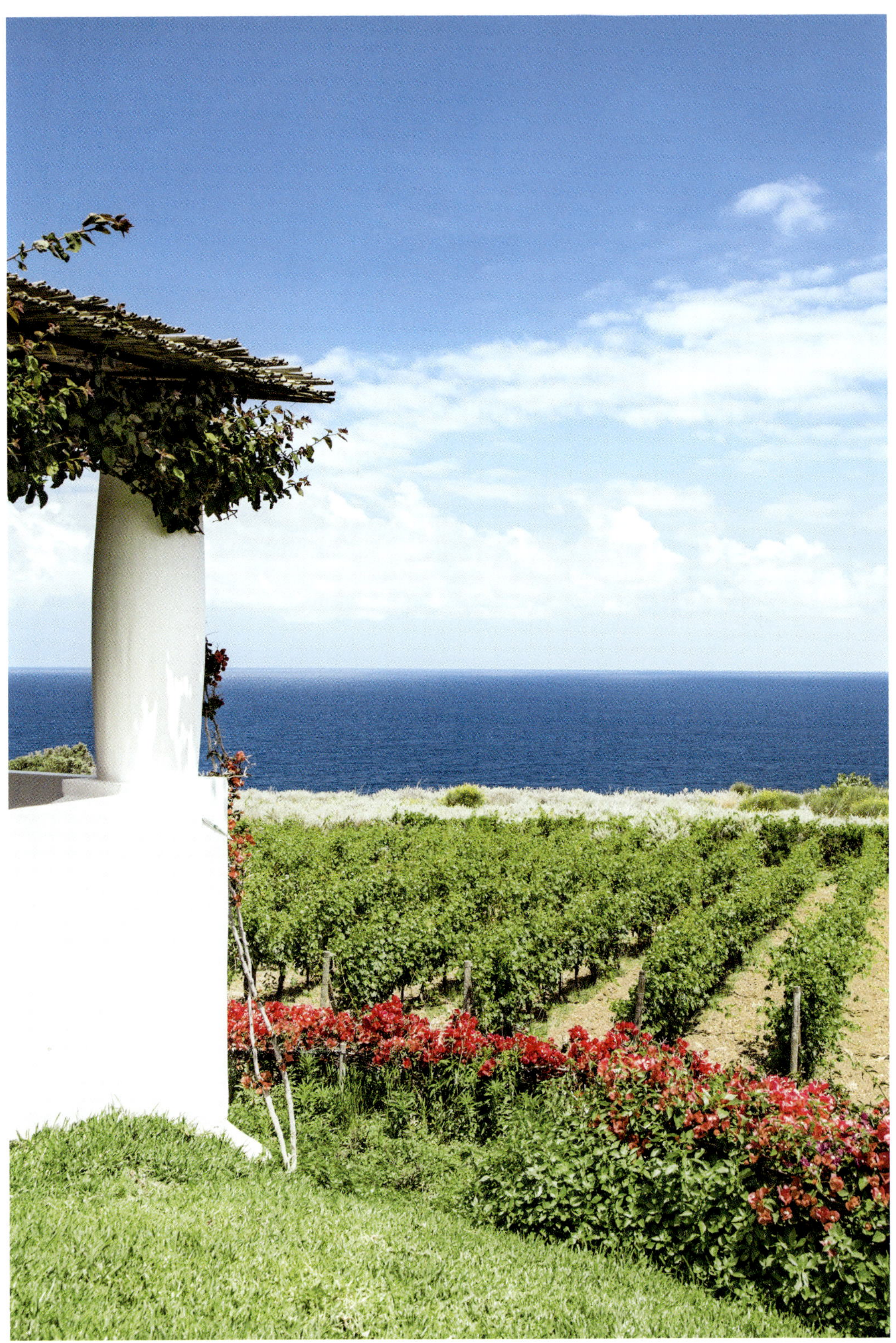

SICILIA

CAPOFARO

Via Faro 3, 98050 Salina
Tel. +39 090 9844 330 · info@capofaro.it
www.capofaro.it
Open from mid-April to late October

A TASTE OF SUMMER The crowning glory of any dinner on Salina is Malvasia, a white wine that gleams golden-yellow in the glass, has a bouquet of raisins, candied fruit and lily of the valley at first, and then unfolds surprisingly, with delicate nuances of citronella and pepper. Only here, on the volcanic soil of the second-largest of the Aeolian Islands, are Malvasia grapes grown, then laid out to dry in the shade on straw mats before the pressing and fermentation takes place. The most elegant Malvasia wine is made by the Tasca d'Almerita family, a Sicilian dynasty whose wine estate has been one of the best in southern Italy for more than 200 years. A fitting place to enjoy this wine is Capofaro Resort, once owned by them and recently sold to another Sicilian family. It lies on the edge of the vineyards and has a view far across the sea to Panarea and Stromboli. When the neighbouring islands shimmer pink and orange at sunset and the volcano spits glowing lava after dark, the sight is quite simply spectacular. The cottages, too, which are scattered around the estate and have flat roofs and terraces with blinds made of rushes in the Aeolian architectural tradition, boast panoramas fit for a painter's canvas. The interiors of the rooms do not even try to steal the show from the overwhelming beauty outdoors, but are white, minimalist and wonderfully soothing. The restaurant follows the same philosophy by concentrating on essentials, which is why it serves such excellent island dishes. The seafood in particular is a real treat for the taste buds – only the Malvasia tastes more of summer, sun and Salina. ◆ Book to pack: "Sicily" by Guy de Maupassant.

SO SCHMECKT DER SOMMER Er ist der krönende Abschluss eines jeden Dinners auf Salina: der Weißwein Malvasia, der goldgelb im Glas glänzt, erst nach Rosinen, kandierten Früchten und Maiglöckchen duftet und dann mit zarten Nuancen von Citronella und Pfeffer überrascht. Seine Trauben werden nur hier kultiviert – auf dem vulkanischen Boden der zweitgrößten Liparischen Insel – und im Schatten auf Strohmatten getrocknet, ehe sie gepresst und vergoren werden. Den elegantesten Malvasia keltert die Familie Tasca D'Almerita, eine sizilianische Dynastie, die seit mehr als 200 Jahren zu den besten Winzern Süditaliens zählt. Ihren Wein genießt man am passendsten im Capofaro Resort, das einst ihnen gehörte und kürzlich an eine andere sizilianische Familie verkauft wurde. Das Resort liegt am Rand der Rebhänge und blickt weit übers Meer bis nach Panarea und Stromboli – wenn die Nachbarinseln bei Sonnenuntergang pink-orange schimmern und der Vulkan nach Einbruch der Dunkelheit glühende Lava spuckt, ist die Sicht schlicht spektakulär. Auch die Cottages, die sich auf dem Grundstück verteilen und nach äolischer Architekturtradition Flachdächer sowie Terrassen mit Schilfrohrmarkisen besitzen, eröffnen leinwandtaugliche Panoramen. Das Interieur der Zimmer versucht erst gar nicht, der überwältigenden Landschaft die Schau zu stehlen, sondern gibt sich ganz in Weiß, minimalistisch und wunderbar wohltuend. Derselben Philosophie folgt das Restaurant, das aufs Wesentliche reduziert ist und genau deshalb so gute Gerichte der Insel serviert. Vor allem die Meeresfrüchte sind echtes Gaumenglück – noch mehr nach Sommer, Sonne und Salina schmeckt nur der Malvasia.
◆ Buchtipp: „Sizilien" von Guy de Maupassant.

LE GOÛT DE L'ÉTÉ Le Malvoisie delle Lipari est le couronnement de tout dîner à Salina : couleur jaune d'or, il embaume les fruits secs, les agrumes confits et le muguet avant de surprendre par ses nuances délicates de citronnelle et de poivre. Ses raisins blancs ne sont cultivés qu'ici, sur le sol volcanique de l'île, la deuxième de l'archipel des Éoliennes par sa superficie, et séchés à l'ombre sur des nattes de paille avant d'être pressés et de fermenter. Le Malvoisie le plus élégant est produit par la famille Tasca D'Almerita, une dynastie sicilienne qui fait partie depuis plus de deux siècles des meilleurs vignerons de l'Italie du Sud. Un endroit idéal pour déguster ce vin est le Capofaro Resort, qui leur appartenait autrefois et qui a récemment été vendu à une autre famille sicilienne. Il est situé à la lisière des vignobles et offre une vue imprenable sur la mer, jusqu'à Panarea et Stromboli. Lorsque les îles voisines se teintent de rose orange au soleil couchant et que le volcan crache sa lave dans l'obscurité, la vue est tout simplement spectaculaire. Éparpillées sur le domaine, les petites maisons qui offrent des vues sublimes sur le paysage alentour sont typiquement éoliennes avec leurs toits plats et leurs terrasses dotées de stores en roseau. L'aménagement intérieur ne cherche pas à rivaliser avec l'extérieur extraordinaire et se contente de blanc minimaliste et merveilleusement bienfaisant. Le restaurant illustre la même philosophie en servant des plats de l'île réduits à l'essentiel, ce qui ne les rend que plus exquis. Les fruits de mer, surtout, sont un vrai délice – il n'y a que le malvoisie pour offrir plus encore le goût de l'été, du soleil et de l'île.
◆ À lire : « En Sicile » de Guy de Maupassant.

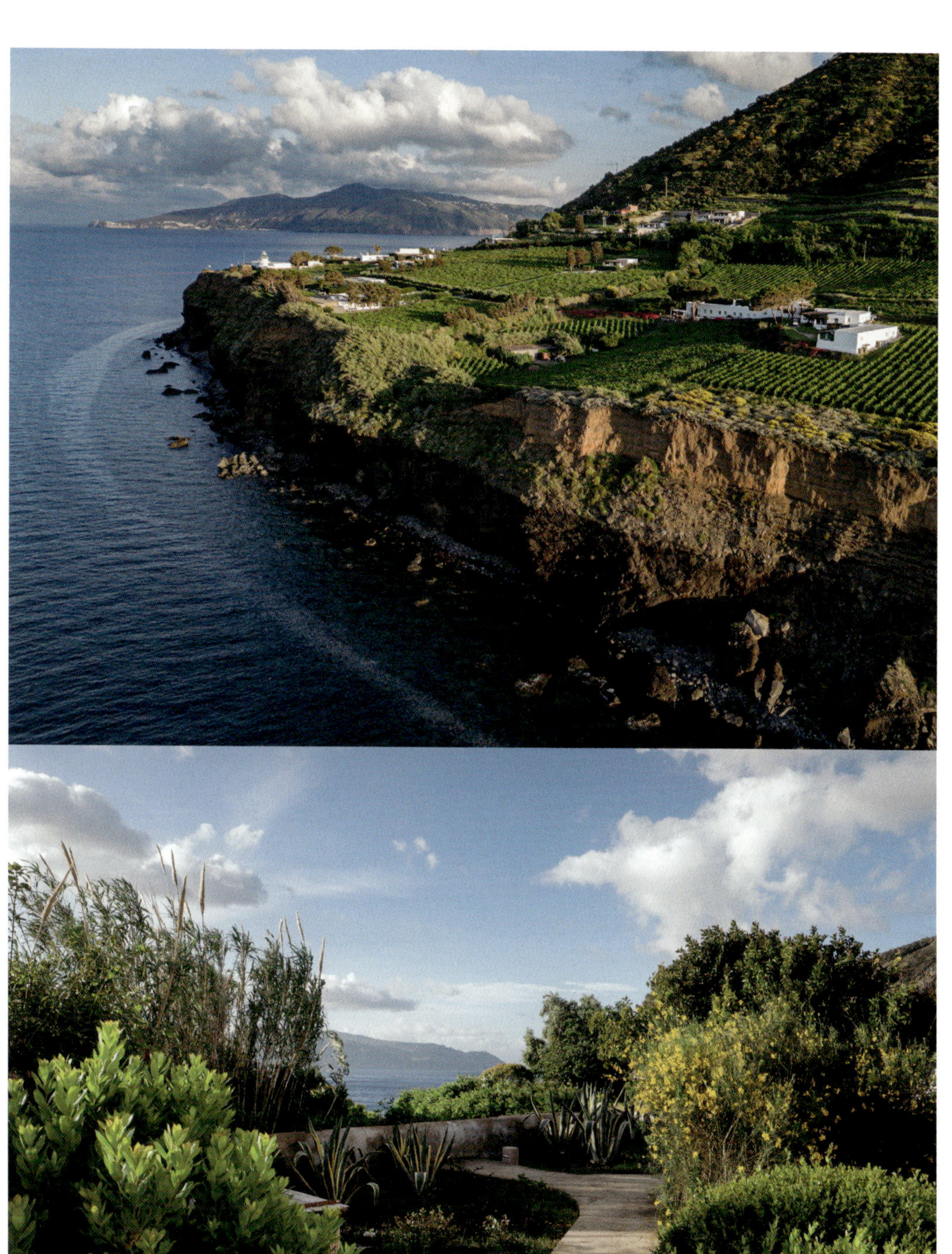

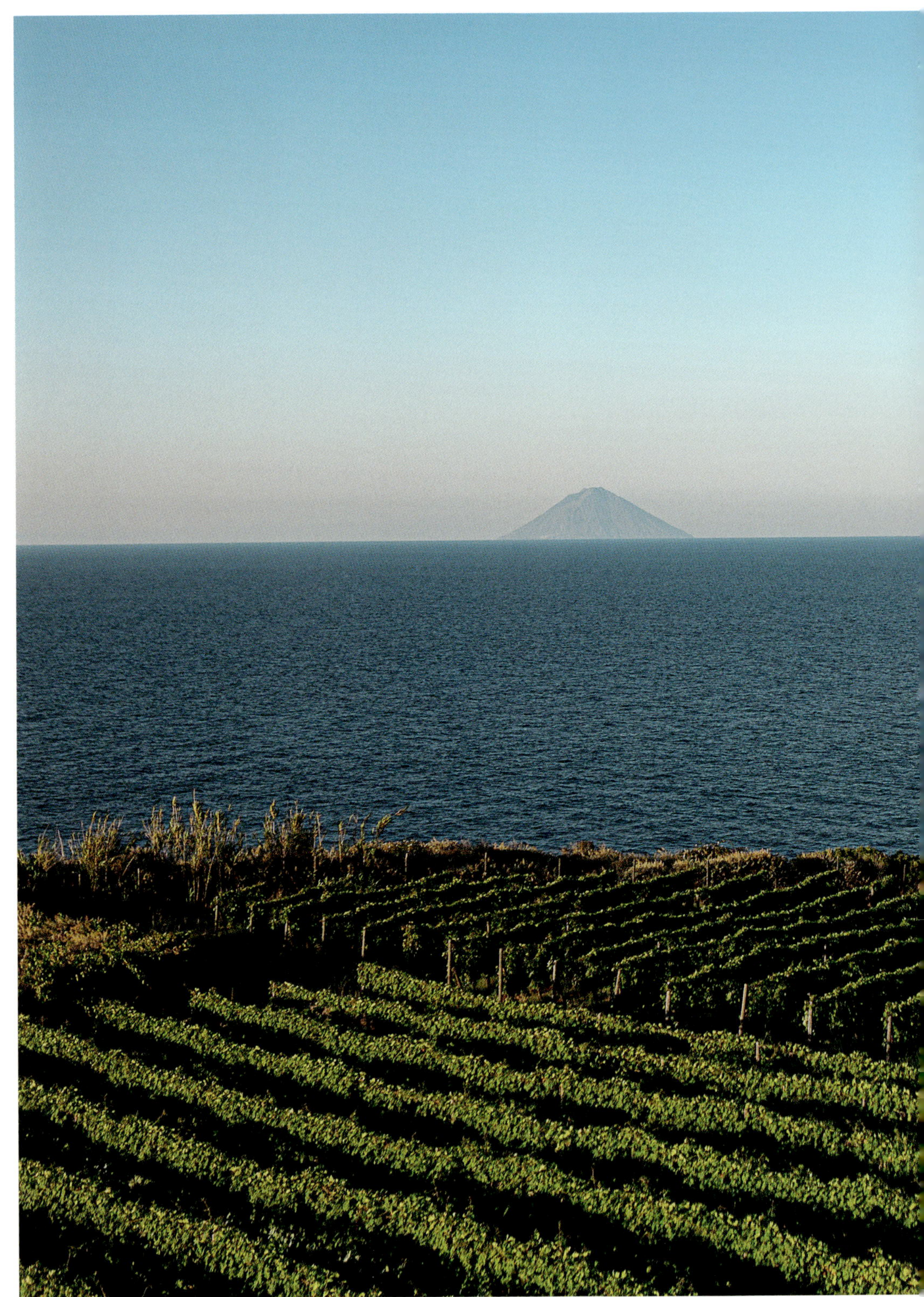

SICILIA

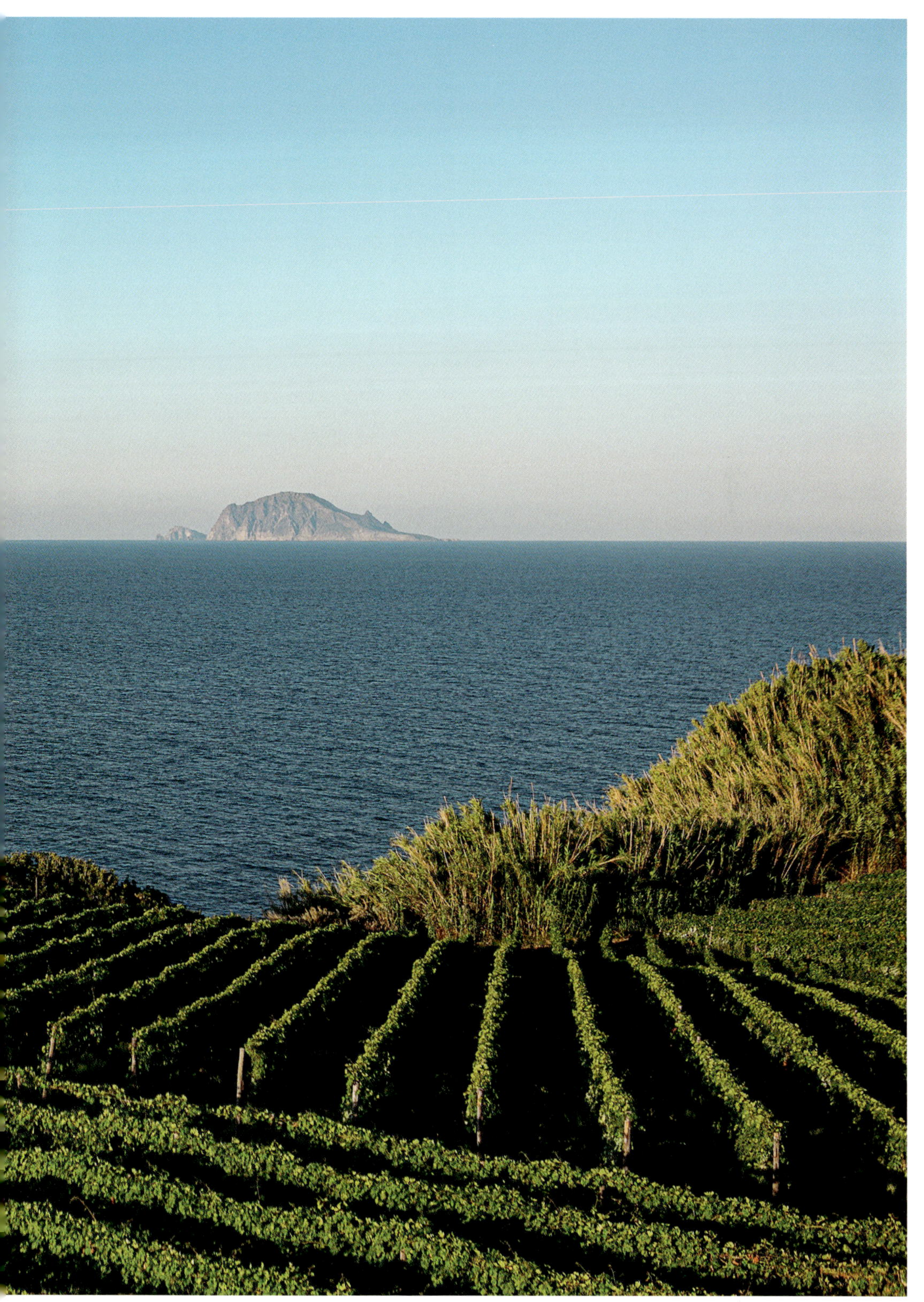

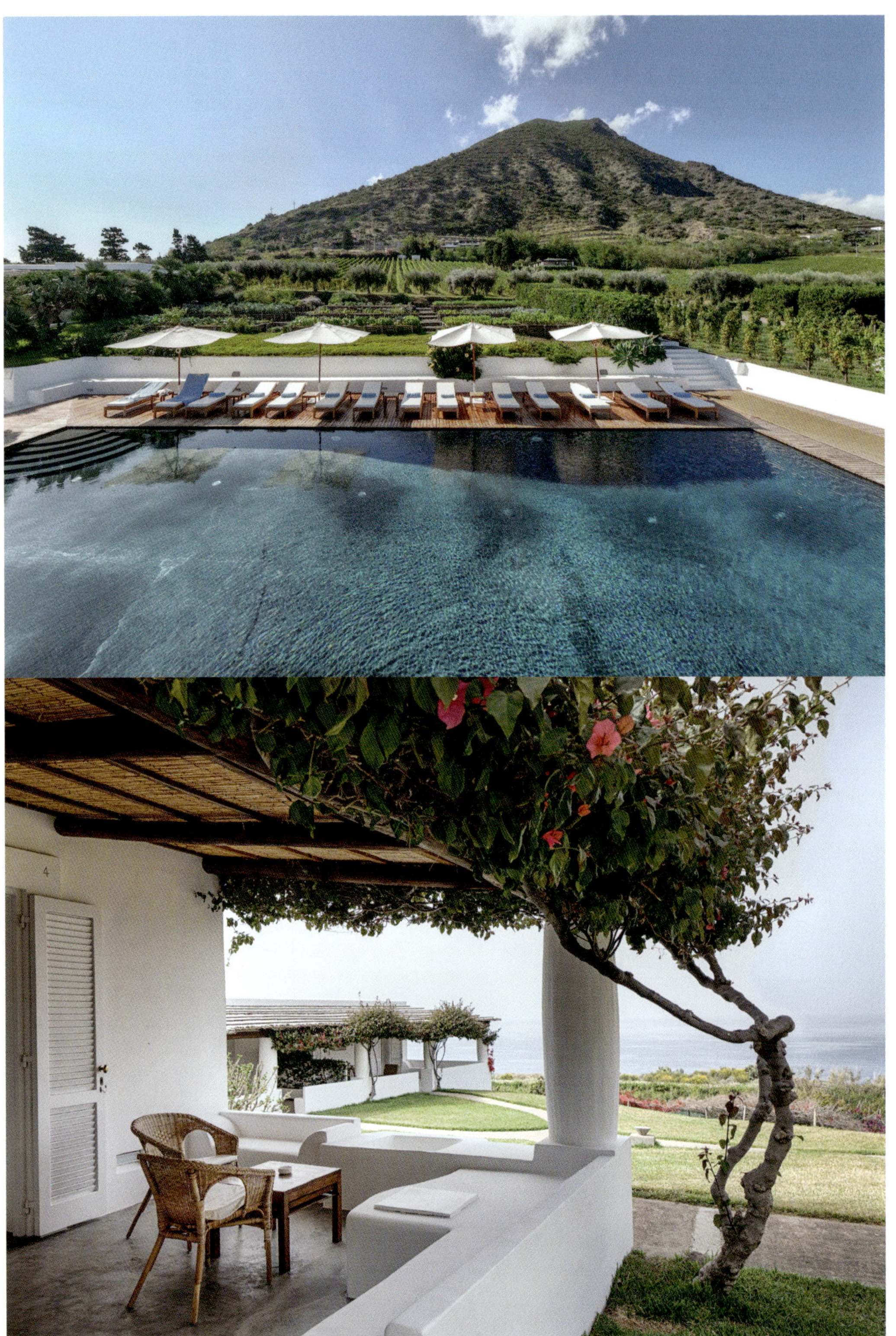

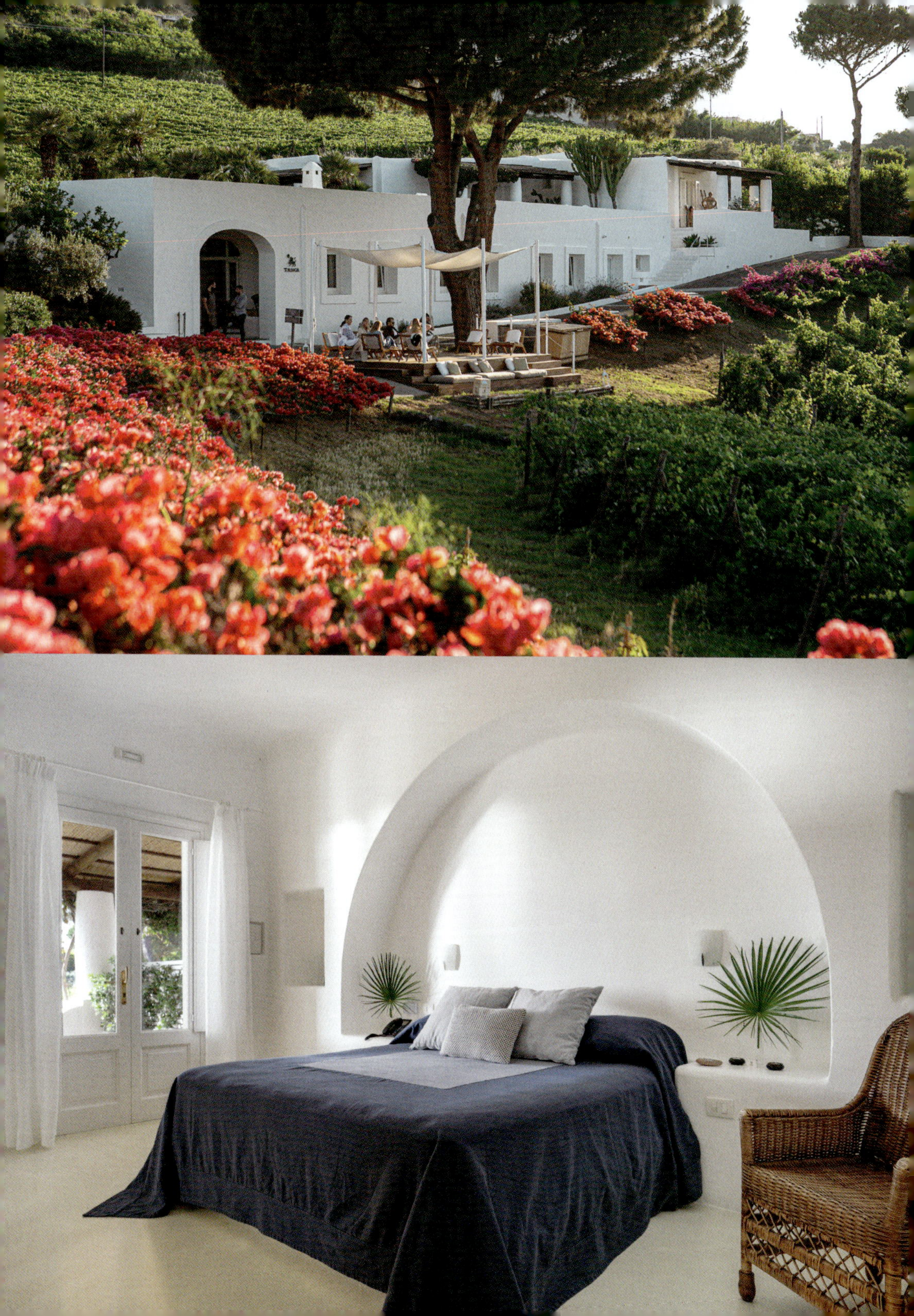

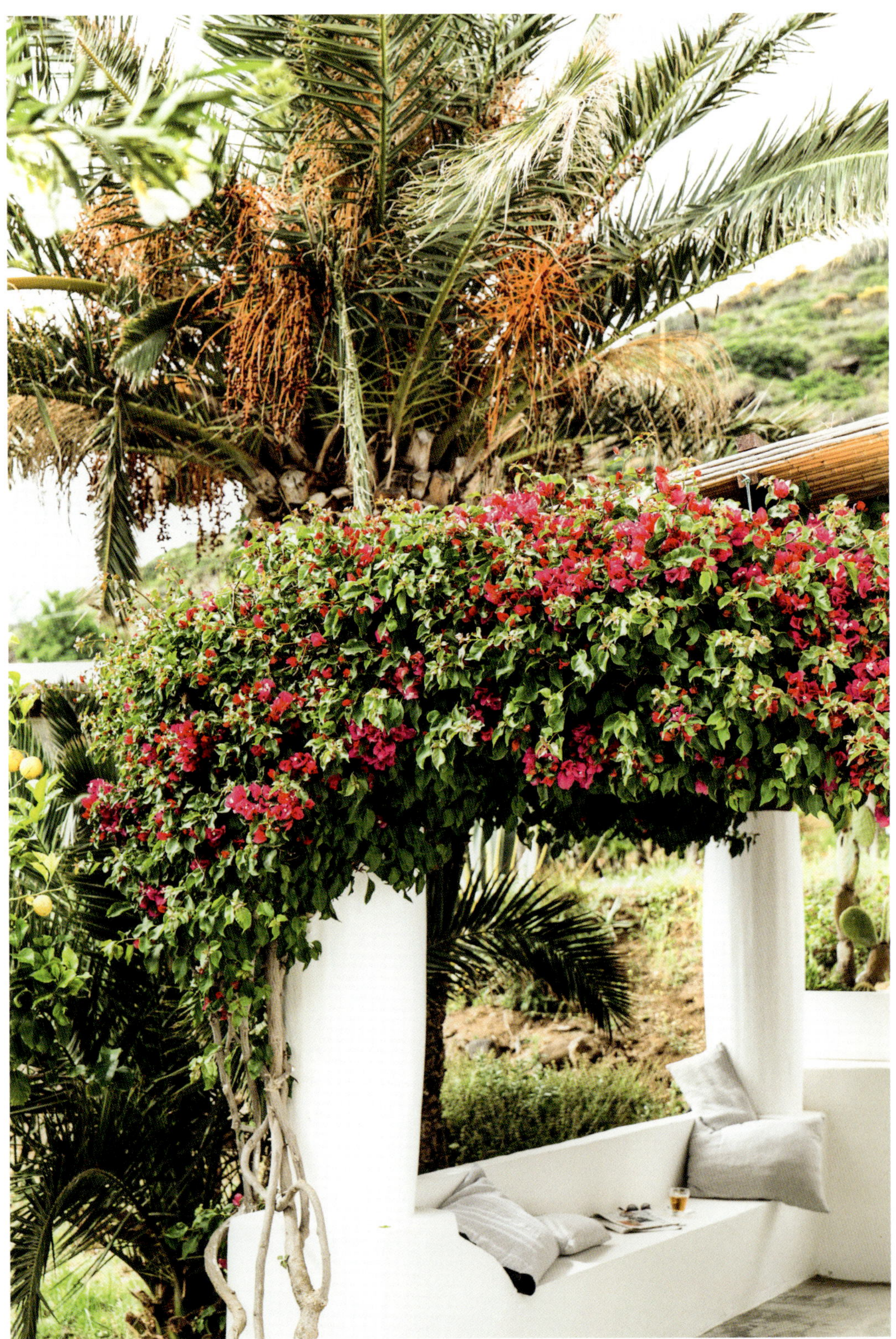

SICILIA

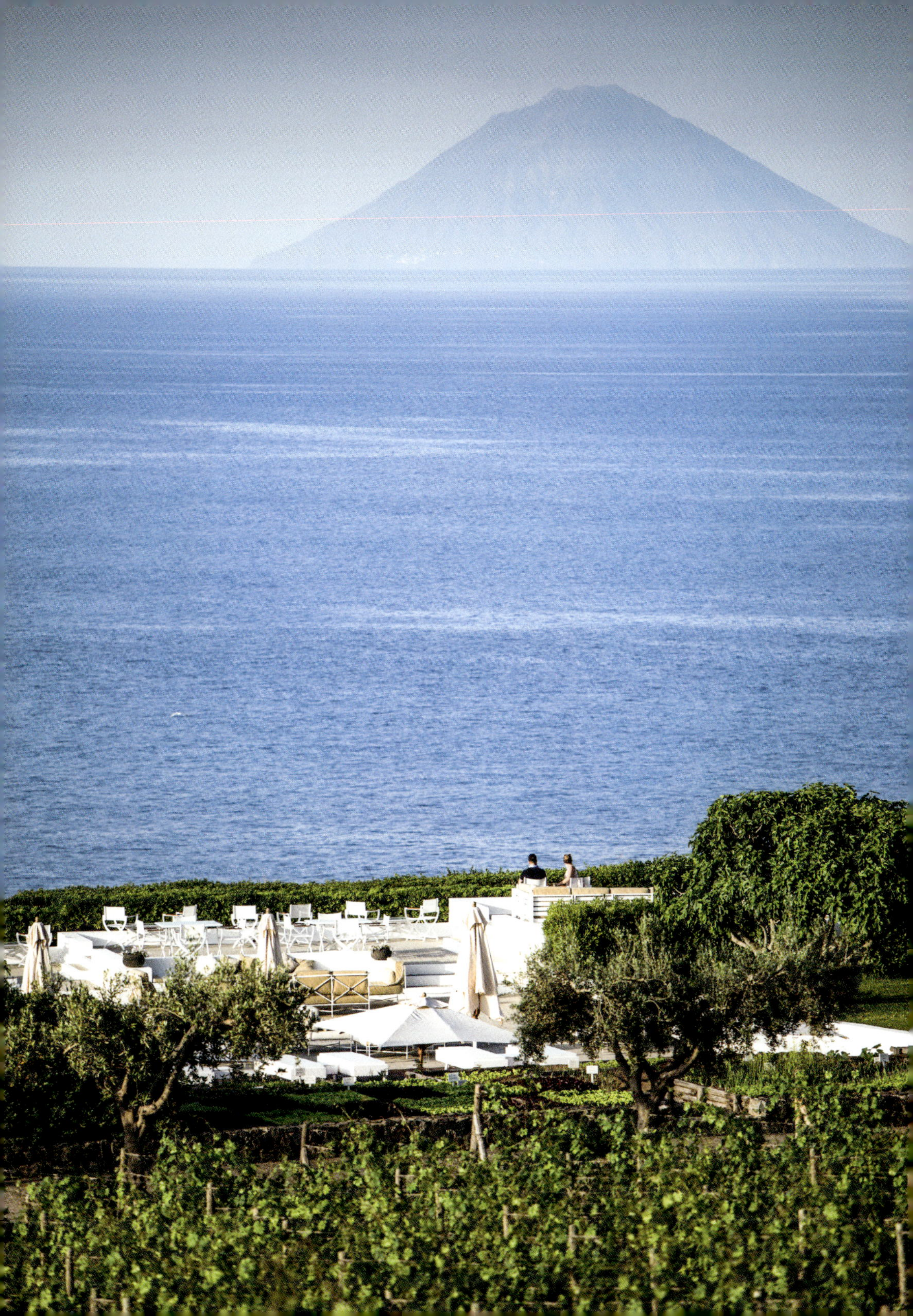

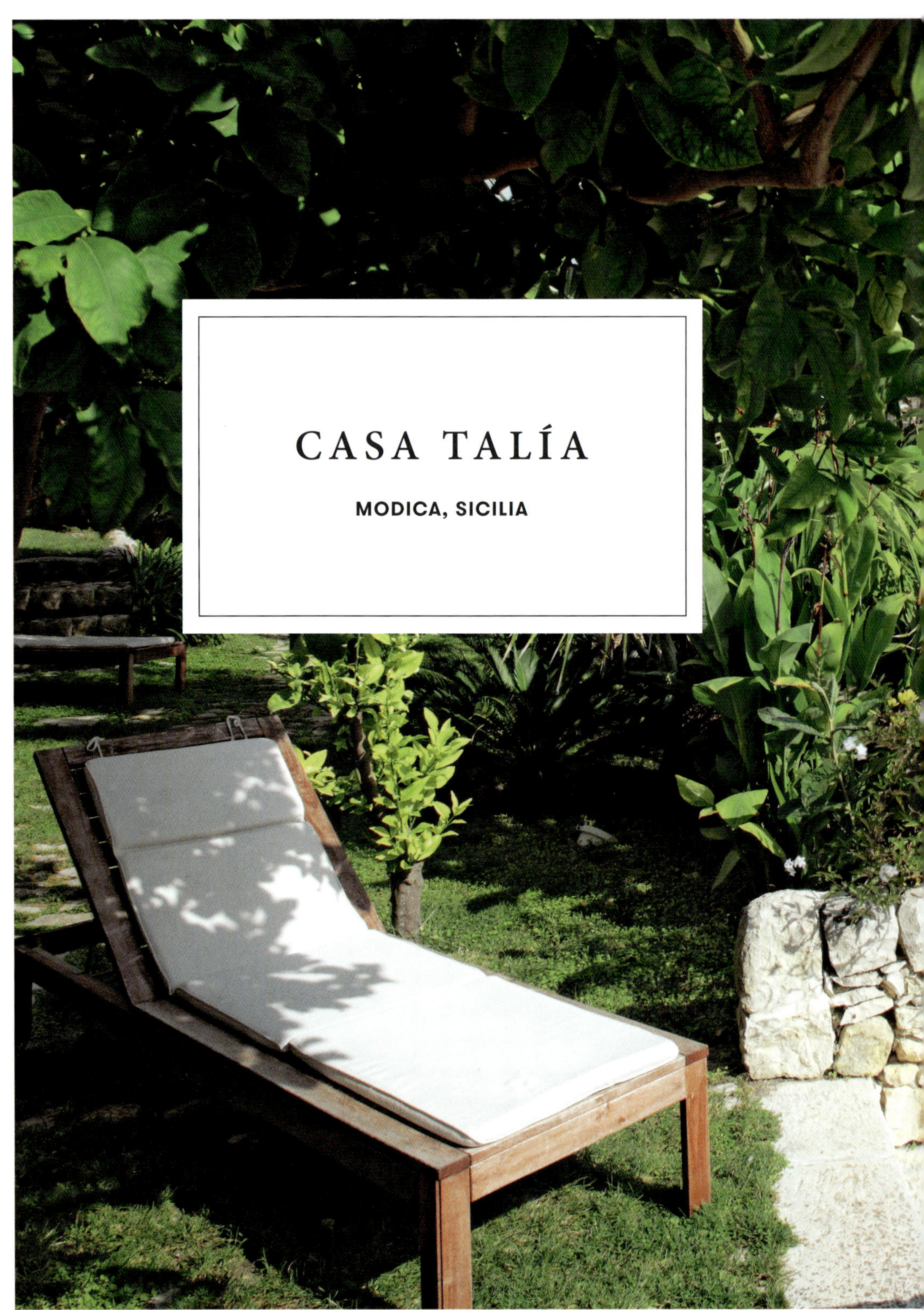

CASA TALÍA

MODICA, SICILIA

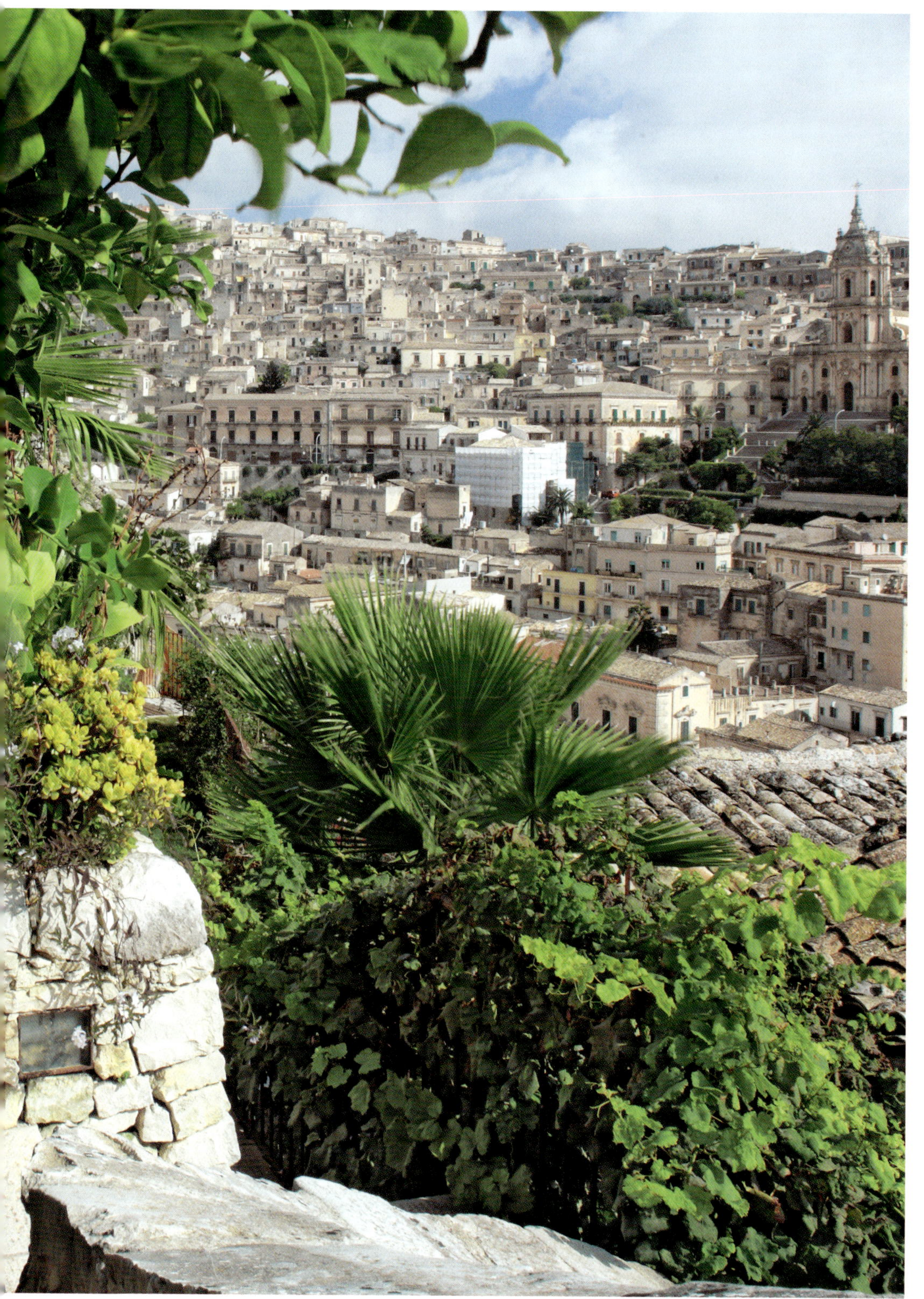

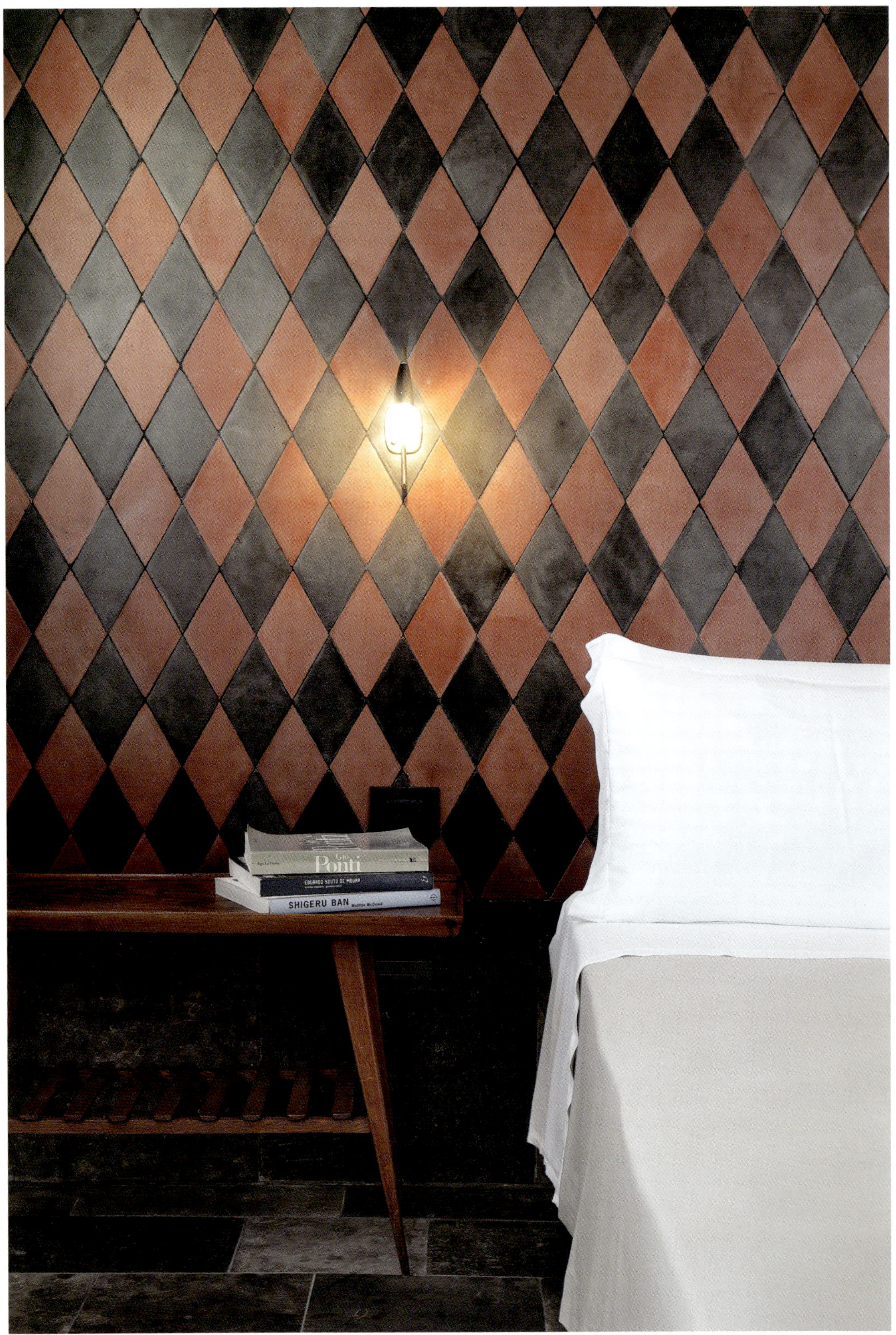

SICILIA

CASA TALÍA

Via Exaudinos 1/9, 97015 Modica
Tel. +39 0932 752 075 · info@casatalia.it
www.casatalia.it

POSTCARD PANORAMA When the ground shook more violently than ever before on 9 and 11 January 1693 in Sicily, the settlements of the Val di Noto in the south-east of the island were almost completely destroyed, and 60,000 people lost their lives. Yet after the catastrophe, those who survived created a work of art: they rebuilt their towns in the finest Sicilian late Baroque style. In Modica, especially, wealthy citizens competed to construct the most magnificent palazzi and the most imaginative façades. Both the lower and the upper town were given their own cathedral, and so many other churches were built that Modica is known today as the "city of 100 bells and churches". An unforgettable view of this scenery, which has UNESCO World Heritage status, is the privilege of guests at Marco Giunta and Viviana Haddad's Casa Talía. An architect couple from Milan, they bought eleven houses that are grouped around a pretty garden on different levels, and renovated them in a simple but stylish way with natural materials. Thus the rooms have walls of unclad stone, wooden or bamboo ceilings, and floors made from lava stone or terracotta. All of this is embellished with Mediterranean accessories and antique tiles. Each room has a balcony, a terrace or direct access to the garden, in which a superb breakfast is served – with a wonderful view of the town, needless to say. "Talía!" ("look!") is a Sicilian exclamation – and the Casa lives up to its name. ◆ Book to pack: "Complete Poems" by Salvatore Quasimodo – a holder of the Nobel Prize for Literature who was born in Modica.

POSTKARTEN-PANORAMA Als am 9. und 11. Januar 1693 die Erde auf Sizilien so heftig bebte wie noch nie zuvor, wurden die Orte des Val di Noto im Südosten der Insel fast völlig zerstört und 60.000 Menschen verloren ihr Leben. Doch die, die überlebten, ließen der Katastrophe ein Kunstwerk folgen: Sie bauten die Städte im schönsten sizilianischen Spätbarock wieder auf. Vor allem in Modica wetteiferten betuchte Bauherren um die prächtigsten Palazzi und fantasievollsten Fassaden. Unter- und Oberstadt bekamen je einen eigenen Dom und man errichtete so viele weitere Gotteshäuser, dass Modica heute auch als „Stadt der 100 Glocken und Kirchen" bekannt ist. Einen unvergesslichen Blick über diese Szenerie, die UNESCO-Weltkulturerbe ist, haben Gäste der Casa Talía von Marco Giunta und Viviana Haddad. Das Mailänder Architektenpaar kaufte elf kleine Häuser, die auf verschiedenen Ebenen um einen hübschen Garten liegen, und renovierte sie schlicht, aber stilvoll und mit natürlichen Materialen. So gibt es in den Zimmern Wände aus rohem Stein, Decken aus Holz oder Bambus, Böden aus Lavastein oder Terrakotta; alles verschönert mit mediterranen Accessoires und antiken Fliesen. Alle Räume besitzen einen Balkon, eine Terrasse oder einen direkten Zugang zum Garten, in dem ein großartiges Frühstück serviert wird, natürlich bei bester Sicht über die Stadt. „Talía!" (Schau mal!): Nicht umsonst verdankt die Casa diesem sizilianischen Ausruf ihren Namen. ◆ Buchtipp: „Gesammelte Gedichte" von Salvatore Quasimodo – der Literaturnobelpreisträger wurde in Modica geboren.

UNE VUE DE CARTE POSTALE Les 9 et 11 janvier 1693, la terre sicilienne a tremblé plus violemment que jamais, les villages de Val di Noto, au sud-est de l'île, ont été presque entièrement détruits et 60 000 personnes ont péri. Mais ceux qui ont survécu ont réagi, créant de l'art après la catastrophe : ils ont reconstruit les villes dans le plus beau style baroque finissant sicilien. À Modica surtout, les bâtisseurs fortunés ont rivalisé à qui aurait les plus beaux palais et les façades les plus inventives. La ville basse et la ville haute avaient chacune leur cathédrale, et tant d'autres lieux de culte ont été construits que Modica est maintenant aussi connue comme la « ville aux 100 cloches et églises ». Les hôtes de la Casa Talía de Marco Giunta et Viviana Haddad ont une vue inoubliable sur ce paysage inscrit au patrimoine mondial de l'UNESCO. Ce couple d'architectes milanais a acheté onze petites maisons sur différents niveaux autour d'un joli jardin et les a rénovées simplement, mais avec goût et des matériaux naturels. Les pièces ont des murs en pierre brute, des plafonds en bois ou en bambou, des sols en pierre de lave ou en terre cuite, le tout agrémenté d'accessoires méditerranéens et de carrelages anciens. Toutes les chambres disposent d'un balcon, d'une terrasse ou d'un accès direct au jardin, où est servi un petit déjeuner grandiose, et qui offre bien sûr la meilleure vue sur la ville. « Talía ! » (« Regarde ! ») : ce n'est pas pour rien que la Casa doit son nom à cette exclamation sicilienne. ◆ À lire : « Poèmes » de Salvatore Quasimodo – le prix Nobel de littérature est né à Modica.

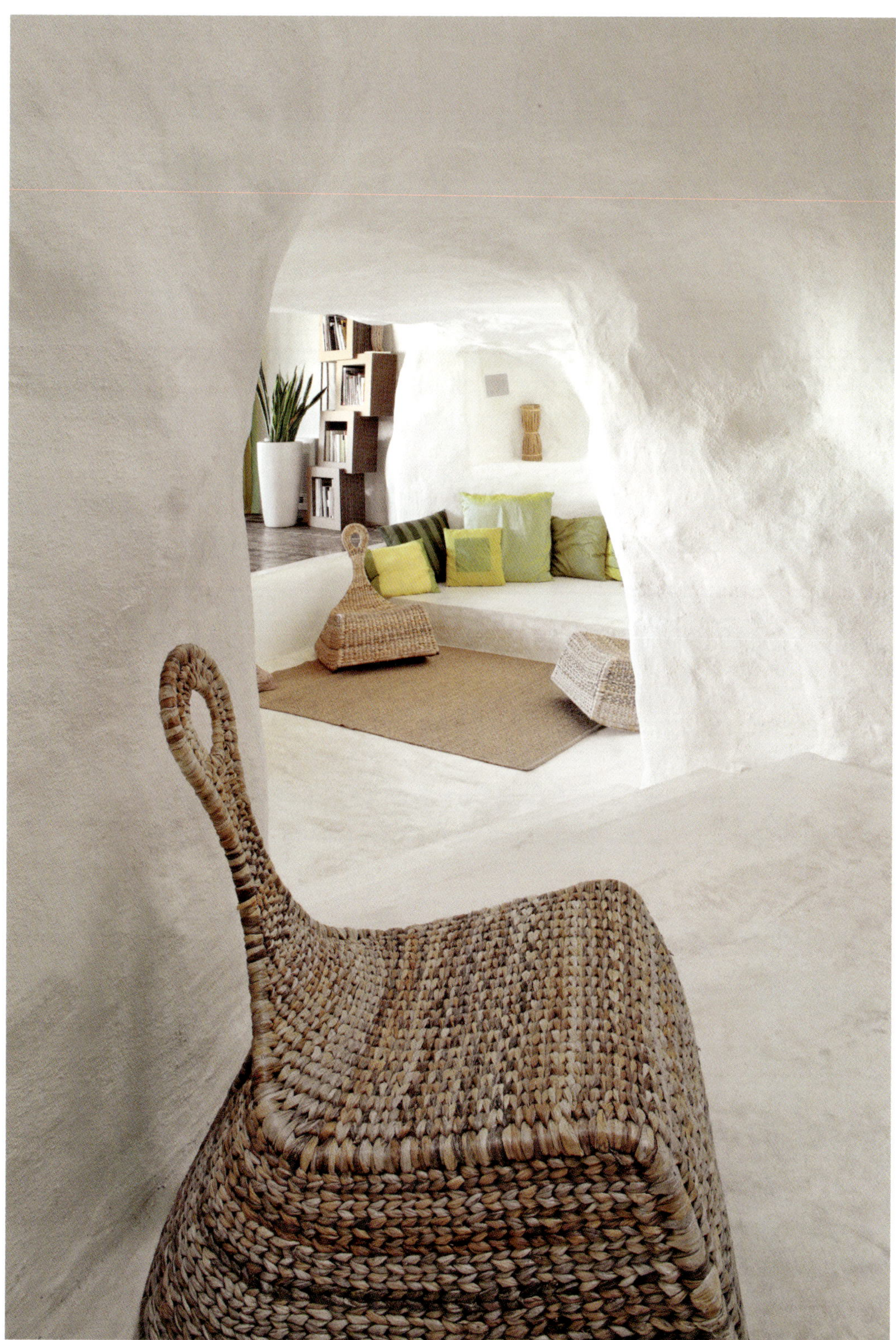

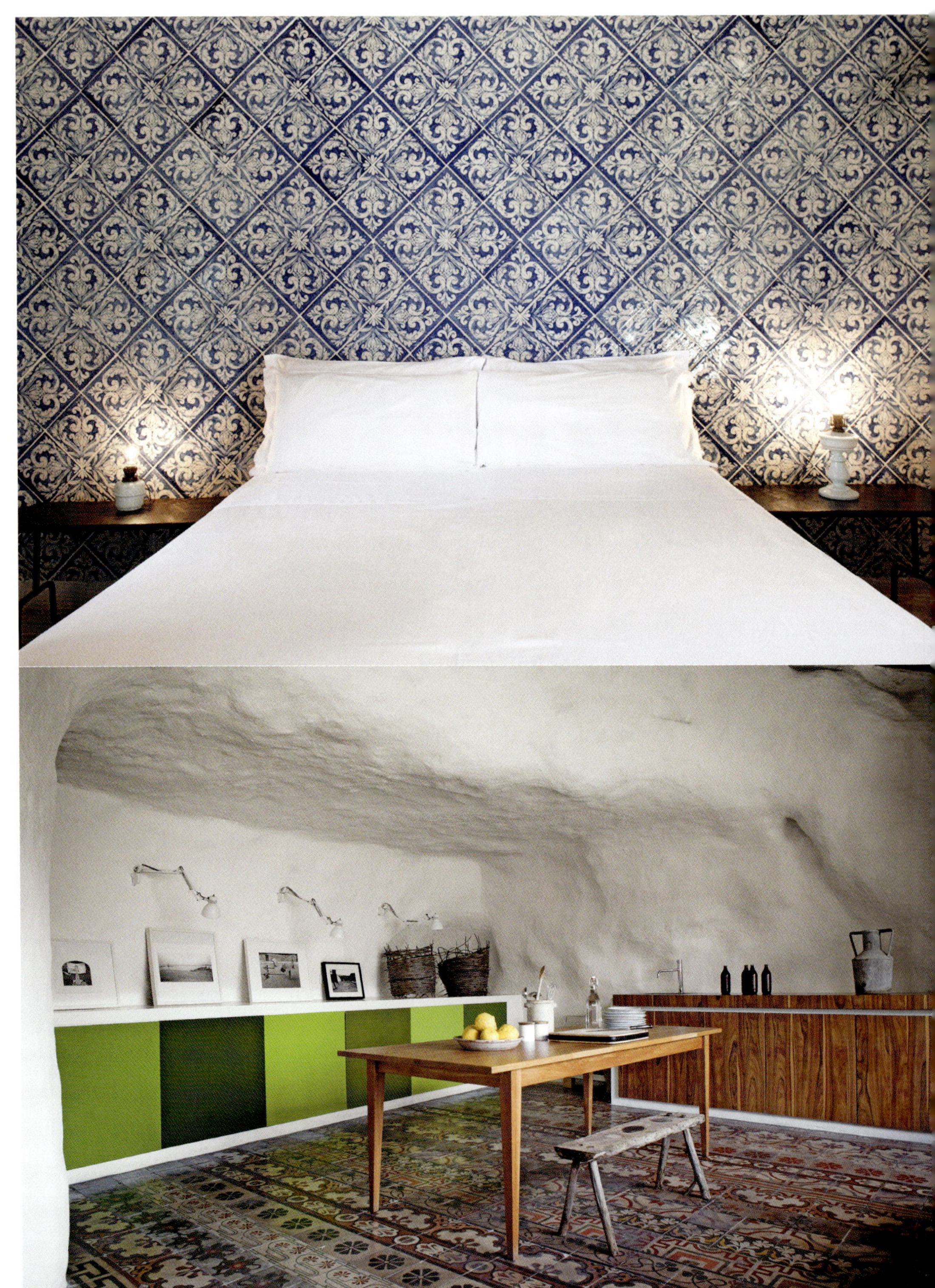

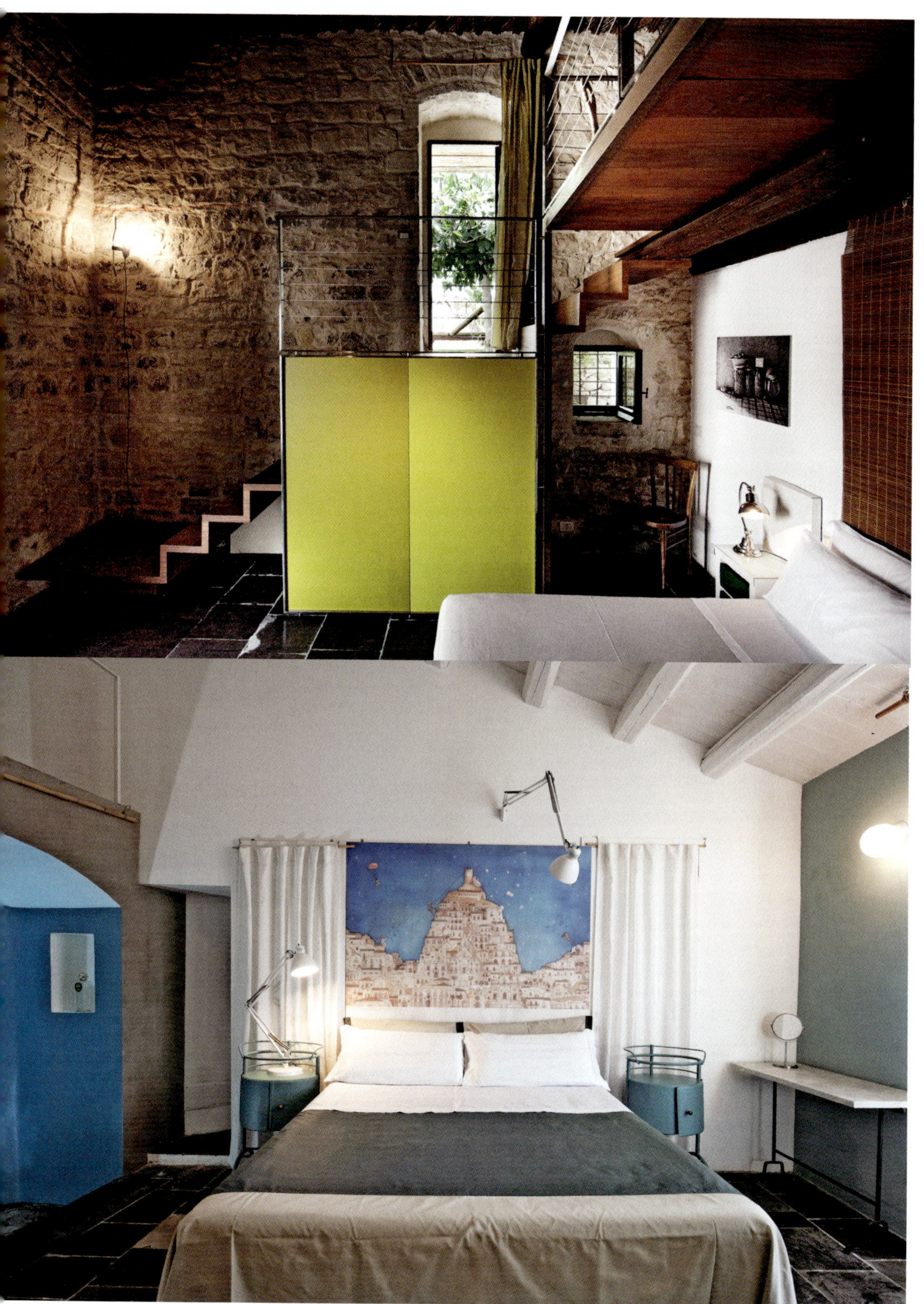

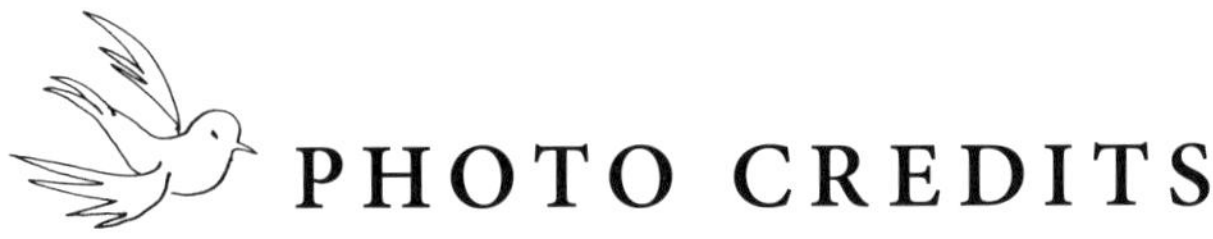

PHOTO CREDITS

6 **Ottmanngut**
Supplied by the hotel

18 **Vigilius Mountain Resort**
pp. 18–19, 20, 22, 24–25, 27–29 by Florian Andergassen; p. 26 by Patricia Parinejade; supplied by the hotel

30 **Pension Briol**
pp. 30–32, 35 by Mathias Michl, pp. 38–41 by Luca Meneghel; supplied by the hotel

42 **Villa d'Este**
Photos courtesy by the hotel

56 **Villa Feltrinelli**
Supplied by the hotel

70 **Villa Cipriani**
pp. 70–71, 72, 76, 77b, 80b,81t by Stefano Scatà; pp. 75, 77t, 78–79, 80t, 81b by Giovanni de Sandre; supplied by the hotel

82 **Hotel Flora**
Valentina Sommariva; supplied by the hotel

92 **Villa Pisani**
Andréa Fazzari

102 **Relais San Maurizio**
Supplied by the hotel

112 **Antico Borgo del Riondino**
Supplied by Interhome

120 **Splendido, A Belmond Hotel**
pp. 120–121, 125b, 128–131 by Mattia Aquila; pp. 122, 128–131 by Salva Lopez; p. 125t by Mary Quincy; pp. 126–131 by Matthieu Salvaing; courtesy of Belmond

132 **La Sosta di Ottone III**
Supplied by the hotel

140 **Villa Lena**
pp. 140–141 by Giacomo Lai; pp. 142, 146–147, 149 by Henrik Lundell/hlvm; p. 145 by Ivan Erofeev; courtesy of Villa Lena

150 **Torre di Bellosguardo**
Supplied by the hotel

166 **Villa Bordoni**
Ernst Barth; supplied by the hotel

172 **Fattoria San Martino**
Supplied by the hotel

180 **Adler Thermae**
pp. 180–181, 186–187 by Mads Mogensen, styling: Martina Hunglinger; supplied by the hotel

190 **Castello di Vicarello**
Supplied by the hotel

204 **Hotel Il Pellicano**
pp. 204–205 by Stephen Ringer; courtesy Pellicano OpCo S.r.L.

216 **Reschio Hotel**
Philip Vile; p. 223t supplied by the hotel

228 **Locanda del Gallo**
Supplied by the hotel

236 **Casa San Ruffino**
Adriano Bacchella/ Photofoyer

244 **Sextantio Santo Stefano**
Mirjam Bleeker

252 **Hotel Locarno**
Supplied by the hotel

262 **Albergo Il Monastero**
Sandra Semburg

270 **Mezzatorre**
p. 276t by Giada Mariani, supplied by the hotel; all other photos by James Widegren

278 **Hotel Parco dei Principi**
Supplied by the hotel

286 **Il San Pietro**
Supplied by the hotel

292 **Villa Cimbrone**
Roberto Vuilleumier; supplied by the hotel

300 **Il Cannito**
Supplied by the hotel

308 **Villa Cenci**
Supplied by the hotel

316 **Borgo Egnazia**
pp. 316/317, 322b by Nicola Cipriani; pp. 321t, 322t by Jacob Sjoman; p. 323 by Giorgio Baroni; supplied by the hotel

324 **Masseria Moroseta**
Supplied by the hotel

338 **Convento di Santa Maria**
Gianni Basso/Vega MG/ TASCHEN GmbH

348 **Relais Histó S. Pietro**
Adriano Bacchella/ Photofoyer

358 **Sextantio Le Grotte della Civita**; Manuel Zublena, styling: Sabine Bouvet; supplied by the hotel

366 **Palazzo Margherita**
Gundolf Pfotenhauer

384 **Faro Capo Spartivento**
Supplied by the hotel

394 **Capofaro**
pp. 394–396, 404–405 by Matteo Carassale; pp. 399–403 by Tommaso Pini; supplied by the hotel

406 **Casa Talía**
pp. 406–407, 412t, 413b by Simone Aprile; p. 411 by Matteo Cirenei; p. 408 Michele Battaglia; p. 412b Simone Aprile; p. 413t Andrea Ferrari; supplied by the hotel

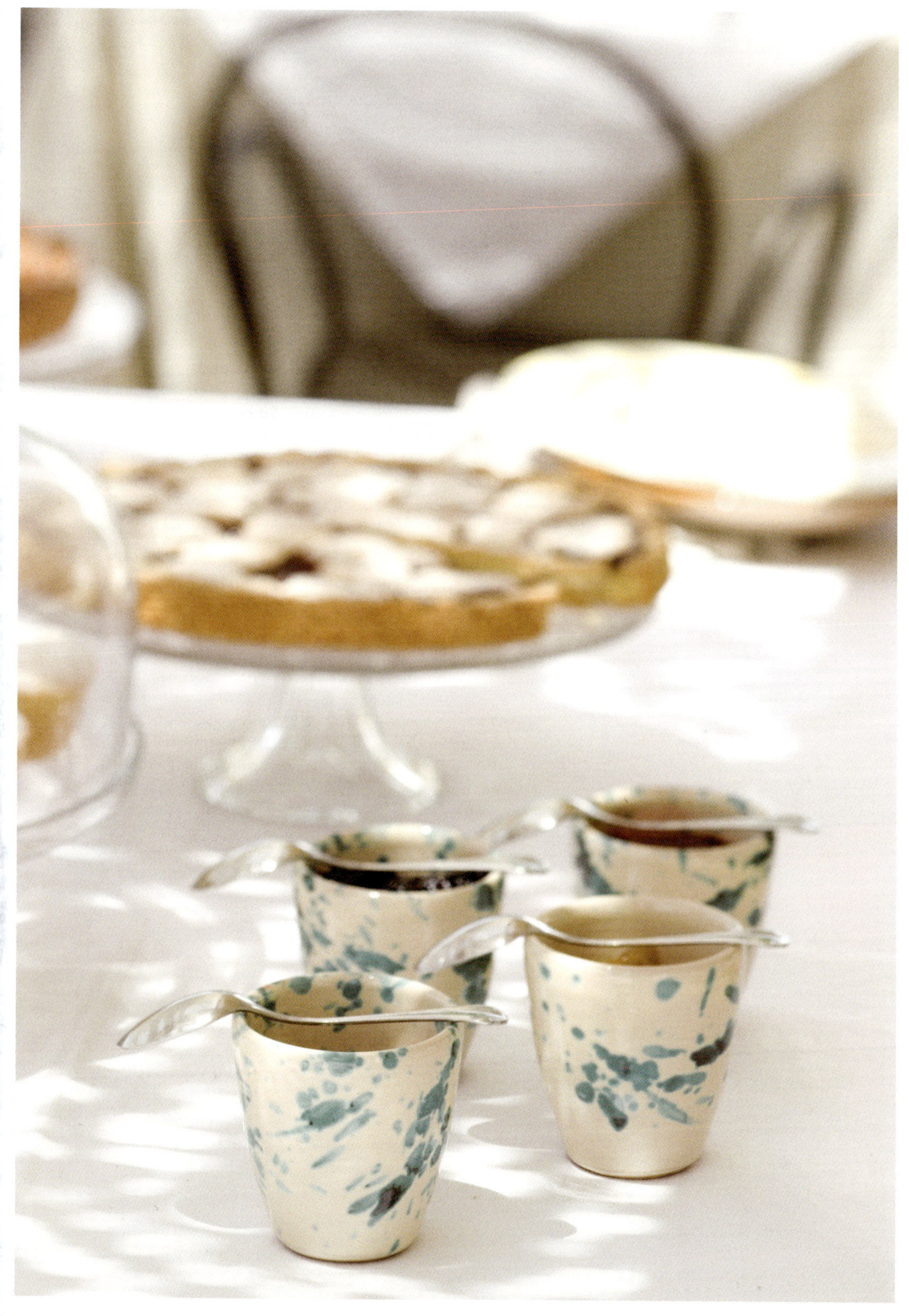

IMPRINT

EDITING, ART DIRECTION AND LAYOUT
Angelika Taschen, Berlin

PROJECT MANAGER
Stephanie Paas, Cologne

DESIGN
Maximiliane Hüls, Cologne

TEXTS
Christiane Reiter, Brussels

ENGLISH TRANSLATION
John Sykes, Cologne

FRENCH TRANSLATION
Michèle Schreyer, Cologne

EACH AND EVERY TASCHEN BOOK PLANTS A SEED!
Each year, we offset our annual carbon emissions with carbon credits at the Instituto Terra, a reforestation program in Minas Gerais, Brazil, founded by Lélia and Sebastião Salgado. To find out more about this ecological partnership, please check: www.taschen.com/institutoterra.
Inspiration: unlimited.
Carbon footprint: (almost) zero.

Want to see more? Visit taschen.com to view our current publications, browse our latest magazine, and subscribe to our newsletter.

Hohenzollernring 53, D-50672 Köln
www.taschen.com

Printed in Bosnia-Herzegovina
ISBN 978-3-7544-0079-1